Métis–Crown Relations

MÉTIS–CROWN RELATIONS

Rights, Identity, Jurisdiction, and Governance

Frederica Wilson & Melanie Mallet
EDITORS

IRWIN LAW

Métis–Crown Relations: Rights, Identity, Jurisdiction, and Governance

Published in 2008 by

Irwin Law Inc.
14 Duncan Street
Suite 206
Toronto, Ontario
M5H 3G8

www.irwinlaw.com

ISBN-13: 978-155221-158-8

Library and Archives Canada Cataloguing in Publication

Métis–Crown relations : rights, identity, jurisdiction and governance / Frederica Wilson & Melanie Mallet, editors.

Includes bibliographical references and index.
ISBN 978-1-55221-158-8

1. Métis—Legal status, laws, etc. 2. Métis—Government relations. 3. Métis—Politics and government. I. Wilson, Frederica II. Mallet, Melanie

FC125.M48 2008 342.7108'72 C2008-904719-2

The publisher acknowledges the financial support of the Government of Canada through the Book Publishing Industry Development Program (BPIDP) for its publishing activities.

We acknowledge the assistance of the OMDC Book Fund, an initiative of Ontario Media Development Corporation.

Printed and bound by CPI Group (UK) Ltd, Croydon, CR0 4YY

1 2 3 4 5 12 11 10 09 08

Table of Contents

Foreword

The relationship between the Métis Nation and the Crown has been both troubling and remarkable.

It has been troubling because even though Aboriginal rights are recognized and affirmed by the Constitution of Canada, Métis harvesters are systematically pursued and prosecuted by the Crown when trying to harvest food to feed their families. It has also been troubling because Métis are the only Aboriginal people that Canada has refused to accept legislative jurisdiction for, arguing that the Crown–Métis relationship should be with the provinces — the same governments that are prosecuting Métis for exercising traditional harvesting rights. The resolution of these issues relating to access to lands and resources, and the question of jurisdiction, is central to establishing an honourable and enduring Crown–Métis relationship. Sadly, these are the very issues we sought to resolve more than 150 years ago and that resulted in the Métis wars and the hanging of Louis Riel.

But the relationship between the Métis and the Crown is also remarkable. We have endured and thrived in this country. While there is still much poverty, many of our people are lawyers, doctors, engineers, and entrepreneurs. And this entrepreneurial spirit helped create the fur industry and was a key factor in establishing settlements in Western Canada. Even more remarkable, Métis remain proud Canadians who truly believe in the honour of the Crown.

The recognition of Métis as an Aboriginal people in Canada and the affirmation of our Aboriginal rights was a high-water mark in the Métis struggle. We assumed that with this recognition, the questions of jurisdiction and access to lands and resources would be resolved as a matter of course. We knew it would not be easy, but we were prepared to invest the time and resources to work cooperatively with the federal and provincial governments to resolve issues central to the Métis struggle. For these reasons, we have worked with both levels of governments, often in coordination with other Aboriginal governments and organizations, with the hope that our issues would be resolved through honourable negotiations. On occasion, we have been successful, but for the most part, our issues remain unresolved: more than a quarter-century after the constitutional recognition of Métis and the Aboriginal rights of Métis, we still find ourselves marginalized, being bounced between different levels of government and treated as the "in-between" people.

Over the last several years, we have turned to the courts to seek redress. In the courts, we have had some success and some failures. The Supreme Court of Canada's decision in *Powley* was an obvious success, but the same Court's decision in *Blais* was a setback. And there have been more successes in the lower courts and some major setbacks, such as the Manitoba Queen's Bench decision in *MMF v. Canada and Manitoba*. It is getting tiresome to have to constantly confront the Crown, either in the courts or on the land, as we exercise our harvesting rights.

The courts are not the preferred forum for the Métis. Métis issues involve matters of history, culture, politics, justice, and human decency. Our issues need to be resolved through a dialogue so that we can create a better understanding of both the Crown and the Métis perspectives. We also need to understand each other's fears. The debate needs to be both technical and political. The technical debate must take place because many of the issues are technical. The question of jurisdiction, and the related matter of interjurisdictional immunity, is complex. Questions linked with Métis identity and the identification of historic Métis communities can also involve a good deal of research and historical data. But ultimately, the solutions will involve political will, or an unusual amount of both courage and clarity from the courts. As the court process is costly, gut-wrenching, and unpredictable, our preference is to resolve Métis issues through negotiations on a nation-to-nation basis.

Unfortunately, there is no ongoing forum in which the Métis can carry on a conversation with the Crown to address these fundamental issues in an open and honest manner. For the most part, our discussions with the Crown are a repeat of the same old, comfortable arguments that lead nowhere. For this reason, I was delighted when the Law Commission of Canada approached the Métis National Council and asked us to join them in sponsoring an open dialogue on Crown–Métis relations in which Métis rights advocates, scholars, and Crown representatives could participate. This open dialogue, or "safe forum," provided an opportunity for the best minds in the country engaged in Métis issues to converse and take part in thoughtful discussion. The outcome of this conversation is the compilation of a number of well-considered papers offered as a small legacy from the joint initiative of the Law Commission of Canada and the Métis National Council.

Clem Chartier
President, Métis National Council
March 2008

Métis–Crown Relations: Rights, Identity, Jurisdiction, and Governance

The years 2003 to 2005 represented a watershed period for the Métis people of Canada, both in terms of affirmation of their constitutionally protected rights and the willingness of government to engage in dialogue needed to move their relationship forward. The paramount development was the 2003 Supreme Court of Canada decision in *R. v. Powley*,[1] widely regarded as a landmark ruling for its affirmation of Métis rights in section 35 of the *Constitution Act, 1982*.[2] In that same year, the federal government announced its commitment to Métis issues in the Speech from the Throne and in 2004 joined the Federal Interlocutor for Métis and Non-Status Indians with the Indian and Northern Affairs portfolio. Less than a year later, the Métis National Council and the federal government entered into the Métis Nation Framework Agreement, detailing their commitment to a process to address the outstanding issues between them. These milestones indicated a place of prominence for the agenda of a long-neglected people and created optimism for an improved and clarified relationship between the Métis and government.

Although these developments indicated momentum in the field of Métis rights, the *Powley* decision, in particular, highlighted several important issues that require resolution. For instance, how should a historic

1 [2003] 2 S.C.R. 207 [*Powley*].

2 *Constitution Act, 1982*, s. 35, being Schedule B to the *Canada Act 1982* (U.K.), 1982, c. 11.

Métis rights-bearing community be defined? What is meant by the term *effective control*? What are the limitations of the historical record in informing these determinations?

R. v. Blais,[3] a decision released concurrently with *Powley*, added to the battery of questions regarding Métis rights. *Blais* stated that the Métis are not "Indians" for the purpose of the *Natural Resources Transfer Agreements*, which regulate Indian wildlife harvesting in the prairie provinces. Since many Métis people live in Western Canada, their exclusion from these agreements raises questions about how their harvesting practices should be regulated and how these regimes would differ from those governing "Indians."

In a broader sense, both *Powley* and *Blais* highlighted the particular position of the Métis vis-à-vis governments. Lurking in the background and as a part of the context of these two cases is the question about jurisdiction for the Métis. While section 91(24)[4] expressly refers to "Indians" and has long been interpreted to include the Inuit, the federal government has never accepted legislative responsibility for the Métis. Nor, with the exception of Alberta, have the provinces. Provinces generally take the view that Canada has legislative responsibility for the Métis pursuant to its jurisdiction over Indians and lands reserved for the Indians under section 91(24) of the *Constitution Act, 1867*. This jurisdictional no man's land in which the Métis find themselves has critical implications, including the differential application of federal and provincial laws and policies, and gaps in the provision of services.

Related to the question of jurisdiction is the constitutional doctrine of interjurisdictional immunity. The doctrine, which protects the core of certain federal subject matters from the application of provincial laws, has developed significantly in relation to section 91(24) of the *Constitution Act, 1867*. If the Métis are not included in the scope of section 91(24), as argued by the federal government, the doctrine of interjurisdictional immunity does not apply to them and they are not shielded from provincial laws of general application. If, however, the Métis are "Indians" for the purposes of section 91(24), as argued by many academics, they would

---

3 [2003] 2 S.C.R. 236 [*Blais*].

4 *Constitution Act, 1867* (U.K.), 30 & 31 Vict., c. 3, s. 91(24), reprinted in R.S.C. 1985, App. II, No. 5.

be protected from the application of provincial laws in the exercise of their section 35 rights under the *Constitution Act, 1982*. The fact that section 88 of the *Indian Act*,[5] which allows provincial laws to apply to status Indians, does not apply to the Métis adds to the complexity of issues.

Recognizing the need for clarity and the potential for law reform generated by these issues, the Law Commission of Canada and the Métis National Council jointly sponsored a national symposium on Crown–Métis relations, held in Winnipeg in February 2006. Bringing together academics, lawyers, government officials, and Métis leaders, the symposium provided a safe forum to discuss and debate these questions. This volume is a compilation of the papers prepared for the symposium. In addition to the authors whose papers appear, John Graham of the Institute on Governance, Brent Cotter, dean of the College of Law, University of Saskatchewan, and Larry Chartrand, then director of the Aboriginal Governance Program and professor in the Department of Politics at the University of Winnipeg, provided thoughtful introductory comments during the symposium to situate the discussions.

The collection opens with an essay by Arthur Ray, a noted scholar of Aboriginal history, commenting on the imperfect fit between accepted historical methodology and expert testimony in Métis litigation. This latter issue will become more and more important as all of the unsettled issues emanating from *Powley* end up in the courts.

In Part II, Paul Chartrand, Brad Morse, Charlotte Bell, Frank Tough, Mark Stevenson, and Jean Teillet examine aspects of Métis identity and the position of the Métis vis-à-vis the *Constitution Act, 1867*, including the implications of their exclusion from section 91(24). Chartrand's paper focuses on one of the central issues arising out of *Powley*, that is, the identification of the Métis. Teillet also tackles this theme, focusing on the identification of Métis collectives. Overwhelmingly, the authors who focus on the exclusion of the Métis from section 91(24) find no sound juridical reason for this omission; rather, they present several compelling reasons why governments and courts should adopt a more purposive and encompassing view of both section 91(24) and section 35. As Dean Cotter explained in his framing remarks, a definitive and affirmative placement of the Métis within section 91(24) would allow for a more "articulated"

5 R.S.C. 1985, c. I-5.

relationship with both orders of government. Speaking at the symposium, he called for a constitutional reference to the Supreme Court to settle this matter. Mark Stevenson, a former commissioner of the Law Commission, also explores an agenda for law reform to address the legal and policy issues faced by the Métis.

In Part III, Dale Gibson, Albert Peeling, Mitch McAdam, and Kent McNeil explore the shifting terrain of interjurisdictional immunity. McAdam and McNeil present divergent viewpoints on the precise effect of provincial wildlife laws on Aboriginal rights, as well as the protections afforded by the doctrine of interjurisdictional immunity. For his part, Gibson suggests how the doctrine might afford protections for the Métis. His analysis hinges on the assumption that the Métis are included in section 91(24), further underlining the importance of reconciling this issue of the constitutional place of the Métis. After examining the scope of section 91(24) through the lenses of arguments that seem to support a finding that the Métis are within the exclusive jurisdiction of the federal government, Peeling looks critically at the waning influence of the doctrine of interjurisdictional immunity. The authors differ in their estimation of the doctrine's importance and on the effect that case law will have on interjurisdictional immunity in relation to Indians and the Métis. This section of the book is enriched by McNeil's thoughtful comments on the positions articulated in the papers of McAdam, Gibson, and Peeling, an aspect of McNeil's paper that reflects its origins as a commentary for the symposium. Added to the commentary, however, is McNeil's own thoughtful analysis of interjurisdictional immunity and its application to the Métis.

Part IV of the collection is a series of papers dealing with governance. As John Graham thoughtfully pointed out in his introductory comments at the symposium, the *Powley* case lays the groundwork for the argument that the Métis have an inherent right to self-government, and it will be the courts that will rule on this issue. As Graham noted, the contours of self-government remain to be defined, as does a common understanding of what good governance means in the Métis context. The Métis generally do not have a defined land base, something that adds further complexity to the self-government question. Speaking to these governance issues are Jason Madden, Fred Caron, Catherine Bell and Harold Robinson, and Harvey Bostrum, Alison Rogan, and Richard Asselin. These papers describe a series of culturally responsive governance success stories and best practices, including the establishment of a Métis child welfare agency in Manitoba and legislation in Alberta establishing Métis Settlement lands.

Since the time the papers were presented, there have been several important decisions with possible repercussions for the Métis. *R. v. Morris*[6] and *Canadian Western Bank v. Alberta*,[7] in which the majority of the Supreme Court of Canada expressed discomfort with interjurisdictional immunity, have an impact on the application of the doctrine to this area. The precise effect of these developments, however, remains to be seen.

Mere days before this manuscript was submitted to the publisher, the Manitoba Court of Queen's Bench released a ruling in *Manitoba Metis Federation Inc. v. Canada (Attorney General)*[8] denying a land claim launched by the Manitoba Metis Federation and seventeen families to huge tracts of land in downtown Winnipeg and along the Assiniboine and Red Rivers. We are grateful to Brad Morse and Frank Tough for their description of the lengthy case. The Métis, notes Morse, were seeking a declaration that federal and provincial legislation and Orders-in-Council passed between 1877 and 1885 that helped land speculators acquire the land scrip promised to the Métis were unconstitutional. In rejecting the claim, MacInnes J. made some findings that have important implications for the issues explored in this volume, including that the Métis had no Aboriginal title as they "did not live in a communal or collective setting," but as individual landholders; they were not and did not regard themselves to be "Indians"; the Crown is not in a fiduciary relationship with the Métis; and none of the legislative instruments challenged were *ultra vires*. The precise impact of these findings remains to be seen particularly given the likelihood of an appeal.

When the Law Commission of Canada was shut down in December 2006, we, both former researchers at the Commission, feared that this valuable collection of papers would never make it to print. These papers embrace the philosophy of the Commission to examine areas of the law that are unfair, that create anomalies, or that fail to reflect the "law as

6 [2006] 2 S.C.R. 915.

7 2007 SCC 22.

8 2002 MBQB 52.

lived" by the people it is meant to govern. Equally significant, this publication provides a forum for diverse voices — those of legal academics, historians, government officials, and members of the private bar — to engage in an exchange of views. All of these constituencies have important perspectives on the relationship between the Métis and the Crown, perspectives that expand both the breadth and depth of the discussion. As the above-mentioned Manitoba case illustrates, the issues explored in this volume remain current and of vital importance.

As a final note, the editors express their appreciation of the determination of Clem Chartier and Dale Leclair of the Métis National Council, and Mark Stevenson, former Commissioner, Law Commission of Canada to have this volume published.

Ethnohistory and the Development of Native Law in Canada: Advancing Aboriginal Rights or Re-inscribing Colonialism?[1]

ARTHUR J. RAY

> While at times it felt like the Court had been sent back to school, the historical information and interpretations presented were always interesting and, on many occasions, quite fascinating. It would have been all too easy to wander down the many well-trod avenues, lesser byways, and faint trails of our history . . .
>
> I have attempted to present, for the most part, an historical chronology, as opposed to drifting into any analytical abstractionism, which is best left to academics, not judges.[2]

Canadian Aboriginal and treaty rights law is a relatively new field of Canadian jurisprudence. It has developed mostly since the landmark *Calder*[3] decision of the Supreme Court. The period after the adoption of the 1982 Canadian Constitution has been particularly productive because section 35 of the *Constitution Act, 1982*,[4] defined Aboriginal peoples broadly to include the Métis and entrenched "existing" Aboriginal and treaty rights

1 This paper is based partly on research support provided by an SSHRC Bora Laskin National Fellowship in Human Rights Research and a Woodrow Wilson Fellowship. The initial draft of this paper was prepared for a workshop, sponsored by the Canadian Department of Justice (Vancouver Office), held in Vancouver 27–28 November 2005.

2 *Samson Indian Nation and Band v. Canada*, 2005 FC 1622 at para. 3, Teitelbaum J. [*Victor Buffalo*].

3 *Calder v. British Columbia (Attorney-General)*, [1973] S.C.R. 313.

4 *Constitution Act, 1982*, being Schedule B to the *Canada Act 1982* (U.K.), 1982, c. 11.

even though the nature and extent of those rights were unknown. Many excellent overviews have been written about the development of Native law since these events.[5] Most have been authored by lawyers and legal scholars and, understandably, they focus on the implications of the growing body of case law for Aboriginal rights in Canada. What is lacking are studies that consider the implications of the fact that this new body of case law is (and continues to be) built on ethnohistorical evidence that experts have presented to the courts. This is my concern here. I will consider the litigation process from the perspective of the issues and questions that arise concerning the use of this line of evidence. These are (1) the different ways scholars and the courts approach and use history; (2) the implications that rights tests developed by the courts have for claims research; and (3) the problems that are associated with using different lines of evidence in court.

A. ACADEMIC AND COURT HISTORIOGRAPHIES

Australian legal scholar Alex Reilly has noted that the historiographies generated by the scholarly community and the courts are fundamentally different because they serve wholly dissimilar objectives.[6] Academic scholarship does not seek to provide finality to historical interpretation. Rather, it is now widely, if not universally, accepted that our perceptions of the past are linked to the present because they are socially constructed and connected to current concerns. An analysis of the ethnohistorical literature regarding North American Aboriginal peoples makes this clear. Succeeding generations of scholars deployed different theoretical and methodological frameworks that have continually altered our understandings of Aboriginal history. In this way, academic scholarship has helped to keep the Aboriginal past alive and connected to the present.

Reilly points out that courts use history to bury the past rather than to continually revisit it. They use historical "evidence" to resolve disputes

---

5 One of the best of these is the *Annual Métis Law Summary*, written by Jean Teillet of Pape, Salter and Teillet, Vancouver. It is available online: www.pstlaw.ca/resources/MLS-2006.pdf. This work is much more comprehensive than the title suggests.

6 Alexander Reilly, "The Ghost of Truganini: Use of Historical Evidence as Proof of Native Title" (2000) 28 Fed. L. Rev. 453.

that arise from the contested past so that parties to litigation can move forward. Given that courts must provide resolutions in a timely fashion, they may have to invent historical "facts" for decision-making purposes. Justice Binnie acknowledged this reality in *R. v. Marshall*,[7] when he responded to criticisms from the academy about the way trial judges used Aboriginal history in their decisions.[8] He pointed out to these critics: "the law sees a finality of interpretation of historical events where finality, according to the professional historian, is not possible. The reality, of course, is that the courts are handed disputes that require for their resolution the finding of certain historical facts. The litigating parties cannot await the possibility of a stable academic consensus."[9]

These different approaches to history have important implications for litigation. Reilly points out that historical evidence enters claims trials from the dynamic context of the academy, but "the law's approach to history is far from dynamic" because it "assumes that the past belongs to another realm of time that can be separated from the present and understood on its own terms."[10] While this may be the case, the law constructs models to imagine the past to suit its needs. In this way, the courts' view of history is presentist. In any event, it is clear that the claims litigation process is an exercise in which Aboriginal peoples' pasts are filtered through multiple sets of academic and legal models, or lenses, and Aboriginal rights are acknowledged (created) or denied on that basis. This means that historiographic discussions of the theoretical models that shaped the evidence presented in court should be a central aspect of expert testimony. It rarely is, however. Usually, most court time is spent addressing the contested details about the past. As a result, too often the trial judge does not gain an adequate understanding of the intellectual

7 [1999] 3 S.C.R. 456.

8 He made specific references to critiques by Robin Fisher and Arthur J. Ray: Robin Fisher, "Judging History: Reflections on the Reasons for Judgment in *Delgamuukw v. B.C.*" (1992) XCV B.C. Studies 43–54; Arthur J. Ray, "Creating the Image of the Savage in Defence of the Crown: The Ethnohistorian in Court" (1990) VI Native Studies Review 13–29.

9 Above note 7 at para. 37.

10 Reilly, above note 6. He was quoting from Bain Attwood, ed., *In the Age of Mabo* (St. Leonards, NSW: Allen & Unwin, 1996) at xvi.

roots of the historical controversies that are expressed in the courtroom or offered an explanation of how "facts" were identified.[11]

The different approaches that the academy and the law take to history also have implications for the ways courts receive expert witnesses. Those experts who approach the past as a detached reality, whose components can be discerned by systematic ("scientific") analysis, are appealing — their approach is in harmony with that of the courts. Indeed, those who make their livelihoods as experts adopt this perspective and go about their litigation research as though it is merely a "fact-finding" exercise. Their objective does not include educating the courts about the nuances of historical interpretation that arise from the inter- and multidisciplinary nature of ethnohistory. Rather, they seek to provide an "objective" interpretation based on carefully (systematically) selected facts. The *Victor Buffalo* case[12] is very interesting and important with respect to this issue. In this instance, the plaintiffs' legal team and experts made a great, but ultimately unsuccessful effort to demonstrate the tentative nature of ethnohistorical understanding in order to provide an opening for the alternative Cree understanding of the history and meaning of Treaty 6. The Crown's experts, Drs. Thomas Flanagan and Alexander von Gernet, essentially advanced the proposition that there was *a single* correct interpretation of Treaty 6 that could be discerned by the application of Western approaches to history that had been developed during and after the Enlightenment.[13] They applied this rationale to legitimate extant scholarship on western Canadian history, particularly the Aboriginal and treaty dimensions, to trump alternative interpretations advanced by

11 The *Bear Island* case provides a good example where groups of opposing experts represented two competing views of post-contact Subarctic history. This underlying cleavage was not discussed at trial.

12 Above note 2.

13 Flanagan outlined his perspective in briefs that he filed in rebuttal to those of the plaintiffs' experts. Thomas Flanagan, "Analysis of the Plaintiffs' Expert Reports in the case of *Chief Victor Buffalo v. Her Majesty et al.*" (21 July 1998), T-2022-89 and T-1254-92 (F.C.T.D.), and "Surrebuttal to the Rebuttal Reports of Bob Beal, Carl Beal, Stan Cuthand, Arthur Ray, and John Tobias" (2 June 2000). Von Gernet's position is articulated in part in Alexander von Gernet, "Aboriginal Oral Documents" and "Comments on Winona Wheeler's Indigenous Oral Tradition Histories: An Academic Predicament" (Report Prepared for the Defendants, 19 October 2001).

the plaintiffs and their experts. The latter essentially held that the treaty was not plain on its face to the Cree's ancestors who signed it in 1876. They also asserted the document did not encompass all of the commitments the two parties had made. In the end, the trial judge preferred the Flanagan–von Gernet approach and interpretation.[14]

An important issue that Binnie J. and Reilly did not address is the fact that the claims litigation process destabilizes knowledge about local Aboriginal history. Typically, one or both of the opposing parties (usually Aboriginal people as plaintiffs or defendants) will undertake new empirical research or advance new interpretive or theoretical models. One reason is that many Aboriginal groups were not the focus of scholarly research before the time they file their claims. The Gitxsan-Wet'suet'en plaintiffs in *Delgamuukw*[15] and the Sault Ste. Marie Métis in the *Powley*[16] case are two excellent examples. The Gitxsan-Wet'suet'en live in the much-studied Northwest Coast culture area, but their territory lies inland in the Skeena River basin. Before the 1980s, most of the extant ethnographic literature focused on their coastal Tsimshian neighbours living to the west, whom anthropologists regarded as being more typical Northwest Coast people, or the Sekani, living to the east, who were considered to have a culture characteristic of the Subarctic cultural area. Historians of the Métis, on the other hand, largely had ignored the Sault Ste. Marie community because they were more interested in the relatives of these people who lived in the western Canadian Prairie region.[17]

Even when there is a literature dealing with the ethnohistory of claimants' ancestors, it often does not deal extensively with the issues at hand.[18]

---

14 *Victor Buffalo*, above note 2, Teitelbaum J. He also noted that the Federal Court of Appeal had opted for von Gernet's approach in *Benoit v. Canada* (2003), 228 D.L.R. (4th) 1 at para. 112 [*Benoit*].

15 *Delgamuukw v. British Columbia* (1993), 104 D.L.R. (4th) 470 (B.C.C.A.), var'd [1997] 3 S.C.R. 1010 [*Delgamuukw*].

16 *R. v. Powley* (2001), 53 O.R. (3d) 35 (C.A.), aff'd [2003] 2 S.C.R. 207 [*Powley*].

17 An example is the work of Jacqueline Peterson, "Prelude to Red River: A Social Portrait of the Great Lakes Métis" (1978) 25 Ethnohistory 41–67; "Many Roads to Red River: Métis Genesis in the Great Lakes Region, 1680–1815" in Jennifer Brown & Jacqueline Peterson, eds., *The New Peoples* (Winnipeg: University of Manitoba Press, 1985) at 37.

18 These deficiencies led the plaintiffs to commission extensive new archival and oral history research, which their elders and experts presented at trial. In reply,

Over a half-century ago, prominent anthropologists A. L. Kroeber and J. Steward noted that their predecessors had not systematically studied Indian tenure systems or the political systems that supported these schemes.[19] Thirty or more years later, many Canadian First Nations, the Gitxsan-Wet'suet'en among them, faced a similar problem, which led them to commission oral and documentary histories of their traditional house-territory system.

Path-breaking claims research usually is presented in court before it is subject to peer evaluation in the academy. There are two reasons for this. First, litigation-oriented research commonly takes place in a more compressed time frame than is typical of scholarly investigations. Second, claims researchers are discouraged (or prevented) from presenting their work at conferences or in academic publications before judges have made rulings. The reason is that the parties to a dispute are loath to have their opponents obtain academic validation for their research, fearing that such approval might adversely affect their case before the courts.

This issue first arose in the 1950s during the earliest days of the United States Indian Claims Commission (USICC) hearings, which operated from 1946–76. Lawyers representing Indian claimants complained that the new *Ethnohistory* journal, which was edited by federal government expert Erminie Wheeler-Voegelin, published some of her research team's reports before the USICC had ruled on the cases for which these briefs had been prepared. The Indians' lawyers protested that Wheeler-Voegelin was trying to give these studies scholarly credibility by having them appear in a peer-reviewed journal. Government lawyers promptly replied that Kroeber and others, who acted as experts for Indian plaintiffs, were attempting to do the same thing. They specifically cited the example of

---

the Crown's experts turned mostly to the published ethnographic literature to make contrary arguments about Gitxsan-Wet'suet'en history (largely by using the technique of ethnographic analogy). This technique has been commonly used by archeologists and ethnographers. It involves looking at groups for which there is solid data and which are thought to have been or are similar societies (occupy similar rungs on cultural-evolutionary ladders) to make inferences about a people for whom information is lacking.

19 Arthur J. Ray, "Kroeber and the California Claims: Historical Particularism and Cultural Ecology in Court," in Richard Handler, ed., *Central Sites, Peripheral Visions: Cultural and Institutional Crossings in the History of Anthropology History of Anthropology*, vol. 11 (Madison, WI: University of Wisconsin Press, 2006).

Kroeber's paper on *tribelets*, which had appeared in *Ethnohistory* in 1955. Kroeber had developed the innovative notion of the *tribelet* on behalf of the plaintiffs in the California Indian Claims (Dockets 31 & 33). His *Ethnohistory* paper appeared before the USICC had ruled on the case.[20]

The foregoing example illustrates that when judges weigh the merits of competing historical interpretations, they often face the difficult task of sorting out pure advocacy from opinions based on current scholarship or from data generated by new claims-oriented research. Complicating the judges' task is the fact that experts have a potpourri of theoretical and methodological approaches to choose from. These include "intellectual artifacts" that have been left behind by previous generations of scholars as the field of ethnohistory moved forward. These artifacts exist in the form of unpublished and published works, many of which may seem legitimate because they have been peer-reviewed and seem to bear the stamp of approval of scholarly journals or institutions. In other words, it is not uncommon for judges to have to choose from a range of theoretical models that include outdated (abandoned) outlooks at one end of the spectrum, through a range of models currently under consideration in the academy, to cutting-edge constructs based on new research. At the extreme other end of the spectrum of possible interpretations are those based on pure speculation. This range of opinion was presented in *Delgamuukw*.[21]

Although it may be clear which interpretations fall on the opposite ends of the range and are mere advocacy, those propositions within the limits of acceptable discourse are harder to identify — these limits are continually shifting. For this reason, the courts need to know the intellectual pedigrees of experts who appear before them and to be aware of the theories they advance to be properly guided when making their choice. Unfortunately, this information is all too often not sufficiently provided, partly because extensive historiographic discussions, such as the plaintiffs attempted in *Victor Buffalo*,[22] add much to the length and expense of trials. *Victor Buffalo*, for example, has cost the parties $100

20 It should be noted that the academy never adopted Kroeber's idea. *Ibid.*

21 I have discussed this in A.J. Ray, "From the United States Indian Claims Commission Cases to *Delgamuukw*" in Louis Knafla, ed., *Aboriginal Title and Indigenous Peoples: Comparative Essays on Australia, New Zealand, and Western Canada* (Vancouver: University of British Columbia Press, forthcoming).

22 Above note 2.

million through the trial phase. Some judges have little interest in what they regard as mere academic debates. Judges may also prefer outdated notions to newer claims research-based ideas. The first reason is the suspicion that new interpretations are mere advocacy. This was the case in *Delgamuukw*,[23] where the trial judge opted for an interpretation based on older, mostly pre-1970s ethnographic literature. Ironically, it turns out that key elements of this literature were rooted in research undertaken for the United States Justice Department in opposition to claims Indian tribes brought before USICC.[24] The second reason why older perspectives can be more attractive to the court is that they suggest less disruptive remedies. Much of the older scholarship, especially that rooted in evolutionary theories, helped legitimate the colonial dispossession and marginalization that Aboriginal peoples are seeking to redress through litigation. For example, if these perspectives are abandoned in favour of newer outlooks, it will be harder to reject Aboriginal people's claims for commercial harvesting rights. The *Van der Peet*[25] fishing rights claim of the Sto:lo peoples of British Columbia is an illustration. One of the several reasons cited at trial for denying full commercial fishing rights to this First Nation was that anthropological experts, including those who appeared for the plaintiffs, had testified that the ancestral Sto:lo had a band rather than a tribal culture. The judge then concluded that they were unlikely to have the capability of engaging in the kind of regular market exchange that was characteristic of more advanced societies.[26]

---

23 Above note 15.

24 Sheree Ronaasen, Richard O. Clemmer, & Mary Elizabeth Rudden, "Rethinking Cultural Ecology, Multilinear Evolution, and Expert Witnesses: Julian Steward and the Indian Claims Commission Proceedings" in Richard Clemmer, Daniel Meyers, & Mary Elizabeth Rudden, eds., *Julian Steward and the Great Basin: The Making of an Anthropologist* (Salt Lake City: University of Utah Press, 1999) at 171–72.

25 *R. v. Van der Peet*, [1996] 2 S.C.R. 507 [*Van der Peet*].

26 Specifically, the Supreme Court of Canada noted at para. 7 that the trial judge concluded there was no trade of salmon "in any regularized or market sense" but only "opportunistic exchanges taking place on a casual basis." He found that the Sto:lo could not preserve or store fish for extended periods of time and that the Sto:lo were a band rather than a tribal culture; he held both of these facts to be significant in suggesting that the Sto:lo did not engage in a market system of exchange. Subsequently, historian Keith Carlson provided linguistic evidence that suggests this First Nation did engage in regular trade. Keith Thor Carlson, "Sto:lo Exchange Dynamics" (1997) 11 Native Studies Review 5–48.

B. RIGHTS TESTS, CLAIMS RESEARCH, AND EXPERT TESTIMONY IN CANADA

The different ways that the academy and the courts approach history also means that scholarly and applied litigation-oriented research differ in significant ways. In the academy, ideally, scholars continually test their theoretical models of Aboriginal societies against data they collect in the field or archives. Ethnohistorical expert witnesses, on the other hand, are retained to find data and offer interpretive frameworks that "prove" claimants do or do not fit the model of Aboriginal culture that the courts have generated for the purpose of determining rights. Experts are not expected to challenge the law's construct of Aboriginal culture, no matter how dubious it might be. The courts' models drive claims research and the presentation of evidence, so it is important to consider what that construct is in Canada and to think about the implications it has for gathering and interpreting ethnohistorical evidence for litigation.

The Supreme Court began constructing its model of Aboriginal culture in 1990, in a series of landmark decisions that have established tests that claimants must meet to have their rights recognized. Viewed from the perspective of their relevance to our understanding of the courts' notions about the nature of Aboriginal culture and ethnohistory, the most important tests are as follows:

1. The concept that Aboriginal peoples' rights are based on traditional practices that were "of central significance to the aboriginal society in question — one of the things which made the culture of the society distinctive" (*R. v. Adams*[27] and *R. v. Van der Peet*[28]). Regarding an

27 [1996] 3 S.C.R. 101.

28 Above note 25. In *Van der Peet*, the Court specified in para. 51: "In assessing a claim to an aboriginal right a court must first identify the nature of the right being claimed in order to determine whether a claim meets the test of being integral to the distinctive culture of the aboriginal group claiming the right." According to the headnote,

> to characterize an applicant's claim correctly, a court should consider such factors as the nature of the action which the applicant is claiming was done pursuant to an aboriginal right, the nature of the governmental regulation, statute or action being impugned, and the practice, custom or tradition being relied upon to establish the right. The activities must be considered at a general rather than specific level. They may be an exercise in modern form of a pre-contact prac-

integral practice, the Court said: "the practice, custom or tradition cannot exist simply as an incident to another practice, custom or tradition. Incidental practices, customs and traditions cannot qualify as aboriginal rights through a process of piggybacking on integral practices, customs and traditions" (*Van der Peet*[29]);

2. The requirement that claimants' ancestors had to have been members of an identifiable organized society that occupied a distinct territory (so-called *Baker Lake* test,[30] *Sparrow*,[31] and *Delgamuukw*[32]); and
3. The doctrine of continuity (*Sparrow*[33] and *Van der Peet*[34]).

Collectively, these rulings amount to a generalized model of Aboriginal cultures that presumes (1) every Aboriginal culture can be meaningfully dissected into *identifiable components*; (2) the *relative significance* of

---

> tice, custom or tradition and the claim should be characterized accordingly. To be integral, a practice, custom or tradition must be of central significance to the aboriginal society in question — one of the things which made the culture of the society distinctive. A court cannot look at those aspects of the aboriginal society that are true of every human society (e.g., eating to survive) or at those aspects of the aboriginal society that are only incidental or occasional to that society. It is those distinctive features that need to be acknowledged and reconciled with the sovereignty of the Crown.

Online: http://scc.lexum.umontreal.ca/en/1996/1996rcs2-507/1996rcs2-507.html.

29 The Court explained in *Van der Peet*, *ibid.* at headnote:

> Courts considering a claim to the existence of an aboriginal right must focus specifically on the practices, customs and traditions of the particular aboriginal group claiming the right. Claims to aboriginal rights are not to be determined on a general basis. In identifying those practices, customs and traditions that constitute the aboriginal rights recognized and affirmed by s. 35(1), a court must ensure that the practice, custom or tradition relied upon in a particular case is independently significant to the aboriginal community claiming the right. The practice, custom or tradition cannot exist simply as an incident to another practice, custom or tradition. Incidental practices, customs and traditions cannot qualify as aboriginal rights through a process of piggybacking on integral practices, customs and traditions.

30 *Baker Lake (Hamlet) v. Canada (Minister of Indian Affairs and Northern Development)*, [1980] 1 F.C. 518 (T.D.) [*Baker Lake*].

31 [1990] 1 S.C.R. 1075 [*Sparrow*].

32 *Baker Lake*, above note 30; *Delgamuukw*, above note 15.

33 Above note 31.

34 Above note 25.

each component for the whole can be clearly established; (3) the *essence* of each trait can be discovered; (4) traits or trait complexes can be ascribed to *historical peoples* who lived in bounded territories, which they occupied to the near exclusion of their neighbours; and (5) the *persistence or disappearance* of any trait or people determined.

1) Aboriginal Culture as a Collection of "Integral Practices" or Traits

The problem with the Supreme Court's conceptualization is that every aspect of its model has been the subject of lengthy and, in most cases, unresolved scholarly debate. For example, the requirement that rights can be derived only from "integral (culturally defining) traditional practices" implies that Aboriginal cultures were fundamentally different from those of European newcomers. While this is no doubt the case, the problem is that, since the birth of their discipline in the 19th century, anthropologists have held very different opinions about what the nature of these differences were or are. Leading historians of anthropology have noted that their field of scholarship initially was conceived of as the study of the "primitive."[35] In other words, "Native others" were thought to be culturally less advanced than Westerners, particularly in terms of their political and economic development. Although the search for the "primitive" has long ceased to be fashionable, echoes of it remain in ethnohistory debates about whether Aboriginal people were more spiritual and less materialistic than Westerners; about whether Aboriginal people engaged in external exchange primarily for ceremonial or political reasons rather than for economic gain[36]; and about whether all Aboriginal people had well-articulated land ownership schemes before Europeans arrived.[37] These are all sensitive issues in rights litigation.

35 Adam Kuper, *The Invention of Primitive Society: Transformations of an Illusion* (London: Routledge, 1988) at 1. Kuper notes that the idea emerged in the 1860s and 1870s, and through various transformations, remains with us today. This persistence is the subject of his book.

36 In economic history and economic anthropology, this is referred to as the "formalist" or "substantivist" controversy. See A.J. Ray & D.B. Freeman, *Give Us Good Measure* (Toronto: University of Toronto Press, 1978).

37 Adrian Tanner, "Who Owns the Beaver?" is an example. "Who Owns the Beaver? A Study of Northern Algonquian Land Tenure Reconsidered" (1986) 28 Anthropologica 7.

The Supreme Court's supposition that "integral," or culturally defining, traditional practices can be readily separated from other traditions for study and the determination of rights raises a host of other old issues. Essentially, it calls for a return to a cultural element approach, a perspective that held sway during the early 20th century. Anthropologists abandoned this outlook long ago, opting instead for more holistic perspectives that treat cultures as integrated and dynamic systems that amount to more than the sums of their components. The idea that certain practices can be defined as being more integral, or culturally defining, than others is even more problematic. Scholars have long recognized that the cultural elements researchers identify mostly reflect their theoretical dispositions and ideas about how the *Native other* is to be defined and cultures classified. One key area of cleavage has been over whether one should emphasize materialistic dimensions or ceremonial/spiritual aspects. Experts drew this old debate into the hearing rooms of the USICC in the United States in the early 1950s, and it is still with us.[38] Because early (pre-claims era) anthropology emphasized ceremonial, religious, and mythical aspects of Aboriginal culture,[39] First Nations often have to confront the old ethnographical literature when they assert Aboriginal and treaty commercial hunting and fishing rights.

Another weakness of the old cultural element approach was that definitions of the scope of a trait were arbitrary and depended on whether the researcher was a "splitter" or a "lumper." For example, should salmon fishing be regarded as a trait or included as a component of the trait of fishing? Issues of this type now are the subject of litigation under the regime that the Supreme Court has established. *Powley*[40] is a good example; I appeared as an expert witness for Steve and Roddy Powley. At trial, I was aggressively cross-examined on the question of whether Métis hunting rights should be determined on a species-by-species basis

38 In the California USICC claims, the case pitted the utilitarian cultural ecology approach against that of the culture area anthropologists. The former stressed the importance of subsistence land use and the latter argued that all uses (economic, ceremonial, and spiritual) were significant. See A.J. Ray, "Kroeber and the California Claims," above note 19.

39 *Ibid.*

40 Above note 16.

(the Crown's position) or defined more broadly as an aspect of the right to make a livelihood from the land (my position).

Undoubtedly, the most controversial aspect of defining the scope of Aboriginal livelihood practices concerns the question of whether these customs included a commercial component. This is often an issue in treaty rights claims. I addressed this question in the first claims case in which I was involved, *Horseman v. Regina*. This case dealt with Treaty 8 hunting rights. I argued that commercial and subsistence practices were inseparable in 1899–1900 when the Northern Alberta[41] Cree signed the treaty. I cited the example of beaver, which was the staple commodity of the pre-Confederation fur trade. Aboriginal people ate the meat, used and sold castorum and the beaver pelt. With the proceeds, they purchased their hunting and trapping outfits.[42] Similar questions about the scope of livelihood practices arise with respect to West Coast fishing rights cases.[43]

In my opinion, Métis claimants pose particular challenges for the "integral trait" approach to rights determination. As the Court acknowledged in *Van der Peet*,[44] Métis communities emerged after contact due to the melding together of Euro-Canadian and local Aboriginal cultural traditions. This reality raises a fundamental question: Can there be any integral cultural practices — perhaps the Mitchif language for some groups — that defines these people (are unique to them), or does their cultural distinctiveness arise from the way they combine these dual traditions? In the economic sphere, for instance, most historic Métis communities had mixed economies that combined making a livelihood off the land through hunting, fishing, trapping, and collecting for commercial and subsistence purposes, with permanent or seasonal wage labour, small-scale farming for commercial and subsistence purposes, and various types of entrepreneurial activities, most notably fur trading and

41 At the time it was part of the North-West Territory.

42 A.J. Ray, "Economy of the Peace River, 1870–1930" (Prepared in 1985 for the Alberta Indian Federation for use in *Regina v. Horseman*. Subsequently, this article was published as A. J. Ray, "Commentary on the Economic History of the Treaty 8 Area" (1995) 10 Native Studies Review 169–95.

43 For example, traditionally Aboriginal people in this region harvested salmon for ceremonial, exchange, and subsistence purposes.

44 Above note 25.

operating transportation services. They were opportunistic economies, or economies where the relative importance of each sector to the whole, and of subsistence to commercially oriented activities, varied regionally according to local ecological circumstances and temporally, in reaction to fish and wildlife population cycles and local markets. Therefore, one cannot determine whether a practice was integral based on a single snapshot in time, or even several of them.

2) An Identifiable Organized Society Occupying a Distinctive Territory

The notion that a claimant's ancestors had to have been members of an identifiable organized society that exclusively used and occupied a distinct territory appears to be an artifact of Lockean-based property theory, American jurisprudence, and the *United States Indian Claims Commission Act* of 1946.[45] Key elements of this notion raise questions about Aboriginal political organization and land tenure practices, particularly the scholarly meanings of such basic terms as *band*, *tribe*, and *nation*; the problems of identifying autonomous groups in documentary records; and searching for evidence that establishes or challenges the existence of territorial boundaries. Ethnohistorians deliberated all of these issues in USICC hearings for almost thirty years. The debate was especially heated in the 1950s, the first decade when cases came before the Commission. In 1955, Kroeber noted two problems associated with using political anthropology terminology in claims cases. First, anthropologists did not use their terms with the degree of consistency that the law required. Second, and more troublesome, some of the terminology biased the presentation of evidence before the USICC. He noted, for instance, that the term *band* implied a nomadic existence and a lower level of socio-political organization than *tribe*. For this reason he proposed that the term *tribelet* be applied to the autonomous land-owning groups of California. Kroeber noted that the latter groups were smaller in size than tribes.[46] He feared

45 Above note 21.

46 Arthur J. Ray, "Constructing and Reconstructing Native History: A Comparative Look at the Impact of Aboriginal and Treaty Rights Claims in North America and Australia" (2005) 16 Native Studies Review 15 at 21. It should be mentioned that the academy never adopted Kroeber's concept.

that if they were referred to as bands, it would predispose the Commission to think of them as having been nomadic and lacking strong notions of territoriality.

The Mid-Western treaty cases that came before the USICC in the 1950s raised other issues about using anthropological models to organize and present evidence in claims cases. In these cases, it became clear that the most basic and persistent of all North American anthropological classification schemes — the culture area approach — filtered information in ways that could affect claims outcomes. In some culture areas, such as that of the Eastern Woodlands, the assumption was that Indians were not nomadic, especially those engaged in horticulture, and that they had well-developed and bounded tenure systems. This was also true of the Southeast culture area. The Subarctic, on the other hand, was regarded as the region of band societies, and the Plains region was considered to have been the domain of nomadic buffalo hunters. In other words, the culture area model implied, among other things, that different regions represented different levels of cultural development and land tenure regimes.[47]

The issues that arose fifty years ago because of the linkage of anthropological terminology with evolutionary notions remain a problem for First Nations litigants in Canada, as the *Van der Peet*[48] case illustrates. It is also likely to surface in future Métis cases because most of the scholarly literature about the Métis is cast in evolutionary perspectives. The common thesis is that the Métis were a people who had one foot in the primitive world of hunter-gatherers and the other in the realm of mercantile capitalism, which was associated with the pre-industrial fur trade. It is widely assumed that Métis communities did not form where conditions were unfavorable for these worlds to mesh; it is also commonly supposed that with the passage of the mercantile age, those communities that had formed dissolved in the latter half of the 19th century.[49]

47 I discussed this in Arthur J. Ray, "Anthropology, History and Aboriginal Rights: Politics and the Rise of Ethnohistory in North America in the 1950s" in Arif Derlik, ed., *From Colonialism to Globalism: Changing Times, Changing Spaces, and Our Ways of Knowing* (Savage, MD: Rowman & Littlefield, forthcoming).

48 Above note 25.

49 A.J. Ray, "Métis Economic Communities and Settlements in the 19th Century" (July 2005) [Unpublished Report for Métis National Council].

Métis communities pose other very difficult challenges for the courts' perception of Aboriginal society as it was expressed in the *Baker Lake* test. *Powley* established that Métis rights had to be linked to specific Métis communities, without defining the nature or limits of the latter. Research makes it clear that no Métis physical settlements were (are) sustained solely by the economic activities that took place within their built-up areas (on-site wage labour, gathering, farming, domestic work, and so on). Rather, community members engaged in spatially extensive activities, such as collecting, fishing, hunting, trapping, trading, and transportation work, which complemented activities based in the settlement. Métis commonly established seasonal out-camps to conduct these extra-settlement livelihood practices. Consequently, communities were spatially dispersed genealogical, sociological, and economic entities anchored at sites where families maintained households. Frequently, these regional communities overlapped one another and the territories of the local First Nations.[50]

3) Cultural Continuity

Although the doctrine of continuity was intended to quash the wrong-headed legal theory that Aboriginal rights could only be derived from practices that had survived in their pure, pre-contact form,[51] the continuity notion remains highly problematic. This doctrine still conceptualizes the issue of rights determination in non-Western/Western terms, which leaves claimants vulnerable to having the courts conclude that their aboriginality has been, to use the phrase of the High Court of Australia,

50 The scholarly literature on this aspect of the Métis offers another example where the scholarly literature likely will be problematic for the litigation of Métis rights. Academics have not used the terms *settlement* and *community* with any consistency. Sometimes, they use the two words to refer to physical places, where Métis lived for extended periods and built permanent structures on the land; at other times, they use them to describe local social groups, which were comprised of related Métis families that interacted with each other enough to have developed a sense of cohesiveness. Ray, "Métis Economic Communities and Settlements in the 19th Century," *ibid.*

51 This is the so-called "frozen rights doctrine."

washed away by the "tide of history."[52] It also leads claims researchers and the courts back to all of the old disagreements mentioned above, and it engages other long-standing ethnohistorical debates about how to study cultural change in post-contact Aboriginal societies. In particular, it raises two related questions that have engaged scholars for many years: Did the key catalysts for change originate inside or outside of Aboriginal cultures? Were changes superficial or fundamental?[53] There are extensive literatures that debate these broad topics from the perspectives of continuity and change, acculturation, assimilation, diffusion, authenticity versus the invention of tradition, migration, and the role of Aboriginal agency. All of these approaches have been and remain the subject of divided opinions.

The continuity doctrine raises another ongoing controversy about how Aboriginal history should be periodized. It is a crucial question because chronologies are based on key Western notions about Aboriginal history. For many years it was common practice for scholars to divide their chronologies into three basic units: the Prehistoric, the Protohistoric, and the Historic periods. This scheme, derived from archeology, was intended to reflect two primary considerations: first, the intensity of Native–European contact and the disruptions that resulted from it; second, the absence or presence of documentary sources to facilitate the study of those processes. The basic premise, of course, was

52 In this case, the trial judge, Olney J. of the Federal Court of Australia, ruled:

> The evidence does not support a finding that the descendants of the original inhabitants of the claimed land have occupied the land in the relevant sense since 1788 nor that they have continued to observe and acknowledge, throughout that period, the traditional laws and customs in relation to land of their forbears. The facts in this case lead inevitably to the conclusion that before the end of the 19th century the ancestors through whom the claimants claim title had ceased to occupy their traditional lands in accordance with their traditional laws and customs. The tide of history has indeed washed away any real acknowledgement of their traditional laws and any real observance of their traditional customs.

The High Court upheld Olney J.'s decision in *Members of the Yorta Yorta Aboriginal Community v. Victoria*, [2002] HCA 58 at para. 107, Online: www.austlii.edu.au/au/cases/cth/HCA/2002/58.html (accessed 18 January 2006).

53 The latter issue, of course, also engaged the debate about how the *Native other* was to be defined.

that Aboriginal cultures had been largely static before European contact. For most Aboriginal peoples, contact influences initially came indirectly (the Protohistoric period), primarily as a consequence of the diffusion of European goods through inter-tribal trade and demographic changes caused by epidemics, migration, and inter-group warfare. European knowledge and writing about these events was based on second-hand reports, or hearsay, that the newcomers received from their Native allies and trading partners. The Historic period, beginning with the arrival of Europeans, supposedly marks the time when the rate of cultural change accelerated. It is also the time these newcomers began writing eyewitness accounts of their interactions with Aboriginal people.[54]

For two main reasons, Native people have long objected to this framework. First, it suggests that they were without history and that their cultures were static before Europeans arrived.[55] Second, it is a Eurocentric perception of their history that does not take into account varied Aboriginal historical traditions. As a partial concession to their objections, it has become a common practice to use the terms *Pre-Contact*, *Proto-Contact*, and *Contact*, but this modification does not address Aboriginal concerns in a fundamental way. These traditional chronologies were used in *Victor Buffalo*[56] and clearly had a major impact on the outcome.

The problem of developing appropriate chronological frameworks is complicated further by the fact that ethnohistorical experts must relate their chronologies to those that the courts are developing. In litigation, the rarefied dates that researchers must consider are the times when contact, effective sovereignty, and treaty signing took place. The courts regard contact as the benchmark time when interaction with Europeans led Aboriginal people to adopt some of their practices that are not eligible for protection as Aboriginal rights. (Hereinafter, I will refer to this time as "effective contact.") As the above discussion makes clear, determining the date of effective contact for many areas of Canada is not simple: it cannot be treated as one event that had an impact on all spheres of an Aboriginal culture equally. Courts do not consider the fact that a given Aboriginal

54 In effect, this time also marks the beginning of the erasure of Aboriginal oral histories.

55 This issue is explored by Eric Wolf, *Europe and the People without History* (Berkeley: University of California Press, 1982).

56 Above note 2.

people might have experienced effective contact at various times depending on the sphere of culture. The date when effective sovereignty was established locally is equally difficult to determine, especially if the courts make an honest effort to accommodate Aboriginal perspectives.

Ethnohistorical experts face a further complication when orienting their research to the law's periodization scheme: the dates of effective contact and Crown sovereignty are often among the findings of "fact" that the court must make based on the evidence presented at trial. Ethnohistorical experts are often asked to present data that helps the court decide when these events happened, while providing a snapshot of a claimant group's ancestral culture that is temporally broad enough in scope to bracket whatever datelines are selected. In *Delgamuukw*,[57] for example, at trial it was uncertain how long after the arrival of Russian fur traders in Alaska (late 18th century) and Captain James Cook on Vancouver Island (1778) that culture-transforming contact began. In the eyes of the law, it also was unknown when Britain/British Columbia established effective sovereignty in Gitxsan-Wet'suet'en territory.[58] Similar difficulties arose in *Powley*.[59] I argued that Métis communities began forming in the upper Great Lakes area sometime after the establishment of the earliest French trading posts in the area in the late 16th century; I also posited that effective British sovereignty was probably established after the merger of the Hudson's Bay Company and the North West Company in 1821,[60] and certainly with the signing of the Robinson treaties in 1850. In Métis cases, the date of effective sovereignty is especially critical because local communities must have been established by that date to validate their claim.

At trial in *Victor Buffalo*, the possible dates for the commencement of effective contact for the Plains Cree ancestors of the Samson Cree that experts advanced ranged from mid-17th century to the late 18th century. Justice Teitelbaum selected 1670, the year the Hudson's Bay Company was founded, as the date. In creating this "fact" for the purposes of the law, Teitelbaum J. stated:

57 Above note 15.

58 The court determined that it was 1846, the time of the Oregon Boundary Treaty.

59 Above note 16.

60 Until that time, the fur trade in the region was very competitive, and no outsiders had effective control.

> of course I do not presume that the practices, customs and traditions of the Cree changed immediately at this point. However, this date marks the beginning of a cultural transformation which saw the Cree become immersed in the European fur trade upon the arrival of the Hudson's Bay Company and the establishment of their post at York Factory.[61]

By picking this date, which predates the establishment of the company on the western shores of Hudson Bay by twelve years,[62] Teitelbaum J. placed the commencement of substantial changes to Plains Cree life due to the fur trade at least 100 years before sustained face-to-face interaction began locally. There is no convincing evidence or scholarly literature that supports this conclusion, however.[63]

The reason why the selection of this date for effective, or transformational, contact was so crucial in *Victor Buffalo* was that it related to a fundamental question at trial about whether it is likely that the ancestors of the Samson Cree had become familiar enough with Western practices and modes of thinking to fully understand the Euro-Canadian legal language and concepts that Treaty 6 (1876) contained. Ethnohistorical researchers have long debated this kind of issue, that is, when Aboriginal people adopt many of the material dimensions of European culture and engage in hybridized ceremonies with the newcomers, such as the gift-exchange ceremony, can it be assumed that they have made parallel changes in the ideological and intellectual spheres of their culture? Scholarly opinions remain divided on this issue, partly because they go to the heart of definitions of the *Native other*. By deciding that Plains Cree culture had undergone major transformations 200 years before treaty-signing as

61 See above note 2 at para. 550 for the rationale in choosing this date; it is at variance with the one used in *Powley*, above note 16. In the latter case, the period 1821–50 was selected because that was when trading company rivalries had largely ended (no European group had control before then). In 1670, the Hudson's Bay Company had no effective control, but Teitelbaum J. concluded that this year marked the beginning of significant cultural change resulting from European contact. He rationalized this by saying that the Supreme Court allowed a modification of the *Van der Peet* test for the Métis because they appeared after contact.

62 The company did not establish the precursor to York Factory, which was Fort Nelson, until 1682.

63 My early work, which emphasized cultural dynamics, would be included in this literature. Arthur J. Ray, *Indians in the Fur Trade* (1974; repr., Toronto: University of Toronto Press, 1998).

a consequence of the European fur trade, Teitelbaum J. warranted his assumption that the Cree who signed the treaty would have understood its terms as they had been explained (translated) at the time.

This case and the above discussion highlight the problems of meshing the chronological schemes of the academy with those of the courts. The former treat post-contact culture change as an ongoing and cumulative process, which is divisible into loosely defined periods, while the latter imagine the process as a series of singular and transformative events that led Indigenous people to acquire exotic cultural elements not eligible for legal protection and to understand, if not think like, the newcomers.

Another problem that bedevils the continuity notion relates to applying it. A key difficulty is that the lines of evidence claimants must rely upon are usually fragmented. Evidentiary gaps commonly are the result of accidental or deliberate destruction of documents,[64] the infrequency of historical observations, forced acculturation, and blatant discrimination. The latter two practices often forced Aboriginal individuals and groups to suppress their identity and engage in cultural practices clandestinely beyond the gaze of outside observers. The *Powley*[65] case demonstrated all of these problems. As I noted above, the case arose as a Métis moose-hunting issue. If the Crown had succeeded in keeping the court narrowly focused on that topic, the Powleys likely would not have succeeded at trial and on appeal for two reasons. First, after an era of over-hunting the moose at the turn of the 19th century, there was an extensive gap in moose hunting mid-century. Second, the severe discrimination Métis experienced after 1870 and 1885, coupled with provincial game laws, forced the local Métis to develop an underground economy in the late 19th century, when moose returned to the area.

64 Perhaps the most glaring example concerns the Chickahominay of Charles City, Virginia. The director of the Bureau of Vital Statistics for the state systematically expunged all references to Indians during the period from 1912 to 1946. His actions were reinforced by the state's *Racial Integrity Act of 1924* [in effect until 1967] and the eugenics movement, which was endorsed by leading state universities. The 1924 law forced people to be registered at birth as either "white or colored." Because they were erased from official records during this period, the Chickahominay were forced to seek recognition through a federal act. Testimony of Chief Adkin before the Senate Indian Affairs Committee, 11 May 2005, online: http://indian.senate.gov/2005hrgs/051105hrg/051105wit_list.htm (accessed 8 January 2005).

65 Above note 16.

Courts, commissions, and other adjudication bodies that deal with history-based rights claims have tried to address these evidentiary problems by being flexible about how they treat breaches in the record that demonstrate claimants' genealogical and cultural links to their ancestors. This accommodating approach can be highly controversial, however, as the Tribal Recognition program of the United States Bureau of Indian Affairs makes clear. The Bureau has established a seven-part test that Indian groups must meet to receive federal recognition as a tribe.[66] A central feature of this scheme is the requirement that claimants prove they have existed as a distinct group since early contact. Recognizing that Indians living in various parts of the United States have had varied post-contact histories, the Bureau has applied this measure flexibly, accepting the fact that some claimant groups have more complete historical records to draw on than others. For this reason, the Bureau has not specified when a gap is so great that a claim must be rejected. Critics of the recognition program[67] argue that because the Bureau accepts evidentiary gaps of different lengths, its scheme is arbitrary and not transparent.[68] It remains to be seen how the Canadian courts will deal with this problem.

C. LINES OF EVIDENCE: ORAL HISTORY

Evidentiary issues inevitably arose as the Supreme Court developed its generalized model of Aboriginal cultures and specified the tests claimants must meet. It came to the fore in *Delgamuukw*.[69] When ruling on the appeal in this case, the Supreme Court of Canada faulted the trial judge for not giving proper weight to the oral history testimony of the Gitxsan-Wet'suet'en elders. Apart from the fact that it requires a substantial relaxation of the hearsay evidence rule, the Court's judgment did not take into account the practical problems this line of evidence poses

---

66 Many benefits flow from such recognition. Most notably and controversially, these include the right to operate casinos in states where gaming is permitted.

67 These commonly include non-Indians who fear the negative economic consequences they will experience if particular claimants are successful, as well as tribes that already have made successful claims. Usually, the latter are tribes that have developed gaming operations and do not welcome new competitors.

68 Some of these critics have called for a codification of the Bureau's guidelines through legislation.

69 Above note 15.

in litigation. A key difficulty is that the veracity of this line of evidence is hotly disputed by parties to litigation, partly because it often juxtaposes Aboriginal (or insider) views of their histories, which I have often found are revisionist, against those of outsiders. In treaty rights cases, as happened in *Victor Buffalo*, these revisionist views of history challenge an older historiography about treaties that uncritically portrayed the government and its agents as acting largely in the best interests of the Aboriginal people.[70] Put simply, the older literature upheld the honour of the Crown, and the First Nations' oral histories challenge it.

There is also a practical reason why oral history evidence has become so contentious: the opposing sides in rights litigation do not have equal access to oral history informants before going to trial. Given the adversarial nature of the process, it is not surprising that Aboriginal claimants are unwilling to let the Crown undertake research in their communities if it will be used against them in court. As a result, the Crown is not normally able to review this evidence until Aboriginal claimants have filed their reports, or their elders and experts have testified in court. The adversarial aspect of the process is heightened because the Crown is limited to questioning the veracity of the oral evidence. The problem is, as Steward noted in the 1950s, elders and the field ethnologists whom Aboriginal claimants retain as their experts, are, to a considerable extent, *the* evidence.[71] This reality makes it very difficult to depersonalize the cross-examination of these experts in court. The inability of the Crown to undertake its own pre-trial oral history research also forces its experts to rely heavily on published ethnographic studies to develop counter-interpretations. As discussed above, all too often this literature is based on fieldwork that was undertaken long ago, for different purposes, and it

70 This issue is discussed at length in Arthur J. Ray, J.R. Miller, & Frank Tough, *Bounty and Benevolence: A History of Saskatchewan Treaties* (Montreal: McGill-Queen's University Press, 2000).

71 Steward remarked: "In using this secondary, or predigested evidence, both from the Indian informant and the historical source, the anthropologist redigests it according to his own point of view. He himself becomes 'evidence' in that his testimony is based to an incalculable extent upon his theory (explicit or implicit), his experiences among the people, his travels over the territory, his reading of the historic documents and his broader knowledge of primitive people." Julian Steward, "Theory and Application in a Social Science" (1955) 4 Ethnohistory 292 at 300.

was directed by or filtered through Eurocentric (colonial/evolutionary) interpretive frameworks.

These problems have meant that ever since *Delgamuukw*, battles over the weight that should be given to oral history vis-à-vis other lines of evidence have been an increasingly central feature of claims cases. Perhaps the best two recent examples are *Benoit*[72] and *Victor Buffalo*.[73] In the former case, the trial judge gave considerable weight to the plaintiff's oral evidence, but he was faulted for doing so on appeal. In the latter instance, the trial judge gave little weight to this line of evidence partly because he concluded that the Cree lacked a systematic way of establishing the veracity of their oral histories. Ironically, he held up the Gitxsan-Wet'suet'en as having the kind of formalized procedure for evaluating their oral traditions that is acceptable to the courts.[74]

It is clear that, unless oral evidence is given significant weight, many of Canada's Aboriginal people will not be able to marshal the historical evidence they need to succeed in litigation if continuity is a key dimension of the claim. This is because the surviving documentary record concerning Aboriginal communities reflects Canada's colonial past, especially its fur-trading past. For example, Hudson's Bay Company records are the critical documentary sources for a majority of Aboriginal claims throughout the north, the Prairies, and portions of British Columbia. The company's posts, and those of its rivals, were, in effect, Euro-Canadian observation stations. Their location and position on lakeshores and riverbanks of fur-trading transportation networks strongly determined the size and quality of the documentary record that traders generated. District headquarters, transportation junction points, and major trading posts often produced vast records. The First Nations and Métis communities that developed adjacent to such places have better prospects of collecting the documentary information they need for their claims than

72 Above note 14.

73 Above note 2. For discussions of this issue in these cases, see: Frank Tough, "Prof v. Prof in the Benoit Treaty Eight Tax Case: Some Thoughts on Academics as Expert Witnesses" (2004) 15 Native Studies Review 53–72, and Arthur J. Ray, "'History Wars' and Treaty Rights in Canada: The Case of *Victor Buffalo et al. v. Regina*" in A. Harmon, ed., *Text, Context and Meaning: Towards a New Understanding of Indian Treaties in the North American West* (Seattle: University of Washington Press, forthcoming).

74 *Victor Buffalo, ibid.* at paras. 456–57.

do those Aboriginal people who lived near small outposts on the extremities of the trading networks. For these more remote communities, oral histories likely will be the prominent, perhaps sole, line of evidence.

The *Powley* case[75] illustrates these kinds of evidentiary problems. In that case, game hunting practices were a key issue at trial. The problem faced was that few documentary records describe the economy of the community's hinterland, primarily because Sault Ste. Marie lay on the major fur-trading route that connected the Northwest with the St. Lawrence Valley. Most visitors arrived during the summer by canoe and boat; consequently, they did not witness inland life during the autumn, winter, and spring when and where hunting and trapping took place. Also, Sault Ste. Marie served mainly as a transportation centre. It therefore produced fewer records pertaining to hunting and trapping than most Hudson's Bay Company posts provide. Finally, the few trading establishments that were located in Sault Ste. Marie's hinterland were small outposts, situated on the northern perimeter.

D. CONCLUSION

In this paper I have focused on the interactive relationship between the courts and ethnohistorical scholarship in Canada during the post-*Calder* era. I have emphasized that litigation-oriented research is driven by the courts' conceptualizations of Aboriginal cultures. These notions are based, at least in part, on old colonial notions that call for outdated approaches to ethnohistorical scholarship. Countering this tendency towards conservative historical interpretations is the fact that the litigation process also destabilizes older understandings. Aboriginal claimants undertake new research and advance fresh perspectives to challenge the scholarship that helped legitimate colonialism. This fundamental tension frequently has led and continues to lead ethnohistorical experts to present trial judges with competing interpretations of local Aboriginal history.

Judges face a great challenge when they try to separate sound research, both old and new, and interpretations from pure advocacy. In weighing the evidence, the courts understandably have taken a conserv-

75 Above note 16.

ative approach for several reasons. When new research challenges extant scholarship, the courts commonly suspect it is mere advocacy. This worry is not unreasonable, given that claims research often has not been subject to prior review in the academy. Moreover, trial judges are often not given enough of the intellectual context of the evidence for them to make sound judgments about its appropriateness. Another explanation for a conservative reading of the evidence is that notwithstanding the Supreme Court's ruling in *Delgamuukw*,[76] Aboriginal oral histories and claims-generated field ethnology are often not given significant weight. The fact that the latter ruling has intensified the battles over the veracity of this line of evidence partially explains this. Indeed, there are now experts who specialize in challenging oral history evidence.

Finally, and perhaps most important, radical new interpretations that overturn the scholarship which legitimated colonization often suggest disruptive remedies; these are upsetting to the economic situation, which is a legacy of colonialism. All of these considerations raise the question about whether ethnohistory in the service of litigation can advance Aboriginal rights to any significant extent or merely help legitimate the current order by altering its minor aspects when remedies do not adversely affect the interests of non-Aboriginal people in significant ways. Certainly, Métis claims will raise this issue because the Métis have been Canada's forgotten people.

76 Above note 15.

‹ 2 ›

Defining the "Métis" of Canada: A Principled Approach to Crown–Aboriginal Relations

PAUL L.A.H. CHARTRAND

A. OUTLINE

1) Object and Subject Matter

This chapter examines the current judicial and political attempts to define the *Métis people* of Canada. Finding these attempts inadequate, it then proposes an alternative approach within which the issue of definition becomes a workable aspect of new Crown–Métis relations. The chapter aims to contribute to the identification of the elements of a new approach to both constitutional and policy development in Crown relations not only with the Métis people, but with all the Aboriginal peoples of Canada whose rights are recognized and affirmed in the law of the Constitution.

An important caveat is required. The analysis and conclusions are tentative, due not only to the limitations of scope and length of a chapter in a book, but also to the relatively immature doctrinal development on the subject. In some cases, necessity has led to the substitution of assertion for argument. The object is to identify a plausible approach for discussion and debate.

The complex subject-matter of this chapter includes both law and policy. It invites a consideration of basic questions that emerge from a historic process where former political relations between the Crown and Aboriginal peoples have now turned primarily into constitutional and legal relations, and the political relations have, by and large, succumbed to these changes.

The historic political relations between the Crown and the Métis people in Western Canada are well known. After the military and political subjugation of the Métis in the late 19th century, a new era of political and constitutional reform in Canada resulted in the constitutional recognition and affirmation of the rights of all Aboriginal peoples, including the Métis, in the *Constitution Act, 1982*. By this time, federal policy and legislation, largely based on the anachronistic and illegitimate recognition policies of the 1876 *Indian Act*, had substantially abandoned recognition of the Métis and their rights. Accordingly, Crown–Métis relations fail to reflect the new constitutional values, principles, and structures that now bind the three branches of government in their relations with the Métis people. The new values and principles require the Crown to recognize, respect, and protect the interests and rights of the Aboriginal peoples. This chapter identifies principles to guide just and practical Crown–Métis relations, within which the Métis people will be identified.

2) Method

The objectives of the chapter, which aim at proposing a basis for Crown–Métis relations that respects the Crown's constitutional obligations, cannot be met with legal or constitutional analysis alone. Canada's obligations engage all three branches of government: executive, legislative, and judicial. The legitimate and proper role of each branch of government is necessarily at issue, something that raises a fundamental question: What standards are to guide the search for appropriate Crown–Métis relations that respect the Crown's constitutional status and obligations?

A comparative approach is adopted. This approach identifies principles from law, policy, and legislation that were applied elsewhere and to other people, and tests their application to the case of Aboriginal peoples. The comparative approach is based on the proposition that Aboriginal peoples, and specifically Métis people, should be treated in the same way as those who are respected. What is thought to be good for those who are respected, whether out of fear or of love, ought also to be good for the Métis people.

Within the limits of this paper, it is not possible to develop each point and argument — that will have to be left to another day. The paper's more modest goal is to briefly identify the conclusions and, as much as possible, identify or outline the arguments and the authorities from which they are drawn.

3) Conclusions

1. Three fundamental elements of a national policy to establish and maintain appropriate Crown–Métis relations are drawn from the principles that are in the following analysis:

    a) The Crown must enter into political relations with Métis representatives, with a view to negotiate and reach agreement on the recognition and protection of the rights of the Métis people.
    b) Legal protection must be provided for the agreements that result from these negotiations by enacting appropriate legislation; legislation is also necessary to implement the agreements.
    c) Special adjudicative bodies with authority to deal with disputes arising from the legislated agreements must be established.

2. The definition of *Métis* would emerge from the negotiations and agreements, and would be given effective protection by legislation.
3. It is essential to note that the applicable principles require that the same approach apply to *all* Aboriginal peoples. In order to make effective the constitutional recognition and affirmation of the rights of all Aboriginal peoples in the *Constitution Act, 1982*, Canada must abandon the *Indian Act* scheme of recognition. What is required by the law of the Constitution which binds governments is a new recognition scheme that respects and protects the rights of all the Aboriginal peoples, in accordance with the applicable constitutional standards.

B. REVIEW OF THE MEMBERSHIP CODES OF MÉTIS POLITICAL REPRESENTATIVE ORGANIZATIONS

A critical review has been made of the criteria for membership in political organizations that represent the Métis for various purposes, particularly in their relations with the federal and provincial governments.[1]

---

1 Not many useful published works concerning these organizations, their membership, and their roles exist. For a dated, but useful anthropological perspective, see

The particular focus was on the approach to the definition of the Métis people in the membership codes. This membership code approach has been critically compared to the approach required to define the Métis for constitutional purposes, and particularly for the purposes of section 35(2) of the *Constitution Act, 1982*.[2] The examination of these approaches to the definition of the Métis advances the purposes of this chapter by identifying particular difficulties in the quest for definitions. Furthermore, a critical analysis will be useful because it has been argued that the definition adopted by the Métis National Council (MNC) ought to be recognized and respected by the government of Canada as reflective of the meaning of section 35(2).[3]

The review is included as an appendix to this chapter. It is sufficient in this section to offer the general comments and conclusions that emerge from the analysis.

1) Observations and Conclusions

1. The two national organizations that purport to represent the Métis people politically have not tried to agree on a definition of *Métis*. Only the MNC has adopted a definition for its purposes.
2. The MNC membership code is imprecise and circular. The primary purpose revealed by its text and structure is to identify individuals who may be eligible for membership in the organization, and its code cannot by itself provide a model for identifying the rights-bearing people and its constituent communities within the meaning of section 35 of the *Constitution Act, 1982*.[4]

Joe Sawchuk, *The Métis of Manitoba: Reformulation of an Ethnic Identity* (Toronto: P. Martin Associates, 1978).

2 Part II of the *Constitution Act, 1982*, being Schedule B to the *Canada Act 1982* (U.K.), 1982, c. 11, is headed "Rights of the Aboriginal Peoples of Canada." Section 35(1), the first provision under the heading, provides: "The existing aboriginal and treaty rights of the aboriginal peoples of Canada are hereby recognized and affirmed." Section 35(2) provides: "In this Act, 'aboriginal peoples of Canada' includes the Indian, Inuit, and Métis peoples of Canada."

3 J. Madden, J. Graham, & J. Wilson, "Exploring Options for Métis Governance in the 21st Century" (September 2005), online: www.iog.ca/publications/2005_metis_gov.pdf (accessed 29 July 2006).

4 Above note 2. The political organizations provide definitions.

3. The MNC has attempted for many years to generate an agreement among all its provincial constituents to adopt a national definition of *Métis* for its members. The provincial codes do not now exactly mirror the MNC definition, except for that of the Métis Nation of Ontario (MNO). It may reasonably be concluded that securing agreement among the Métis regarding their own self-definition is a difficult political challenge.
4. A formidable challenge faced by any Canadian Aboriginal community seeking political unity within itself is the power of the provinces. It is evident that the constituents of the MNC have been persuaded to organize themselves along provincial boundaries. Some of them have gone so far as to assume names that identify them as distinct "nations" that occupy provincial boundaries, regardless of the geographic extent of traditional homelands.

This preference for organization along provincial lines can be explained as a practical step for a number of reasons. First, the organizations are funded by governments and rely in part on funds from the provincial treasuries. Second, successive federal governments have persistently taken the political stance that, notwithstanding the recognition of the Métis as an Aboriginal people in section 35, the Métis people are not included within the exclusive federal heads of power over "Indians, and Lands reserved for the Indians" in the *Constitution Act, 1867*.[5] Federal government representatives assert that the Métis must deal with the provinces, and the provinces have generally responded by treating the Métis *qua* provincial residents, and not *qua* historic nations with distinct constitutional status. The federal political stance on this issue is not constitutionally defensible. However, that matters little because ultimately, political power shapes the substance of constitutional power and authority. Métis representatives in the provinces have been forced to deal with provincial governments as provincial residents and not as federal entities whose primary constitutional relationship is with the federal Crown.

This situation reflects the fact that in Canada, provincial power, by and large, trumps Aboriginal and treaty rights. The power of provinces in the Canadian federal system provides a formidable challenge

5 (U.K.), 30 & 31 Vict., c. 3, reprinted in R.S.C. 1985, App. II, No. 5.

to the design of any legal and policy regime that could provide a constitutionally defensible basis for Crown–Métis relations.

5. Similarly, the federal distribution of legislative powers between the federal and provincial governments is a formidable challenge to implementing an effective and valid scheme to recognize, respect, and protect the interests and rights of the Aboriginal peoples in Canada.

   In the *Powley*[6] case, the Court commented on the lack of a uniform definition among Métis organizations, stating that "[a]s Métis communities continue to organize themselves more formally and to assert their constitutional rights, it is imperative that membership requirements become more standardized so that legitimate rights-holders can be identified."[7] In the next section, the approach of the Court is reviewed to see if the judges' approach might provide a useful foundation for official recognition in the context of just and workable Crown–Métis relations.

C. JUDICIAL DEFINITION OF THE MÉTIS PEOPLE

1) Introduction

Aboriginal rights were affirmed and recognized by the Constitution in 1982. Neither the substantive rights nor the Aboriginal peoples that have them were identified or defined in the constitutional text. The cases in which the Court began to develop its doctrine of Aboriginal rights involved mostly Indian "bands" within the meaning of the *Indian Act*,[8] or other Indian groups that have long been officially recognized by federal legislation and policy. In these cases, the Court was not asked and did not undertake to define the rights-bearing groups. Presumably, the government was not inclined to challenge its own recognition laws and policies in its own courts. A second group recognized in the *Constitution Act, 1982*,[9] the Inuit, has been recognized mainly by executive action and policy, although the Inuit are not included in the federal *Indian Act*[10] that provides the legal basis for Indian policy.

6 [2003] 2 S.C.R. 207 [*Powley*].

7 *Ibid.* at para. 29.

8 R.S.C. 1985, c. I-5 [*Indian Act*].

9 Above note 2.

10 Above note 8.

In the Indian cases, it does not appear to have been argued, and it certainly was not decided, that each Indian rights-bearing community must demonstrate that it constituted a part or all of an Indian "people." Neither were the litigants required to prove they were not Inuit people or Métis people. The Court developed tests for proof of Aboriginal rights and began to describe the contents of the rights, without regard to the particular identity of the Aboriginal party in the rights dispute at issue.

That approach changed in the *Powley*[11] case where the Court was asked to decide the claims of two individuals who asserted membership in a rights-bearing Métis community.[12]

2) The *Powley* Definition

It is unnecessary to review the facts and decision of this case, which has been critically reviewed elsewhere and which will be well known to most readers.[13] For present purposes, it may be recalled that the facts related to the city of Sault Ste. Marie, in Ontario, which is far from the western prairie and northern rivers and lakes region where Crown–Métis relations is a well-known part of Canadian history. A case from that region would have provided a less challenging set of facts upon which to decide a case of first impression.

11 Above note 6.

12 It is remarkable, given the collective nature of Aboriginal rights — a point decided by the Court itself — that the Court has, from the beginning, accepted that individuals have the status, standing, and competence to prove the existence of the collective rights of the community to which they belong. In the result, individual members of Aboriginal rights-bearing communities are required to prove, not their own personal rights, but the rights of their community. The Court has not found it necessary to require the participation of the community in this exercise, or to afford the community the requisite status and standing in court to prove its own rights

13 Andrea Horton & Christine Mohr, "*R. v. Powley*: Dodging *Van der Peet* to Recognize Métis Rights" (2005) 30 Queen's L.J. 772–824 ["Dodging *Van der Peet*"]. See also the review of the case at the Ontario Court of Appeal level in Paul L.A.H. Chartrand, "The Hard Case of Defining 'the Métis People" and Their Rights: A Comment on *R. v. Powley*" (2003) 12 Const. Forum Const. 84, since most of the issues considered there were not addressed by the Supreme Court. See also Paul L.A.H. Chartrand, ed., *Who Are Canada's Aboriginal Peoples: Recognition, Definition and Jurisdiction* (Saskatoon: Purich, 2002).

The Court decided that the definition of the individual members of a Métis community is to be determined by applying a three-pronged test consisting of self-identification, ancestral connection, and community acceptance.

The Court was able to arrive at a definition of individual Métis persons without deciding how to identify the Métis people in section 35. It focused instead on the small community that was thought to have the local or "site-specific" right at issue, that of hunting for food. The Court, in essence, presumed that this little community belonged to the Métis people, a task assisted by the circular character of its treatment of the question of defining a human group. As for the definition of the little community, the Court stated that it was "a group of Métis with a distinctive collective identity, living together in the same geographic area and sharing a common way of life."[14] The vagueness of the criteria and the tenuous evidence that led to the finding of a relevant community in this case has been the subject of critical commentary.[15]

3) Right of Self-Definition of the People Usurped

The *Powley*[16] decision involved an unprecedented and unabashed arrogation of political power to itself by the Court, which in effect emphatically rejected the legitimacy of the Métis people's right to define itself. Opening an era of political control by appointed judicial public servants over the political representatives of the Métis people, who are now the new wards of the Court, the judges stated, in a *per incuriam* decision:[17]

---

14 *Powley*, above note 6 at para. 12. The circularity is evident in this statement, which purports to define a Métis community by using the idea of "Métis," which is not defined.

15 "Dodging *Van der Peet*," above note 13, particularly at 810.

16 *Powley*, above note 6.

17 The decision was given *per incuriam* on the basis that the common-law authorities that bind the Court were not applied. On this issue, see the text accompanying note 59, below in this chapter. On the application of the *per incuriam* test, see *Huddersfield Police Authority v. Watson*, [1947] 2 All E.R. 193 (K.B.D.), *Young v. Bristol Aeroplane Co.*, [1944] K.B. 718 (C.A.), *Morelle, Ltd. v. Wakeling*, [1955] 1 All E.R. 708 (C.A.); *Re Hardy Trusts*, [1955] 5 D.L.R. 10 (Ont. C.A.), *Farrell v. Alexander*, [1976] 1 All E.R. 129 (H.L.), *Greater Montreal Protestant School Board v. Quebec (Attorney General)*, [1989] 2 S.C.R. 167, *British Columbia (Attorney General) v. Canada (Attorney General)*, [1994] 2 S.C.R. 41. For decisions particular to Aboriginal people,

> ... no matter how a contemporary community defines membership, only those members with a demonstrable ancestral connection to the historic community can claim a s. 35 right. [18]

The Court failed to consider the right of self-definition of the Métis people itself, presuming instead to accord a right to every little community to decide who will have the constitutionally protected rights of a people. It arrogated to itself the right to define, as a matter of law, the identity of the members of a Métis rights-bearing community. It did so without deciding how an Aboriginal "people" in section 35 is to be identified, an issue that remains an open question in Canadian constitutional law.[19]

The issue of deciding how an Aboriginal "people" in section 35 is to be identified is better described as an issue of identification as opposed to a definition. Section 35 affirms the rights of peoples, but this alone does not mean that the judicial branch of government has a valid constitutional mandate to decide the identity of those peoples. Every good reason, including the precepts that emerge from the right of self-determination recognized by international law,[20] require that the identity of

---

see *R. v. George*, [1966] S.C.R. 267; *Canada (Minister of Indian Affairs and Northern Development) v. Ranville*, [1982] 2 S.C.R. 518; *R. v. Paul and Polchies* (1984), 58 N.B.R. (2d) 297 (Prov. Ct.); *British Columbia (Attorney General) v. Mount Currie Indian Band* (1991), 54 B.C.L.R. (2d) 156 (C.A.); *Tseshaht Indian Band v. British Columbia* (1992), 94 D.L.R. (4th) 97 (B.C.C.A.); and *R. v. Grumbo*, [1998] 3 C.N.L.R. 172 (Sask. C.A.).

18 *Powley*, above note 6 at para. 34. It may be argued that the Court only decided a test for determining the membership of Métis rights-bearing communities, and not a definition of the Métis people. This argument is shallow because a judicial determination of which individuals are entitled to belong to Métis communities with fundamental constitutional rights in Canada will inevitably affect the Métis people's own views on the matter of self-identity, particularly where the Métis people have little of the political power required to be able to overcome the Court's decision.

19 Brent Olthius, *The Constitution's Peoples: A Robust and Group-Centred Interpretation of the Constitution Act, 1982* (LL.M. Thesis, University of Victoria, 2005) [unpublished].

20 See Erica-Irene A. Daes, "Striving for Self-Determination for Indigenous Peoples" in Y.N. Kly & D. Kly, eds., *In Pursuit of the Right of Self-Determination: Collected Papers & Proceedings of the First International Conference on the Right to Self-Determination & the United Nations, Geneva 2000* (Atlanta, GA: Clarity Press, 2001)

the Aboriginal peoples in section 35 be decided as a political issue and not as a justiciable issue.[21]

Canada, unlike the United States, which has a mature doctrine of "political questions" that the Court will not decide, has yet to address the full implications of the fundamental constitutional changes worked by the 1982 constitutional amendments. While the new Constitution grants new roles to the Court, there seems to be little valid reason to conclude that the Court now has the power to decide each and every constitutional question under the guise of construing the text of the Constitution.

The identity of "the Métis people" in section 35 is a matter for discussion and agreement between the legitimate political representatives of the Métis people and the Crown's legitimate representatives on the other side — it is not a matter for the Court. Nor is it the responsibility of every little community that has that authority foisted upon it as a result of litigation by individuals whose immediate interest is to avoid penalties under provincial legislation, and in judicial proceedings in which the community is not required to participate.

Some issues of fundamental constitutional and political importance emerge from a situation where the membership of Aboriginal communities may be decided in litigation between the Crown and individuals. What is the proper and legitimate role of the lawyers and judges in making decisions about who belongs to a people with specially recognized constitutional rights? In the context of the present judicial approach, what is the justification for lawyers and judges to decide who belongs to particular little communities?

The current situation, where these issues of community membership are debated in courtrooms, presents a real dilemma which pits the interests of the community against the interests of litigants. In the *Laviolette*[22] case, for example, L identified himself to the Crown's representatives who

---

["Striving for Self-Determination"] and *Reference re Secession of Quebec*, [1998] 2 S.C.R. 217 [*Quebec Secession Reference*].

21 On justiciability see, generally, Lorne M. Sossin, *Boundaries of Judicial Review: The Law of Justiciability in Canada* (Scarborough, ON: Carswell, 1999). See also *Quebec Secession Reference*, *ibid.* at para. 31 where the Court discusses the concept of justiciability and concludes, in effect, that the Court will decide what it believes it ought to decide.

22 *R. v. Laviolette*, [2005] 3 C.N.L.R. 202 (Sask. Prov. Ct.) [*Laviolette*].

questioned him in the field, as a member of Flying Dust First Nation, an Indian band located in northern Saskatchewan. He resided there and was married into the community of Flying Dust. He was fishing with Flying Dust community members. These criteria would satisfy most reasonable observers that the man belonged to Flying Dust. However, as a result of the litigation where L was anxious to avoid the penalties of the law, the trial-level provincial court, following the tests laid down in *Powley*, decided that L was a member of the Green Lake Métis community. L did not reside in the Green Lake community; nevertheless, the judge assigned him to it because an ancestor had belonged to the community and he had relatives there at the time of the incident. To reach this decision, the judge defined the Green Lake community to include more than the actual community of residents.

4) Racist Criterion Condemned by the Royal Commission on Aboriginal Peoples Adopted by the Court

It is regrettable that the Court chose to adopt a racist standard for identifying members of Métis communities. It did this by deciding that only persons biologically descended from a Métis ancestor could belong to a Métis rights-bearing community and enjoy the benefit of membership.[23] The focus on personal antecedents, which is more appropriate to the identification of specimens for the purposes of animal husbandry, implies that, in the opinion of the judges on the Court, biological descent is more important than such factors as residence and family and community relations, an issue that is starkly demonstrated by the facts in the *Laviolette*[24] case, which purported to apply the *Powley*[25] definition.

In concluding that personal descent was essential to Métis definition, the Court took a view that contrasts sharply with that of the Royal Commission on Aboriginal Peoples (RCAP). In its final report, the royal commission argued that official state recognition of the Aboriginal peoples

---

23 *Powley*, above note 6 at para. 34. The Court did not apply that criterion to the "ancestor," who could belong to the community for reasons other than being descended from a community member. No explanation was given for the different treatment.

24 *Laviolette*, above note 22.

25 *Powley*, above note 6.

must not be based upon fictitious ideas of "race" and that "Aboriginal peoples are not impoverished racial minorities whose interests need to be served better by the Canadian state. They are political entities that, because of their treaties, the recognition of their rights in Canada's constitution, and the nature of their social and cultural cohesion, need to be recognized as nations, negotiated with as nations, and thereby empowered to implement their own solutions within a flexible Canadian federation."[26]

The reasoning and conclusions of the Court suggest that it believes a community is but the sum of its parts. This conception is an error. People acting as a community can accomplish much more than individuals acting in solitude. A community is more than the sum of its parts. It involves collective authority and dynamic social relations that do not exist within the individuals alone.

5) *Powley* Test Is Not Useful, Necessary, or Legitimate

Prof. Brian Slattery has demonstrated that the test in *Powley*[27] cannot be practically applied so as to distinguish between Indian and Métis communities.[28] Others have shown that it is impossible to arrive at a definition of the Métis people without at the same time deciding on a definition of the Indian people.[29] There is no good legal or policy reason to attach a label of "Métis" or "Indian" to an Aboriginal community in order to recognize, respect, and protect its constitutional rights. That label is an internal political matter and is not justiciable. In order to acquire official recognition for particular purposes, the representatives of the people can negotiate the issues of membership without the assistance of judges.

---

26 Canada, Royal Commission on Aboriginal Peoples, *Report of the Royal Commission on Aboriginal Peoples: Restructuring the Relationship*, vol. 2, part 2 (Ottawa: Minister of Supply and Services Canada, 1996) at 1016. [RCAP vol. 2].

27 *Powley*, above note 6.

28 Brian Slattery, Speaking Notes, "The Significance of the *Powley* Case" (19 December 2003) [unpublished, in the possession of the author] ["The Significance of the *Powley* Case"]. The opinion was delivered at a conference in Edmonton on that date.

29 John Giokas & Paul L.A.H. Chartrand, "Who Are the Métis? A Review of the Law and Policy Relating to Métis and 'Mixed-Blood' People in Canada" in Chartrand, ed., *Who Are Canada's Aboriginal Peoples*, above note 13.

6) No Constitutional Warrant to Create Distinct Tests for Proof of Métis Rights

Prof. Slattery has also argued convincingly that the judicial development of particular tests for proof of Métis rights, which are different from the tests for proof of the rights of other Aboriginal peoples, is not required or defensible on the basis of the applicable constitutional principles.[30] The law of Aboriginal rights ought to be developed on the basis of general tests that apply to all the Aboriginal peoples. There is no need to search for particular tests to apply to any one Aboriginal people.

7) The Relevant Date in the Test for Proof of Aboriginal Rights

The date for proof of Aboriginal rights is at the heart of the reason why the Court seemed to feel compelled to design a distinct test for proof of Métis Aboriginal rights. The Court had already established two distinct dates for proving Aboriginal rights and Aboriginal title, a subset of Aboriginal rights. In *Powley*[31] the Court applied the date of "effective control," which had in an earlier case been described by the Court as the correct way to describe the "contact date" test that had been developed in previous cases. The Court did not give any compelling reasons for these different tests, and commentators have suggested that in time, the Court may well settle on one test date for proof of all types of Aboriginal rights.[32] The dates adopted so far do not seem just or practical.

As will be explained below, it is not right to require proof of customs with origins that lie that far back in history. In comparison, the test for proof of custom at common law is easier and more just. Furthermore, the facts that must be proved relate to a concept — that of culture — which is not certain enough to operate as a legal test. Consider as a comparison that the culture of French-Canadians has been presumed as something worthy of protection without the need to prove elements of it as matters of fact or law. In clear contradiction, such proof is required of Aboriginal people who claim constitutional rights.

---

30 "The Significance of the *Powley* Case," above note 28.

31 *Powley*, above note 6.

32 "Dodging *Van der Peet*," above note 13 at 34. See also "The Significance of the *Powley* Case," above note 28.

It is tentatively suggested that the relevant date for proof of Aboriginal rights is the date at which the courts of law were brought "to every man's door," so that the protection of the law was made available to the Aboriginal people. This suggestion about the relevant date concept applies well-established constitutional principles. The Crown enters into a constitutional fiduciary relationship at a certain date, and when it does so, it undertakes to extend its protection to the Aboriginal people, who owe the Crown allegiance as the *quid pro quo* in this new relationship.[33] The courts — the courts of the Crown — have been established to protect the rights and interests of the Crown's subjects. Were this test for proof of Aboriginal rights to be adopted, then it would be sufficient for claimants to prove that they had Aboriginal rights; there would be no reason to assign a label such as "Métis," "Indian," or "Inuit" to the rights-bearing community.

8) "Culture" Not a Useful Concept in Developing Doctrine of Aboriginal Rights

In *Powley*[34] the Court said that the purpose of section 35 included the protection of the culture of the Métis people:

> The purpose and the promise of s.35 is to protect practices that were historically important features of these distinctive communities and that persist in the present day as integral elements of their Métis culture.[35]

It seems, however, that the concept of culture has an uncertain and indefinite content and accordingly cannot be an adequate basis for developing the doctrine of Aboriginal rights.

A legal test must be defined with the precision necessary for it to operate as a practical guide for those who have to apply it to particular facts. An examination of the concept of culture as developed and used by anthropologists is instructive. According to Michael Asch, a leading scholar and anthropologist with interests in Aboriginal rights issues:

---

33 Albert Peeling & Paul Chartrand, "Sovereignty, Liberty and the Legal Order of the 'Freeman' (Otipahemsu'uk): Towards a Constitutional Theory of Métis Self-Government" (2004) 67 Sask. L. Rev. 339. ["Sovereignty, Liberty and the Legal Order"].

34 *Powley*, above note 6.

35 *Ibid.* at para. 13.

> ... anthropology represents the primary approach developed in the western intellectual tradition to understand cultures other than one's own. It has developed its approach on the basis of over a century of purposive enquiry into the nature of culture ....[36]

If the concept of culture has a precise meaning, then, it can reasonably be expected to be found in the work of anthropologists. A classic study published in 1952 contained more than 164 definitions of culture. Many more have been developed since then. New ones are being proposed. No one definition has succeeded in gaining general acceptance among anthropologists. Some anthropologists contend that the concept is too ambiguous, broad, and contentious to be of any use and argue that academic discourse should abandon it.[37] For instance, it has been stated, "Once we locate the reality of society in historically changing, imperfectly bounded, multiple and branching social alignments ... the concept of fixed, unitary, and bounded culture must give way to a sense of the fluidity and permeability of cultural sets."[38]

9) Judicial Respect for the "Culture" of French-Canadians in Minority Rights Cases

Relying on the work of Vallance,[39] this section compares the approach taken by the Court in its use of the concept of culture in Aboriginal

---

36 Michael Asch, "Errors in *Delgamuukw*: An Anthropological Perspective" in Frank Cassidy, ed., *Aboriginal Title in British Columbia: Delgamuukw v. The Queen* (Lantzville, BC: Oolichan Books, 1992) 221 at 223. See also Michael Asch, "The Judicial Conceptualization of Culture after *Delgamuukw* and *Van der Peet*" (2000) 5 Rev. Const. Stud. 119–37 ["The Judicial Conceptualization"].

37 The following authorities are cited in the works by Vallance, below note 39: Adam Kuper, *Culture, the Anthropologists' Account* (Cambridge, MA: Harvard University Press, 1999); Fredrik Barth, "Rethinking the Object of Anthropology" (2001) 103 American Anthropologist 435–37; A.L. Kroeber *et al.*, *Race, Science and Politics*, rev. ed. (New York: Viking Press, 1945).

38 Eric Wolf, *Europe and the People without History* (Berkeley: University of California Press, 1982) at 387.

39 Neil Vallance, *The Use of the Term "Culture" by the Supreme Court of Canada: A Comparison of Aboriginal and Non-Aboriginal Cases since 1982* (M.A. Thesis, University of Victoria, 2003) [unpublished] [*Use of the Term "Culture"*]; Neil Vallance, "The Misuse of "Culture" by the Supreme Court of Canada" in Avigail Eisenberg, ed., *Diversity and Equality: The Changing Framework of Freedom in Canada* (Van-

rights cases with its approach in French-Canadian rights cases. Vallance searched about 2000 Supreme Court cases decided since 1982 for a judicial definition of "culture." He found 165 cases that contained 714 uses of the term *culture*. None contains a definition.[40]

The *Mahe*[41] case can serve to demonstrate the approach taken by the Court in relation to the concept of culture in French-Canadian language rights, and to exemplify how the approach differs from the Court's approach to culture in Aboriginal rights cases. In the *Mahe* case, the Court had to decide the meaning of section 23 of the *Charter*.[42] While section 23 makes no express reference to culture, it deals with French-language minority rights. Chief Justice Dickson explained why culture was relevant. The purpose of section 23 is "to preserve and promote the two official languages of Canada and their respective cultures."[43]

The Chief Justice did not explain what he meant by culture. He did not inquire into the content of French language culture. He presumed the existence of such a culture, and decided that it was worthy of constitutional and judicial recognition, respect, and protection. He did not ex-

---

couver: UBC Press, 2006) 97–113 ["Misuse of Culture"]. Vallance is an expert in both law and anthropology.

40 Vallance, *Use of the Term "Culture," ibid.*

41 *Mahe v. Alberta*, [1990] 1 S.C.R. 342 [*Mahe*].

42 Section 23 of the *Canadian Charter of Rights and Freedoms*, Part I of the *Constitution Act, 1982*, being Schedule B to the *Canada Act 1982* (U.K.), 1982, c. 11, provides:

> (1) Citizens of Canada (a) whose first language learned and still understood is that of the English or French linguistic minority population of the province in which they reside, or (b) who have received their primary school instruction in Canada in English or French and reside in a province where the language in which they received that instruction is the language of the English or French linguistic minority population of the province, have the right to have their children receive primary and secondary school instruction in that language in that province.
>
> (2) Citizens of Canada of whom any child has received or is receiving primary or secondary school instruction in English or French in Canada, have the right to have all their children receive primary and secondary school instruction in the same language.

43 *Mahe*, above note 41 at 362. It is remarkable that the languages of the two groups of Europeans who took the lands from the Indigenous peoples are officially promoted and protected, but not those of the Indigenous peoples. If the latter die, they die absolutely; if the former die, they live in their homelands.

plain the relationship between language and culture, which would have been helpful since language is not usually regarded as synonymous with culture, although it is undoubtedly a part of it.

10) "Culture" of Aboriginal Peoples Is Not Judicially Treated in the Same Way: Unequal Value and Respect?

In the *Van der Peet*[44] case, Lamer C.J. announced, without citing any relevant authority, a new test to determine what constitutes an Aboriginal right:

> . . . in order to be an aboriginal right an activity must be an element of a practice, custom or tradition integral to the distinctive culture of the aboriginal group claiming the right.[45]

Parenthetically, it is difficult to reconcile this test with the Court's characterization of Aboriginal rights as group or collective rights. Perhaps what the extract means is that an individual member of the rights-bearing group is acting in the enjoyment of the group right when the individual engages in an activity that is part of a practice, custom, or tradition of the group. As mentioned earlier, the Court's view seems to be predicated on the notion that the group is the sum of its parts and no more.

The case and the new test have been vigorously criticized elsewhere[46] and do not require elaboration for present purposes. It is sufficient to identify the test and to conclude that a concept that is being tossed away by social scientists because it is uselessly indefinite is not the best way to develop a new jurisprudence for the most fundamental rights of Aboriginal peoples.

In Aboriginal cases, the Court has viewed culture as a fact to be proved, whereas in French-Canadian minority rights cases, the Court has treated culture as a concept that does not require proof, but can be presumed as the basis for legal decisions. If the approach to the Court's

44 *R. v. Van der Peet*, [1996] 2 S.C.R. 507 [*Van der Peet*].

45 *Ibid*. at para. 46.

46 "The Judicial Conceptualization," above note 36; Russel L. Barsh & James Y. Henderson, "The Supreme Court's *Van Der Peet* Trilogy: Naive Imperialism and Ropes of Sand" (1997) 42 McGill L.J. 993; John Borrows, "The Trickster: Integral to a Distinctive Culture" (1997) 8 Const. Forum Const. 27.

use of the concept of culture in French language cases is good, then it ought to be good for Aboriginal rights cases, unless for good reason. There is no apparent reason for the different approaches. The Court has not explained the reasons for this difference. The Court has leaned on the idea that Aboriginal rights are of a unique kind, or *sui generis*. The Court's explanation is less than convincing, however. In one of its latest Aboriginal rights decisions, the Court has shown that it can retreat from the notion that Aboriginal rights are unique, requiring instead that they mirror English rights if they are to be worthy of judicial recognition.[47]

Vallance concludes, "by comparison of the cases . . . [we find] that the court uses the term [culture] in a manner that confers a benefit upon Canada's official language minorities and confers an unjust burden upon the First Nations of Canada."[48]

11) Test for Proof of Aboriginal Rights More Onerous than Common-Law Tests Applied in Britain

The conclusion reached by Vallance in respect to judicial treatment of culture in Canada applies to the differences between the cases on proof of Aboriginal rights in Canada, on the one hand, and the common-law cases that recognized the customs and practices of distinct British peoples, on the other hand.

The history of common-law recognition of the *lexi loci* [49] or customary laws of Celtic peoples, such as the Cornish people of Britain, shows that the common law developed a sophisticated set of rules for recognizing, respecting, and protecting local laws or customs.[50] At common law a

47 *R. v. Marshall; R. v. Bernard*, [2005] 2 S.C.R. 220. For a critical commentary, see Paul L.A.H. Chartrand, "*R. v Marshall; R. v. Bernard*: The Return of the Native" (2006) 55 U.N.B.L.J. 135.

48 "Misuse of Culture," above note 39 at 97.

49 See, particularly, Russel L. Barsh, "Indigenous Rights and the *Lex Loci* in British Imperial Law" in Kerry Wilkins, ed., *Advancing Aboriginal Claims* (Saskatoon: Purich, 2004).

50 See, generally, *Hammerton v. Honey* (1876), 24 W.R. 603 (C.A.) [*Hammerton*]. See Mark D. Walters, *The Continuity of Aboriginal Customs and Government under British Imperial Constitutional Law as Applied in Colonial Canada, 1760–1860* (Ph. D. Dissertation, Oxford University, 1996) [unpublished]. See also *The Case of the Stannaries* (1606), 12 Co. Rep. 9, *Trelawny v. Williams* (1704), 2 Vern. 483, *Crease v. Barrett* (1835), 1 Cr. M. & R. 919, *Doe d. Falmouth (Earl) v. Alderson* (1836), 1 M.

custom is described as "a particular rule which has existed either *actually or presumptively* from *time immemorial* and obtained the force of law in a particular locality although contrary to, or not consistent with, the general common law of the realm . . . . *Custom is unwritten law* peculiar to particular *localities*."[51]

At common law, a valid custom must have the following essential attributes:

> (1) it must be immemorial; (2) it must be reasonable; (3) it must be certain in respect of its nature generally, as well as in respect of the locality where it is alleged to obtain and the persons who it is alleged to affect; and (4) it must have continued without interruption since its immemorial origin.[52]

The first attribute — that a custom must date from time immemorial — can be gauged by the British date for proof of local custom, set at 1189.[53] This date of legal memory can be equated with the extension of regal power throughout the kingdom by Richard I's father, Henry II, who established the King's Courts. As previously mentioned, in Canada, legal memory should, in principle, date from the time of the establishment of the courts, which extended the protection of the Crown to the Aboriginal peoples, in exchange for their allegiance.

Sir George Jessel explained the method for proving the existence of a custom at the date of legal memory, or to time immemorial, by testimony of living memory:

& W. 210, *R. v. Crease* (1840), 11 Ad. & El. 677, *Vice v. Thomas* (1842), 1 L.T.O.S. 312, *Crease v. Sawle* (1842), 2 Q.B. 862, *Rogers v. Brenton* (1847), 10 Q.B. 26, *Carlyon v. Lovering* (1857), 1 H. & N. 784, *Ivimey v. Stocker* (1865), 2 Drew. & Sm. 537, *Behrens v. Richards*, [1905] 2 Ch. 614. It is unnecessary for present purposes to decide whether the English respected the Celtic peoples out of fear or love, or both. The case of the Celtic Cornish may be compared and contrasted with the case of the Celtic Irish: see, for example, Robert A. Williams, Jr., *The American Indian in Western Legal Thought: The Discourses of Conquest* (New York: Oxford University Press, 1990) at 136*ff.* for a discussion of the English treatment of the Gaelic tribes in Ireland.

51 *Halsbury's Laws of England*, 4th ed., vol. 12 (London: Butterworths, 1980) at para. 401 [emphases added].

52 *Ibid.* at para. 406.

53 See the discussion of legal memory in "Sovereignty, Liberty and the Legal Order," above note 33 at 348.

> The usual course taken is this: persons of middle or old age are called, who state that in their time, usually at least half a century, the usage has always prevailed. That is considered, in the absence of countervailing evidence, to show that the usage has prevailed from all time.[54]

It will be recalled that the Court has decided that Aboriginal people must prove, as matters of fact, particular elements of practices, customs, or traditions as existing at either the date of assertion of sovereignty, or the date of contact, meaning the exercise by the Crown of effective control over the local population. In light of this judicial requirement that is applied only to proof of Aboriginal rights, the following statement is instructive as to what is just and reasonable:

> Then, as to the proof of the custom, you cannot, indeed, reasonably expect to have it proved before you, that such a custom did in fact exist before time of legal memory, that is, before the first year of the reign of Richard 1; *for if you did, it would in effect destroy the validity of almost all customs*, but you are to require proof, as far back as living memory goes, of a continuous, peaceable, and uninterrupted user of the custom, and then you should inquire whether any document, or memorial, of more ancient times, is produced, tending to disprove the existence of the custom at that early period to which the law looks back.[55]

To do justice to its own people in Britain, the common-law courts designed a legal presumption to facilitate proof of custom going back to the dawn of legal memory.[56]

Of particular significance to Aboriginal rights cases are the early common-law cases dealing with non-literate Indigenous societies in Britain. The common law has extensive experience dealing with unwritten law:

> The common law of England was itself unwritten, and has been described as "an ancient collection of unwritten maxims and customs." *In order to ascertain what it is when there are no decisions to guide the Court, we have regard to the wisdom of our ancestors, and to their view of the law . . . .*[57]

---

54 *Hammerton*, above note 50 at 604.

55 *Bastard v. Smith and others*, [1835–42] All E.R. Rep. 201 at 203 [emphasis added].

56 *Halsbury's Laws of England*, above note 51 at para. 608.

57 *Ward v. Dwelley*, [1902] 2 Ch. 488 at 493 [*Ward*] [emphasis added].

If this principle were applied in Aboriginal rights cases, then the unwritten law of the Aboriginal peoples would be found in the oral evidence of living witnesses, testifying as to the wisdom of their ancestors. Where there are no authoritative sources in the case law, the Court must have regard "to the wisdom of our ancestors," probing the wisdom of the Aboriginal people whose law is being discovered. Since Aboriginal laws predate Canadian society, Aboriginal law can be found only in the wisdom of Aboriginal ancestors.

In this search for principles to guide Crown–Aboriginal relations of justice, further reference will be made below to the common-law cases relating to non-literate British local peoples.

12) Common Law and Aboriginal Rights Law: Reflections and Conclusions

Should the Court adopt the common-law rules instead of creating new ones for Aboriginal rights? What is suggested here is that the common-law cases provide a very rich source of authority that is directly relevant to the issues that arise in Aboriginal rights litigation, and that the Court ought to consider, and where appropriate, distinguish those cases, so that the law may be better known. The Court will do better justice, as revealed by the above comparisons, and will contribute more to the certainty that the law must promote, if it will consider and distinguish, where appropriate, the law as applied to non-Aboriginal people.

The Court is required, as a common-law court, to follow and apply, or distinguish, cases that have established the rules and principles of law. The Court has chosen not to follow the common law as it develops the doctrine of Aboriginal rights.[58] Decisions given without any reference to authoritative sources do not have the character of judicial decisions: they are merely the personal opinion of the judge or judges. The legal legitimacy of judicial decisions depends upon their being based on legitimate authority. Courts are bound to follow relevant common-law precedents

58 See, generally, Mark D. Walters, *The Continuity of Aboriginal Customs and Government under British Imperial Constitutional Law as Applied in Colonial Canada, 1760–1860* (Ph.D. Dissertation, Oxford University, 1996) [unpublished]; Mark D. Walters, "The Golden Thread of Continuity: Aboriginal Customs at Common Law and under the *Constitution Act, 1982*" (1998) 44 McGill L.J. 711–52.

and principles, and the decisions in which they fail to do so are rendered *per incuriam* and do not correctly state the law.[59] All this may be trite, but it must be emphasized in light of the Court's penchant in Aboriginal rights cases, including *Powley*,[60] to arrive at decisions directly without citing and distinguishing relevant cases.

Whether the common law or other sources of authority are appropriate for deciding Aboriginal rights cases, there are good reasons to challenge the view that there is a legitimate role for the judges in defining the Aboriginal peoples. The concept of culture being adopted as a foundational element of the doctrine of Aboriginal rights is inadequate for the task of definition. Too imprecise to be a legal concept, it fails to address the real policy reason for recognizing that Aboriginal peoples have a right to define themselves and their public interest.

Aboriginal people do not so much fear changes in their culture as they abhor the transgression of human rights by the state that forces upon them social and political change that transforms their culture. It is the ability to determine their own destiny — the right to develop, maintain, and protect their own vision of the good society — that is valued by Aboriginal people, and indeed, by all peoples. The core of the right of self-determination, it includes the right of self-definition. That is what deserves the protection of the law. In this context, the right of self-identification is a political, not a cultural issue.[61] Aboriginal peoples must define themselves in order to pursue their human and constitutional rights to survive as distinct peoples in Canada. What the law must protect is the political right and capacity of Aboriginal peoples to govern cultural and political change within Aboriginal society. That their right to determine their own identity and self-definition is usurped by the judicial branch, as in the *Powley* case, rather than by the executive or legislative branches, as in the case of the *Indian Act*, [62] does not transform a wrong into a right.

The essential task of Aboriginal rights law, as stated by Binnie J., in *Mikisew Cree*,[63] is to reconcile the competing interests of Aboriginal

59 See, generally, *per incuriam* decisions, above note 17.

60 *Powley*, above note 6.

61 Tim Schouls, *Shifting Boundaries: Aboriginal Identity, Pluralist Theory, and the Politics of Self-Government* (Vancouver: UBC Press, 2003).

62 Above note 8.

63 *Mikisew Cree First Nation v. Canada (Minister of Canadian Heritage)*, [2005] 3 S.C.R. 388 at para. 1 [*Mikisew Cree*].

peoples and the rest of the Canadian population. The interests of either side in particular cases may be substantial and compelling. Their legal protection may require urgent action to avoid their being irretrievably eroded or consumed. Is the common law, which develops slowly on a case-by-case basis, the best way to accomplish this contemporary reconciliation in Canada?

The British cases considered below show that modifications to the customary laws were effected by legislation, being careful to ensure the continuing participation of the local people whose law was at issue in the continuing administration and adjudication of the law. The need for legislative changes to ancient laws in order to reconcile them with contemporary interests, including the interests of both Aboriginal people and the Canadian public, invites a search for principles that might guide Crown–Aboriginal relations where judicial decisions alone are incapable of rendering substantial justice to all. This search is the focus in the next section.

It is worth emphasizing that the need to alter the law by legislation as found by the common-law courts does not mean that the approach of the common law as it extends its recognition, respect, and protection to the laws of Aboriginal peoples ought to be different from its approach to its own British peoples. On the contrary, what is asserted is that creating differences in common-law tests, rules, and principles is unnecessary and may be unjust unless these are shown to be inapplicable. Thus, the courts ought to examine the common-law cases and distinguish them as necessary in deciding Aboriginal rights cases. Justice then may be seen to be done. It has been shown above that there are instances where unjustifiable distinctions have been made.

D. POLITICAL PARTICIPATION: PRINCIPLES FOR LEGITIMATE CROWN–ABORIGINAL RELATIONS

1) Introduction

In a democracy, participation is the key to legitimacy. The principle that Aboriginal people must have effective participation in Canadian public life if Canada is to have a legitimate governing order has support from domestic and international sources. It was urged as the basic principle to guide Crown–Aboriginal relations by the Royal Commission on Aboriginal Peoples.[64] In the *Quebec Secession Reference* the Court viewed the participation by the French-Canadians of Quebec in the public life of Canada as evidence that they are not an oppressed people and therefore on that basis entitled to exercise their international-law right of self-determination by secession.

It is instructive to apply those indicators to the Aboriginal people, for so doing leads to the opposite conclusion.[65] These factors convinced the Court that the French-Canadians in Quebec were not an oppressed people:[66]

- the Prime Minister for nearly forty of the last fifty years has been from Quebec;
- Quebecers have held from time to time in this period all the most important positions in the federal Cabinet;
- the Prime Minister and the Leader of the Opposition for eight years prior to 1997 were from Quebec;
- presently, all the following officials are from Quebec: the Prime Minister, the Chief Justice, two other members of the Supreme Court of Canada, the Chief of Staff of the Canadian Armed Forces, the Canadian Ambassador to the United States, the Deputy Secretary-General of the United Nations;
- Quebecers occupy prominent positions within the government of Canada,
- Quebecers freely make political choices and pursue economic, social and cultural development within Quebec, across Canada, and throughout the world,
- Quebecers are equitably represented in legislative, executive, and judicial institutions.

The principle that participation is essential to democracy emerges from a number of other distinct sources and thereby establishes itself as a

---

64 Canada, Royal Commission on Aboriginal Peoples, *Report of the Royal Commission on Aboriginal Peoples: Looking Forward, Looking Back*, vol. I (Ottawa: Supply and Services, 1996) "Opening the Door."

65 For a discussion of the non-participation of Aboriginal people in Canadian public governance, see Paul L.A.H. Chartrand, "Canada and the Aboriginal Peoples: From Dominion to Condominium" in F. Leslie Seidle & David C. Docherty, eds., *Reforming Parliamentary Democracy* (Montreal and Kingston: McGill-Queen's University Press, 2003) at 99–127.

66 *Quebec Secession Reference*, above note 20 at paras. 135–36.

universal principle that must be respected. Some of those sources will be identified in the following sections. For present purposes it is sufficient to assert that in the above circumstances that have revealed the non-participation of Aboriginal peoples, Canada's governance over the Aboriginal peoples is not constitutionally legitimate and must be legitimized by the effective participation of Aboriginal peoples. The principle of participation applies along with the other principles that are identified below, and further references to it will be made in the following discussion.

2) Principle of Consent

In the *Manitoba Language Reference*[67] the Court stated that constitutional legitimacy depends upon the consent of the governed:

> The Constitution of a country is a statement of the will of the people to be governed in accordance with certain principles held as fundamental and certain prescriptions restrictive of the powers of the legislature and government. It is, as s. 52 of the *Constitution Act, 1982* declares, the "supreme law" of the nation, unalterable by the normal legislative process, and unsuffering of laws inconsistent with it. The duty of the judiciary is to interpret and apply the laws of Canada and each of the provinces, and it is thus our duty to ensure that the constitutional law prevails.[68]

From this principle of consent, it may be deduced that the consent of the Aboriginal peoples is necessary to the legitimacy of the constitutional order of Canada. Such consent can be inferred from effective and legitimate participation in the governance of Canada. The representatives of Canada who agreed to the original Constitution did not represent the Aboriginal peoples as such. Today, the consent and participation of the Aboriginal peoples, *qua* constitutional rights-bearing peoples, is essential to legitimize the laws of Canada that apply to them, judge-made law as well as legislation. The political fortunes of the Aboriginal peoples, or, in other words, the "public interest" of each Aboriginal people, cannot be left in the hands of the appointed judges to determine and protect. That task is required, by the law of the Constitution, to be performed by the people and the people's representatives.

---

67 *Reference re Manitoba Language Rights*, [1985] 1 S.C.R. 721.

68 *Ibid.* at para. 48 [emphasis added].

3) Rule of Law

This other fundamental principle of the Constitution is relevant in identifying the elements of constitutionally defensible Crown–Aboriginal relations. The principle was described in the *Manitoba Language Reference*:

> "The rule of law" means literally what it says: the rule of the law . . . . It has two aspects: (1) that people should be ruled by the law and obey it, and (2) that the law should be such that people will be able to be guided by it (The Authority of Law, (1979), at pp. 212–13). The rule of law simply cannot be fulfilled in a province that has no positive law.[69]

The Court elaborated as follows:

> Additional to the inclusion of the rule of law in the preambles of the Constitution Acts of 1867 and 1982, the principle is clearly implicit in the very nature of a Constitution. The Constitution, as the Supreme Law, must be understood as a purposive ordering of social relations providing a basis upon which an actual order of positive laws can be brought into existence. The founders of this nation must have intended, as one of the basic principles of nation building, that Canada be a society of legal order and normative structure: one governed by rule of law. While this is not set out in a specific provision, the principle of the rule of law is clearly a principle of our Constitution.[70]

This principle is an important guide that compels the Crown to act in its executive and legislative functions in response to judicial decisions on Aboriginal rights, as will be explained below.

4) Duty to Consult and Participation

In the *Haida Nation*[71] case, the Court enunciated another principle to guide constitutionally defensible Crown–Aboriginal relations: the duty of the Crown to consult Aboriginal peoples in order to recognize, respect, and protect not only their rights, but also their interests.

---

69 *Ibid.* at para. 62.

70 *Ibid.* at para. 64.

71 *Haida Nation v. British Columbia (Minister of Forests)*, [2004] 3 S.C.R. 511 [*Haida Nation*].

> Put simply, Canada's Aboriginal peoples were here when Europeans came, and were never conquered. Many bands reconciled their claims with the sovereignty of the Crown through negotiated treaties. Others, notably in British Columbia, have yet to do so. The *potential rights* [which are broader than rights and here called "interests": emphasis added] embedded in these claims are protected by s. 35 of the Constitution Act, 1982. The honour of the Crown requires that these rights be determined, recognized and respected. This, in turn, requires the Crown, acting honourably, to participate in processes of negotiation. While this process continues, the honour of the Crown may require it to consult and, where indicated, accommodate Aboriginal interests.[72]

This particular duty that binds the Crown applies to the case where the interests of Aboriginal peoples indicate the potential existence of Aboriginal or treaty[73] rights.

An examination of yet another constitutional duty to consult that the Court identified in the *Quebec Secession Reference* will broaden the scope of this duty to consult Aboriginal peoples. That "other duty to consult" is linked with the principles of participation, democracy, and the rule of law that were identified above. It is addressed in the next section.

5) The Constitutional Duty to Negotiate: *Quebec Secession Reference*

In the *Quebec Secession Reference* the Court explained that to find the rights and obligations that flow from the law of the Constitution,

> it is necessary to make a . . . profound investigation of the underlying principles that animate the whole of our Constitution, including the principles of federalism, democracy, constitutionalism and the rule of law, and respect for minorities . . . .[74]

In that reference, the Court found that where a participant in the federation, in this instance a province, democratically expresses its will to negotiate the terms of the Constitution to which its consent will attach,

---

72 *Ibid.* at para. 25.

73 In *Mikisew Cree*, above note 63 at paras. 33–34, the Court found that the duty attaches to treaty rights.

74 *Quebec Secession Reference*, above note 20 at para. 148.

then there is a positive constitutional obligation requiring the other participants to enter into negotiations.

A profound investigation[75] into the fundamental principles of the Constitution would lead to the argument that Aboriginal peoples are also constitutionally relevant federal participants, as are the provinces, and that where an Aboriginal people democratically expresses its will to negotiate the terms of the Constitution to which its consent will attach, then there is a positive obligation for the other federal participants to enter into negotiations. Each of the federal participants in theory derives its constitutional authority from the role and status of the Crown. The honour of the Crown requires it to enter into negotiations in the circumstances just mentioned, just as it does whenever it contemplates action that might infringe the interests or rights of the Aboriginal peoples.[76]

6) Duties of the Crown Exercising Executive Power

First, the Crown acting through its elected advisers has a general duty to act in order to protect the interests and rights of the Aboriginal peoples. To do so, the government must renounce its current approach in which Aboriginal issues are "managed," or where it takes action only when, and to the extent that, circumstances generate a political imperative to act.

Second, the Crown must act in accordance with the law of the Constitution. Attacks by the Harper Conservative minority government on Aboriginal rights[77] demonstrate the value of constitutional protection against the unconscionable actions of temporary governments. Constitutional protection is not sufficient to safeguard the rights of politically weak minorities. However, some political leverage is available in a constitutional democracy because public opinion can be persuaded that a government that tramples the constitutional rights of one minority to-

75 This profound investigation is beyond the scope of this paper.

76 An additional principle of the Constitution would support this argument. The right of self-determination of all peoples, including the Aboriginal peoples of Canada, is a human right. In *R. v. Demers*, [2004] 2 S.C.R. 489 at paras. 79–85, Le Bel J. opined that "respect for human rights" was also a fundamental principle of the Constitution of Canada.

77 These attacks were widely covered in the public media. See, for example, Doug Cuthand, "PM Boiling Native Rights into Question of Race" *Saskatoon Star Phoenix* (28 July 2006) A11.

day might trample the rights of another tomorrow. Popular elections and a functioning democracy are important to safeguard the interests and rights of Aboriginal peoples within powerful states.

Third, where the Courts have found rights vested in Aboriginal peoples, the Crown in its executive capacity and authority must act to recognize, respect, and protect those rights without delay. This principle is found in the French language minority rights cases. It should be clarified that there is no need for executive recognition of rights that have been judicially found because such rights are the law, which is binding upon governments.[78] In particular, the Aboriginal and treaty rights of the Aboriginal peoples require positive action by not only the executive, but also by the legislative and judicial branches to make them effective.[79]

Fourth, the Crown has a duty to ensure that representatives of the Aboriginal peoples participate in governance on matters encompassed by their rights. This principle is evident in recent constitutional cases on French minority rights[80] and also in the actions of the British Crown in relation to the ancient rights of the Cornish people.[81]

Finally, it is instructive to note a basic dilemma that complicates the role of the Crown in respecting, recognizing, and protecting the interests and rights of the Aboriginal peoples. Aboriginal persons are, in law at least, citizens of Canada, as well as members of rights-bearing Aboriginal peoples. The Crown owes duties that emerge from the *Charter* and from Canada's international-law obligations to safeguard human rights to the Aboriginal citizens. The Crown also has a duty to safeguard the collective interests of the Aboriginal peoples, and in addition to that, to reconcile all of these with the public interest of Canadians generally. The Crown represents the public interest and at the same time has a duty to safeguard the public interest of each Aboriginal people. The only legitim-

78 In *Ward*, above note 57 at 492, the court explained that unwritten laws based on local custom do not require executive recognition: "[i]t is plain that the continuance of this custom in Kent stood in no need of any confirmation from the Conqueror, since it was in his time the common law of the kingdom…."

79 This principle was explained by the Court in *Canada (Combines Investigation Acts, Director of Investigation and Research) v. Southam Inc.*, [1984] 2 S.C.R. 145.

80 See, for example, *Reference re Public Schools Act (Man.), ss. 79(3), (4), and (7)*, [1993] 1 S.C.R. 839.

81 These executive actions are evident from the actions taken by the Crown in Parliament, which are discussed below; see text accompanying note 84.

ate way to perform the latter duty is to seek the views of the Aboriginal people about the nature and scope of its public interest. The Crown cannot act unilaterally. Aboriginal participation is the key that legitimizes Crown executive action when the Crown acts in its duties towards Aboriginal peoples and their interests.

7) The Crown in Parliament: Legislation to Regulate Crown–Aboriginal Relations

While legislation is not needed to validate the treaty, common law, and constitutional rights of the Aboriginal peoples, legislation is required to make the Crown's duties of respect and protection effective. For example, money must be appropriated and civil servants must have their lawful instructions and authority to act.

Furthermore, legislation will be needed to reconcile the interests of the public with the interests of the Aboriginal peoples. Yet another reason for legislation is to create a regime that provides remedies where unwritten law no longer seems to promote the best interests of the Aboriginal and non-Aboriginal publics, as it may be concluded in the course of consultations and negotiations.

The legislative regimes established in response to the need to expand upon and protect the interests of the Cornish people that had been recognized as the *lex loci* based on their ancient customs provide an example of what was thought to be right in the case of a distinct Celtic people in Britain.[82] Under the rule of Edward IV, after a dispute arose between the people and Lord Benfield as to which rights and customs should be applied to miners, a royal inquiry was instituted and the customary laws of the miners were embodied in a code of written law.[83]

82 See the following legislation: *Stannary Act*, 1836, 6 & 7 Wm. IV, c. 106; *Stannary Act*, 1855, 18 & 19 Vic., c. 32. See also Robert Pennington, *Stannary Law: A History of the Mining Law of Cornwall and Devon* (Newton Abbot: David and Charles, 1973) [*Stannary Law*]; G.R. Lewis, *The Stannaries: The Tin Miners of Cornwall and Devon* (Cambridge, MA: Harvard University Press, 1924) [*The Stannaries*].

83 *The Stannaries, ibid.* at 80.

The principle of participation was also evident in the creation of special local legislative assemblies, the consent of which was essential to validate any applicable legislation.[84]

8) The Crown as the Fountain of Justice: Adjudicative Bodies to Resolve Disputes Arising under Legislation

Further evidence of the right way for the Crown to respect rights found to exist at common law can be found in the special courts that were created to adjudicate disputes arising from the administration of the Stannary laws in Cornwall.[85] According to Robert Pennington,

> [t]he system of law which governed metalliferous mining in Cornwall and Devon was unique in two ways. In the first place the tin mining and smelting industries were subject to comprehensive regulating by laws different in origin and content from the common law of England, which governed all other industries; these special laws were enforced by specialised local courts, whose jurisdiction was confined at first to tin mining and miners, but was extended in 1836 to metalliferous mining and miners generally. Secondly, the system of law governing tin mining and smelting was universal in that it related not only to operations and transactions necessarily occurring in the industries . . . but also extended to all aspects of the lives of those who were engaged in tin affairs.[86]

More recently, in Canada, the Royal Commission on Aboriginal Peoples proposed the establishment of special tribunals to adjudicate disputes relating to the rights of Aboriginal peoples.[87]

84 Alan Wharam, "Judicial Control of Delegated Legislation: The Test of Reasonableness" (1973) 36 Mod. L. Rev. 611 at 611–12; John Murray, *A Hand-book for Travellers in Devon & Cornwall* (London: J. Murray, 1851) at xxxiv.

85 *The Stannaries*, above note 82 at 118.

86 *Stannary Law*, above note 82 at 7.

87 RCAP vol. 2, above note 26 at 591–612.

E. A PRINCIPLED APPROACH TO GUIDE CROWN–ABORIGINAL RELATIONS

From the above principles, the following course is proposed to establish and maintain Crown–Aboriginal relations of justice and reconciliation:

a) Enter into political relations with Aboriginal (Métis) representatives, with a view to negotiate and reach agreement on the recognition and protection of the rights of the Aboriginal (Métis) people.
b) Provide legal protection for the political recognition of the Aboriginal (Métis) people that results from these negotiations by enacting appropriate recognition and implementation legislation.
c) Establish, by legislation, special adjudicative bodies with authority to deal with disputes arising from the legislated agreements.

1) Métis Definition

The definition of "Métis" appropriate for Crown–Métis relations would result from the negotiations and agreements, and would be given effective protection by legislation.

2) General Principles

It is essential to note that the applicable principles require that the same approach apply to *all* the Aboriginal peoples. In order to make effective the constitutional recognition and affirmation of the rights of all Aboriginal peoples in the *Constitution Act, 1982*, it is imperative that Canada abandon the *Indian Act* scheme of recognition. What is required by the law of the Constitution which binds governments is a new recognition scheme that respects and protects the rights of all the Aboriginal peoples, in accordance with the applicable constitutional standards.

APPENDIX

A. REVIEW OF THE MEMBERSHIP CODES

1) Métis National Council

The Métis National Council (MNC) was created by the leaders of the three prairie provincial organizations representing Métis just before the start of the national first ministers' conferences on Aboriginal constitutional reform in 1983. Later on, organizations from the Northwest Territories, British Columbia, and Ontario were added. Today, the MNC has one provincial affiliate in each of the five provinces of British Columbia, Alberta, Saskatchewan, Manitoba, and Ontario.

The MNC website contains the following information related to the national definition of its membership that was adopted at a meeting in Edmonton on 27 September 2002.[88]

> *National Definition of Métis*
>
> 1. "Métis" means a person who self-identifies as Métis, is distinct from other Aboriginal peoples, is of Historic Métis Nation ancestry, and is accepted by the Métis Nation.
>
> *Defined Terms within National Definition of Métis*
>
> 1.2 "Historic Métis Nation" means the Aboriginal people then known as Métis or Half-breeds who resided in the Historic Métis Nation Homeland.
>
> 1.3 "Historic Métis Nation Homeland" means the area of land in west central North America used and occupied as the traditional territory of the Métis or Half-breeds as they were then known.
>
> 1.4 "Métis Nation" means the Aboriginal people descended from the Historic Métis Nation which is now comprised of all Métis Nation citizens and is one of the "aboriginal peoples of Canada" within the meaning of s.35 of the *Constitution Act, 1982*.
>
> 1.5 "Distinct from other Aboriginal peoples" means distinct for cultural and nationhood purposes.[89]

88 Métis National Council, "Who Are the Métis," online: www.metisnation.ca/who/definition.html (accessed 29 July 2006).

89 *Ibid.*

It is immediately apparent from the text and structure of this definition that the primary concern of the MNC is to identify individual members of its organization: the definition begins by addressing the definition of "persons" who may be accepted as members, and not "the Métis people," or nation, that has constitutional rights.

For the purposes of section 35, the primary issue is to identify the "people" whose rights are affirmed and recognized. Since the purpose of section 35 is to affirm and recognize ancestral rights of peoples, and because those rights are collective, not individual rights, the initial task is to identify the descendant communities of the historic people whose rights are affirmed and recognized in the Constitution of Canada. Once the people or nation is identified, its constituents may then be identified by reference to the applicable rules, practices, or conventions of the people. A "people" is more than the sum of its parts or, more properly, a people is more than merely the aggregation of individuals of which it is comprised. This principle will have further relevance in the analysis of the case law that follows the analysis of the political organizations' definitions in this section.

The MNC definition of individual members, in substance, purports to assert that an individual member must be "distinct from other Aboriginal peoples." This comparison is not rational since it purports to compare individual persons to "peoples." Individuals and groups are not in comparable categories. The distinction that is mentioned in section 35 is between various peoples, including the Indian, Métis, and Inuit peoples. That distinction, an objective factor to be determined as a matter of fact, will be considered more fully below.

The MNC definition begins by identifying the necessary subjective element of self-identification by its members. At first blush, this provision in a membership code is odd since potential members will necessarily identify themselves as Métis in their applications for membership if they are willingly making application. Reflecting upon the role of the MNC, however, the self-identification element is presumably linked to the requirements of domestic and international law in reconciling individual and collective rights. Section 35 affirms and recognizes group rights. International law recognizes the group rights of all "peoples."[90]

90 For a discussion of the right of self-determination of Indigenous peoples, see "Striving for Self-Determination," above note 20 at 50–62. See also the discussion

Collective or group rights cannot be exercised or enjoyed without societal institutions of the group that perform such roles as identifying members and maintaining the group's existence. Thus the individual member of the rights-bearing community or group will be linked to the group by binding social and legal relations. Members have a special set of rights and obligations that distinguish them from other citizens in Canada. This set of unique rights and obligations flows from the special constitutional status of Aboriginal peoples in Canada, and from international standards. By the introduction of the self-identification element, the general principle that the law will not foist a distinct legal status upon an unwilling individual is also respected in the MNC definition. This proposition is subject to the exception of children who acquire the status of their parents. They, however, are entitled to exercise their right to divest themselves of a legal status upon attaining the age of majority.

Parenthetically, it is arguable that the current *Indian Act* offends the principle of free association by not allowing individuals who are registered under its authority to opt out of *Indian Act* status if they so choose. The Act therefore may offend the constitutionally guaranteed freedom of association of individual Indians.[91]

The third element examined here is the requirement that an MNC member must be of "Métis Nation ancestry." The definition purports to create a closed category of members, all of whom must be descended from ancestors who belonged to the Métis Nation. Nothing is provided in the definition to determine how this ancestral belonging is to be identified. In principle, persons who formed part of the Métis ancestral community, however defined, would be included.

---

in the *Quebec Secession Reference*, above note 20 at paras. 109–46.

91 Section 2 of the *Charter of Rights and Freedoms*, above note 42, provides: "Everyone has the following fundamental freedoms: (a) freedom of conscience and religion; . . . (d) freedom of association. The issue has not been settled. Most of the cases on the freedom of association deal with union membership." See, for example, *Lavigne v. O.P.S.E.U.*, [1991] 2 S.C.R. 211, and *Advance Cutting & Coring Ltd.* (2001), 205 D.L.R. (4th) 385 (S.C.C.), where the negative right not to associate is also examined. For a discussion of freedom of association in the context of Indians within the *Indian Act*, above note 8, see, for example, *Sawridge Band v. Canada*, [1995] 4 C.N.L.R. 121 (F.C.T.D.). At least one past attempt by the MNC to get the federal government to amend the *Indian Act* to allow Indians who wish to opt out to join Métis organizations went nowhere.

The MNC definition approach, which attempts to link individuals with an ancestral community, may be contrasted with the particular inquiry that is appropriate to identify the Métis people in section 35. There, *it is the rights-bearing community* that must be descended from the ancestral Métis community or people. In that case, the personal antecedents of each and every member of the rights-bearing community are not material. To identify the relevant group involves identifying the relevant characteristics of the group, *not* the characteristics of its individual members. To argue otherwise is to lean on the thin-reed presumption that a people is no more than the sum of its parts or members.

The next element of the MNC definition requires acceptance of the individual member by the Métis Nation. Use of the term *Métis Nation* raises ambiguities. These ambiguities will now be examined in light of the definitions provided in the definition section of the MNC code.

> 1.2 "Historic Métis Nation" means the Aboriginal people then known as Métis or Half-breeds who resided in the Historic Métis Nation Homeland.[92]

The focus again is on individuals. The definition does not refer to collectivities, such as villages or communities identified by their distinct geographic, political, economic, and social characteristics, but rather, to individuals who themselves were called "Métis" or "Half-breeds."[93]

This focus on the individual accords with the ostensible purpose of the MNC code: to register individual members. The language of the code reveals the purpose of identifying individual applicants on the basis of their personal antecedents, whether they belong to a Métis community

92 "Who Are the Métis," above note 88.

93 Unless it has been adopted by and is used by the people designated by the term, which is the case in some parts of the Prairies, especially among the English linguistic group of Métis, then the term *Half-breed* is pejorative. It may be an appropriate term for discussions of animal husbandry, but not to refer to human beings. For a general description of the pejorative connotations, see, for example, Jerome Loving, *Walt Whitman: The Song of Himself* (Los Angeles: University of California Press, 1999) at 89. "In the nineteenth century as in most of the twentieth, the term 'half-breed' was pejorative . . . . Its negative connotation in this century has hinged on the lack of white purity, but in the nineteenth century 'half-breed' alluded almost exclusively to ethnically mixed Americans whose Native identity was tainted with European blood . . . ."

today or not. For example, persons who would generally be considered as members of a community, such as long-time residents and persons who have married into or been adopted by families within the community, are excluded on account of their personal antecedents, regardless of community acceptance.

By way of comparison and emphasis, to fulfill the purposes of section 35, which includes the affirmation and recognition of the *collective* rights of Aboriginal communities, a definition of an Aboriginal people would emphasize the character and the historical antecedents of the community itself, and not those of its residents or other members, as previously explained.

The next point is the characterization in the MNC code of the Historic Métis Nation, the nation whose members resided in a place called the Historic Métis Nation Homeland. This distinction seems to imply the acceptance by the MNC that there are other Métis nations. If there were only one, it would be unnecessary to stipulate the particular region it occupied. It might be added here that the term *resided* used in this definition is more appropriate to describe individuals than a people or nation. Ostensibly, it reflects the MNC object of registering individual applicants. An Aboriginal people within the meaning of section 35 would better be described as *occupying* a homeland rather than *residing* in it. Indeed, the terms *used* and *occupied* are used in 1.3, where the MNC is explicit in referring to a people.

> 1.3 "Historic Métis Nation Homeland" means the area of land in west central North America used and occupied as the traditional territory of the Métis or Half-breeds as they were then known.[94]

Following the MNC code's approach requires an examination of the term *Métis Nation Homeland*, since the meaning of the MNC concept Historic Métis Nation depends upon it. Use of the term *Métis* as an adjective creates a tautology that does not advance the purpose of a definition, since it repeats the term it sets out to define. As a matter of fact, other Aboriginal peoples also occupied the same region as the Métis people, so on this account the reference seems unhelpful.

---

94 "Who Are the Métis," above note 88.

There are other problems with precision in this part of the MNC definition. The phrase "then known" cannot have meaning without more. When is then? And known by whom? By themselves? By others?

"West central North America" is, by itself, unhelpful. "North America" rather than "Canada" reflects the fact that the historic Métis people occupied regions in what is now the United States as well as parts of Canada. The phrase cannot refer usefully to contemporary provincial boundaries except in a rough way, such as suggesting that the relevant area is that now included within the boundaries of certain named provinces. The definition refers to a historic people whose existence predates the establishment of the provinces.

It is useful next to consider a possible geographical meaning. The geographical centre of Canada, measured from east to west only, is located east of Winnipeg, Manitoba. The geographical interpretation of the definition implies that the homeland is west of that point. Assuming that the phrase was intended to capture a portion of central North America, that would include the Red River region, just a few kilometres west of the centre of Canada, but communities within Ontario — and certainly one as far east as Sault Ste Marie, the site of the hunting rights in the *Powley*[95] case — would be excluded.

The basic problem is that the Homeland cannot be defined more specifically without deciding more specifically who the Métis are. Rather than assisting that task, the term *Homeland* is purportedly used to define the Métis. This portion of the definition provides only unhelpful circularity.

> 1.4 "Métis Nation" means the Aboriginal people descended from the Historic Métis Nation which is now comprised of all Métis Nation citizens and is one of the "aboriginal peoples of Canada" within the meaning of s.35 of the *Constitution Act, 1982*.[96]

If the definition of the Historic Métis Nation is not clear, which is the case, then it will be impossible to determine what contemporary community descends from it today.

---

95 *Powley*, above note 6.

96 "Who Are the Métis," above note 88.

The reference to citizenship is not helpful since the citizens are not identified. The reference to section 35 of the *Constitution Act, 1982*, in the code leads to the implication that the term *citizen* refers to Canadian citizenship.[97] In this regard it is useful to note that all Canadian Aboriginal persons who belong to rights-bearing Aboriginal peoples are entitled to act so as to enjoy the collective rights of their people, in addition to being citizens of Canada. By virtue of their Canadian citizenship, they enjoy all the civil rights and bear all the responsibilities of citizens. Thus, Aboriginal people have both individual citizenship rights and Aboriginal group rights.[98]

The reference to section 35 does not add to a definition unless it is the intention of the MNC to adopt prospectively the definitions that the courts will give to its terms. This would mean that the MNC purports to adopt whatever meaning appointed judicial servants decide; however, there is no apparent reason to believe that the MNC would intend that in drafting this code.

> 1.5 "Distinct from other Aboriginal peoples" means distinct for cultural and nationhood purposes.[99]

Each Aboriginal people, including the Métis people, is presumptively distinct for multiple purposes, and to limit the distinctiveness of the Métis to cultural and nationhood purposes can be problematic. Applying the canon of construction *expressio unius est exclusio alterius* results in the meaning that the Métis are only distinct from other Aboriginal

97 It is beyond the scope of this chapter to assess the implications of an alternative interpretation that members of the MNC have "citizenship" in a Métis nation. Citizenship usually refers to the civil rights of persons who belong to states. For a useful discussion of the ideals of citizenship in Western thought, see J.G.A. Pocock, "The Ideal of Citizenship since Classical Times" (1992) 99 Queen's Quarterly 35–55.

98 This feature is the frequent target of racist political attacks which seek to use the concept of race to oppose the dual-constitutional status of persons who belong to Aboriginal communities. The distinction between Aboriginal rights and citizenship rights is obscured for political purposes. Such attacks cannot be effective to absolve governments from respecting, recognizing, and protecting Aboriginal rights since they are enshrined in the Constitution, which binds governments. Only a constitutional amendment can do that. See also above note 78 and accompanying text.

99 "Who Are the Métis," above note 88.

peoples "for cultural and nationhood purposes." Other purposes, such as those of section 35, are excluded. However, this construction directly conflicts with the definition of the contemporary Métis Nation in 1.4, which is discussed above.

In summary, the MNC definition is circular and imprecise.[100]

2) The Congress of Aboriginal Peoples

The Congress of Aboriginal Peoples (CAP) has succeeded the Native Council of Canada that, for more than two decades, represented many Aboriginal persons not included within the federal government's recognition scheme based on the *Indian Act*. The CAP does not purport to define the Métis people. Its website notes the following:

> Métis people are located in all of the provinces and territories of Canada. These persons, who may or may not be entitled to status under the *Indian Act*, are Métis culturally, historically, and for purposes of constitutional recognition. Some of this group are a distinctive mixed blood population, others are closely identified with the history and culture of the French/Cree Métis in southern Manitoba and central Saskatchewan in the 1860s.[101]

It appears from this that the CAP conception of Métis focuses on individuals who may belong to the organization. The idea that Métis people are "located" in all parts of Canada may be taken to mean individuals who may reside anywhere in Canada, even though their domicile, or their ancestral community and territory, may be elsewhere.

In conclusion, the information provided by the CAP does not seem to assist an inquiry into the meaning of *Métis people* for constitutional or policy purposes. It is also evident that the two national political representative organizations do not agree on the issue of defining the Métis people.

---

100 To be fair, some of the kinds of problems that have been considered are expected to be found in texts produced in a complex political process, as was the MNC definition.

101 Congress of Aboriginal Peoples, "The Forgotten People and the *Indian Act* System," online: www.abo-peoples.org/background/indianact.html (accessed 29 July 2006).

3) The Métis Nation of Alberta

The Métis Nation of Alberta (MNA), a member of the MNC, offers its own definition of its members.[102]

> "Métis" means a person who self-identifies as a Métis, is distinct from other aboriginal peoples, is of historic Métis Nation ancestry, and is accepted by the "Métis Nation."
>
> Historic Proof: refers to the evidence of an ancestor who received a land grant or a scrip grant under the *Manitoba Act* or the *Dominion Lands Act*, or who was recognized as a Métis in other government, church or community records.
>
> Historic Métis Nation: refers to the Aboriginal people then known as Métis or Half-breeds who occupied the traditional territory of the Métis.
>
> Métis Nation Homeland: is the area of land in west central North America used and occupied as the traditional territory of the Métis.
>
> Métis Nation: means the Aboriginal people descended from the Historic Métis Nation, which [is] now comprised of all Métis Nation peoples [*sic*] and is one of the "aboriginal peoples" of Canada as defined in s.35 of the *Constitution Act*, 1982.
>
> Distinct from other Aboriginal peoples means distinct for cultural and nationhood purposes.[103]

The MNA definition closely resembles the MNC definition analyzed above. The above review of the MNC definition provides a complete analysis of the features that are shared by the MNC and MNA definition codes.

One salient distinction in the Alberta code is the attempt to define historic proof, where there is no use of this phrase in the definition itself. A second difference is that the term citizen has been replaced with "peoples" in the statement that mirrors 1.4 in the MNC code. While this change provides a rational comparator with other Aboriginal peoples, it

---

102 The Métis Nation of Alberta, "Who Are the Métis?," online: www.metisnation.ca/who/index.html (accessed 29 July 2006). The definition was adopted at a meeting in Edmonton in August 2003.

103 *Ibid.*

does not provide an explanation for the recognition of a multiplicity of distinct Métis peoples that must now be taken to have merged into one people called the "Métis Nation." Further, there is no explanation how this Métis Nation is related to the Alberta Métis Nation. The typographical omission of the word "is" following "which" in the definition of Métis Nation supports the speculation that the plural form of "peoples" may not have been deliberate.

4) Manitoba Metis Federation

The Manitoba Metis Federation (MMF) constitution adopted in September 2005 contains a definition of its members under Article III headed "Definitions and Applications for Membership."[104] This definition closely follows the MNC definition considered earlier. Like the MNA code, it too offers a definition of a term which does not appear in the definition itself, namely, that of *children*.

The MMF code reproduces the MNC definitional element that refers to the meaning of *Métis* in section 35 of the *Constitution Act*,[105] thus indicating an abdication of the right of self-definition to the courts of Canada. The same statement appears also in a preambular statement in the MMF code. This approach is contradicted, however, by the emphatic assertion that has appeared above the president's name on the MMF website: that the MMF and the Métis people will determine who is Métis and who is not.[106]

5) Métis Nation of Ontario

The purpose of the Métis Nation of Ontario (MNO) Registry is to list Métis people in the province of Ontario who meet the standards for

104 Manitoba Metis Federation, "Manitoba Metis Federation Constitution" (11 September 2005), online: http://mmf.mb.ca/images/stories/departments/Federation/MMFConstitution-11-09-07.PDF.

105 Above note 2.

106 See, for example, the message of the president of the Manitoba Metis Federation, online: http://mmf.mb.ca/index.php?option=com_content&task=view&id=273&Itemid=41 (accessed 25 February 2008).

registration in accordance with criteria established by the Métis National Council which represents the historic Métis Nation in Canada.[107]

The MNO has adopted the MNC definition reviewed earlier in this chapter.

6) Métis Nation — Saskatchewan

The definition of membership to the Saskatchewan Métis organization differs from those of the other MNC provincial constituents in that it does not purport to adopt the substance of the MNC code. The constitution of the organization provides:

> ARTICLE 10: CITIZENSHIP
>
> "Métis" means an Aboriginal person who self-identifies as Métis, who is distinct from Indian and Inuit, and:
>
> is a descendant of those Métis who received or were entitled to receive land grants and/or (sic) Scrip under the provision of the *Manitoba Act, 1870* or the *Dominion Lands Act*, as enacted from time to time; or
>
> a person of Aboriginal descent who is accepted by the Métis Nation and/or Métis Community. (Amended Dec. 13/97)
>
> Any Métis who is a member of a duly registered Local is a member of the Métis Nation of Saskatchewan.[108]

"Métis" is defined by the term *Aboriginal person*, but it fails since the latter term is not defined. Two factors may entitle applicants to membership. The first relies on the historic recognition of individuals in federal legislation; it therefore seeks to mirror federal recognition rather than providing criteria developed by the Métis people for acceptance as a member. The second basis for acceptance is also imprecise: "Aboriginal descent" is too imprecise to identify individuals, and the two bodies who are entitled to provide official acceptance — the Métis Nation and the Métis Community — are not defined.

---

107 Métis Nation of Ontario, online: www.metisnation.org (accessed 29 July 2006).

108 Métis Nation — Saskatchewan, "Constitution of the Métis Nation of Saskatchewan," online: http://metna.sasktelwebhosting.com/governance/acts/const.html#link10 (accessed 29 July 2006).

It is possible that an imprecise and circular definition such as this may have been practically workable because of popular understandings and practices adopted by the organization, but it is concluded that the membership code cannot provide a useful model for official recognition of the Métis people for policy purposes that respect the law of the Constitution of Canada.

Federal and Provincial Crown Obligations to the Métis

JEAN TEILLET

A. INTRODUCTION

The language and purpose of section 35 in the *Constitution Act, 1982*, imported equity into the federal common law of Aboriginal rights. The Supreme Court of Canada has held that equity governs the relationship of the Crown to the Aboriginal peoples of Canada because the language of section 35 establishes that the Crown is in a fiduciary relationship with the "aboriginal peoples of Canada." The equitable oversight has been supported by the continuing iterations of the federal common law[1] with respect to the fiduciary relationship between the Crown and Aboriginal peoples,[2] and the honour of the Crown.

This paper explores whether the Crown has equity-based obligations to Métis as one of the "aboriginal peoples of Canada" in section 35 and concludes that the Crown indeed has such obligations. The Crown's obligations to the Métis arise from a purposive, equitable, and remedial

1 *Roberts v. Canada*, [1989] 1 S.C.R. 322, where the Supreme Court of Canada found that Aboriginal title was federal common law. For more on federal common law, see Peter Hogg, "Constitutional Law — Limits of Federal Court Jurisdiction — Is There a Federal Common Law?" (1977) 55 Can. Bar Rev. 550.

2 *R. v. Sparrow*, [1990] 3 C.N.L.R. 160 at 180 (S.C.C.) [*Sparrow*], where the Court found that "the Government has the responsibility to act in a fiduciary capacity with respect to aboriginal peoples. The relationship between the Government and aboriginals is trust-like, rather than adversarial, and contemporary recognition and affirmation of aboriginal rights must be defined in light of this historic relationship."

analysis of section 35, which calls for the recognition, affirmation, and protection of the Métis. It also calls for the Crown to determine, recognize, and respect their Aboriginal and treaty rights. None of this can be achieved by silence or inaction. The conclusion is that these obligations can be implemented only by positive actions.

Many have proposed that Métis must be, along with Inuit,[3] considered "Indians" within the meaning of section 91(24) of the *Constitution Act, 1867*, with the result that the federal Crown would have jurisdiction for all Aboriginal peoples.[4] Some have proposed that this jurisdiction is exclusive and ousts the provinces from legislating with respect to Aboriginal rights.[5] However, section 35 is not limited in its application to federal jurisdiction. This paper proposes the more compelling argument that with respect to the Crown's obligations to determine, recognize, and protect the Métis and their rights, the Crown is indivisible and that both the federal and provincial Crowns carry these obligations.

B. A PURPOSIVE, EQUITABLE, AND REMEDIAL READING OF SECTION 35

In 1982, the Canadian Constitution was amended to include section 35, which recognized and affirmed the Aboriginal and treaty rights of the

3 *Reference re Eskimos*, [1939] S.C.R. 104.

4 Peter Hogg, *Constitutional Law of Canada*, 4th ed. (Scarborough, ON: Carswell, 1997) at 27-4. Also see Clem Chartier, "Indians: An Analysis of the Term They Used in s. 91(24) of the *British North America Act, 1867*" (1978–1979) 43 Sask. L. Rev. 37; B.W. Morse & J. Giokas, "Do Métis Fall within Section 91(24) of the *Constitution Act, 1867*?" in Canada, Royal Commission on Aboriginal Peoples, *Aboriginal Self-Government: Legal and Constitutional Issues* by Patrick Macklem (Ottawa: Royal Commission on Aboriginal Peoples, 1995) [*Aboriginal Self-Government*]. For the opposite view, see Thomas Flanagan, "The Case against Métis Aboriginal Rights" (1983) 9 Can. Pub. Pol'y 314; Bryan Schwartz, *First Principles: Constitutional Reform with Respect to the Aboriginal Peoples of Canada* (Kingston, ON: Institute of Intergovernmental Relations, 1985). For discussion as to whether it matters, see McMahon and Martin, "The Métis and 91(24): Is Inclusion the Issue?" in *Aboriginal Self-Government, ibid.*

5 Kent McNeil, "Aboriginal Title and the Division of Powers: Rethinking Federal and Provincial Jurisdiction" in Kent McNeil, *Emerging Justice: Essays on Indigenous Rights in Canada and Australia* (Saskatoon: Native Law Centre, 2001) at 248–80.

Aboriginal peoples of Canada. Section 35 of the *Constitution Act, 1982*, reads as follows:

> s. 35(1) The existing aboriginal and treaty rights of the aboriginal peoples of Canada are hereby recognized and affirmed.
>
> s. 35(2) In this Act, "aboriginal peoples of Canada" includes the Indian, Inuit and Métis peoples of Canada.

As a result of this constitutional recognition and affirmation, Aboriginal and treaty rights in Canada, previously subject without restriction to federal and provincial legislation, now have constitutional protection. Although this constitutional recognition was unique at the time, several other countries have now amended their constitutions to recognize and protect the rights of Indigenous peoples.[6] Indeed, such constitutional recognition appears to be emerging as a customary international-law norm.[7] While the general constitutional recognition of Aboriginal and treaty rights is no longer unique to Canada, at least one aspect of it is: the constitutional recognition of the Métis.

Since 1982, the appropriate interpretive approach to section 35(1) has been an evolving theme of Canadian courts. The Supreme Court of Canada has held that the proper interpretative approach to section 35(1) is derived from general principles of constitutional interpretation, principles relating to Aboriginal rights and the purposes behind the constitutional provision itself.[8] These can be best understood by examining the shortcomings of the common law in terms of protecting Aboriginal peoples and their rights before 1982. Setting out these deficiencies provides an explanation for why section 35 was entrenched in the Constitution and why its interpretation must be equitable and remedial.[9]

---

6 For example, see the Bolivian Constitution, amended in 1994; the Brazilian Constitution, amended in 1988; the Colombian Constitution, amended in 1991; the Ecuadorian Constitution, amended in 1998; and the Political Constitution of Nicaragua, amended in 1995.

7 S. James Anaya & Robert A. Williams, Jr., "The Protection of Indigenous Peoples' Rights over Lands and Natural Resources under the Inter-American Human Rights System" (2001) 14 Harv. Hum. Rts. J. 33.

8 *Sparrow*, above note 2 at 178.

9 A brief account of this history is set out in *Sparrow*, *ibid.* at 177–78.

Before 1982, Aboriginal and treaty rights were governed by common law. Had the claims of Aboriginal peoples been treated as equitable claims, remedies might have been available, because as McLachlin C.J. explained, "equity offered relief where the common law shoe pinched."[10] However, before the enactment of section 35, the doctrine of equity had little influence on Aboriginal rights. By the late 1970s, the common law had pinched Aboriginal and treaty rights into virtual non-existence, even restricting Indians from hunting on reserves.

In the 1960s, in *R. v. George* and *Daniels v. White*, the Supreme Court held that treaty rights were subordinate to federal legislation.[11] Following these decisions, lower courts and governments assumed that legislation overruled Indian treaty rights. By the late 1970s, *George* and *Daniels* represented the general state of Aboriginal rights law in Canada. Aboriginal peoples were being charged for practising their traditional way of life on the land. Indian harvesting rights, protected by treaties or the *Natural Resources Transfer Agreements*, could be ignored or overridden by either level of government by legislative enactment. No equitable relief was available.

> If the claim in equity exists it must be shown to have an ancestry founded in history and in the practice and precedents of the courts administering equity jurisdiction. It is not sufficient that because we may think

---

10 The Honourable Beverley McLachlin, "The Place of Equity and Equitable Doctrines in the Contemporary Common Law World: A Canadian Perspective" in Donovan W.M. Waters, ed., *Equity, Fiduciaries and Trusts* (Scarborough, ON: Carswell, 1993) at 38.

11 *R. v. George* (1966), 55 D.L.R. (2d) 386 (S.C.C.); *Daniels v. White*, [1968] S.C.R. 517. For a more complete discussion on the history of the Ontario regulatory regime with respect to Aboriginal harvesting, see Jean Teillet & Frank Tough, "Aboriginal Harvesting: The 19th and 20th Century Battle for Access to Fish and Wildlife" in *The Role of the Natural Resources Regulatory Regime in Aboriginal Rights Disputes in Ontario*, Report for the Ipperwash Inquiry (31 March 2005), online: www.ipperwashinquiry.ca/policy_part/research/pdf/Teillet.pdf. See also Frank Tough, *A Review of the History of Indian Resource Rights and Conservation Regulations in Ontario ca. 1880–1945* [unpublished, 1995]; and see Frank Tough, *Ontario's Appropriation of Indian Hunting: Provincial Conservation Polices vs. Aboriginal Treaty Rights, ca. 1892–1930*, report for the Ontario Native Affairs Secretariat [unpublished, January 1991].

> that "justice" of the present case requires it, we should invent such a jurisdiction for the first time.[12]

Against this backdrop of shortcomings in the common law, section 35 of the *Constitution Act, 1982*, was enacted. At the time, there was a consensus that the Aboriginal peoples of Canada had "old and difficult grievances" that required reconciliation.[13] Section 35 was to be a guarantee that "no government or individual will again be able to put aside or disregard the rights of Canada's original peoples" because Parliament had taken the "opportunity of redressing their claims in the Constitution and to provide a legal basis for it."[14] In this way, Canadians wrote a remedial and equitable statement of purpose about Aboriginal peoples and their rights into the *Constitution Act, 1982*, and thereby provided what was thought at the time to be an appropriate remedy pursuant to section 52(1).[15] Thereafter, a law inconsistent with section 35 would be declared of no force and effect.

If events in 1982 established a new constitutional order, they also mandated new approaches to the interpretation of the newly entrenched constitutional rights of the Aboriginal peoples of Canada. Such rights were hereafter to be interpreted in a purposive, remedial, and equitable manner.

The purposive approach to constitutionally guaranteed rights was set out in one of the earliest *Charter* cases, *Hunter v. Southam*. In that case, the Supreme Court of Canada, in examining the reasonableness of a statute authorizing a search, held that the purpose of the *Charter* was to "guarantee and to protect" rights and freedoms, and one way to accomplish this was by constraining government action that was inconsistent

---

12 McLachlin C.J., above note 10 at 38, quoting the English Court of Appeal in *Re Diplock*, [1948] Ch. 465 at 481–82 (C.A.).

13 Canada, House of Commons and Senate, *Hansard*, Senate Debates 1980–1982 at 3317 (Statement by Senator Austin re inclusion of s. 35).

14 *Hansard*, Senate Debates, *ibid.* at 1921–22 and 3318; see also *Hansard*, House of Commons Debates 1980–1982 at 3889, 4044–45, 7448, 7519–21, 9403, 13276, and 13280.

15 Section 52(1) of the *Constitution Act, 1982*, being Schedule B to the *Canada Act 1982* (U.K.), 1982, c. 11, reads, in part, as follows: "The Constitution of Canada is the supreme law of Canada, and any law that is inconsistent with the provisions of the Constitution is, to the extent of the inconsistency, of no force or effect."

with protected rights and freedoms.[16] Shortly afterwards, the Supreme Court of Canada reaffirmed the purposive approach to interpretation of the *Charter* in *R. v. Big M Drug Mart Ltd.*

> ... the proper approach to the definition of the rights and freedoms guaranteed by the *Charter* was a purposive one. The meaning of a right or freedom guaranteed by the *Charter* was to be ascertained by an analysis of the purpose of such a guarantee; it was to be understood, in other words, in the light of the interests it was meant to protect.
>
> In my view *this analysis is to be undertaken, and the purpose of the right or freedom in question is to be sought by reference to the character and the larger objects of the* Charter *itself, to the language chosen to articulate the specific right or freedom, to the historical origins of the concepts enshrined, and where applicable, to the meaning and purpose of the other specific rights and freedoms with which it is associated within the text of the* Charter. The interpretation should be, as the judgment in Southam emphasizes, a generous rather than a legalistic one, aimed at fulfilling the purpose of the guarantee and securing for individuals the full benefit of the *Charter's* protection. At the same time it is important not to overshoot the actual purpose of the right or freedom in question, but to recall that the *Charter* was not enacted in a vacuum, and must therefore, ... be placed in its proper linguistic, philosophic and historical contexts.[17]

Like the *Charter*, section 35(1) is to be construed in a purposive fashion. In *R. v. Sparrow*, the first case that dealt with section 35(1), the Supreme Court determined that in addition to a purposive analysis, section 35 is to be interpreted in a remedial manner:

> The nature of s. 35(1) itself suggests that it be construed in a purposive way. When the purposes of the affirmation of aboriginal rights are considered, it is clear that a generous, liberal interpretation of the words in the constitutional provision is demanded. When the Court of Appeal below was confronted with the submission that s. 35 has no effect on aboriginal or treaty rights and that it is merely a preamble to the parts

16 *Hunter v. Southam Inc.*, [1984] 2 S.C.R. 145, 1984 CanLII 33 at paras. 19 –20.

17 *R. v. Big M Drug Mart Ltd.*, [1985] 1 S.C.R. 295, 1985 CanLII 69 at paras. 116–17 [*Big M Drug Mart*] [emphasis added].

of the *Constitution Act, 1982*, which deal with aboriginal rights, it said the following, at p. 322:

> This submission gives no meaning to s. 35. If accepted, it would result in denying its clear statement that existing rights are hereby recognized and affirmed, and would turn that into a mere promise to recognize and affirm those rights sometime in the future. . . . To so construe s. 35(1) would be to ignore its language and the principle that the Constitution should be interpreted in a liberal and remedial way. We cannot accept that that principle applies less strongly to aboriginal rights than to the rights guaranteed by the *Charter*, particularly having regard to the history and to the approach to interpreting treaties and statutes relating to Indians . . . .[18]

As Kerans J.A. stated in reference to minority language protections in the *Charter*, "the very existence of the section implies the inadequacy of the present regime."[19] The same could be said of section 35; it was not to be considered a "mere promise . . . sometime in the future." Instead, a remedial interpretation to section 35 was required. In order to implement the remedial purpose of section 35, the Supreme Court held, in *Sparrow*, that there was an obligation on the Crown to reconcile its powers under section 91(24) with its section 35 duties.[20]

> Rights that are recognized and affirmed are not absolute. Federal legislative powers continue, including, of course, the right to legislate with respect to Indians pursuant to s. 91(24) of the *Constitution Act, 1867*. These powers must, however, now be read together with s. 35(1). In other words, *federal power must be reconciled with federal duty and the best way to achieve that reconciliation is to demand the justification of any government regulation that infringes upon or denies aboriginal rights.*[21]

---

18 *Sparrow*, above note 2 at 179.

19 *Mahe v. Alberta*, [1990] 1 S.C.R. 342 at para. 34, 1990 CanLII 133.

20 Later, reconciliation was more often described as reconciliation between Aboriginal peoples and the sovereignty of the Crown. See *R. v. Van der Peet*, [1996] 2 S.C.R. 507, 1996 CanLII 216 at para. 31 [*Van der Peet*].

21 *Sparrow*, above note 2 at 181 [emphasis added].

Subsequent case law has affirmed that the same principles apply to provincial powers.[22] Therefore, with respect to recognition of Aboriginal peoples and affirmation of their rights, Crown powers — both federal and provincial — need to be reconciled with their duties. As the Chief Justice noted in her comments with respect to the need to reconcile equitable remedies with "other rule systems," where the equitable goals are different from the goals of other rule systems, the remedies may also need to be different.[23] This is helpful in understanding the remedial purpose of section 35. It confirms that one remedial obligation arising out of section 35 is the need to reconcile the Crown's constitutional obligations with the rule systems embodied in statute, regulations, and policy.[24] It also aligns with the Court's conclusions in *Charter* cases that the protection of rights and freedoms would need to be accomplished by constraining inconsistent government action.[25]

In *Sparrow*, the Supreme Court also established that the relationship between Aboriginal peoples and the Crown was to be governed by equity. The relationship between the government and Aboriginal peoples is trust-like rather than adversarial, and the recognition and affirmation of Aboriginal rights must be defined in light of this historic relationship.[26] While the fiduciary concept in *Guerin* was held to have originated in Aboriginal title, in *Sparrow*, the source was the language of section 35.

> Yet, we find that the words "recognition and affirmation" incorporate the fiduciary relationship referred to earlier and so import some restraint on the exercise of sovereign power.[27]
>
> The "historic powers and responsibility assumed by the Crown" in relation to Indian rights, although spoken of in *Sparrow*, at p. 1108, as a "general guiding principle for s. 35(1)", is of broader importance. All members of the Court accepted in *Ross River* that potential relief by way of fiduciary remedies is not limited to the s. 35 rights (*Sparrow*) or exist-

22 *R. v. Powley*, 2003 SCC 43 [*Powley*], *Game and Fish Act*, R.S.O. 1990, c. G.1, ss. 46 and 47(1). *R. v. Sappier*, [2006] 2 S.C.R. 686, where the defendants were charged pursuant to the *Crown Lands and Forests Act*, S.N.B. 1980, c. C-38.1.

23 McLachlin C.J., above note 10 at 40.

24 *R. v. Adams*, [1996] 4 C.N.L.R. 1 at para. 54 (S.C.C.) [*Adams*].

25 *Hunter v. Southam Inc.*, above note 16 at paras. 19–20.

26 *Sparrow*, above note 2 at 180–81.

27 *Ibid.* at 181.

> ing reserves (*Guerin*). The fiduciary duty, where it exists, is called into existence to facilitate supervision of the high degree of discretionary control gradually assumed by the Crown over the lives of aboriginal peoples.[28]

After *Calder v. Attorney-General of British Columbia*,[29] where the Court recognized that Indian title was a legal interest, it became clear that recognition of Aboriginal rights could not be treated "merely as an act of grace and favour on the part of the Crown."[30] The concept that the duty of the Crown to Aboriginal peoples was merely a political trust, meaning that its obligations were unenforceable at law, was dismissed in *Guerin*[31] and the fiduciary relationship was subsequently reaffirmed in *Sparrow*.[32] It is now clear that equity supervises the fiduciary relationship between Aboriginal peoples and the Crown and that equity holds the fiduciary to a strict standard of conduct.[33]

We know that not every action of the Crown in its relationship with Aboriginal peoples triggers fiduciary obligations.[34] However, it is trite law that one of the first duties of any fiduciary is to ascertain the beneficiaries.[35] It is important when looking at a fiduciary relationship to distinguish between the duties and discretion of the fiduciary.

> Sometimes the line between duty and discretion is not easy to discover, but a trustee who interprets himself to have a discretion when in fact he has a duty does so at his peril.[36]

Ascertaining the beneficiaries is not a discretionary activity. A fiduciary has an obligation to carry out her obligations and if she does not, the courts will ensure that the duty is discharged. Further, if a fiduciary

28 *Wewaykum Indian Band v. Canada*, [2002] 4 S.C.R. 245 at para. 79 [*Wewaykum*]; and see *R. v. Marshall*, 1999 CanLII 665, [1999] 3 S.C.R. 456 at para. 17; and W.R. McMurtry & A. Pratt, "Indians and the Fiduciary Concept, Self-Government and the Constitution: *Guerin* in Perspective," [1986] 3 C.N.L.R. 19 at 31.

29 *Calder v. British Columbia (Attorney General)*, [1973] S.C.R. 313.

30 *Wewaykum*, above note 28 at para. 75.

31 *R. v. Guerin*, [1984] 2 S.C.R. 335 at 375–76, 1984 CanLII 25 [*Guerin*].

32 *Sparrow*, above note 2 at 180–81.

33 *Guerin*, above note 31 at 384.

34 *Wewaykum*, above note 28 at paras. 80, 81, and 83.

35 D.W.M. Waters, *Law of Trusts in Canada* (Toronto: Carswell, 1974) at 113–19.

36 *Ibid*. at 664.

knows that an exercise of her discretion will adversely affect the rights or interests of a vulnerable party to whom she may owe fiduciary obligations, she has a duty to make appropriate inquiries, and to inform herself about the possibility of such a duty.[37] These are the minimum fiduciary obligations on the Crown under section 35.

The trust-like relationship between the Crown and the Aboriginal peoples of Canada includes the Métis. This assumption arises from the reasoning of the Court in applying the fiduciary relationship to First Nations. In *Sparrow*, the Court held that the words "recognize" and "affirm" in section 35 of the *Constitution Act, 1982*, incorporated the fiduciary duty.[38] Those words apply to the "aboriginal peoples of Canada," which section 35(2) defines as including the Métis.

If the Crown is in a fiduciary relationship with the Métis, then arguably, it has an obligation, as a fiduciary, to recognize and affirm this relationship. The recognition and affirmation of Aboriginal and treaty rights in section 35 is meaningless if the Aboriginal peoples who hold the rights are not also recognized and affirmed. This suggests, and the court of appeal in Ontario has affirmed, that the Crown has a positive obligation to work with the Métis to recognize their collectives.[39]

In *Haida Nation v. British Columbia (Minister of Forests)*[40] and *Taku River Tlingit First Nation v. British Columbia (Project Assessment Director)*,[41] the Supreme Court of Canada began to articulate new Crown duties based on its trust-like relationship with Aboriginal peoples. These cases reflect the Court's continuing commitment to the remedial and equitable purposes that underlie section 35 in the *Constitution Act, 1982*. They establish new positive duties owed by all Crown actors to Aboriginal peoples.

---

37 J.M. Gautreau, "Demystifying the Fiduciary Mystique" (1989) 68 Can. Bar Rev. 1 at 4–5 and 25; Waters, *Law of Trusts in Canada*, above note 35 at section 19(i); Philip Pettit, *Equity and the Law of Trusts*, 8th ed. (London: Butterworths, 1997) cc. 17 and 20.

38 *Sparrow*, above note 2 at 180.

39 *R. v. Powley*, 2001 CanLII 24181 at para. 166 (Ont. C.A.).

40 *Haida Nation v. British Columbia (Minister of Forests)*, [2004] 3 S.C.R. 511, 2004 SCC 73 [*Haida*].

41 *Taku River Tlingit First Nation v. British Columbia (Project Assessment Director)*, [2000] B.C.J. No. 1301 (S.C.), aff'd [2002] B.C.J. No. 155 (C.A.), rev'd [2004] 3 S.C.R. 550 [*Taku River*].

The duties of consultation and accommodation recognized in *Haida Nation* and *Taku River* are based on the honour of the Crown and are not fiduciary duties. However, that does not mean that they lack equitable character. The duties are designed to complement the fiduciary relationship already articulated by the Court, which requires the protection of defined Aboriginal and treaty rights within section 35. By confirming that the Crown has positive duties triggered by an *assertion* of Aboriginal rights, the Court has required governments to acknowledge and act on the original purpose for section 35, and to alter their conduct as necessary to ensure the achievement of that purpose.[42]

This very significant development in the section 35 jurisprudence builds on earlier principles articulated by the Court. In her dissent in *Van der Peet*, McLachlin J. (as she then was) explained the fundamental importance of territorial lands and resources as the foundation for Aboriginal rights, what she described as "the *grundnorm* of settlement in Canada."[43] In *Sparrow*, the Court stated that the inclusion of section 35 in Canada's constitution represented a substantial promise that must be given remedial effect,[44] and in *Adams*, the Court said that governments are obliged to take affirmative steps designed to avoid infringing Aboriginal rights.[45] Those cases form the backdrop for the positive duty to consult, which has an important purpose: to transform the relationship between the Crown and Aboriginal peoples from one tainted by colonialism to a new one based on a just settlement and reconciliation.[46]

C. POSITIVE OBLIGATIONS

The traditional view of the Crown's obligations to legislate pursuant to its jurisdiction has generally been characterized as negative.[47] Under this analysis, the Crown need only refrain from unjustifiably interfering (either in purpose or effect) with Aboriginal and treaty rights. The argu-

42 *Haida*, above note 40 at paras. 26, 27, and 33.

43 *Van der Peet*, above note 20 at paras. 272 and 275.

44 *Sparrow*, above note 2 at 180.

45 *Adams*, above note 24 at para. 54.

46 *Haida*, above note 40 at para. 20.

47 Morse & Giokas, "Do the Métis Fall within Section 91(24) of the *Constitution Act, 1867*?" above note 4 at 231–32.

ment goes that neither section 91(24) of the *Constitution Act, 1867*, nor section 35 of the *Constitution Act, 1982*, oblige the state to take affirmative action to safeguard or facilitate rights.

In light of this, does the equitable and remedial purpose of section 35 impose positive obligations on the Crown to extend recognition and protective legislation to the Métis as an unprotected group in order to determine, recognize, and affirm their rights? More broadly, does the distinction between positive and negative state obligations justify the exclusion of Métis from a protective regime and contribute to the violation of Métis rights?

Questions with respect to positive obligations have been discussed by the courts in the context of *Charter* guarantees, such as freedom of association and freedom of religion. In *Delisle*,[48] an employment case, L'Heureux-Dubé J. recognized that freedom of association may require protection against unfair labour practices in certain circumstances:

> It may also be that there is a positive obligation on the part of governments to provide legislative protection against unfair labour practices or some form of official recognition under labour legislation, because of the inherent vulnerability of employees to pressure from management, and the private power of employers, when left unchecked, to interfere with the formation and administration of unions.[49]

In the context of freedom of religion, the court held that "protection of one religion and the concomitant non-protection of others imports disparate impacts destructive of the religious freedom of the collectivity."[50] Recognition that government action with respect to one group can have this effect leads logically to the conclusion that legislation and policy that are under-inclusive may have a substantial impact on the exercise of a constitutional right or freedom. It may also mean that there is a constitutional right to protective legislation.

48 *Delisle v. Canada (Deputy Attorney General)*, [1999] 2 S.C.R. 989, 1999 CanLII 649 at para. 7.

49 *Ibid.*

50 *Big M Drug Mart*, above note 17 at 337.

> [A] situation might arise in which, in order to make a fundamental freedom meaningful, a posture of restraint would not be enough, and positive governmental action might be required.[51]

In *Reference re Public Service Employee Relations Act*, Dickson C.J. held that positive obligations may be required "where the absence of government intervention may in effect substantially impede the enjoyment of fundamental freedoms."[52]

Despite these observations about the need for government action, courts have been reluctant to speak about legislative silence and have held that the doctrine of under-inclusion does not, on its own, oblige the state to act where it has not already legislated in a certain area. In examining the boundaries that separate the areas where constitutional norms apply and where they do not, Prof. Hogg noted:

> The effect of the governmental action restriction is that there is a . . . realm in which . . . constitutional norms do not intrude. The boundaries of that realm are marked, not by an *a priori* definition . . . but by the absence of statutory or other governmental intervention.[53]

Can excluding Métis from regimes that recognize and protect other Aboriginal peoples and their institutions constitute a substantial interference with their rights?[54] The answer to this question is yes. Is the relationship between the Métis and the Crown impervious to court review simply because there has been legislative silence with respect to Métis institutions? The answer to this question must be no.

The federal Crown does not include Métis in section 91(24). It restricts that Aboriginal recognition regime to First Nations and Inuit. In the case of First Nations, the collective institutions recognized by govern-

---

51 *Haig v. Canada; Haig v. Canada (Chief Electoral Officer)*, [1993] 2 S.C.R. 995 at 1039.

52 *Reference re Public Service Employee Relations Act (Alta.)*, [1987] 1 S.C.R. 313, 1987 CanLII 88 at para. 77.

53 Peter Hogg, *Constitutional Law of Canada*, above note 4 at 34-27.

54 There are two exceptions to this. In Saskatchewan, see the *Métis Act*, S.S., c. M-14.01, which is *An Act to recognize contributions of the Métis and to deal with certain Métis Institutions*. In Alberta, several acts collectively deal with the Métis settlements: *Métis Settlements Accord Implementation Act*, S.A. 1990, c. M-14.5; *Métis Settlements Land Protection Act*, S.A. 1990, c. M-14.8; and the *Metis Settlements Act*, S.A. 1990, c. M-14.3.

ments are the chiefs, bands, and councils created long ago by the Crown, which gradually replaced the traditional Indian forms of governance and are now defined terms in the *Indian Act*.[55] The Crown has never created such entities for the Métis and has refused to recognize Métis-created organizations for constitutional purposes. It has then used that Métis absence from its recognition regime to deny Métis the opportunity to defend their Aboriginal rights in court. The Crown's position was starkly expressed in *The Labrador Metis Nation v. Newfoundland and Labrador (Minister of Transportation and Works)*:

> . . . the Labrador Metis Nation is a political organization and a stakeholder on a political level only and does not constitute a community for constitutional purposes obliging the government of the province to consult with it. He argues that the honour of the Crown requires the Crown to consult with the community, not a political organization and that a corporate body can not represent the aboriginal people. He argues further that for a community of people to fit the Section 35 constitutional reference to Metis people, those people must be represented by a governing body of the community. Such a governing body, he argues, can be a Band Council, or a Council of Elders, or even a person appointed by the community such as a chief, but it can never be a corporate person because the corporation can never be the holder of aboriginal rights and can not be assigned such rights.[56]

Whether Métis corporate organizations are legally capable of representing the Métis for the purposes of asserting their constitutional rights *qua* Métis was also considered in the case of *Manitoba Metis Federation*

---

55 *Indian Act*, R.S.C. 1985, c. I-5. See s. 2 for definitions of "band" and "council of the band." For a discussion with respect to the legal capacity of bands, see Shin Imai, *The 2007 Annotated Indian Act and Aboriginal Constitutional Provisions* (Scarborough, ON: Thomson Carswell, 2006) at 6–10.

56 *Labrador Metis Nation v. Newfoundland and Labrador (Minister of Transportation and Works)*, 2006 NLTD 119 at para. 57 [*Labrador Metis Nation*]. While the Court of Appeal disputed the use of the *Powley* test because it determined that these people were not Métis, it emphatically upheld that there was sufficient evidence to show that the applicants were Aboriginal and that there was an obligation to consult with them — whether they are Métis or Inuit.

v. Canada.[57] In his dissenting opinion, O'Sullivan J.A. of the Manitoba Court of Appeal addressed the difficulties facing the Métis in asserting their collective Aboriginal rights:

> It is difficult for common lawyers to understand what the rights of a "people" can mean. Indeed, at a hearing before a parliamentary committee on the 1987 Constitution Accord (of Meech Lake) held August 27, 1987, the distinguished constitutional expert, the Right Honourable Pierre Elliott Trudeau said:
>
> > "In my philosophy, the community, an institution itself, has no rights. It has rights by delegation from the individuals. You give equality to the individuals and you give rights to the individuals. Then they will organize in societies to make sure those rights are respected."
>
> This is an approach with deep roots in the British tradition . . . . But, as far as I can see, what we have before us in court at this time is not the assertion of bundles of individual rights but the assertion of the rights and status of the half-breed people of the western plains.
>
> The problem confronting us is how can the rights of the Métis people as a people be asserted . . . the rights of the Métis people must be capable of being asserted by somebody. If not by the present plaintiffs, then by whom?
>
> . . . One of the difficulties in enforcing the rights of native peoples is that they are difficult to define in common-law terms. Even the question of membership in a people may provide perplexing issues. But that a half-breed people existed as a people in the western plains of British North America in 1869 can hardly be doubted by those familiar with the history of this country.
>
> . . . I add some comments on the need to develop the rule of law so as to make possible a legal solution to minority claims . . . it is evident that since the advent of the age of nationalism and democracy world society

57 *Dumont v. Canada (Attorney General)*, [1990] 2 C.N.L.R. 19 (S.C.C.), rev'g (*sub nom. Manitoba Metis Federation Inc. v. Canada (Attorney General)*) (1988), 52 D.L.R. (4th) 25 (Man. C.A.), rev'g [1987] 2 C.N.L.R. 85 (Man. Q.B.); on the merits, see *Manitoba Metis Federation Inc. v. Canada (Attorney General)*, [2007] M.J. No. 448 (Q.B.).

> has failed to develop satisfactory rules for the recognition of communal minority rights and for the balancing of such rights with the common good of society as a whole .... Constitutional protections have been largely ineffective because of our failure to develop a jurisprudence capable of dealing adequately with the issues.
>
> Our courts have become expert at determining facts in individual cases and of applying agreed rules to them. In the protection of minority interests, however, the courts as now constituted face an almost insuperable hurdle, that of determining constitutional facts which depend so much on historical interpretations and social and political analysis ....
>
> Nevertheless, I think it is important to accept that the claims asserted by the plaintiffs in the present action are justiciable and not merely political. The plaintiffs have status to assert their claims in the Court of Queen's Bench. I am sure the judge assigned to try the case will have a difficult time and will have to be able to adapt the process of the court to suit the nature of the case. But, in the end, in my opinion it is in the development of law to deal with claims of "peoples" that lies the best hope of achieving justice and harmony in a world full of minority groups.[58]

The Supreme Court unanimously overturned the majority decision of the Manitoba Court of Appeal,[59] which appeared to leave O'Sullivan J.A.'s finding that the Manitoba Metis Federation was the appropriate legal entity to represent Métis with respect to their rights. However, when the case returned to the Court of Queen's Bench on the merits, MacInnes J. agreed with counsel for Manitoba and Canada that the Manitoba Metis Federation had no standing to pursue the claims of the Métis.[60]

The court in *Labrador Metis Nation* noted that the Crown's policy on this issue is inconsistent:

> ... I am more in agreement with Counsel for the Applicant when he argues ... that the aboriginal community can be represented by an agent, in this case the Labrador Metis Nation or LMN .... Clearly in the instant case the Metis people of Labrador have chosen the LMN as their agent to make their case for them. I should add that it has not gone unnoticed by the court that at the same time that the Province of New-

58 *Ibid*. at 28–34 (C.A.).

59 *Ibid*. (S.C.C.).

60 *Ibid*. at paras. 400–407 (Man. Q.B. 2007).

> foundland and Labrador was preparing its response to the present Metis case before this court it was completing the final stages of a Treaty with the Labrador Inuit. What is remarkable about that Treaty . . . is that the signatories to that Treaty were (1) The Inuit of Labrador as represented by Labrador Inuit Association; (2) Her Majesty the Queen in Right of Newfoundland and Labrador; and (3) Her Majesty the Queen in Right of Canada. Under part 1.1.1 of the Treaty; "Labrador Inuit Association" means the body corporate of that name organized and existing under the "*Corporations Act*."
>
> It seems to me therefore that for the Crown to have been engaged in complex negotiations on a Constitutional level concerning aboriginal rights issues with a corporate person representing the Inuit people on the one hand and now take the position that it is improper to do so when dealing with the Labrador Metis people on the other hand is simply confusing and not in keeping with the high principled honour of the Crown.[61]

The Court of Appeal agreed with the trial judge and also rejected the Crown's submission that a corporate plaintiff could not be the vehicle for enforcement of an Aboriginal right to consultation. It noted that the Crown provided no authority for its submission that section 35 rights could not be asserted and protected by an agent, and also rejected the Crown's submission that in order for an agent to so assert and protect, the rights would have to be transferred, which is impossible with section 35 rights. The court held that it knew of "no proposition in the law of principle and agent which requires that rights be transferred to an agent before the agent can act to protect them."[62]

The appeal court found that the trial judge erred in concluding that the Crown should be estopped from questioning the authority of a corporation to deal with Aboriginal rights because the Crown had signed a treaty with the Labrador Inuit Association, also a corporation, dealing with Inuit rights in northern Labrador. The court agreed with the Crown that the Crown has the authority to create new constitutionally protected

61 *Labrador Metis Nation*, above note 56 at paras. 60 and 68.

62 *Labrador Métis Nation v. Newfoundland and Labrador (Minister of Transportation and Works)*, [2007] N.J. No. 421 at paras. 46–49 (C.A.).

rights through the treaty process.[63] The Crown's recognition of Inuit corporate bodies for the purposes of treaty negotiations may not be grounds for estoppel, but is evidence of the Crown's inconsistency in this regard.

The Métis situation has become a game of denial. The federal and provincial Crowns have made the following claims about the Métis: they are not within either federal or provincial jurisdiction; there is no definition of who they are; the Crowns do not know where Métis communities are; and Métis corporate organizations cannot defend Métis rights or be consulted. All of this amounts to affirmative interference, much of which is based on denial of jurisdiction. The Crown simply will not exercise its discretion to recognize the Métis and protect their Aboriginal rights. As Evans notes, discretionary power is commonly defended by denial of its existence.[64] The Court rejected this kind of submission in *Powley*:

> This theory in effect would deny to Métis their full status as distinctive rights-bearing peoples whose own integral practices are entitled to constitutional protection under s. 35(1).[65]

This jurisdictional vacuum is also a situation that the Métis themselves cannot fix. The Métis cannot force the Crown to accept jurisdiction or to enact recognition legislation, yet in *Haida Nation v. British Columbia (Minister of Forests)*,[66] the Court found:

> The potential rights embedded in these [asserted] claims are protected by s. 35 of the *Constitution Act, 1982*. The honour of the Crown requires that these rights be determined, recognized and respected.[67]

Here, the Court did not limit the obligation to rights claims already determined in treaty or bylaw. The finding applies to asserted or "potential rights" and the Court notes that the honour of the Crown requires it to ensure that these claimed rights are "determined." This cannot be understood as anything other than a positive obligation.

---

63 *Ibid.* at para. 48.

64 Robert G. Evans, "Illusions of Necessity: Evading Responsibility for Choice in Health Care" (1985) 10 J. Health Pol. 439–67.

65 *Powley*, above note 22 at para. 38.

66 *Haida*, above note 40.

67 *Ibid.* at para. 25.

Entitlement to constitutional protection as a rights-bearing people therefore implies that the Crown has a positive duty with respect to the Métis. It implies the need for a relationship and if there is to be an effective relationship with the Métis, the Crown will need to implement a profound change in its policies and law. It must take steps to inform itself about the Métis, and identify and work with the representatives of Métis collectives. Positive obligations to act exist even in the face of uncertainty, as stated by the Ontario Court of Appeal:

> . . . I do not accept that uncertainty about identifying those entitled to assert Métis rights can be accepted as a justification for denying the right . . . . There is an element of uncertainty about most broadly worded constitutional rights. The government cannot simply sit on its hands and then defend its inaction because the nature of the right or the identity of the bearers of the right is uncertain.[68]

D. DIVISION OF POWERS

Can the Crown evade its positive obligations to the Métis with a division-of-powers argument? Can the provinces continue to claim that the Métis are a federal responsibility while the federal government claims that responsibility for the Métis falls to the provinces? The answer to both these questions is no. The Crown cannot evade its responsibilities by shifting them back and forth between provincial and federal jurisdictions.

The courts have already found that the Crown is indivisible with respect to two aspects of its relationship to Aboriginal peoples: the fiduciary relationship and the duty to consult and accommodate flowing from the Crown's honour.[69] In *Gitanyow First Nation v. Canada*, Willliamson J. held that the fiduciary obligation to Aboriginal peoples resides in both the federal and provincial Crowns.

> From the perspective of Aboriginal peoples, then, the fiduciary obligations of the Crown remain whether they were dealing with the Crown

68 *R. v. Powley*, above note 39 at para. 166.

69 *Gitanyow First Nation v. Canada*, [1999] 3 C.N.L.R. 89 at paras. 45–49 (B.C.S.C.) [*Gitanyow*]; *Haida*, above note 40 at paras 57–59.

> of colonial times, or are dealing with the Crown in Right of Canada or the Crown in Right of British Columbia.[70]

In *Haida*, British Columbia argued that the obligation to consult or accommodate rested with Canada and not with the Crown in right of the province. The Supreme Court of Canada did not agree.

> The Province of British Columbia argues that any duty to consult or accommodate rests solely with the federal government. I cannot accept this argument.
>
> The Province's argument rests on s. 109 of the *Constitution Act, 1867*, which provides that "[a]ll Lands, Mines, Minerals, and Royalties belonging to the several Provinces of Canada . . . at the Union . . . shall belong to the several Provinces." The Province argues that this gives it exclusive right to the land at issue. This right, it argues, cannot be limited by the protection for Aboriginal rights found in s. 35 of the *Constitution Act, 1982*. To do so, it argues, would "undermine the balance of federalism" . . . .
>
> The answer to this argument is that the Provinces took their interest in land subject to "any Interest other than that of the Province in the same" (s. 109). The duty to consult and accommodate here at issue is grounded in the assertion of Crown sovereignty which pre-dated the Union. It follows that the Province took the lands subject to this duty. It cannot therefore claim that s. 35 deprives it of powers it would otherwise have enjoyed. As stated in *St. Catherine's Milling and Lumber Co. v. The Queen* (1888), 14 App. Cas. 46 (P.C.), lands in the Province are "available to [the Province] as a source of revenue whenever the estate of the Crown is disencumbered of the Indian title" (p. 59). The Crown's argument on this point has been canvassed by this Court in *Delgamuukw, supra*, at para. 175, where Lamer C.J. reiterated the conclusions in *St. Catherine's Milling, supra*. There is therefore no foundation to the Province's argument on this point.[71]

In light of this, it seems reasonable to propose that all of the Crown's equitable and remedial obligations to all Aboriginal peoples, including

70 *Gitanyow, ibid.* at paras. 45–49.

71 *Haida*, above note 40 at paras. 57–59.

the Métis, reside in both federal and provincial governments. As noted by the Supreme Court of Canada in *R. v. Côté*,

> The text and purpose of s. 35(1) do not distinguish between federal and provincial laws which restrict aboriginal or treaty rights, and they should both be subject to the same standard of constitutional scrutiny.[72]

The trust-like relationship and its obligations bind the Crown as a whole, including all officials who exercise Crown authority. Applying this doctrine in *Taku River*, the courts rejected the Crown's argument that the minister's responsibilities were limited to those set out in the specific statute and that he was not responsible for positions taken by other ministers of the Crown who were engaged in treaty negotiations with the Tlingits.[73] A fiduciary must ensure that all those who act on its behalf do so according to the requirements of equity.[74]

A related concept is that a fiduciary cannot rely on its own internal structure or distribution of authority to avoid its obligations.[75] It follows that a fiduciary should not be able to use the beneficiaries' internal structure or distribution of authority to avoid its obligations; therefore, the Crown should not be able to avoid its obligations to Aboriginals by pointing to its particular arrangements. The Crown should also be precluded from arguing that it has no obligations to Aboriginal peoples whose internal governing structures are not set up to its liking. The Crown, as a fiduciary, should be precluded from taking the position that the internal structure of its beneficiaries — for example, Métis who are structured as corporations — is a reason for avoiding its obligations. That is neither equitable nor honourable.

---

72 *R. v. Côté*, 1996 CanLII 170 at para. 74 (S.C.C.).

73 *Taku River*, above note 41.

74 *Lloyds Bank Ltd. v. Bundy*, [1974] 3 All E.R. 757 at 768 and 770–71 (C.A.).

75 *W.K. v. Pornbacher*, [1997] B.C.J. No. 57 at para. 54 (S.C.). The Catholic Church was found to be in a fiduciary relationship with the students in its schools. The Church was found vicariously liable for the sexual assaults on students carried out by its priests. The court held that "the church cannot insulate itself from the laws and sanctions of the secular community through the implementation of its own internal law. The church must be, and is, subject to the laws of the secular community in its dealings with the members of that community."

E. CONCLUSION

The lack of recognition for Métis organizations affects almost every aspect of Métis life. The Crowns — both federal and provincial — seem willing enough to recognize Métis organizations for the purposes of program and service delivery; however, for the purposes of rights recognition, protection, or litigation, the Crown has consistently denied recognition for Métis organizations south of the 60th parallel.[76] While there have always been departments and ministries at the federal and provincial levels for Indians, historically no such institutions of the Crown existed for the benefit of the Métis. Only after *Powley* did the Minister of Indian Affairs acknowledge the Métis for some purposes other than program and service delivery.[77] Notwithstanding this development, the Métis remain excluded from many of the protections of the law, government policies, programs, services, and benefits made available to Indians and Inuit because the federal and provincial governments deny recognition and jurisdiction and lawful obligations for Métis.

In *Sparrow*, the Supreme Court explained why it was necessary to protect Aboriginal rights in the Constitution, noting that we "cannot recount with much pride the treatment accorded to the native people of this country."[78] This reality prompted the inclusion of Aboriginal and treaty rights in the *Constitution Act, 1982*. Perhaps O'Neill J. stated the reasons best:

> The purposes underlying the aboriginal rights recognized and affirmed by s. 35(1) of the *Constitution Act, 1982* relate to both prior occupation, and reconciliation. What, however, are the reasons underlying the protection that s. 35(1) gives, and what is the basis for the special protection that aboriginal peoples generally, and Métis people specifically, have within Canadian society? Surely, at the heart of s. 35(1), lies a recognition that aboriginal rights are a matter of fundamental justice protecting the survival of aboriginal people, as a people, on their lands. The Métis have aboriginal rights, as people, based on their prior use and occupation as a people. It is a matter of fairness and fundamental justice that the aborig-

76 The exception is Alberta, but even its recognition does not include rights recognition.

77 For more on the creation of the Métis Interlocutor, see Morse & Giokas, above note 4 at 230–31.

78 *Sparrow*, above note 2 at 177.

inal rights of the Métis which flow from this prior use and occupation, be recognized and affirmed by s. 35(1) of the *Constitution Act, 1982*.[79]

In *Powley*, Ontario urged the court not to treat the Métis as a people but rather as individuals who are descendants of Indians, with their rights and existence determined by their Indian ancestors, their Indian blood quantum, and their Indian lifestyle. There would have been no reason, in fact, to include the Métis in section 35 if they were to be treated as individuals who are part Indian rather than a distinct people. *Powley* affirmed that the Métis are an Aboriginal collective with their own distinctive practices, customs, and traditions. The court set out a test for identifying section 35 harvesting rights of the Métis. It held that the purpose of including Métis in section 35 was to enhance "their survival as distinctive communities" and to "protect practices that were historically important."[80]

To give meaning to the constitutional recognition and affirmation of Métis rights, section 35 must be interpreted in light of the interests it was meant to protect. Courts must be mindful of the trust-like relationship between the Crown and the Métis peoples of Canada. As the Supreme Court of Canada noted in *Sparrow*, Aboriginal peoples are justifiably suspicious of "neutral" rules that, in reality, place insurmountable obstacles that bar the exercise of their rights.[81]

The constitutional protection of Métis rights places positive duties on the Crown federal and the Crown provincial. After all, non-interference may be achieved by inaction, but protection cannot be implemented in the abstract or in the negative. Protection also cannot be achieved by denial of jurisdiction, by a policy and law vacuum, or by the enactment of policies and laws that affect, but do not recognize and affirm Métis collectives, their representative organizations, and their Aboriginal rights.

79 *R. v. Powley*, [2000] O.J. No. 99 at para. 18 (S.C.J.).

80 *Powley*, above note 22 at para. 13.

81 *Sparrow*, above note 2 at 181.

‹ 4 ›

Beyond Space and Time — A Purposive Examination of Section 91(24) of the *Constitution Act, 1867*

CHARLOTTE A. BELL

> When great causes are on the move in the world . . . we learn that we are spirits, not animals, and that something is going on in space and time, and beyond space and time, which, whether we like it or not, spells duty.
>
> —*Winston Churchill, in a radio broadcast to the United States, 16 June 1941*

A. INTRODUCING THE TOPIC

From 1867 to 1982, the relationship between the Crown and "Indians" was mediated primarily by section 91(24)[1] of the *British North America Act, 1867*,[2] which authorized Parliament to "legislate for the benefit of the Indian population in a preferential, discriminatory, or distinctive fashion vis-à-vis others."[3]

Then in 1982, section 35 of the *Constitution Act, 1982*,[4] affirmed the rights of all of Canada's Aboriginal peoples: Inuit, Métis, and Indians.

---

1 Section 91(24) granted to the Parliament of Canada the exclusive right to legislate with respect to "Indians, and lands reserved for the Indians."

2 Now the *Constitution Act, 1867* (U.K.), 30 & 31 Vict., c. 3, reprinted in R.S.C. 1985, App. II, No. 5.

3 *Reference re Bill 30, An Act to amend the Education Act (Ont.)*, [1987] 1 S.C.R. 1148 at 1206, Estey J.

4 Being Schedule B to the *Canada Act 1982* (U.K.), 1982, c. 11.

This step was profoundly important in strengthening and protecting the rights of Aboriginal peoples in Canada and demanded a new model for the relationship between governments and Aboriginal peoples.

The question this paper addresses is whether section 35 has superseded section 91(24) in terms of mediating the relationship of Aboriginal peoples with the Crown — including rights protection — or whether section 91(24) of the *Constitution Act, 1867* remains relevant in this relationship.

This paper begins with an analysis of the purpose and effect of section 35, and then examines the history of the Crown's relationship with First Nations to determine the purpose and effect of section 91(24).

From there, it is argued that section 91(24) preserves a relationship, begun centuries ago by the imperial Crown, that means as much today as it did when first enacted. In particular, section 91(24) provides the federal Crown with the authority to promote reconciliation by legislating programs aimed at ameliorating the disadvantage suffered by "Indians" while at the same time making the necessary and inevitable adjustments to the sovereignty of the Crown.

B. SECTION 35

1) A Historical Perspective

In the opening statement at the 1983 First Ministers Conference,[5] a meeting held to identify and define section 35 rights, Prime Minister Pierre Trudeau observed:

> We are dealing for the first time with a Constitution which is finally our own, close now to all Canadians, to the many peoples and ethnic groups who make their home in this broad land. We are dealing with a constitution that still needs to define the place of our Aboriginal peoples in Canadian society.

In referring to "Aboriginal peoples," the prime minister included First Nations, Métis, and Inuit peoples whose rights were now recognized and affirmed in section 35 of the *Constitution Act, 1982*.

The distinctness of these constitutionally recognized Aboriginal societies was to be recognized and protected. Moreover, Aboriginal rights

5 Ottawa, 15–16 March 1983.

were to be defined in a way that preserved diversity. The prime minister's keynote address characterized Canadian society as one that had always respected and nurtured differences; the new Constitution merely codified this approach and made it legally enforceable. Trudeau's address expressed this in the following way:

> For two hundred years fundamental political changes in Canada have, in the main, been brought about through peaceful accommodation and compromise, which have found expression in our constitutional laws and conventions. As Canadian society grew and diversified, political evolution in this country increasingly reflected attitudes of respect for distinctiveness in fellow Canadians. In significant ways, Canadians seem as much concerned with preserving their diversities as with safeguarding their political freedoms and legal equality.

While the prime minister acknowledged that Aboriginal peoples were a distinct group in Canadian society, he also acknowledged that groups of Aboriginal peoples were distinct from each other.

> Clearly our Aboriginal peoples each occupied a special place in history. To my way of thinking, this entitles them to special recognition in the Constitution and to their own place in Canadian society, distinct from each other and distinct from other groups who, together with them, comprise the Canadian citizenry.

Over the next two decades, much of the business of the Supreme Court of Canada involved identifying and defining the rights that had been constitutionalized by section 35 of the *Constitution Act, 1982*.

First Nations peoples were the first Aboriginal peoples in Canada to seek the assistance of the courts in defining and enforcing their constitutionally enshrined rights. In cases such as *Sparrow*,[6] *Horseman*,[7] and *Delgamuukw*,[8] the Supreme Court struggled to give substance to the rights protected under section 35, and to place those rights in the broader political and economic landscape. The Court, consistent with the underlying theory of section 35 of the *Constitution Act, 1982*, articulated the

6 *R. v. Sparrow*, [1990] 1 S.C.R. 1075 [*Sparrow*].

7 *R. v. Horseman*, [1990] 1 S.C.R. 901.

8 *Delgamuukw v. British Columbia*, [1997] 3 S.C.R. 1010 [*Delgamuukw*].

scope and content of the section in a way that preserved distinctness and recognized the proper place of Aboriginal peoples. Later, in *Powley*,[9] the Supreme Court of Canada defined the nature of the Aboriginal rights of the Métis people of Canada.

2) The Judicial Perspective

The seminal judicial pronouncements on the purpose of section 35 of the *Constitution Act, 1982*, are those of Lamer C.J. In *Delgamuukw*, he expressed the purpose of the rights guaranteed under section 35 as "preserving the integral and defining features of distinctive Aboriginal societies."[10] He went on to explain that "the purpose of s.35 is to reconcile the prior presence of Aboriginal peoples in North America with the assertion of crown sovereignty."[11]

The practical effect of this interpretation is that Aboriginal rights protected under section 35 cannot be unilaterally infringed by any government. However, governments can infringe Aboriginal rights for justifiable reasons grounded in substantial and compelling public objectives.[12]

In *Sparrow*,[13] the Court observed that section 35 applied to all of Canada's Aboriginal peoples — Indians, Inuit, and Métis — and that it did more than preserve diversity and safeguard political freedom and legal equality. The section provided a "solid constitutional base" upon which negotiations of rights claims could take place.

> Section 35 calls for a just settlement for aboriginal peoples. It renounces the old rules of the game under which the Crown established courts of law and denied those courts the authority to question sovereign claims made by the Crown.[14]

The Supreme Court concluded that the Crown had failed to preserve the diversity and safeguard the political freedom and equality of

9 *R. v. Powley*, [2002] S.C.R. 207.

10 *Delgamuukw*, above note 8 at paras. 136 and 141, quoting *R. v. Côté*, [1996] 3 S.C.R. 139 at para. 52.

11 *Delgamuukw*, *ibid.* at para. 141.

12 *Mitchell v. Canada (Minister of National Revenue)*, [2001] 1 S.C.R. 911 at para. 11.

13 *Sparrow*, above note 6.

14 *Ibid.* at para. 54, quoting Prof. Lyon in "An Essay on Constitutional Interpretation" (1988) 26 Osgoode Hall L.J. 95.

Canada's First Nations peoples and looked to a new way of protecting the interests of Canada's Aboriginal peoples: a way that focused on the settlement of claims and the protection of rights. This new way placed the Court in the role of balancing the preservation of diversity and the accommodation of the interests and aspirations of all of the people in the broader Canadian society.

In *Haida Nation*, McLachlin C.J. articulated the principles that the Court would apply in drawing this line. The Chief Justice saw section 35 as the Crown's promise to respect Aboriginal rights. A necessary corollary of this promise, she noted, was the responsibility to recognize and define those rights, and to attempt to reconcile them with the rights of others. She wrote:

> Section 35 represents a promise of rights recognition, and "[i]t is always assumed that the Crown intends to fulfill its promises"... This promise is realized and sovereignty claims reconciled through the process of honourable negotiation. It is a corollary of s. 35 that the Crown act honourably in defining the rights it guarantees and in reconciling them with other rights and interests. [15]

Since then, Binnie J., in *Mikisew Cree First Nation v. Canada (Minister of Canadian Heritage)*, explained that section 35 corrected the Crown's historic indifference to the concerns of Aboriginal peoples:

> The management of these relationships [between aboriginal peoples and non-aboriginal peoples] takes place in the shadow of a long history of grievances and misunderstanding. The multitude of smaller grievances created by the indifference of some government officials to aboriginal people's concerns, and the lack of respect inherent in that indifference has been as destructive of the process of reconciliation as some of the larger and more explosive controversies.[16]

In Binnie J.'s view, the Crown has failed to consistently respect the rights of Aboriginal peoples. Like other Supreme Court justices, he saw the purpose of section 35 as obligating the Crown "to respect the existing treaty

---

15 *Haida Nation v. British Columbia (Minister of Forests)*, [2004] 3 S.C.R. 511 at para. 20.

16 *Mikisew Cree First Nation v. Canada (Minister of Canadian Heritage)*, [2005] S.C.J. No. 71 at para. 1 [*Mikisew Cree*].

rights of aboriginal peoples."[17] The extent and application of this obligation will be determined in context and then enforced by the courts.

While Binnie J.'s comments might well be taken to be equally applicable to all Aboriginal peoples of Canada, he specifically addressed the relationship between First Nations and the Crown, referring to the Crown's obligations to "Indians."[18]

The Supreme Court has consistently explained that section 35 engages the honour of the Crown in preserving the diversity of Canada's Aboriginal peoples. The section obliges the Crown to respect the existing rights of all Aboriginal peoples of Canada and requires that these rights be defined and reconciled with the rights of others.

Given the purpose and effect of section 35, does section 91(24) still contribute to the content of the constitutional relationship between the Crown and First Nations? The answer lies in the relationship between the Crown and First Nations, the policy of the Crown towards Indians as expressed in the *Royal Proclamation of 1763*, and the ability of the Crown to realize that policy by means of section 91(24) of the *Constitution Act, 1867*.

C. SECTION 91(24)

1) A Historical Perspective

a) Forging a Political Alliance with the Imperial Crown

The British Crown asserted sovereignty over "the Canadas"[19] in 1763. However, the relationship between the British Crown and the First Nations peoples with whom it came into contact in America had developed a century before then. An abundance of historical documents describe the factors that shaped that relationship.

One of the most poignant of these historical documents is the transcript of a speech given by Sachems, of the "Onnondage" and "Cajouga," on 2 August 1684 to the governor of New York.[20] In the speech,

17 *Ibid.* at para. 4.

18 *Ibid.* at para. 51.

19 "The Canadas" was the term used in the Treaty of Paris to describe Canadian territories ceded in that treaty by France.

20 Peter Wraxall, *An Abridgment of the Indian Affairs Contained in Four Folio Volumes, Transacted in the Colony of New York, from the Year 1678 to the Year 1751*, ed.

the orator reminds the listener of the past and foreshadows what was to come:

> You are a Mighty Sachem and we but a Small People. When the English first came to New York to Virginia and Maryland, they were but a small People and we a large Nation; and we finding they were good People gave them Land and dealt Civilly by them; Now that you are grown Numerous and we decreased, you must protect us . . . from the French, which if you don't we shall loose all our Hunting and Beavers; The French want all the Beavers and are Angry that we bring any to the English.
>
> We have put all our Land and our Persons under the Protection of the Great Duke of York Brother to your Mighty Sachem. The Susquahanna River which we won with our Sword, we have given to this Government; And we desire it may be a Branch of that Great Tree which is Planted here, whose Top reaches to the Sun and under whose Branches We Shelter our Selves from the French or any other Enemy: Our Fire burns in your Houses and Your Fire in Ours . . . and we desire it may ever so continue . . . .
>
> We will not consent that the Great Penn's People should settle on the Susquhanna River; Our Young Warriors are like the Wolves of the Forest as you Great Sachem of Virginia know, besides, we have no other Land to leave our Wives and Children . . . .
>
> . . . we are a Free People and unite our Selves to the English . . . .

The speech might have been the archetype for imperial Crown relations with First Nations peoples throughout North America. A political pact had been forged, its genesis being the nation-to-nation alliance that had been built initially during times of war out of the need for protection from a common external enemy. The speech also provides evidence of the effect of the gradual movement of the now larger European community into the shrinking territory of the First Nations.

It is significant that the speaker petitions the Crown for protection and justice.

By the 1750s, almost a century after this appeal, First Nations peoples in what is now the United States continued to petition the British Crown

---

by Charles Howard McIllwain (New York: Benjamin Blom, 1968) at 11–12. Speech at Albany (2 August 1684).

for justice and for protection of their lands against the encroachment of settlers. England's Indian Affairs policy was to reserve and protect the land rights of the Indigenous peoples. This policy, however, was not embraced by the colonists.

The difficulty the British Crown experienced in enforcing its policy is demonstrated in a story set out in correspondence between the Lords of Trade and the governor of New York. The story illustrates the tension between British policy and colonial ambitions; it also demonstrates the efforts made by the British Crown to honour its policy of respecting First Nations land rights.

The story begins in 1753, when a deputation of Mohawk Indians came to New York to complain that they had been defrauded of some of their lands: lands that had been patented by the province. The deputation was dismissed by officials of the province of New York in an "abrupt and hasty manner."[21] The Mohawks then complained directly to the King.

The King took up their cause. He directed the Lords of Trade to write to the governor of New York, expressing surprise that the council and assembly of New York had been "so little attentive to His Majesty's interests, and to their own security," to treat the Mohawks in this fashion. The Lords of Trade instructed the governor to inform the assembly

> in the strongest manner of how great importance it is to the Province of New York to preserve the friendship and affection of the Indians and the fatal consequences which must inevitably follow a neglect of them.[22]

In order to amend the insult, the governor was to "immediately" send "a person of character and integrity" to ask for a meeting with the Indians, at a location of their choosing, as Albany was now "obnoxious to them."[23] The messenger was to promise the Indians that the king had ordered presents for them in the hope that their friendship could be renewed. The concerns of the Indians were to be listened to "carefully and respectfully."

---

21 John R. Brodhead, ed., *Documents Related to the Colonial History of the State of New York Procured in Holland England and France*, vol. 7 (Albany: Weed, Parsons, 1856) at 800. Lords of Trade to Sir Danvers Osborne (18 September 1753).

22 *Ibid.*

23 *Ibid.*

The Lords of Trade and, of course, the Crown hoped that the result of this meeting would be to take all proper and legal methods to redress the wrong done to the Indians.

Unfortunately, there was little that the governor, as the King's representative, could do. His authority was limited to that which had been delegated to him by his commission from the King; that is, it was limited to the residue of discretionary authority left to the King himself.[24] All other powers and authorities had vested in the assembly — the assembly was not responsible to the King.

With respect to the setting aside of patents of land, neither the King nor the governor had the authority to set aside improperly issued patents, not even those obtained by fraud. Only the Legislative Assembly of New York had jurisdiction to set aside patents.[25]

All that was left to the governor was the art of persuasion. The Lords of Trade directed him to prevail upon the legislature of New York to revoke the patents. Unfortunately, in this he was unsuccessful.

Although the Lords of Trade were unable to do justice in this instance, they took measures to prevent similar injustices. The governor was instructed that in the future, he was not to issue patents to any persons who had purchased lands directly from the Indians. If the Indians were inclined to sell their lands, the purchase was to be made only by His Majesty, and the lands were to be paid for out of the public treasury.

This experience with the Mohawk patents was one factor that resulted in what later came to be known as "the surrender provisions" of the *Royal Proclamation of 1763*.

A further policy was also established as a result of the experience of the Mohawk patents. The Lords of Trade concluded that it would be improper for a province to enter into a treaty in its own name. In the future, when agreements were needed, there was to be only one general treaty, in His Majesty's name, with the affected Indians. There was to be no patchwork of treaty rights across the territories, but rather consistent and uniform dealings.

---

24 *Attorney-General v. De Keyser's Royal Hotel*, [1920] A.C. 526 (P.C.). See also *Campbell v. Hall* (1774), 98 E.R. 1045 (K.B.).

25 See Brodhead, above note 21 at 377, Lords of Trade to Governor Hardy (19 March 1756).

b) The Political Alliance Extends into Canada

As seen above, the British Crown had extensive experience in Indian Affairs diplomacy before 1763. It had interacted with the First Nations peoples in North America for more than a century. Sir William Johnson, a leading figure in the development of Indian Affairs policy, was commissioned in 1756 by King George III to be "colonel, agent, and sole superintendent of the affairs of the Six Nations and other northern Indians."[26]

Johnson had experienced first-hand the shortcomings of local provincial control over Indian Affairs in both his personal and professional lives. He also had a keen understanding of the special relationship between the Crown and First Nations, and the harmony both fiscally and socially that could be the consequence of such a relationship.

In 1759, in anticipation of the defeat of the French in North America, Johnson wrote to the Lords of Trade on how to best improve and extend His Majesty's interests in America, "should the French be absolutely extirpated, and much more if they should not."[27] Johnson urged that the Indians be redressed for all of their reasonable and well-founded complaints against the issuance of fraudulently obtained patents. Treaties were to be made with Indians, setting out the limits of their territories, and these treaties were to be strictly observed by the provinces. The superintendency and direction of Indian Affairs and Trade were to be under the direct authority of the Crown.

Proclamations[28] containing Johnson's themes were issued pursuant to Royal instruction by Governor Monckton of New York in December 1761,[29] by Henry Bouquet, the colonel of Foot and Commanding at Fort Pitt and Dependencies, October 1761,[30] and by Cadwallader Colden, the lieutenant governor of New York, on 17 February 1762.[31]

---

26 Commission of Johnson (March 1756), in Brodhead, *ibid.* at 76–77, Fox to Johnson (13 March 1756).

27 Brodhead, *ibid.* at 377. Sir William Johnson to the Lords of Trade, Fort Johnson (17 May 1759).

28 There well may be more, but these ones came immediately to hand. [The author]

29 M.W. Hamilton, ed., *The Papers of Sir William Johnson*, vol. 10 (Albany: University of the State of New York, 1951) at 340–42.

30 Douglas Brymner, ed., *Report on Canadian Archives 1889* (Ottawa: B. Chamerlin, 1890).

31 Library and Archives Canada, Reel C13159, CO5/284 at 14-9.

After the Treaty of Paris in 1763, the King turned his "Royal Attention" to "the next important Object of securing to His Subjects, and extending the Enjoyment of the Advantages, which Peace has secured."[32] One of his principal secretaries of state, Charles, Earl of Egremont, wrote to the Lords of Trade, seeking their opinion on what regulations would encourage the best commercial advantage for His Majesty's trading subjects. He posed three questions:

> "What new governments should be established and what form should they take?"
>
> "What military establishments would be sufficient?"
>
> "What would be the most palatable mode of seeking contribution for the support from the Colonials of the additional expenses of the military and civil establishments?"

The second question, relating to the security of North America, called for the lords' immediate attention and recommendations. While seeking the advice of the Lords of Trade, the Earl of Egremont expressed his own inclinations in this matter, which accorded with the policy that Johnson had urged. He wrote:

> Tho' in order to succeed effectually in the Point, it may become necessary to erect some Forts in the Indian country, with their Consent, yet His Majesty's Justice & Moderation inclines Him to adopt the more eligible Method of conciliating the Minds of the Indians by the Mildness of His Government by protecting their Persons & Property & securing to them all the Possessions, Rights and Privileges they have hitherto enjoyed, & are entitled to, most cautiously guarding against any Invasion or Occupation of their Hunting Lands, the Possession of which is to be acquired by fair Purchases only; and it has been thought so highly expedient to give them the earliest and most convincing Proofs of His Majesty's Gracious and Friendly Intentions on this Head, that I have already received and transmitted the King's Commands to this Purpose to the Governors of Virginia, the Two Carolinas & to the Agent for Indi-

32 Parliament, "Documents Relating to the Constitutional History of Canada 1759–1791" by A. Shortt & A. Doughty in *Sessional Papers*, No. 18 (1907) at 93, Egremont to Lords of Trade (5 May 1763).

> an Affairs in the Southern department, as Your Lordships will see fully in the enclosed Copy of my Circular Letter to them on this subject.[33]

The themes of military alliance, respect of territories and rights, and the relationship as between friends characterized the Crown's inclinations from the first formative days of Crown–First Nations relations in Canada.

But honour was also engaged. The relationship was to develop in an atmosphere of friendship and mutual obligations of protection and support. There was to be a fair bargain. Title was to rest upon the political relationship forged through pacts of friendship and mutual assistance, and the generous cessions of land that allowed the British to expand into North America. The Lords of Trade explained the foundation of British sovereignty in Canada this way:

> a Colour might be taken on some future Occasion, for supposing that Your Majesty's Title to [this Country] had taken its rise, singly from the Cessions made by France, in the late Treaty, whereas Your Majesty's Title to the Lakes and circumjacent Territory as well as to the Sovereignty over the Indian Tribes, particularly of the six Nations, rests on a more solid and even a more equitable Foundation; and perhaps nothing is more necessary than that just Impressions on this subject should be carefully preserved in the Minds of the Indians . . . .[34]

The Lords of Trade recommended that a proclamation be immediately issued, declaring His Majesty's intentions.

c) The Formal Declaration of the Terms of the Political Alliance

On 7 October 1763, King George III issued Canada's foundational constitutional document, the *Royal Proclamation of 1763*. It announced the assertion of sovereignty over British North America, established the geographic parameters and the political structure of the new governments, and became the cornerstone of Indian policy in Canada. Indian Affairs would remain under the authority of the Royal Prerogative.

Under the regime established by the *Royal Proclamation of 1763*, the Indians' rights in their lands were to be respected. Any alienation of Indian lands was to take place only under the auspices and with the approval

---

33 *Ibid.*

34 *Ibid.* at 110–11, Lords of Trade to the King (5 August 1763).

of the Crown, and most important, with the consent of the Indians. Because First Nations had no authority to issue patents recognized at law,[35] as long as the authority to issue patents remained exclusively with the Crown, fraud in the purchase of Indian lands would be avoided.

The King's first instructions,[36] given on 7 December 1763, to James Murray, commander of His Majesty's forces in Quebec, and therefore in charge of Indian Affairs, were crafted so as to secure the Crown's friendship with those nations living in the newly acquired territory. These instructions convey the Crown's deference towards Canada's First Nations and need for their good will and friendship. It is only when read with knowledge of modern history that they also communicate a sense of foreboding.

> And Whereas Our Province of Quebec is in part inhabited and possessed by several Nations and Tribes of Indians, with whom it is both necessary and expedient to cultivate and maintain a strict Friendship and good Correspondence, so that they may be induced by Degrees, not only to be good Neighbours to Our Subjects, but likewise themselves to become good Subjects to Us; You are therefore, as soon as you conveniently can, to appoint a proper Person or Persons to assemble, and treat with the said Indians, promising and assuring them of Protection and Friendship on Our part, and delivering to them such Presents, as shall be sent to you for that purpose.
>
> And you are to inform yourself with the greatest Exactness of the Number, Nature and Disposition of the several Bodies and Tribes of Indians, of the manner of their Lives, and the Rules and Constitutions, by which they are governed or regulated. And You are upon no Account to molest or disturb them in the Possession of such Parts of the said Province, as they at present occupy or possess: but to use the best means You can for conciliating their Affections, and uniting them to Our Government, reporting to Us, by Our Commissions for Trade and Plantations, whatever Information you can collect with respect to these People, and the whole of your Proceedings with them.

---

35 *Johnson and Graham's Lessee v. William McIntosh*, 21 U.S. 543 (1823).

36 Given at Court at St. James 7 December 1763, to Governor Murray, captain general and governor-in-chief in and over [Our Province of] Quebec in America, and [of] all Our Territories dependent thereupon. See above note 32 at 181–205.

And so the first instructions given to the first British authority over what is now Canada called for "conciliation," reconciling the sovereignty of the Crown with the sovereignty of the First Nations.

d) Indian Affairs, 1764–1860

In 1764, the imperial Crown codified the first comprehensive plan for the conduct of the Indian Department[37] in the colonies. In the early years, the Indian Department was under military control, and the principal concern of Indian Affairs was the maintenance of the military assistance of the Indians in order to protect the colony from American incursion (a spectre that loomed with the coming of the American Revolution).

In subsequent decades, as the colony grew, Indian Affairs became more concerned with the acquisition of Indian lands for settlement. The acquisition of Indian lands was to be accomplished in accordance with the British policy expressed in the *Royal Proclamation of 1763*.

By the late 1820s, the threat of war with the United States was beginning to recede. Indian Affairs, while still under the control of the military, became increasingly less focused on the defence of the realm. Much of Lower Canada and Upper Canada was filling with white settlements. Indian Affairs became more concerned with the effects of European society on the Indians and the concomitant problem that maintaining a relationship with them was having a negative impact on the treasury. From the time of first contact, presents had been given to the Indians as tokens of respect and friendship, and in order to bind them in loyalty to the Crown.

Much discussion of the cost of the presents, and the considerations for maintaining or discontinuing them, can be found in the correspondence of the military, still responsible for Indian Affairs in the first decades of the 1800s. The dispatch written 16 May 1829, by Sir James Kempt, commander of the forces, to Sir George Murray, secretary of state for the colonies, is typical of the debate.

Kempt began his correspondence with a discourse on the expense and lack of efficiency in distribution and value to the Crown of the long-

37 *Plan for Management of Indians, 1764, Lords of Trade,* attached as part of s. 32 of Instructions to Governor Carleton (3 January 1775). See *ibid.* at 594–637, especially 614–20.

standing practice of issuing presents to the Indians. Despite this he recommended no immediate change in this Crown policy:

> Were any sudden and immediate reduction made in the Indian presents, it would doubtless excite great suspicion and dissatisfaction amongst them; and as their issue is generally guaranteed by treaty, it would be alike impolitic and unjust to discontinue them at present, though I have no doubt that object may be hereafter gradually attained. [38]

As well, as Kempt observed, "their alliance in war is considered important."

Kempt next turned to the task that would become the central issue for Indian Affairs until today: how best to reconcile First Nations peoples with the new sovereignty. He opined that the settling of the Indians would gradually relieve His Majesty's government from the expense of these presents and eventually from the expense of the Indian Department. His plan was to gather the Indians in "considerable numbers" and settle them in villages, giving them a sufficient portion of land for cultivation so that they could support themselves by farming.

To whatever degree Kempt's plan was carried out, by 1845 it had not had the desired effect. The impact of British settlement on the First Nations of central Canada was described by Sir Charles Bagot, a later governor general, in his report to the Legislative Assembly of the Province of Canada on 29 March 1845.[39]

> Experience has shown that Indians can no longer lead a wild and roving life, in the midst of a numerous and rapidly increasing white population. Their hunting grounds are broken up by settlements; the game is exhausted; their resources as hunters and trappers are cut off; want and disease spread rapidly among them, and gradually reduce their numbers. To escape these consequences, no choice is left, but to remove beyond the pale of civilization, to settle and cultivate the land for a livelihood. From this cause, and under the influence of the Missionaries, few Indians remain settled in the inhabited parts of Canada.

---

38 U.K., H.C., *Accounts and Papers*, vol. 2, No. 617 in *Parliamentary Papers*, vol. 44 (1834) at 37–53. Kempt to Murray (16 May 1829).

39 Canada, Legislative Assembly, "Report on the Affairs of the Indians in Canada, Appendix C, Section 3" in *Journals* (1844–1845) Appendix EEE [Bagot Report].

> But the settled and partially civilized Indians, when left to themselves, become exposed to a new class of evils. They hold large blocks of lands, generally of the most valuable description, which they can neither occupy nor protect against the encroachments of the white squatters, with whom, in the vain attempt to guard their lands, they are brought into a state of constant hostility and collision .... these (Indian) reserves are serious obstacles to the settlement and improvement of the surrounding country, and their possessors become objects of jealousy and dislike to their neighbours; of these the unprincipled are always on the alert, to take advantage of the ... Indians, ... in order to plunder them of their improvements and property.

Bagot recommended that Indian Affairs remain under the immediate control of the representative of the British Crown within the province and that efforts to educate the First Nations peoples in Christianity and the ways of the Europeans continue.

By 1850, the provinces of British North America were enacting legislation that touched upon Indians. Legislation directed at settlers, forbidding encroachment on Indian lands, and invalidating contracts made with Indians for the sale of their lands, were passed in both Canada West (formerly Upper Canada) and Canada East (formerly Lower Canada).[40] These acts were directed at the settlers and did not purport to exercise legislative authority over Indians or Indian lands directly. In 1857, *An Act to encourage the gradual Civilization of the Indian Tribes in this Province, and to amend the Laws respecting Indians* was passed by the legislature of the Province of Canada and received Royal assent on 10 June 1857.

The preamble to this latter legislation reflects the British melting pot policy that was, the approach that colonial governments were taking towards reconciling Indian peoples with European settler communities by the 1850s.

> Whereas it is desirable to encourage the progress of Civilization among the Indian Tribes in this Province, and the gradual removal of all legal distinctions between them and Her Majesty's other Canadian Subjects ....

The Act defined the term *Indian* for the purpose of the legislation. Generally, it meant persons of Indian blood, or intermarried with Indians,

40 13-14 Vict., c. 74 (C.W.) and 13-14 Vict., c. 42 (C.E.).

who were acknowledged as members of tribes or a band of Indians living on unsurrendered land or land reserved by treaty. The Act provided that individuals considered appropriate by the government could cease to be Indians and would be entitled to parcels of land that had been reserved for their tribes or bands.

In 1842[41] and 1859,[42] the colony of Nova Scotia passed legislation appointing a commissioner of Crown lands whose duties included the supervision of reserve lands.

In 1857, the Pennefather Royal Commission of Inquiry[43] recommended that Indian peoples remain under the "special care and protection" of the Crown.

In 1860, the Province of Canada gained complete legislative control over Indians and Indian lands with the passage of *An Act respecting the Management of the Indian Lands and Property.*[44] From this time until near the end of the next century, civilization, equally referred to as "assimilation," became the dominant theme of Indian Affairs policy.

e) From the Imperial Crown to the Crown in Right of Canada

In 1867, three[45] of the colonies in what became Canada joined together in a federation, and responsibility for Indian Affairs passed to the Crown in right of Canada. In pre-Confederation debates, there is scant discussion that sheds light on why the federal Crown was given responsibility for Indian Affairs. However, it is obvious that this exceptional section of the Constitution of Canada had its beginning in the political relationship between the British Crown and the First Nations of North America.

The earliest experience of the British Crown demonstrated that justice would be best served if the authority to purchase Indian lands was not with the ultimate beneficiary of the freed-up interest in the lands. One of the primary functions of Indian Affairs was always to protect

---

41 S.N.S. 1842, c. 16.

42 S.N.S. 1859, c. 14.

43 Canada, Legislative Assembly, "Report of the Special Commissioners Appointed on 8 September 1856 to Investigate Indian Affairs in Canada" in *Sessional Papers* (1858) Appendix 21 at 120 [Pennefather Report].

44 C. 1860, c. 151 (23 Vict.).

45 New Brunswick, Nova Scotia, and the Province of Canada (made up of Upper Canada and Lower Canada and reconstituted as Ontario and Quebec).

Indians and Indian lands from the encroachments of the European colonial society. Thus, while the provinces were allocated the benefits of the surrender of Indians lands that would accrue pursuant to section 109 of the *Constitution Act, 1867*, the ability to purchase these lands remained exclusively with the federal Crown under section 91(24).

The first *Indian Act* was passed by Parliament in 1868.[46] In the opinion of the deputy superintendent of Indian Affairs, the Act was intended to reconcile First Nations and European communities by using self-government as a tool to effect integration.[47]

> The Acts framed in the years 1868 and 1869 relating to Indian Affairs, were designed to lead the Indian people by degrees to mingle with the white race in the ordinary avocations of life. It was intended to afford facilities for electing, for a limited period, members of bands to manage, as a Council, local matters; that intelligent and educated men, recognized as chiefs, should carry out the wishes of the male members of mature years in each band, who should be fairly represented in the conduct of their internal affairs.

The allocation of legislative authority over Indian lands to the federal Crown by means of section 91(24) arguably resulted in a voluntary and fair land cession process, partially fulfilling the promise of the early political relationship. However, the purpose of reconciling First Nations communities with non-Indian society was not achieved. The condition of the Indians throughout Canada remained unacceptable for at least the century following Confederation (many would say, until present times). Numerous royal commissions[48] recommended that the Crown abandon its failed assimilation policy.

In 1964, the Hawthorn Report concluded:

---

46 *An Act providing for the organization of the Department of the Secretary of State of Canada, and for the management of Indian and Ordnance Lands*, S.C. 1868, c. 42 (31 Vict.).

47 William Sprague (2 February 1871), as quoted in P. G. McHugh, *Aboriginal Societies and the Common Law* (Oxford: Oxford University Press, 2004) at 183. Pierre Trudeau also envisioned self-government as the route to reconciliation. See opening speech at the First Ministers Conference, above note 5.

48 Special Joint Committees in 1948 and 1961. See *Final Report of the Special Joint Committee (1946–1948) of the Senate and House of Commons Appointed to Examine and Consider Indian Affairs* at 187, and *Final Report of the Special Joint Committee*

> . . . it is worth reiterating clearly and simply that [we] do not think that the Indian should be required to assimilate . . . Ordinary respect for what values and institutions, languages, religions and modes of thought, persist in their own small societies, which were once fully viable and to varying extents are so today, calls for maintenance of principle . . . . Continuation of the present situation of internal colonialism is unacceptable.

Not until 1982 did constitutional arrangements attempt to preserve diversity by recognizing and affirming Aboriginal rights. One must ask, then, whether section 91(24) has accomplished any part of the original Indian Affairs policy that promised a nation-to-nation political alliance that would benefit all.

2) The Judicial Perspective

Throughout the last century and a half, many judges have commented on the purpose of section 91(24) of the Constitution.

In *St. Catherine's Milling and Lumber Co. v. The Queen*,[49] Lord Watson wrote that section 91(24) was enacted from a policy of ensuring uniformity of administration of Indian lands and Indian Affairs generally.

In 1909, in *Ontario v. Canada*, the Supreme Court of Canada commented on the purpose of section 91(24):

> The case as it presents itself to my mind is that the Dominion was assigned by the "*British North America Act*," sec. 91, sub-sec. 24, quoted above, the high, honourable, and onerous duties of the guardians of the many races of Indians then within or that might at any future time fall within the borders of Canada; that these duties were to be discharged as occasion called for, having in mind always the peace, order and good government of Canada and, as part and parcel thereof and not the least factor in promoting all implied therein, the due observance of those duties towards the Indians, which the policy of the British Crown had rendered of paramount importance; that the discharging, in a states-

---

(1959–1961) of the Senate and House of Commons on Indian Affairs at 605 [Hawthorn Report].

49 *St. Catherine's Milling and Lumber Co. v. The Queen* (1888), 14 App. Cas. 46 at 59 (J.C.P.C.). The case was a dispute between Canada and Ontario over which government would have the benefit of surrendered Indian lands. It decided that the beneficial interest in surrendered lands accrued to Ontario.

> manlike way, when the several occasions I have recited called for, these high duties of national importance they were discharged all the better by being freed from the trammels of being confined within the narrow views that the provincial range of vision might have restricted action to, if the needs and wishes of a single province were to be considered, or even the dominant factor used as a guide, perhaps to the detriment of national interests. [50]

The "high, honourable, and onerous duties" attached to section 91(24) referred to in this case were those of ensuring compliance with the imperial policy requiring that Indian land could be obtained only on consent, and then by means of a fair bargain. For Idington J., this protective function was the focus of section 91(24): jurisdiction over Indians and their lands was fixed in a government other than that which had an interest in making lands available for settlement.

In the same case, Duff J. also commented on the purpose of section 91(24). His observation focused on the duties[51] that had been cast upon the federal Crown to reconcile First Nations with the effects of colonization. He wrote:

> The traditional policy in Canada respecting the Indians themselves pointed in the same direction. That policy was that when the progress of advancing settlement brought with it danger of collision between white settlers and Indians still in a savage and pagan state, to induce, if possible, the Indians to settle on limited areas and by slow degrees to lead them into the ways of civilized life. The responsibility in respect of all these matters is by the "*British North America Act*" cast upon the Dominion . . . .[52]

Justice Duff saw that the mechanism that had been used for achieving reconciliation was the "civilization" policy — assimilation and loss of diversity. Undoubtedly, he would not have seen the policy in those terms.

---

50 *Ontario v. Canada* (1909), 42 S.C.R. 1 at 117–18, Idington J., aff'd without comment on this point [1910] A.C. 637 (J.C.P.C.).

51 The sentiment misses the mark in another respect: subsequent decisions of the Supreme Court of Canada have held that a grant of legislative authority does not impose a justiciable obligation to use it. *Kwong v. Alberta* (1978), 96 D.L.R. (3d) 214 (Alta. S.C.A.D.), aff'd [1979] 2 S.C.R. 1010.

52 *Ontario v. Canada*, above note 50. at 124 (S.C.R.).

These early cases demonstrate that, within the first fifty years of Confederation, the Court's understanding of the purpose of section 91(24) was consistent with the historical record.

Section 91(24) enabled the federal government to realize Indian Affairs policy as it had developed consistently from the time of the first interactions between the British and First Nations communities. This policy reflected the need for peace and order, the protection of Indigenous land and other rights, and a response to the stresses imposed on Indigenous culture by colonization.

History had taught the British imperial Crown that these needs could best be met by vesting ultimate power over Indian Affairs in a central government without direct financial interest in promoting Indian land sales and that was not responsible for enabling the exploitation of natural resources.

But history has also shown that the Crown blundered seriously in its response to the stresses imposed on indigenous culture by colonization. The various "civilization" policies adopted by Indian Affairs from the 1800s through to the 1980s were not successful. Nor did these policies reflect the spirit of the political nation-to-nation relationship captured in the words of the Sachem, "Our Fire burns in your Houses and Your Fire in Ours . . . and we desire it may ever so continue."[53]

Naturally, early jurisprudence around Confederation was concerned with the scope and division of powers granted by the *British North America Act, 1867*[54] to the federal and provincial governments. As social issues evolved in the 1960s and 1970s, section 91(24) again fell to judicial scrutiny, this time in the context of cases placing "Indians" within a constitutional framework that would protect their civil liberties.

In 1970, *R. v. Drybones*[55] came before the Supreme Court. This case called into question the validity of section 94(b) of the *Indian Act*, which made it an offence for an Indian person to be intoxicated off reserve. The provision was challenged as violating the *Canadian Bill of Rights*. On the purported federal legislative power to support such legislation, Pigeon J., in dissent, commented:

---

53 See above note 20.

54 Now titled the *Constitution Act, 1867*.

55 [1970] S.C.R. 282.

> [Section] 91(24)'s very object in so far as it relates to Indians . . . is to enable the Parliament of Canada to make legislation applicable only to Indians as such and therefore not applicable to Canadian citizens generally . . . . Outside the territories, provincial jurisdiction over education and health facilities would make it very difficult for federal authorities to provide such facilities to Indians without "discrimination" as understood in the courts below.[56]

Justice Pigeon was concerned that if the *Canadian Bill of Rights* could render federal legislation invalid, it would indirectly alter the status of Indians and endanger future ameliorative federal legislation enacted pursuant to section 91(24).

Justice Ritchie, writing for the majority, viewed the section more narrowly: while section 91(24) could support legislation that treated Indians distinctly, the section only supported protective purposes.

> It appears to me to be desirable to make it plain that these reasons for judgment are limited to a situation in which, under the laws of Canada, it is made an offence punishable at law on account of race, for a person to do something which all Canadians who are not members of that race may do with impunity . . . .[57]

The decisions of Pigeon and Ritchie JJ. are an expression of the discussion about the boundary between appropriately recognizing a special status for First Nations — for example, for the purpose of granting access to government ameliorative programs — and inappropriately singling them out.[58]

Since 1982, the rights of Aboriginal peoples have been protected by section 35 of the *Constitution Act, 1982*. The Supreme Court of Canada appears to have expanded the content of this protection beyond the initial parameters, that is, the reconciliation of the power of the Crown and the duty of the Crown to Aboriginal peoples, as articulated in *Sparrow*.[59] Could the Supreme Court now be imputing a much broader objective to

56 *Ibid.* at 303.

57 *Ibid.* at 298.

58 See, for example, *Lovelace v. Ontario*, [2000] 1 S.C.R. 950.

59 *Sparrow*, above note 6 at 1109.

section 35? This objective is described by Binnie J. in *Mikisew Cree*, where he wrote:

> The fundamental objective of the modern law of aboriginal and treaty rights is the reconciliation of aboriginal peoples and non-aboriginal peoples and their respective claims, interests and ambitions.[60]

It is unlikely that these objectives will be accomplished by the Court through its enforcement of section 35 alone. Section 35 is fundamentally a mechanism that is engaged to protect against government activity that infringes Aboriginal rights. Absent government action that infringes or threatens to infringe Aboriginal rights, section 35 would appear to have no application. The section's purpose is limited to setting parameters around the Crown's ability to infringe or extinguish Aboriginal rights.

The scope of section 35 may not be sufficient to permit the courts to accomplish the reconciliation of the claims, interests, and ambitions of the Aboriginal and non-Aboriginal peoples of Canada. If it is not, then the power to accomplish the reconciliation of which Binnie J. wrote must be found elsewhere. Historically, the Crown's role was to define and reconcile the relationship between First Nations and others. Arguably, the Crown has the same role, even today.

If so, there still seems to be a role for section 91(24).

D. THE POLITICAL RELATIONSHIP

As the historical development of First Nations–Crown relations demonstrates, section 91(24) reflects centuries of policy designed to protect and advance the interests of First Nations peoples because of the political relationship that had been forged.

This relationship continues today, in part, because of the *Indian Act*.[61] The *Indian Act* facilitates First Nations communication with government by establishing a structure that is cognizable to the Canadian system of governance. Although exchanges of promises of political alliance and mutual support predate the *Indian Act*, in an increasingly complex legal

60 *Mikisew Cree*, above note 16 at para. 1.

61 R.S.C. 1985, c. I-5.

environment, certainty and predictability of statutorily based government is essential.

The political alliance has always taken place on a government-to-government basis. The governance provisions of the *Indian Act*, and the governance provisions of the *Constitution Act, 1867*, foster this relationship by prescribing how, and through whom, one party can communicate with the other.

Canada has a continuing role to play in honouring the terms of the relationship. The political obligation to sustain efforts to remove the stresses on First Nations societies caused by colonization falls to Canada. That, after all, was the deal at the beginning, and no one has called a halt. Justice Pigeon recognized this when he observed that section 91(24) permits the federal Crown to provide facilities to First Nations communities without the necessity of providing them equally to a broader community.

Indeed, the Federal Court of Appeal has already linked section 91(24) and ameliorative programs designed by Indian Affairs. That court determined that, notwithstanding the authorization of a program under Parliament's spending power, if it is directed at "Indianness," it is supported by section 91(24). In *Shubenacadie Indian Band v. Canada*, Isaac J. wrote:

> . . . a programme designed to promote Indianness and limited territorially to the Reserve is one that is constitutionally supportable under section 91(24) of the *Constitution Act, 1867*, as being a programme relating to Indians and lands reserved for the Indians.[62]

Ameliorative programs, such as the social assistance program at issue in *Shubenacadie*, meet the fundamental objective of Indian Affairs policy: the reconciliation of the interests and ambitions of First Nations with those of others.

While the inclusion of Indians within section 91(24) does not obligate the federal government to establish socio-economic programming for First Nations, it does permit it the opportunity to do so, without requiring that such programming be offered equally towards the advancement of others.

---

62 *Shubanacadie Indian Band v. Canada (Human Rights Commission)*, [2000] F.C.J. No. 702 at para. 60 (C.A.).

The political relationship between the Crown and First Nations communities predates the Canadian nation. The aspect of the political relationship that requires the Crown "to use the best means You can for conciliating their Affections, and uniting them to Our Government,"[63] if it is a constitutional responsibility, is Canada's to fulfill because of section 91(24) of the *Constitution Act, 1867*.

Canada and the courts have difficult decisions to make in the future. There are many equally worthy needs competing for government resources. This paper suggests that political alliances endure and are to be honoured

beyond space and time, which, whether we like it or not, spells duty.

63 The King to Commander Murray (7 December 1763). See above note 36.

‹ 5 ›

Are the Métis in Section 91(24) of the *Constitution Act, 1867*? An Issue Caught in a Time-Warp

BRADFORD W. MORSE

A. INTRODUCTION

Addressing the question posed in the title of this paper has proven to be particularly difficult for me on a personal level. In some senses, I have been wrestling with the uncertainty implicit in the query for much of my professional life. I have authored and co-authored a variety of legal articles on varied aspects of this topic for many years;[1] I have prepared internal briefing notes and legal opinions for the Native Council of Canada (now known as the Congress of Aboriginal Peoples) and for other

1 See, for example, Bradford W. Morse, "Government Obligations, Aboriginal Peoples and Section 91(24)" in David C. Hawkes, ed., *Aboriginal Peoples, Government Responsibility: Exploring Federal and Provincial Roles* (Ottawa: Carleton University Press, 1989) at 59; also Bradford W. Morse & Robert K. Groves, "Canada's Forgotten Peoples: The Aboriginal Rights of Métis and Non-Status Indians" (1987) 2 Law & Anthropology 139; Bradford W. Morse, *Aboriginal Self-Government in Australia and Canada* (Kingston: Institute of Intergovernmental Relations, Queen's University, 1984); Bradford W. Morse & John Giokas, "Do the Métis Fall within Section 91 (24) of the *Constitution Act, 1867*?" in Royal Commission on Aboriginal Peoples, *Aboriginal Self-Government: Legal and Constitutional Issues* (Ottawa: Supply and Services Canada, 1995) at 140; Bradford W. Morse & Robert K. Groves, "Constituting Aboriginal Collectivities: Avoiding New Peoples 'In Between'" (2004) 67 Sask. L. Rev. 257; Bradford W. Morse & Robert K. Groves, "Métis and Non-Status Indians and Section 91(24) of the *Constitution Act, 1867*" in Paul Chartrand, ed., *Who Are Canada's Aboriginal Peoples? Recognition, Definition and Jurisdiction* (Saskatoon: Purich Publications, 2002) at 191–229.

Indigenous peoples' organizations in Canada. For well over two decades, I have also advocated in favour of either a reference to our highest court or a constitutional amendment to resolve this debate. The governments of Canada and the Northwest Territories had each seriously contemplated making a reference for resolution of this constitutional issue in the mid-1980s, but never proceeded with the plan. Agreement was reached among all prime ministers, premiers, and leaders through the Charlottetown Accord[2] in 1992. That accord would have led to a constitutional overhaul. It would have decided this matter conclusively in favour of expressly including all Aboriginal peoples within a renewed section 91(24), along with a justiciable commitment to negotiate self-government agreements, entrenching the inherent right of self-government and other constitutional provisions. There was as well a complementary political commitment, called the Métis Nation Accord, by the federal government with the five western provinces, the Northwest Territories, and the Métis National Council, to develop a new relationship with the Métis Nation. That consensus, however, died with the rest of the accord's defeat in separate, but simultaneous national and Quebec referenda in October of 1992. As a result, the government of Canada continues to treat the Métis as outside its section 91(24) jurisdiction.

The jurisdictional question itself has not died. It continues to plague the very core of the political and legal position of the Métis people of Canada. Section 91(24), a provision dating back to Confederation in 1867, remains the single largest stumbling block to welcoming the Métis people, and especially those of the Métis homeland, into the circle of Confederation in the 21st century. Over the years, many federal ministers and senior officials have proposed putting the question aside and focusing on efforts to achieve practical measures to address socio-economic imbalances between the Métis and other Canadians. Although this approach has helped spur some tangible gains, creating federally funded

---

2 The accord was signed on 28 August 1992 by the first ministers and national Aboriginal leaders, with the draft legal text released on 9 October. It proposed to amend s. 91(24) to replace "Indians" with "Aboriginal Peoples of Canada." It also would have protected the long-standing unique relationships established for specified Métis settlements in Alberta by enacting s. 95E through which the province of Alberta would have received concurrent yet subordinate jurisdiction to the federal government concerning the Métis people within its borders.

employment training programs and other initiatives, the absence of a definitive resolution as to whether the Métis are, constitutionally speaking, "Indians" in the same sense as the Inuit has caused many practical difficulties in moving forward.

This situation remains unresolved due to the unwillingness of all provinces to agree with the federal interpretation of section 91(24). Instead, they unanimously agree with the political and legal positions taken by the Métis National Council and the Congress of Aboriginal Peoples, both of which assert that the Métis are within the parameters of section 91(24). Unfortunately for the Métis, this agreement has meant that provincial governments, with the notable exception of Alberta, have refused to respond to the real needs of the Métis for land, natural resources, economic opportunity, and self-determination. The provinces argue that the federal government is shirking its fiscal and legislative responsibilities by refusing to accept its jurisdiction for the Métis under section 91(24). The predominant provincial view is that the government of Canada should bear the cost for Métis programs, services, and the fulfillment of outstanding Aboriginal rights obligations, as it does with federally recognized First Nations and Inuit peoples.[3] It is the Métis who have suffered from the jurisdictional vacuum caused by the failure of either of the two orders of government to accept responsibility. In many ways, the worst aspect of this is that governments are fighting to avoid accepting constitutional jurisdiction for the Métis rather than trying to include them within their constitutional ambits.

---

3 The provincial governments have also been criticizing the federal government actively over the past thirty-five years for failing to respect many of its financial obligations to Indian and Inuit peoples. The provinces complain that the federal interpretation of its mandate continues to shrink such that it denies any responsibility at all for non-status Indians (even though the *Indian Act* regulates the definitional dividing line), while seeking to limit its authority solely to those status Indians residing on a reserve. The federal government has also consistently sought to limit its responsibility solely to those Inuit living north of the 60th parallel except when it is directly negotiating land claims settlements. This pattern of federal reluctance to assume its constitutional obligations regarding Indians is outlined in greater detail in Morse, "Governmental Obligations, Aboriginal Peoples and Section 91(24) of the *Constitution Act, 1867*," above note 1 at 59–91.

The net result of this unresolved dimension to the *Constitution Act, 1867*,[4] is political and legal limbo for the Métis. They are largely unable to persuade either the federal or provincial governments to engage in meaningful negotiations on land claims, hunting or fishing rights, the development of Métis political institutions, or other section 35 collective Aboriginal or treaty rights issues arising from the *Constitution Act, 1982*.[5] The two levels of government will talk only when the other one is present, if at all. When governments do sit down to talk, their biggest precondition to reaching agreement is resolving who will pay for whatever might come out of the negotiations.

Equally frustrating, no government has been prepared to force a judicial determination through a reference to its appellate court. None of the jurisprudence that has dealt with Métis rights has yet been compelled to rule on this question. Even the latest efforts by Métis leaders and organizations to litigate this matter directly have yet to bear fruit. One federal court judge, in dealing with a federal motion to strike out litigation that would respond to this question, was moved to say:

> **24** Finally, there is the issue of whether there is some other reasonable and effective manner in which the Plaintiffs' issue may be brought before the Court. Clearly, neither the federal Crown nor the provincial Crown are the least bit interested in negotiating with the Métis and with non-status Indians who, as a result, are trapped in a jurisdictional vacuum between Canada and the Provinces. Therefore, even though "... the Crown is under a moral, if not a legal, duty to enter into and conduct those negotiations in good faith," as Chief Justice Lamer pointed out in *Delgamuukw v. B.C.*, [1997] 3 S.C.R. 1010 at 1123, the issues in this proceeding are highly unlikely to come before the Court in the context of a suit over a specific right. Given the track record of the Crown in refusing to negotiate, it could well be generations before this issue could come before the Court in some other suitable fact situation. That is in no one's interest. To urge, at this point, that the litigation is premature, when there is no prospect of negotiation, is to throw unreasonable difficulty in the way of this proceeding, for there is a real point of difficulty

4 *Constitution Act, 1867* (U.K.), 30 & 31 Vict., c. 3, reprinted in R.S.C. 1985, App. II, No. 5.

5 *Constitution Act, 1982*, being Schedule B to the *Canada Act 1982* (U.K.), 1982, c. 11.

which requires a timely judicial decision. Here I acknowledge that the *Dumont* case is perhaps headed for some sort of a determination under section 91(24) of the *Constitution Act of 1867*, however the parties have been litigating for over 20 years and perhaps will never reach a conclusion, let alone a timely conclusion. Thus the present proceeding is an appropriate vehicle.[6]

B. BACKGROUND

More than 140 years ago, the Fathers of Confederation actively negotiated among competing visions for a new country. Regional politics and interests were paramount. Clearly missing from these debates was any discussion of the legitimacy of the imperial Crown's claim to sovereignty over the original Indigenous nations and their territories, never surrendered to the Crown or seized through military victory. Moreover, affected Indigenous peoples were not invited to participate in or even comment on the proposed federation. There are no records of any serious consideration of the terms on which the Crown–Aboriginal relationship would be reaffirmed or recast. The apparent, almost complete silence on this matter is particularly ironic given that so many of the important discussions among colonial leaders occurred in the Maritime colonies that had a treaty history with the Mik'maq, Malecite, and Passamoquoddy Nations that extended over two centuries. The overwhelming majority of the people living in the four colonies that contained a land base larger than most of Europe were members of other nations and yet these peoples were never invited to take part in the negotiations.

This failure to consider the pre-existing claims of Indigenous peoples persisted when colonial powers fantasized about the riches that would accrue to the new state if Great Britain and the Hudson's Bay Company could be enticed to transfer Rupert's Land. Even when a clause was negotiated for inclusion in the proposed *British North America Act*[7] to facilitate this purchase and assignment, no thought seems to have been given

---

6 *Daniels v. Canada (Minister of Indian Affairs and Northern Development)*, [2002] 4 F.C. 550, 220 F.T.R. 41 (Fed. Ct.).

7 (U.K.), 30 & 31 Vict., c. 3. Also included in s. 146 were other imperial lands unilaterally claimed and relabelled as the "North-western Territory." This Act was renamed as the *Constitution Act, 1867*, by the Schedule to the 1982 reforms.

to the views of those most affected. In retrospect, it may seem surprising that political leaders could debate the shape of a new state to be founded on democratic principles while never considering that the majority population in British Columbia and the unorganized rest of Western Canada might have different perspectives or aspirations for the future.

As a result of what can only be labelled as blindness and prejudice, there is no record of any discussions about the views of these negotiators regarding the place of Indian, Inuit, and Métis peoples within — or outside of — the new Canada. Similarly, there is no transcript or *travaux préparatoire* that gives even a glimmer of the true intention of those negotiating the terms of the *British North America Act* when they agreed to include the following sections:

> **91.** It shall be lawful for the Queen, by and with the Advice and Consent of the Senate and House of Commons, to make Laws for the Peace, Order, and good Government of Canada, in relation to all Matters not coming within the Classes of Subjects by this Act assigned exclusively to the Legislatures of the Provinces; and for greater Certainty, but not so as to restrict the Generality of the foregoing Terms of this Section, it is hereby declared that (notwithstanding anything in this Act) the exclusive Legislative Authority of the Parliament of Canada extends to all Matters coming within the Classes of Subjects next hereinafter enumerated; that is to say, . . .
>
> **24.** Indians, and Lands reserved for the Indians.
>
> . . .
>
> And any Matter coming within any of the Classes of Subjects enumerated in this Section shall not be deemed to come within the Class of Matters of a local or private Nature comprised in the Enumeration of the Classes of Subjects by this Act assigned exclusively to the Legislatures of the Provinces.[8]

Section 91(24) has had a profound impact upon the evolution of the Crown–Aboriginal relationship since 1867. Its very existence generated the ready presumption that all of the major responsibilities that had been held exclusively by the Colonial Office, including obligations under pre-

8 Above note 7.

Confederation treaties and the power to negotiate new ones, were simply transferred to the government of Canada. As this passage is the only one expressly addressing legislative jurisdiction concerning "Indians," and thereby implicitly including executive authority, it was clear that imperial power was not being transferred to the provinces. The only remaining interpretation would have been that the United Kingdom retained responsibility under existing treaties and the power to negotiate new treaties with First Nations as it did for all international treaties on Canada's behalf until after the First World War. Although a possible legal interpretation, such a view was never advocated, and the federal government did begin negotiating the numbered treaties in Kenora in 1870. Despite its extraordinary influence in the westward and northward expansion of this fragile new country, little parliamentary guidance as to the scope of section 91(24) has been provided.

Similarly, the judiciary has had few occasions to determine the precise meaning of this constitutional language. Even then, as Prof. Peter Hogg has cautioned: "The main problem is that it is not possible to be confident as to the 'intention of the framers' or the 'original understanding' . . . who are to count as framers? Whose original understanding or intention is important?"[9] This is not to say that turning to legislative history is entirely inappropriate, as it can often provide guidance and some understanding of what has influenced lawmakers. This history can present an excellent point of departure in the search for legislative meaning. As Beetz J. put it, "legislative history provides a starting point," [10] but it cannot be conclusive in interpreting essential dynamic provisions. Other members of the Supreme Court, however, have suggested that legislative history is deserving of only little weight.[11] In either assessment, there is significant added concern when it comes to deducing the meaning of constitutional language due to its greater importance, difficulty in amending, and necessity to continually be speaking in the present so as to address the exigencies of an ever evolving world.

The ambiguity surrounding section 91(24) is compounded by the lack of any documentation or other evidence that illuminates what was in the

---

9 Peter W. Hogg, *Constitutional Law of Canada*, looseleaf, vol. 2 (Scarborough, ON: Carswell, 1992–) at 57-7.

10 *Martin Service Station v. M.N.R.*, [1977] 2 S.C.R. 996 at 1006.

11 *Re B.C. Motor Vehicle Act*, [1985] 2 S.C.R. 486, Lamer J.

minds of the drafters when they crafted "Indians, and Lands reserved for the Indians." If there is no definitive legislative history, then one must turn to the historical information available at the time, as well as the jurisprudence, for whatever guidance may be provided. The most useful guide is likely the Supreme Court of Canada's one opportunity to reflect upon the meaning of the term *Indians* in section 91(24).

C. *REFERENCE RE ESKIMOS*[12]

The only time the Supreme Court has been asked to deliberate on the scope of section 91(24) was in the context of another federal–provincial battle to avoid fiscal obligations. During the Depression, the Quebec government decided to provide emergency relief to help Inuit families on the brink of starvation. The province sought reimbursement for its expenditures from the federal government, which quickly declined. After lengthy, but ultimately futile, correspondence, it was agreed that the dispute would be remitted to the Supreme Court of Canada.[13] A formal reference was made by Order-in-Council P.C. 867, issued on 2 April 1935.

---

12 *In the Matter of a Reference as to Whether the Term "Indians" in Head 24 of Section 91 of the* British North America Act, 1867, *includes Eskimo Inhabitants of the Province of Quebec*, [1939] S.C.R. 104, commonly referred to as *Reference re Eskimos*, although it is indexed by the S.C.C. as *Reference re British North America Act, 1867 (U.K.), s. 91*.

13 Wakeling J., in dissent in *R. v. Grumbo* (1998), 159 D.L R. (4th) 577 (Sask. C.A.), rev'g [1996] 3 C.N.L.R. 122 (Sask. Q.B.), had a particularly critical cast on the motives of the parties when he stated at para. 83:

> I view it as unfortunate that there appears to be a considerable amount of tactical manoeuvring involved in the positions taken by the federal and provincial authorities with respect to issues of this nature. This does not assist in reaching the appropriate judicial interpretation of the legislation and agreements which are before this court. For example, in the reference to the Supreme Court of Canada to determine whether Eskimos were included in the word Indian in s. 91(24) of the *Constitution Act, 1867*, the federal government took the position they were not included and the Province of Quebec took the position they were. I do not believe it had gone unnoticed that if the Eskimos were in fact included as Indians, a significant increase in the federal budget for the Department of Indian Affairs was inevitable. Nor was the Province of Quebec unaware that it was in their best interests to see that Eskimos were a Federal responsibility.

Despite the opinion of the lawyers for the federal Crown that the Inuit (then referred to as "Eskimos") were indeed Indians for the purposes of section 91(24), the government persisted in opposing Quebec's argument until it was confirmed by the Supreme Court of Canada after several years of preparation.[14]

The Order-in-Council transmitting the reference is worthy of quoting in detail for its discrete treatment of the cause of the reference:

> The Committee of the Privy Council have had before them a report, dated April 1, 1935, from the Minister of Justice, representing that under the terms of the *British North America Act, 1867*, section 91 "the exclusive legislative authority of the Parliament of Canada extends to all matters coming within the classes of subjects next hereinafter enumerated," and that among these subjects is number "24. Indians, and Lands reserved for the Indians."
>
> The Minister states that in parts of the province of Quebec there are Eskimo inhabitants, and
>
> That a controversy has arisen between the Dominion Government and the Government of the province of Quebec in relation to the question whether the legislative and executive power of the Dominion Government under the above provision of the *British North America Act, 1867*, extends to the Eskimo inhabitants of the province of Quebec.
>
> The Committee, on the recommendation of the Minister of Justice, advise that Your Excellency may be pleased, in the exercise of the powers conferred by section 55 of the *Supreme Court Act*, to refer to the Supreme Court of Canada for hearing and consideration the following question:
>
> Does the term "Indians," as used in head 24 of section 91 of the *British North America Act, 1867*, include Eskimo inhabitants of the Province of Quebec?[15]

The case was heard over two days in June of 1938, some thirty-eight months after the Order-in-Council was issued. The only participant

---

14 The case is discussed in Richard Diubaldo, "The Absurd Little Mouse: When Eskimos Became Indians" (1981) 16 J. Can. Studies 34. The author informs us (at 36) that the Justice Department, and especially its external counsel, was of the opinion that the federal case was weak enough that it seemed unwise to incur the expense of arguing it before the Supreme Court and favoured a settlement.

15 *Reference re Eskimos*, above note 12 at 104–5.

other than the federal government was the province of Quebec.[16] The Inuit were not involved in any way and appear never to have been asked to comment. As there was no regional Inuit political representative or other organization at that time, it would have been exceedingly difficult for an Inuit perspective to have been presented to the Court.

The Court was unanimous in answering the question in the affirmative, almost ten months later. The majority judgment was written by Duff C.J. (with Hudson, Davis, and Crocket JJ. concurring), who described the task before the Court in these terms:

> The *British North America Act* is a statute dealing with British North America and, in determining the meaning of the words "Indians" in the statute, we have to consider the meaning of that term as applied to the inhabitants of British North America. In 1867 more than half of the Indian population of British North America were within the boundaries of Rupert's Land and the North-Western Territory; and of the Eskimo population nearly ninety per cent were within those boundaries. It is, therefore, important to consult the reliable sources of information as to the use of the term "Indian" in relation to the Eskimo in those territories. Fortunately, there is evidence of the most authoritative character furnished by the Hudson's Bay Company itself.[17]

As Duff C.J. makes clear through this passage, the Court was required to assess what was encompassed within the term *Indians*, not just through pre-Confederation experience within the three colonies, as the Inuit presence in the limited territorial extent of these colonies at that time was minimal. Rather, the Court had to be cognizant of the fact that the *British North America Act*, through its preamble and section 146, expressly envisaged territorial expansion. Furthermore, the Quebec that argued this Reference in 1938 was dramatically different in size than it was in 1867, when most of its current territory was still part of Rupert's Land.

Chief Justice Duff reviewed the historical record, such as it was, that had been presented to the Court by both participants. In addition to the

16 The province of Newfoundland and Labrador did not yet exist, such that the colonial government in St. John's would have had no interest in an interpretation of a matter internal to Canada's division of powers.

17 *Reference re Eskimos*, *ibid.* at 124–25.

reports provided by the Hudson's Bay Company to the British Parliamentary Committee that investigated Aboriginal affairs in 1856–57, the record consisted of reports from colonial governments and missionaries, as well as proclamations and descriptions of the process of acquiring the new western and northern lands in 1870. The Chief Justice was quite prepared to be persuaded by the documentary record of how the Inuit of Labrador were viewed prior to 1867, even though Labrador was not part of Canada when this Reference was determined. Chief Justice Duff was particularly struck by the repeated usage of "savages" as a synonym for "Indians" in many of the documents and how both words seemed to include the "Esquimaux." Occasionally, the expression was the "Esquimaux Indians."

Chief Justice Duff had little difficulty in coming to this conclusion:

> Nor do I think that the fact that British policy in relation to the Indians, as evidenced in the Instructions to Sir Guy Carleton and the Royal Proclamation of 1763, did not contemplate the Eskimo (along with many other tribes and nations of British North American aborigines) as within the scope of that policy is either conclusive or very useful in determining the question before us. For that purpose, for construing the term "Indians" in the *British North America Act* in order to ascertain the scope of the provisions of that Act defining the powers of the Parliament of Canada, the Report of the Select Committee of the House of Commons in 1857 and the documents relating to the Labrador Eskimo are, in my opinion, far more trustworthy guides.
>
> Nor can I agree that the context (in head no. 24) has the effect of restricting the term "Indians." If "Indians" standing alone in its application to British North America denotes the aborigines, then the fact that there were aborigines for whom lands had not been reserved seems to afford no good reason for limiting the scope of the term "Indians" itself.
>
> For these reasons I think the question referred to us should be answered in the affirmative.[18]

Justice Kerwin wrote a further judgment (to which Cannon and Crocket JJ. concurred) agreeing in the result. While he placed far greater weight on dictionary definitions and correspondence after 1867 than his

18 *Ibid.* at 134–35.

peers, his view was nonetheless clear when he said in his opening lines, "In my opinion, when the Imperial Parliament enacted that there should be confided to the Dominion Parliament power to deal with 'Indians and Lands reserved for the Indians,' the intention was to allocate to it authority over all the aborigines within the territory to be included in the confederation."[19]

Justice Cannon wrote a short judgment in which he indicated he agreed with Kerwin J. Justice Cannon felt, however, that there was little need to go beyond noting that the official French translation of the original proposed wording for what would become section 91(24) used the phrase "Les Sauvages et les terres réservées pour les Sauvages." In his view, this signified the following understanding:

> The Upper and Lower Houses of Upper and Lower Canada petitioners to the Queen, understood that the English word "Indians" was equivalent to or equated the French word "Sauvages" and included all the present and future aborigines native subjects of the proposed Confederation of British North America, which at the time was intended to include Newfoundland.[20]

It is noteworthy that in Duff C.J.'s review of these many documents, he frequently quoted passages that spoke of "Half-breeds," "half Indians," intermarriage with non-Aboriginal men, and the inclusion of the children within the Indigenous community. At the same time, the judgments of both Duff C.J. and Kerwin J. placed great weight on the information derived from the report of the Select Committee on the Hudson's Bay Company to the Houses of Parliament of Great Britain and Ireland, presented in 1857. The population estimates generated by the many company managers and local factors of the individual Hudson's Bay trading posts resulted in a listing of "Indian Races," after which was included the following:

> Total Indians 147,000
>
> Whites and half-breeds in Hudson's Bay Territory 11,000
>
> Souls 158,000

19 *Ibid.* at 137.

20 *Ibid.* at 136.

The identification of "Half-breeds" in the same population pool as "whites" in this report has been relied upon heavily by some commentators as evidence that the Métis were not seen in the same way as First Nations and the Inuit. Therefore, it is argued, the Métis were never meant to be included within section 91(24).[21] This view is not shared by the majority of scholars, including Métis scholars, who have come to a different conclusion.[22]

Something that is often overlooked when considering the statistics set out above is the nature, composition, and precise location of many families resident in Rupert's Land in the 1850s. There were virtually no European women anywhere in the north or west. Thus, the men of the Hudson's Bay Company would marry women from local Indian Nations or Métis women. Their children would be "Half-breeds" or Métis who stayed with their family and the Company. Other Métis families also gathered near the trading posts as they subsisted by trapping, interpreting, and participating in other aspects of the trading economy.

How would the male employees of the Company—those who developed these local estimates—likely perceive their situation so as to define themselves, their wives, their children, and their grandchildren? Would it be logical for them to divide up their families into different categories? Or, would they more likely lump their family members in with themselves under the vaguer, yet more comprehensive, category of "Whites and Half-breeds in Hudson's Bay Territory"? Little attention seems to have been given to this very human element in the scholarly

---

21 See, for example, Thomas Flanagan, "The Case against Métis Aboriginal Rights" (1983) 9 Can. Pub. Pol'y 314; Thomas Flanagan, "The History of Métis Aboriginal Rights: Politics, Principle, and Policy" (1990) 5 C.J.L.S. 71; Bryan Schwartz, *First Principles, Second Thoughts: Aboriginal Peoples, Constitutional Reform and Canadian Statecraft* (Montreal: The Institute for Research on Public Policy, 1986).

22 For the earliest study of this topic by a Métis expert, see Clem Chartier, "'Indian': An Analysis of the Term as Used in Section 91(24) of the *British North America Act, 1867*" (1978–79) 43 Sask. L. Rev. 37. For another excellent and thorough study, see Mark Stevenson, "Section 91(24) and Canada's Legislative Jurisdiction with Respect to the Métis" (2002) 1 Indigenous L.J. 237; see also Mark Stevenson, "Métis Aboriginal Rights and the 'Core of Indianness'" (2004) 67 Sask. L. Rev. 301; Lionel Chartrand, "Are Métis Persons 'Indians'? Challenging Manitoba's Natural Resources Transfer Agreement" (2004) 67 Sask. L. Rev. 235; and for the most recent critique of the views of Thomas Flanagan, see Darren O'Toole, "La revendication du titre 'indien' par les Métis" (2006) 39 Canadian Journal of Political Science 529.

debate over what interpretation should be assigned to this demographic data description.

From a legal perspective, what matters is whether by 1867 the constitutional language and structure of federalism would have intended to include Métis within "Indians" as the Supreme Court concluded it did regarding the Inuit. Were the Métis, as Duff C.J. and Kerwin J. asked in *Reference re Eskimos*, considered within the common meaning of "aborigines" or were they seen as "whites," at least for constitutional purposes?

D. SUBSEQUENT JURISPRUDENCE

In recent years, much jurisprudence dealing with the Métis has arisen in the context of hunting and fishing cases in which a Métis accused has mounted a defence to a regulatory charge by asserting an Aboriginal right, a treaty right, or a right confirmed by one of the *Natural Resources Transfer Agreements*.[23] While those who practise a "traditional" Aboriginal lifestyle, in the courts' view, and those with a clear tie to the Métis Nation have had growing success in recent years, none of these cases has directly answered whether the Métis are included within section 91(24). The Supreme Court has definitively declared in *R. v. Powley*[24] that the Métis possess Aboriginal rights and that the inclusion of the Métis in section 35(1) of the *Constitution Act, 1982*, was not a hollow promise.

In *R. v. Blais*,[25] released concurrently with *Powley*, the Court determined that the Métis were not constitutional Indians in the context of the *Manitoba Natural Resources Transfer Agreement* (NRTA) and the *Constitution Act, 1930*.[26] The Court explicitly avoided the section 91(24) jurisdictional question when it rejected a continuity of language argu-

---

23 See, for example, *R. v. McPherson*, [1992] 4 C.N.L.R. 144 (Man. Prov. Ct.), rev'd [1994] 2 C.N.L.R. 137 (Man. Q.B.); *R. v. Morin*, [1996] 3 C.N.L.R. 157, [1996] S.J. No. 262 (Prov. Ct.), aff'd [1998] 1 C.N.L.R. 182 (Sask. Q.B.); *R. v. Maurice*, [2002] 2 C.N.L.R. 244 (Sask. Prov. Ct.), aff'd [2002] 2 C.N.L.R. 273 (Sask. Q.B.); *R. v. Grumbo*, above note 13; *R. v. Castonguay*, [2003] 1 C.N.L.R. 177 (N.B. Prov. Ct.); and *R. v. Blais*, [1997] 3 C.N.L.R. 109 (Man. Prov. Ct.), aff'd [1998] 4 C.N.L.R. 103 (Man. Q.B.), aff'd [2001] M.J. No. 168 (C.A.), aff'd 2003 SCC 44.

24 [2003] 2 S.C.R. 207.

25 Above note 23.

26 *Constitution Act, 1930*, 20-21 Geo. V, c. 26 (U.K.), formerly called the *British North America Act, 1930*.

ment submitted by the Crown. This argument had suggested that the term *Indians* should be interpreted in all constitutional enactments in the same manner as referenced most recently in the *Constitution Act, 1982*. In other words, the Crown suggested that the term *Indians* as being just one of three groups within the overall definition of "aboriginal peoples" in section 35(2) should acquire the same meaning when used in the NRTA. The Court stated:

> [w]e do not find this approach persuasive. To the contrary, imposing a continuity requirement would lead us to conclude that "Indians" and "Métis" are different, since they are separately enumerated in s. 35(2) of the Constitution Act, 1982. *We emphasize that we leave open for another day the question of whether the term "Indians" in s. 91(24) of the Constitution Act, 1867 includes the Métis* — an issue not before us on this appeal.[27]

This argument would also have indirectly required an overruling of the *Reference re Eskimos* decision as the Inuit are also distinctly identified within section 35(2) yet included within section 91(24). In avoiding this question, the Court must have been aware that it had done the same thing three years earlier in *Lovelace v. Ontario* [28] when it advised:

> 4 At the outset, I wish to note that this appeal has raised collateral issues which are of great importance; among them are the constitutionality of the Indian Act and the scope of the federal jurisdiction with respect to Métis and non-registered First Nation peoples pursuant to s. 91(24) of the *Constitution Act, 1867*. Although the substantive equality analysis obliges the Court to consider the circumstances of these appellant aboriginal communities, including the social realities relating to their exclusion from, or non-participation in, the *Indian Act* regime, these important collateral issues are not properly raised in this appeal and, therefore, cannot be decided herein. Similarly, it is neither necessary nor appropriate for this Court to decide or comment upon the responsibilities of provincial governments with respect to these matters.

27 *Blais*, above note 23 at para. 36 [emphasis added].

28 *Lovelace v. Ontario*, [2000] 1 S.C.R. 950, 188 D.L.R. (4th) 193, 2000 SCC 37.

No other case dealing with Métis issues that has touched on this matter can be viewed as decisive in this regard. Efforts have been made to set the question squarely before Canadian courts, but the task has proven to be surprisingly difficult. Most recently, Métis leader Harry Daniels filed a statement of claim in the Federal Court to force a resolution to this issue, but the matter has yet to go to trial due at least in part to procedural challenges brought by the federal Justice Department. In *Daniels v. Canada* the Crown unsuccessfully challenged the appropriateness of the action.[29] After the tragic death of Harry Daniels, the federal government challenged the addition of Daniel's son Gabriel as a plaintiff, a move necessary to maintain the cause of action. The government was unsuccessful before the case management judge and then again on appeal.[30] These procedural obstacles are hardly a vigorous display of adherence to the "honour of the Crown" standard that has been declared by our highest court as "always at stake in its dealings with Aboriginal peoples."[31]

At present, the best prospect of obtaining judicial direction on the scope of section 91(24) lies in the *Dumont* case,[32] which was originally launched solely to pursue Métis land rights. The intention was to challenge the constitutionality of legislation enacted after 1870 that is alleged to have been intended to undermine the implementation of the scrip entitlements set out in the *Manitoba Act*. The litigation had languished for many years following its filing in 1980 due to budgetary problems. These problems stemmed, in part, from the numerous federal motions that led the case all the way to the Supreme Court of Canada on preliminary matters in 1990,[33] then back to the Court of Appeal.[34] Since then, the case has become re-energized and has begun to move forward to trial. On 15 March 2000,

29 *Daniels v. Canada (Minister of Indian Affairs and Northern Development)*, [2002] 4 F.C. 550 (T.D.).

30 *Daniels v. Canada (Minister of Indian Affairs and Northern Development)*, 2005 FC 1109, [2005] 4 C.N.L.R. 156.

31 *Haida Nation v. British Columbia (Minister of Forests)*, [2004] 3 S.C.R. 511 at para. 16.

32 *Dumont v. Canada (Attorney General)*, [1990] 2 C.N.L.R. 19 (S.C.C.), rev'g (*sub nom. Manitoba Metis Federation Inc. v. Canada (Attorney General)*), [1988] 3 C.N.L.R. 39 (Man. C.A.), rev'g [1987] 2 C.N.L.R. 85 (Man. Q.B.). See also *Dumont v. Canada (Attorney General)* (1991), [1992] 2 C.N.L.R. 34 (Man. C.A.), rev'g [1991] 3 C.N.L.R. 22 (Man. Q.B.).

33 *Ibid.*

34 *Dumont v. Canada (Attorney General)* (1991), 91 D.L.R. (4th) 654 (Man. C.A.).

the plaintiffs filed an amended statement of claim in which they asserted for the first time that the Métis are Indians within the meaning of section 91(24). Efforts by the Attorneys General of Manitoba and Canada to have these amendments struck out were rejected.[35] After a lengthy trial in 2006, a decision by the Manitoba Court of Queen's Bench is eagerly awaited.

In *R. v. Laviolette*,[36] a Métis accused raised the jurisdictional question as part of a defence to a fishing charge in Saskatchewan. The Crown prosecutor conceded the section 91(24) issue and the argument then became that this concession had rendered the matter moot. Although agreeing with the Crown in this regard, the judge stated:

> While the Crown argues that this is an attempt to turn this case into a private reference case and that this ruling is sought for larger political purposes, the same argument of "playing politics" could be levelled against the Crown for continuing to make this admission, as it appears to have done consistently beginning with the decision of our Court of Appeal in *Grumbo* [1998] 3 C.N.L.R. 172, thereby avoiding a judicial determination of this issue. Where there [is] no other way of making this judicial determination, I would agree that it was appropriate that the Accused be permitted to call evidence on this issue, and have the Court rule on it, despite the Crown's concession.[37]

While there is still hope that either the *Dumont* case (renamed *Manitoba Metis Federation Inc.*) or the *Daniels* case will ultimately lead to a judicial resolution of this issue, neither of these cases promises attractive resolution. Any decision by the trial judge will clearly need to be appealed to serve as an authoritative answer to the question. The willingness of the Saskatchewan government to concede the section 91(24) jurisdictional debate in *Laviolette* and similar cases so as never to appeal its defeats

---

35 *Manitoba Metis Federation Inc. v. Canada (Attorney General)*, 2002 MBQB 52. See a discussion of this case in the Introduction to this book.

36 *R. v. Laviolette*, 2004 SKPC 102.

37 *Ibid.* at para 4. The accused appealed this ruling unsuccessfully: *R. v. Laviolette*, [2005] SKQB 61, 260 Sask. R. 121. The trial court later held that the accused possessed Aboriginal rights and acquitted him; however, it was unnecessary to address the s. 91(24) issue as well as a variety of other legal arguments to reach the conclusion regarding the presence of s. 35(1) rights in this case, 2005 SKPC 70. This latter decision has recently been followed and applied to a different region of Saskatchewan in *R. v. Belhumeur*, 2007 SKPC 114.

demonstrates only too vividly that appellate decisions are essential. However, pursuing an appeal can be as much as a six- to ten-year process after a trial decision and is hardly a speedy or inexpensive resolution.

One could also readily argue that litigation is the absolutely worst way to proceed and that negotiation should be the preferable strategy to resolve this matter. Indeed, our highest court has frequently encouraged negotiation as the preferred approach to settle major Aboriginal legal disputes. Resorting to litigation is a last resort that reflects the complete unwillingness on the part of the federal government to concede the point and accept that its interpretation is contrary to that of every provincial and territorial government in Canada as well as the Aboriginal associations involved. Alternatively, if it is so confident in the strength of its legal arguments, the government of Canada could expedite obtaining judicial direction by pressing ahead to a determination through a reference to the Supreme Court. Instead, the message conveyed by trying to avoid the issue, or even settling the matter in Court, is similar to that sent in 1936. At that time, the government's legal advice was that winning the *Reference re Eskimos* matter seemed unlikely so it was wiser not to proceed; this led the government to slow the preparation of the submission down without seeking a negotiated resolution. However, in 1936, the Quebec government was insistent upon proceeding and had the benefit of the 1935 federal Order-in-Council directing the Reference. These factors made it too politically embarrassing for the federal government to retreat. When delay was no longer sustainable, the government had to go through with its legal arguments. Clearly, a negotiated solution today would be a preferable way to build a country, while also respecting the unique political and legal history of the Métis Nation within Canada.

E. ROYAL COMMISSION ON ABORIGINAL PEOPLES

The Royal Commission on Aboriginal Peoples declared its conclusion on the section 91(24) interpretation question after carefully considering its own research, holding community hearings, listening to presentations from Métis organizations, and contracting research[38] in these terms:

---

38 I wish to advise readers that I co-authored a research paper with John Giokas for the Commission on this precise topic, which was subsequently published by the

1.5 Coverage under Section 91(24)

> We are convinced that all Métis people, whether or not they are members of full-fledged Aboriginal nations, are covered by section 91(24). There are several reasons for that conclusion. The first is that at the time of Confederation, use of the term "Indian" extended to the Métis (or "halfbreeds" as they were called then). This can be seen, for example, in section 31 of the *Manitoba Act, 1870* and in section 125(e) of the *Dominion Lands Act 1879*, both of which made provision for land grants to "halfbreed" persons ("Métis" in the French versions) or in connection with the "extinguishment of *Indian* title." The Supreme Court of Canada held as early as 1939 that Inuit ("Eskimos") are included within the scope of section 91(24) because the section was intended to refer to "all the aborigines of the territory subsequently included in the Dominion" and there is every reason to apply the same reasoning to Métis people. Most academic opinion supports the view that Métis are Indians under section 91(24), and a recent commission of inquiry [referencing the Aboriginal Justice Inquiry] in Manitoba reached the same conclusion. We support this view.[39]

In light of this assessment, the Royal Commission then proceeded to recommend the following action to the federal government:

> 4.5.3 The government of Canada either
> (a) acknowledge that section 91(24) of the *Constitution Act, 1867* applies to Métis people and base its legislation, policies and programs on that recognition; or
> (b) collaborate with appropriate provincial governments and with Métis representatives in the formulation and enactment of a constitutional amendment specifying that section 91(24) applies to Métis people.

Commission: "Do the Métis Fall within Section 91(24) of the *Constitution Act, 1867*?" in Royal Commission on Aboriginal Peoples, *Aboriginal Self-Government: Legal and Constitutional Issues*, above note 1 at 140–276; also published in French as "Les Métis sont-ils visés par le paragraphe 91(24) de la *Loi Constitutionnelle de 1867*?" in *L'autonomie Gouvernemental des Autochtones: Questions juridiques et constitutionnelles* (Ottawa: Supply and Services Canada, 1995) at 159–313.

39 Canada, Royal Commission on Aboriginal Peoples, *Report of the Royal Commission on Aboriginal Peoples: Perspectives and Realities*, vol. 4 (Ottawa: Supply and Services Canada, 1996) c. 5 at 209 [emphasis in original; footnotes omitted].

If it is unwilling to take either of these steps, the government of Canada make a constitutional reference to the Supreme Court of Canada, asking that court to decide whether section 91(24) of the *Constitution Act, 1867* applies to Métis people.

Of the many measures needed to ensure that Métis people receive fair treatment in the future, one of the most fundamental is the elimination of discrimination in all forms. The refusal by the government of Canada to treat Métis as full-fledged Aboriginal people covered by section 91(24) of the constitution is the most basic current form of governmental discrimination. Until that discriminatory practice has been changed, no other remedial measures can be as effective as they should be.[40]

F. CONCLUSION

We have passed the eleventh anniversary of the Final Report of the Royal Commission on Aboriginal Peoples without any action on either of the two main recommendations or any willingness shown to accept the fall-back choice of a reference. One wonders if the jurisdictional question will remain unanswered at the twentieth anniversary of the Royal Commission's groundbreaking work. One can only hope that this will not be the case. While the matter seems anachronistic, given the developments through section 35 and land claims settlements in the North, its lack of resolution prevents significant progress in addressing the real needs and aspirations of the Métis people. As long as federal and provincial governments in Canada focus so heavily on who pays before being willing to move forward and continue to abdicate responsibility in the interim, one cannot expect a decision as to whether the Métis are inside or outside of section 91(24) of the *Constitution Act, 1867*.[41] This jurisdictional ambiguity will continue to retard the legitimate progress of the Métis people in achieving their goals well into the 21st century.

40 *Ibid.* at 210.

41 Above note 4.

‹ 6 ›

Reconciling Differences between the Métis Nation and the Crown: An Agenda for Law Reform[1]

MARK L'HIRONDELLE STEVENSON

A. INTRODUCTION

Since the time of first contact, Indigenous peoples have been engaged in a constant struggle to protect their communities and their lands and resources from encroachment. This struggle is well documented in Canadian history,[2] which for the Métis, began only after the emergence of distinct Métis communities, particularly on the Prairies. This struggle has been documented in numerous accounts of the war between the followers of Louis Riel and Gabriel Dumont and the Canadian troops sent by Sir John A. Macdonald and others. The Métis struggle was marked by two significant and seemingly contradictory events: the first was the successful establishment of the Métis provisional government in Manitoba, along with negotiations for the inclusion of Manitoba in Confederation. Coinciding with this was the subsequent election of Louis Riel as a federal member of Parliament. The second significant event was the Battle of Batoche and the subsequent hanging of Louis Riel. These events, however, were followed by a long period of inaction and indifference: never before and never since has the battle for Aboriginal rights and autonomy been waged so fiercely against the Canadian government, only to be so quickly forgotten.

---

1 This article represents the personal views of the author and is not to be reproduced in any way without permission.

2 See, for example, Robin Fisher, *Contact and Conflict* (Vancouver: UBC Press, 1997).

Although the Métis struggle continued, it was not until the *Constitution Act, 1982*, with its recognition of Aboriginal and treaty rights, and the constitutional conferences that followed, that Métis rights once again became a national issue.[3] But the constitutional euphoria was short lived. The issues around the recognition of the Métis as a people, and the recognition and affirmation of Métis rights, quickly faded into the background of political discourse. The Métis were left to their own devices and to the creative arguments of their lawyers to advance the Métis rights agenda. The Crown was ever present, however, as Crown prosecutors and armed game wardens ignored the constitutionally guaranteed rights of the Métis. But the Crown was not to have the last word.

The last words were to come from the Métis and their Métis lawyers, and the final say from the Supreme Court of Canada, which in 2003 recognized that the Métis have Aboriginal rights that are protected by section 35 of the *Constitution Act, 1982*.[4] Although the question of jurisdiction over the Métis remains unresolved[5], the Court's affirmation of the existence of Métis Aboriginal rights has given meaning—at least in the judicial realm—to the constitutional promises made more than twenty-five years ago. The task for those who cherish their rights is to oblige governments to do more than honour those rights in the breach. If governments are to be honourable, they must recognize Métis Aboriginal rights and ensure that legislative regimes, including those governing wildlife harvesting, respect those rights and accord them the protection guaranteed by the Constitution. To do so, decision makers will require a purposive and principled approach to identification of Métis Aboriginal rights. Decision makers must be mindful of the purpose of section 35 rights: to protect the customs, practices, and traditions of Métis communities. While keeping this purpose in mind, both the courts and government decision makers will have to approach the interpretation of Métis Aboriginal rights based upon a set of rational principles.

---

3 *Constitution Act, 1982*, being Schedule B to the *Canada Act 1982* (U.K.), 1982, c. 11; *Ibid.*, s. 37.1; and "Consensus Report on the Constitution: Final Text" (Charlottetown, 28 August 1992) [Charlottetown Accord].

4 See *R. v. Powley*, [2003] 4 C.N.L.R. 321 (S.C.C) [*Powley*]; *R. v. Blais*, [2003] 4 C.N.L.R. 219 (S.C.C.) [*Blais*].

5 The jurisdiction question refers to the debate on which level of government has the legislative jurisdiction for the Métis.

This paper will discuss the principles that must guide the development of Métis Aboriginal rights. From there, it will discuss the law reform imperatives that result from the development of these rights.

B. OVERARCHING PRINCIPLES

What principles should guide courts and legislators in honouring Métis Aboriginal rights? Based upon principles of constitutional interpretation and the jurisprudence since *Sparrow*, *Van der Peet*, and now *Powley*,[6] a framework that will assist in the interpretation of these rights has emerged. This framework must take into account broader, overarching principles that have guided Crown–Indigenous relationships since the arrival of settler nations. These principles include the recognition of the rights of Indigenous peoples, the assertion of Crown sovereignty and the exclusive nature of that assertion, and the special relationship between Indigenous peoples and the Crown.

The first principle, the recognition of the rights of Indigenous peoples, was embodied in the language of the *Royal Proclamation of 1763*[7] and has subsequently become a constitutional imperative through the recognition and affirmation of Aboriginal and treaty rights in section 35.[8] While the Royal proclamation recognized Indigenous rights in land and resources, section 35 provided the constitutional protection necessary to give those rights meaning.

The second principle — exclusivity — arises by virtue of the doctrine of discovery and the assertion of sovereignty. Under this latter doctrine, the imperial Crown claimed the exclusive right to buy and sell Indigenous lands and to have the exclusive monopoly with respect to any dealings with Indigenous nations. Consequently, Indigenous nations could alienate their lands only by way of "surrender" to the Crown. This exclusivity or monopoly in favour of the discovering nation was eventually reflected in Canada's exclusive jurisdiction over Indians and Indian lands as set out in section 91(24) of the *Constitution Act, 1867*.[9]

---

6 *R. v. Sparrow*, [1990] 3 C.N.L.R. 160 (S.C.C.); *R. v. Van der Peet*, [1996] 4 C.N.L.R. 177 (S.C.C.) [*Van der Peet*]; *Powley*, above note 4.

7 *Royal Proclamation, 1763*, reprinted in R.S.C. 1985, App. II, No. 1.

8 *Constitution Act, 1982*, above note 3, s. 35.

9 *Constitution Act, 1867* (U.K.), 30 & 31 Vict., c. 3, reprinted in R.S.C. 1985, App. II, No. 5.

A third principle governing the Crown–Indian relationship is "the honour of the Crown," including any fiduciary duties that may arise from the Crown's discretion over established rights.[10] The Crown's fiduciary duty is rooted in the discretion exercised by the Crown over Indigenous lands and their governing structures, and the vulnerability of Indigenous peoples to that discretion.

These overarching principles remain the bedrock of the relationship between Indigenous peoples and the Crown, and inform the Métis Aboriginal rights framework.

C. MÉTIS ABORIGINAL RIGHTS FRAMEWORK

While the principles set out above are germane to the Métis Aboriginal rights framework, Métis rights are unique. The Métis Aboriginal rights framework emerges primarily from the Supreme Court of Canada decision in *Powley*[11] and from basic principles of constitutional law. It can be summarized as follows: the Métis are a distinct Aboriginal people, with Aboriginal rights that are independent from those of the Indians and the Inuit. The approach used in the interpretation of Métis Aboriginal rights should be purposive. A test for Aboriginal rights based upon a rigorous requirement to demonstrate continuity with pre-contact practices, customs, and traditions would ignore the fact that Métis are a distinct Aboriginal people that emerged in the post-contact era. A distinct test is required to accommodate Métis needs. A test for Métis Aboriginal rights that requires continuity with customs, practices, and traditions of historic Métis communities that emerged in the period after contact, but before the "exercise of control" by the colonizers accommodates Métis Aboriginal rights in a manner consistent with section 35. This has now been established as a principle of law. Consequently, courts and decision makers will no longer be able to slavishly apply the *Van der Peet* pre-contact test respecting Métis Aboriginal rights.[12]

A principled approach to the Métis Aboriginal rights framework suggests that the Métis fall under federal jurisdiction. The federal govern-

10 *Haida Nation v. British Columbia (Minister of Forests)*, 2004 SCC 73.

11 Above note 4.

12 *Van der Peet*, above note 6 at para. 44.

ment has the exclusive legislative jurisdiction over Indians and lands reserved for the Indians by virtue of section 91(24) of the *Constitution Act, 1867*. The term *Indians* as used in section 91(24) is broad in scope and includes the Inuit.[13] It should also be read to include the Métis. Such an interpretation is consistent with the analysis used by the Supreme Court of Canada in *Re the term "Indians,"*[14] and with the purposive approach required in interpreting constitutional documents.

The jurisdictional point is important, as within the scope of Canada's jurisdiction over Indians and lands reserved for the Indians is a core of Indianness that is protected from provincial laws by the doctrine of interjurisdictional immunity. According to that doctrine, provincial laws cannot apply in a way that impairs federal subject matters. The content of the core of Indianness, or the heart of section 91(24), includes rights protected by section 35, Métis Aboriginal rights among them. Provincial laws that impair this core of Indianness must be read down. As Métis Aboriginal rights fall within the core of Indianness, or the heart of section 91(24), they would be protected from the application of some provincial laws.[15]

This view was reaffirmed in the Supreme Court of Canada in *R. v. Morris*[16] where the Court stated at paragraphs 90 and 91:

> Under the doctrine of interjurisdictional immunity, valid provincial legislation is constitutionally inapplicable to the extent that it intrudes or touches upon core federal legislative competence over a particular matter. Thus, exclusive federal jurisdiction under s. 91(24) protects "core Indianness" from provincial intrusion: *Delgamuukw v. British Columbia*, [1997] 3 S.C.R. 1010, at para 177. Valid provincial legislation which does not touch on "core Indianness' applies *ex proprio vigore*. If a law does go to "core Indianness" the impugned provincial legislation will not apply unless it is incorporated into federal law by s. 88 of the *Indian Act*.

13 For a detailed analysis, see Clem Chartier, "'Indians': An Analysis of the Term as used in Section 91(24) of the *British North American Act, 1867*" (1978–1979) 43 Sask. L. Rev. 37; See also Mark L. Stevenson, "Section 91(24) and Canada's Legislative Jurisdiction with Respect to the Métis" (2002) 1 Indigenous L.J. 237.

14 *Reference re Eskimos*, [1939] S.C.R. 104.

15 See Mark L. Stevenson, "Métis Aboriginal Rights and the 'Core of Indianness'" (2004) 67(1) Sask. L. Rev. 301.

16 *R. v. Morris*, [2006] 2 S.C.R. 915.

> Indian treaty rights and aboriginal rights have been held to fall within the protected core of federal jurisdiction: *Simon v. The Queen*, [1985] 2 S.C.R. 387, at p 411; *Delgamuukw*, at para 178. It follows that provincial laws of general application do not apply *ex proprio vigore* to the hunting activities of Indians that are protected by a treaty.

Obviously, the Aboriginal rights of Indians also fall within the core of Indianness, or the heart of section 91(24). Section 88 of the *Indian Act*, however, incorporates by reference provincial laws of general application that cannot apply *ex proprio vigore* because of their effects on Indians and land reserved for Indians. Section 88 makes such laws applicable to status or registered Indians as federal laws.[17] Consequently, those aspects of provincial wildlife regimes that affect the core of Indianness to the requisite degree apply to status Indians by operation of section 88, subject, of course, to the section 35 justification analyses.[18] Métis rights must be treated differently than those of status Indians because the Métis are not captured by the terms of the *Indian Act*: section 88 therefore does not apply to them. Therefore, the Métis are subject to different treatment under provincial natural resources laws.

These elements of the Métis Aboriginal rights framework, while not universally agreed to, flow from an analysis of the meaning of the term *Indians* as used in section 91(24) of the *Constitution Act, 1867*, a purposive approach to the interpretation of section 35 Métis Aboriginal rights, a review of the Supreme Court of Canada's decision in *Powley*, and the doctrine of interjurisdictional immunity.

D. LAW REFORM

Legislative change is required when the law no longer reflects the norms, values, and conduct of society. The law reform process should also respond to injustices or anomalies in the law. This vision of law reform, as articulated by the Law Commission of Canada, gives priority to the law as lived, as opposed to the law as written in statutes. The disparity between

---

17 *Indian Act*, R.S.C. 1985, c. I-5.

18 For a discussion of *R. v. Morris*, above note 16, and its impact on this area of the law, please refer to papers by Mitch McAdam and Kent McNeil (see Chapters 10 and 11).

the law as written and the law as lived by the Métis makes this area ripe for law reform. Métis harvesters, for instance, continue to practise their traditional way of life by exercising their Aboriginal rights, even though the law as written in the statute books has not provided sufficient space to do so, notwithstanding the decision in *Powley*. As a consequence, even though the Supreme Court of Canada has recognized the Métis Aboriginal right to hunt for food, the various provincial wildlife regimes do not, and Métis rights harvesters continue to be prosecuted.

Several areas of the law relating to the Métis require re-examination.

1) Section 91(24) of the *Constitution Act, 1867*

The scope of section 91(24) should be clarified to confirm that it includes the Métis. With this clarification, it would be important to ensure that the Métis Settlements legislation in Alberta, which assumes provincial authority over the Métis, would not be struck down.[19] The failed Charlottetown Accord proposed to clarify section 91(24) and to protect the Alberta Métis Settlement legislation from any adverse consequences that flowed from this process. This aspect of the Charlottetown Accord needs to be revisited by law and policy makers.

To provide greater clarity with respect to jurisdiction over the Métis, changes to section 91(24) ought to become a part of a constitutional reform package. If this is not possible, the government of Canada must at least exercise its jurisdiction with respect to the Métis in a manner consistent with the "honour of the Crown." Hiding behind the lack of jurisdictional clarity is no longer acceptable. If these changes do not happen, governments will return to ignoring Métis issues and using the appearance of jurisdictional uncertainty as an excuse for maintaining the status quo.

2) Wildlife Harvesting and the *Natural Resources Transfer Agreements*

The decision in *Powley*, coupled with the doctrine of interjurisdictional immunity, requires changes to the manner in which the provincial fish

19 For a discussion of the Métis Settlements legislation in Alberta, please refer to Catherine Bell and Harold Robinson's paper (see Chapter 15).

and wildlife regimes are enforced in each province. In addition, as a result of the Supreme Court of Canada's decision in *Blais*,[20] further law reform is required to resolve anomalies related to the *Natural Resources Transfer Agreements* (NRTAs). Before the decision in *Blais*, it was undetermined whether Métis were Indians for the purposes of the agreements, which govern natural resource harvesting for Indians resident in the prairie provinces. In *Blais*, however, the Court held that the term *Indian* in the NRTAs does not include the Métis. If the Métis had been considered Indians for the purposes of those agreements, there would have been two results. First, under the NRTAs, the Métis could pursue their traditional activities of hunting, trapping, and fishing for food, in the same manner as do Indians: on unoccupied Crown land, throughout the year, and on private lands to which they have a right of access. Second, those activities could not have been exercised without restrictions. Indians carrying out their traditional harvesting activities under the NRTAs are subject to laws respecting game in force in the province from time to time.

In other words, the NRTAs define what rights may be exercised and place restrictions on how they may be exercised by allowing for the application of provincial laws. Had *Blais* been decided differently, the provincial regulatory regime would have applied to Métis harvesters because of the NRTAs, subject to the section 35 justification. *Blais* made clear that this is not the case, causing a conundrum for the provinces. The Métis have Aboriginal harvesting rights, but these are subject to different regulation than similar rights exercised by Indians.

The regulatory regime needed to fill these anomalies in the application of the NRTAs might be federal or might involve a federal–provincial agreement. Perhaps the cleanest solution would be to amend the NRTAs in each of the prairie provinces to ensure that the Indian provisions apply to the Métis. In the interim, the Métis will have to ensure that their traditional practices conform to Métis wildlife harvesting regimes developed by the Métis in each Prairie province.

However, care must be taken in amending natural resource harvesting regimes. If the Crown intends to establish a regime that would interfere with the exercise of Métis Aboriginal rights, a meaningful consultation process related to the development of such regulations needs to be put

20 Above note 4.

in place. This imperative, which flows from the section 35 justification analysis already established by the courts, ought not to be the subject of great debate. One need only recall the words of the Supreme Court of Canada in *Delgamuukw*,[21] which made it quite clear that the duty to consult may require consent, particularly when the provinces are trying to enact hunting and fishing regulations:

> Moreover, the other aspects of aboriginal title suggest that the fiduciary duty may be articulated in a manner different than the idea of priority. This point becomes clear from a comparison between Aboriginal title and the aboriginal right to fish for food in *Sparrow*. First, aboriginal title encompasses within it a right to choose to what ends a piece of land can be put. The aboriginal right to fish for food, by contrast, does not contain within it the same discretionary component. This aspect of aboriginal title suggests that the fiduciary relationship between the Crown and aboriginal peoples may be satisfied by the involvement of aboriginal peoples in decisions taken with respect to their lands. There is always a duty of consultation. Whether the aboriginal group has been consulted is relevant to determining whether the infringement of aboriginal title is justified, in the same way that the Crown's failure to consult an aboriginal group with respect to the terms by which reserve land is leased may breach its fiduciary duty at common law: *Guerin*. The nature and scope of the duty of consultation will vary with the circumstances. In occasional cases, when the breach is less serious or relatively minor, it will be no more than a duty to discuss important decisions that will be taken with respect to lands held pursuant to aboriginal title. Of course, even in these rare cases when the minimum acceptable standard is consultation, this consultation must be in good faith, and with the intention of substantially addressing the concerns of the aboriginal peoples whose lands are at issue. In most cases, it will be significantly deeper than mere consultation. *Some cases may even require the full consent of an aboriginal nation, particularly when provinces enact hunting and fishing regulations in relation to aboriginal lands.*[22]

---

21 *Delgamuukw v. British Columbia* (1997), [1998] 1 C.N.L.R. 14 (S.C.C.) [*Delgamuukw*].

22 *Ibid.* at para. 168 [emphasis added].

Equally important, any regime that is put in place to regulate wildlife harvesting must provide clear criteria for statutory decision makers to exercise their discretion consistently with the Crown's honour and fiduciary duties, as required in *Adams*.[23] The Crown cannot simply adopt an unstructured administrative regime that risks infringing Aboriginal rights. The Supreme Court of Canada has clearly recognized this:

> . . . Parliament may not simply adopt an unstructured discretionary administrative regime which risks infringing Aboriginal rights in a substantial number of application sin the absence of some explicit guidance. If a statute confers an administrative discretion which may carry significant consequences for the exercise of an Aboriginal right, the statute or its delegate regulations must outline specific criteria for the granting or refusal of that discretion which seek to accommodate the existence of Aboriginal rights.[24]

3) Claims Process

Ultimately, the reconciliation of Aboriginal rights with Crown sovereignty involves a formal process of resolution. The historic treaty process was intended to reconcile the assertion of Crown sovereignty with Aboriginal rights and title. The modern-day land claims process was put in place after the *Calder* decision to resolve the claims that were not addressed through the historic treaties.

The modern claims process, however, has a glaring omission, and this needs to be rectified. Now that it is clear that Métis have Aboriginal rights that are constitutionally protected, a process of reconciliation needs to be put in place to resolve the outstanding matters relating to these rights. To begin with, the process should address Métis harvesting rights similar to the manner in which both the historic and modern treaties address the harvesting rights of the Indians and the Inuit. Issues of Métis Aboriginal title and of governance also need to be addressed. This claims process would best be established through legislation, would likely have to be tripartite, and should be established in each province of the Métis Homeland. This will happen neither immediately nor easily. It

---

23 *R. v. Adams*, [1996] 3 S.C.R. 101 [*Adams*].

24 *Ibid.* at para. 54.

took significant litigation on the part of First Nations to put the modern-day treaty process in place, and it is likely to take further litigation to put a Métis claims process in place. The Crown needs to be made aware of the inevitability of this process, but for this to occur, Crown officials and politicians must shed their indifference. This will take time and further litigation, as indifference towards the Métis and their issues is deeply imbedded in the culture of governments.

Such indifference was the subject of comments from the Supreme Court of Canada in *Mikisew Cree First Nation v. Canada (Minister of Canadian Heritage),* where Binnie J. stated:

> The fundamental objective of the modern law of aboriginal and treaty rights is the reconciliation of aboriginal peoples and non-aboriginal peoples and their respective claims, interests and ambitions. The management of these relationships takes place in the shadow of a long history of grievances and misunderstanding. The multitude of smaller grievances created by the indifference of some government officials to aboriginal people's concerns, and the lack of respect inherent in that indifference has been as destructive of the process of reconciliation as some of the larger and more explosive controversies. And so it is in this case.[25]

E. CONCLUSION

Powley and *Blais* have highly significant implications for the Métis and for governments, particularly in relation to wildlife harvesting. Both the Crown and the Métis have much work to do if there is to be a sensible response to the decisions in *Powley* and *Blais.* Both parties must also work together to address the jurisdictional vacuum left by the failure of the federal government to exercise its authority in a manner consistent with the obligations attached to "the honour of the Crown." A starting point would be for the Crown to adopt a law reform agenda that includes clarification of the scope of section 91(24), the development of a wildlife harvesting regime that takes into account a proposed Métis Aboriginal rights framework, and the establishment of a Métis claims process.

25 *Mikisew Cree First Nation v. Canada (Minister of Canadian Heritage),* 2005 SCC 69 at para. 1.

Of course, this agenda needs to be carried out in cooperation with the Métis and in a process involving good faith negotiations and meaningful consultation. Unless this happens, Métis Aboriginal rights will become forgotten promises, honoured only in the breach.

‹ 7 ›

"Neither Fish nor Indians": Pursuing Crown–Métis Relations through Historical Evidence Concerning Policies and the *Constitution Act, 1930*[1]

FRANK J. TOUGH

A. INTRODUCTION: "MUST BE READ GENEROUSLY"

The question of the recognition of federal responsibility for the Métis under section 91(24) of the *Constitution Act, 1867*, can be pursued by considering the relationship between the Crown and the Métis. That relationship can be pondered by considering legal doctrines and principles or it can be carefully reconstructed through historical evidence. Of course, the interpretation of historical evidence can be informed by the values of justice and equity, or it can draw on absurdities, formalities, and false dichotomies to come to the aid of antagonistic views, for instance, those who regret that Métis rights were ever recognized in the first instance.[2] By being cognizant of the surrounding circumstances of legal and political processes, this analysis will attempt to demonstrate the value of a nuanced approach for utilizing records.

1 This title borrows from a centuries-old idiom used to describe difficult categories, "Neither fish nor fowl," or, more accurately, "Neither fish, nor flesh, not fowl, nor good red herring." It serves as a subtle reminder about the many "red herrings" that are offered to counter a recognition of federal jurisdiction concerning the Métis due to the problem of classifying this Aboriginal people.

2 For those contemplating the relevance of historical evidence, such as questions of fact, selection, and interpretation, see E.H. Carr, *What Is History?* (Harmondsworth: Penguin Books, 1964; original 1961) at 7–30. See Thomas Flanagan, "The Case against Métis Aboriginal Rights," *Canadian Public Policy* vol. 9, no. 3 (1983) at 314–25.

While the intention is not to relentlessly pursue all the problems of law and historical fact that frequently emerge in Aboriginal and treaty rights litigation, the analysis here contradicts several aspects of the large historical conclusions deriving from the *Blais* decision.[3] In *Blais*, the Supreme Court found:

> The *NRTA* [Natural Resources Transfer Agreement] is a constitutional document which must be read generously within its contextual and historical confines and yet in such a way that its purpose is not overshot. Here, the appellant is not entitled to benefit from the protection accorded to "Indians" in the *NRTA*. First, the *NRTA*'s historical context suggested that the term "Indians" did not include the Métis. The historical documentation indicated that, in Manitoba, the Métis had been treated as a different group from "Indians" for purposes of delineating rights and protections. Second, the common usage of the term "Indian" in 1930 did not encompass the Métis. The terms "Indian" and "half-breed" had been used to refer to separate and distinguishable groups of people in Manitoba from the mid-19th century through the period in which the *NRTA* was negotiated and enacted. The location of para. 13 in the *NRTA* under the heading "Indian Reserves" further supports this interpretation. Third, the purpose of para. 13 of the *NRTA* was to ensure respect

3 Most of the recent litigation concerns the effect of the NRTAs on the treaties covering the prairie provinces. The NRTA Indian livelihood right provided:

> 12. [13] In order to secure to the Indians of the Province the continuance of the supply of game and fish for their support and subsistence, Canada agrees that the laws respecting game in force in the Province from time to time shall apply to the Indians within the boundaries thereof, provided, however, that the said Indians shall have the right, which the Province hereby assures to them, of hunting, trapping and fishing game and fish for food at all seasons of the year on all unoccupied Crown lands and on any other lands to which the said Indians may have a right of access.

In the Alberta and Saskatchewan agreements, the Indian hunting right is found in paragraph 12, whereas the same wording is found in paragraph 13 in the Manitoba agreement. Three Memoranda of Agreement were made: (1) Dominion of Canada and the Province of Manitoba (14 December 1929); (2) Dominion of Canada and the Province of Alberta (14 December 1929); and, somewhat later (3) Dominion of Canada and Province of Saskatchewan (20 March 1930). By convention, these agreements are referred to as the *Natural Resources Transfer Agreements, 1930* [NRTAs]. The content of these agreements is very similar.

> for the Crown's obligations to "Indians" with respect to hunting rights, who were viewed as requiring special protection and assistance. This view did not extend to the Métis, who were considered more independent and less in need of Crown protection.[4]

And more specifically, the Court asserted: "We find no reason to disturb the lower courts' findings that neither the Crown nor the Métis understood the term 'Indians' to encompass the Métis in the decades leading up to and including the enactment of the *NRTA*."[5] Based on the evidence before the Court, this finding may have been reasonable; however, this chapter will present historical evidence that directly contradicts this legal conclusion. There are many large issues involved in the NRTA, most of which have been ignored or handled badly.[6] It is not possible here to argue the inclusion of the Métis in the Indian livelihood rights provision in each of the NRTAs (paragraph 12 in the Alberta and Saskatchewan agreements; paragraph 13 in the Manitoba agreement), although the analysis offered here challenges some of the assumptions that were devised for interpreting the "hunting" rights paragraph).[7] Nonetheless, it is my impression that the arguments made in the *Blais* case and the actual de-

---

4 *R. v. Blais*, [2003] 2 S.C.R. 236 at 237. Recall, that the essential issue concerned a Métis constitutional right to hunt under the NRTA.

5 *Ibid.* at 256.

6 Only recently are historical analyses of the Indian interests in the NRTAs developing. See Robert Irwin, "'A Clear Intention to Effect Such a Modification': The *NRTA* and Treaty Hunting and Fishing Rights," *Native Studies Review* vol. 13, no. 2 (2000) at 47–89; and Frank J. Tough, "The Forgotten Constitution: The Natural Resources Transfer Agreements and Indian Livelihood Rights, ca. 1925–1933," *Alberta Law Review* vol. 41, no. 4 (2004) at 999–1048. Neither Erwin nor Tough found evidence of clear and plain intent on the part of the Crown to modify treaty rights with paragraph 12/13. The assumption that treaties were modified by the NRTAs is a historically unproven foundation adopted for all court decisions concerning the "Indian livelihood right" provided by NRTAs. For the broader political context relating to process, see Nicole Colleen O'Byrne, "The Answer to the 'Natural Resources Question': A Historical Analysis of the *Natural Resources Transfer Agreements*," LL.M. thesis (Montreal: McGill University, 2005).

7 A first step in making an argument for an inclusion of the Métis as Indians in the livelihood right provisions of the NRTAs requires the correction of the historical hypotheses in the existing case law with respect to the modification, consolidation, merger, or cutting down of treaty rights. This task is beyond the scope of the present analysis.

cision indicate an extremely problematic use of historical records as extrinsic evidence.

The key historically-oriented assertions deriving from the *Blais* decision are these:

1. Historical context does not suggest that Indians included Métis.
2. Métis rights are different from Indian rights.
3. Common usage of Indian did not include Métis.
4. Half-breed and Indian were used to separate and distinguish people in Manitoba since the mid-19th century through to the period of the negotiation and enactment of the *NRTA*.
5. The purpose of the hunting rights provision was to ensure respect for the Crown's obligations to Indians.
6. The Métis were considered independent and not in need of Crown protection.[8]

Moreover, the Court found that "A requirement for 'continuity of language' should not be imposed on the Constitution as a whole and, in any event, such an interpretation would not support the contention that the term 'Indians' should include the Métis."[9] Taken together, these findings of "fact" amount to a simple conclusion, namely, that the categories "Halfbreed" and "Indian" were fixed historically and thus, legally impermeable. However, such claims to historical conclusion should be able to demonstrate vastly dissimilar economies and patterns of resource use. Several of these historical assertions in *Blais* relate directly to the general topic of the history of Crown–Métis relations and to the question of the undefined use of the term *Indian* in the Constitution Acts of 1867 and 1930. However, other issues (such as the common usage of the terms *Halfbreed* and *Indian*, and protection of hunting rights limited to the Crown's obligations to Indians) relate directly to the Indian livelihood rights paragraph in the NRTA in the specific circumstances of the history of southern Manitoba and cannot be discussed here. In essence, though, several of these claims seek to dichotomize "Indian" and "Métis" in a way that negates the possibility of the category "Aboriginal" ever

8 *R. v. Blais*, above note 4, at 237 and 246–53.

9 *Ibid.* at 237.

existing in the past. My purpose here is to balance some of these legalistic assertions and mindsets with some historical facts and analysis.

Whether or not Indians and Métis were separate and distinct in all respects after 1850 (which they were not, anyway) does not really address the fact that the expression "Indian" had been used in a generic way in the past, even after 1870, and in the same way that "Aboriginal" is used today. Even the use of the compound expression "Indians and Half-breeds" in some instances does not negate the fact that "Indians" in other situations could be used as a generic category for Natives or Aboriginals. The use of the compound or phrase implies something of a common quality and not a divisive separation. The coupling of "Half-breed" with Indian as an idiomatic concept provides assurance that the Métis are included in the categories of many things that relate to "Indian."

The scope of the historical evidence and interpretation of the interchangeability of the terms *Indian*, *Native*, *Non-Treaty*, *Half-breed*, and *Métis* are too large for this paper. And as will be demonstrated, some of the perpetrators of this "ambiguity" — or use of *Indian* to mean Métis — were agents of the Crown. With respect to the topic at hand, how do we get beyond this secure, but one-dimensional dichotomy of "Indian" and "Métis"? This research might be a useful step towards a more historically anchored analysis of Crown–Métis relations, and a challenge to the *a priori* position which holds that the really contentious issues in Aboriginal and treaty rights are strictly a matter of law and cannot be informed by history.

Nonetheless, for my purposes, an introduction to Crown–Métis relations can be pursued by looking at each end of an imaginary spectrum of legal and historical indicators: (1) important policies, as implemented on the ground; and (2) constitutional and property issues addressed by authoritative legal minds.

I will confine this analysis to an era (1869 to 1934) that corresponds to the period that the *Blais* decision lays claim to a historical-evidentiary certainty. The geographical scope of this paper is limited to a region presently known as the "prairie provinces." Crown–Métis relations can be viewed up close, that being how policies and regulations concerning the Aboriginal harvesting of fish were devised and implemented, which, in turn, affected people's livelihoods and customs. Fish were integral to an Aboriginal mode of life throughout much of the historical Métis

Homeland.[10] However, this sort of dogged survey of mundane archival sources — the administrative papers of common fisheries overseers, Indian agents, and Mounties — is not very persuasive to those minds steeped in skepticism about inductive reasoning and historical knowledge. Fortunately, then, historical relations between the Métis and Crown can also be considered from a more exalted constitutional perspective. Historical records, relating to the meanings and the origins of property or the tenure making up "Halfbreed scrip," generated by those officials involved with the *Natural Resources Transfer Agreements*, before and after 1930, do exist.[11] For the simple fact that Métis scrip was one of the categories of land grants that emerged from the Dominion government's control over prairie provincial lands, it did not go unnoticed in discussions about compensation owed to the prairie provinces during this constitutional process. While it is often intellectually satisfying and convenient to treat constitutional issues as situated in some sort of seminar of the serious minded — above and beyond the murk of history, politics, and geography — there are good archival sources for both the history of policy and the history of the *Constitution Act, 1930*. Again, a complete analysis of all the documents relating to Métis interests and NRTA is not possible here. Although I have separated the question of policies and regulations from the constitutional imperatives, both really concern property. In the case of fishing resources, recognition of a right of access would have been regarded at the time, at the very least, as some sort of usufructuary right. In the case of Métis scrip, this potential grant of fee simple title was rescued from the obscurity of short-term collective memory lapse and became a topic that informed the NRTA process.[12] Consequently, an examination of these documents provides insight, if

10 Frank Tough, "'The Storehouses of the Good God': Aboriginal Peoples and Freshwater Fisheries in Manitoba," *Manitoba History* No. 39 (2000) at 2–14.

11 From what I can determine, these records were not made available to the court.

12 Two basic sources concerning this arcane topic are these: Gerhard J. Ens, "Métis Scrip," in *The Recognition of Aboriginal Rights*, Samuel W. Corrigan and Joe Sawchuk, eds. (Brandon: Bearpaw Publishing, 1996) at 47–57; and Frank Tough and Erin McGregor, "'The Rights to the Land May Be Transferred': Archival Records as Colonial Text — A Narrative of Métis Scrip," in *Natives and Settlers: Now and Then: Historical Issues and Current Perspectives on Treaties and Land Claims in Canada*, Paul W. DePasquale, ed. (Edmonton: University of Alberta Press, 2007) at 33–63.

not some clarity, concerning the foundation, scope, and meaning of the expression "Indian" in the Constitution.

Both approaches suggest that the assertions by the Supreme Court claiming that (1) historical context excludes the Métis from the term *Indian*; (2) Métis rights are necessarily different from Indian rights; (3) "the terms 'Indian' and 'half-breed' had been used always to refer to separate and distinguishable groups of people in Manitoba from the mid-19th century through the period in which the *NRTA* was negotiated and enacted"; or (4) the Métis did not benefit from special consideration from the Crown are not valid generalizations that can be readily applied outside of the postage stamp province of Manitoba, and with additional research, interpretation, and analysis may prove to be imprecise for southern Manitoba. The historical evidence here not only provides some general background on Crown–Métis relations, but also challenges, and may even refute, specific historical findings in *Blais* so as to caution against a similar line of argument being applied to section 91(24) of the *British North America Act, 1867*.[13]

B. DISTINCTLY ABORIGINAL: "SO CALLED INDIANS OF THE NORTH ARE ALL HALF-BREEDS"

A few general observations provide some introductory guidance towards grasping an understanding of the meaning of "Indians" in Crown–Métis relations. Records generated by the Department of Indian Affairs provide a clear indication of a close association between Métis individuals and Treaty Indians. Annual reports on the Manitowapah Indian Agency, located in what is now the Manitoba Interlake, show that federal officials acknowledged that the Métis were strongly associated with Indians, occasionally even to the point of a continuing identification of a number of mixed-bloods as status "Indians." Over nearly twenty years, the population of this agency was generally described as being Ojibwa, but with the qualification that "in fact there are very few pure-blooded Indians"[14] and the bands included "many French, English and Scotch

13 Now known as the *Constitution Act, 1867* (U.K.), 30 & 31 Vict., c. 3, reprinted in R.S.C. 1985, App. II, No. 5.

14 Canada, *Sessional Papers*, 1903, Annual Report of the Department of Indian Affairs, 1902, Paper No. 27, at 91 [CSP, 1903, Indian Affairs].

half-breeds."[15] Descriptions of the populations of other Indian agencies on the Prairies also reveal a spectrum of Métis presence, ranging from bands that consisted entirely of mixed-bloods to bands with some mixture of "white blood." For example, the population of the Portage La Prairie Agency was characterized as "all of the Ojibbewa [*sic*] tribe, with more or less strain of white man's blood."[16] At the other end of the spectrum stood the Clandeboye Indian Agency, where the status Indian population was described in this way: "a great many of them have white blood in their veins, and are very little different from the half-breed population . . . ."[17] Similarly, the Indians of The Pas Agency, which today includes portions of northwest Manitoba and northeast Saskatchewan, were depicted: "nearly all the Indians of this agency are of the Cree family, with a goodly admixture of white blood."[18] Such official descriptions hardly indicate that officials could disassociate or would always distinguish the Métis from the Indians. In fact, when agents depicted reserve populations in the post-1870 era, the descriptor "Half-breed" was often as important as tribal labels, such as Cree or Ojibwa. Such descriptions do not suggest that once an individual Métis decided to opt for Indian status, all "Metis-ness" quickly disappeared, any more than the state's legal "Indian" status necessarily wiped out being Cree or Ojibwa.

Officials were also aware that the categories of Métis and Indian were not exclusive. Fisheries Overseer O.T. Stone provided a description of the Long Lake (Saskatchewan) fishery in 1889, in which he indicated that belonging to a treaty did not erase the category Half-breed:

> Since the opening of the season for whitefish, viz.: 10th November, there have been engaged in the fishery four outfits of whitemen and twenty families, and about one hundred Indians and Half-breeds. Of these there is but a small percentage of Half-breeds; all of whom, *both Indians and Half-breeds, belong to Treaty No. 4.*[19]

---

15 CSP, 1901, Indian Affairs, 1900, No. 27, at 88; see also CSP, 1904, Indian Affairs, 1903, No. 27, at 98; CSP, 1905, Indian Affairs, 1904, No. 27, at 94; CSP, 1907–8, Indian Affairs, 1907, No. 27, at 100; CSP, 1909, Indian Affairs, 1908, No. 27, at 104; and CSP, 1910, Indian Affairs, 1909, No. 27, at 108.

16 CSP, 1904, Indian Affairs, 1903, No. 27, at 95.

17 *Ibid.* at 115–16.

18 CSP, 1905, Indian Affairs, 1904, No. 27, at 89.

19 CSP, 1890, Fisheries, 1889, No. 17, at 246 [emphasis added].

Thus, some fifteen years after Treaty 4 had been signed, the pre-treaty mixed-blood population continued to be identified as "Half-breeds" despite treaty status. While documents may have distinguished Indians and "Half-breeds," they were not necessarily separate in other respects, especially as they may have belonged to the same treaty or band.

While it is often suggested that individuals could simply choose between treaty and scrip, outside of Manitoba, the Northwest scrip commissions did not deal with the Métis until 1885. It should be understood that the treaty and scrip process was not synchronized until the 1889 Adhesion to Treaty 6, and thus, the timing of the implementation of section 31 of the *Manitoba Act, 1870*[20] (the Métis land grant), Treaties 1 to 7, and the granting of Northwest scrip, did not mean that "self-identification" was unrestricted. In 1887 alone, some 321 claims were allowed for "Treaty Half-Breeds" by the North-West Half-Breed scrip commission.[21] The category Treaty Half-Breed referred to "the applications made by the half-breeds attached to Indian bands to withdraw from treaty in order to participate in the half-breed grant . . . ."[22] This official category, employed by the commissioners to describe former Treaty Indians that participated in the scrip process, does not suggest that the federal government necessarily cared about separating and distinguishing the "Métis" from the "Indians." What it did care about was the same individual claiming both Métis and Indian entitlements—*Manitoba Act* land grants and treaty entitlements, respectively.

Similarly, when it later came to treaty-making and scrip claims in the northern fur country, the concomitant categorization of "Indians" and "Half breeds" (Métis) was perplexing. O.C. Edwards, a doctor and member of the 1899 Treaty 8 party, stated:

> It seems absurd to classify the dark skinned people of the north under the separate heads of Indians and half breeds. I have not seen an Indian as he is popularly known or depicted since I left Calgary. *These so called Indians of the north are all half breeds* and in dealing with them, the

20 33 Vict., c. 3.

21 CSP, 1888, Annual Report of the Department of the Interior, 1887, Paper No. 14, Part 5: Report of the North-West Half-Breed Claims Commission (10 January 1888) at 6–7 [CSP, 1888, Interior].

22 *Ibid.* at 3.

> Commissioners have allowed them to choose under which head they shall be paid. If they choose "treaty" then they are written down as Indians, if they select "scrip" then they are called half breeds.[23]

For outsiders, such as Dr. Edwards, similarities overshadowed the differences between the Indian and Métis populations in the Treaty 8 territory. Based on his participation as secretary to the Treaty 8 Scrip Commission, and in the company of Dr. Edwards, Charles Mair observed the traditional economy of northern Alberta and he later recalled: "the Indians and half-breeds of Athabasca Lake did not seem to differ in any way from those of the Middle and Upper Peace River, save that the former were all hunters and fishermen, pure and simple, there being little or no agriculture."[24] Similarly, J.A.J. McKenna, the 1906 commissioner for Treaty 10, made an interesting observation about the Aboriginal population of the Isle a la Crosse area in northwest Saskatchewan, stating: "It is difficult to draw a line of demarcation between those who classed themselves as Indians and those who elected to be treated with as half-breeds. *Both dress alike and follow the same mode of life.*"[25] These observations are significant for the simple reason that treaty officials commented on the striking similarities between Indians and Métis, indicating an awareness that their modes of living at the time of treaty signing were not so very distinct from each other. This is particularly true of the north, in which the fur-trade economy continued to define a common mode of existence for both Aboriginal populations. Significantly, these observations occurred after 1850.

For the 1901 Census of Canada, Indian and Métis individuals might variously be enumerated as "Cree Indian," "French Breed," "Scottish Cree Breed," and so on under the heading of Racial or Tribal Origin, but both were described by the letter *R*, standing for Red, under the head-

---

23 David Leonard and Beverly Whalen, eds., *On the North Trail: The Treaty 8 Diary of O.C. Edwards* (Calgary: Alberta Records Publication Board, 1999) at 53 [emphasis added]. Edwards also described the Native population of northern Alberta as "dark skinned people pure and half breeds" and "dark skinned breeds and Indians" (at 66, 86).

24 Charles Mair, *Through the Mackenzie Basin: A Narrative of the Athabasca Peace River Treaty Expedition of 1899* (Toronto: William Briggs, 1908) at 117.

25 CSP, 1909, Indian Affairs, 1908, No. 27, at xliii [emphasis added].

ing Colour.[26] Although many subclasses of Aboriginal peoples can be discerned from this national count — Chipeway, English Breed, Chipeway-Scotch Breed — for national purposes, census officials conflated the categories "Indian" and "Métis" by giving both populations an *R*. In a basic demographic sense — racial categorization — the Canadian state did not distinguish between the Métis and Indians.

Descriptions of the Aboriginal population of the Northwest in historical documents of the Department of Indians Affairs support several conclusions about federal officials' views of the Métis. The federal government took little exception to "mixedbloods" or "half-breeds" belonging to bands as "Indians," and in some instances, mixedbloods were said to dominate the makeup of "Indian" bands.[27] At the time of treaty-making in northern Alberta (1899) and northern Saskatchewan (1906), treaty officials did not detect a separate mode of life or contrast in the general appearance of the Indian and Métis populations. The perseverance of this mode of livelihood of Indian and Métis peoples is far more significant to the discussion than the fact that the Crown allowed individuals to exercise some choice, often though not apprised of the implications, about legal categories of Indian and Half-breed. The lifestyle of the Métis was part of a widespread Aboriginal mode of life (hunting, trapping, and fishing) which had been shaped by the fur trade.[28] The central and significant place of fishing in the culture and economy of the Métis closely resembled Indian societies in the Northwest Territories, and thus, as dull a topic as fish can be, it is a relevant approach for considering the factual interface between the Crown and the Métis.

---

26 Library and Archives Canada, public records of Statistics Canada RG 31, Census of Canada: 1901; for examples, see microfilm reels T-6435, T-6553, and T-6555.

27 Above note 25 at 81. The Account for the St. Peter's Band stated that "[t]he Indians of the reserve are all half-breeds."

28 Arthur J. Ray, *Indians in the Fur Trade: Their Role as Trappers, Hunters, and Middlemen in the Lands Southwest of Hudson Bay, 1660–1870* (Toronto: University of Toronto Press, 1998; original 1974).

C. ABORIGINAL ACCESS TO FISHERIES AND FEDERAL REGULATORY POLICIES PRIOR TO 1930: "LEAVE THE HALF-BREEDS IN THE HANDS OF THE QUEEN"

A review of federal freshwater fisheries records, regulations, and policies in the Canadian Northwest and Manitoba from the late 1800s up to the passing of the *Constitution Act, 1930*,[29] supports four conclusions: (1) Indians and Métis were understood by federal fisheries officials to belong to essentially the same category of persons ("Natives," or Aboriginal peoples); (2) acknowledgment was made by federal officials that the Métis had expectations and a mode of life closely resembling that of the Indians — both groups fished out of necessity; (3) as a result of their livelihood needs, the Métis expressed their interests and rights in the fishery; and (4) the federal government's fisheries policies and regulations treated Indians and Métis in a similar manner because federal officials frequently affirmed that the Métis were "Native" in much the same sense as the Indians, and because federal officials were well aware that fishing was a vital component of an Aboriginal mode of living.

A few examples will illustrate the interrelationship of these specific conclusions. In 1894, F.C. Gilchrist, inspector of Fisheries for the Northwest Territories, reported to the deputy minister of Marine and Fisheries upon Special Guardian D. Villebrun's account of the Jackfish Lake fishery in the Battleford area: "Those whom he reports fishing are widows[,] an old destitute halfbreed and his wife and two or three families of Saulteaux Indians all of whom are fishing under *free permits*, and several settlers who are fishing under license."[30] In other words, settlers were licensed, while Natives held free permits. Similarly, when the Depart-

29 The *Constitution Act, 1930* (U.K.), 20–21 George V, c. 26, constitutionalized the *Alberta Natural Resources Act*, S.C. 1930, c. 3; *Manitoba Natural Resources Act*, S.C. 1930, c. 29; and *Saskatchewan Natural Resources Act*, S.C. 1930, c. 41. These Acts transferred most federal Crown lands in the prairie provinces to their respective governments, and the provinces became responsible for administering fishing regulations.

30 Library and Archives of Canada, Public Records of the Department of Marine and Fisheries, Record Group 23, vol. 273, file 2029 pt. 1, Gilchrist to deputy minister of Marine and Fisheries (21 February 1895) [emphasis added] [LAC, RG 23]. Library and Archives Canada is a new name for the National Library and the National Archives of Canada. For most of its history, the national archives were known as the Public Archives of Canada.

ment of Indian Affairs requested an exclusive fishing reserve of Dawson Bay on Lake Winnipegosis for the Fort Pelly Band, Deputy Minister of Fisheries John Tilton responded, noting: "there exists strong objections to granting the Indians 'exclusive' rights in localities fast filling with Settlers, and where their claims as well of those the Half-Breeds are also entitled to consideration."[31]

From the late 1800s in the Northwest Territories until 1930 in the prairie provinces, federal regulation of freshwater fisheries frequently made special provisions with respect to licence and closed-season exemptions for both Indians and Métis. By the early 1890s, exemptions for Aboriginal communities to the application of closed seasons were evident. For example, Inspector Gilchrist was able to state in his report to Sir Charles Hibbert Tupper, minister of Marines and Fisheries, for the Lac La Biche District: "The *Indians and half-breeds* . . . fished as usual during the close season."[32] Moreover, throughout the 1890s and into the 1920s, it became common practice to provide both Indians and Métis with free fishing licences in order to feed themselves and their families.[33] For the Qu'Appelle fishery, however, a two-dollar licence fee was charged to both Indians and Métis in 1903.[34] Significantly, when fisheries officials deemed it necessary to regulate the fishery through a closed season, the department took enforcement actions against both Indians and Métis. For example, in 1893, Special Guardian J. Teader of the Qu'Appelle District reported to Inspector Gilchrist that he had "seized, and delivered over to the Inspector, during 1893 in all twenty-seven gill nets. Of these eleven belonged to half-breeds and sixteen to Indians."[35] In this particular case, it would seem that Indians were not afforded any special exemption or protection.

---

31 LAC, Public Records of the Department of Indian Affairs, RG 10, vol. 3807, file 52,936, Tilton to Deputy Superintendent of Indian Affairs L. Vankoughnet (28 July 1891).

32 CSP, 1894, Fisheries, 1893, No. 11, at 271 [emphasis added].

33 *Ibid.* at 271 and 274. For additional discussions of licences and permits, see CSP, 1893, Fisheries, 1892, No. 10A, at 143; CSP, 1895, Fisheries, 1894, No. 11A, at 359; CSP, 1899, Fisheries, 1897, No. 11A, at 213; CSP, 1901, Fisheries, 1900, No. 22, at 153; CSP, 1905, Fisheries, 1904, No. 22, at 207; and CSP, 1911, Fisheries, 1909–10, No. 22, at 224.

34 For example, see LAC, RG 23, vol. 99, file 86, pt. 3, Form D, Schedule of Applications for Fishing Licenses for Qu'Appelle, NWT, February/March/April/December 1903.

35 CSP, 1894, Fisheries, 1893, No. 11, at 274.

The granting of free licences and permits to Indians and Métis became an established procedure by the Department of Marine and Fisheries. In fact, the link between these two groups was a standard characteristic of federal fisheries policy, suggesting an awareness that the Métis belonged to the same class of persons as Indians. As will be demonstrated, free permits and exemptions from the closed season for Métis and Indians endured during the period of direct federal administration of fisheries management.[36] With the exception of the question of special, exclusive fishing reserves for Indians, federal government records with respect to fisheries regulations or policies tended to couple the term *Half-breed* with "Indian."[37] The reasons federal officials might regard the Indians and Métis as belonging to the category of "Native" include these: (1) they followed a similar mode of life; (2) the Métis expressed concern about fishing rights; and consequently, (3) regulations treated the Métis and Indians similarly, but usually distinct from settlers. The nitty-gritty of sweeping claims about big concepts such as special protection comes down to issues of fact relating to policy and regulations: how such policies might be modified by those subjected to the regulations and how those charged with implementing such policies and regulations may have exercised practical discretion.

In the era in which the Dominion government held considerable jurisdiction over the old Northwest, federal officials acknowledged that fish were important to both Indian and Métis livelihoods. In 1893, Inspector Gilchrist reported to Sir Charles Hibbert Tupper, the minister of Marine and Fisheries, noting: "The population is native, either half-breed or Indian, and lives very largely, and in the majority of cases, almost wholly on fish throughout the year."[38] Nothing in this observation provides a meaningful distinction between the two categories of Natives. Similarly, in his report to the minister of Marine and Fisheries for 1894,

36 To illustrate, see LAC, RG 23, vol. 764, file 716-12-4, pt. 1, Found to McLean (19 May 1921).

37 In Manitoba and the Northwest Territories, requests and suggestions to establish special fishing reserves for Indians were not acted upon. See Frank Tough, *"As Their Natural Resources Fail": Native Peoples and the Economic History of Northern Manitoba, 1870–1930* (Vancouver: University of British Columbia Press, 1996) at 184, 238–39.

38 CSP, 1894, Fisheries, 1893, No. 11, at 269.

Gilchrist again attested to the significance of the fisheries for the Métis in the Northwest:

> At present the half-breeds, as a whole are paupers.... As a means to assist [them] in the settlement of this serious question the fisheries are not to be lost sight of. If they are well protected and kept up to the standard, and where they are now depleted, if they are, by means of protection and restocking, when possible, brought back to a condition of plentifulness, there will never be a failing supply of wholesome food for these people.[39]

In 1897, the minister of Marine and Fisheries laid before the Privy Council the broad generalization that "the Indians and Half-breeds on the lands around certain lakes in the North West Territories are in great measure dependent upon the supply of fish they catch."[40] Similarly, in 1901, the deputy minister of Marine and Fisheries reported to the minister: "In the northern districts [of the Northwest Territories] the Indian and half-breed population . . . generally more or less depends on fish for their livelihood."[41]

In 1896, Frank Oliver,[42] writing in his capacity as a member of Parliament from the Northwest Territories to the minister of Marine and Fisheries, also confirmed the dependence of the Métis on fishing for subsistence purposes. Oliver, although favouring enforcement of a closed season for conservation reasons, advocated for a better treatment of the Métis, stating:

---

39 CSP, 1895, Fisheries, 1894, No. 11A, at 346.

40 Privy Council Order Number 2890 (20 October 1897) copy found in LAC, RG 23, vol. 126, file 170, pt. 1 [PC No. 2890].

41 CSP, 1902, Fisheries, 1901, No. 22, at xxxv.

42 Frank Oliver was a central figure in the political life of the NWT and later the prairie provinces. One biographer, E. Holmgren, stated: "He brought the first printing press to Edmonton and in 1880 founded the Edmonton *Bulletin* which he published until 1923. He was a member of the North-West Council 1883–85 for Edmonton and was elected to the Legislative Assembly of the North-West Territories in 1888 and 1894. He sat in the House of Commons as a Liberal under Sir Wilfrid Laurier 1896–1917 and was minister of the interior and superintendent general of Indian affairs 1905–11." Eric J. Holmgren, "Frank Oliver" in *The Canadian Encyclopedia*, 2d ed., vol. 3 (Edmonton: Hurtig Publishers, 1988) at 1564.

> I would be very glad to agree to the strict requirements of the close season on this condition, adding the words "half-breed" to the word "Indian." It is because the Government will not agree to [provide assistance to the Métis during the close season] that the necessity of allowing the half-breeds considerable liberty in the matter of fishing, is necessary.[43]

His objection demonstrates that the Métis relied on fishing to the extent that, like the Indians, they either had to fish for food or be supported somehow while the fisheries were closed. Oliver also rebutted the contention of some officials that it was possible for the Métis to replace fishing and hunting with wage labour, offering further support to the view that the Métis relied heavily on fishing.[44] This is an instance when a territorial politician intervened to add the word "half-breed" to the word "Indian" because of the need to pursue and secure a similar livelihood.

Federal records pertaining to the region that now constitutes the province of Manitoba also support the view that Métis communities continued to rely upon fisheries.[45] In 1872, the first Fisheries Department report on Manitoba noted "that white fish [*sic*] forms a staple article of food with the Indians and half-breeds."[46] In 1885, Alex McQueen, inspector of Fisheries for Manitoba and the Northwest Territories, commented in his annual report to the minister that in the Lake Winnipeg District "the catch is principally used by the Indians and half-breeds for home consumption."[47] The following year, H. Martineau, a fisheries official and Indian agent, reported the same type of information for the Lake Manitoba region, stating that the people "in this vicinity, with very few exceptions, fish for their own use."[48] In 1889, McQueen included in his annual report to the minister details relayed to him from Martineau regarding the practice of smoking fish and making fish pemmican, which consti-

---

43 LAC, RG 23, vol. 126, file 170, pt. 1, Oliver to Minister of Marine and Fisheries (Sir Louis Henry Davis) (1 October 1896). Because Treaty Indians were provided with relief and rations when required, the application of the closed season would not have the same effect.

44 *Ibid.*

45 The boundaries of the original province of Manitoba were expanded westward and northward in 1881.

46 CSP, 1873, Fisheries, 1872, No. 8, at 194.

47 CSP, 1886, Fisheries, 1885, No. 11, at 332.

48 CSP, 1887, Fisheries, 1886, No. 16, at 317.

tuted the "principle food supply for both Indians and half-breeds."[49] And in 1891, Guardian William Archer at Fairford informed Inspector McQueen that "Fish is the chief food used by Indians and half-breeds in this district, during the summer and winter."[50] The reliability of the fisheries in this region contrasts sharply with the fate of Aboriginal peoples that ensued with the demise of the bison on the plains. In Manitoba after 1870, both the Indians and Métis fished. The fact that both Métis and Indians ate fish is not earth shattering; however, the implication that this activity might have something to do with a livelihood, and perhaps livelihood rights, creates the controversy.

Moreover, correspondence and reports generated by other government officials and employees in regions that later became the prairie provinces provide significant support for the view that Métis and Indians throughout most of the Northwest continued to depend heavily on the fisheries for support and sustenance. J.D. Moodie of the North West Mounted Police (NWMP) reported this to his commanding officer at Battleford in 1893: "The Indians and breeds at Lac La Beiche [Biche] . . . receive no assistance . . . from the Government, and were it not for the fishing . . . they would be destitute."[51] Shortly thereafter, in 1895, Inspector Gilchrist commented in his report to the minister that in the Lac La Biche District "there are about 300 resident half-breeds there who live very largely on fish."[52]

Senior fisheries officials for the region that now constitutes the province of Saskatchewan recorded details regarding the central and significant place of the fisheries in the livelihood of the Métis communities. E.W. Miller, inspector of Fisheries, reported to the minister of Marine and Fisheries in 1897 that the "vast district [Cumberland] lying along the lower Saskatchewan River has a population of from 4,000 to 5,000 Indians and half-breeds, who, with the gradual decline of the quantity of game and fur, have now become almost entirely dependent on the fisheries for their subsistence."[53] While the mixed economy traditionally in-

49 CSP, 1890, Fisheries, 1889, No. 17, at 242.

50 CSP, 1892, Fisheries, 1891, No. 11A, at 158.

51 LAC, RG 23, vol. 126, file 170, pt. 1, Moodie to The Officer Commanding, "C" Division, Battleford (4 November 1893).

52 CSP, 1896, Fisheries, 1895, No. 11A, at 191.

53 CSP, 1899, Fisheries, 1897, No. 11A, at 215.

volved fishing, hunting, and trapping, the capacity to draw more heavily on one particular component was essential to the long-term viability of communities. Two years later, Inspector Miller reported to the minister that with respect to the "lakes north of the Saskatchewan River," fisheries were significant "sources of food to the resident half-breeds and Indians."[54] For the Lower Saskatchewan River District, Miller also observed that the "fisheries of the lower Saskatchewan valley" were of particular value because they provided "an ample fish supply for food requirements" for the "resident Half-breeds and Indians."[55] Similarly, in 1895, an unsigned letter to D.H. MacDowall, member of Parliament representing the District of Saskatchewan constituency, stated: "It is true the Indians and half-breeds mainly depend upon the fish supply for food . . . ."[56] In the year prior to Saskatchewan becoming a province, Inspector Miller reported on the more remote lakes of the Prince Albert District: "the Indian and Half-breed residents fish for their own food supply."[57] Inspector Miller suggested in 1900 that an overseer be appointed to the "Lower Saskatchewan District" where commercial fishing had become appealing "to the resident Half-breeds and Indians" due to the rise in the price of sturgeon.[58] And in 1910, he recorded: "In the Green Lake, Lac la Plonge, Ile a la Crosse, and Lac La Rouge [Ronge] and other northern waters an enormous catch of fish is annually made, it forming the staple food of the resident Indians and half-breeds and of their dogs."[59] Numerous observations about the fisheries throughout Saskatchewan establish that fishing for subsistence purposes was clearly, as it had been before 1870, a central and significant element in the lives of both the Métis and Indians. Thus, after 1870, fishing remained central to the Aboriginal mode of life.

With the appearance of a regulatory regime designed to limit fishing effort, Aboriginal concerns arose about access to traditional fisheries. For example, in the early 1890s, the chief and council of The Pas Band wrote to officials regarding the proposed regulation of the fisheries, stating: "We all, both Indians and Half-breeds residing in this part of the

54 CSP, 1900, Fisheries, 1899, No. 11A, at 186.

55 CSP, 1901, Fisheries, 1900, No. 22, at 150, 153.

56 LAC, RG 23, vol. 126, file 170, pt. 1, Unsigned letter to MacDowall (28 November 1895).

57 CSP, 1905, Fisheries, 1904, No. 22, at 207.

58 CSP, 1901, Fisheries, 1900, No. 22, at 150.

59 CSP, 1911, Fisheries, 1909–10, No. 22, at 224.

country, will find it very hard to make a living if this law is enforced . . . fish has been our staple article of food. Deprived of the privilege of fishing in the fall we are actually deprived of what is to us our harvest."[60] From the perspective of the Métis and Indians of this region, fishing was their birthright, a fact that was recognized by the federal government "at the time of the first Treaty."[61]

Much earlier, the Métis of Lake Qu'Appelle made a similar appeal on 11 September 1874 when they petitioned Lieutenant-Governor Alexander Morris:

> The half-breeds of the Lakes Qu'Appelle and environs . . . submit to you the following petitions, which they present in their name and in the name of all their brethren scattered over the prairies, and beseech you to give them a favourable hearing, and to remember them in the various arrangements that the Government may make with the Indians . . . . The right of fishing in all lakes of the above mentioned river [River Qu'Appelle]. The right of hunting freely in the prairies west and south-west of the Lakes Qu'Appelle, without being arbitrarily hindered by the Indians, but only in virtue of the regulations that the Indians in concert with the half-breeds and the Government shall establish hereafter for the good of all . . . .
>
> That the Government, in concert with the Indians and the half-breeds, do make, with regard to winter quarters and buffalo hunting, laws which will be of great use to all, such as to prevent wintering too far out in the prairies and to compel every one to start together for the chase, &c., &c . . . .
>
> In all these demands the half-breeds have no intention of depriving the Indians of their rights, but merely claim the recognition and respect of their own, and are disposed to live with the Indians as with brothers and with friends.[62]

In the face of external encroachment, these petitioners sought a continuation of their way of life; however, they also recognized the need for

60 LAC, RG 23, vol. 126, file 170, pt. 1, Letter from the Chief and Councillors of The Pas Band (undated, ca. 1894).

61 *Ibid.*

62 CSP, 1885, No. 116, Department of the Interior, Papers and Correspondence in Connection with Half-breed claims and other matters relating to the North-West Territories, at 7.

regulation and were willing to work with the government and Indians to develop the terms of resource management. Moreover, this Métis petition asserted that their rights were analogous to the Indian rights that were being considered by pending treaty negotiations. The Métis concern for livelihood rights provides little support for the assertion that the Métis were necessarily independent and incorrigibly individualistic.

The unfolding of the treaty process in this region provides an essential historical context for understanding the 11 September 1874 Métis petition. Commencing on 8 September 1874, the treaty talks that would eventually lead to the signing of Treaty 4 opened at Fort Qu'Appelle. Several issues, some of which involved protocol, stood in the way of the proceedings.[63] On the fifth day of the gathering (12 September 1874) The Gambler or *Otahaoma*, son of *Peicheto*, told Lieutenant-Governor Alexander Morris, the senior negotiator for the Crown, some of his concerns:

> I told the soldier master you did not set your camp in order, you came and staid beyond over there, that is the reason I did not run in over there. Now when you have come here, you see sitting out there a mixture of Half-breeds, Crees, Saulteaux and Stonies, *all are one*, and you were slow in taking the hand of a Half-breed. All these things are many things that are in my way. I cannot speak about them.[64]

Of interest is that one of the leading negotiators of Treaty 4 classified the Métis, Cree, Ojibwa, and Assinboine as one. Moreover, The Gambler suggested that Morris had slighted a Métis person. The dichotomous conceptualization of Métis and Indians in *Blais* does not permit the relevance of such a crucial fact.

On the issue of a Métis presence at the treaty talks, Morris responded:

> We have here Crees, Saulteaux, Assiniboines and other Indians, they are all one, and we have another people, the Half-breeds, they are of your blood and my blood. *The Queen cares for them*, one of them is here an of-

---

63 For details on the negotiations of Treaty 4, see Arthur J. Ray, Jim Miller, & Frank J. Tough, *Bounty and Benevolence: A History of Saskatchewan Indian Treaties* (Montreal: McGill-Queen's University Press, 2000) at 105–20.

64 Alexander Morris, *The Treaties of Canada with the Indians of Manitoba and the North-west Territories* (Toronto: Belfords, Clarke and Co., 1880) at 98 [emphasis added]. The treaty party camped at the Hudson's Bay Co. post, which was of concern to The Gambler.

> ficer with a Queen's coat on his back. At the Lake of the Woods last winter [Treaty 3] every Half-Breed who was there with me was helping me, and I was proud of it, and glad to take the word back to the Queen, and her servants, and you may rest easy, *you may leave the Half-breeds in the hands of the Queen who will deal generously and justly with them.*[65]

To indicate that the Crown did not harbour ill will towards the Métis, Morris acknowledged the crucial role that several Red River Métis played at the Treaty 3 talks in securing a treaty with the Ojibwa of northwestern Ontario in 1873. The uncertainty about the future of the Métis in the post-treaty era was addressed by Morris when he pointed to his personal relations with several prominent Métis individuals as evidence of good intentions on the part of the Crown. The Métis petition of 11 September 1874, which raised concerns about future livelihood, coincided with strong assurances by Lieutenant-Governor Morris at a treaty-negotiation meeting which resulted in a treaty that the Métis would be dealt with "generously and justly" by the Crown and that the Queen "cares for them." This issue needed to be cleared up before The Gambler was willing to talk about the treaty with the Crown.

The records documenting federal fisheries policies, practices, and regulations do not employ present-day, commonly used terminology to define "rights." Nonetheless, F.C. Gilchrist,[66] inspector of Fisheries from 1891 to 1896 and an official in the Department of Marine and Fisheries for more than a decade, believed that the Métis should have a "right" to

---

65 *Ibid.* at 98–99 [emphasis added]. It is not clear which Métis with "the Queen's Coat" Morris was referring to; however, Pascal Breland signed the treaty as a witness.

66 Perhaps it was his intricate knowledge of the region that led him to raise the suggestion of a Métis "legal and moral right" to fish. A summary of Bocking's biography of Frederick Charles Gilchrist demonstrates that he was one of the first fisheries officials to advocate for the application of scientific research methods in the management of the fisheries. During his time with the department, Gilchrist published three works on the fisheries and freshwater lakes of the Northwest and contributed preserved specimens of fish species to the Smithsonian Institute. In addition to his scientific interests, Gilchrist also travelled throughout the Northwest by canoe and was intimately familiar with the land and its people. He served as the fisheries overseer and inspector from 1884 to 1896. D.H. Bocking, "Frederick Charles Gilchrist" in *Dictionary of Canadian Biography, 1891–1900*, vol. 12 (Toronto: University of Toronto Press, 1990) at 365–66.

fish. In a letter to the minister of Marine and Fisheries dated 3 June 1895, Gilchrist wrote:

> It is a well known fact that a large number of the halfbreeds are worse off than the Indians . . . the unfortunate halfbreed is left to his own resources, and greatly does he suffer in consequence. Claiming an inherent right in the soil that no "taking of scrip" has extinguished, he bitterly resents the giving of a privilege to the Indians that is not also extended to him. *In my opinion the legal and moral rights of the halfbreed in regard to the fisheries are quite as worthy of consideration as are those of the Indian.*[67]

In Gilchrist's informed view, the needs of the Métis to fish should have resulted in a treatment similar to that of the Indians. He also repeated the Métis' view that their rights, which were similar to Indian rights, were being overlooked. In another letter to the deputy minister of the department, also in 1895, Inspector Gilchrist took issue with the *ad hoc* and inconsistent treatment of the Métis by the Department of Marine and Fisheries, arguing:

> The halfbreeds at lake [*sic*] La Biche, Green Lake, and other places have only the fur game and fish to depend upon, and yet the Department is insisting upon their observing the close seasons. In the light of this, what reason is there for granting to the halfbreeds of the Qu'Appelle District the very privileges that are refused to the northern, and in many ways worse off, natives?[68]

In this instance, he suggested that the northern Métis, and not just the southern Métis, needed year-round access to the resource. Clearly, Gilchrist understood the importance of fishing to Métis livelihood and this logically resulted in his observations about "legal and moral rights." Similarly, Inspector McQueen reported a concern expressed by Guardian William Archer about the fishing needs of a particular group of Aboriginal people: "some provision be made for those half-breeds, who have recently quitted treaty. They might be allowed like the Indians, to

67 LAC, RG 23, vol. 126, file 170, pt. 1, Gilchrist to Deputy Minister of Marine and Fisheries (William Smith) (3 June 1895) [emphasis added].

68 *Ibid.*, Gilchrist to W. Smith (16 February 1895).

catch fish for their own use, during the close season. If not allowed this privilege they will suffer, as they have no other means of subsistence."[69]

A royal commission, chaired by Professor E.E. Prince, on the fisheries of Alberta and Saskatchewan in 1911, recorded some observations on Aboriginal fishing. Under the heading Indians and Halfbreeds the commission stated: "One important point in dealing with the fisheries of these two Provinces, is the claim of Indians and Halfbreeds to special consideration."[70] Had Prince stated instead "the claim of Aboriginal peoples to special consideration," the statement would have remained valid. At Lac La Loche in northern Saskatchewan, the commission's inquiries learned: "Scrip Commissioners told the Indians they would not be interfered with fishing and hunting."[71] This observation may appear perplexing and might not agree with contemporary sensibilities or indeed to the Supreme Court's reasoning in *Blais*. However, it should be appreciated that J.A.J. McKenna was appointed commissioner for both the treaty and scrip interests.[72] Moreover, neither a treaty nor treaty adhesion was signed at La Loche.[73] In 1906, however, some 205 claims were made for Halfbreed scrip.[74] Nonetheless, why would a scrip commissioner assure "Indians" that their livelihood rights would not be interfered with? Recall that Commissioner McKenna made a point of reporting that in Treaty 10, those that took treaty and those who applied for scrip could not be distinguished. And in keeping with past recognition by the fisheries department, the inland fisheries commission report recognized the overall category "Indian" as including both Indians and Métis, stating:

69 CSP, 1892, Fisheries, 1891, No. 11A, at 158.

70 Canada, *Final Report: Alberta and Saskatchewan Fishery Commission: 1911* by Commissioners Professor Edward E. Prince, Honourable Thomas H. McGuire, & Dr. Huston Sisley, presented to Honourable J.D. Hazen, minister of Marine and Fisheries (30 December 1911) at 62 [Fishery Commission: 1911].

71 *Ibid.*, at 16. Meetings were held at the HBC post and the Revillon Company post. The commissioners received their information from Lamuel Janvier, Michel Lamerge, Angus McLean, Reverend Père Pinard, Joseph Janvier, Piere [*sic*] Maurice and J. Pickering.

72 PC No. 1459 (20 July 1906), copy found in LAC, RG 15, vol. 227, part 5.

73 For details on Treaty 10, see Ray *et al.*, *Bounty and Benevolence*, above note 63 at 170–86.

74 This total is based on an examination of claims registers. LAC, RG 15, vols. 1487–89, 1492, 1494, 1498–1504, 1508, 1515, 1516, 1537, and 1594, claims registers.

> To intelligently handle this question it will be necessary to go into the subject more fully than at first sight may appear desirable, and for the sake of brevity *the term "Indian" is meant to include Halfbreed as well*, and one term might include them both, for it has been repeatedly stated to the Commissioners that there are few, if any, pure bred Indians in existence at the present time, referring especially to those living in the North.[75]

Clearly, a federal royal commission on inland fisheries would not refer to the Métis as Indians if their fisheries were separate and distinct from the Indian interest in the same resource. Special consideration applied to both Métis and Indians because their modes of living were indistinguishable in many respects. Here, federal officials have used the term *Indian* in a generic way to include the Half-breed, a usage that constitutes a historical fact that does not align with the *Blais* decision.

The observations and comments made by fisheries officials are interesting for several reasons. Their observations attested to the fact that fishing was of crucial importance to the Métis, in much the same way as it was for the Indians of the Northwest. Additionally, Gilchrist contended that the "legal and moral rights" of the Métis were, on some level, similar to those of the Indians; and finally, McQueen expressed concern that "Treaty Half-Breeds" (those that had quit the treaty) should be permitted, "like the Indians," to fish for subsistence reasons during closed seasons. The positions adopted by Inspectors Gilchrist and McQueen, both experienced Department of Marine and Fisheries officials who had advocated for, and approved, special exemptions from fishing regulations for the Métis, were at least partially motivated by their understanding that the Métis, like the Indians, had a need to fish for food. Finally, a federal royal commission on inland fisheries identified the particular needs and interest of Indians which, to their way of thinking, logically included the Métis.

Insights about Crown–Métis relations can be discerned not only from suggestions on policy, but also from observations on how the law was applied. Similarly, the necessity of facilitating Métis subsistence fishing was also recognized by members of the NWMP, who were responsible for enforcing fishing regulations. While unsympathetic to the idea of exemptions for closed seasons in the Battleford area, and concerned

75 Fishery Commission: 1911, above note 70, at 62 [emphasis added].

about declining fish stocks, NWMP Inspector J.D. Moodie recommended a shutting down of the fishery "for a year or two, excepting the actual half-breed settlers and that these be allowed to catch for their own requirements and not for sale or barter."[76] He also recommended that licences

> . . . be free to the Indians and Half-breeds for waters where fishing was not prohibited, as they are almost without exception, quite unable to pay the license fee and therefore must run the chance of being prosecuted for infraction of the law. I fancy few men would be found willing to become fish guardians if compelled to enforce the law on these poor people. If prosecuted they could not pay a fine and imprisonment to the head of the family would practically mean starvation to the others.[77]

A.H. Greisbach, in command of the "G" Division at Fort Saskatchewan, Alberta, was also unsympathetic regarding special considerations for the Métis, yet he recognized that for "a large number of Half-breeds . . . fish were their principle means of support" and consequently, having no special exemption in 1893 at Lac La Biche, the Métis "being without food proceeded to break the law by taking fish during the close season . . . from information which I received I believe if the law had then been strictly enforced, trouble of a serious nature would have ensued, as these people were absolutely dependent upon the fish for food."[78] With respect to the Métis, a discrepancy was acknowledged in the difference between regulation and enforcement by those charged with the responsibility of enforcing the law. The policy recommendations by regional fisheries officials that recognized Aboriginal fishing practices were consistent with the views of those charged with the problem of enforcement.

In light of the difficulties of enforcement and the needs and customary uses of fish by the Aboriginal populations in the 1890s, frequent revisions to fisheries regulations are understandable. Consolidated fisheries regulations in May 1894 made several provisions with respect to access to fisheries by Aboriginal people:

---

76 LAC, RG 23, vol. 126, file 170, pt. 1, Moodie to The Officer Commanding, "C" Division (4 November 1893).

77 *Ibid.*

78 *Ibid.*, Griesbach to The Commissioner, NWMP (1 December 1893).

> 6. Every farmer, settler, or bonâ fide fisherman, Indian or Half-breed, who is an actual resident of the locality where he proposes to fish, shall be entitled to a "domestic license." . . . A fee of $2 shall be paid for each "domestic license."
>
> 10. Fishing by means of nets or other apparatus, without leases or licenses, is prohibited in the waters of Manitoba and the North West Territories.
>
> 16. These regulations shall apply to Indians and Half-breeds, as well as to settlers and all other persons; provided always, that the Minister of Marine and Fisheries may from time to time set apart for the exclusive use of the Indians, such waters as he may deem necessary, and may grant to Indians or their bands, free licenses to fish during the close seasons, for themselves or their bands, for the purposes of providing food for themselves, but not for the purpose of sale, barter or traffic.
>
> 17. . . . Provided always, that special licenses may be issued to Indians or Indian bands permitting them to catch and kill fish in the manner specified in such license for the sole purpose of providing themselves or their bands with food.[79]

On the face, these regulations did not distinguish between Aboriginal and non-Aboriginal domestic licences. Domestic licences cost two dollars for all fishers. The general regulations were specifically applied to Métis and Indians, and at the discretion of the Minister, the exemption for the closed season and free licences applied only to Indians. Notwithstanding these written regulations, the regulatory regime that was implemented proved to be somewhat different.

Out of necessity, these regulations were modified. The Legislative Assembly of the Northwest Territories took measures to address the sub-

79 Regulations Relating to Fishing in Manitoba and the North West Territories (8 May 1894) *Canada Gazette*, vol. 27, no. 48 (26 May 1894) at 2107–8. These regulations rescinded the regulations adopted by Orders-in-Council (28 December 1893, 7 February 1894, 8 March 1894, and 12 March 1894). For some discussion of early federal regulations in the old North West, see Frank Tough, "The Establishment of a Commercial Fishing Industry and the Demise of Native Fisheries in Northern Manitoba," *Canadian Journal of Native Studies* vol. 4, no. 2 (1984) at 303–19.

sistence fishing needs of the Métis by passing a resolution on 5 September 1894, which recommended to the Privy Council that

> ... the Fishery Regulations for the Territories be so modified as to permit of residents around lakes LaBiche [*sic*], St. Ann, Pigeon, Jackfish, Green and other lakes in the northern part of the Territories to fish for Whitefish during the close season, for the purpose of procuring supplies of fish sufficient for their wants, and that the Regulations regarding fishing for Sturgeon in the Saskatchewan and Battle Rivers be amended, so as to permit of Half-Breeds catching these fish for their own use.[80]

Territorial politicians were also aware of the significance of the fishery to Métis communities. The year after the Legislative Assembly's resolution, W. Sutherland, the member for Fort Qu'Appelle, wrote to T.M. Daly, the minister of the Interior, to draw his attention to a "subject of importance to the Half-breed population" requesting that "instructions be sent to the Inspector of Fisheries of the N.W. to issue free licenses to fish to the extent of one net for each family and for their own use."[81] The responses of regional fisheries officials, Mounties, and territorial assembly were mindful of the needs and customs of Métis and Indian fishing practices.

Fisheries officials established and maintained a system of free licences for both Indians and Métis. In the annual report prepared for the minister of Marine and Fisheries, Inspector Gilchrist observed the following in the Prince Albert District in 1893: "Forty-five free permits have been issued to destitute half-breeds; 10 free licenses to Indian bands."[82] Gilchrist, for the Lac La Biche District, reported in the same year, "The Indians and half-breeds in this district ... fished as usual during the close season" and the following year (1894) Overseer Cook stated, "One hundred and thirty-six permits have been issued to destitute half-breeds and Indians to fish for their own use, as compared with 55 for last year."[83] Although the regulations of May 1894 made no provision for free licences for the Métis in practice, free fishing licences for both Indian and Métis fishers were

80 PC No. 502 J (10 October 1894), copy found in LAC, RG 23, vol. 126, file 170, pt. 1.

81 LAC, RG 23, vol. 126, file 170, pt. 1, Extract from a letter from W. Sutherland Esq. M.L.A. to Minister of the Interior T. Mayne Daly (2 January 1895).

82 CSP, 1894, Fisheries, 1893, No. 11, at 271.

83 CSP, 1895, Fisheries, 1894, No. 11A, at 359.

issued before and after Privy Council Order No. 502 J (10 October 1894). In some instances, a misleading view of the historical past is created when only readily accessible library materials are called up for consultation.

The acknowledgment of the need for access for Aboriginal fishers endured. In 1897, Fisheries Inspector E.W. Miller recorded in his annual report that, in the Prince Albert District, "One hundred and thirteen free permits were issued to Indians and half-breeds, allowing them to fish for their own use only."[84] Also in 1897, Overseer H. Young of the Edmonton District commented in his report to Inspector Miller: "The destitution prevailing among the half-breed population . . . led to the necessity of some relaxation in their favour, of the regulations regarding the close season."[85] And for the Cumberland District, Inspector Miller commented: "Indians and half-breeds . . . have now become almost entirely dependent on the fisheries for their subsistence. It has not been deemed expedient to enforce the regulations."[86] Also in 1897, the minister of Marine and Fisheries informed the Governor General in Council that "the Indians and half-breeds on the lands around certain lakes in the North West Territories are in a great measure dependent upon the supply of fish"; subsequently, the minister relayed his approval for "granting ten days fishing during the close season in certain lakes there."[87]

While regulations changed frequently, the impression exists that discretion was practised because of the well-established needs and customs of the Aboriginal population. The categories of licences were important for the management of fisheries, as a 1903 letter from Inspector Miller to the deputy minister of Marine and Fisheries noted: "The applicants for licenses as per schedule are all recommended favorably by the Overseer but he has neglected to state whether they are residents and whether they are white, Halfbreed or Indian."[88] In the Prince Albert District in 1909, Inspector Miller reported: "An increasing number of licenses is now being taken out

84 CSP, 1899, Fisheries, 1897, No. 11A, at 213.

85 *Ibid.* at 214.

86 *Ibid.* at 215.

87 LAC, RG 23, vol. 126, file 170, pt. 1, Minister of Marine and Fisheries to Governor General in Council (5 October 1897).

88 LAC, RG 23, vol. 99, file 86, pt. 3, Miller to Deputy Minister of Marine and Fisheries (9 September 1903). There would be little purpose to collecting this information if all fishers were the same.

as all persons selling or dealing in portions of their catch are required to have licenses, but in these as yet distant districts residents are allowed to fish for their own family consumption without procuring a license."[89] Even as fishing pressure increased, it was still the practice to permit domestic fishing without a licence. By officially advising the minister of local licensing practices, the discretion afforded the Métis was evident.

The policy of making special consideration for the Métis so they were able to fish for subsistence purposes, like the Indians, without following licence requirements or closed seasons, became common or regular practice in the Northwest Territories. Confirmation of this conclusion concerning the similar treatment of Indians and Métis also stems from the fact that in 1921, William A. Found, the assistant deputy minister of Marine and Fisheries, stated that "for years our regulations have definitely provided that any Indian or half-breed in that portion of the country is eligible for a free permit authorizing fishing by him, and that this permit even allows fishing for current need during the usual close season."[90] Given this acknowledgment by the assistant deputy minister, the Fisheries Department regulated in favour of exceptional fisheries because the closed season and licence fee exemptions ensued for decades. The special exemptions afforded to Indians and Métis were reaffirmed by regulations passed by the Privy Council on 26 April 1922 and 27 May 1927. These regulations granted free licences for "any Indian or half-breed resident . . . which shall entitle him or a member of his family to fish with not more than sixty yards of gill-net for domestic use, but not for sale or barter."[91] Fishing for daily consumption was permitted during the close season with the only qualification being "if more fish be taken in any one day during any such close season than are needed for consumption of the permittee and his family that day the net shall not be again placed in the water until the fish taken have been used."[92] These regulations are significant because

89 CSP, 1911, Fisheries, 1909–10, No. 22, at 225.

90 LAC, RG 23, vol. 764, file 716-12-4, pt. 1, Found to J. D. McLean (19 May 1921).

91 "Special Fishery Regulations for the Provinces of Saskatchewan and Alberta and the Northwest Territories North Thereof" (27 May 1927) *Canada Gazette*, vol. 60, no. 49 (4 June 1927) at 3750; see also "Special Fishery Regulations for the Provinces of Saskatchewan and Alberta, and the Territories North Thereof," *Statutes of Canada*, 1922, 12–13 Geo. V, Vols. I–II, at cxxxi–cxxxvi.

92 "Special Fishery Reglations" (1927), *ibid.*

of the appearance that Métis and Indians were placed in a separate class, distinct from all other fishers in Saskatchewan and Alberta.

Given the historical evidence that Indian and Métis populations depended largely on fish for subsistence, the government continued to recognize that the enforcement of a closed season would cause undue hardship for these communities. The importance of fishing to Aboriginal livelihood is generally taken for granted or ignored; however, it was integral to the way of life of Aboriginal peoples. Important, if somewhat unglamorous, insights into Crown–Métis relationships are afforded by a historical analysis of archival records. During the Dominion government's administration of fisheries (1870–1930), the recognition of the importance of Aboriginal fish-resource use for both Indian and Métis resulted in a management system that often provided for fishing during what was otherwise a closed season and a licensing system that generally provided free licences. In this sense, the "protection" afforded the Métis for the maintenance of a livelihood was, for all intents and purposes, identical to that provided to Indians. Because federal policies and officials had provided Indians and Métis with similar access to freshwater fisheries for several decades, the currently accepted claim that paragraph 12/13 of the NRTAs captured a historical continuity based on dichotomizing groups of Aboriginal people is certainly wrong with respect to the fishery.

D. THE JUSTICE DEPARTMENT PREPARES FOR THE NRTAS: "THE LANDS SET APART FOR INDIANS IN THE SHAPE OF SCRIP"

Some relatively unknown historical records concerning the NRTAs demonstrate (1) scrip policies originated with the obligations arising out of the constitutional instrument that allowed Canada to acquire Rupertsland and the Northwest; (2) Halfbreeds were considered to be Indians; (3) Indians were issued scrip; (4) the authority to issue scrip and to deal with Halfbreeds also derived from section 91(24) of the *Constitution Act, 1867*; and (5) scrip was an important land tenure that needed to be understood in order to properly assess the compensation that the federal government owed the provinces of Saskatchewan and Alberta. These findings run counter to the far-reaching claims made by the Court in *Blais*.

Although Indian interests continue to be litigated in relation to the *Natural Resources Transfer Agreements*, the process that resulted in the negotiation, drafting, and enactment of the NRTAs involved a variety of interests and rights. As a result of the Dominion's administration of prairie lands and resources for a sixty-year period, a large number of land tenures and rights were entangled with the transfer of resources in 1930. Consequently, complex disagreements existed in respect of the compensation owed to the provinces for the loss of the enjoyment of those lands and resources. What has not always been appreciated is that each NRTA is not simply an agreement between two levels of government, but an amendment to the *British North America Acts, 1867–1916*.[93] The preamble to the Alberta agreement scheduled with the *Alberta Natural Resources Act, 1930*, identified the purpose: "And Whereas it is desirable that the Province should be placed in a position of equality with the other provinces of Confederation with respect to the administration and control of its natural resources . . . ."[94] With the transfer of public lands and resources from the Dominion to the prairie provinces achieved by the *British North America Act, 1930*, continuing Indian interests were understandably related to this political/legal process.[95]

---

93 These agreements were enacted concurrently at the provincial, federal, and imperial levels. See the *Manitoba Natural Resources Act*, S.M. 1930, c. 30 [assented to 19 February 1930]; the *Alberta Natural Resources Act*, S.A. 1930, c. 21 [assented to 3 April 1930]; the *Saskatchewan Natural Resources Act*, S.S. 1930, c. 87 [assented to 10 April 1930]; the *Alberta Natural Resources Act*, S.C. 1930, c. 3; the *Manitoba Natural Resources Act*, S.C. 1930, c. 29; the *Saskatchewan Natural Resources Act*, S.C. 1930, c. 41 [all assented to on 30 May 1930]; and the *British North America Act, 1930* (U.K.), 20–21 Geo. V, c. 26 [assented to 10 July 1930]. The Manitoba and Alberta agreements were made in 1929, but these agreements were not enacted until 1930. The long title of the imperial statute is "An Act to confirm and give effect to certain agreements entered into between the Government of the Dominion of Canada and the Governments of the Provinces of Manitoba, British Columbia, Alberta and Saskatchewan respectively." The agreement with British Columbia involved the railroad lands and the Peace River block which had been administered by the Department of the Interior. The *British North America Act, 1930*, has been retitled as *Constitution Act, 1930*. The Canadian statute was also referred to as having the following effect: *An Act to Amend the British North America Acts, 1867 to 1916*.

94 *The Alberta Natural Resources Act*, S.C. 1930, c. 3, preamble.

95 Significantly, the term *Indian* is undefined in the NRTA, and on this point Justice Department legal opinions of that era by Deputy Minister W. S. Edwards raise doubts about the intention to modify treaties by paragraph 12/13 of the NRTA. Edwards argued that Indians of the province included Treaty and Non-Treaty Indians.

The controversy concerning the expressed provisions in the NRTAs is becoming better known; however, records documenting the circumstances that shaped the negotiations, drafting, and legislating of the *Constitution Act, 1930*, have not been fully appreciated. For many decades, these records were not consulted by historians, lawyers, or the courts. In order to place the prairie provinces in a position of equality in Confederation, which entailed not only the return of lands and resources, but also compensation for losses, an appraisal of the Dominion lands policies was required. Consequently, the absence of the word "Halfbreed" or "Métis" in the plain text of the agreements does not mean that the NRTAs are irrelevant to a discussion of Crown–Métis relations, as some wish to surmise. In contrast to the rather mundane historical examination of fishing policy and regulations, which happens to demonstrate a similarity of Métis and Indian access for resource harvesting, constitutional and property issues usually generate heady excitement.

The NRTAs represented a full-blown constitutional process that began in earnest in 1918.[96] Manitoba's claims and the federal government's analysis of the question of specific policies and compensation were developed in the early 1920s.[97] One compensation calculation was related to "land scrip issued to half-breeds for the extinguishment of their title" which was analyzed in an internal Justice Department memorandum, prepared for Deputy Minister of Justice E.L. Newcombe.[98] Significant-

---

For published versions of these opinions, see Frank Tough, "Introduction: Indian Hunting Rights, *Natural Resources Transfer Agreements* and Legal Opinions from the Department of Justice," *Native Studies Review* vol. 10, no. 2 (1995) at 121–67.

96 For an account of this early process in relation to the province of Manitoba, see Jim Mochoruk, *Formidable Heritage: Manitoba's North and the Cost of Development, 1870 to 1930* (Winnipeg: University of Manitoba Press, 2004) at 211–14, 230–38, 296–98, 344–54, 376–77.

97 For Manitoba's position, see Chester Martin, *The Natural Resources Question* (Winnipeg: King's Printer, 1920). The federal government's response was developed by the minister of Railways, John Reid, in a series of substantive memoranda. The main memorandum was titled: "In re Financial Questions involved in the proposal of the Prairie Provinces for transfer of the control of their Natural Resources" (18 April 1921), copy found in Archives of Manitoba, Premier John Bracken Papers, G550, file 232 ([AM, Bracken Papers]; formerly catalogued as Provincial Archives of Manitoba, MG13 I2, Box 20, File 232.

98 LAC, RG 13, vol. 1949, file 1921-854, J. C. [John Chisholm] to Newcombe (5 August 1921). This memorandum was initialled J. C. In 1926, the only senior official in the

ly, this analysis not only related unequivocally the land scrip policy to Indian title, but also to the imperial Order-in-Council of 23 June 1870, a constitutional instrument that is seldom consulted today because its existence and historical and political context are generally unknown.[99] This 1870 imperial Order is the mechanism by which the Dominion of Canada acquired a vast region then known as the Hudson's Bay Company Territory.[100] This Justice Department memorandum cited one of the conditions that Canada and the HBC had agreed to:

> 14. "Any claims of Indians to compensation for lands required for the purposes of settlement, shall be disposed of by the Canadian Government in communication with the Imperial Government; and the Company shall be relieved of all responsibility in respect of them."[101]

The wording of this clause provided justification for the land scrip policy, stating: "This evidently enables the Canadian Government in communication with the Imperial Government to extinguish the Indian title" and this "is done by issuing land scrip to them as mentioned."[102] A rather direct connection was made between Métis scrip policies and the 1870 imperial Order.[103]

---

employ of the Justice Department was John Chisholm, K.C., assistant deputy minister. LAC, RG 13, vol. 2187, file 1926-635, Chief Officials — Department of Justice (26 March 1926). In memorandum of 18 April 1921, Reid erred by stating that the extinguishment of Indian title "is not a Federal obligation but one particularly belonging to the Provinces" and therefore ". . . not considered to be lands 'used for the purpose of the Dominion', and are not taken into account in any computations to be made hereafter." AM, Bracken Papers, G550, file 232, Reid Memorandum on Financial Questions (18 April 1921) at 25–26.

99 The "Order of Her Majesty in Council admitting Rupert's Land and the North-Western Territory into the Union" (23 June 1870) is printed in E. H. Oliver, ed., *The Canadian North-West: Its Early Development and Legislative Records*, vol. 2 (Ottawa: Government Printing Bureau, 1915) at 939–63. [1870 imperial Order]. This instrument is now known as "Rupert's Land and North-Western Territory Order."

100 For a historical background on what is usually referred to as the Rupertsland Transfer, see Frank J. Tough, "Aboriginal Rights versus the Deed of Surrender: The Legal Rights of Native Peoples and Canada's Acquisition of the Hudson's Bay Company Territory," *Prairie Forum* vol. 17, no. 2 (1992) at 225–50.

101 LAC, RG 13, vol. 1949, file 1921-854, Chisholm to Newcombe (5 August 1921).

102 *Ibid.*

103 That the Justice Department of the day was well aware of this imperial Order and that it held an enduring relevance in the early 20th century was an unexpected find.

The immediate and practical significance to the balancing of claims to compensation was that "the province can have no claim whatever on account of such settlement with the Indians."[104] Thus, the analysis expressed the conclusion that "the lands set apart for Indians in the shape of scrip, which give[s] a right to the holder to dispose of the lands referred to in such scrip."[105] The reasonable premise here, even if unstated, is that only Indians could possess Indian title. In fact, without this premise, the actions of the Crown with respect to the obligations acquired by the 1870 imperial Order would be irrational.

A few weeks later, Newcombe provided a legal opinion for James A. Calder, president of the Privy Council, stating:

> The other point raised in Mr. Reid's letter relates to land scrip issued to half-breeds for the extinguishment of their title. The clause in the surrender relating to Indian claims is as follows:
>
> > 14. "Any claims of Indians to compensation for lands required for the purposes of settlement, shall be disposed of by the Canadian Government in communication with the Imperial Government; and the Company shall be relieved of all responsibility in respect of them."
>
> This enables the Canadian Government in communication with the Imperial Government to extinguish the Indian title and if this be done by issuing land scrip to them as mentioned, the Province can have no legal claim whatever on account of such settlement with the Indians.[106]

Newcombe's opinion followed the Justice Department's memorandum of 5 August 1921. Significantly, the Justice Department justified the federal government's authority to issue scrip, not on the basis of the provisions of the *Dominion Lands Act* or even the *Manitoba Act, 1870*, but more directly on the basis of the instrument that established a foundation for Canadian sovereignty in what had been the Hudson's Bay Company Territory — the 1870 Imperial Order by which the Canadian government had committed to deal with the "claims of the Indians." And significant-

104 Above note 101.

105 *Ibid.*

106 *Ibid.*, legal opinion, Newcombe to Calder (20 August 1921).

ly, all those that took scrip were "Indians."[107] In effect, the Department of Justice was using "Indians" to apply to the Métis/Half-breeds as we would today use the term *Aboriginal* to include the Métis. The Justice Department was advising the Privy Council on the question of Indian title, which had already been "extinguished," but the foundation for the opinion accepted the priority of the obligations and commitments that came with the Dominion's acquisition of the Hudson's Bay Company Territory. Consequently, the source for Canadian Crown–Métis relations was not the various *Dominion Lands Acts* or even the *Manitoba Act, 1870*, which interested scholars never tire of citing, but the imperial Order-in-Council of 23 June 1870. As with the NRTAs, the 1870 imperial Order has received little empirical analysis, by either historians or legal scholars, and yet these instruments are fundamental to understanding changing property relations sanctioned by constitutional instruments.

There is little doubt about the significance of this analysis. The legal position opined by the federal Justice Department expressed several sound assertions: Indian title existed; the Métis held Indian title; the Métis could be referred to as Indians; and recognition was given to an obligation acquired by Canada to deal with Indian title — the terms of which were expressed through the results of the negotiations between the Hudson's Bay Company and the Canadian delegates in London, supervised by the Colonial Office. From the view of the Justice Department, scrip was issued to "Indians." Emphatically in 1921, which simple arithmetic tells us is fully seven decades after the supposed 1850 threshold of differentiation between Métis and Indian, senior Justice Department officials regarded Half-breeds as Indians because of how a grant of title based on scrip figured into the compensation question. No great angst or handwringing was expressed about Half-breeds, Indians, Indian title, scrip, or the "claims of the Indians to compensation" by the Justice Department. Significantly then, at the commencement of the NRTA process, the federal government did not distinguish the Métis from Indians — the Métis were classified as Indians. This document is not an off-the-cuff comment or idle musing; it represented a position on all-important issues relating

107 This category applied to all those that were issued scrip, not simply to a special subcategory of scrip recipients officially known as Treaty Half-Breeds who, especially in the period 1885–1889, withdrew from the treaty to apply for Northwest Halfbreed Scrip.

to compensation during a constitutional process and it was presented by the deputy minister of Justice to the president of the Privy Council. The Métis were not distinguished and separated from Indians in this drawn-out constitutional process. Clearly, some of the political history claims made in *Blais* cannot account for the existence of this straightforward analysis by the Justice Department or that such a legal analysis would prove to be practical and influential.

Perhaps, though, the documentation concerning the Newcombe opinion of 29 August 1921 lacks any real legal significance. After all, an opinion is merely an opinion, and perhaps one written by a deputy minister of Justice would have no more weight than that drafted by an earnest articling student. To place this record in a more precise context, a contemporary record of the Justice Department described the competence and authority of the department:

> Since 1867, when the union of the provinces was effected, the duties of the law officers of the Crown have been constantly augmented, and to-day the Department of Justice is the largest law office of the Dominion. Its head (the Minister of Justice) is *ex-officio.* His Majesty's Attorney General of Canada and his functions are not exceeded in importance by those of any of his colleagues. He is the official legal adviser of the Governor General and the legal member of His Majesty's Privy Council for Canada. It is his especial duty to see that the administration of public affairs is in accordance with law, and he has the superintendence of all matters connected with the administration of justice in Canada not under the jurisdiction of the governments of the provinces. He has to advise upon the legislative Acts and proceedings of each of the legislatures of the provinces of Canada, and generally to advise the Crown upon all matters of law referred to him by the Crown .... He has to advise the heads of the several departments of the Government upon all matters of law connected with these departments. It is his duty to settle and approve all instruments issued under the Great Seal of Canada and to regulate and conduct all litigation for or against the Crown or any public department of any subject within the authority or jurisdiction of Canada ....
>
> The law officers of the Crown attached to this department have to draft all government contracts, often involving many millions of dol-

> lars. They have to give legal opinions on almost every conceivable subject to the other departments of the Government . . . [108]

This description indicates that the position and duties of the federal department were large and that the department generated unique sources of legal analysis. The importance of the Department of Justice is seen in these ways: (1) it is described as the largest law firm in the country and its head, the minister of Justice served as (2) attorney general for Canada, (3) legal adviser to the governor general, and (4) legal member of Privy Council, along with responsibilities that included (5) ensuring that the administration of public affairs is legal; (6) superintending justice administration; (7) advising on provincial and federal legislation; (8) advising on all matters of law referred to the Crown; (9) settling and approving all instruments issued under the Great Seal; (10) litigating all cases involving the Crown; (11) drafting contracts; and (12) writing a variety of legal opinions to government departments.

Such authority also had a basis in statute. For example, the *Department of Justice Act, 1906*, provided that the minister of Justice serve as "Ex officio His Majesty Attorney General of Canada" and that the first duty of the minister of Justice was to

> 4 (a) be the official legal advisor of the Governor General and the legal member of His Majesty's Privy Council for Canada;
> (b) see that the administration of public affairs is in accordance with law;
> (c) have the superintendence of all matters connected with the administration of justice in Canada, not within the jurisdiction of the governments of the provinces;
> (d) . . . and generally advise the Crown upon all matters of law referred to him by the Crown.[109]

Perhaps not all legal opinions are equal. Clearly, an opinion from the deputy minister of Justice had institutional, legal, and historical influence. In light of this authority, the views expressed by Deputy Minister Newcombe about the connection between the 1870 Imperial Order and Métis scrip should not be ignored. Overall, Justice Department records

108 LAC, RG 13, vol. 2187, file 635-1926, History of the Department (1926).
109 *Department of Justice Act*, R.S.C. 1906, c. 21.

constitute important, even if seldom consulted, historical sources concerning Crown–Aboriginal relationships.[110]

E. THE SASKATCHEWAN NRTA AND THE ALLOCATION OF MÉTIS SCRIP: "IT IS COMPLICATED"

The imperial Parliament's enactment of the *British North America Act, 1930*, which was given Royal assent on 10 July 1930, did not terminate the NRTA process. Alberta and Saskatchewan had signed NRTAs without an exact understanding of the value of compensation owed for the loss of the beneficial interests in lands and resources. Paragraph 24 of the Saskatchewan agreement provided for an inquiry to report upon the financial compensation. The resulting royal commissions on Saskatchewan and Alberta natural resources provided an opportunity to document and analyze the purposes to which the Dominion government had put the lands and resources of the prairie provinces. This was no idle historical interest; the amount of compensation owed to the provinces would be determined by the analysis of these administrative records.

The Saskatchewan Resources Commission sought to determine what compensation was owed to the Province of Saskatchewan as a result of the loss of beneficial interest in lands and resources after 1905, and transcripts of the commission's deliberations exist. In the course of examining the records of federal land policies, Halfbreed scrip became a topic of interest, as it had been in the 1921 legal opinion of Newcombe. On 14 May 1934, the Commission met in Ottawa with the representatives of Canada and Saskatchewan.[111]

---

110 Although federal Justice Department legal opinion file material was destroyed in accordance with Treasury Board 6545563 (25 April 1966), the surviving material provides fascinating insights into legal history.

111 The commissioners included the Honourable A.K. Dysart, chairman (Judge of the Court of King's Bench, Manitoba), the Honourable H.V. Bigelow (Judge of the Court of King's Bench, Saskatchewan), George C. McDonald, C.A., and Oliver Master, who served as secretary of the Commission. Counsel for the province of Saskatchewan included P.H. Gordon, K.C., and Major John Bennett, deputy minister of Natural Resources. The representatives for Canada included James McGregor Stewart, K.C.; T.A. Hunt, K.C.; C.P. Plaxton, K.C. (Department of Justice); K.R. Daly (Department of the Interior); and K.R. McIntyre (Department of Finance). These individuals were present on 14 May 1934. LAC, Public Records

Counsel for the Dominion, James McGregor Stewart, K.C.,[112] described some of the documentation concerning Métis scrip by using some examples from northern Manitoba. The discussion continued:

> THE CHAIRMAN: Now it will be necessary there to refer us to the Act and these treaty provisions, in order to check up with you.
>
> MR. STEWART: The Act, my Lord, is 7-8 Edward VII — or the revisions of the Act—
>
> THE CHAIRMAN: Dominion? What year?
>
> MR. STEWART: This is the Dominion [Lands] Act, Chapter 20 of the Statutes of 1908, Section 76.
>
> THE CHAIRMAN: That lays the foundation for all you say?
>
> MR. STEWART: Yes, and that is simply a revision again, a consolidation. It goes right back, and the provision is simply this: the Governor in Council may grant lands in satisfaction of claims of half-breeds arising out of the extinguishment of Indian title. *And throughout the history of Canada the term "Indian" has been held to include half-breeds.*[113]

Stewart then read into the record the Order-in-Council (29 May 1909), an instrument that established the terms of scrip for the Treaty 5 Adhesion in northern Manitoba. After that, P.H. Gordon, K.C., counsel for the Province of Saskatchewan, declared, "It is complicated," to which Stewart agreed by responding emphatically: "It *is* complicated."[114] Stewart then elaborated:

---

of the Saskatchewan Natural Resources Commission, RG 33/50 vol. 21, Saskatchewan Resources Commission, "Report of Proceedings," vol. 5 (14 May 1934) at 1050 [Report of the Saskatchewan Proceedings, vol. 5]. The Saskatchewan government's copies of Proceedings are found at Saskatchewan Archives Board NR.1 1-A.

112 For a biography on Stewart, see Barry Cahill, *The Thousandth Man: A Biography of James McGregor Stewart* (Toronto: University of Toronto Press and Osgoode Society for Canadian Legal History, 2000). I appreciate Nicole O'Byrne bringing this source to my attention.

113 Report of the Saskatchewan Proceedings, vol. 5, at 1167–68 [emphasis added].

114 *Ibid.* at 1170 [emphasis in original].

> This does not come into our claim at all; this does not come into the province's claim; but it is simply a concrete illustration showing on what basis the scrip was issued — why it was issued.
>
> Now, as regards the 96,740 acres in respect of which the province is claiming, I have this submission to make, that from the commencement of Canada and by the agreement between the Hudson's Bay Company and Canada, the rights of the aboriginal population were regarded as existing. It was considered that they had rights in this Western country. Canada proceeded to treat with the aboriginal population on principles of decency and justice. The policy was to procure the surrender of their nomadic rights or their floating rights, by acceptance of definite reservations, and regards half-breeds by the allocation of scrip giving them the right to a farm or to a part purchase price on a farm. By so doing the Dominion extinguished the floating charge on the Territories. If the Dominion had not retained control and administration of these lands in 1905 the problem would have been one for the provinces to deal with. The provinces would have to face the Indian claim. They would have to make their reservations. They would have to provide for half-breed scrip or compensate the half-breed in some way.[115]

After that, the commissioners and counsels looked at the *Saskatchewan Act*, the *Manitoba Act*, and the NRTA, and then puzzled briefly over the absence of a section 31 of the *Manitoba Act* in the legislation that created Alberta and Saskatchewan.[116] While Stewart was somewhat distracted, Gordon, counsel for Saskatchewan, pronounced: "Under the *British North America Act* Indians and Indian reservations are in the exclusive jurisdiction of the Dominion."[117] Counsel for Saskatchewan, in effect,

115 *Ibid.* at 1171. *Corpus Juris* defined this concept of floating rights with "respect to land grants or certificates" to indicate "a certain quantity out of a larger quantity of land, as where the grant is of a certain number of sections to the mile out of swamp lands then belonging to, or that might thereafter belong to, the state, without any limitations or restrictions as to sections or locality." William Mack, ed., *Corpus Juris Being a Complete and Systematic Statement of the Whole Body of the Law as Embodied in and Developed by All Reported Decisions*, vol. 26 (New York: American Law Book Company, 1921) at 741.

116 Report of the Saskatchewan Proceedings, vol. 5, at 1171–74. Section 31 of the *Manitoba Act* provided a land grant to the Métis.

117 *Ibid.* at 1172.

connected Métis scrip policies with the federal government's constitutional jurisdiction concerning Indians.

Then Stewart summarized: "Now, if the Dominion had not done this, the problem of taking care of half-breeds on the signing of the adhesion to the treaty, or on being dealt with on the extinguishment of the half-breed's recognized floating charge, would have been a problem on the doorstep of the province after 1905, necessarily."[118] On the question of the charge of Métis scrip, Stewart concluded: "we can rely for the proposition that the issuance of half-breed scrip would have been considered by any province as a proper charge out of the lands administered by them — a very proper charge."[119] He explained more fully:

> . . . the province would been compelled to grapple with the problem of settlement with the half-breed in order to extinguish the Indian claims, the Indian floating charge on the lands generally, in order to acquire a complete title to its natural resources. We have no suggestion from any source that that right would have been extinguished in any other way except the one the Dominion followed, namely, by the issue of half-breed scrip. We claim, therefore, that there should be no credit allowed the province on this score.[120]

Thus, the policy of issuing scrip, which was converted into titles to lands (to which the province might, in the absence of any Indian title, have had a beneficial interest in), was not a claim that either the province or the Dominion could make towards a balancing of the amount of compensation owed — it simply had to be done.

Several significant assertions are evident in the federal government's position at the Saskatchewan Resources Commission: (1) the term *Indian* was always held to include Half-breeds; (2) Aboriginal people had existing rights; (3) the agreement with the HBC recognized their "floating" rights; (4) principles of decency and justice were required in the treatment of Aboriginal people; and (5) reserves and scrip were the result of the recognition of the "floating" title. Here Stewart has used "Indian" to include "Half-breed," but once he had done so, he employed the term

118 *Ibid.* at 1174.
119 *Ibid.* at 1175.
120 *Ibid.* at 1177.

Aboriginal people to refer to both Indians and Métis and their rights. With the exception of references to reserves and scrip, no separation of the Métis from the Indians occurred in his submission to the royal commission. Stewart's argument in 1934 was consistent with the position expressed by Newcombe in 1921. At no point did any participant at the commission's proceedings jump up to suggest that the 1870 Imperial Order was irrelevant to the Métis, or that the Métis lacked the "floating" rights of Aboriginal title, or that the Métis were not Aboriginal people, or that throughout the history of Canada the Métis were not Indians. None of this discussion during the Saskatchewan Resources Commission is helpful for the dichotomizing exercise that led the Court in *Blais* to dismiss a Métis interest in the NRTAs.

Saskatchewan's position on scrip was provided by Gordon:

> Now it is interesting to note, too, that the Dominion government has exclusive jurisdiction over Indians and Indian reserves. Under subsection 24 of section 91 . . . the right to legislate with respect to Indians rests entirely with the Dominion government . . . .
>
> My learned friend's [James McGregor Stewart] argument, although very cogent, comes down to this: that although there was no trust still the halfbreeds were, so to speak, sitting on the doorstep of the government of Saskatchewan and in all decency, in view of the traditions of the British people in dealing with the aboriginal inhabitants of a country, the people recognized in the circumstances a compelling duty, a moral on it is true, if not legal, to provide for them.[121]

Again, scrip was related to traditions of British decency in dealing with the title of Natives or Aboriginal inhabitants. On the question of provincial jurisdiction, Stewart confirmed: "They have no right to protect Indians but they have a right to make land grants."[122] Gordon continued with his presentation:

> But as we say, we wish to get away from the legal point of view. If we were getting to be a matter of strict law, as so many of the statesmen have said, it would be referred to the courts of the Dominion. But it is not a matter of strict law. The principles on which you gentlemen, I submit, will

121 *Ibid.* at 1315–16.

122 *Ibid.* at 1319.

> proceed, are those of the widest natural justice — what is fair, in view of the circumstances, as between the Dominion and the province. If you come to the conclusion that the province had a duty towards these half-breeds then you will probably give effect to it. I submit that under the British North America Act — and that, no doubt, is the only thing that will stand, although we should like to change it in many respects — you will come to decision as to what is fair in the view of the liability of the Dominion to look after their wards, the Indians of the prairies. Now, that is all I have to say in reference to halfbreed scrip.[123]

Of course, Aboriginal interests could not be easily accommodated by the Law, but British views of natural justice could inform the Crown's dealings and relationships with Aboriginal peoples. Gordon did not separate the *British North America Act*, Indians, Half-breeds, and Métis scrip.

Understandably, discussions got more involved with the recognition that the federal government was responsible for Indians, but that for the provinces that confederated in 1867, provincial governments controlled the Crown lands.

> MR. GORDON: We agreed to give the reserves at any time.
>
> MR. STEWART: That is not restricted to reserves. Now, in further dealing with the halfbreed scrip, one of the chief difficulties we have in this case, is, to use the expression that Mr. Meighen [former Prime Minister] used in this very connection, to unscramble the egg that was scrambled in 1905. That shows up particularly in connection with halfbreed scrip, but my learned friend gives me the cue, and I submit that the proper cure for the determination of a question of this kind is to be found in his remarks this morning. He said that a matter of this sort had to be settled on the broad principles of natural justice. It is in conformity with the broad principles of natural justice that the Dominion, in handing back the natural resources to Saskatchewan, which has been relieved of the encumbrances — that is, the floating charge of the Indians as a result of Dominion policies, and as a result of the Dominion becoming obligated to the halfbreeds — is it in conformity with the broad principles of natural justice, because the egg was scrambled then and has to

123 *Ibid.* at 1321.

> be unscrambled now, that the Dominion should have to pay for it out of its own pocket.[124]

The federal position seems to assert that the province would have to pay directly or indirectly. The positions of the federal and Saskatchewan governments differed on how to account for scrip for the purposes of compensation owed, but on the essentials concerning the Indian status of the Métis, the connection between scrip and Indian title, and the obligations to deal with Métis deriving from the *Constitution Act, 1867*, and the 1870 Imperial Order, there was no disagreement.

F. THE ALBERTA RESOURCES COMMISSION: "A TRUST IN FAVOUR OF THE HALF-BREED"

With respect to the Alberta NRTA, the question of compensation for the loss of the beneficial interests in land covered the period from 1 September 1905 to 30 September 1930. Compensation was required to put Alberta in a position of equality with other provinces, and paragraph 22 of the Alberta agreement provided for an inquiry.[125] Dominion counsel Stewart had assumed that the arguments made before the Saskatchewan Resources Commission would hold for the Alberta situation; however, because Alberta's position on its compensation was based on an assertion that its resources were "expropriated" by the federal government after 1905, the Dominion brief had to address this far-reaching provincial claim: that compensation owed would be equal to the capital value of the resources in 1905, less the subsidies paid to Alberta by the Dominion.[126] Consequently, the question of Halfbreed scrip also was considered by the Alberta Resources Commission. In his pursuit of unscrambling "the egg" that was scrambled in 1905, Stewart was guided by this view: "No *ex*

---

124 *Ibid.* at 1380–81.

125 See LAC, RG 33/51, Alberta Resources Commission 1933–43, vol. 2, Exhibit 251-D, Brief on Behalf of the Dominion of Canada, submitted by James McGregor Stewart (November 1934) [Dominion Brief to Alberta Commission].

126 Apparently, the National Energy Policy of the 1970s is not the first time that Alberta took exception to federal resource policies. In contrast, Manitoba had based its claim to compensation on a fiduciary argument. The Dominion's response to the expropriation claim and the basis for assessing the compensation were well developed in this brief at pages 3–11b.

post facto appraisal of any policy or act can be very helpful in the enquiry. Each item must be viewed in the light of surrounding circumstances and conditions."[127] This approach would prove to be sensible in dealing with the complication that scrip represented.

The Dominion's brief dealt with "North West Half Breed Grants," calculated as entailing 128,250 acres that were of interest to the Alberta claim.[128] As during the Saskatchewan Resources Commission hearings, Canada predicated scrip entitlements in terms of clause 14 of the 1869 Deed of Surrender from the HBC, but the Dominion's brief also cited the Canadian Parliamentary Address of December 1867, which provided:

> And furthermore that, upon the transference of the territories in question to the Canadian Government, the claims of the Indian tribes to compensation for lands required for purposes of settlement will be considered and settled in conformity with the equitable principles which have uniformly governed the British Crown in its dealings with the aborigines.[129]

Stewart's brief continued by providing the foundations for the issuing of Métis scrip and the historical particulars relating it to the province of Alberta:

> The Dominion Government has, throughout, recognized the Half Breed as an Indian within the meaning of these obligations and has consequently treated him as entitled to some share or interest in the lands. As each treaty was made with the Indian Tribes, the Government appointed one or more Commissioners to enquire into the claims of Half

127 Dominion Brief to Alberta Commission, above note 125, at 7. Indeed, lacking access to the extrinsic evidence concerning the drafting of the agreement, courts generated precedents on the Indian hunting rights paragraph through an *ex post facto* reading of paragraph 12/13.

128 *Ibid.* at 32–33b. Brief discussion in Ottawa of Métis scrip had occurred prior to this brief; see LAC, Public Records of the Alberta Natural Resources Commission, RG 33/51 "Report of Proceedings," vol. 1, at 270; and again at vol. 2, at 425, 449–51.

129 This 1867 address can be found in the "Order of Her Majesty in Council admitting Rupert's Land and the North-Western Territory into the Union" (23 June 1870), which is printed in Oliver, *The Canadian North-West*, above note 99, at 946. The relevance of the 1870 Imperial Order was also made in an earlier memorandum; see LAC, RG 33/51, vol. 7, Exhibit 124-D, Memorandum: Alberta Resources Commission: RE: Half-Breed Scrip (4 October 1934).

> Breeds resident in the territory at the time of the treaty. The measure of relief took the form either of cash scrip for $240.00 or land scrip for 240 acres of land.
>
> In all, four of such Indian Treaties have been signed covering lands in Alberta, namely Treaties 6, 7, 8 and 10 . . . .
>
> In the first instance it was apparently thought that the scrip should be issued only to Half Breeds who were born prior to the 15th July 1870 when the Dominion acquired control over the North West Lands. Against this view the Legislature of the North West Territories protested. Several resolutions were passed by that body and submitted to the Dominion Government, urging that recognition be given to Half Breeds who had been born prior to 1885 in which year the scrip was first issued. In this view the Dominion Government ultimately concurred . . . .
>
> The obligation to provide for the Indian (including the Half Breed) was considered as applying without distinction to the whole of Ruperts [*sic*] Land and the North West Territories. Consequently the scrip issued entitled the Half Breed to locate it in any Dominion Lands available for settlement. For the same reason the Commissions appointed to adjudicate on the rights of the Half Breeds visited the various settlements and reported and issued the scrip without keeping any data that would enable one to determine the number of Half Breeds resident in the various provinces.[130]

Here again, scrip was related to the question of Indian title and the treaty process, and "Half-breeds" were at that time, and in 1934, classified as Indians.

In determining the relevance of scrip to the Alberta claims, the Dominion's brief advanced several important conclusions:

> (a) That the Province can have no claim in respect of any scrip issued prior to September 1st 1905 whether located before or after that date. The right conferred by the scrip to locate on Dominion Lands generally should be regarded as a trust in favour of the Half Breed, which Alberta would have been bound to respect if it had received the Re-

130 Dominion Brief to Alberta Commission, above note 125, at 32–33a. Stewart also provided a plan of the areas covered by the treaties and 23 Orders-in-Council relating to scrip claims.

sources on September 1st 1905 on a basis of equality with the other provinces.

(b) In all cases in which scrip was issued whether before or after 1905 in respect of Indian Treaties entered into prior to 1905 the right of the Half Breed to receive his scrip and to locate it anywhere in Dominion Lands should be recognized as a vested right and as a "trust" within the meaning of Section 109 of the B.N.A. Act.

(c) As to scrip issued after 1905 in respect of Indian Treaties entered into after that date, the Province should have no claim in cases where the Half Breed was resident in Alberta at the time of the Treaty or the issue of the scrip, but where the Half Breed was not resident in Alberta the province may be regarded as entitled to claim against the Dominion.[131]

A significant elaboration of the Dominion's position in the Alberta Resources Commission, which did not appear in the Saskatchewan submission, was the identification of Halfbreed scrip as a trust in favour of the Métis, a vested right, and a trust within the meaning of section 109 of the *Constitution Act, 1867*.[132]

After relating the relevance of Northwest Halfbreed scrip to the compensation questions before the Commission, the Dominion brief concluded:

> It is submitted that it is inconceivable, at least for the purposes of this Commission, that the Province would have declined to extinguish the Indian title (including Half Breed claims) "in conformity with the equitable principles which have uniformly governed the British Crown in its dealing with the aborigines". If it had so declined, it is submitted that the Dominion could have taken the necessary steps under Section

---

131 *Ibid.* at 33a. By distinguishing the residency of a Métis grantee after the creation of the Province of Alberta in 1905, Stewart allowed for some compensation against the Dominion.

132 Section 109 provides: "All Lands, Mines, Minerals, and Royalties belonging to the several Provinces of Canada, Nova Scotia, and New Brunswick at the Union, and all Sums then due or payable for such Lands, Mines, Minerals, or Royalties, shall belong to the several Provinces of Ontario, Quebec, Nova Scotia, and New Brunswick in which the same are situate or arise, subject to any Trusts existing in respect thereof, and to any Interest other than that of the Province in the same." *Constitution Act, 1867* (U.K.), 30 & 31 Vict., c. 3.

> 91(24) of the B.N.A. Act to compel equitable treatment to Indians and Half Breeds.[133]

Essentially, Canada again argued that in order to act upon British equitable principles reflected in the commitments of the 1870 Imperial Order, it issued scrip to Halfbreed Indians. Notwithstanding this imperial instrument, Canada would still have had to act on section 91(24) — Indians, and Lands reserved for Indians — of the *Constitution Act, 1867*. These obligations to follow equitable principles based on constitutional principles and definitions negated any compensation claims that the provinces of Saskatchewan and Alberta might have advanced against the Dominion on account of their lands being taken up by scrip.

The question of Métis scrip and the province's claims for a loss necessitated a discussion of what exactly was entailed by the Dominion's grant of this unique tenure. This tenure was explained in terms of federal jurisdiction with regards to Indians and lands reserved to Indians, the extinguishment of Indian title, the floating rights of Indians and Halfbreeds in the prairie provinces, and the obligation that Canada acquired with the transfer of the Hudson's Bay Company Territory through the 1870 imperial Order. Throughout this informed legal discourse, the term *Indian* included "Half-breed." At no point did any of the distinguished participants suggest that the inclusion of Half-breeds with Indians was passé or that they existed as separate entities since 1850. These records could have informed the Court in *Blais* about the continuity of language, but that would have required recognition of the usefulness of historical evidence to understanding Crown–Métis relations.

G. CONCLUSION: "THE EGG WAS SCRAMBLED THEN AND HAS TO BE UNSCRAMBLED NOW"

In terms of the historical records documenting federal fisheries policies and the property foundational issues raised by the transfer of land and resources from the Dominion to prairie provincial administration, a very different relationship between the Métis and the Crown was evident than that constructed by the attorney general for Manitoba and the Court in *Blais*. With respect to accessing fisheries in accordance with need and

133 Dominion Brief to Alberta Commission, above note 125, at 33a–33b.

custom, no essential differences existed between the Métis and Indians for the period examined (ca. 1890s–1920s). When the British principles for dealing with Aboriginal populations are recognized, the NRTA constitutional process did not differentiate the Métis from Indians. Given the historical records documenting federal fisheries policies and the development of the NRTAs, would it have been unduly generous today to recognize that the historical usage of "Indian" often means Aboriginal and is, therefore, inclusive of the Métis? A crude binary has been constructed without recognizing that the two parts (Indian and Métis) constitute a single class — Aboriginal — throughout a geographical region now known as the Métis Homeland by the Métis Nation. If the Métis were "independent," lacking any need for protection of livelihood rights, and were not "Indians," then what justification could the federal government have for granting scrip or for providing special considerations with respect to harvesting fish?

From the perspective of an Aboriginal mode of life and a concomitant access to much-needed fishing resources, considerable historical and archival evidence demonstrates that routine relations between agents of the Crown and the Métis were not all that different from those with the Indian population. The term *Halfbreed* is extensively used in close association with references to "Indians" throughout federal fisheries regulations, correspondence, and reports, as it had been employed in descriptions of the demographic makeup of Treaty Indian bands. The rather consistent union of the terms *Halfbreeds* and *Indians* by government officials suggested that, with respect to access to fisheries, the Métis were considered to be "Natives" in the same way as Indians and for the same reason that Indians are "Aboriginal." The prevalence of the strong connection between the terms *Halfbreeds* and *Indians* provides real support to the view that the federal government and its officials, particularly in the Department of Marine and Fisheries, and for the purpose of accessing fish resources, clearly understood the Métis to be "Natives," or Aboriginal, in the same sense as Indians. Departmental records from Marine and Fisheries, along with other correspondence of government officials, reveal that government officials recognized that the Métis, like the Indians, required exemptions from closed seasons and often made provision for free licences simply because fishing was essential to the Métis. The Métis were not independent of fish.

If one gets beyond the modern-day readings of the plain text of the NRTAs, largely restricted to interpretation of the livelihood rights provision (paragraph 12/13), an examination of the processes that brought them into being, along with consideration of the question of trusts, obligations, and compensation for the loss of beneficial interests are fundamental to providing a modern-day meaning to the Indian interests specifically protected by this constitutional process. Given that this compensation had real financial consequences, the question of Métis scrip was given a serious turn of the mind. To satisfy this imperative of determining the federal compensation owed to Alberta and Saskatchewan, Halfbreed scrip, a land grant provided by the *Dominion Lands Acts*, and numerous federal Orders-in-Council, required sound justification by the commissions. This explanation was provided by some authoritative legal minds that had the advantage of developing an understanding of the entire system of Dominion lands and tenures (ca. 1870–1930) and had developed a thorough familiarity with the NRTAs. Well before the final drafting of the NRTAs, back in 1921, the Department of Justice explained the granting of scrip to the Métis (as Indians) in terms of obligations arising from the 1870 imperial Order. The accepted argument was that scrip was granted to Indians (that is, Halfbreeds) because of an obligation to "extinguish" their Indian title. The "compensation" due to this floating title was based on British equitable principles according to the federal Department of Justice. And then a few years later, after the NRTAs had been enacted, the nature of Métis scrip was scrutinized by two royal commissions. The Justice Department's position remained unchanged, and if anything, the discussions contributed to the view that defined Métis as Indians for the purpose of the Constitution. Furthermore, the entitlement that was represented by Métis scrip was defined as a trust within the meaning section 109 of the *British North America Act, 1867*.

None of the participants during the commissions' discussions differentiated the Indian from the Half-breed. Again, "Indian" was used to the same effect that we use "Aboriginal" since that era. The federal government's jurisdiction over Indians was combined with the principles of natural justice to justify the policy of issuing scrip to the Métis. While the federal government's position was more elaborate in 1934, it still rested squarely on the argument made to the Privy Council by the Justice Department in 1921. With respect to the NRTAs, much anchoring of the plain text of the agreements to the historical context, and to the surrounding circumstances of the negotiation, drafting, and enactment, still needs to be done. Eventually, a more definitive assessment of the use of history to make law in *Blais* will be completed, along an empirical re-examination of the problematic belief that the NRTAs set out to alter treaty rights.

Significantly, if the provinces wanted to find an opportunistic and unprincipled means to bump-up the compensation owed by the federal government, their counsels should have argued loudly that the Métis were not Indians, and thus scrip policies could not be supported by "the claims of the Indian tribes" that "the equitable principles which have uniformly governed the British Crown in its dealings with the aborigines" never applied to the Métis, or that federal jurisdiction for Indians excluded the Métis. As of yet, I have found no indications of any such unlikely sophistry; instead, it would seem that a measure of good sense prevailed then.

Archival sources have provided information for this analysis that would not have been possible if research was confined to obtaining published primary sources from libraries. An examination of the May 1894 fishing regulations, without the benefit of the trail of archival records, would not have identified the measure of defence that the Crown gave to the Métis during that period. The documentation concerning the negotiation, drafting, and enactment of the *Natural Resources Transfer Agreements* is integral to understanding the meaning of this part of our Constitution. Clearly, archival research is an essential method for reconstructing Aboriginal–Crown relations.

Where does this evidence-based analysis of fisheries policies and constitutional development leave the historical findings of *Blais*? Table 1, at the end of this paper, provides a succinct summary of the empirical findings of this research relative to the historical/legal determinations of *Blais*. (Two of the historical assertions in *Blais* — that is, common usage of Indian and Métis, and the intent of the hunting rights provision of the NRTAs — are unrelated to the issues discussed here and will require research.) Clearly, most of the historical claims made in *Blais*, especially in respect to the prairie provinces outside the original 1870 borders of Manitoba, do not stand up to empirical scrutiny. With respect to the NRTA, the reconstruction of a more nuanced historical context of this constitutional process is not as the Court has determined. The Justice Department stated rather forthrightly that Indians were issued scrip. And significantly, protection that was obtained in the 1870 Imperial Order with respect to Indian tribes and their lands was deemed to have included the Métis. Thus, if one broadens the search for archival records beyond the files of the Department of Indian Affairs, a limitation evident in the application of history in *Blais*, and looks up to the Justice Department, then what emerges is a historical context that defines the Métis as "Indians" with rights deserving Crown protection. In 1921 and 1934, the federal Justice Department seemed to have employed a continuity of language approach that defined the Métis (Half-breed) as Indian by reaching back to the *British North America Act, 1867*, Canadian Parliamentary Address of 16 and 17 December 1867, and the 1870 Imperial Order. Certainly, the reasoning in *Blais* is at odds with the legal analysis promoted by the Justice Department at the time, for whom the NRTA process was a lived experience.

Blais, aided by sous-chefs *Horseman*[134] and *Badger*,[135] has scrambled an egg in order to serve up a rather uninteresting omelet, which today, like the Saskatchewan and Alberta acts of 1905, desperately needs to be unscrambled. Conceptually, unscrambling this egg is possible. If we read "Aboriginal" in place of "Indian," then many problems disappear. The Crown could then direct state agencies to pursue a relationship with the Métis Nation sanctioned by the Constitution. Such clarity would curtail the need for producing academic exegeses, such as the one that I am now concluding, and instead energy could be focused on reconciling the past. With all due respect, from my point of view, the discussion in May 1934 between Gordon and Stewart at a royal commission, which admittedly may have been naively predicated on elements of self-congratulatory claims about British principles of natural justice, along with the Dominion's brief of November 1934, demonstrate more generosity towards Aboriginal peoples than the Supreme Court did for the Métis in *Blais* some seven decades later. And if we persist in turning historical experience into artifact, masked by pedantry and literalism, then our naïveté con-

134 *R. v. Horseman*, [1990] 3 C.N.L.R. 95 (S.C.C.), aff'g [1987] 4 C.N.L.R. 99 (Alta. C.A.), aff'g [1986] 2 C.N.L.R. 94 (Alta. Q.B.), rev'g [1986] 1 C.N.L.R. 79 (Alta. Prov. Ct.).

135 *R. v. Badger*, [1996] 2 C.N.L.R. 77 (S.C.C.).

cerning our own generosity about dispensing justice will surely exceed that of the legal positivists of another, "less enlightened," era.

Table 7.1: Historical Assertions Deriving from Federal Fisheries Policies and the NRTA Constitutional Process Relative to the Historical Findings in R. v. Blais

	Fish Policies	**NRTA Process**
Federal Fisheries Policies		
Indians and Métis are Native/Aboriginal	✓	–
Indians and Métis share a similar mode of life	✓	–
Métis expressed an interest in protecting fishing rights	✓	–
Federal fisheries policies and regulations treated the Métis and Indians as a group	✓	–
NRTA Constitutional Process		
Half-breeds are Indians for the purpose of the Imperial Order-in-Council 23 June 1870	–	✓
Federal government was obligated to deal with the existing Indian title in the west	–	✓
Scrip lands were justified as necessary outcome for extinguishing Indian title	–	✓
Half-breeds held Indian title	–	✓
Dealing with Indian title was a federal obligation under section 91(24)	–	✓
Findings in *Blais*		
Historical context does not suggest that Indians include Métis	X	X
Métis rights are different from Indian rights	X	X
Common usage of "Indian" did not include Métis	NA	NA
Half-breeds and Indians separate and distinct from 1850-1930	X	X
Purpose of hunting rights ensures respect to Crown's obligation to Indians	NA	NA
Métis were independent and did not need protection	X	X

X = historical records and analysis are inconsistent with the historical claims in *R. v. Blais*

NA = the historical records do not apply to this particular finding from *R. v. Blais*

Acknowledgments

I am deeply grateful to Clayton Leonard, a former student and now a treaty rights lawyer, for his significant insights into federal fisheries records on the question of the usage of the terms *Métis* and *Indian*. I would also like to thank the following who, under my supervision, assisted with various past research efforts associated with this analysis: Erin McGregor, Raylene Whitford, and Meika Taylor. Moreover, this type of research would not be possible without the existence of publicly funded archival facilities.

< 8 >

Métis Interjurisdictional Immunity: A Third Way to Protect Métis Constitutional Rights?[1]

DALE GIBSON

A. INTRODUCTION

In 2003, Métis constitutional rights were the subject of both a monumental victory and a serious disappointment, both at the hands of the Supreme Court of Canada. In *R. v. Powley*,[2] the Court upheld the existence of Métis Aboriginal rights under section 35 of the *Constitution Act, 1982*.[3] In *R. v. Blais*,[4] on the other hand, which was argued and decided at the same time as *Powley*, the Court rejected a second asserted constitutional basis for Métis rights by holding that Métis are not entitled to the rights guaranteed to "Indians" by the *Natural Resources Transfer Agreements*.

The task of this essay is to examine a third possible way in which Métis rights might be protected: by the somewhat obscure, but important constitutional principle known as interjurisdictional immunity.

---

1 This paper is a revised version of a presentation to the Law Commission of Canada and Métis National Council National Symposium, "Crown–Métis Relations and Section 91(24) of the *Constitution Act, 1867*," held in Winnipeg, Manitoba, 5–7 February 2006. Subsequent to the original presentation, the Supreme Court released its decision in *Canadian Western Bank v. Alberta*, 2007 SCC 22 [*Canadian Western Bank*], which affects some of the comments I originally made about the doctrine of interjurisdictional immunity. I have inserted references to that case where relevant.

2 (2003), 230 D.L.R. (4th) 1 (S.C.C.) [*Powley*].

3 Being Schedule B to the *Canada Act 1982* (U.K.), 1982, c. 11.

4 (2003), 230 D.L.R. (4th) 22 (S.C.C.) [*Blais*].

B. GENERAL PRINCIPLES

Interjurisdictional immunity is an invisible constitutional cloak worn by those who fall within the constitutional jurisdiction of the Parliament of Canada. The cloak shields federally regulated persons, entities, and activities from provincial or local laws that would otherwise apply to them if such laws would crucially affect the aspect of their identity or activity that is subject to federal control.[5] To put it another way, federally regulated persons, entities, and enterprises are said to have, to that extent, a "constitutional exemption" from the provincial and local laws in question.[6]

Earlier jurisprudence determined that airports, for example, are immune from municipal or provincial zoning laws that would otherwise affect their location or design, because the location and design of airports is part of the essence of aviation, a matter under the constitutional jurisdiction of the federal order of government.[7]

It is important to understand that this immunity exists in the absence of relevant federal legislation. If Parliament has spoken on the subject, the applicable constitutional principle is federal paramountcy, and the only question to be determined is whether the provincial law is inconsistent with the federal law. Interjurisdictional immunity, by contrast, operates even when no federal legislation has been enacted. The mere *potential* law-making power of Parliament is sufficient to create a constitutional exemption.[8]

---

5 See D. Gibson, "Interjurisdictional Immunity in Canadian Federalism" (1969) 47 Can. Bar Rev. 40; P. W. Hogg, *Constitutional Law of Canada*, looseleaf (Scarborough, ON: Carswell, 2007–) at 15-28 and 15-33; J. Woodward, *Native Law*, looseleaf (Toronto: Carswell, 1989–) at 121 *ff.* In *Canadian Western Bank*, above note 1, Binnie and LeBel JJ., writing for eight members of the Court, indicated that the threshold for application of the doctrine should be "impairment."

6 The principle is not reciprocal. Provincially regulated persons, entities, and enterprises have no equivalent immunity from valid federal legislation that affects their core components because the principle of federal paramountcy, which dictates that statutes of the Parliament of Canada trump inconsistent provincial statutes, would apply, with even greater force, in the absence of applicable provincial legislation.

7 *Johannesson v. West St. Paul*, [1952] 1 S.C.R. 292.

8 "The abstinence of the Dominion Parliament from legislating to the full limit of its powers could not have the effect of transferring to any provincial legislature the legislative power which had been assigned to the Dominion by s. 91 of the Act of

Failure to appreciate that distinction has occasionally led to confusion. It is sometimes suggested, for example, that courts have a *choice* as to whether to apply paramountcy or inter-jurisdictional immunity, depending on which is more convenient in the circumstances. Doing this is not possible, however, because paramountcy cannot operate in the absence of pre-emptive federal legislation, and when it does operate, there is no need for interjurisdictional immunity.

The misunderstanding seems to have originated in a separate concurring opinion of Dickson C.J. in *O.P.S.E.U. v. Ontario (Attorney General)*.[9] In that case, the other members of the Supreme Court of Canada simply found interjurisdictional immunity to be inapplicable on the facts. The Chief Justice, however, expressed the opinion that it is "not a particularly compelling doctrine," and that courts should exercise "caution" about its scope and not "extend [it] . . . into a field . . . which is unrelated to . . . the historical roots of the doctrine." With the greatest respect to one of Canada's greatest judges, Chief Justice Dickson's analysis on that occasion showed little understanding of either the nature of the principle or its constitutional usefulness. In any event, he spoke only for himself; the Court has continued to apply, and to extend, the principle in appropriate circumstances.[10]

The Dickson critique nevertheless continues to fuel frontal assaults on interjurisdictional immunity from time to time. Most recently, in *Canadian Western Bank*, the majority judgment expressed concern about the detrimental consequences of an overly generous reliance upon the doctrine. These judges did not, however, reject the legitimacy or logic of the principle.[11] Interjurisdictional immunity plays a uniquely useful role in Canadian constitutional law, providing a mechanism by which courts can prevent impermissible applications of provincial laws to federally regulated entities and activities without having to strike down otherwise valid legislation altogether, and without requiring the enactment of conflicting federal legislation.

1867." *Union Colliery v. Bryden*, [1899] A.C. 580 at 588 (P.C.). In *Canadian Western Bank*, above note 1, the Court was critical of this feature of the doctrine.

9 (1987), 41 D.L.R. (4th) 1 at 10–12 (S.C.C.).

10 Notably, in the present context, in *Delgamuukw v. British Columbia* (1997), 153 D.L.R. (4th) 193 (S.C.C.) [*Delgamuukw*].

11 See *Canadian Western Bank*, above note 1.

The cloak of interjurisdictional immunity does not provide those who are subject to federal jurisdiction with *total* protection from provincial laws; it does so only with respect to those matters that go to the heart of the federal concern. As Dickson J. (as he then was) once observed on behalf of the Supreme Court of Canada, the immunity applies only to those matters that are "vital, essential or integral" to the "core federal undertaking."[12] Thus, airports must abide by provincial and local laws concerning garbage disposal and wages paid to airport coffee-shop cooks, newsstand clerks, and even those who construct airport runways.[13] Because the serving of liquor on in-flight aircraft is not integral to aeronautics, it is subject to provincial regulation.[14]

C. APPLICATION OF INTERJURISDICTIONAL IMMUNITY TO ABORIGINAL MATTERS

The application of interjurisdictional immunity to the realm of Aboriginal matters has never been clearly understood. In principle, since "Indians, and Lands reserved for the Indians" is a legislative responsibility of the Parliament of Canada under section 91(24) of the *Constitution Act, 1867*,[15] provincial laws should not apply to any matter that goes to the heart of "Indianness." For example, in *Natural Parents v. British Columbia (Superintendent of Child Welfare)*[16] Laskin C.J. expressed his view and that of three other members of the Supreme Court of Canada[17] that absent federal legislation, provincial adoption laws would not apply to status Indians.

The immediate issue in the *Natural Parents* case was whether a provincial law could validly permit Indian children to be adopted by non-Indian parents. In the course of dealing with that question, Laskin C.J.

12 *Northern Telecom Ltd. v. Communications Workers of Canada* (1979), 98 D.L.R. (3d) 1 at 13–14 (S.C.C.).

13 The Supreme Court of Canada explained the principle and applied it to airport construction workers in *Montcalm Construction Inc. v. Quebec (Minimum Wage Commission)*, [1979] 1 S.C.R. 754 [*Montcalm Construction*].

14 *Air Canada v. Ontario (Liquor Control Board)* (1997), 148 D.L.R. (4th) 193 (S.C.C.).

15 (U.K.), 30 & 31 Vict., c. 3, reprinted in R.S.C. 1985, App. II, No. 5.

16 (1975), 60 D.L.R. (3d) 148 at 152–54 (S.C.C.) [*Natural Parents*].

17 Including Dickson J.

made some general observations about the applicability of provincial laws to Indians:

> It cannot be said . . . that because a provincial statute is general in its application, in the sense that its terms are not expressly restricted to matters within provincial competence, it may embrace matters within exclusive federal competence . . . .
>
> . . . [T]he *Adoption Act* [of the province] did not purport to extend to areas of exclusive federal competence, *e.g.*, Indians. It could only embrace them if the operation of the Act did not deal with what was integral to that head of federal legislative power, there being no express federal legislation respecting adoption of Indians. It appears to me to be unquestionable that for the provincial *Adoption Act* to apply to the adoption of Indian children of registered Indians, who could be compelled therefore to surrender them to adopting non-Indian parents, would be to touch "Indianness," to strike at a relationship integral to a matter outside of provincial competence . . . .
>
> Counsel for the respondents cited a number of cases holding Indians to be subject to provincial legislation . . . . These . . . are simply illustrative of the amenability of Indians off their reservations to provincial regulatory legislation, legislation which, like traffic legislation, does not touch their "Indianness." Such provincial legislation is of a different class than adoption legislation which would, if applicable as provincial legislation *simpliciter*, constitute a serious intrusion into the Indian family relationship. It is difficult to conceive what would be left of exclusive federal power in relation to Indians if such provincial legislation was held to apply to Indians.[18]

At the time those remarks were made, it could not be said with complete certainty that they accurately described the applicability of provincial laws to Aboriginal peoples. Chief Justice Laskin spoke for only four of the Court's nine members. Four other judges, represented by Martland and Ritchie JJ., expressed the view that statutes like the provincial *Adoption Act* in question applied to Indians "of their own force,"[19] as Ritchie

18 *Natural Parents*, above note 16 at 153–54.

19 *Ibid.* at 174.

J. put it. The ninth member of the Court, Beetz J., chose not to address the question.

Justice Beetz was technically justified in remaining silent about general principles of interjurisdictional immunity in the *Natural Parents* case because the outcome of the specific dispute did not hinge on those principles. The Court was unanimous in finding the provincial legislation to be applicable, and since the provincial Act permitted adoption by non-Indians, the challenge was rejected by all nine judges. The disagreement between the blocs of the Court, those represented by Laskin C.J. and by Martland and Ritchie JJ., related to general principles not pertinent to the specific appeal, and Beetz J. therefore chose to ignore them.

The reason that general principles were not applicable in that case was that Parliament long ago inserted a provision in the *Indian Act* that explicitly subjects status Indians to the general laws of the provinces where they reside:

> 88. Subject to the terms of any treaty and any other Act of Parliament, all laws of general application from time to time in force in any province are applicable to and in respect of Indians in the province, except to the extent that those laws are inconsistent with this Act or the *First Nations Fiscal and Statistical Management Act*, or with any order, rule, regulation or law of a band made under those Acts, and except to the extent that those provincial laws make provision for any matter for which provision is made by or under those Acts.[20]

In view of this provision, which has not changed since the date of the *Natural Parents* decision, general principles of interjurisdictional immunity have limited applicability to the situation of Aboriginal persons, activities, or enterprises that are subject to the *Indian Act*. For the same reason, judicial decisions about the impact of provincial laws on such matters provide little guidance to understanding the Métis situation, since Métis are not subject to the *Indian Act*.[21]

Although the foregoing observations of Laskin C.J. in *Natural Parents* were made only in passing and on behalf of a minority of the Court, they eventually became the basis of the principle upon which interjur-

20 R.S.C. 1985, c. I-5, s. 88.

21 Refer to Chapter 10 (Mitch McAdam) and Chapter 11 (Kent McNeil).

isdictional immunity applies to all Aboriginal peoples, including, in my opinion, the Métis. As Lamer C.J. stated on behalf of a majority of the Supreme Court of Canada almost a quarter century later: "[S]ection 91(24) protects a 'core' of Indianness from provincial intrusion, through the doctrine of interjurisdictional immunity."[22]

Justice Beetz, who displayed no interest in interjurisdictional immunity in *Natural Parents*, became the chief articulator of the principle in *Montcalm Construction*[23] only a few years later. Shortly after deciding *Montcalm*, when he applied the doctrine to an Aboriginal setting in *Four B Manufacturing Ltd. v. United Garment Workers of America*,[24] his reasoning echoed that in Laskin C.J.'s remarks on *Natural Parents*.

The *Four B Manufacturing* case considered the applicability of provincial labour relations legislation to employees of a shoe factory located on an Indian reserve. The factory was owned by four members of the band, all status Indians, but was a private operation, not carried out under band auspices. All but ten of its sixty-eight employees were Indians, however. Neither the *Indian Act* nor the *Canada Labour Code* purported to apply to labour relations on Indian reserves. An application to certify the employees' union under provincial legislation was resisted on the ground that provincial labour law was inapplicable. Chief Justice Laskin, supported by Ritchie J., agreed with that objection, holding that provincial laws did not, of their own force, extend to Indian reserves except with respect to non-Indians thereon.[25]

Justice Beetz, for the majority, rejected that conclusion as embodying a long-since discredited "enclave" approach to Indian reserves. He turned instead to a "functional" analysis similar to that which he had applied in *Montcalm Construction* and that Laskin C.J. had used in *Natural Parents*. Justice Beetz drew upon language taken from the earlier Laskin analysis:

> The functional test is a particular method of applying a more general rule, namely, that exclusive federal jurisdiction over labour relations

22 *Delgamuukw*, above note 10 at 269.

23 Above note 13.

24 (1979), 102 D.L.R. (3d) 385 (S.C.C.) [*Four B Manufacturing*].

25 *Ibid.* at 391–92. He does not appear to have considered s. 88 of the *Indian Act*, above note 20, because the decision appealed from held that the provincial statute applied of its own force: *ibid.* at 387.

> arises only if it can be shown that such jurisdiction forms an integral part of primary federal jurisdiction over some other federal object . . . . Given this general rule . . . the first question which must be answered in order to deal with appellant's submissions is whether the power to regulate the labour relations in issue forms an integral part of primary federal jurisdiction over Indians and lands reserved for the Indians . . . .
>
> . . . The matter . . . involves the rights of Indians and non-Indians to associate with one another for labour relations purposes, purposes which are not related to "Indianness"; it involves their relationship with the United Garment Workers of America or some other trade union about which there is nothing inherently Indian; it finally involves their collective bargaining with an employer who happens to be an Ontario corporation, privately owned by Indians, but about which there is nothing specifically Indian either . . . .[26]

Even if the non-Indian aspects were disregarded, he held, there would be no reason to exclude the provincial law:

> [N]either Indian status is at stake nor rights so closely connected with Indian status that they should be regarded as necessary incidents of status such for example as registrability, membership in a band, the right to participate in the election of chiefs and band councils, reserve privileges, etc. For this reason, I come to the conclusion that the power to regulate the labour relations in issue does not form an integral part of primary federal jurisdiction over Indians or lands reserved for the Indians.[27]

Although Beetz J. did refer to section 88 of the *Indian Act*, almost in passing, later in his reasons,[28] he appears to have concluded[29] that, in this case, the provincial statute applied of its own force.

Several Supreme Court of Canada decisions since the *Four B Manufacturing* case have added to our understanding of interjurisdictional immunity as it applies to Aboriginal matters.

---

26 *Ibid.* at 396–97.

27 *Ibid.* at 397.

28 *Ibid.* at 398.

29 This can also be said of the decision under appeal.

Dick v. The Queen[30] concerned provisions of the British Columbia *Wildlife Act*. These provisions were held to be applicable to Indians by reason of section 88 of the *Indian Act*. Justice Beetz, writing for the Court, indicated that he was "prepared to assume, without deciding" that the provisions would "impair the Indianness" of the affected Indians, and drew favourable attention to the conclusions of the court below to that effect. Provincial motor vehicle laws were held applicable of their own force to an Indian reserve in *R. v. Francis*.[31]

In the landmark *Delgamuukw* decision, the Court held that provincial legislation of general application that purported to extinguish Aboriginal rights before 1982 was not effective because it affected "the occupation of land and the activities which are integral to the distinctive aboriginal of the group . . . [which] aboriginal rights are part of the core of Indianness at the heart of s. 91(24)."[32]

Kitkatla Band v. British Columbia (Minister of Small Business, Tourism and Culture),[33] a 2002 decision of the Supreme Court, held that a provincial *Heritage Preservation Act*, which permitted Aboriginal and non-Aboriginal heritage items to be removed if an assessment process so recommended, applied to some trees that an Aboriginal group claimed were of cultural significance. Justice Le Bel, who wrote for the Court, was careful to point out, however, that the evidence was weak as to the cultural worth of these particular trees, that the legislation exempted resources in which Aboriginal rights were claimed, and that the assessment process established by the statute provided for a careful balancing of the interests involved.

---

30 (1985), 23 D.L.R. (4th) 33 at 55 (S.C.C.) [*Dick*].

31 (1988), 51 D.L.R. (4th) 418 (S.C.C.).

32 Above note 10 at 271.

33 (2002), 210 D.L.R. (4th) 577 at 604–5 (S.C.C.) [*Kitkatla*]. In 2006, the Court held in *R. v. Morris* (2006), 274 D.L.R. (4th) 193 (S.C.C.) that a provincial prohibition on night-light hunting did not apply to members of the Saanich First Nation because the relevant treaty contemplated such hunting methods. Although only the dissenters referred to interjurisdictional immunity by name, all judges accepted the applicability of the principle to this situation. Little was added to prior analyses of the principle, and the decision turned on differing views of whether the provincial law constituted a substantial violation of the treaty right.

In *Paul v. British Columbia (Forest Appeals Commission)*,[34] a 2003 ruling, the Court held that provincial legislation empowering a provincial administrative tribunal to determine, in the course of its duties and subject to judicial review by the courts, the existence of Aboriginal rights, did not, in substance, affect the core of Indianness.

Although these decisions have put a few more pieces of the jigsaw puzzle in place, the relatively narrow scope of each, and the fact that most were complicated by the effect of section 88, has resulted in a far-from-complete picture of interjurisdictional immunity as it applies to "Indians." They provide sufficient clues, however, to support some informed speculation, especially with respect to Métis, to whom section 88 of the *Indian Act* does not apply.

D. APPLICATION TO MÉTIS MATTERS: GENERAL

How do these principles apply to Canada's Métis population? The Métis situation differs from that of First Nations Canadians in one, and possibly two, respects. First, section 88 of the *Indian Act* has no application to Métis. Second, it cannot be unequivocally asserted that the two groups are in constitutionally identical positions because the key question as to whether section 91(24) of the *Constitution Act, 1867*, applies to Métis remains unanswered by the courts. Since the latter question is examined at length by others,[35] I will address it only briefly.

Assuming that Métis do wear the cloak of interjurisdictional immunity, four further questions arise for consideration: (1) Does it matter? Has section 35 supplanted the principle?; (2) Which matters qualify for its protection as being "vital, essential or integral" to Métis culture?; (3) Does such immunity deprive Métis of the *benefit* of statutes that bestow culturally significant entitlements on other provincial residents?; (4) Does it prevent provinces from enacting Métis-specific legislation, such as Alberta's trail-blazing *Metis Settlements Act*?[36]

---

34 (2003), 231 D.L.R. (4th) 449 (S.C.C.) [*Paul*].

35 Refer to the work of Brad Morse (see Chapter 5).

36 R.S.A. 2000, c. M-14.

E. ARE MÉTIS "INDIANS" UNDER SECTION 91(24)?

Because this question is dealt with by others in this volume, I will not dwell on it; I will simply proceed on the assumption that the answer is yes. I wish to say in passing, however, that I consider the historical evidence in support of an affirmative conclusion compelling.

The 1996 *Report of the Royal Commission on Aboriginal Peoples* expressed the view that Métis, broadly defined, fall within the constitutional jurisdiction of the Parliament of Canada with respect to "Indians" under section 91(24) of the *Constitution Act, 1867*.[37] The Royal Commission noted that the Parliament of Canada stated in both section 31 of the *Manitoba Act, 1870*, and section 125(e) of the *Dominion Lands Act, 1879*, that the land grants to "halfbreeds" ("Métis" in the French versions) were made for "extinguishment of Indian title." The Commission also considered the Supreme Court of Canada's observation, in a 1939 decision on the status of Inuit ("Eskimos"), that section 91(24) applies to "all the aborigines in the territory subsequently included in the Dominion."[38] A similar conclusion was reached in 1991 in the *Report of the Aboriginal Justice Inquiry of Manitoba*.[39]

F. SECTION 35: A SUBSTITUTE BASIS FOR MÉTIS CONSTITUTIONAL IMMUNITY?

If the widely held view that section 91(24) applies to Métis is correct, the principle of interjurisdictional immunity unquestionably affects the application of provincial statutes to Métis people and activities to at least some extent. But what if the Supreme Court of Canada decides that view is mistaken and that the Parliament of Canada has no legislative jurisdiction over Métis matters under the authority of section 91(24)?

---

37 *Perspectives and Realities*, vol. 4 (Ottawa: Supply and Services Canada, 1996) c. 5 at 209. The present writer authored that section of the report on behalf of the Royal Commission. See also Dale Gibson, "When Is a Métis an Indian? Some Consequences of Federal Constitutional Jurisdiction over Métis" in Paul Chartrand, ed., *Who Are Canada's Aboriginal Peoples?* (Saskatoon: Purich, 2002) at 258.

38 *Reference re Eskimos*, [1939] S.C.R. 104. Brad Morse discusses this decision in Chapter 5.

39 Vol. 1 (Winnipeg: Public Inquiry into the Administration of Justice and Aboriginal People, 1991).

In my opinion, in practical terms, the situation might not be much different than if section 91(24) and interjurisdictional immunity applied. I believe that Métis Aboriginal rights under section 35 of the *Constitution Act, 1982*, provide a cloak of constitutional immunity where Aboriginal rights are involved that is as effective as that provided by interjurisdictional immunity. In some respects, section 35's protections are more effective, since the section unquestionably protects against federal as well as provincial legislation, and operates outside of the context of the division of governmental powers between Ottawa and the provinces. Section 35 deals with fundamental constitutional rights.

The Supreme Court of Canada established in the *Powley* case, for instance, that a province may not, by reason of section 35, apply legislation that would restrict traditional Métis hunting rights.[40] In such circumstances, there is no need to consider interjurisdictional immunity.

Yet interjurisdictional immunity is not necessarily a meaningless concept for the Métis. In the first place, it will be a long time before the full extent of the rights entrenched for Métis by section 35 is known. It is possible, too, that the Aboriginal rights guaranteed for the Métis people by section 35 may be judicially defined to be narrower than the core legislative jurisdiction of Parliament with respect to Métis. In the *Paul* case,[41] Bastarache J. remarked: "The 'core' of Indianness has not been exhaustively defined." He then stated, "It encompasses the whole range of aboriginal rights that are protected by s. 35(1)," but offered no comment as to how far it might extend *beyond* Aboriginal rights. In the meantime, and perhaps always, section 91(24) and the principle of interjurisdictional immunity will remain major bulwarks of constitutional protection for the Métis way of life.

G. HOW LARGE IS THE CLOAK?

The cloak of interjurisdictional immunity is not an all-encompassing garment. It protects only that which is "vital, essential or integral" to the core federal undertaking. In this context, the core federal undertaking is Parliament's legislative responsibility for the Aboriginal ("Indian") aspects of the lives of Canada's Métis.

---

40 Above note 2.

41 Above note 34.

Of what does that Métis Aboriginal core consist? Which matters are "vital, essential or integral" to it? As one who is neither Métis nor Aboriginal, I am poorly qualified to answer those questions. The speculation that follows is therefore offered tentatively, and purely for the purpose of illustrating the general principles involved and stimulating discussion of their possible practical implications by those who are better informed than I.

What lies at the interjurisdictionally immune core, or heart, of Parliament's constitutional jurisdiction over Métis matters, in my opinion, is Métis culture in the broadest sense: the practices, ideas, and values that confer a unique identity on those Aboriginal social groupings that are called "Métis" or cognate names. Although those practices, ideas, and values had their origins in the ways of the past, and still pay respectful heed to those traditional ways, the Métis are contemporary Canadians, and their cultures, like all cultures, have evolved over time. What the cloak of interjurisdictional immunity protects against, in my view, is provincial legislation that would significantly threaten the preservation or perpetuation of the key cultural practices, ideas, and values, generously and contemporaneously defined, of Canada's Métis.

To understand what that generalization means on the ground, it will be necessary to consider a few practical illustrations. They will be grouped for convenience into four categories: family, community, harvesting, and economics.

1) Family

No social unit or educational influence is more important to the propagation of culture than the family, nuclear and extended. I once had the chilling experience of hearing a Manitoba government official proudly explain that he was implementing a policy of assimilation in remote Aboriginal communities by luring their most promising young people from their families to schooling in the south. His goal, expressed as a kind of "tough love," was to undermine communities that the government perceived as having no future — "to drag them into the 20th century."

In my view, interjurisdictional immunity would apply to provincial laws that would adversely affect the membership and protection of Métis families in "vital, essential or integral" ways. A law that would, for example, permit the adoption of a Métis child by non-Métis parents, without adequate regard to the cultural advantage of adoption by a Métis family, would, in my opinion, be inapplicable to Métis children.[42]

This is not to say that provincial adoption laws must require Métis children to be adopted by only Métis parents. If, after consideration of all relevant factors, it is determined that no appropriate Métis applicant parents are available and that the child would be better off with a non-Métis family than in an institutional setting, I doubt that interjurisdictional immunity would stand in the way of the preferable solution. In the *Kitkatla* decision,[43] the Supreme Court of Canada took account of the fact that the statute in question provided for a *balancing* of Aboriginal and other interests in its decision that "core Indianness" was not affected. In my view, a provincial law that permitted non-Métis adoption of Métis children after full and fair consideration of possible adoption by suitable Métis families, would not affect core Métis Aboriginalness ("Métisness") to a "vital, essential or integral" extent.

Precisely what a court would regard as a full and fair consideration of Métis cultural factors in an adoption situation is not easy to predict, of course. In my home province of Alberta, the relevant legislation requires those who make adoption decisions to consider, as the last of seven specified factors:

> in the case of an aboriginal child, the uniqueness of aboriginal culture, heritage, spirituality and traditions, and the importance of preserving the child's cultural identity.[44]

While this factor might be seen as sufficient to ensure an adequate balancing of cultural and other factors, it should be noted that, in the case of an Indian child who is subject to the *Indian Act*, the same Act provides that a person designated by the band in question must, in most cases, be "involve[d] . . . in decisions relating to the adoption of the child."[45] This discrepant treatment of Indian and Métis children might well be considered discriminatory under section 15(1) of the *Canadian*

42 This conclusion would seem to be warranted, in the absence of legislation equivalent to s. 88 of the *Indian Act*, by the *Natural Parents* and *Four B Manufacturing* decisions, above notes 16 and 24 respectively.

43 Above note 33.

44 *Child, Youth and Family Enhancement Act*, R.S.A. 2000, c. C-12, s. 58.1(g).

45 *Ibid.*, s. 67.

Charter of Rights and Freedoms.[46] Whether it would also cause a court to find that interjurisdictional immunity applies because Métis cultural considerations are not given enough weight is a moot question.

2) Community

Community influences are also vital to cultural survival. Provincial laws that impair the establishment or operation of Métis community organizations, be they social, cultural, educational, or philanthropic, should be inoperative. That certainly does not mean that Métis organizations can generally ignore provincial laws. It does mean, however, that they can invoke interjurisdictional immunity where provincial legislation would impair their existence and the promotion of Métis Aboriginal culture.

For example, many provinces have legislation that regulates money-raising activities by charitable organizations.[47] If such legislation presented an insurmountable hurdle to fund-raising by an organization operating in the province for the purpose of preserving and promoting Métis culture,[48] I think a strong legal argument could be made in support of a constitutional exemption. Reasonable restrictions on the methods employed to solicit donations would be applicable, however.

There are many other areas in which culturally significant activities of Métis community organizations could be sterilized by provincial laws. A nursing home for Métis seniors might be denied an operating licence because of bureaucratic concerns remote from the needs or interests of the Métis community. Provincial authorities might lay claim to a historic resource of peculiar interest or value to a Métis people.[49] Provincial cemeteries legislation might pose a barrier to the burial of a Métis leader at a site of cultural significance to his or her people, or the establishment of

---

46 Part I of the *Constitution Act, 1982*, being Schedule B to the *Canada Act 1982* (U.K.), 1982, c. 11.

47 See, for example, *Charitable Fund-Raising Act*, R.S.A. 2000, c. C-9.

48 Providing social services for a Métis community, for instance.

49 Although the *Kitkatla* case, above note 33, permitted the application of provincial heritage resources legislation to trees in which an Aboriginal group claimed a cultural interest, that decision seems to have hinged on evidentiary issues and on the fact that the legislation provided for a balancing of competing interests.

a cemetery for Métis persons generally.[50] Provincial privacy laws might impose unreasonable restrictions and requirements on a small communal Métis organization. School legislation might unduly restrict the operation of Métis educational programs. In such situations, the doctrine of interjurisdictional immunity could overcome such legislative or regulatory barriers. The question, of course, would be to persuade a court that the law in question would impair Métis cultural interests.

3) Harvesting

Historically, a central characteristic of the Métis and their Aboriginal ancestors was their dependence on the bounty of the wilderness for sustenance, trade, and spirituality. Hunting, fishing, trapping, and gathering were vital to Métis life for all of those purposes. For some Métis in the 21st century, this remains the case; for others, wildlife harvesting has ceased to be of major significance for sustenance or economic purposes.

For most Métis, however, the third essential element of natural harvesting — the learning, enlightenment, spiritual refreshment, and traditional continuity that comes from ongoing contact with the land and its cycles — persists, and will continue to do so in the foreseeable future. For the Métis, no less than for other Aboriginal peoples, experiencing and partaking of the fruits of the natural environment lie at the heart of their Aboriginal heritage.

Does the importance of natural harvesting to past and present Métis mean that it is so much a part of "Métisness" that it is protected from provincial laws by interjurisdictional immunity? In principle, I think it should, though there is as yet no closely relevant case law.[51]

The most helpful analogous precedent, *Dick v. The Queen*,[52] dealt inconclusively with the issue in the case of a non-treaty member of a British Columbia Indian band who shot a deer on traditional hunting lands off the band's reserve, and was charged under the provincial *Wildlife Act*.

---

50 For example, s. 3 of the *Cemeteries Act*, R.S.A. 2000, c. C-3, states: "No new cemetery may be established except by a religious auxiliary, religious denomination or municipality." Section 5 states: "No person shall bury a dead human body in any place other than a cemetery . . . ."

51 Refer to comments above at note 33.

52 Above note 30.

The Supreme Court of Canada upheld the accused's conviction on the ground that section 88 made the *Wildlife Act* applicable to Indians. Before reaching that conclusion, however, Beetz J., who spoke for a unanimous Supreme Court, gave sympathetic consideration to the contention that, apart from section 88, interjurisdictional immunity would shield Indians from the provincial Act. Justice Lambert had so held, in dissent, in the Court of Appeal, and Beetz J. said he was "prepared to assume, without deciding, that Lambert J.A. was right on this point."[53] More than that, Beetz J. noted that the assumption was "strengthened" by the following passage from Lambert J.A.'s reasons concerning the impact of the legislation on "Indianness":

> The question of whether provincial legislation affects Indians as Indians, or Indians in their Indianness, to put it another way, is at the root of both arguments that I have considered in this appeal. I think it is worth adding that I have derived some sense of the nature of Indianness from the fact that the Indians in Alberta, Saskatchewan and Manitoba have the right to hunt and fish for food at all seasons of the year (see the Natural Resources Agreements and the *Constitution Act, 1930*, R.S.C. 1970, Appendix No. 25), and the treaty Indians in British Columbia also have the right: see *R. v. White and Bob* (1965), 52 D.L.R. (2d) 481*n*, [1965] S.C.R. vi. I think that those rights are characteristic of Indianness, at least for those Indians, and if for those Indians, why not for the Alkali Lake Band of the Shuswap people?[54]

"On the basis of that assumption," Beetz J. continued, "and subject to [s. 88], it follows that the *Wildlife Act* could not apply to the appellant *ex proprio vigore*."

Consider the situation of a Métis person, say a resident of an Alberta Métis Settlement, who, like the accused in the *Dick* case, hunts for food out of season on unoccupied Crown land off the settlement forming part of traditional Métis hunting territory. If the reasoning that led Lambert J.A. to conclude, in *Dick*, that such hunting affects "Indianness" is valid, would "Métisness" not be similarly affected in our hypothetical? Admit-

53 *Ibid.* at 55.

54 *Ibid.*

tedly, Beetz J. merely *assumed* the validity of the Lambert reasoning, but he gave the distinct impression that he found it compelling.

In my view, the *Dick dictum* and the generally accepted principles on which it is based provide a strong basis for asserting that the cloak of interjurisdictional immunity shields Métis persons from provincial wildlife legislation that would impair their pursuit of traditional hunting, fishing, trapping, and gathering activities.

How can that conclusion be reconciled with existing case law concerning Métis rights? For example, given that *Powley*[55] has already established the existence of Aboriginal Métis hunting rights in appropriate circumstances, what useful additional role can interjurisdictional immunity play? As noted earlier, the existence of Aboriginal rights are distinct from the question of interjurisdictional immunity. Aboriginal rights are group rights that are seldom easy to prove and that do not necessarily have to be proven in order to shield individuals from the brunt of provincial laws. In the *Dick* case, Beetz J. made it clear that "[o]ne issue that does not arise is that of aboriginal title or rights . . . . [T]he case has been argued as if the Indians' right to hunt were a personal one."[56] It is quite possible, therefore, that Métis who could not prove the existence of Aboriginal harvesting rights could still be entitled to exemption from provincial wildlife legislation.

What about the *Blais* case,[57] in which it was held that Métis are not entitled to the hunting rights of "Indians" under the *Natural Resources Transfer Agreements*? That decision, which shattered the hopes of many Prairie Métis, has made it all the more important to explore the validity and implications of the third way that interjurisdictional immunity offers for protection of Métis rights.

If this third way is viable with respect to harvesting rights, how far does it go? Would it, for example, protect sports hunting by Métis persons who genuinely pursue it in search of the Aboriginal spirituality described above? I doubt it. In other contexts, we have seen that interjurisdictional immunity applies only with respect to legislation that goes to the very heart of the federally regulated matter in question; it is highly doubtful that restricting Métis sports hunting activities to the seasons

55 Above note 2.

56 Above note 30 at 51.

57 Above note 4.

and circumstances prescribed for all other hunters would be considered to impair Métis spirituality to so vital an extent.

Little purpose would be served by enquiring in what other respects the application of the principle to harvesting activities might be constrained. Each situation would be governed by its particular facts. But at least in circumstances comparable to those in *Dick*, that is to say harvesting for sustenance on unoccupied Crown land where the individuals' Métis ancestors traditionally did likewise, I believe there is a good chance that the cloak of interjurisdictional immunity could be effectively worn by Métis hunters, fishers, trappers, and gatherers.

4) Economics

Natural harvesting has economic aspects. How might interjurisdictional immunity apply to other economic activities?

Economics can trump culture, and often does. The inability of many Indian reserves to support their populations adequately has, for example, driven many First Nations Canadians to the cities, where the preservation and perpetuation of their Aboriginal traditions is much more difficult than on the reserve. The Aboriginal heritage of Métis, who lack a land base apart from a few exceptions like Alberta's Métis Settlements, is even more at the mercy of economics.

If culture is dependent upon, or heavily influenced by, economic considerations, one would expect, on the basis of the general principles examined above, that interjurisdictional immunity would provide some protection for economic enterprises that bring and hold Aboriginal communities together. The sparse case law that exists suggests that while this may be the case for those enterprises that are of an inherently cultural nature, it may not be so for those which, although not culturally oriented in themselves, help to ensure the community cohesion that is vital to cultural survival.

Consider a paper mill, cooperatively owned, operated, and managed by the members of a Métis community in the north of one of the prairie provinces. Suppose that, to gain a competitive market edge, the management of the mill decides that its employees should be treated less generously than provincial laws relating to minimum wage, hours of work, and other employment standards require. Could it successfully resist the application of those laws?

The most apposite precedent is the *Four B Manufacturing* case[58] where, it will be recalled, the question was whether provincial labour relations legislation applied to a shoe factory on an Indian reserve that was owned and largely staffed by band members, but was a private enterprise rather than a band undertaking. The Supreme Court of Canada concluded that since the dispute concerned the relationship of the employees to a general trade union, a question "about which there is nothing inherently Indian,"[59] there was no reason not to apply the provincial law to the operation.

The breadth of the *Four B Manufacturing* rationale remains in doubt. Justice Bastarache described it too sweepingly, I believe, when he said in passing in *Paul*[60]: "The core has been held not to include labour relations." There is nothing in Beetz J.'s careful analysis of the shoe factory situation in *Four B Manufacturing*, I submit, that suggests the entire subject of labour relations is beyond the protection of interjurisdictional immunity.

Justice Beetz's words could possibly, however, be construed to mean that the protection extends only to those economic enterprises that directly relate, in themselves, to culture narrowly defined: say, for example, a factory owned and operated by an Indian band that manufactured moccasins intended primarily for sale to other Indians for ceremonial purposes, or to a bannock bakery owned and operated by a Métis organization for communal benefit.

In my opinion, so narrow an interpretation would be mistaken. If interjurisdictional immunity is to provide an effective protective cloak for the core, or essence, of "Métisness" from the corrosive influences of the 21st century, it must be applicable to those economic activities, such as the hypothetical paper mill described above, that aim to create or preserve viable communities within which Métis culture can be nurtured. A time-frozen moccasin-and-bannock approach to Métis culture would be useless.

58 Above note 24.

59 *Ibid.* at 397.

60 Above note 34 at para. 33.

H. IMPACT ON PROVINCIAL LEGISLATION OF BENEFIT TO MÉTIS

If provincial legislation that affects vital aspects of Métis Aboriginal culture is rendered inoperative by the principle of interjurisdictional immunity, does it deprive Métis Canadians of the benefit of general provincial statutes that bestow *entitlements* on all residents of the province? What are the implications for Métis-specific provincial statutes, such as Alberta's *Metis Settlements Act*?

In my opinion, the principle has no negative implications for the Métis. Métis persons residing in Alberta, to use my province as an illustration, are Albertans, just like their non-Métis neighbours, and are equally entitled to the full benefit of all provincial laws. A right to which any Albertan is entitled by reason of any statutorily authorized scheme of the province, whether it relates to health care, education, social assistance, matrimonial matters, or adoption, is as available to Métis persons as to anyone else. The fact that their Métis status, coupled with interjurisdictional immunity, entitles them to a constitutional exemption from the obligations of provincial laws that would seriously affect their Aboriginal heritage does not alter that entitlement.

This situation is not peculiar to Métis and other Aboriginal Canadians; it is shared by all persons and enterprises, such as military personnel, airports, banks, and interprovincial railways that are subject to federal legislative jurisdiction, but reside or are located within particular provinces. The situation is a consequence of the unavoidable functional overlap that exists between the federal and provincial spheres of constitutional jurisdiction. In the case of Métis, Parliament's legislative jurisdiction over "Indians, and Lands reserved for the Indians" (section 91(24)) overlaps with the law-making authority of provincial legislators derived from such powers as "Property and Civil Rights in the Province" (section 92(13)) and "Generally all Matters of a merely local or private Nature in the Province" (section 92(16)).[61]

Admittedly, two lines of constitutional attack are open to those who might wish to challenge the validity of such legislation as Alberta's *Metis Settlements Act*. I believe, however, that both would fail.

---

61 *Constitution Act, 1867* (U.K.), 30 & 31 Vict., c. 3, reprinted in R.S.C. 1985, App. II, No. 5.

Although it might be contended that such statutes are *ultra vires* because they relate in essence to the exclusive federal domain of "Indians, and Lands reserved for the Indians," I am of the opinion that the courts would hold that, under the hoary dual aspect doctrine of Canadian federalism, the legislation concerns property and civil rights, or some other overlapping head of provincial jurisdiction.

Another possible ground for attacking the *Metis Settlements Act* and similar legislation would be that it violates the equality guarantees of the *Canadian Charter of Rights and Freedoms*[62] by discriminating on the basis of race and ethnic origin against Albertans who are not Métis. In my view, such a challenge would also be rejected by the courts. There is nothing discriminatory about the Alberta legislation. Like special statutes that are often enacted for the benefit of particular groups or organizations — resource development corporations, municipalities, benevolent associations, universities, and so on — after negotiation and agreement between the Crown and the organization in question, Alberta's *Metis Settlements Act* was the product of negotiations between the provincial government and representatives of the Métis community. In the case of the Alberta Métis, the impetus for the negotiations was a mutual desire to settle a major lawsuit against the province.[63] The *Metis Settlements Act* is no more discriminatory than, say, legislation implementing an agreement to convey Crown land to a religious or ethnic organization, or a statute creating special rules for landholding by religious organizations.[64] Even if I were mistaken in that conclusion, the *Metis Settlements Act* would seem to be immune from attack by reason of section 15(2)[65] or section 1 of the *Charter*.[66]

---

62 [*Charter*], s. 15(1), Part I of the *Constitution Act, 1982*, being Schedule B to the *Canada Act 1982* (U.K.), 1982, c. 11.

63 Fred V. Martin, "Alberta Métis Settlements: A Brief History" in R. Connors & J.M. Law, eds., *Forging Alberta's Constitutional Framework* (Edmonton: University of Alberta Press, 2005) at 345.

64 See, for example, *Religious Societies' Land Act*, R.S.A. 2000, c. R-15. See, especially, s. 11, which applies only to Presbyterian congregations.

65 Section 15(2) protects laws, programs, or activities that have as their object the amelioration of conditions of disadvantaged individuals or groups. Here, the ground would be the historic racial discrimination against the Métis.

66 Above note 62. If the legislation did not withstand scrutiny under s. 15(2), s. 1 might save it as a "reasonable limit" demonstrably justified in a free and democrat-

I. CONCLUSIONS

I summarize my thoughts about the "third way" of protecting the Métis as follows. I believe the Parliament of Canada has legislative jurisdiction, under section 91(24) of the *Constitution Act, 1867*, with respect to the Aboriginal aspects of Métis culture.

Even if Parliament never legislates on that subject, Métis persons and organizations are, by reason of Parliament's potential power to do so, interjurisdictionally immune from provincial legislation that would affect a "vital, essential or integral" aspect of Métis Aboriginal culture. This immunity is more extensive in practice than that which applies to First Nations Canadians because section 88 of the *Indian Act*, which extends provincial statutes to the latter group, does not apply to Métis.

Even if interjurisdictional immunity did not protect Métis from provincial legislation, substantial protection would exist by virtue of the constitutional entrenchment of Métis constitutional rights in section 35 of the *Constitution Act, 1982*. However, section 35 may not protect as many areas of Métis endeavours as would interjurisdictional immunity.

Although it is not easy to predict with confidence what constitutes "vital, essential or integral" aspects of Métis culture, they appear to include adoption, marriage, and other family relations; the activities of Métis social and cultural organizations; and wildlife harvesting and economic activities that are culturally significant.

Interjurisdictional immunity does not operate to deprive Métis persons or organizations of any benefits otherwise available under provincial legislation in the provinces where they reside. Moreover, neither that principle nor the *Charter* affords a basis for striking down beneficial Métis-specific provincial legislation, such as Alberta's *Metis Settlements Act*.

As a gloss on the arguments set out in this paper, I would direct readers to the *Canadian Western Bank* case.[67] The case includes an extensive and important restatement of the principle of interjurisdictional immunity. Although the lengthy discussion on the doctrine was not necessary to resolve the case, eight of the Court's justices chose to comment

---

ic society. I should note that my comments are not meant to say that *every* aspect of such legislation is valid. For example, provisions *detrimental* to Métis culture might be open to challenge.

67 Above note 1.

at length. The majority, in reasons jointly authored by Binnie and LeBel JJ., explained what they perceived to be the doctrine's proper place in Canadian constitutional law.

Justices Binnie and LeBel urged a restrained application of the doctrine. Possibly signalling judicial reluctance to rely upon the doctrine, their comments could result in narrower implications for Métis rights than contended for in the body of this chapter.

Although Bastarache J. agreed with his colleagues as to the result of their decision, he did not concur in their general comments about the scope of the interjurisdictional immunity principle. So far as the general constitutional role of interjurisdictional immunity was concerned, he saw no reason to deviate from classic articulations of the principle. Friends of Métis rights have reason to hope that this attitude will prevail in the future.

Fiddling with Head 91(24): Métis Interjurisdictional Immunity

ALBERT C. PEELING

Whether the Métis in Canada are "Indians" within the meaning of head 91(24) of the *Constitution Act, 1867*,[1] has never been conclusively determined by any court.[2] The question is an important one: if the Métis are Indians and within the scope of head 91(24), it follows that they are entitled to a degree of immunity from provincial legislative and executive authority under the doctrine of interjurisdictional immunity. Interjurisdictional immunity is a doctrine of constitutional law which establishes a core of federal jurisdiction in each class of subjects assigned to the federal government by section 91 of the *Constitution Act, 1867*. This core is beyond the reach of provincial authority. In this paper I propose to examine the application of the doctrine of interjurisdictional immunity to Métis people.

The paper begins with an examination of whether the Métis are "Indians" within the meaning of the phrase "Indians, and Lands reserved for the Indians" as it is used in head 91(24) of the *Constitution Act, 1867*. I then consider the sorts of activities that might be protected from the

1 (U.K.), 30 & 31 Vict., c. 3, reprinted in R.S.C. 1985, App. II, No. 5.

2 For an in-depth discussion of the issue, see Clem Chartier, "'Indian': An Analysis of the Term as Used in Section 91(24) of the *British North America Act, 1867*" (1978–1979) 43 Sask. L. Rev. 37; Mark L. Stevenson, "Section 91(24) and Canada's Legislative Jurisdiction with Respect to the Métis" (2002) 1 Indigenous L.J. 237; Mark L. Stevenson, "Métis Aboriginal Rights and the 'Core of Indianness'" (2004) 67 Sask. L. Rev. 301.

reach of provincial laws by the doctrine of interjurisdictional immunity. Finally, I look briefly at the differences between Métis people and Indians with respect to provincial legislative authority in light of section 88 of the *Indian Act*.[3]

A. DO THE MÉTIS FALL WITHIN EXCLUSIVE FEDERAL JURISDICTION UNDER HEAD 91(24) OF THE *CONSTITUTION ACT, 1867*?

In this part of the paper, I set out some of the arguments relating to the Métis people and the reach of head 91(24). The arguments are doctrinal and historical, textual and structural, prudential and ethical. I have borrowed the classification of arguments used here from Phillip Bobbitt's helpful work on constitutional argumentation, *Constitutional Fate*.[4] In addressing the question of whether the Métis are Indians within the meaning of head 91(24) of the *Constitution Act, 1867*, I propose to draw heavily upon Bobbitt's typology and will define each archetype of argument as I discuss and apply them.

The first archetype Bobbitt sets out is *historical*, which he defines as argument that relies on the intent of the constitutional drafters and the beliefs and attitudes prevalent at the time of ratification.[5]

Historical argument is argument based on legislative intention. In terms of the question of the scope of head 91(24) of the *Constitution Act, 1867*, one must consider the intention of both the Fathers of Confederation and the imperial Parliament. It is also necessary to consider what the intention was in 1867 and whether that original intention was altered by the amendment of the Constitution in 1982.

Textual argument relies on the current understanding of the words of the text.

The words in head 91(24), "Indians, and Lands reserved for the Indians," do not provide us with an obvious answer to the questions we are asking: "Who are Indians?" and specifically, "Are Métis Indians?" Furthermore, the quest for meaning is not helped by the *Confederation*

---

3 *Indian Act*, R.S.C. 1985, c. I-5.

4 Philip Bobbitt, *Constitutional Fate: Theory of the Constitution* (New York: Oxford University Press, 1982, 1984).

5 *Ibid.* at 7.

Debates,[6] which have been referred to by the Supreme Court of Canada in several cases[7]. Head 91(24) was mentioned, according to my review of those debates, only twice: once at the beginning of the debates when the draft of the Confederation legislation was read and once at the end, when it was read again.

It seems that the assignment of Indians to the federal government was a continuation of the imperial policy of removing jurisdiction over Aboriginal people from local legislatures, on the theory that the federal government was more removed from the influence and interests of local majorities. Prof. Peter Hogg notes two reasons for placing responsibility for Indians in the central government. One was premised on the perceived lack of self-interest that this entity would exercise in dealing with Indians and their lands. The second related to a desire for similar policies to be implemented across the country.[8]

Hogg's arguments are essentially *structural* in character, that is, they are based upon an idea that principles can be traced to the structure and institutions of government.[9]

The first of Hogg's arguments can be supported historically by a report made to the imperial House of Commons in 1837, which stated:

> The protection of the Aborigines should be considered as a duty peculiarly belonging and appropriate to the Executive Government, as administered either in this country or by the Governors of the respective Colonies. This is not a trust which could conveniently be confided to the local Legislatures. In proportion as those bodies are qualified for the right discharge of their proper functions, they will be unfit for the performance of this office .... Whatever may be the legislative system of any Colony, we therefore advise that, as far as possible the Aborigines be withdrawn from its control. In the formation of any new colonial constitution, or in the amendment of any which now exist, we think that

6 *Parliamentary Debates on the Subject of the Confederation of the British North American Provinces* (Quebec: Hunter, Rose & Co., 1865; Ottawa: King's Printer, 1951).

7 See, for example, *Reference re Manitoba Language Rights*, [1985] 1 S.C.R. 721 at 739; and *Re B.C. Motor Vehicle Act*, [1985] 2 S.C.R. 486.

8 Peter Hogg, *Constitutional Law of Canada*, 3d ed. (Scarborough, ON: Carswell, 1992) s. 27.1(a) (references omitted).

9 Bobbitt, above note 4 at 7.

> the initiative of all enactments affecting the Aborigines should be vested in the officer administering the Government; that no such law should take effect until it had been expressly sanctioned by the Queen except in cases of evident and extreme emergency; that copies of all such laws should he communicated to both Houses of Parliament with all convenient dispatch; and that the Governor of each Colony should he invested by Her Majesty, so far as the Royal Prerogative should be adequate to the Purpose, with authority for the decision of all questions affecting the interests of the native tribes.[10]

It is noteworthy that the report includes a discussion of the people of Red River as Aborigines.

While not all of the recommendations of the report were adopted, it does show clearly that British politicians before and at the time of Confederation were aware of a fundamental conflict of interest between Aboriginal peoples and settlers. Although the drafters of the Constitution chose to protect the Aboriginal peoples from the settlers by assigning power and responsibility for Aboriginal peoples to the federal government rather than reserving it for the imperial government, their choice still is reflective of an idea inherent in and fundamental to federalism: liberty of peoples is promoted by dividing sovereignty and authority. As Lord Acton wrote:

> Of all checks on democracy, federalism has been the most efficacious and the most congenial .... The Federal system limits and restrains sovereign power by dividing it, and by assigning to government only certain defined rights. It is the only method of curbing not only the majority but the power of the whole people ....[11]

It is troubling that, in the wake of the *Charter* and section 35,[12] the protections inherent in federalism are often forgotten.

---

10 *Report from the Select Committee on Aborigines: British Settlements* (1836; repr., Shannon: Irish University Press, 1968) at 77.

11 John E.E. Dalberg Acton, First Baron Acton, *The History of Freedom and Other Essays*, ed. by J. N. Figgis & R. V. Laurence (London: Macmillan, 1907) at 98, online: http://oll.libertyfund.org/index.php?option=com_staticxt&staticfile=show.php%3Ftitle=75&Itemid=27.. See also F.A. Hayek, *The Constitution of Liberty* (London: Routledge, 1960) at 184, where the point is discussed.

12 *Constitution Act, 1982*, being Schedule B to the *Canada Act 1982* (U.K.), 1982, c. 11.

If a perceived conflict of interest between Aboriginal peoples and settlers lay behind the assignation of head 91(24) by the imperial Parliament to the federal government rather than to the local legislatures, that supports the conclusion that the Métis should be included within its reach. The historical record shows that, like other Aboriginal peoples, the Métis were in conflict with settlers and were prejudiced by the encroachment of settlers. The events leading up to the two uprisings of the Métis led by Louis Riel provide ample proof of this.

Hogg suggests that another reason for the assignment of jurisdiction over Indians to the federal government was the desire to maintain uniform national policies with respect to Aboriginal peoples. This argument also supports the conclusion that Métis should fall within the scope of head 91(24) and receive the same constitutional treatment as other Aboriginal peoples.

There is doctrinal support that the desire for uniform treatment of Aboriginal peoples in Canada explains why head 91(24) is a head of federal power. Bobbitt defines *doctrinal* argument as that which can be derived from precedent.[13] In no less an authority than the *St. Catherine's Milling and Lumber* case, Lord Watson said:

> It appears to be the plain policy of [head 91(24) of the *Constitution Act, 1867*] that, in order to ensure uniformity of administration, all such lands, and Indian affairs generally, shall be under the legislative control of one central authority.[14]

In terms of doctrinal argument, academically one would be hard pressed to find a serious contention that the Métis are not within the scope of head 91(24). There are however two cases concerning the meaning of the term *Indians* which must be commented upon: *Reference re Term "Indians,"*[15] and *R. v. Blais.*[16]

In *Reference re Term "Indians"* the Supreme Court decided that Inuit were Indians within the meaning of head 91(24). The issue arose out of a

13 Bobbitt, above note 4 at 7.

14 *St. Catherine's Milling and Lumber Co. v. The Queen* (1888), 14 App. Cas. 46 at 59 (J.C.P.C.).

15 [1939] S.C.R. 104. Elsewhere in this volume, this case is referred to as *Reference re Eskimos.*

16 [2003] 2 S.C.R. 236 [*Blais*].

dispute between the federal government and the government of Quebec, neither of which wanted constitutional responsibility for the Inuit. This reluctance to accept constitutional responsibility, rooted in a desire to avoid the duty to spend money on the Inuit for their benefit and on the administration of laws and policies in relation to them, led to a constitutional reference before the Court. A similar reluctance on the part of federal and provincial governments with respect to the Métis probably explains why their status under head 91(24) has never been conclusively determined. For our purposes, *Reference re Term "Indians"* is important because all of the judges agreed that the meaning of "Indians" in head 91(24) was synonymous with the Aboriginal peoples of Canada.

The judges tended to adopt a historical approach to interpretation of the term *Indians* as can be seen from this excerpt from the judgment of Duff C.J.:

> The *British North America Act* is a statute dealing with British North America, and, in determining the meaning of the word "Indians" in the statute, we have to consider the meaning of that term as applied to the inhabitants of British North America. In 1867 more than half of the Indian population of British North America were within the boundaries of Rupert's Land and the North-Western Territory; and of the Eskimo population nearly ninety per cent. were within those boundaries. It is, therefore, important to consult the reliable sources of information as to the usage of the term "Indian" in relation to the Eskimo in those territories. Fortunately, there is evidence of the most authoritative character furnished by the Hudson's Bay Company itself.[17]

The Chief Justice then referred to a census prepared for a committee of the House of Commons in 1856 and 1857.[18]

> The Indian Races shown in detail in the foregoing census may be classified as follows:

Thickwood Indians on the east side of the Rocky Mountains	35,000
The Plain Tribes (Blackfeet, etc.)	25,000
The Esquimaux	4,000

17 Above note 15 at 106.

18 *Ibid.* at 107.

Indians settled in Canada	3,000
Indian in British Oregon and on the North West Coast	80,000
Total Indians	147,000
Whites and half-breeds in Hudson's Bay Territory	11,000
Souls	158,000

The census did not treat Half-breeds as Indians, but they are not really treated as whites either. It may have been written in this way to enhance the European presence in the territories. The fact that Métis participation in the fur trade was of particular importance to the Hudson's Bay Company, as governor of Rupert's Land and fur-trade monopolist, may also have contributed to the characterization of the Métis. I note that in other documents Half-breeds are counted along with Indians. For example, in his reasons, Duff C.J. also emphasized the following sentence from an 1869 report:

> In this number about 300 Indians and half-breeds of the Esquimaux and Mountaineer races are included.[19]

In considering whether the Inuit are included within the meaning of "Indians," the Chief Justice also referred to an 1849 report by the Bishop of Newfoundland:

> With the exception of Mrs. Saunders, there is not an Englishwomen on the coast, from Battle Harbour to Sandwich Bay; all, or nearly all, are Indians (Esquimaux or mountaineer), or half Indians, and of course the children are the same mixed race.[20]

Chief Justice Duff concluded from these examples that the Inuit are indeed Indians for the purposes of head 91(24):

> Thus it appears that, through all the territories of British North America in which there were Eskimo, the term "Indian" was employed by well established usage as including these as well as the other aborigines; and I repeat the *British North America Act*, in so far as it deals with the subject of Indians must, in my opinion, be taken to contemplate the Indians of British North America as a whole.

19 *Ibid.* at 112.

20 *Ibid.* at 113.

> . . .
>
> Nor can I agree that the context (in head no. 24) has the effect of restricting the term "Indians." If "Indians" standing alone in its application to British North America denotes the aborigines, then the fact that there were aborigines for whom lands had not been reserved seems to afford no good reason for limiting the scope of the term "Indians" itself.[21]

This statement seems to forecast the rulings in *Cardinal v. Alberta (Attorney General)*[22] and *Four B Manufacturing Ltd. v. United Garment Workers of America*[23]; particularly that head 91(24) enumerates two subjects of exclusive federal jurisdiction and is not to be interpreted conjunctively as Indians on lands reserved for the Indians. It seems clear that for Duff C.J., the term *Indians* was synonymous with Aboriginal peoples. The same can be said of the other judgments in the case. Justice Cannon wrote:

> The correspondence between Sir John Macdonald and Sir Hector Langevin with reference to the relief to be given to the Montagnais and Eskimo Indians of the Lower St. Lawrence would show that these two Fathers of the Confederation always understood that the English word "Indians" was to be construed and translated as "sauvages" which admittedly did include *all* the aborigines living within the territories in North America under British authority, whether Imperial, Colonial, or subject to the administrative powers of the Hudson Bay Company.[24]
>
> . . .
>
> This, I think, disposes of the very able argument on behalf of the Dominion that the word "Indians" in the *British North America Act* must be taken in a restricted sense. The Upper and Lower Houses of Upper and Lower Canada petitioners to the Queen, understood that the English word "Indians" was equivalent to or equated the French word "Sauvages" and included all the present and future aborigines native subjects of the proposed Confederation of British North America, which at the time was intended to include Newfoundland.[25]

---

21 *Ibid.* at 114–17.

22 [1974] S.C.R. 695.

23 [1980] 1 S.C.R. 1031.

24 Above note 15 at 117.

25 *Ibid.* at 118.

A similar approach is evident in the concurring judgment of Kerwin J.:

> There are also a few other publications to which our attention has been called where "Indians" and "Esquimaux" are differentiated but the majority of authoritative publications, and particularly those that one would expect to be in common use in 1867, adopt the interpretation that the term "Indians" includes all the aborigines of the territory subsequently included in the Dominion.[26]

Justice Kerwin also referred to the fact that in 1924, the *Indian Act* was specifically amended to confirm that the superintendent general of Indian Affairs had jurisdiction over "Eskimo affairs." I note that the *Indian Act* has also referred to Métis people in earlier times, something that allows us to make a specific type of historical argument: it is based on the canon of construction *contemporanea exposito,* explained in *Campbell College, Belfast (Governors) v. Commissioner of Valuation for Northern Ireland*, in the following terms:

> As to *contemporanea exposito*, this doctrine is I believe truly confined to the construction of ambiguous language used in very old statutes where indeed the language itself may have had a different meaning in those days. As Mr. Baron Martin said in *Morgan v. Crawshay*, [1871] L.R. 5 304, 315, in delivering the opinion of the judges to your Lordships' House: "In construing old statutes it has been usual to pay great regard to the construction put on them by the judges who lived at or soon after the time when they were made because they were best able to judge of the intention of the makers at the time."[27]

Thus, one clue to the meaning of the term *Indians* as a head of power lies in the way in which that power was exercised soon after Confederation. It is important to note that in its earliest form, the *Indian Act* dealt specifically with the Métis in defining Indians:

> 3. The term "Indian" means
>
> First. Any male person of Indian blood that is reputed to belong to a particular band;
>
> Secondly. Any child of such person;

26 *Ibid.* at 121.

27 [1964] 1 W.L.R. 912 at 941 (H.L. (Northern Ireland)).

> Thirdly. Any woman who is lawfully married to such person;
>
> . . .
>
> [e] provided also that no half breed in Manitoba who has shared in the distribution of half-breed lands shall be accounted an Indian; and no half-breed head of a family [except the widow of an Indian, or a half-breed who has already been admitted into a treaty], shall, unless there are very special circumstances, to be determined by the superintendent general or his agent, be accounted an Indian or entitled to be admitted into any Indian treaty.
>
> 4. The term "non-treaty Indian" means any person of the Indian blood who is reputed to belong to any regular band, for whom follows the Indian mode of life even though such person be only a temporary resident in Canada.[28]

From this, it can be seen that the project of the Department of Indian Affairs was from the very beginning to limit the scope of its jurisdiction. It also demonstrates that the definition of "Indian" was uncertain and based on reputation.[29] But in the earliest *Indian Act*, in any event, it seems that the only thing separating Métis from Indians was the fact that they took scrip, a separation based not on the natural limits of the term "Indians" in head 91(24), but on administrative convenience. I would emphasize that the definition of "Indian" in the earliest *Indian Act* confirms that the term "Indians" in head 91(24) included Métis, but that any Métis who took scrip lost the right to be considered an Indian.

For the act of taking scrip to extinguish Indian status (apart from arguments about the clear and plain intention of the legislature), Parliament would have to have the jurisdiction to define the scope of head 91(24). It does not. In a federal state such as Canada, the legislative branches of both the federal and provincial governments are incapable of exercising judicial or definitional functions where a constitutional question is involved. This is a limitation on the British tradition of the supremacy of Parliament. As Kerwin C.J. said in *British Columbia Power Corporation v. British Columbia Electric Company*:

---

28 *Indian Act*, S.C. 1876, c. 18.

29 See Frank Tough's discussion of this issue in Chapter 7.

> In a federal system, where legislative authority is divided, as are also the prerogatives of the Crown, as between the Dominion and the Provinces, it is my view that it is not open to the Crown, either in right of Canada or of a Province, to claim a Crown immunity based upon an interest in certain property, where its very interest in that property depends completely and solely on the validity of the legislation which it has itself passed, if there is a reasonable doubt as to whether such legislation is constitutionally valid. To permit it to do so would be to enable it, by the assertion of rights claimed under legislation which is beyond its powers, to achieve the same results as if the legislation were valid. In a federal system it appears to me that, in such circumstances, the Court has the same jurisdiction to preserve assets whose title is dependent on the validity of the legislation as it has to determine the validity of the legislation itself.[30]

This statement is a federalist extension of a fundamental constitutional principle limiting the power of the executive in the United Kingdom, put in these terms by Lord Wilberforce:

> Legislation . . . is passed by Parliament, and put in the form of written words. This legislation is given legal effect upon subjects by virtue of judicial decision, and it is the function of the courts to say what the application of the words used to particular cases or individuals is to be. This power which has been devolved upon the judges from the earliest times is an essential part of the constitutional process by which subjects are brought under the rule of law — as distinct from the rule of the King or the rule of Parliament; and it would be a degradation of that process if the courts were to be merely a reflecting mirror of what some other interpretation agency might say. The saying that it is the function of the courts to ascertain the will or intention of Parliament is often enough repeated, so often indeed as to have become an incantation. If too often or unreflectingly stated, it leads to neglect of the important element of judicial construction; an element not confined to a mechanical analysis of today's words, but, if this task is to be properly done, related to such matters as intelligibility to the citizen, constitutional propriety, con-

30 [1962] S.C.R. 642 at 644–45.

> siderations of history, comity of nations, reasonable and non-retroactive effect and, no doubt, in some contexts, to social needs.
>
> It is sound enough to ascertain, if that can be done, the objectives of any particular measure, and the background of the enactment: but to take the opinion, whether of a Minister or an official or a committee, as to the intended meaning in particular applications of a clause or a *phrase,* would be a stunting of the law and not a healthy development.[31]

Effectively, the power of constitutional definition belongs only to one who has the power to amend the Constitution. The role of the courts is to construe the language of the Constitution. Executive or administrative understanding of the law must be used cautiously; in this case, it certainly does not undermine the argument that Métis are Indians within the meaning of head 91(24).

The issue in *Blais* was whether the Métis are Indians within the meaning of the *Natural Resources Transfer Agreements* (NRTAs). These agreements between the federal government and each of the provinces of Manitoba, Saskatchewan, Alberta, and British Columbia transferred land owned by the federal government to the provinces, to bring those provinces into symmetry with the eastern provinces that own the land. The NRTAs were given constitutional force by the *Constitution Act, 1930.* Those of Manitoba, Saskatchewan, and Alberta contain a provision which gives to Indians some specific immunity from provincial laws, but also broaden the power that a province may bring to bear upon Indians. Paragraph 13 of the Manitoba NRTA reads as follows:

> In order to secure to the Indians of the Province the continuance of the supply of game and fish for their support and subsistence, Canada agrees that *the laws respecting game in force in the Province from time to time shall apply to the Indians within the boundaries thereof,* provided, however, that the said Indians shall have the right, which the Province hereby assures to them, of hunting, trapping and fishing game and fish for food at all seasons of the year on all unoccupied Crown lands and on any other lands to which the said Indians may have a right of access.[32]

---

31 *Black-Clawson International Ltd. v. Papierwerke Waldhof-Aschaffenburg,* [1975] A.C. 591 at 629–30 (H.L.).

32 *Manitoba Natural Resources Transfer Act,* C.C.S.M. c. N30, Sch.

This is an exception to the general rule under the doctrine of interjurisdictional immunity that provincial game laws do not apply to Indians under head 91(24) of their own force. Though the courts have tended to describe the NRTA as a *quid pro quo*, it certainly seems to be more *quo* than *quid*. I note that *R. v. Horseman*[33] and *R. v. Badger*[34] decided that one effect of the NRTA was to take away the commercial element in their hunting, fishing, and trapping rights. The benefit to Indians derived from the NRTA was the territorial extension of their treaty rights throughout the province in which they resided. However, most recently in *Mikisew Cree First Nation v. Canada (Minister of Canadian Heritage)*,[35] Binnie J. questioned whether it really is a benefit. Writing for the Court, he said:

> [The Minister asserts], at para. 96 of her factum, that the test ought to be "whether, after the taking up, it still remains reasonably practicable, *within the Province as a whole*, for the Indians to hunt, fish and trap for food [to] the extent that they choose to do so" (emphasis added). This cannot be correct. It suggests that a prohibition on hunting at Peace Point would be acceptable so long as decent hunting was still available in the Treaty 8 area north of Jasper, about 800 kilometres distant across the province, equivalent to a commute between Toronto and Quebec City (809 kilometres) or Edmonton and Regina (785 kilometres). One might as plausibly invite the truffle diggers of southern France to try their luck in the Austrian Alps, about the same distance as the journey across Alberta deemed by the Minister to be an acceptable fulfilment of the promises of Treaty 8.[36]

And further:

> The arguments of the federal and Alberta Crowns simply ignore the significance and practicalities of a First Nation's traditional territory. Alberta's 23 square kilometre argument flies in the face of the injurious affection of surrounding lands as found by the trial judge. More significantly for aboriginal people, as for non-aboriginal people, location is important. Twenty-three square kilometres alone is serious if it

---

33 [1990] 1 S.C.R. 901.

34 [1996] 1 S.C.R. 771.

35 2005 SCC 69 at para. 45 [emphasis in original].

36 *Ibid.* at para. 45.

> includes the claimants' hunting ground or trap line. While the Mikisew may have rights under Treaty 8 to hunt, fish and trap throughout the Treaty 8 area, it makes no sense from a practical point of view to tell the Mikisew hunters and trappers that, while their own hunting territory and traplines would now be compromised, they are entitled to invade the traditional territories of other First Nations distant from their home turf (a suggestion that would have been all the more impractical in 1899 .... *Badger* recorded that a large element of the Treaty 8 negotiations were the assurances of *continuity* in traditional patterns of economic activity. Continuity respects traditional patterns of activity and occupation. The Crown promised that the Indians' rights to hunt, fish and trap would continue "after the treaty as existed before it" (p. 5). This promise is not honoured by dispatching the Mikisew to territories far from their traditional hunting grounds and traplines.
>
> ...
>
> The "meaningful right to hunt" is not ascertained on a treaty-wide basis (all 840,000 square kilometres of it) but in relation to the territories over which a First Nation traditionally hunted, fished and trapped, and continues to do so today. If the time comes that in the case of a particular Treaty 8 First Nation "no meaningful right to hunt" remains over *its* traditional territories, the significance of the oral promise that "the same means of earning a livelihood would continue after the treaty as existed before it" would clearly be in question, and a potential action for treaty infringement, including the demand for a *Sparrow* justification, would be a legitimate First Nation response.[37]

Given the fact that the NRTA is a wolf in sheep's clothing, it is no great loss that the Métis are not "protected" by it; instead, since it does not apply to them, they may be able to assert commercial hunting and trapping rights. The history of the Métis and their involvement in the fur trade certainly makes it possible that they have commercial rights. This wolfish aspect of the NRTA was recognized in *Blais*:

> Paragraph 13 both affirmed and limited the Province's regulatory power: *Frank v. The Queen*, [1978] 1 S.C.R. 95, at p. 100; *Moosehunter v. The Queen*, [1981] 1 S.C.R. 282, at p. 285; *R. v. Horseman*, [1990] 1 S.C.R. 901,

37 *Ibid.* at paras. 47 & 48.

> at pp. 931–32; *R. v. Badger*, [1996] 1 S.C.R. 771, at para. 45. It affirmed the Province's power to regulate hunting for conservation purposes (see *Badger*, *supra*, at para. 71) but it carved out a protected space for hunting by Indians on unoccupied Crown lands and on lands to which the Indians have a right of access. Other potential sources of aboriginal hunting rights exist outside of the para. 13 framework, such as time-honoured practices recognized by the common law and protected by s. 35 of the *Constitution Act, 1982*. However, because Mr. Blais grounds his claim exclusively in para. 13 of the *NRTA*, we must confine our reasoning to this provision.[38]

Later in the paper, another wolf in sheep's clothing, section 88 of the *Indian Act*, will be discussed.

In *Blais*, the Supreme Court concluded that the historical record did not support a finding that the Métis were considered Indians at the time the NRTA was entered into. The following excerpts from the decision illustrate the Court's approach and its findings:

> The difference between Indians and Métis appears to have been widely recognized and understood by the mid-19th century. In 1870, Manitoba had a settled population of 12,228 inhabitants, almost 10,000 of whom were either English Métis or French Métis. Government actors and the Métis themselves viewed the Indians as a separate group with different historical entitlements; in fact, many if not most of the members of the Manitoba government at the time of its entry into Confederation were themselves Métis.[39]
>
> . . .
>
> It could be argued that the ability of individual Métis to identify themselves with Indian bands and to claim treaty rights on this basis weighs against a view of the two groups as entirely distinct. However, the very fact that a Métis person could "choose" either an Indian or a white identity supports the view that a Métis person was not considered Indian in the absence of an individual act of voluntary association.
>
> The Canadian government's response to an 1877 petition from a group of Métis further illustrates the perceived difference between the

38 *Blais*, above note 16 at para. 13.

39 *Ibid.* at para. 21.

Indians and the Métis, and the exclusion of the Métis from the purview of Indian treaties. The Métis petitioners requested a grant of farming implements and seeds, and the relaxed enforcement of game laws to enable them to recover economically from the small-pox epidemic of 1870. David Laird, the Lieutenant-Governor of the North-West Territories, responded to the petition. He concluded by declaring:

> I can assure you that the Government feel[s] a kindly interest in your welfare, and it is because they desire to see you enjoying the full franchise and property rights of British subjects, and not laboring under the Indian state of pupilage, that they have deemed it for the advantage of half-breeds themselves that they should not be admitted to the Indian treaties. (W. L. Morton, ed., *Manitoba: The Birth of a Province* (1984), vol. I, at p. 23)

Without commenting on the motivations underlying the government's policy or on its ultimate wisdom, we take note of the clear distinction made between Indians and "half-breeds", and the fundamentally different perception of the government's relationship with and obligations towards these two groups. We also note that counsel for the intervener, the Métis National Council, told the Court of Appeal: "the Métis want to be 'Indian' under the *NRTA*, but for no other purpose" (para. 75).[40]

. . .

The common usage of the term "Indian" in 1930 also argues against a view of this term as encompassing the Métis. Both the terms "Indian" and "half-breed" were used in the mid-19th century. Swail Prov. Ct. J. cites a North American census prepared by the Hudson's Bay Company in 1856-57 (pp. 146–47). The census records 147,000 "Indians", and breaks this down into various groups, including "The Plain Tribes", "The Esquimaux", "Indians settled in Canada", and so forth. A separate line indicates the number of "Whites and half-breeds in Hudson's Bay Territory", which is estimated at 11,000, for a total of 158,000 "souls". This document illustrates that the "Whites and half-breeds" were viewed as an identifiable group, separate and distinct from the Indians.

The Red River Métis distinguished themselves from the Indians. For example, the successive Lists of Rights prepared by Métis leaders at the

40 *Ibid.* at paras. 24–25.

> time of the creation of the Province of Manitoba excluded "the Indians" from voting. This provision could not plausibly have been intended to disenfranchise the Métis, who were the authors of the Lists and the majority of the population. The Third and Fourth Lists of Rights emphasized the importance of concluding treaties "between Canada and the different Indian tribes of the Province", with the "cooperation of the Local Legislature" (Morton, *supra*, at pp. 246 and 249). The Local Legislature was, at that time, a Métis-dominated body, underscoring the Métis' own view of themselves and the Indians as fundamentally distinct.
>
> There might not have been absolute consistency in the use of the terms "Indian" and "half-breed", and there appears to have been some mobility between the two groups. However, as evidenced by the historical documents statement cited above, the prevailing trend was to identify two distinct groups and to differentiate between their respective entitlements. Dr. Ens indicated in his report: "By 1850 'Half-Breed' was the most frequently used term among English-speaking residents of the North West to refer to all persons of mixed ancestry. It was a term that clearly differentiated between Indian and Metis populations" (respondent's record, at p. 176). At trial, the appellant's expert, Dr. Shore, could not cite any source in which the Canadian government used the term "Indian" to refer to all Aboriginal peoples, including the Métis.[41]

The Court's finding in *Blais* is peculiar in light of its decision in *Reference re Term "Indians"* that "Indians" as used in head 91(24) means all Aboriginal people.

In rejecting the "continuity of language" argument advanced by the appellant, the Court in *Blais* made clear that it was not ruling on whether the Métis fall within the scope of head 91(24).

> The appellant asks us to impose a "continuity of language" requirement on the Constitution as a whole in order to support his argument that the term "Indians" in the *NRTA* includes the Métis. We do not find this approach persuasive. To the contrary, imposing a continuity requirement would lead us to conclude that "Indians" and "Métis" are different, since they are separately enumerated in s. 35(2) of the *Constitution Act, 1982*. We emphasize that we leave open for another day the question of

41 *Ibid.* at paras. 27–29.

> whether the term "Indians" in s. 91(24) of the *Constitution Act, 1867* includes the Métis — an issue not before us in this appeal.[42]

It is difficult to accept that the term *Indians* should be given the same meaning throughout all constitutional documents. Certainly "Indians" as used in head 91(24) is more general (embracing both Indians and Inuit) than it is in section 35(2) of the *Constitution Act, 1982*. In my view the uncertainty over the scope of head 91(24) was removed by the enactment of section 35.

In defining Aboriginal peoples in section 35(2) as Indians, Inuit, and Métis, the drafters of the *Constitution Act, 1982*,[43] must have been cognizant of the ruling of the Supreme Court in *Reference re Term "Indians"* that "Indians" in head 91(24) meant all Aboriginal people. I think that is perhaps the strongest argument in favour of the conclusion that Métis are within the scope of head 91(24). The fact that section 35.1(b) requires that Métis representatives be consulted before head 91(24) of the *Constitution Act, 1867*, can be amended provides further support for this conclusion. If the Métis have no stake in head 91(24), that provision would make no sense.

For the sake of completeness, I will briefly comment on the remaining two archetypes identified by Bobbitt: *prudential* and *ethical*.

The main concern in *prudential* arguments seems to be the protection of the legitimacy of the courts. A typical prudential argument would not answer the question of whether the Métis come within the scope of head 91(24) if the question before the courts could be answered in another fashion. Thus, if Métis hunting rights can be protected under the auspices of section 35, a court likely will not find it necessary to answer questions concerning the scope of head 91(24). I note that the vigour of arguments based on the division of powers has declined since section 35 came into being. I will provide some examples of this constitutional atrophy in the next section of this paper.

Perhaps the most difficult archetype in Bobbitt's typology to grasp is *ethical* argument. Ethical arguments suggest that the national character of Canadians should be reflected in their institutions of government. Ethical arguments are not, however, moral, but are based upon the ab-

42 *Ibid*. at para. 36.

43 Above note 12.

straction of a Canadian identity to which Canada's government should conform.

An example of the use of ethical arguments can be seen in *Reference re Secession of Quebec*, where the Supreme Court held:

> These supporting principles and rules, which include constitutional conventions and the workings of Parliament, are a necessary part of our Constitution because problems or situations may arise which are not expressly dealt with by the text of the Constitution. In order to endure over time, a constitution must contain a comprehensive set of rules and principles which are capable of providing an exhaustive legal framework for our system of government. Such principles and rules emerge from an understanding of the constitutional text itself, the historical context, and previous judicial interpretations of constitutional meaning. In our view, there are four fundamental and organizing principles of the Constitution which are relevant to addressing the question before us (although this enumeration is by no means exhaustive): federalism; democracy; constitutionalism and the rule of law; and respect for minorities. The foundation and substance of these principles are addressed in the following paragraphs. We will then turn to their specific application to the first reference question before us.[44]

These defining principles are expressive of the fundamental quality of the Canadian character, though it seems to me there is also a high degree of overlap with structuralism. In terms of the position of Métis, an ethical argument could be made that differentiating between Aboriginal peoples by not affording them all the same constitutional protections represents a departure from the principle of equality and should be avoided.

B. IMPLICATIONS

If the Métis are within the exclusive jurisdiction of the federal government under head 91(24), provincial legislative authority is limited in two ways:

1. The legislature of a province may not pass legislation that overtly or colourably intends to regulate a federal subject.

44 [1998] 2 S.C.R. 217 at para. 32.

2. Provincial laws are limited in their reach and may not apply to a federal subject with respect to that which makes the subject specifically of federal jurisdiction.

Legislation of the first type, whose pith and substance is federal, is invalid and void *ab initio*. Legislation of the second type is valid, but inapplicable to the federal subject-matter. The second type of limit refers to the doctrine of interjurisdictional immunity.

The Supreme Court gave this explanation of the doctrine of interjurisdictional immunity in *Derrickson v. Derrickson*:

> When otherwise valid provincial legislation, given the generality of its terms, extends beyond the matter over which the legislature has jurisdiction and over a matter of federal exclusive jurisdiction, it must, in order to preserve its constitutionality, be read down and given the limited meaning which will confine it within the limits of the provincial jurisdiction.[45]

A leading case on interjurisdictional immunity is *Bell Canada v. Quebec (Commission de la santé et de la sécurité du travail du Québec)*,[46] where Beetz J. held:

> It should however be noted that the rules stated in this third proposition appear to constitute only one facet of a more general rule: works, such as federal railways, things, such as land reserved for Indians, and persons, such as Indians, who are within the special and exclusive jurisdiction of Parliament, are still subject to provincial statutes that are general in their application, whether municipal legislation, legislation on adoption, hunting or the distribution of family property, provided however that the application of these provincial laws does not bear upon those subjects in what makes them specifically of federal jurisdiction. [47]
>
> . . .
>
> [T]his theory does not confer on Parliament any power that it does not already have, since it is an integral and vital part of its primary legislative authority over federal undertakings. If this power is exclusive, it

45 [1986] 1 S.C.R. 285 at 296.

46 [1988] 1 S.C.R. 749. The criticism of other aspects of this case in *Canadian Western Bank v. Alberta*, 2007 SCC 22 [*Canadian Western Bank*], is noted.

47 *Bell Canada*, *ibid*. at 762 (references omitted).

> is because the Constitution, which could have been different but is not, expressly specifies this to be the case; and it is because this power is exclusive that it pre-empts that of the legislatures both as to their legislation of general and specific application, in so far as such laws affect a vital part of a federal undertaking. The exclusivity rule is absolute and does not allow for any distinction between these two types of statute. However, the pith and substance doctrine does require a distinction to be made between these two types of statute, as well as between laws of general application and their application to particular institutions.[48]

Beetz J.'s reasons are expressly limited to federal subjects. Interjurisdictional immunity is not reciprocal. The reason for this is that, as Beetz J. notes, there is a

> presumption created by s. 91 *in fine*, under which . . . any Matter coming within any of the Classes of Subjects enumerated in this Section shall not be deemed to come within the Class of Matters of a local or private Nature comprised in the Enumeration of the Classes of Subjects by this Act assigned exclusively to the Legislatures of the Provinces.[49]

Because of this constitutional presumption, which is rooted in the constitutional text and supported by case law, if a federal law is valid, and the intention of Parliament is that it apply to subjects that are at the core of provincial heads of power, then the federal law will apply. However, there may be instances where a court will not lightly attribute to Parliament the intention to affect those subjects. The remarks made by the Supreme Court of Canada in *Canadian Western Bank*[50] concerning a theoretical reciprocal provincial immunity are based on cases that illustrate this point. There is a distinction between the reading down of legislation due to an absence of legislative intention (or out of respect for the legislative intention) and the reading down of legislation in spite of the legislative intention. Only the second type is properly interjurisdictional immunity.

One problem with interjurisdictional immunity is that the identification of what makes a subject-matter specifically of federal jurisdiction is inherently vague. The concept of interjurisdictional immunity developed

---

48 *Ibid.* at 840–41.

49 *Ibid.* at 816.

50 *Canadian Western Bank*, above note 46 at para 35.

first in the cases concerning provincial jurisdiction over federal companies, where it has been held that provincial laws apply to those companies, but may not sterilize them or impair their status and capacities. One example that I think is particularly useful to make note of is the application of the principle of interjurisdictional immunity in the case of the Royal Canadian Mounted Police (RCMP). Provincial jurisdiction over the federal police force seems to me to be extremely limited. The protection the RCMP has is especially peculiar given the fact that policing is specifically a provincial responsibility under head 92(14).

In head 91(24), the terms used to describe that federal core jurisdiction are not particularly helpful. Typically, phrases such as "that which affects Indians *qua* Indian" and "that which touches Indians in their Indianness" tend to be used, but to define the core of head 91(24) in such a manner is circular. It provides no real indication of what that core is.[51] Furthermore, to define the core of head 91(24) as in Indianness where the person concerned is a Métis is at least confusing and probably outright misleading. I propose to look at a few cases where the core of head 91(24) is discussed.

In *Dick v. the Queen*[52] Beetz J., writing for the majority of the Supreme Court, appeared to adopt the findings of Lambert J.A. of the British Columbia Court of Appeal concerning the core of head 91(24):

> And, before concluding at p. 495, Lambert J.A. wrote:
>
>> Indeed, I would add that if the facts in this case do not place the killing of the deer within the central core of Indianness, if there is one, or within the boundary that outlines the status and capacities of the Alkali Lake Band, then it is difficult to imagine other facts that would do so.
>
> In *Cardinal v. Attorney General of Alberta*, [1974] S.C.R. 695 at p. 706, it had already been held, apart from any evidence, that provincial game laws do not relate to Indians *qua* Indians. In the case at bar, there was considerable evidence capable of supporting the conclusions of Lambert J.A. to the effect that the *Wildlife Act* did impair the Indianness of

51 The Supreme Court of Canada made similar observations in *Canadian Western Bank*, *ibid.* at para. 43.

52 [1985] 2 S.C.R. 309.

the Alkali Lake Band, as well as the opposite conclusions of the courts below.

I am prepared to assume, without deciding, that Lambert J.A. was right on this point and that appellant's submission on the first issue is well taken.

I must confess at being strengthened in this assumption by what Lambert J.A. said at p. 493:

> The question of whether provincial legislation affects Indians as Indians, or Indians in their Indianness, to put it another way, is at the root of both arguments that I have considered in this appeal. I think it is worth adding that I have derived some sense of the nature of Indianness from the fact that the Indians in Alberta, Saskatchewan and Manitoba have the right to hunt and fish for food at all seasons of the year (see the Natural Resources Agreements and the *Constitution Act, 1930*, R.S.C. 1970, Appendix No. 25), and the treaty Indians in British Columbia also have that right: see *R. v. White and Bob* (1965), 52 D.L.R. (2d) 481 *n.*, [1965] S.C.R. vi. I think that those rights are characteristic of Indianness, at least for those Indians, and if for those Indians, why not for the Alkali Lake Band of the Shuswap people?

On the basis of this assumption and subject to the question of referential incorporation which will be dealt with in the next chapter, it follows that the *Wildlife Act* could not apply to the appellant *ex proprio vigore*, and, in order to preserve its constitutionality, it would be necessary to read it down to prevent its applying to appellant in the circumstances of this case.[53]

In this case, the core of head 91(24) was identified by the concept of impairment of status and capacities, a concept drawn perhaps inappropriately from company law. It will be noted also that the concept was extended to the impairment of hunting and fishing rights of Indians; the *Dick* case concerned events that occurred in 1980, before the patriation of the Constitution and the enactment of section 35. The decision of the Supreme Court of Canada however was rendered in 1985. In my view, it

53 *Ibid.* at 320–21. For more on this issue, please refer to Chapter 10 by Mitch McAdam and Chapter 11 by Kent McNeil.

is one of the great misfortunes of Canadian Aboriginal law that the application of the doctrine of interjurisdictional immunity to Indians was worked out in the shadow of the dialogue on Aboriginal rights. After the enactment of section 35, I think the courts have tended to take a prudential approach to the division of powers as it applies to Aboriginal people. Because section 35 can be used to protect Aboriginal rights, other methods of protection seem to be ignored.[54]

The identification of the core of head 91(24) with Aboriginal rights was reiterated explicitly *in Delgamuukw v. British Columbia* by Lamer C.J.:

> What must be answered, however, is whether the same principle allows provincial laws of general application to extinguish aboriginal rights. I have come to the conclusion that a provincial law of general application could not have this effect, for two reasons. First, a law of general application cannot, by definition, meet the standard which has been set by this Court for the extinguishment of aboriginal rights without being *ultra vires* the province. That standard was laid down in *Sparrow, supra*, at p. 1099, as one of "clear and plain" intent. In that decision, the Court drew a distinction between laws which extinguished aboriginal rights, and those which merely regulated them. Although the latter types of laws may have been "necessarily inconsistent" with the continued exercise of aboriginal rights, they could not extinguish those rights. While the requirement of clear and plain intent does not, perhaps, require that the Crown "use language which refers expressly to its extinguishment of aboriginal rights" (*Gladstone, supra*, at para. 34), the standard is still quite high. My concern is that the only laws with the sufficiently clear and plain intention to extinguish aboriginal rights would be laws in relation to Indians and Indian lands. As a result, a provincial law could never, *proprio vigore*, extinguish aboriginal rights, because the intention to do so would take the law outside provincial jurisdiction.
>
> Second, as I mentioned earlier, s. 91(24) protects a core of federal jurisdiction even from provincial laws of general application, through the operation of the doctrine of interjurisdictional immunity. That core has been described as matters touching on "Indianness" or the "core of Indianness" (*Dick, supra*, at pp. 326 and 315; also see *Four B, supra*, at p. 1047 and *Francis, supra*, at pp. 1028-29). The core of Indianness at the

54 On this topic, refer to the work of Charlotte Bell in Chapter 4.

> heart of s. 91(24) has been defined in both negative and positive terms. Negatively, it has been held to not include labour relations (*Four B*) and the driving of motor vehicles (*Francis*). The only positive formulation of Indianness was offered in *Dick*. Speaking for the Court, Beetz J. assumed, but did not decide, that a provincial hunting law did not apply *proprio vigore* to the members of an Indian band to hunt and because those activities were "at the centre of what they do and what they are" (at p. 320). But in *Van der Peet*, I described and defined the aboriginal rights that are recognized and affirmed by s. 35(1) in a similar fashion, as protecting the occupation of land and the activities which are integral to the distinctive aboriginal culture of the group claiming the right. It follows that aboriginal rights are part of the core of Indianness at the heart of s. 91(24). Prior to 1982, as a result, they could not be extinguished by provincial laws of general application. [55]

It will be noted that the Chief Justice said that Aboriginal rights are part of the core of head 91(24). This opinion implies that the core of that head of power is not exhausted by the concept of Aboriginal rights. In my view, the distinction made in *R. v. Sparrow*,[56] referred to by Lamer C.J., is fraught with difficulty because it draws between laws that extinguish Aboriginal rights and those laws that merely regulate them. To extinguish Aboriginal rights, a law must be expressed in a way that clearly and plainly expresses the legislative intention to extinguish the right. Any such law passed by a provincial legislature is invalid since, by definition, it would affect a subject-matter of exclusive federal jurisdiction. But surely the regulation of Aboriginal rights that are at the core of a federal head of power would also be beyond provincial competence. This line of reasoning is supported in *R. v. Morris*.[57]

One final note with respect to the core of head 91(24) is that "Indianness" is a misleading term. *Reference re Term "Indians"* established that "Indians" means Aboriginal people in the context of head 91(24). The core of head 91(24) would thus be better described as the aboriginality of Aboriginal peoples. But we know from *R. v. Powley*[58] that aboriginality is

---

55 [1997] 3 S.C.R. 1010 at paras 180–81.

56 *R. v. Sparrow*, [1990] 1 S.C.R. 1075 at 1099.

57 [2006] 2 S.C.R. 915.

58 (2003), 230 D.L.R. (4th) 1 at paras. 37–39 (S.C.C.).

different for the Métis than for Indians. At least until the Supreme Court reconsiders its position, the Aboriginal rights of Indians are determined with respect to pre-contact practices. The Aboriginal rights of Métis are determined in relation to practices existing prior to effective control by the settlers. In my view, the core of head 91(24) in relation to Métis people cannot be confined to "Indianness" except insofar as "Indianness" is given a broad and encompassing meaning that includes all Aboriginal peoples — Indian, Inuit, and Métis.

The term *Indianness* also does not seem to me to reflect the core of the second class of subjects contained within head 91(24): "Lands reserved for Indians."

Despite the ruling in *Delgamuukw*, the doctrine of interjurisdictional immunity has been given little application in more recent cases, particularly with respect to head 91(24). In *Paul v. British Columbia (Forest Appeals Commission)*[59] and in *Kitkatla Band v. British Columbia (Minister of Small Business, Tourism and Culture)*,[60] for example, the Court declined to invoke interjurisdictional immunity to provide any protection to Aboriginal peoples from provincial law. Recently, it seems that interjurisdictional immunity is found to be applicable only where Aboriginal rights can be proven (which, in the eyes of the Court, appears to make application of the doctrine unnecessary) or the incidental effect rule has been applied to save the offending provincial legislation. These developments, although consistent with modern approaches to Canadian federalism, do violence to the protective value of federalism when it comes to Indians. As was mentioned earlier, one key feature of a federal system of government is that it provides limits on a government's power. The drift away from exclusive powers and towards concurrency means that the protections of federalism are lost in the name of effective government. The decline of federalism may be an unintended consequence of the adoption of the *Charter*, which to some extent rationalizes and stabilizes the protections of federalism, but may also diminish them. In some respects, it marks the transition from the liberty of Lord Acton's federalism to the cold efficiency of Weberian bureaucracy. It is interesting in this regard to bear in mind how well interjurisdictional immunity

59 [2003] 2 S.C.R. 585.

60 [2002] 2 S.C.R. 146.

protects the RCMP from provincial oversight, even though the Constitution assigns police to the provincial governments.[61]

Section 88 of the *Indian Act* has served to distort federalist lines of authority, something that is particularly troubling in light of the dictum of Rand J. in *Saumur v. City of Quebec*:

> Legislation . . . must be sufficiently definite and precise to indicate its subject matter. In our political organization, as in federal structures generally, that is the condition of legislation by any authority within it: the courts must be able from its language and its relevant circumstances, to attribute an enactment to a matter in relation to which the legislature acting has been empowered to make laws. That principle inheres in the nature of federalism; otherwise, authority, in broad and general terms, could be conferred which would end the division of powers.[62]

I conclude with a brief note concerning the application of section 88. It was established in *Dick v. The Queen* that section 88 of the *Indian Act* referentially incorporates provincial laws of general application as federal laws so that even those provincial laws that touch on the core of "Indianness" may apply to Indians as long as they are otherwise valid and come within the terms of section 88 itself.[63] Section 88 has limited application to Métis people, however, as the *Indian Act* in subsection 2(1) defines the Indian to which section 88 refers as, "a person who pursuant to this act is registered as an Indian or is entitled to be registered as an Indian."[64] Section 88 thus applies only to those few Métis people who are also entitled to be registered as Indians. As a result, provincial laws of general application that would interfere with the rights of the Métis cannot apply to the Métis. It is noteworthy, though, that, as we have seen since the earliest *Indian Act*, Métis people have not been entitled to be registered.

---

61 See *Alberta (Attorney General) v. Putnam*, [1981] 2 S.C.R. 267.

62 [1953] 2 S.C.R. 299 at 333.

63 The complexities concerning the relationship between s. 88 of the *Indian Act*, R.S.C. 1985, c. I-5, and s. 35 of the *Constitution Act, 1982*, being Schedule B to the *Canada Act 1982* (U.K.), c. 11, have been addressed most recently in *R. v. Morris*, [2006] 2 S.C.R. 915.

64 *Indian Act*, *ibid.*, s. 2(1).

C. CONCLUSION

Applying the various forms of argument articulated by Bobbitt makes it clear that Métis people are "Indians" within the meaning of head 91(24) of the *Constitution Act, 1867*. Under the principles of constitutional law, particularly interjurisdictional immunity, provincial laws may not either overtly or colourably regulate Métis.[65] Nor can provincial laws impair the core of the Métis as a federal subject-matter. As the core of federal jurisdiction over the Métis includes, at a minimum, all matters concerning their Aboriginal rights, provincial laws that interfere with the exercise by Métis people of these rights must be either invalid or inapplicable to Métis people and are, in that sense, unconstitutional and may not be justified under section 35 of the *Constitution Act, 1982*.

65 Please refer to Chapter 10 by Mitch McAdam and Chapter 11 by Kent McNeil for a discussion of s. 88 of the *Indian Act* on this area.

‹ 10 ›

Interjurisdictional Immunity and Métis Aboriginal Rights: A Provincial Perspective[1]

P. MITCH McADAM

A. INTRODUCTION

In *R. v. Powley*,[2] the Supreme Court recognized for the first time that contemporary Métis communities can possess Aboriginal hunting and fishing rights that fall within the protection of section 35(1) of the *Constitution Act, 1982*.[3] In a companion case, *R. v. Blais*,[4] the Court held that Métis people are not "Indians" for the purpose of exercising the hunting, fishing, and trapping rights set out in the *Natural Resources Transfer Agreements* (NRTAs) applicable in the prairie provinces, which were confirmed by the *Constitution Act, 1930*.[5] Although the reasoning of the Court in *Blais* suggests that Métis people are not "Indians" for the purpose of section 91(24) of the *Constitution Act, 1867*,[6] that issue was not directly addressed — it remains highly contentious. It will undoubtedly be addressed in other cases, one of which will make its way to the Supreme

1 The arguments set out in this paper with respect to interjurisdictional immunity and Métis rights reflect the position taken by the attorney general of Saskatchewan in *Paul v. British Columbia (Forest Appeals Commission)*, [2003] 2 S.C.R. 585 [*Paul*] and in *R. v. Morris*, [2006] 2 S.C.R. 915 [*Morris*].

2 [2003] 2 S.C.R. 207 [*Powley*].

3 Schedule B to the *Canada Act 1982* (U.K.), 1982, c. 11.

4 [2003] 2 S.C.R. 236 [*Blais*].

5 20-21 Geo. V, c. 26 (U.K.).

6 Above note 4 at para. 21. *Constitution Act, 1867* (U.K.), 30 & 31 Vict., c. 3, reprinted in R.S.C. 1985, App. II, No. 5.

Court. In this paper, I do not intend to address the broader issue concerning whether Métis people are Indians for the purpose of section 91(24) of the *Constitution Act, 1867*. Rather, I will assume that Métis people are, constitutionally, "Indians" and will then examine the implications of the constitutional doctrine known as interjurisdictional immunity for ongoing provincial regulation of the exercise of Métis Aboriginal hunting and fishing rights, referring to recent developments in the jurisprudence. It must, however, be kept in mind that the jurisprudence with respect to the recognition of Métis Aboriginal rights remains in an embryonic state and the jurisprudence with respect to interjurisdictional immunity as it applies to Aboriginals is complicated. The convergence of these two issues results in a complex constitutional conundrum.

B. WHAT IS INTERJURISDICTIONAL IMMUNITY?

The doctrine of interjurisdictional immunity is one of the most poorly understood concepts in Canadian constitutional law. The basic idea can be stated quite simply: each of the various heads of federal jurisdiction set out in section 91 of the *Constitution Act, 1867*, carries with it a basic, minimum, and unassailable core that is off limits or immune from the application of provincial laws that affect the federal subject-matter. The Supreme Court recently clarified that for the doctrine to be applicable, the provincial law must "impair" the federal matter.[7] The application of the doctrine is not dependent upon the existence of a contradictory federal law.

In his textbook, *Constitutional Law of Canada*, Prof. Peter Hogg indicates that the general rule is that provincial laws apply to Indians and lands reserved for Indians, subject to five important exceptions, one of which is interjurisdictional immunity. He describes the doctrine in this context as follows:

> The second exception to the general rule that provincial laws apply to Indians and lands reserved for the Indians is "Indianness". A provincial law that affects "an integral part of primary federal jurisdiction over Indians and lands reserved for the Indians" will be inapplicable to Indians

7 *Canadian Western Bank v. Alberta*, 2007 SCC 22 at para. 48 [*Canadian Western Bank*].

> and lands reserved for the Indians, even though the law is one of general application that is otherwise within provincial competence. This vague exception, which has been framed as precluding laws that impair the "status or capacity" of Indians, or that affect "Indianness", has its analogy in the immunity from provincial laws that affect a vital part of undertakings within federal jurisdiction.[8]

Interjurisdictional immunity is an exception to what is understood to be the norm in Canadian constitutional law reflected in doctrines like double aspect. The courts have long recognized that particular subjects can fall under provincial powers for some purposes, but under federal powers for other purposes. In these cases, there is room for both federal and provincial laws to apply — jurisdiction is essentially concurrent. Another related rule is the incidental effect rule, according to which a valid provincial law can touch on something within federal jurisdiction, as long as the effects are simply incidental or secondary. Both of these rules reflect a view of Canadian federalism that recognizes overlapping jurisdiction. People and lands — or to use the constitutional jargon, "matters" — can be the subject of both federal and provincial laws at the same time. When both federal and provincial laws apply, the doctrine of federal paramountcy is used to sort out conflicts. In cases of conflict, the federal law prevails and the provincial law, while remaining valid in its provincial applications, is inoperative vis-à-vis the federal matter. In the ordinary situation, the Canadian Constitution recognizes that where there is both a federal interest and a provincial interest in a matter, both federal and provincial laws can apply, subject to paramountcy rules. Interjurisdictional immunity is really a remnant of an earlier era in the development of Canadian constitutional law, which is often referred to as the age of watertight compartments. During this era, the courts took a very different view of Canadian federalism and saw federal and provincial powers as largely exclusive. The courts did not countenance the significant overlapping of jurisdiction which has become prevalent in more recent years. The Supreme Court's recent decision in *Canadian Western Bank* affirms that interjurisdictional immunity is contrary to trends in modern constitutional interpretation and should be invoked only exceptionally.

---

8 Peter W. Hogg, *Constitutional Law of Canada*, looseleaf (Scarborough, ON: Carswell, 1997–) at 27-10 to 27-11.

Notwithstanding the Court's restriction of the doctrine, when invoked, interjurisdictional immunity remains an all-or-nothing proposition. Anything that falls on the federal side of the fence is off limits to the application of provincial laws, without exception. According to this characterization of the doctrine, there is no consideration of the effect of the provincial law. In my opinion, the doctrine is too stark. It precludes an examination of the purpose of the provincial law, its real or practical effect on the federal matter, and how the two legislative schemes potentially fit together. This is at odds with modern approaches to interpretation that afford a wide scope for the application of both federal and provincial laws.

C. WHAT DOES INTERJURISDICTIONAL IMMUNITY MEAN FOR MÉTIS ABORIGINAL RIGHTS?

The doctrine of interjurisdictional immunity is relevant to issues concerning Métis Aboriginal rights only if it is accepted that Métis are "Indians" for the purposes of section 91(24) of the *Constitution Act, 1867*, and they are, accordingly, a federal subject-matter. For the purposes of this paper, I will assume that Métis are section 91(24) Indians and examine the question of what, if any, implications the doctrine of interjurisdictional immunity has for the application of provincial laws to Métis people who are exercising Aboriginal rights to hunt and fish. In order to answer this question, it is necessary to determine what matters are at the core of section 91(24) and what the doctrine of interjurisdictional immunity really means for the application of provincial laws to these matters.

I do not intend to deal with the scope of Métis Aboriginal rights in this paper. In *Powley*, the Supreme Court set out the test that must be satisfied to establish the existence of a Métis Aboriginal right. The test consists of two distinct stages. The first stage concerns the community and reflects the fact that Métis Aboriginal rights, like all Aboriginal rights, are communal rights. The person asserting the right must show that a contemporary Métis community exists and that it is the modern emanation of a historic Métis community that existed at the date when a European or Canadian government asserted effective control over the area. This community must have persisted with at least some degree of continuity over the years, and hunting and fishing for food must have been important cultural practices in the historic community and in the community today.[9] The second stage focuses on the individual and determines whether the individual is someone who is entitled to exercise the Aboriginal rights of the contemporary community. The individual must establish Métis identity, membership in the contemporary community, and an ancestral connection to the historic community.[10] It remains to be seen how many rights-bearing Métis communities exist in Canada, what geographical areas their rights can be exercised within, what sort of priorities, if any, Métis Aboriginal rights have vis-à-vis First Nation Aboriginal and treaty rights, and what other Métis Aboriginal rights might exist.

In order to determine what matters concerning Métis people potentially fall within the core of section 91(24), we can examine the case law concerning Indians and the core of section 91(24). There have, however, been few cases about the core of section 91(24). The lack of jurisprudence on this issue can be traced to section 88 of the *Indian Act*.[11] In *R. v. Dick*,[12] the Supreme Court held that section 88 was intended to overcome the doctrine of interjurisdictional immunity vis-à-vis Indians by declaring that otherwise inapplicable provincial laws are incorporated by reference and so apply to Indians. As a result, the courts have not had to grapple with interjurisdictional immunity issues in the context of Indians: provincial laws will either apply directly or will apply indirectly through the operation of section 88, subject only to the exceptions set out in section 88 itself.

Section 88 applies only to "Indians" as defined by the *Indian Act*. It does not apply generally to the Métis, although individual Métis may be entitled to registration as "Indians" under the Act if otherwise qualified.[13] The extent to which provincial laws apply to Métis must accordingly be

9 Above note 2 at paras. 30–33.

10 See, generally, *R. v. Norton*, [2005] 3 C.N.L.R. 268 (Sask. Prov. Ct.); *R. v. Laviolette*, [2005] 3 C.N.L.R. 202 (Sask. Prov. Ct.); *R. v. Willison*, 2006 BCSC 985; and *R. v. Kelley*, 2006 ABPC 17.

11 R.S.C. 1985, c. I-5.

12 [1985] 2 S.C.R. 309 [*Dick*].

13 See, for example, *Canada (Registrar of Indian Register) v. Sinclair*, [2001] 4 C.N.L.R. 11 (F.C.T.D.).

measured solely by interjurisdictional immunity and without consideration of section 88.[14]

The limited jurisprudence on section 91(24) and interjurisdictional immunity does tell us that provincial laws will not apply if they affect the "status and capacities" of Indians,[15] if they regulate "Indians *qua* Indians," or if they touch "Indianness."[16] These concepts are vague, nebulous, and in my opinion, almost meaningless. They tell us little that is helpful in determining whether a particular matter falls within the core of section 91(24).

The case law with respect to interjurisdictional immunity and other heads of federal power is similarly unhelpful. No principles that assist us in defining the core for any particular federal power have emerged. The cases appear to turn more on the court's view of federalism than anything else.[17]

One thing that has been established is that Aboriginal rights fall within the core of section 91(24). The Supreme Court decided this in *Delgamuukw v. British Columbia*[18] which, prior to *Morris*,[19] was undoubtedly the leading case with respect to the application of the doctrine of interjurisdictional immunity and federal power over "Indians, and Lands reserved for the Indians." The precise issue regarding section 91(24) that the Court considered in *Delgamuukw* was whether provincial laws of general application could extinguish Aboriginal title. Chief Justice Lamer's discussion of this issue is summed up at paragraph 181 of his judgment:

> Second, as I mentioned earlier, s. 91(24) protects a core of federal jurisdiction even from provincial laws of general application, through the operation of the doctrine of interjurisdictional immunity. That core has

14 See, generally, *R. v. Alphonse*, [1993] 4 C.N.L.R. 19 (B.C.C.A.).

15 *R. v. Kruger*, [1978] 1 S.C.R. 104 at 110 [*Kruger*].

16 *Natural Parents v. British Columbia (Superintendent of Child Welfare)*, [1976] 2 S.C.R. 751 at 760–61; *Dick*, above note 12 at 326. But see *Canadian Western Bank*, above note 7.

17 This remains so after *Canadian Western Bank*, *ibid*. At para. 43 of that decision, the majority commented that the "development of an abstract definition of a 'core' is not compatible with the tradition of Canadian constitutional interpretation, which favours an incremental approach."

18 [1997] 3 S.C.R. 1010 [*Delgamuukw*].

19 Above note 1.

> been described as matters touching on "Indianness" or the "core of Indianness" (*Dick, supra*, at pp. 326 and 315; also see *Four B, supra* at p. 1047 and *Francis, supra*, at pp. 1028–29). The core of Indianness at the heart of s. 91(24) has been defined in both negative and positive terms. Negatively, it has been held to not include labour relations (*Four B*) and the driving of motor vehicle (*Francis*). The only positive formulation of Indianness was offered in *Dick*. Speaking for the Court, Beetz J. assumed, but did not decide, that a provincial hunting law did not apply *proprio vigore* to the members of an Indian band to hunt and because those activities were "at the centre of what they do and who they are" (*supra*, at p. 320). But in *Van der Peet*, I described and defined the aboriginal rights that are recognized and affirmed by s. 35(1) in a similar fashion, as protecting the occupation of land and the activities which are integral to the distinctive aboriginal culture of the group claiming the right. *It follows that aboriginal rights are part of the core of Indianness at the heart of s. 91(24). Prior to 1982, as a result, they could not be extinguished by provincial laws of general application.*[20]

In *Delgamuukw*, Lamer C.J. draws a distinction between provincial laws that infringe Aboriginal rights and those that extinguish Aboriginal rights. In his view, only provincial laws that extinguish Aboriginal rights either directly or indirectly cross the interjurisdictional immunity boundary-line and are constitutionally inapplicable. Provincial laws that infringe those rights and that are justifiable according to the *Sparrow* test[21] can apply without invoking interjurisdictional immunity concerns.

This view is consistent with other decisions from the Supreme Court which have held that provincial hunting and fishing laws that satisfy the *Sparrow* justificatory test can apply to Indians exercising constitutionally protected hunting rights. For example, in *R. v. Côté*, Lamer C.J. held as follows:

> In *Sparrow*, the Court set out the applicable framework for identifying the infringement of an aboriginal right or treaty right under s. 35(1) of the *Constitution Act, 1982*. It should be noted that the test in *Sparrow* was originally elucidated in the context of a federal regulation which al-

20 Above note 18 [emphasis added].

21 [1990] 1 S.C.R. 1075 [*Sparrow*].

> legedly infringed an aboriginal right. The majority of recent cases which have subsequently invoked the *Sparrow* framework have similarly done so against the backdrop of a federal statute or regulation. See, e.g., *Gladstone*. But it is quite clear that the *Sparrow* test applies where a provincial law is alleged to have infringed an aboriginal or treaty right in a manner which cannot be justified: *Badger, supra*, at para. 85 (application of *Sparrow* test to provincial statute which violated a treaty right). *The text and purpose of s. 35(1) do not distinguish between federal and provincial laws which restrict aboriginal or treaty rights, and they should both be subject to the same standard of constitutional scrutiny.*[22]

This point was made again in *R. v. Marshall No. 2* when, in reference to its earlier decision in *Marshall No. 1*, the Court stated:

> At para. 64, the majority judgment again referred to regulation permitted by the *Badger* test. *The Court was thus most explicit in confirming the regulatory authority of the federal and provincial governments within their respective legislative fields to regulate the exercise of the Treaty right* subject to the constitutional requirement that restraints on the exercise of the Treaty right have to be justified on the basis of conservation or other compelling and substantial public objectives.[23]

The recognition that valid provincial laws can infringe Aboriginal and treaty rights in certain circumstances is simply a reflection of a well-established and long-standing principle of Canadian constitutional law, namely, that legislation within the jurisdiction of one level of government may have an impact on or affect matters within the jurisdiction of the other level. This principle has been applied many times to uphold the applicability of provincial laws to "Indians, and Lands reserved for the Indians." The principle was fully discussed by the Supreme Court in *Cardinal v. Attorney General of Alberta*, a case dealing with the application of a provincial law prohibiting trafficking in wildlife to an Indian on an Indian reserve. Justice Martland, who wrote the majority judgment, described the principle as follows:

---

22 [1996] 3 S.C.R. 139 at para. 74 [*Côté*] [emphasis added]; see also *R. v. Badger*, [1996] 1 S.C.R. 771 at para. 85 [*Badger*], and *R. v. Sundown*, [1999] 1 S.C.R. 393 at para. 38.

23 [1999] 3 S.C.R. 533 at para. 24 [*Marshall No. 2*] [emphasis added], referring to [1999] 3 S.C.R. 456 [*Marshall No. 1*]; see also *Paul*, above note 1 at paras. 24 and 25.

> I am not prepared to accept this initial premise. Section 91(24) of the *British North America. Act, 1867*, gave exclusive legislative authority to the Canadian Parliament in respect of Indians and over lands reserved for the Indians. Section 92 gave to each province, in such province, exclusive legislative power over the subjects therein defined. It is well-established, as illustrated in *Union Colliery Co. of British Columbia Ltd. v. Bryden*, that a province cannot legislate in relation to a subject matter exclusively assigned to the federal Parliament by section 91. *But it is also well-established that Provincial legislation enacted under a heading of section 92 does not necessarily become invalid because it affects something which is subject to Federal legislation.*
>
> . . .
>
> A Provincial Legislature could not enact legislation in relation to Indians, or in relation to Indian Reserves, but this is far from saying that the effect of section 91(24) of the *British North America Act, 1867*, was to create enclaves within a Province within the boundaries of which Provincial legislation could have no application. In my opinion, the test as to the application of provincial legislation within a reserve is the same as with respect to its application within the Province and that is that it must be within the authority of section 92 and must not be in relation to a subject-matter assigned exclusively to the Canadian Parliament under section 91. Two of those subjects are Indians and Indian Reserves, but *if Provincial legislation within the limits of section 92 is not construed as being legislation in relation to those classes of subjects (or any other subject under section 91) it is applicable anywhere in the Province, including Indian Reserves, even though Indians or Indian Reserves might be affected by it.* My point is that section 91(24) enumerates classes of subjects over which the Federal Parliament has the exclusive power to legislate, but it does not purport to define areas within a Province within which the power of a Province to enact legislation, otherwise within its powers, is to be excluded.[24]

Furthermore, several cases in the Supreme Court and in provincial appellate courts have held that the application of provincial hunting laws to Indians does not affect their "Indianness," does not regulate them *qua*

---

24 [1974] S.C.R. 695 at 702–3 [*Cardinal*] [emphasis added]; see also *Rex v. Martin* (1917), 39 D.L.R. 635 at 638–39 (Ont. S.C.A.D.).

Indians, and accordingly, does not raise interjurisdictional immunity concerns.[25]

It has been suggested that provincial game laws apply to Indians in the prairie provinces only because the numbered treaties specifically provide for government regulations and the *Natural Resources Transfer Agreements* (NRTAs) give the provinces specific constitutional authority to apply these laws to Indians. I do not believe that this is a correct interpretation of either the treaties or the NRTAs. First, the Supreme Court held in *Marshall No. 2* that treaty rights are subject to regulations[26] that satisfy the *Sparrow* test whether or not the written text of the treaty expressly acknowledges the possibility of those regulations.

Second, prior to 1930, the prairie provinces could impose their game laws on Indians off-reserve even in the face of treaty rights. The true effect of the NRTAs was not to bestow new powers on the prairie provinces — powers that are not possessed by the other provinces — but rather, to reduce the scope of provincial powers by requiring respect for treaty rights, as modified by the NRTAs. This effect was described by Laskin J. in his dissenting judgment in *Cardinal* as follows:

> It [the *Alberta Transfer Agreement*] is concerned rather with Indians as such, and with guaranteeing to them a continuing right to hunt, trap and fish for food regardless of provincial game laws which would otherwise confine Indians in parts of the province that are under provincial administration. *Although inelegantly expressed, s. 12 does not expand provincial legislative power but contracts it.* Indians are to have the right to take game and fish for food from all unoccupied Crown lands (these would certainly not include reserves) and from all other lands to which they may have a right of access. There is hence, by virtue of the sanction of the *British North America Act, 1930,* a limitation upon provincial authority regardless of whether or not Parliament legislates.[27]

This view of the constitutional effect of the NRTAs was subsequently adopted by Cory J. in his majority judgment in *Horseman* and, therefore,

---

25 See *Kruger*, above note 15 at 110; *R. v. Horseman*, [1990] 1 S.C.R. 901 at 936 [*Horseman*]; *R. v. Paul and Copage*, [1978] 4 C.N.L.B. 43 (N.S.S.C.A.D.); and *R. v. Julian*, [1979] 1 C.N.L.R. 66 (N.S.S.C.A.D.).

26 Above note 23 at para. 14.

27 *Cardinal*, above note 24 at 722 [emphasis added].

should be considered as the authoritative statement on the true effect of the NRTAs with regard to provincial powers.[28] The constitutional authority that the prairie provinces have to apply their game laws to Indians is accordingly not greater, but more limited than that of other provinces.

My conclusion that the doctrine of interjurisdictional immunity prevents the extinguishment of Métis Aboriginal hunting and fishing rights by provincial laws, but not the infringement of those rights, is consistent with the Supreme Court's jurisprudence concerning interjurisdictional immunity and other matters within federal jurisdiction, such as federally incorporated companies. In these cases, the Court determined that provincial laws can apply to federal entities provided that they do not "sterilize," "paralyze," or "impair" their operations, a standard affirmed in *Canadian Western Bank.*[29] Although later decisions, like *Bell Canada v. Quebec (Commission de la santé et de la sécurité du travail du Québec)*,[30] took a somewhat broader view of interjurisdictional immunity, I believe that those cases could be better rationalized with the other jurisprudence if they had been decided on the basis of an expanded view of paramountcy, not interjurisdictional immunity. Accordingly, it is my view that interjurisdictional immunity should not be seen as a fence which hives off certain subjects, like treaty rights, from the effect of provincial laws in all cases. Rather, in each case, courts should determine the effect that the provincial law has on the exercise of the right. Effects that amount to extinguishment of the right will cross the interjurisdictional immunity boundary-line, while others short of extinguishment will not. It is the effect of the provincial law that is determinative, not the fact that a federal matter is affected. In cases falling short of extinguishment, the *Sparrow* justificatory test and the doctrine of paramountcy will still be relevant, but interjurisdictional immunity will not.

The Supreme Court considered the application of provincial laws to matters falling within federal jurisdiction over "Indians, and Lands reserved for the Indians" in *Kitkatla Band v. British Columbia (Minister of*

28 *Horseman*, above note 25 at 934; see also *Kruger*, above note 15 at 111–12.

29 *Canadian Western Bank*, above note 7. See *John Deere Plow Company Ltd. v. Wharton*, [1915] A.C. 330 at 726 (J.C.P.C.); *Great West Saddlery Company Ltd. v. The King* (1921), 2 A.C. 91 at 200 (J.C.P.C.); Hogg, above note 8 at 15-25 to 15-34.

30 [1988] 1 S.C.R. 749.

Small Business, Tourism and Culture).[31] The issue in that case concerned the application of a provision of British Columbia's heritage property legislation that authorized the alteration or destruction of Aboriginal artifacts, such as culturally modified trees. Justice LeBel, for a unanimous Court, held that the legislation applied and confirmed several important principles that support my thesis. First, the basic assumption in Canadian constitutional law is that provincial laws apply to Indians and on Indian reserves. Second, merely incidental effects will not disturb the constitutional applicability of an otherwise valid provincial law. Third, provincial laws that treat Indians and non-Indians alike will not be rendered constitutionally inapplicable simply because they have a disproportionate effect upon Indians. The constitutional principles recognized in *Kitkatla* must apply to Aboriginal and treaty hunting and fishing rights just as they do to reserve lands and Indian artifacts. There is no juristic reason to distinguish between different aspects of federal jurisdiction under section 91(24).

D. DOES THE CORE OF SECTION 91(24) INCLUDE LAND USES?

To fully understand the implications of interjurisdictional immunity on the ability of provinces to apply their fish and game laws to Métis people exercising Aboriginal hunting and fishing rights, it is also necessary to examine the extent to which interjurisdictional immunity limits the ability of provinces to regulate the use of lands that fall within section 91(24) of the *Constitution Act, 1867*. In *Delgamuukw*, the Supreme Court held that section 91(24) embraces both reserve lands and Aboriginal title lands. The Métis Nation — Saskatchewan has commenced legal proceedings against Canada and Saskatchewan, claiming unextinguished Aboriginal title to a large part of northwestern Saskatchewan.[32] The Métis Nation claims that these lands were historically occupied by Métis people and were used for hunting, fishing, trapping, and gathering. If the claim is successful, these lands, or at least the Métis interest in the lands, would potentially fall within section 91(24) and might, therefore, raise a broader question about the Métis and their relationship to that section.

31 [2002] 2 S.C.R. 146 [*Kitkatla*].

32 *Morin et al. v. Canada et al.*, Saskatoon, File No. 619/1994 (Sask. Q.B.).

The question would be whether the province could continue to apply its fish and game laws to Métis people on these lands or otherwise regulate use of the land.

It is often stated that provincial laws cannot affect the use of reserve lands. The genesis for this proposition appears to be the decision of the British Columbia Court of Appeal in *Peace Arch Enterprises Ltd. v. Surrey*.[33] That case determined that municipal zoning bylaws and provincial construction standards did not apply to a development on a surrendered Indian reserve. In my opinion, the broad proposition is simply wrong and *Peace Arch* should no longer be considered as authoritative. I take this position for several reasons.

First, *Peace Arch* was decided before *Cardinal* and is premised upon the enclave theory that was clearly rejected by the Supreme Court in *Cardinal*. While *Peace Arch* has been referred to by the Supreme Court, it has never been approved or affirmed. More recent case law from several jurisdictions has held that bright-line distinctions between land use and other types of activities are no longer relevant in determining the application of provincial laws on Indian reserves.[34]

Second, there is a logical inconsistency in treating section 91(24) lands different than section 91(24) people. The courts have clearly recognized that section 91(24) people are not immune from the application of all provincial laws. Section 91(24) lands should not be treated any differently. However, if it is accepted that any provincial laws which touch on land use are excluded by interjurisdictional immunity, then that is precisely the effect. Any such conclusion is contrary to the decision in *Cardinal* and would, in effect, revive the enclave theory.

Third, it is practically impossible to distinguish between laws affecting[35] people and laws affecting land. For example, the courts have held that building specifications relate to a use of land[36] but store hours[37] and

33 (1970), 74 W.W.R. 380 (B.C.C.A.) [*Peace Arch*].

34 See, for example, *Rempel Brothers Concrete Ltd. v. Chilliwack (District)*, [1994] 5 W.W.R. 122 (B.C.C.A.); *Brantford (Township) v. Doctor*, [1996] 1 C.N.L.R. 49 (Ont. Ct. Gen. Div.); and *Oka (Municipality) v. Simon*, [1999] 2 C.N.L.R. 205 (Que. C.A.).

35 To the degree of severity stipulated in *Canadian Western Bank*, above note 7.

36 *Peace Arch*, above note 33.

37 *R. v. Duncan Supermarket Ltd.*, [1982] 4 W.W.R. 181 (B.C.S.C.).

rent controls[38] do not. Hunting has been recognized as a use of land in one case[39] but not in others. The lack of a clear line of demarcation between these two categories of laws suggests that no constitutional distinctions should be made between them.

In my opinion, the proper test for determining the application of interjurisdictional immunity with respect to section 91(24) lands should be the same test as is employed with respect to section 91(24) people. The issue is not whether the provincial law affects or touches upon some use of the land any more than the test is whether the provincial law touches upon the activities of people. A proper characterization of the test would be whether the provincial law affects the Indian lands *qua* Indian lands or whether it affects the Indianness of the lands. Such a characterization would focus the inquiry on what is distinctive about the lands and what really is at the heart of section 91(24).

The decision of the Saskatchewan Court of Queen's Bench in *R. v. Fiddler*[40] illustrates this thesis. The accused in that case was an Indian who was charged with two offences under provincial law as a result of a fire he started on an Indian reserve which escaped and damaged nearby properties on and off the reserve. The accused argued that the law did not apply to him because it purported to regulate the use of reserve lands. The attorney general successfully argued that there was no constitutional impediment to the application of the law. The court accepted that interjurisdictional immunity could not be invoked in the case because the accused was a farmer who was burning stubble like any other farmer in the province. While he was clearly using the land, there was nothing uniquely "Indian" about what he was doing. The attorney general acknowledged that the situation may well have been different if the fire had been started as part of some cultural activity or religious ceremony and the provincial law provided a complete ban on these sorts of activities. However, even if the activity had been elevated to the status of an Aboriginal or treaty right, it was the attorney general's position that the exercise of the right, like the exercise of hunting and fishing rights, was subject to safety con-

38 *Re Park Mobile Home Sales Ltd. and Le Greely* (1978), 85 D.L.R. (3d) 618 (B.C.C.A.).

39 *R. v. Isaac* (1975), 13 N.S.R. (2d) 460 (S.C.A.D.).

40 [1993] 3 W.W.R. 594 (Sask. Q.B.).

siderations and the provincial law constituted a justified infringement of any right in issue. It remained constitutionally applicable.

In conclusion, even if the Métis Nation is ultimately able to establish Aboriginal title or some other Aboriginal interest in lands in Saskatchewan, it is my opinion that the nature of the interjurisdictional immunity argument does not change. When it comes to applying the doctrine of interjurisdictional immunity, there is no logical reason to treat section 91(24) lands differently than section 91(24) people. Section 91(24) lands are no more immune from the application of provincial laws than are section 91(24) people. Describing Aboriginal hunting rights as a use of the land, as an aspect of Aboriginal title, or as a reflection of any other interest in the land should not change the essence of the debate or the test to be applied. There still remains constitutional authority for the application of provincial hunting and fishing laws to the same extent as exists in the absence of any underlying Aboriginal title or interest in the land.

E. SASKATCHEWAN CASES DEALING WITH INTERJURISDICTIONAL IMMUNITY AND MÉTIS RIGHTS

Interjurisdictional immunity issues have arisen in a number of cases in Saskatchewan concerning Métis hunting and fishing. In *R. v. Grumbo*,[41] the accused was a Métis man who was charged with unlawful possession of a whitetail deer carcass under the *Wildlife Act*. A defence argument was that hunting and sharing the bounty of the hunt is an important cultural activity for Métis people and falls within the core of section 91(24) of the *Constitution Act, 1867*; therefore, the provincial Act did not apply. The accused did not attempt to portray his possession of the deer as the exercise of an Aboriginal right. The case ultimately made its way to the Saskatchewan Court of Appeal, where the interjurisdictional immunity argument was rejected without much discussion. Justice Sherstobitoff, for the majority, held as follows:

> The division of powers argument was treated by both parties as a secondary argument. Mr. Grumbo argues that, the Crown having stipulated that Métis are Indians within the meaning of s. 91(24) of the *Constitution Act, 1867*, then the provisions of *The Wildlife Act* cannot

41 [1998] 3 C.N.L.R. 172 (Sask. C.A.) [*Grumbo*].

> apply to them as it would be legislation relating to Indians *qua* Indians. The weight of authority clearly says that provincial legislation relating to game is provincial law of general application affecting Indians not *qua* Indians but as inhabitants of the province, and is applicable to them, subject of course to s. 12 of the *Natural Resources Transfer Agreement*; *Cardinal v. The Attorney General of Alberta*, [1974] S.C.R. 695 [[1973] 6 W.W.R. 205, 40 D.L.R. (3d) 553, 13 C.C.C. (2d) 1]; *R. v. Horseman*, at p. 934 [S.C.R.; pp. 104-5 C.N.L.R.]; *R. v. Kruger and Manuel*, [1978] 1 S.C.R. 104, [[1977] 4 W.W.R. 300, 75 D.L.R. (3d) 434, 34 C.C.C. (3d) 377, 14 N.R. 495]. The principle is not affected by the judgment of the Supreme Court in *R. v. Dick*, [1985] S.C.R. 309 [69 B.C.L.R. 184, 23 D.L.R. (4th) 33, [1986] 1 W.W.R. 1, [1985] 4 C.N.L.R. 55, 22 C.C.C. (3d) 129, 62 N.R. 1], where the court was prepared to assume, for the purpose of the judgment, that the legislation in issue affected the Indianness of the accused, because it was specifically said that the court was not deciding the issue. Mr. Grumbo cannot succeed on this ground.[42]

R. v. Maurice,[43] dealing with the Métis and interjurisdictional immunity, followed *Grumbo*. The accused in this case were two Métis men, charged under the *Wildlife Regulations* for hunting at night with lights in an area in northern Saskatchewan where Métis people are recognized to have Aboriginal hunting and fishing rights. One issue in the case was whether the accused could exercise these rights given that they did not live in the area. The Provincial Court held that they could, as they were originally from a Métis community in the area and they maintained a substantial connection to the community. The Crown, however, argued that the Aboriginal right did not include the right to hunt at night with lights or, if it did, the provincial regulations constituted a justifiable infringement of that right for safety purposes.[44] One argument advanced by the defence was interjurisdictional immunity. In brief detail, the defence argued that the provincial law could not apply because of interjurisdictional immunity and that only Parliament could regulate the exercise of Métis Aboriginal hunting and fishing rights. The defence said

---

42 *Ibid* at 185.

43 (2001), [2002] 2 C.N.L.R. 244 (Sask. Prov. Ct.), aff'd [2002] 2 C.N.L.R. 273 (Sask. Q.B.) [*Maurice*].

44 This was prior to the Supreme Court's determination in *Morris*, above note 1.

that whether the *Sparrow* justificatory test could be satisfied in this case was irrelevant because the division-of-powers issue had to be addressed first and the law could not apply because of interjurisdictional immunity. This argument was rejected. The court accepted that interjurisdictional immunity does not prevent provincial laws from infringing Aboriginal rights as long as the infringement is justified. It relied upon the comments of Lamer C.J. in *Delgamuukw*[45] for this proposition and concluded that interjurisdictional immunity only prevents the extinguishment of Aboriginal rights by the provinces.

The law in Saskatchewan therefore appeared to be settled on this point: Métis people exercising Aboriginal rights to hunt and fish were not immune from the application of provincial laws. As long as they could be justified under the *Sparrow* test, provincial fish and game laws were constitutionally applicable even if they infringed upon the right. Interjurisdictional immunity could be invoked only where the effect of the provincial law was to extinguish the right.

F. *R. v. MORRIS*

Not so long ago, the Supreme Court decided a case concerning interjurisdictional immunity and hunting rights. *R. v. Morris*[46] dealt with two treaty Indians from British Columbia charged with a provincial offence for hunting at night with lights. As in *Maurice*, the defence argued that provincial law could not apply to the accused while they were exercising their treaty hunting rights because of the doctrine of interjurisdictional immunity.

The attorney general for Saskatchewan intervened in *Morris* and took a position similar to what had been advanced in *Maurice*. Saskatchewan's position can be summed up in the following five points.

First, cases dealing with hunting by First Nations people pursuant to Aboriginal or treaty rights fall within the double aspect doctrine. Provinces have jurisdiction over hunting and hunting safety. The province's authority to enact such laws is derived from various heads of power under section 92 of the *Constitution Act, 1867*, such as subsection (13) "Prop-

45 Above note 20.

46 Above note 1.

erty and Civil Rights" and subsection (16) "Local Matters,"[47] and from the province's ownership of the resources. This jurisdiction has been recognized for many years.[48] Parliament has jurisdiction over Indians. Hunting by Indian people pursuant to Aboriginal and treaty rights or otherwise accordingly falls squarely within the double aspect doctrine. There is a role or at least a potential role for both levels of government to regulate these activities. Parliament can, of course, always legislate and trump the application of provincial laws by invoking paramountcy. However, there are currently no federal laws with respect to Indians who are hunting off-reserve.

Second, the courts must also recognize that the provinces have an ownership interest in wildlife resources: in the Prairies, the provinces own the wildlife and the fish. Although Parliament may have jurisdiction to regulate hunting or fishing by Indians, this power cannot extend to allocating provincially owned resources. Parliament cannot enact a comprehensive code dealing with hunting and fishing by Indians in the prairie provinces as it cannot allocate provincially owned resources[49] or guarantee access to provincially owned lands for hunting and fishing. Parliament cannot determine the sorts of priorities that, in *Sparrow*,[50] the Supreme Court said were necessary between Aboriginal rights-holders and others. The recognition of provincial ownership reflects a very real provincial interest in the "matter," one that goes beyond legislative jurisdiction.

Third, it was Saskatchewan's submission that the Court should provide a narrow interpretation of the core of section 91(24) and of interjurisdictional immunity generally. This would be consistent with the trend of recent jurisprudence. It would also reflect the fact that interjurisdictional immunity should reflect only the basic minimum and unassailable core of each of the heads of power set out in section 91. Such an interpretation is consistent with the existing jurisprudence on interjurisdictional

47 Above note 6.

48 See, generally, *R. v. Robertson* (1886), 3 Man. L.R. 613 (C.A.); *R. v. Chiasson* (1982), 135 D.L.R. (3d) 499 (N.B.C.A.), aff'd [1984] 1 S.C.R. 266; and *R. v. Custer*, [1998] S.J. No. 567 (Q.B.).

49 *Attorney General for Canada v. Attorneys General for Ontario, Quebec, and Nova Scotia*, [1898] A.C. 700 (J.C.P.C.).

50 Above note 21.

immunity in other areas and with the nature of Canadian federalism. For example, in *O.P.S.E.U. v. Ontario (Attorney General)*,[51] it was argued that a provincial law limiting the political activities of provincial civil servants during federal election campaigns intruded upon the core of exclusive federal jurisdiction over federal elections. After discussing the history of interjurisdictional immunity, Dickson C.J. said that it was "not a particularly compelling doctrine."[52] He accepted the criticisms of the doctrine set out by Prof. Hogg in his textbook and concluded as follows:

> I favour both of these arguments of caution about the scope of the interjurisdictional immunity doctrine. The history of Canadian constitutional law has been to allow for a fair amount of interplay and indeed overlap between federal and provincial powers. It is true that doctrines like interjurisdictional and Crown immunity and concepts like "watertight compartments" qualify the extent of that interplay. But it must be recognized that these doctrines and concepts have not been the dominant tide of constitutional doctrines; rather they have been an undertow against the strong pull of pith and substance, the aspect doctrine and, in recent years, a very restrained approach to concurrency and paramountcy issues.
>
> . . .
>
> I am not prepared to extend the doctrine of interjurisdictional immunity into a field — federal elections — which is unrelated to either the company law cases or the federal undertakings cases, the two historical roots of the doctrine.[53]

More recently, in *Reference re Firearms Act (Can.)*, this Court made the following statement:

> In a federal system, each level of government can expect to have its jurisdiction affected by the other to a certain degree. As Dickson C.J. stated in *General Motors of Canada Ltd. v. City National Leasing*, [1989] 1 S.C.R. 641, at p. 669, "overlap of legislation is to be expected and accommodated in a federal state". Laws mainly in relation to the jurisdiction of

51 [1987] 2 S.C.R. 2.

52 *Ibid.* at para. 21.

53 *Ibid.* at para. 22 [citations omitted]; see also *Westbank First Nation v. British Columbia Hydro and Power Authority*, [1999] 3 S.C.R. 134 at para. 18.

> one level of government may over-flow into, or have "incidental effects" upon, the jurisdiction of the other level of government. It is a matter of balance and of federalism: no one level of government is isolated from the other, nor can it usurp the functions of the other.[54]

In *Law Society of British Columbia v. Mangat*,[55] the Supreme Court had to determine whether agents appearing before the Immigration and Refugee Board were required to comply with British Columbia's *Legal Profession Act*. Justice Gonthier, for the Court, rejected the argument that the provincial legislation could not apply because of the doctrine of interjurisdictional immunity. His comments suggest a narrow role for the doctrine and imply that it is preferable to rely upon the doctrine of paramountcy in attempts to exclude the application of provincial laws. In particular, he held as follows:

> There was much argument submitted by the parties regarding the respective preferability of the doctrines of paramountcy and interjurisdictional immunity in determining the manner in which federal provisions would prevail over the provincial legislation. The latter doctrine has received its classical application in *Bell Canada, supra*. The authority for the former is *Multiple Access, supra*.
>
> I believe Mackenzie J.A. disposed of this question in a satisfactory manner. Paramountcy is the more appropriate doctrine in this case. *The existence of a double aspect to the subject matter of ss. 30 and 69(1) favours the application of the paramountcy doctrine rather than the doctrine of interjurisdictional immunity.* While the role for provincially regulated lawyers is non-exclusive, it is nonetheless inconsistent with interjurisdictional immunity, which would exclude provincial legislation, even if Parliament did not legislate in the area. The application of the interjurisdictional immunity doctrine in such a context might lead to a bifurcation of the regulation and control of the legal profession in Canada. The application of the paramountcy doctrine safeguards the control by Parliament over the administrative tribunals it creates.[56]

54 [2000] 1 S.C.R. 783 at para. 26.

55 [2001] 3 S.C.R. 113.

56 *Ibid.* at paras. 51–52 [emphasis added].

A narrow interpretation of interjurisdictional immunity would recognize a wide scope for overlapping federal and provincial powers and greater possibility for conflict. Saskatchewan argued that disputes concerning the application of federal and provincial laws should be resolved through a broader and more flexible paramountcy rule. Saskatchewan also argued that an enhanced role for paramountcy was justified by the Supreme Court's most recent pronouncement in *Rothmans, Benson and Hedges Inc. v. Saskatchewan*.[57] In the past, paramountcy has been held to apply only in very limited circumstances where citizens are being told to do incompatible things: one law says "yes" and the other law says "no" and it is impossible to comply with both.[58] The Supreme Court expanded the meaning of conflict, increasing the cases in which the doctrine might be invoked. Paramountcy may also apply where the strict "impossibility of dual compliance" test is not met, but where the application of the provincial law would thwart the purpose of the federal law. Paramountcy is a much more flexible tool as a result. While interjurisdictional immunity is a hammer, paramountcy permits a more nuanced analysis to constitutional issues and permits the Court to examine how the federal and provincial schemes fit together. Paramountcy is accordingly the preferable way for resolving all disputes between federal and provincial legislation.

Fourth, in order for paramountcy to apply, there must be a federal law that is either inconsistent with the provincial law or whose purpose would be thwarted by the application of the provincial law. Paramountcy cannot be invoked where Parliament has jurisdiction, but has not acted upon it. The advantage of relying on paramountcy as opposed to interjurisdictional immunity is that it avoids gaps in the law. The *Maurice* and *Morris* cases are perfect examples of the flaw in relying on interjurisdictional immunity. There is no federal law regulating hunting practices by Indians off-reserve or by Métis people generally. Therefore, accepting the application of interjurisdictional immunity in either *Maurice* or *Morris* would result in the individuals involved being constitutionally entitled to hunt without regard for broader public concerns except to the extent that those limits are imposed by their own communities.

---

57 [2005] 1 S.C.R. 188.

58 See, for example, *Multiple Access Ltd. v. McCutcheon*, [1982] 2 S.C.R. 161, and *Bank of Montreal v. Hall*, [1990] 1 S.C.R. 121.

There were two corollary points to this submission. First, if the matter of hunting pursuant to Aboriginal and treaty rights is so important to federal jurisdiction that it must be considered to fall within the core of section 91, it is difficult to explain why Parliament has never chosen to legislate with respect to the matter. Second, relying on paramountcy rather than interjurisdictional immunity will not lead to unwarranted intrusions of provincial law into matters otherwise considered to be within federal jurisdiction because Parliament always retains the option of enacting legislation that can trigger paramountcy and push the provinces out of the field.

Fifth, it is also important to keep in mind that the protection in section 35(1) of the *Constitution Act, 1982*,[59] remains and the provinces cannot run roughshod over Aboriginal or treaty hunting and fishing rights. To begin with, any potentially applicable provincial law must be general in its application, or else it would run afoul of section 91(24). A narrow view of interjurisdictional immunity does not enhance provincial powers under section 92 of the *Constitution Act, 1867*, and does not authorize provinces to enact Indian-specific legislation or legislation that is "in relation to" Indians. If the law infringes upon an Aboriginal right, it must still be justified under the *Sparrow* test. The law must have a valid legislative objective, and this objective must be achieved in a way that upholds the honour of the Crown in its dealings with Aboriginal peoples. The protection of section 35 is substantial.

The Supreme Court released its decision in *Morris* on 21 December 2006[60] and, I think it is fair to say, rejected my arguments completely. I will briefly outline the Court's decision and its reasoning, including the reasons for rejecting the position advanced by myself and others on behalf of provincial attorneys general. Finally, I will set out what I believe to be the implications of the decision for the application of provincial laws to Indian and Métis people who are exercising Aboriginal and treaty rights to hunt and fish for food. I will also highlight the issues that may be raised in future cases dealing with this topic. I will comment briefly on the Supreme Court's decisions in *Canadian Western Bank*[61]

59 Above note 3.

60 Above note 1.

61 Above note 7.

and *British Columbia (Attorney General) v. Lafarge Canada Inc.*[62] which were released six months after *Morris* and which, in my opinion, take a very different approach to interjurisdictional immunity, an approach that is much more in line with what I argued in *Morris.*

1) The Majority Decision in *Morris*

The majority decision in *Morris* was written by Deschamps and Abella JJ., with Binnie and Charron JJ. concurring. The majority accepted that the appellants had a treaty right to hunt on the lands in question, including the right to hunt at night with lights. The Court found that the Saanich Nation had a long tradition of hunting at night with illumination; this tradition existed before the time the treaty was signed.[63] While the majority expressly acknowledged that the treaty right did not include the right to hunt dangerously,[64] they rejected the argument that hunting at night with lights was an inherently dangerous activity and suggested that it could be safely carried out in remote and uninhabited areas.[65] Accordingly, the majority was of the view that the complete ban on hunting at night with lights, contained in British Columbia's legislation, was over-broad and did not constitute a justifiable infringement of the treaty right. In my view, this is the *ratio decidendi* of the decision. The majority's reasons suggest that the law could not apply to the appellants because of its inconsistency with section 35(1) of the *Constitution Act, 1982.*[66] It was unnecessary for the majority to go on and consider the division-of-powers issues; I would argue that the Court's comments on this issue are *obiter dictum.*

The majority provided only a cursory discussion of the applicable principles regarding the division-of-powers questions. The majority accepted that treaty rights are within the core of exclusive federal legislative

---

62 2007 SCC 23 [*Lafarge Canada*].

63 Above note 1 at paras. 25–26.

64 *Ibid.* at para. 35.

65 *Ibid.* at para. 40. This conclusion is contrary to the finding of the trial judge, who held that the evidence in the case supported the conclusion that hunting at night with lights was "inherently unsafe." It is also inconsistent with the conclusion reached by many courts across the country, as noted by McLachlin C.J. in her dissenting opinion at para. 128.

66 Above note 3.

jurisdiction at the heart of section 91(24) of the *Constitution Act, 1867*[67]; this was not seriously disputed, given the Court's earlier pronouncement in *Delgamuukw*.[68] The majority went on to decide that any provincial law which interfered with exercise of a treaty right was constitutionally inapplicable because of interjurisdictional immunity. In reaching this conclusion, the Court did not discuss the competing theories of interjurisdictional immunity that had been presented by the parties and the interveners. The Court obviously rejected the approach to interjurisdictional immunity suggested by Saskatchewan, as set out above. In my view, the majority accepted an all-or-nothing vision of interjurisdictional immunity without providing a rationale for their decision grounded in constitutional principles and without specifically outlining their reasons for refuting a more nuanced approach. In doing so, they provided little or no guidance with respect to the application of the doctrine in future cases, particularly in cases dealing with subjects other than "Indians, and Lands reserved for Indians."

The majority concluded that interjurisdictional immunity applied in this case and then quickly turned their attention to section 88 of the *Indian Act*.[69] After noting that the purpose of section 88, as enunciated in *Dick*,[70] was to override interjurisdictional immunity in the context of Indians, the majority concluded that the opening words of section 88 — "subject to the terms of any Treaty" — meant that provincial laws which interfered in any significant way with the exercise of treaty rights could not be saved by section 88. In *Delgamuukw*, the Court held that Parliament did not intend section 88 to authorize provincial laws that would extinguish Aboriginal rights or title and relied upon the proposition that to extinguish such rights Parliament's intention must be clear and plain. The same principle, however, does not apply to legislation that merely infringes rights as opposed to extinguishing them.

In the majority's view, treaty rights have an absolute protection from the impact of provincial laws. This view seems to be at odds with the Court's pronouncements in several earlier cases such as *Côté*[71] in which

67 (U.K.), 30 & 31 Vict., c. 3, reprinted in R.S.C. 1985, App. II, No. 5.

68 Above note 18.

69 Above note 11.

70 Above note 12.

71 Above note 22.

it was expressly acknowledged that provincial laws which satisfied the *Sparrow/Badger* justificatory test[72] could be applied to Indians exercising Aboriginal and treaty rights. Similar statements were made in *Marshall No. 2*[73] where the Court said it had been "most explicit" in *Marshall No. 1*[74] in confirming the regulatory authority of the federal and provincial governments within their respective legislative fields to regulate the exercise of treaty rights. The majority attempted to distinguish the *Marshall* decisions in paragraph 46 by drawing a distinction between commercial rights and sustenance rights. In my opinion, this distinction makes no juristic sense. It is simply illogical to draw distinctions between the extent to which provincial laws can apply to the exercise of treaty rights by characterizing the right as either a commercial or a subsistence right. Both are treaty rights. The extent to which provincial laws apply cannot depend on such distinctions. In attempting to explain away the Court's comments in *Marshall No. 2*, the majority said that in the case of provincially regulated resources, like wildlife and timber, the Court was not prepared to read commercial rights as being subject to parallel and potentially conflicting federal and provincial oversight. By this, I take the Court to be saying that provincial regulatory powers remain applicable and there is no necessity to establish a separate federal regulatory regime to deal with the Aboriginal and treaty rights issues that arise in connection with the commercial exploitation of these resources. This conclusion, though, seems to be completely at odds with the majority's ultimate decision which will require the establishment of separate federal regulatory regimes to deal with all limits on the exercise of sustenance rights that fall outside of "internal limits" and are required for justifiable purposes, such as the preservation of endangered species.

In my opinion, the majority further confused the issue in its attempt to reconcile *R. v. Côté*. Deshamps and Abella JJ. stated that in non-commercial cases, a distinction could be drawn between provincial laws that insignificantly interfere with treaty rights and provincial laws that constitute *prima facie* infringements of the right. The former could apply without invoking interjurisdictional immunity, while the latter could

72 See *Sparrow*, above note 21, and *Badger*, above note 22.

73 Above note 23.

74 *Ibid.*

not. *Côté* was offered as an example of a law in the first category, as it dealt with the application of a small access fee to enter a controlled harvest zone to fish pursuant to section 35 rights. The Court commented that this fee did not interfere with the exercise of the rights in any significant way. The majority's discussion of insignificant interference versus *prima facie* infringement, which is also reflected in the minority decision, is confusing and unnecessarily complicates the law.

I believe that the Court is saying is that a provincial law which interferes with the exercise of a treaty right in only an "insignificant way" does not trigger the application of interjurisdictional immunity and can apply *ex proprio vigore* without any need to rely upon section 88. A provincial law which interferes with the exercise of a treaty right in more than an insignificant manner constitutes a *prima facie* infringement of the right; in these cases, the provincial law cannot apply *ex proprio vigore*. According to the Court's interpretation, these laws cannot be saved by section 88. The Court may be suggesting that there are three categories of provincial laws to consider: laws that interfere with the exercise of treaty rights in only an insignificant manner, which can apply *ex proprio vigore*; laws that interfere in more than an insignificant manner, but come up short of a *prima facie* infringement, which cannot apply *ex proprio vigore* but could apply through the operation of section 88; and laws that constitute a *prima facie* infringement which cannot apply under any circumstances. However, in my view, such an interpretation of the *Morris* judgments unnecessarily and arbitrarily complicates the law.

2) Implications

The implications of *Morris* with respect to the application of provincial laws to both Indians and Métis who are exercising Aboriginal or treaty rights to hunt can be summed up in the following propositions:

The decision will have no impact on the extent to which provincial hunting and fishing laws can apply to Indians in the prairie provinces because Manitoba, Saskatchewan, and Alberta can rely upon the provisions of the *Natural Resources Transfer Agreements* (NRTAs), affirmed by the *Constitution Act, 1930*,[75] as specific constitutional authorization for the application of provincial game laws to Indians. Nothing in *Morris*

75 Above note 5.

suggests that the principles laid down in *Badger*, namely, that provincial game laws can apply to Indians through the NRTAs provided that they are justified under a *Sparrow*-type test, are no longer good law. Provincial powers derived through the NRTAs, however, have no application to Métis given the Supreme Court's decision in *Blais*.[76]

Second, in cases not covered by the NRTAs, the legal debate will undoubtedly shift away from questions concerning *prima facie* infringement and justification and will instead focus on things like internal limits and significant versus insignificant interference. It may well be argued that both Aboriginal and treaty rights are subject to an internal limit with respect to conservation, which would allow the provinces to apply laws aimed at, for example, the protection of endangered local populations of certain wildlife species not endangered on a national scale and not protected under federal legislation.

Third, to the extent that Métis are considered to be section 91(24) Indians and can establish Aboriginal rights to hunt and fish under the test laid down by the Supreme Court in *Powley*,[77] the decision clearly means that the scope for the application of provincial laws is limited. This will result in the somewhat anomalous situation of the Métis having a greater insulation from the application of provincial fish and game laws than Indians.

Fourth, the *Morris* decision should not change the law with respect to hunting at night with lights in Saskatchewan. First Nations remain subject to the law through the NRTAs either as something that does not interfere with the exercise of their rights or as a justifiable infringement. The evidence in *Maurice* established that the Métis in this province did not historically hunt at night with lights; therefore, in my view, it can be argued that this particular hunting method should not be considered as falling within the Métis Aboriginal right to hunt for food, which is recognized in this province. More significantly, I believe that the conclusion that hunting at night with lights is an inherently dangerous activity which cannot be engaged in safely under any circumstances and which warrants a blanket prohibition remains valid. This conclusion, based upon unequivocal expert evidence, was reached by both the trial judge and the summary conviction appeal court judge in *Maurice*. The expert

---

76 Above note 4.

77 Above note 2.

in *Maurice* expressly rejected the notion that hunting at night with lights can safely occur in isolated or uninhabited areas. Accordingly, in my view, *Maurice* remains good law in Saskatchewan. I suspect that other jurisdictions, when faced with challenges to the application of their night hunting legislation by Indians or Métis, will seek to call expert evidence about the dangers of night hunting that is more in line with the evidence adduced in *Maurice*, as opposed to the more equivocal views expressed by the conservation officer who testified in *Morris*.

The *Morris* decision may also lead to calls for legislative changes to section 88 to provide for equal treatment of Aboriginal and treaty rights, either by extending the protection from incorporated provincial laws to Aboriginal rights or by removing the protection from treaty rights. This latter proposition would allow the extent of interference to both Aboriginal and treaty rights to be determined solely by interjurisdictional immunity and section 35 of the *Constitution Act, 1982*.

I think the decision may also lead to calls for the re-examination of the provisions of the *Natural Resources Transfer Agreements* given that these agreements now appear to put the prairie provinces in a preferential position vis-à-vis the other provinces in regards to the application of their fish and game laws to Indians exercising Aboriginal or treaty hunting and fishing rights.

Finally, the judgment entrenches a stark view of interjurisdictional immunity vis-à-vis section 91(24) which, as I set out above, is inconsistent with broader trends in constitutional interpretation. The judgment also runs counter to the trend of recent Supreme Court jurisprudence which limits the application of interjurisdictional immunity, recognizes overlapping federal and provincial jurisdiction in many areas and resolves disputes between federal and provincial laws by the application of the paramountcy rules. However, in the Supreme Court's subsequent decisions in *Canadian Western Bank* and *Lafarge Canada*, the Court engaged in the full discussion of all the various issues related to interjurisdictional immunity, something that was lacking in *Morris*. The Court confirmed that the scope of the doctrine is quite limited and its application should be confined to cases where interjurisdictional immunity has already been recognized.

The majority judgment in both cases was written by Binnie and LeBel JJ. A key point that emerges from the majority decisions is that interjurisdictional immunity should be applied with restraint and that most cases of potential conflict between the application of federal and provincial laws should be resolved by a vigorous application of the pith and substance doctrine and by paramountcy rules. The majority also noted that a broad application of interjurisdictional immunity would create uncertainty given the difficulties associated with defining the core content associated with the various heads of federal and provincial legislative power.[78] Justices Binnie and LeBel did not try to lay down any firm rules about how to define the core content of the various legislative powers set out in the Constitution; rather, they determined that it was best to define the core powers on a case-by-case basis.[79] They did, however, note that core powers should be defined narrowly and embrace only those aspects of jurisdiction that are vital and essential to the exercise of the legislative power.[80] The majority specifically pointed out that the core of a legislative power is not co-extensive with the full scope of the power, and legislation enacted pursuant to a particular head of power does not necessarily relate to the core of that power.[81] As noted above, Binnie and LeBel JJ. held that the fact a provincial law touches upon or affects the core of federal powers is not sufficient to invoke interjurisdictional immunity. A provincial law should be displaced only where its application impairs or has some adverse impact on core federal powers: the impact need not go so far that it can be characterized as sterilizing or paralyzing the core powers.

Further on in their judgment for *Canadian Western Bank*,[82] Binnie and LeBel JJ. discuss some of the interjurisdictional immunity case law relating to Indians and Indian lands. They refer to such cases as *Paul* and *Kitkatla* as examples of their preferred approach to interjurisdictional immunity. Interestingly, they do not cite *Morris*. However, the decision in *Morris* is reflected in their comment that interjurisdictional immunity will apply in the context of section 91(24) whenever the Court discerns a need for federal exclusivity as a result of Parliament's special responsibilities for Aboriginal peoples.

78 Above note 7 at para. 43.

79 *Ibid.*

80 *Ibid.* at para. 48.

81 *Ibid.* at para. 51.

82 *Ibid.* at paras. 60–61.

Thus, a final implication of *Morris*, which *Canadian Western Bank* points to, is that, as far as Métis Aboriginal rights are concerned, some jurisdictions might reconsider their position on the Métis and section 91(24). Provinces might feel compelled to argue more vigorously that the Métis are not section 91(24) Indians in order to avoid the whole interjurisdictional immunity issue.

G. CONCLUSION

In conclusion, I think that it is fair to say that while interjurisdictional immunity has been restricted with respect to most heads of federal power set out in the *Constitution Act, 1867*, it will remain relevant in the context of section 91(24), particularly where Aboriginal or treaty rights are involved. Much of what I argued on behalf of the attorney general for Saskatchewan in *Morris* about the limited nature of interjurisdictional immunity, while not adopted by the Court in *Morris*, is reflected in the Court's decisions in *Canadian Western Bank* and *Lafarge Canada*. Therefore, I still think I had the right arguments — I was just arguing the wrong case!

The Métis and the Doctrine of Interjurisdictional Immunity: A Commentary

KENT McNEIL

Dale Gibson, Mitch McAdam, and Albert Peeling correctly conclude that the issue of the application of the doctrine of interjurisdictional immunity to the Métis arises only if the Métis are under exclusive federal jurisdiction as "Indians" within the meaning of that term in section 91(24) of the *Constitution Act, 1867*.[1] I think the Métis are so included for the reasons that Albert Peeling and others have already explained, and so I will proceed on that assumption.[2]

---

1 (U.K.), 30 & 31 Vict., c. 3. Section 91(24) gives the Parliament of Canada exclusive jurisdiction over "Indians, and Lands reserved for the Indians."

2 In *R. v. Blais*, [2003] 2 S.C.R. 236 [*Blais*], the Supreme Court explicitly left the s. 91(24) issue open when it decided that the Métis are not "Indians" for the purposes of the *Natural Resources Transfer Agreements*, Schedules 1–3 of the *Constitution Act, 1930* (U.K.), 20 & 21 Geo. V, c. 26 (for recent commentary on these Agreements, see the articles in (2007) 12 Rev. Const. Stud.). However, the provisions in those Agreements relating to "Indians" were specifically intended to protect rights set out in the Indian treaties that were thought to cover the whole of the prairie provinces. As the Métis were generally not included in the treaties, it is not surprising that their rights were not included in the Agreements. See also *Lovelace v. Ontario*, [2000] 1 S.C.R. 950 at paras. 109–11 [*Lovelace*]. There, the Court addressed an argument that a casino revenue-sharing arrangement between First Nations and Ontario violated s. 91(24) because it "undermined the 'Indianness' or aboriginality of non-status and Métis aboriginal communities" (para. 109). Justice Iacobucci, for the Court, held that "there is nothing in the casino program affecting the core of the s. 91(24) federal jurisdiction" because the "province has done nothing to impair the status or capacity of the appellants as aboriginal peoples.

The application of the doctrine of interjurisdictional immunity to the Métis is a matter of great importance. As pointed out by Gibson, McAdam, and Peeling, provincial laws are not made applicable to the Métis by section 88 of the *Indian Act* because they do not come within that statute's definition of "Indian."[3] To the extent, therefore, that the interjurisdictional immunity doctrine encompasses them, the Métis should receive more protection from it than status Indians who have been subjected by section 88 to provincial laws that would not otherwise apply to them.[4]

Therefore, I disagree with Dale Gibson on the significance of interjurisdictional immunity for the Métis. He states that, even if he is wrong about the Métis being within section 91(24), it may not make much difference "in practical terms" because "Métis Aboriginal rights under s. 35 of the *Constitution Act, 1982*[5] provide a cloak of constitutional immunity where Aboriginal rights are involved that is as effective as that provided by interjurisdictional immunity." While Gibson is correct that section 35 provides protection against *federal* as well as provincial legislation and so is more comprehensive than interjurisdictional immunity in that regard, section 35 may provide significantly less protection against *provincial* infringement of Métis rights than section 91(24). The reason is that the Supreme Court has said, in a number of cases, that section 35 rights can be infringed for a wide range of legislative objectives by both the federal and provincial governments.[6] In contrast to this, in situations where

---

Furthermore, in *Pamajewon*, [*R. v. Pamajewon*, [1996] 2 S.C.R. 821], this Court found that gambling, or the regulation of gambling activities, is not an aboriginal right. Consequently, this casino program cannot have the effect of violating the rights affirmed by s. 35(1) of the *Constitution Act, 1982*, and does not approach the core of aboriginality" (para. 111). The Court did not address the issue of whether the Métis come within s. 91(24).

3 R.S.C. 1985, c. I-5, ss. 2 and 6–7.

4 See *R. v. Dick*, [1985] 2 S.C.R. 309 [*Dick*], where the Supreme Court held that those provincial laws of general application that would not apply to status Indians of their own force because they affect "Indianness" are referentially incorporated into federal law by s. 88. For discussion, see Kerry Wilkins, "'Still Crazy after All These Years': Section 88 of the *Indian Act* at Fifty" (2000) 38 Alta. L. Rev. 458; Kent McNeil, "Aboriginal Title and Section 88 of the *Indian Act*" (2000) 34 U.B.C. L. Rev. 159.

5 Schedule B to the *Canada Act 1982* (U.K.), 1982, c. 11.

6 See *R. v. Sparrow*, [1990] 1 S.C.R. 1075 [*Sparrow*]; *R. v. Gladstone*, [1996] 2 S.C.R. 723 [*Gladstone*]; *R. v. Côté*, [1996] 3 S.C.R. 139 [*Côté*]; *Delgamuukw v. British Columbia*,

the doctrine of inter-jurisdictional immunity applies, the protection it provides against provincial laws appears to be absolute: that protection arises from the constitutional division of powers, rather than from the constitutional recognition and affirmation of Aboriginal rights.[7] As Albert Peeling concludes, "[p]rovincial laws that interfere with the exercise by Métis people of these rights must be either invalid or inapplicable to Métis people [due to s. 91(24)] and are in that sense unconstitutional and may not be justified under section 35 of the *Constitution Act, 1982*."

But I am getting ahead of myself. Let me go back and consider the doctrine of interjurisdictional immunity, and then return to its application to Aboriginal peoples, including the Métis.

A. THE DOCTRINE OF INTERJURISDICTIONAL IMMUNITY

The three presenters whose work I am commenting on correctly explain the doctrine and its general application. There is no need for me to repeat what they say. However, while Gibson and Peeling regard the doctrine as providing the core of federal heads of power with complete protection against provincial laws, McAdam advocates for a more fluid application of the doctrine. Taking an explicitly provincial perspective that would extend provincial authority, he argues against applying interjurisdictional immunity in an all-or-nothing way so that "[a]nything that falls on the federal side of the fence is off limits to the application of provincial laws, without exception." He writes:

> According to this characterization of the doctrine, there is no consideration of the effect of the provincial law. In my opinion, the doctrine is too stark. It precludes an examination of the purpose of the provincial law, its real or practical effect on the federal matter, and how the two legislative schemes potentially fit together. This is at odds with modern

---

[1997] 3 S.C.R. 1010 [*Delgamuukw*]. Provincial power to infringe s. 35 rights will be questioned later: see text following note 45, below in this chapter.

7 The Supreme Court has held that those rights are not absolute, as they have to be reconciled with Crown sovereignty: see *R. v. Van der Peet*, [1996] 2 S.C.R. 507 [*Van der Peet*] and the cases cited in the previous note. For confirmation that the division of powers provides greater protection to Aboriginal peoples than s. 35 of the *Constitution Act, 1982*, see *R. v. Morris*, [2006] 2 S.C.R. 915 at para. 55 [*Morris*].

approaches to interpretation that afford a wide scope for the application of both federal and provincial laws.

McAdam describes the doctrine of interjurisdictional immunity as "an exception" to two other division-of-powers rules: double aspect and incidental effect. Those rules allow for overlapping and concurrent federal and provincial jurisdiction, subject always to federal paramountcy, whereby in the event of conflict, constitutionally valid federal laws trump provincial laws. He sees the doctrine of interjurisdictional immunity as "a remnant of an earlier era in the development of Canadian constitutional law, which is often referred to as the age of watertight compartments."

The major problem I see with McAdam's interpretation of the doctrine of interjurisdictional immunity is that it would appear to weaken the doctrine to the point where the concept of *exclusive* federal jurisdiction over section 91 heads of power would lose much of its force.[8] Instead of identifying the core of federal jurisdiction in relation to specific heads of power and then determining whether the provincial law in question impinges on that core, McAdam would ask courts to examine the purpose and effect of the provincial law. His approach appears to me to be a substantial modification of the doctrine that would make the interjurisdictional immunity fence permeable, allowing provinces to effectively breach it by deftly framing their legislation in terms of provincial purposes. I think this approach is inconsistent with the Supreme Court's jurisprudence on interjurisdictional immunity, both generally and in relation to Aboriginal peoples,[9] and is an unabashed attempt to expand provincial jurisdiction. Most of the decisions cited by McAdam that allegedly reveal judicial uneasiness with the doctrine relate instead to the

8 As Albert Peeling points out, it is the exclusiveness of federal jurisdiction that gives rise to the doctrine of interjurisdictional immunity: see *Bell Canada v. Quebec (Commission de la santé et de la sécurité du travail du Québec)*, [1988] 1 S.C.R. 749 at 762 [*Bell Canada*].

9 See, for example, *Bell Canada*, *ibid.*; *Dick*, above note 4; *Alberta (Attorney General) v. Putnam*, [1981] 2 S.C.R. 267; *Derrickson v. Derrickson*, [1986] 1 S.C.R. 285 [*Derrickson*]; *Ordon Estate v. Grail*, [1998] 3 S.C.R. 437 [*Ordon Estate*]. For a useful overview of the doctrine, see Peter Hogg, *Constitutional Law of Canada*, looseleaf (Scarborough, ON: Carswell, 1997–) at 15-25 to 15-34.

definition of the core of federal jurisdiction.[10] While the Supreme Court may have decided to limit that core in favour of concurrency of jurisdiction in specific instances where it found that to be appropriate, before 2007, at least, the Court had not suggested that identifiable cores of federal jurisdiction could be invaded by the provinces.

Since McAdam wrote his original paper and I first drafted this commentary, however, the Supreme Court has handed down two decisions that have reassessed the doctrine of interjurisdictional immunity: *Canadian Western Bank v. Alberta*[11] and *British Columbia (Attorney General) v. Lafarge Canada Inc.*[12] In his revised paper, McAdam accurately observes that one key point made in the majority judgments of Binnie and LeBel JJ. in these two cases is that "interjurisdictional immunity should be applied with restraint and that most cases of potential conflict between the application of federal and provincial laws should be resolved by a vigorous application of the pith and substance doctrine and by paramountcy rules." Moreover, as McAdam notes, Binnie and LeBel JJ. held that the doctrine of interjurisdictional immunity should be invoked only where a provincial law impairs or has an adverse impact on the core of an exclusive federal power. Provincial laws that touch on or affect the core without impairing federal jurisdiction will not run afoul of the doctrine.[13] Whether this standard will have an impact on the application of the doctrine where Aboriginal peoples are concerned remains to be seen.[14]

---

10 See, for example, *Law Society of British Columbia v. Mangat*, [2001] 3 S.C.R. 113, especially at paras. 51–52.

11 2007 SCC 22 [*Canadian Western Bank*].

12 2007 SCC 23 [*Lafarge Canada*].

13 In theory, at least, this works both ways, so that federal laws generally cannot impair the core of exclusive provincial powers either: see *Canadian Western Bank*, above note 11 at para. 35. Note, too, that, in setting "impairs" rather than "affects" as the standard, Binnie and LeBel JJ. explicitly rejected the language used by Beetz J. in *Bell Canada*, above note 8 at 859–60: see *Canadian Western Bank*, *ibid.* at para. 48.

14 In revisions to his paper made in light of *Canadian Western Bank*, Dale Gibson observes that the Court's comments "could result in narrower implications for Métis rights than contended for in the body of this chapter." We will return to this question later: see text following note 117, below in this chapter.

In *Canadian Western Bank*, Binnie and LeBel JJ. also said that the doctrine of interjurisdictional immunity "should in general be reserved for situations already covered by precedent."[15] As we are about to discuss, the application of the doctrine in the context of section 91(24) of the *Constitution Act, 1867*, which assigned exclusive jurisdiction over "Indians, and Lands reserved for the Indians" to Parliament, had already been established by leading Supreme Court decisions, several of which were referred to with apparent approval in *Canadian Western Bank*.[16] Moreover, in *R. v. Morris*,[17] decided just five months before *Canadian Western Bank* and *Lafarge Canada*, the Court reaffirmed the application of the doctrine in the Aboriginal context by using it to protect treaty rights against provincial game laws.[18] We will return to the *Morris* decision after discussing other cases involving section 91(24).

B. ABORIGINAL PEOPLES AND INTERJURISDICTIONAL IMMUNITY

McAdam contends that Supreme Court decisions in relation to Aboriginal peoples prior to *Morris* support his approach. In my opinion, this contention depends on selective reading of the case law and questionable interpretation of the judgments. McAdam suggests that the Supreme Court has been consistent in its application of the doctrine of interjurisdictional immunity in the context of Aboriginal rights, particularly hunting and fishing rights. He goes back to *Cardinal v. Alberta (Attorney General)*,[19] where Martland J. rejected the suggestion that Indian reserves are federal enclaves where provincial laws do not apply, and uses that decision to support his argument that "valid provincial laws can infringe Aboriginal and treaty rights in certain circumstances." In that case, however, Martland J. expressed doubt over whether the provincial game law in question would have applied of its own force on Indian re-

15 *Canadian Western Bank*, above note 11 at para. 77.

16 *Ibid.* at paras. 34, 40–41, 48, 60–61.

17 Above note 7.

18 Significantly, Binnie J., who co-authored the majority judgments in *Canadian Western Bank* and *Lafarge Canada* with LeBel J., also concurred in the majority judgment in *Morris*. Justice LeBel did not participate in the *Morris* appeal.

19 [1974] S.C.R. 695 at 702–3 [*Cardinal*].

serves, absent the constitutional authority conferred on Alberta by its *Natural Resources Transfer Agreement.*[20] The decision does not support the contention that the provinces have general constitutional authority to infringe Aboriginal hunting or fishing rights, especially where "Lands reserved for the Indians" are concerned.

The core of federal jurisdiction in relation to section 91(24), "Indians" has been described as involving Indian status and capacities, or "Indianness."[21] In *Dick v. The Queen,*[22] evidence was presented on the impact of a provincial game law on a member of the Alkali Band of Shuswap Indians who had been accused of hunting deer out of season. Although Lambert J.A. of the British Columbia Court of Appeal found on the evidence that the game law impaired the status and capacity of the accused and so affected his Indianness, Beetz J. for the Supreme Court was only willing to assume that the provincial law would have this effect. On that factual assumption, though — and this is vital — he held that the provincial law could not apply to the accused of its own force because it would impinge on exclusive federal jurisdiction over "Indians" in section 91(24). He went on to determine that the accused was nonetheless subject to the provincial law because it had been referentially incorporated into federal law by section 88 of the *Indian Act.*[23] The following year, the Supreme Court concluded, in *Derrickson v. Derrickson,*[24] that provincial matrimonial property legislation could not apply to reserve lands because they come within exclusive federal jurisdiction over "Lands reserved for the Indians," the other component of section 91(24). In *Derrickson,* the Court also decided that section 88 did not referentially incorporate the provincial legislation because that legislation was in direct conflict with provi-

20 *Ibid.* at 708. The Agreement was given constitutional force by the *Constitution Act, 1930,* above note 2.

21 In *Natural Parents v. British Columbia (Superintendent of Child Welfare),* [1975] 2 S.C.R. 751 at 760–61 [*Natural Parents*], Laskin C.J. held that provincial adoption laws that would impair "Indianness" could not apply to status Indian children: see *Canadian Western Bank,* above note 11 at para. 61, apparently accepting this aspect of Laskin C.J.'s judgment. *Natural Parents* is discussed by Dale Gibson in Chapter 8.

22 Above note 4.

23 Above note 3. Recall that this would not have happened had the accused been Métis: see text accompanying note 3.

24 Above note 9.

sions of the *Indian Act* relating to possession of reserve lands, and so its application was excluded by an express proviso in section 88.[25]

Together, *Dick* and *Derrickson* are clear rulings on the application of the doctrine of interjurisdictional immunity in the context of section 91(24).[26] If provincial laws impair the status or capacities of Indians or have an adverse impact on Indianness, or if they relate to possession or use of lands,[27] they cannot apply of their own force to "Indians" or "Lands reserved for the Indians" within the meaning of those terms in section 91(24). This is due to exclusive federal jurisdiction over those subject matters and the application of the doctrine of interjurisdictional immunity. This division-of-powers doctrine is not connected to and so does not depend on constitutional recognition and affirmation of Aboriginal and treaty rights by section 35 of the *Constitution Act, 1982*.[28] Any uncertainty over the scope of the doctrine's application to "Indians" and "Lands reserved for the Indians" arises from lack of clarity over either

---

25 See also *Paul v. Paul*, [1986] 1 S.C.R. 306. Note that in *Derrickson*, *ibid.*, the general issue of whether s. 88 provides for referential incorporation of provincial laws relating to *land* was left open: see detailed discussion in the articles cited above in note 4. For a recent holding that it does not, see *Tsilhqot'in Nation v. British Columbia*, 2007 BCSC 1700 at paras. 1033–40 [*Tsilhqot'in Nation*].

26 Significantly, *Dick* and *Derrickson* were referred to with approval by Binnie and LeBel JJ. in their judgment in *Canadian Western Bank*, above note 11 at paras. 48 and 61.

27 While *Derrickson* focused on possession of reserve lands, in *Cardinal*, above note 19 at 705, Martland J. stated in reference to *Peace Arch Enterprises Ltd. v. Surrey* (1970), 74 W.W.R. 380 (B.C.C.A.): "Once it was determined that the lands remained lands reserved for the Indians, Provincial legislation relating to their use was not applicable." Other court of appeal decisions have also held that provincial laws in relation to land use are inapplicable to the Indian interest in reserve lands: see *R. v. Isaac* (1975), 13 N.S.R. (2d) 460 at 469 (S.C.A.D.); *Re Stoney Plain Indian Reserve No. 135*, [1982] 1 C.N.L.R. 133 at 151 (Alta. C.A.); *Paul v. Paul*, [1985] 2 C.N.L.R. 93 (B.C.C.A.), aff'd S.C.C., above note 25. Compare *Oka (Municipality) v. Simon*, [1999] 2 C.N.L.R. 205 (Que. C.A.), where the Court (wrongly, in my opinion) distinguished between "Indian" and "non-Indian" uses. For further discussion, see Kent McNeil, "Aboriginal Title and the Division of Powers: Rethinking Federal and Provincial Jurisdiction" (1998) 61 Sask. L. Rev. 431, reprinted in Kent McNeil, *Emerging Justice? Essays on Indigenous Rights in Canada and Australia* (Saskatoon: University of Saskatchewan Native Law Centre, 2001) 249. Compare Mitch McAdam's contrary views in Chapter 10.

28 See *Morris*, above note 7 at para. 55.

the meaning of those terms (e.g., are the Métis "Indians" for the purposes of section 91(24)?[29]) or the extent of the core of section 91(24) jurisdiction (e.g., what is meant by Indian status and capacities or Indianness?). But once it is determined that a matter comes within that core, the doctrine operates to protect it against provincial legislation that would have an adverse impact on it.

The relevance of the doctrine of inter-jurisdictional immunity to Aboriginal peoples was affirmed by the Supreme Court in *Delgamuukw v. British Columbia*.[30] In a passage quoted at length by Mitch McAdam and Albert Peeling, Lamer C.J. said that "s. 91(24) protects a core of federal jurisdiction even from provincial laws of general application, through the operation of the doctrine of interjurisdictional immunity."[31] After referring to the *Dick* decision,[32] Lamer C.J. determined that "aboriginal rights are part of the core of Indianness at the heart of s. 91(24). Prior to 1982, as a result, they could not be extinguished by provincial laws of general application."[33] But because Lamer C.J. drew a distinction between provincial laws that would infringe and those that would extinguish Aboriginal rights, McAdam interprets his judgment to mean that

> . . . only provincial laws that extinguish Aboriginal rights either directly or indirectly cross the interjurisdictional immunity boundary-line and are constitutionally inapplicable. Provincial laws that infringe those rights and that are justifiable according to the *Sparrow* test can apply without invoking interjurisdictional immunity concerns. [References omitted]

McAdam must be wrong in this regard. Provincial laws do not have to *extinguish* rights in order to cross the line into exclusive federal jurisdic-

---

29 See text accompanying notes 1–2, above in this chapter.

30 Above note 6.

31 *Ibid.* at para. 181. In *Lovelace*, above note 2, Iacobucci J. quoted this passage with the apparent approval of a unanimous Court.

32 Above note 4. He also referred to *Four B Manufacturing Ltd. v. United Garment Workers of America*, [1980] 1 S.C.R. 1031 [*Four B Manufacturing*], and *R. v. Francis*, [1988] 1 S.C.R. 1025 [*Francis*], where provincial laws in relation to labour relations (*Four B Manufacturing*), and in relation to traffic laws (*Francis*), were held to be applicable on Indian reserves. For discussion of *Four B Manufacturing*, see Chapter 8 by Dale Gibson.

33 *Delgamuukw*, above note 6 at para. 181.

tion. The *Dick* decision, relied upon by Lamer C.J.,[34] clearly reveals this. In *Dick*, the provincial law in question imposed seasonal restrictions on deer hunting. If applied to the Shuswap people, it would have *regulated*, not *extinguished*, any Aboriginal right they might have to hunt deer.[35] And yet Beetz J. was ready to assume that this law would affect their Indianness so as to make it inapplicable to them of its own force, as a result of the operation of the doctrine of interjurisdictional immunity. Justice Beetz clearly thought, therefore, that provincial laws that regulate hunting would not apply to Indians of their own force if, as a matter of fact, hunting is an aspect of their Indianness. So, provincial laws evidently do not need to extinguish rights for the doctrine of interjurisdictional immunity to apply.[36]

Moreover, in *Delgamuukw* Lamer C.J. gave another reason why provincial laws cannot extinguish Aboriginal rights. After affirming that the test for extinguishment is "clear and plain" legislative intent, he continued:

> . . . the only laws with sufficiently clear and plain intention to extinguish aboriginal rights would be laws in relation to Indians and Indian lands. As a result, a provincial law could never, *proprio vigore*, extinguish aboriginal rights, because the intention to do so would take the law outside provincial jurisdiction.[37]

Here, the Chief Justice was relying on the distinction in constitutional law between provincial laws that relate to "Indians" or "Lands reserved for the Indians" and provincial laws of general application that do not so relate and that have been validly enacted under a section 92 head of provincial power. The former are unconstitutional because they are directly within federal section 91(24) jurisdiction and so are *ultra vires* the provinces, whereas the latter are constitutionally valid and can apply to

34 McAdam does refer to *Dick*, but only to explain why there has not been more case law on the core of s. 91(24). (*Dick* decided that s. 88 makes provincial laws of general application that would not apply of their own force to status Indians apply to them as federal law.)

35 See *Sparrow*, above note 6, where the Court held that extensive regulation of West Coast fisheries, including the imposition of seasonal restrictions, did not extinguish Aboriginal rights to fish.

36 *Morris*, above note 7, confirmed this in the context of treaty rights to hunt.

37 *Delgamuukw*, above note 6 at para. 180.

"Indians" and "Lands reserved for the Indians" if they do not adversely affect the core of federal jurisdiction over these matters.[38] If provincial laws of the latter class do adversely affect that core, they have to be read down in accordance with the doctrine of interjurisdictional immunity to avoid that unconstitutional effect, as was held in *Dick* and *Derrickson*.[39]

Given Lamer C.J.'s conclusion that, to extinguish Aboriginal rights, provincial laws would have to be in relation to Indians or Indian lands and thus *ultra vires* the province, there is no need to apply the doctrine of interjurisdictional immunity in the context of extinguishment. The doctrine applies only to constitutionally valid provincial laws, not to laws that are invalid because they are *ultra vires*. So if the doctrine of interjurisdictional immunity is relevant to Aboriginal rights — as the Chief Justice clearly thought it was — it must operate in the context of infringement, not extinguishment, of those rights.

Recall as well that the provincial hunting law that was held in *Dick* to be inapplicable of its own force (on the factual assumption that it affected the "Indianness" of the Shuswap people) was referentially incorporated into federal law by section 88 of the *Indian Act*. The Supreme Court interpreted section 88 as incorporating only those provincial laws that cannot apply to Indians of their own force. But to be constitutionally valid, those laws cannot be in relation to "Indians" or "Lands reserved for the Indians" because the Court has clearly held that provincial laws in relation to those matters would not be available for referential incorporation by section 88 because they would be *ultra vires* the provinces.[40] Therefore, an additional problem with McAdam's argument that the doctrine of interjurisdictional immunity shields Aboriginal rights only from provincial laws that would extinguish them is that it leaves section 88 with no work to do where Aboriginal rights are concerned. On his argument, provincial laws that merely *infringe* Aboriginal rights do not require section

38 See *ibid.* at para. 179, where Lamer C.J. articulated this distinction. See also Chapter 9 by Albert Peeling. For cases where provincial laws were held to apply to Indians because they did not affect that core, see *Four B Manufacturing* and *Francis*, above note 32.

39 See Wilkins, above note 4 at 465–69.

40 See *Dick*, above note 4 at 322; *Delgamuukw*, above note 6 at para. 182; *Morris*, above note 7 at para. 41 (Deschamps and Abella JJ.), and para. 85 (McLachlin C.J. and Fish J.).

88 to make them apply to section 91(24) "Indians." But in *Delgamuukw*, Lamer C.J. held that provincial laws that would *extinguish* Aboriginal rights would be constitutionally invalid, and so those laws would not be referentially incorporated either. Consequently, if McAdam is right, section 88 is irrelevant where Aboriginal rights are concerned because provincial laws either apply of their own force to infringe them (if the infringement can be justified under the *Sparrow* test) or are invalid because they would extinguish the rights. There are no laws in-between to be referentially incorporated by section 88 in this context. This seems inconsistent with the result in *Dick* because the Shuswap Indians probably do have an Aboriginal right to hunt (this point was not argued in that case, though, likely because the hunting occurred before the enactment of section 35 of the *Constitution Act, 1982*). This conclusion is also contrary to two decisions of the British Columbia Court of Appeal, *R. v. Alphonse*[41] and *R. v. Dick*,[42] which held that provincial laws that infringe Aboriginal rights can be referentially incorporated into federal law by section 88, provided the infringement is justified in accordance with the *Sparrow* test.[43]

My main point, however, is that McAdam's argument that interjurisdictional immunity protects Aboriginal rights from extinguishment, but not infringement, is inconsistent with the *Dick* decision. Given that Lamer C.J. cited that decision with approval in *Delgamuukw*, he cannot have intended to overrule it, as McAdam's argument would require. This understanding is confirmed by the following passage from *Delgamuukw*, coming immediately after a reference to *Dick*:

> . . . s. 88 extends the effect of provincial laws of general application which cannot apply to Indians and Indian lands because they touch on the Indianness at the core of s. 91(24). For example, *a provincial law which regulated hunting may very well touch on this core*. Although such a law

41 [1993] 4 C.N.L.R. 19 [*Alphonse*].

42 [1993] 4 C.N.L.R. 63 [*Dick* 1993].

43 See also *R. v. Sundown*, [1997] 8 W.W.R. 379 (Sask. C.A.), aff'd without reference to this issue, [1999] 1 S.C.R. 393 [*Sundown*]. For criticism of these decisions that does not accept McAdam's argument, questioning instead the constitutional validity and scope of s. 88 in light of s. 35(1) of the *Constitution Act, 1982*, see Kerry Wilkins, "Of Provinces and Section 35 Rights" (1999) 22 Dalhousie L.J. 185 at 226–33; McNeil, above note 4 at 164–70.

> would not apply to aboriginal people *proprio vigore*, it would still apply through s. 88 of the *Indian Act*, being a law of general application.[44]

Here, Lamer C.J. clearly envisaged that a provincial law *regulating*, but *not extinguishing*, hunting could touch on the core of Indianness, and he concluded, as had Beetz J. in *Dick*, that if that occurred the law would not apply to Indians *ex proprio vigore*. The Chief Justice therefore cannot have taken the view that provincial laws that justifiably infringe Aboriginal rights to hunt, but that do not extinguish them, apply to Indians of their own force.[45] In my respectful view, however, there is still a fundamental inconsistency in Lamer C.J.'s judgment in *Delgamuukw*: it arises from his treatment of the doctrine of interjurisdictional immunity on the one hand and provincial authority to infringe Aboriginal rights on the other. Rather than try to interpret this inconsistency out of existence, as McAdam attempts to do, I think it has to be confronted.

I have already discussed Lamer C.J.'s analysis of interjurisdictional immunity and concluded that it affirmed the holding in *Dick*: provincial laws that touch on the Indianness at the core of section 91(24) cannot apply to Indians of their own force. Chief Justice Lamer also held that Aboriginal rights lie within this core. It should therefore follow that Aboriginal rights cannot be infringed by provincial laws, unless those laws are referentially incorporated into federal law by section 88 of the *Indian Act*.[46] And yet Lamer C.J. stated in another part of his judgment in *Delgamuukw* that Aboriginal rights "may be infringed, both by the federal (e.g., *Sparrow*) and provincial (e.g., *Côté*) governments," as long as the infringement can be justified.[47] He then went on to discuss general principles in relation to infringement and justification, and their application to Aboriginal title, without explicitly mentioning provincial infringement or *Côté*[48] again. Chief Justice Lamer drew the principles and his explanation of their application from *Sparrow*[49] and *Gladstone*,[50]

---

44 *Delgamuukw*, above note 6 at para. 182 [emphasis added].

45 Recall that Lamer C.J. held as well that Aboriginal rights are within the core of s. 91(24): see text accompanying note 33, above in this chapter.

46 See *Alphonse*, *Dick* 1993, and *Sundown*, above notes 41–43.

47 *Delgamuukw*, above note 6 at para. 160.

48 Above note 6.

49 *Ibid.*

50 *Ibid.*

two cases that involved federal fisheries legislation rather than provincial legislation. This is a weak basis for concluding, as McAdam does, that Lamer C.J. held that provincial laws can infringe Aboriginal rights of their own force, provided the infringement is justified. My respectful opinion is that the Chief Justice either meant that the infringement could occur through the operation of section 88 or, more likely, he failed to take section 91(24) and interjurisdictional immunity into account in concluding that the provinces can infringe Aboriginal rights because he relied unreflectively on his own judgment in *Côté*. We therefore need to turn our attention to this problematic aspect of the *Côté* decision itself.

The *Côté* case involved charges against members of the Desert River Band of Algonquin Indians for fishing in contravention of regulations made under the federal *Fisheries Act*,[51] and for entering a controlled harvest zone without paying the fee required by regulations made under a Quebec statute.[52] The accused relied on both an Aboriginal and a treaty right to fish. In framing the questions to be considered in relation to the charges under the provincial legislation, Lamer C.J. said that the appeal

> . . . implicates the constitutionality of a *provincial* regulation which allegedly infringes a *treaty* right to fish. Therefore, in the context of this appeal, this Court is additionally asked to consider the overlapping statutory and constitutional protection extended to treaty rights from inconsistent provincial legislation under both s. 35(1) of the *Constitution Act, 1982*, and s. 88 of the *Indian Act*.[53]

What is not mentioned here or, indeed, anywhere in the judgment is section 91(24) of the *Constitution Act, 1867*; therefore, the relevance of interjurisdictional immunity to the application of the provincial legislation to both the treaty right and the Aboriginal right does not appear to have been considered. Instead, Lamer C.J. framed the issue of the application of the provincial statute in this way:

> In *Sparrow*, the Court set out the applicable framework for identifying the infringement of an aboriginal right or treaty right under s. 35(1) of the *Constitution Act, 1982*. It should be noted that the test in *Sparrow*

51 R.S.C. 1985, c. F-14.

52 *An Act Respecting the Conservation and Development of Wildlife*, S.Q. 1983, c. 39.

53 *Côté*, above note 6 at para. 5 [emphasis in original].

> was originally elucidated in the context of a federal regulation which allegedly infringed an aboriginal right. The majority of recent cases which have subsequently invoked the *Sparrow* framework have similarly done so against the backdrop of a federal statute or regulation. See, e.g., *Gladstone*. But it is quite clear that the *Sparrow* test applies where a provincial law is alleged to have infringed an aboriginal or treaty right in a manner which cannot be justified: *Badger, supra*, at para. 85 (application of *Sparrow* test to provincial statute which violated a treaty right). The text and purpose of s. 35(1) do not distinguish between federal and provincial laws which restrict aboriginal or treaty rights, and they should both be subject to the same standard of constitutional scrutiny.[54]

With all due respect, I think that before deciding whether the *Sparrow* justification test applies to provincial legislation, Lamer C.J. should have asked whether the provinces have the constitutional authority to infringe Aboriginal rights, given section 91(24) and the doctrine of interjurisdictional immunity. Had he done so and concluded, as he did in *Delgamuukw*, that Aboriginal rights are within the core of section 91(24), he should have applied the *Dick* case and held that the provincial law could not apply of its own force if it infringed an Aboriginal right.[55] The Chief Justice appears to have missed this division-of-powers issue because he relied on *R. v. Badger*,[56] which he apparently regarded as authority that provincial laws can infringe Aboriginal and treaty rights of their own force. However, *Badger* does not support any general provincial authority to infringe these rights, and can be distinguished because it involved the application of the *Natural Resources Transfer Agreements*.[57] These agreements give the three prairie provinces explicit constitutional authority in relation to Indian hunting, trapping, and fishing, and provide the context in which provincial infringement of a treaty right to hunt was considered in the case.[58] *Badger* should not have been relevant in

54 *Ibid.* at para. 74.

55 It was not even necessary for Lamer C.J. to decide this issue in *Côté* because he concluded that the provincial law did not infringe the Aboriginal or treaty rights of the accused: *ibid.* at paras. 77–80 and 88.

56 [1996] 1 S.C.R. 771 [*Badger*].

57 *Constitution Act, 1930*, above note 2.

58 In his judgment in *Badger*, above note 56 at para. 69, Cory J. relied expressly on the fact that "[b]oth the Treaty and the NRTA specifically provided that the right

Quebec where *Côté* arose because only the prairie provinces have explicit constitutional authority to apply their game laws to Indians, subject to the limitations set out in the *Natural Resources Transfer Agreements*.[59] So instead of *Badger*, Lamer C.J. should have considered and applied the *Dick* decision.

Two more recent Supreme Court decisions are relevant to the issue of the application of provincial laws to section 91(24) "Indians": *Kitkatla Band v. British Columbia (Minister of Small Business, Tourism and Culture)*[60] and *Paul v. British Columbia (Forest Appeals Commission)*.[61] McAdam contends that *Kitkatla*, upholding the application of British Columbia's heritage property legislation to culturally modified trees,

---

would be subject to regulation pertaining to conservation." See Wilkins, above note 43 at 215–16.

59 In Chapter 10 Mitch McAdam disputes this for two reasons. First, "the Supreme Court held in *Marshall No. 2* [*R. v. Marshall*, [1999] 3 S.C.R. 533] that treaty rights are subject to regulations that satisfy the *Sparrow* test whether or not the written text of the treaty expressly acknowledges the possibility of those regulations" [references omitted]. This is correct, but in *Marshall*, the Court was dealing with *federal*, not *provincial*, regulations. In reference to *Badger*, it was stated in *Marshall* at para. 24 that the "Court was thus most explicit in confirming the regulatory authority of the federal and provincial governments within their respective legislative fields to regulate the exercise of the treaty right." The key words here, "within their respective legislative fields," explain the application of the provincial law in *Badger* because the case involved the *Natural Resources Transfer Agreements*. No such explanation exists for the application of the provincial law in the *Côté* decision, where Lamer C.J. neglected to inquire into the respective legislative fields of the federal and provincial governments. Second, McAdam says that "prior to 1930, the prairie provinces could impose their game laws on Indians off-reserve even in the face of treaty rights." As authority for this, he cites a passage from Laskin J.'s dissenting judgment in *Cardinal*, above note 19, cited with approval by Cory J. in *R. v. Horseman*, [1990] 1 S.C.R. 901 [*Horseman*]. However, while Cory J. accepted Laskin J.'s general assessment that the *Natural Resources Transfer Agreements* contracted rather than expanded provincial legislative power, the pre-1930 applicability of provincial game laws to Indian hunting in the prairie provinces had never been resolved, as Martland J., for the majority, pointed out in *Cardinal*: see text accompanying note 20, above in this chapter. Moreover, the *Dick* decision, above note 4, is clear authority that provincial game laws cannot apply of their own force so as to affect Indianness; this would have been as much the case in the prairie provinces before 1930 as in British Columbia where the *Dick* case arose in 1980.

60 [2002] 2 S.C.R. 146 [*Kitkatla*].

61 [2003] 2 S.C.R. 585 [*Paul*].

confirmed several important principles supporting his thesis. He lists three of these principles: (1) the basic assumption that "provincial laws apply to Indians and on Indian reserves," (2) "merely incidental effects will not disturb the constitutional applicability of an otherwise valid provincial law," and (3) "provincial laws that treat Indians and non-Indians alike will not be rendered constitutionally inapplicable simply because they have a disproportionate effect upon Indians." On the basis of these principles, McAdam arrives at this conclusion:

> The constitutional principles recognized in *Kitkatla* must apply to Aboriginal and treaty hunting and fishing rights just as they do to reserve lands and Indian artifacts. There is no juristic reason to distinguish between different aspects of federal jurisdiction under section 91(24).

I disagree emphatically. Interjurisdictional immunity is precisely the juristic reason for distinguishing the core from other elements of section 91(24) jurisdiction,[62] and for treating otherwise valid provincial laws that impinge on that core differently from provincial laws that do not. While *Kitkatla* did decide that provincial laws of general application can apply of their own force to section 91(24) "Indians" even if they have a disproportionate effect upon them, it did not hold that those laws can so apply where Aboriginal or treaty rights, or reserve lands, are concerned. The culturally modified trees in question were not on reserve lands.[63] Any Aboriginal title or other Aboriginal right that would have brought them within the core of federal jurisdiction as identified in *Delgamuukw* was not proven. Moreover, the cultural significance of the trees was not demonstrated. Therefore, the evidential basis for concluding that the provincial law impaired the status or capacity of the Kitkatla or affected their Indianness was insufficient.[64] Delivering the unanimous judgment of the Court, LeBel J. found "no intrusion on a federal head of power" because it had "not been established that these provisions affect the essential and

---

62 For example, in *Francis*, above note 32, the Supreme Court upheld the validity of federal regulation of traffic on Indian reserves, but decided that traffic regulation is not within the *core* of federal jurisdiction and so provincial traffic laws can also apply of their own force on reserves.

63 *Kitkatla*, above note 60 at para. 74.

64 See Kent McNeil, "Culturally Modified Trees, Indian Reserves, and the Crown's Fiduciary Obligations" (2003) 21 Sup. Ct. L. Rev. (2d) 105 at 106–15.

distinctive core values of Indianness which would engage the federal power over native affairs and First Nations in Canada."[65] But if sufficient evidence to that effect had been presented, or an Aboriginal right regarding the trees proven, apparently the outcome would have been different.[66] LeBel J. stated:

> Heritage properties and sites may certainly, in some cases, turn out to be a key part of the collective identity of people. In some future case, it might very well happen that some component of the cultural heritage of a First Nation would go to the core of its identity in such a way that it would affect the federal power over native affairs and the applicability of provincial legislation.[67]

Given the lack of such evidence in this case, LeBel J. concluded that it would "not be useful to discuss the doctrine of interjurisdictional immunity. It would apply only if the provincial legislation went to the core of the federal power."[68] He then referred to the discussions of interjurisdictional immunity in *Ordon Estate*[69] and *Delgamuukw*,[70] confirming its applicability in the context of section 91(24).

The *Paul* case involved a challenge to the authority of the British Columbia legislature to confer jurisdiction on a quasi-judicial tribunal, the Forest Appeals Commission, to determine questions of Aboriginal rights and title. The British Columbia Court of Appeal applied the doctrine of interjurisdictional immunity. It held this attempted conferral of jurisdiction to be unconstitutional because the provincial law would intrude on the Indianness at the core of section 91(24).[71] The Supreme Court reversed this decision, holding that the doctrine does not apply to the exercise of adjudicative, as opposed to legislative, functions. In so doing, however,

---

65 *Kitkatla*, above note 60 at para. 75. See also para. 70.

66 See Jean Leclair, "The Supreme Court of Canada's Understanding of Federalism: Efficiency at the Expense of Diversity" (2003) 28 Queen's L.J. 411 at para. 56.

67 *Kitkatla*, above note 60 at para. 78.

68 *Ibid.* at para. 77. For this reason, he also said that "no discussion of the principle governing the application of s. 88 of the *Indian Act* would be warranted": *ibid.* This confirms the holding in *Dick*, above note 4, that s. 88 is irrelevant if the provincial law in question applies of its own force.

69 Above note 9 at para. 81.

70 Above note 6 at paras. 177–78.

71 [2001] 4 C.N.L.R. 210 (B.C.C.A.).

the Court affirmed the basic tenets of the doctrine, both generally and in the context of section 91(24). After referring to the discussions of the application of the doctrine in *Bell Canada*,[72] *Ordon Estate*,[73] *Delgamuukw*,[74] and *Kitkatla*,[75] Bastarache J., speaking for the whole Court, said:

> The question, then, is whether, in a valid law of general application, provisions that empower a provincially constituted administrative tribunal to hear and rule upon arguments relating to aboriginal rights as they arise in execution of its provincial mandate trench upon the core of Indianness. *If so, those provisions will be inapplicable to Indians.*[76]

Justice Bastarache concluded that the provincial law did not trench on the core of Indianness, or "have a substantial impact upon Indians *qua* Indians," because it did not "alter the substance of any federal rule or aboriginal right."[77] He stated:

> Legislation that triggers the doctrine of interjurisdictional immunity purports to regulate indirectly matters within exclusive federal competence, that is, to alter rights and obligations . . . . The Commission's enabling provisions do not attempt to supplement or amend the constitutional and federal rules respecting aboriginal rights. Indeed, the question is whether the legislature may empower the Commission to take cognizance of existing constitutional rights and rights under federal rules, not to alter or supplant them.[78]

Justice Bastarache was thus of the opinion that provincial laws that would "regulate indirectly matters within exclusive federal competence" or "alter rights and obligations" are subject to the doctrine of interjurisdictional immunity. As Aboriginal rights are at the core of federal jurisdiction under section 91(24),[79] it follows that provincial laws that would regulate or alter them must be inapplicable of their own force. There is

72 Above note 8.

73 Above note 9.

74 Above note 6.

75 Above note 60.

76 *Paul*, above note 61 at para. 16 [emphasis added].

77 *Ibid.* at para. 6.

78 *Ibid.* at para. 19.

79 *Delgamuukw*, above note 6 at para. 181. See text accompanying note 33, above in this chapter.

no need for those laws to try and extinguish the rights for them to be inapplicable in this context.

At one point in his judgment, however, Bastarache J. did envisage provincial infringement of Aboriginal rights. He said that "*Sparrow* stands for the proposition that government regulation, including provincial regulation may, by legislation, infringe an aboriginal right if that infringement is justified."[80] This statement, not backed by other authority, followed these comments on the interplay between section 91(24) of the *Constitution Act, 1867*, and section 35 of the *Constitution Act, 1982*:

> Unless otherwise specified, such as official language rights in the *Charter* particular to New Brunswick, every right in the *Constitution Act, 1982* applies to every province as well as to the federal government. It is also established that one part of the Constitution cannot abrogate another: *Adler v. Ontario*, [1996] 3 S.C.R. 609. By virtue of s. 35, then, laws of the province of British Columbia that conflict with protected aboriginal rights do not so apply to limit those rights, unless the limitation is justifiable according to the test in *Sparrow, supra*.[81]

But if one part of the Constitution cannot abrogate another, section 35 should not have limited the scope of the protection against provincial laws already afforded by section 91(24) and the doctrine of interjurisdictional immunity. It would be absurd for section 35, which was inserted in the Constitution to protect Aboriginal rights from legislative extinguishment and infringement,[82] to have had the effect of reducing the protection those rights already enjoyed through the division of powers.[83] The correct approach to the issue of the application of an otherwise-valid provincial law to an Aboriginal right is therefore to begin with section 91(24) and determine whether the provincial law, in Bastarache J.'s words, "trench[es] upon the core of Indianness."[84] If the answer is yes, then the provincial law cannot apply of its own force, as was held in *Dick*[85] and af-

80 *Paul*, above note 61 at para. 25.

81 *Ibid*. at para. 24.

82 See *Van der Peet*, above note 7 at para. 28; *Mitchell v. Canada (Minister of National Revenue)*, [2001] 1 S.C.R. 911 at para. 11.

83 See Wilkins, above note 43 at 217–19.

84 *Paul*, above note 61 at para. 16. See text accompanying note 76, above in this chapter.

85 Above note 4. See text accompanying notes 22–45, above in this chapter.

firmed in *Paul*[86] (although, as in *Dick*, it might be referentially incorporated into federal law by section 88 of the *Indian Act*). The provincial law would certainly trench upon Indianness if it would extinguish the Aboriginal right. Indeed, in *Delgamuukw*, Lamer C.J. said that to have that effect it would have to be a law "in relation to Indians and Indian lands," taking it completely outside provincial jurisdiction.[87] Yet in *Paul*, Bastarache J. said a provincial law that regulates or alters rights within exclusive federal jurisdiction — and this includes Aboriginal rights — would trigger the doctrine of interjurisdictional immunity.[88] Such a law would still be valid if otherwise within provincial jurisdiction, but would have to be read down so as not to apply of its own force to regulate or alter the Aboriginal right. This issue of whether the provincial law applies of its own force would have to be decided before section 35 is even considered.[89] That section, and the issue of justification, would come into play only if the provincial law could apply to infringe the right, either of its own force or as a result of section 88 of the *Indian Act*.[90]

This analysis follows from Bastarache J.'s comments on the doctrine of interjurisdictional immunity in *Paul*.[91] But like Lamer C.J. in *Delgamuukw*, he assumed that Aboriginal rights can be infringed by some provincial laws without those laws trenching on Indianness by regulat-

---

86 Above note 61. See text accompanying note 76, above in this chapter.

87 *Delgamuukw*, above note 6 at para. 180. See text accompanying note 37, above in this chapter.

88 *Paul*, above note 61 at para. 19. See text accompanying note 78, above in this chapter.

89 In *Paul*, *ibid.* at para. 49, Bastarache J. answered the question of whether the provincial law could apply in this way: "Yes. As a law of general application, the *Forest Practices Code of British Columbia* applies *ex proprio vigore* to Indians, to the extent that it does not touch on the 'core of Indianness' *and* is not unjustifiably inconsistent with s. 35 of the *Constitution Act, 1982*" [emphasis added]. I think it significant that he placed the division-of-powers matter first, as it logically comes before consideration of s. 35: see *Alphonse*, above note 41 at para. 51, where Macfarlane J.A. stated that the s. 35 analysis "stands as a separate and subsequent review, which is properly done after division of powers issues have been resolved."

90 Note, however, that the issue of justification of provincial laws referentially incorporated by s. 88 raises complex constitutional issues not yet addressed by the Supreme Court: see the cases and articles cited in notes 41–43, above in this chapter.

91 Note that Mitch McAdam in Chapter 10 makes no reference to these comments, citing only the passages in *Paul*, above note 61 at paras. 24–25, relating to provincial authority to infringe Aboriginal rights.

ing or altering those rights. However, in neither case was this assumption backed up by analysis, either generally or in the context of a particular provincial law.[92] And we have seen that in *Côté*,[93] the decision relied upon in *Delgamuukw*, the issue of interjurisdictional immunity, though directly relevant, was not even considered due to the Court's misguided reliance upon the *Badger* decision.[94] In my respectful opinion, the Court therefore needs to consider how alleged provincial authority to infringe Aboriginal rights can be reconciled with the doctrine of interjurisdictional immunity; it also needs to explain how a provincial law can infringe an Aboriginal right that is within the core of section 91(24) by regulating or altering the right, without trenching on exclusive federal jurisdiction.

The Supreme Court had the opportunity to consider this matter in the context of treaty rights in *R. v. Morris*.[95] This case involved charges against two members of the Tsartlip Band of the Saanich Nation of violating British Columbia's *Wildlife Act*[96] by hunting at night with lights.[97] The accused contended that they have a treaty right to hunt for food at night using lights, and that the provincial prohibition of night hunting does not apply to them because it violates this right. Justices Deschamps and Abella, writing for the majority of the Court, agreed.[98] After concluding that night hunting is not necessarily dangerous and is within the treaty's scope when conducted safely, they briefly turned their attention to section 91(24) and the constitutional division of powers:

> By virtue of s. 91(24), Parliament has exclusive power to make laws in relation to "Indians, and Lands reserved for the Indians". Provincial laws whose "pith and substance" relates to this head of power are *ultra vires* and

---

92 In *Paul*, *ibid.* at para. 24, Bastarache J. seems to have been concerned with the necessity for the infringement to be justified, without considering the prior issue of whether a provincial law could infringe an Aboriginal right without trenching on Indianness: see text accompanying notes 81–82, above in this chapter.

93 Above note 6.

94 See text accompanying notes 50–59, above in this chapter.

95 Above note 7.

96 S.B.C. 1982, c. 57.

97 This case is discussed at length by Mitch McAdam in Chapter 10 in this volume.

98 Justices Binnie and Charron concurred; McLachlin C.J. and Fish J., Bastarache J. concurring, dissented.

> invalid (*Kitkatla Band* . . . at para. 67). However, provincial laws of general application that affect Indians only incidentally and are enacted under a provincial head of power will be found to be *intra vires* and valid.[99]

Justices Deschamps and Abella went on to affirm that,

> . . . where a valid provincial law [such as the *Wildlife Act*] impairs "an integral part of primary federal jurisdiction over Indians or Lands reserved for the Indians" (*Four B Manufacturing* . . . at p. 1047), it will be inapplicable to the extent of the impairment. Thus, provincial laws of general application are precluded from impairing "Indianness."[100]

Regarding the application of these principles to treaties, they held that "[t]reaty rights to hunt lie squarely within federal jurisdiction over 'Indians, and Lands reserved for the Indians,'" and so "provincial laws of general application that interfere with treaty rights to hunt are inapplicable to particular Aboriginal peoples."[101] The last passage clearly entails the doctrine of interjurisdictional immunity, though Deschamps and Abella JJ. did not refer to it by name.[102]

Chief Justice McLachlin and Justice Fish dissented in *Morris* because they were of the view that night hunting is inherently dangerous, and so cannot be a treaty right. After agreeing that "Aboriginal and treaty rights fall squarely within Parliament's jurisdiction under s. 91(24)" and that "[p]rovincial legislation that, in pith and substance, relates to 'Indians' or 'Lands reserved for the Indians' . . . is *ultra vires*,"[103] they discussed the application of the doctrine of interjurisdictional immunity. They decided that the *Wildlife Act* is within provincial jurisdiction, is not directed at "Indians," and does not conflict with any federal legislation. Turning to interjurisdictional immunity, they stated:

---

99 *Morris*, above note 7 at para. 41.

100 *Ibid.* at para. 42, relying on *Four B Manufacturing*, above note 32, and *Dick*, above note 4 at 326.

101 *Ibid.* at para. 43, relying on *R. v. Simon*, [1985] 2 S.C.R. 387 at 411 [*Simon*], and *Sundown*, above note 43.

102 Later, however, they stated that s. 88 of the *Indian Act*, above note 3, "reflects Parliament's intention to avoid the effects of the immunity imposed by s. 91(24) by incorporating certain provincial laws of general application into federal law": *Morris*, above note 7 at para. 44.

103 *Ibid.* at paras. 83 and 85.

> Under the doctrine of interjurisdictional immunity, valid provincial legislation is constitutionally inapplicable to the extent that it intrudes or touches upon core federal legislative competence over a particular matter. Thus, exclusive federal jurisdiction under s. 91(24) protects "core Indianness" from provincial intrusion: *Delgamuukw* ... at para. 177. Valid provincial legislation which does not touch on "core Indianness" applies *ex proprio vigore* ....
>
> Indian treaty rights and aboriginal rights have been held to fall within the protected core of federal jurisdiction: *Simon* ... at p. 411; *Delgamuukw* ... at para. 178. It follows that provincial laws of general application do not apply *ex proprio vigore* to the hunting activities of Indians that are protected by a treaty.
>
> If, however, a provincial law of general application does not affect a treaty right, and does not otherwise touch upon core Indianness, that law applies *ex proprio vigore*, without recourse to s. 88 [of the *Indian Act*]. Legislation that falls outside the internal limits on the treaty right that the parties to the treaty would have understood and intended would not encroach on the treaty right.[104]

The minority and majority judgments in *Morris* thus appear to be in accord with one another,[105] and in agreement with earlier decisions, on the matter of the application of the doctrine of interjurisdictional immunity in the context of section 91(24), with this difference: the minority preserved the "touch upon" and "affect" language from earlier cases as the standard for determining the inapplicability of provincial laws to "Indians,"[106] whereas the majority used "impair" (in the context of treaty

104 *Ibid.* at paras. 90–92, relying on *Delgamuukw*, above note 6, and *Simon*, above note 101.

105 Justice Vickers reached the same conclusion in *Tsilhqot'in Nation*, above note 25 at para. 1023. Applying the principles from *Morris* to Aboriginal title, he concluded that, due to s. 91(24) and the doctrine of interjurisdictional immunity, the provisions of the *Forest Act*, R.S.B.C. 1996, c. 157, involving acquisition, removal, and sale of timber, cannot apply to Aboriginal title lands.

106 See *Dick*, above note 4 at 326, where Beetz J. stated that "a distinction should be drawn between two categories of provincial laws. There are, on the one hand, provincial laws which can be applied to Indians without touching their Indianness, like traffic legislation; there are on the other hand, provincial laws which cannot apply to Indians without regulating them *qua* Indians." In *Paul*, above note 61 at para. 49, Bastarache J., delivering the unanimous judgment of a nine-member

rights, "interfere with"). The latter anticipates the explicit shift in *Canadian Western Bank* of the standard for invoking the doctrine generally from "touch upon" and "affect" to "impair."[107]

In *Morris*, both the majority and the minority discussed the relevance of section 88 of the *Indian Act*.[108] That section makes provincial laws of general application that do not apply to Indians *ex proprio vigore* apply to them as referentially incorporated federal law, subject to "the terms of any treaty" and other statutory exceptions.[109] Justices Deschamps and Abella, for the majority, decided that section 88 shields non-commercial treaty rights to hunt from *prima facie* infringement, but not from insignificant interference, by provincial laws.[110] Using the test for *prima facie* infringement developed by the Court in the context of section 35 of the *Constitution Act, 1982*, they stated:

> Essentially, therefore, a *prima facie* infringement requires a "meaningful diminution" of a treaty right. This includes anything but an insignificant interference with that right. If provincial laws or regulations interfere insignificantly with the exercise of treaty rights, they will not be found to infringe them and can apply *ex proprio vigore* or by incorporation under s. 88.[111]

As an example of insignificant interference, Deschamps and Abella JJ. referred to *Côté*, where a provincial access fee to a controlled zone was held not to infringe a treaty right to fish because the fee was used to pay for maintenance of roads and facilities in the zone, and the financial bur-

---

bench, provided this answer to the constitutional question: "As a law of general application, the *Forest Practices Code of British Columbia* applies *ex proprio vigore* to Indians, to the extent that it does not touch on the 'core of Indianness' and is not unjustifiably inconsistent with s. 35 of the *Constitution Act, 1982*." See also *Delgamuukw*, above note 6 at para. 178; *Kitkatla*, above note 60 at paras. 75 and 78.

107 See text accompanying note 13, above in this chapter.

108 Above note 3.

109 See *Dick*, above note 4.

110 Justices Deschamps and Abella left the matter of commercial rights to be determined in a case where they are directly in issue: *Morris*, above note 7 at para. 46. In so doing, they avoided coming to terms with an *obiter* statement in *Marshall No. 2*, above note 59, regarding the application of provincial laws in the context of treaty rights that, as Mitch McAdam points out Chapter 10, seems to conflict with their decision in *Morris*.

111 *Morris*, *ibid.* at para. 53.

den it imposed was modest.[112] They contrasted this with the licensing scheme in *Badger*, which infringed a treaty right to hunt because it imposed conditions on "hunting method, the kind and numbers of game, the season and the permissible hunting area."[113]

Justices Deschamps and Abella went on to hold that, while the test for *prima facie* infringement that was developed in the context of section 35 of the *Constitution Act, 1982*, is helpful in determining whether a provincial law infringes a treaty right for the purposes of section 88 of the *Indian Act*, the *Sparrow* test for justifying infringements of section 35 rights does not apply to section 88 treaty rights. The reason is that the "justification analysis does not alter the division of powers, which is dealt with in s. 88."[114] More precisely, the justification test does not apply in the context of section 88 because federal jurisdiction and paramountcy completely exclude the application of provincial laws that would infringe treaty rights.

In conclusion, Deschamps and Abella JJ. decided that the provincial law prohibiting hunting at night and with lights constituted a *prima facie* infringement of the appellants' treaty rights. As a result, the provincial law could not apply to them, either of its own force or through section 88.

Although McLachlin C.J. and Fish J. dissented in *Morris* on the existence of a treaty right to hunt at night, their analysis of section 88 is consistent with that of the majority. Adopting Beetz J.'s interpretation of section 88 in the *Dick* decision, they said the section "incorporates provincial laws of general application that are otherwise constitutionally inapplicable to Indians — laws that are precluded from applying to Indians by the doctrine of interjurisdictional immunity because they affect core Indianness, a matter under federal jurisdiction."[115] They agreed with the majority that "a *prima facie* infringement test best characterizes the degree of conflict required to engage the protection of the treaty exception. Legislation that places no real burden on the treaty right does not

112 *Ibid*. at para. 48, citing *Côté*, above note 6 at para. 88.

113 *Ibid*. at para. 49, quoting *Badger*, above note 56 at para. 92.

114 *Ibid*. at para. 55. This holding resolved the issue, left hanging by Lamer C.J. in *Côté*, above note 6 at para. 87, of whether the justification test should apply to s. 88.

115 *Morris*, *ibid*. at para. 96.

constitute a *prima facie* infringement and would not trigger the treaty exception."[116]

A final matter to be considered before discussing the situation of the Métis is whether the more recent Supreme Court decisions in *Canadian Western Bank*[117] and *Lafarge Canada*[118] will have an impact on the application of the doctrine of interjurisdictional immunity in the context of section 91(24). Remembering that Binnie and LeBel JJ., in *Canadian Western Bank*, said the doctrine "should in general be reserved for situations already covered by precedent,"[119] and that they referred with approval to leading decisions involving its application where Aboriginal peoples are concerned,[120] I do not expect the impact to be significant. However, the shift in that decision of the standard for invoking the doctrine from "touch upon" and "affect" to "impair" may mean that provincial laws that affect, but do not interfere with "Indian status or capacity" or "Indianness," or with possession and use of Indian lands, could apply of their own force to "Indians, and Lands reserved for the Indians." In this context, the Supreme Court might use the distinction between insignificant interference and *prima facie* infringement that it drew in relation to section 88 of the *Indian Act* in *Morris*.[121] As was held in *Morris*, though, provincial laws that would cause *prima facie* infringements of *treaty* rights would be excluded from application by the doctrine of interjurisdictional immunity. If this ruling is logically extended, provincial laws that would cause *prima facie* infringements of *Aboriginal* rights would suffer the same fate (though they might be referentially incorporated into federal law by section 88[122]). However, as argued by Dale Gibson in Chapter 8 in this volume, provincial laws that affect "Indians, or Lands reserved for the Indians" in *positive* ways would not necessarily run afoul of the doctrine.

116 *Ibid.* at para. 99.

117 Above note 11.

118 Above note 12.

119 *Canadian Western Bank*, above note 11 at para. 77.

120 For example, *Dick*, above note 4, and *Derrickson*, above note 9: see above note 16 and accompanying text.

121 The use by Deschamps and Abella JJ., in *Morris*, of the provincial access fee at issue in *Côté* as an example of insignificant interference (see text accompanying note 112, above in this chapter) may be an indication that this will happen.

122 See *Dick*, above note 4, and text accompanying notes 40–43, above in this chapter.

C. THE MÉTIS AND THE DOCTRINE OF INTERJURISDICTIONAL IMMUNITY

Assuming again that the Métis are within the scope section 91(24) of the *Constitution Act, 1867*,[123] the issue of the application of the doctrine of interjurisdictional immunity is potentially of much greater significance for them than it is for status Indians (Aboriginal persons who are under the *Indian Act*). The reason is that, subject to the provisos contained therein, section 88 makes provincial laws of general application that would not apply of their own force to status Indians apply to them as federal laws.[124] Provincial laws may therefore be able to infringe the Aboriginal rights of status Indians through section 88, if the infringement can be justified in accordance with the *Sparrow* test.[125] No such provision exists for making provincial laws that are not applicable to the Métis of their own force, due to the doctrine of interjurisdictional immunity, apply to them through referential incorporation into federal law.[126] So, assuming the Métis are within section 91(24), all provincial laws that impinge on the core of their "Indianness" — or, more appropriately, their "Aboriginality"[127] or "Métisness" — should be inapplicable to them, as Dale Gibson and Albert Peeling have concluded. The potentially large scope of "Métisness" encompasses everything related to the distinctive culture of the Métis people. It would certainly include their Aboriginal rights[128] and should also include broader cultural matters, such as family, community, and economic interests, as Gibson has convincingly argued.[129]

---

123 See above notes 1–2 and accompanying text.

124 See *Dick*, above note 4.

125 See *Alphonse*, *Dick* 1993, and *Sundown*, above notes 41–43. Note, however, the criticisms of these decisions in the articles cited in note 43, above in this chapter.

126 See text accompanying note 3, above in this chapter.

127 The term *Aboriginality* was used by the Supreme Court in relation to the Métis in *Lovelace*, above note 2 at paras. 109 and 111.

128 Recall that in *Delgamuukw*, above note 6 at para. 181, Lamer C.J. held that Aboriginal rights are within the core of s. 91(24): see text accompanying note 33, above in this chapter. Of course, the leading case on Métis Aboriginal rights is *R. v. Powley*, [2003] 2 S.C.R. 207, decided on the basis of s. 35 of the *Constitution Act, 1982*, without considering the issue of s. 91(24) and the application of the doctrine of interjurisdictional immunity.

129 See *Przybyszewski v. Métis Nation of Ontario*, [2004] F.C.J. No. 1238, where Russell J. decided there was sufficient evidence for an adjudicator acting under the *Canada*

In his discussion, Mitch McAdam refers to two Saskatchewan cases, *R. v. Grumbo*[130] and *R. v. Maurice*,[131] where the issue of the protection against provincial game laws afforded to the Métis by federal jurisdiction under section 91(24) and the doctrine of interjurisdictional immunity was argued. The Crown admitted that the Métis are "Indians" for the purposes of section 91(24), but in each case the court held the doctrine to be inapplicable. From these decisions, McAdam concludes that, prior to the more recent Supreme Court decision in *Morris*,

> The law in Saskatchewan therefore appeared to be settled on this point: Métis people exercising Aboriginal rights to hunt and fish were not immune from the application of provincial laws. As long as they could be justified under the *Sparrow* test, provincial fish and game laws were constitutionally applicable even if they infringed upon the right. Interjurisdictional immunity could be invoked only where the effect of the provincial law was to extinguish the right.

In *Grumbo*, the main issue was whether the Métis are Indians for the purposes of the *Natural Resources Transfer Agreements*, an issue since resolved by the decision of the Supreme Court in *Blais* that they are not.[132] Justice Sherstobitoff, for the majority of the Court of Appeal, paid scant attention to the interjurisdictional immunity argument. He dismissed it on the basis that the "weight of authority clearly says that provincial legislation relating to game is provincial law of general application affecting Indians not *qua* Indians but as inhabitants of the province, and is applicable to them, subject of course to s. 12 of the *Natural Resources Transfer Agreement*."[133] After referring to *Cardinal*,[134] *Horseman*,[135] and *R. v. Kruger*,[136] he continued:

Labour Code to conclude that an Aboriginal Healing and Wellness Strategy program, administered by the Métis Nation of Ontario exclusively for Métis persons, to promote the well-being of the Métis people, was sufficiently linked to "Métisness" to come within federal jurisdiction under s. 91(24), if the Métis are "Indians" for the purposes of that provision.

130 [1998] 3 C.N.L.R. 172 (Sask. C.A.) [*Grumbo*].

131 [2002] 2 C.N.L.R. 273 (Sask. Q.B.) [*Maurice*].

132 See above note 2.

133 *Grumbo*, above note 130 at para. 38.

134 Above note 19.

135 Above note 59.

136 [1978] 1 S.C.R. 104.

> The principle is not affected by the judgment of the Supreme Court in *R. v. Dick*, [1985] 2 S.C.R. 309 . . . , where the court was prepared to assume, for the purpose of the judgment, that the legislation in issue affected the Indianness of the accused, because it was specifically said that the court was not deciding the issue. Mr. Grumbo cannot succeed on this ground.[137]

With all due respect, this view is wrong, as the assumption made in *Dick* was *factual*.[138] Justice Beetz clearly was of the view that, as a matter of *law*, a provincial game law shown by the evidence to cross the line into the core of Indianness would not apply of its own force. This interpretation has been affirmed by the Supreme Court in *Delgamuukw*, where Lamer C.J. stated, in reference to *Dick*, that "a provincial law which regulated hunting may very well touch on this core" of Indianness.[139] In *Kitkatla* as well, LeBel J. clearly thought there would be intrusion on federal jurisdiction if the evidence established that a provincial law affected "the essential and distinctive core values of Indianness which would engage the federal power over native affairs and First Nations in Canada."[140] So, Sherstobitoff J.A.'s cursory dismissal of the application of the doctrine of interjurisdictional immunity in the context of provincial game laws should not be regarded as authoritative, even in Saskatchewan.

In *Maurice*,[141] two Métis men were charged with hunting at night with a light, contrary to a provincial game law. The Crown admitted that they had an Aboriginal right to hunt for food, but argued that the right does not include night hunting, and even if it does, the right could be infringed by provincial legislation of general application if the infringement was justified. The Crown contended that, in this instance, infringement was justified by strong safety considerations. Counsel for the accused relied on the *Saskatchewan Natural Resources Transfer Agreement*, as well as on the doctrine of interjurisdictional immunity. Relying on the Crown's admission that the Métis are "Indians" within the meaning of

137 *Grumbo*, above note 130 at para. 38.

138 See text accompanying notes 22–23, above in this chapter.

139 *Delgamuukw*, above note 6 at para. 182: see text accompanying note 44, above in this chapter.

140 *Kitkatla*, above note 60 at para. 75: see text accompanying notes 65–68, above in this chapter.

141 Above note 131.

section 91(24) of the *Constitution Act, 1867*, he contended that the provincial prohibition against night hunting could not apply to them because it touched on the core of their Indianness. It thereby ran afoul of the doctrine of interjurisdictional immunity. Justice Krueger of the Court of Queen's Bench rejected this argument. He referred to the trial judge's factual finding that "night hunting with artificial lights is not a tradition of the Métis of Northwest Saskatchewan" and accepted that it followed from this that a provincial law "prohibiting such hunting does not touch their core of Indianness."[142] Although Krueger J. also held that provincial laws of general application can infringe Aboriginal hunting rights if the infringement is justified,[143] he agreed with the trial judge that laws having a safety objective do not infringe those rights,[144] rendering a decision on provincial power to infringe unnecessary. The crux of his decision, therefore, was that night hunting lay outside the core of Indianness as well as outside the admitted Aboriginal right.[145] The case is thus weak authority indeed for McAdam's assertion that "Métis people exercising Aboriginal rights to hunt and fish were not immune from the application of provincial laws."

D. CONCLUSION

So far, most of the case law on the application of the doctrine of interjurisdictional immunity in the context of Aboriginal peoples has arisen in relation to Indians who come within the scope of the *Indian Act*. Those cases have consistently held that provincial laws affecting "Indianness"

---

142 *Ibid.* at para. 25.

143 As authority for this, he relied primarily on *Sparrow*, above note 6, which involved federal rather than provincial laws, and *Delgamuukw*, above note 6, which contains serious inconsistencies in relation to this issue: see text accompanying notes 44–59, above in this chapter. He also relied on the problematic passage from *Grumbo*, above note 130 at para. 38: see text accompanying notes 137–40, above in this chapter.

144 *Maurice*, above note 131 at paras. 16 and 19.

145 Compare *R. v. Laviolette*, [2005] S.J. No. 454 (Prov. Ct.), where the issue of interjurisdictional immunity was raised as a defence, but not addressed because the court found that the accused had an Aboriginal right as a Métis person to fish for food, and the Crown had presented no evidence to justify infringement of that right by the province.

cannot apply to Indians of their own force without trenching on the core of exclusive federal jurisdiction provided by section 91(24) of the *Constitution Act, 1867*. However, those laws may apply to status Indians if referentially incorporated into federal law by section 88 of the *Indian Act*.

Section 88 does not encompass the Métis because they are excluded by definition from the scope of the *Indian Act*. Assuming the Métis are "Indians" for the purposes of section 91(24), this means that the doctrine of interjurisdictional immunity should have greater significance for them than for status Indians who have been denied some of the doctrine's protection by section 88. If a provincial law affects or at least impairs[146] their "Aboriginality" or "Métisness," it cannot apply to the Métis of its own force. This results from the constitutional division-of-powers and has nothing to do with section 35 of the *Constitution Act, 1982*.

Obiter statements by Supreme Court judges have nonetheless suggested that provincial laws infringing Aboriginal rights can apply of their own force if the infringement can be justified.[147] In making these statements, the judges appear to have leapfrogged over section 91(24) and the doctrine of interjurisdictional immunity, and thus acted *per incuriam*.[148] They have gone straight to justifiable infringement under section 35 of

146 See discussion of *Canadian Western Bank* in text accompanying notes 11–14 and 117–22, above in this chapter.

147 The statements are *obiter* because in no case, other than the exceptional case of *Badger*, above note 56, has the Supreme Court been obliged to decide the issue. In *Côté*, above note 6, Lamer C.J. found there was no infringement, so he did not have to decide whether the province had the constitutional authority to infringe: see above note 55. In *Delgamuukw*, above note 6, and *Paul*, above note 61, there was no question of infringement for the Court to decide. Only in *Badger* was provincial infringement really an issue, but as we have seen, one cannot derive a general provincial authority to infringe from that case because it involved the *Alberta Natural Resources Transfer Agreement*: see text accompanying notes 56–59, above in this chapter. See also note 148 below.

148 The *per incuriam* doctrine applies where judges inadvertently overlook a relevant precedent, statutory provision, or legal principle, bringing their decision on the point into question and undermining its value as a precedent: see *Halsbury's Laws of England*, 4th ed., vol. 26 (London: Butterworths, 1973–) at para. 578, and the authorities listed there. Justice Lambert of the B.C.C.A., in "*Van der Peet* and *Delgamuukw*: Ten Unresolved Issues" (1998) 32 U.B.C. L. Rev. 249 at para. 55, wrote this in relation to provincial authority to infringe Aboriginal title: "But *Côté* is an aboriginal sustenance rights case and not a title case. Neither in *Côté* nor in *Delgamuukw*, does Chief Justice Lamer consider the question of the legislative compe-

the *Constitution Act, 1982*, without considering the prior question of how provincial laws can infringe Aboriginal rights that are clearly within the core of section 91(24), and at the same time avoid violating the doctrine of interjurisdictional immunity. Fortunately, in its decision in *Morris*,[149] the Supreme Court clarified that treaty rights, because they are within the core of section 91(24) jurisdiction and thus protected by interjurisdictional immunity, cannot be infringed by provincial laws, either of those laws' own force or by their referential incorporation into federal law by section 88. Given that Aboriginal rights are also within the core of federal jurisdiction, they must likewise be protected from provincial infringement by interjurisdictional immunity.[150] However, the Supreme Court has not yet decided whether provincial laws that justifiably infringe Aboriginal rights can apply to status Indians through referential incorporation by section 88.[151]

The *Morris* decision provides authoritative support for the arguments made in this commentary that Métis Aboriginal rights and other significant aspects of Métis culture,[152] which should come within the core of federal jurisdiction if the Métis are under section 91(24), are protected by the doctrine of interjurisdictional immunity against infringement or impairment by provincial laws of general application. Moreover, federal jurisdiction should make provincial laws that are aimed at or in relation to the Métis and their rights *ultra vires* and thus unconstitutional.[153] So, if the Métis are within section 91(24), their Aboriginal rights have division-of-powers protection against provincial laws that may be as substantial and extensive as the protection accorded to treaty rights in the *Morris*

---

tence of the province to infringe on aboriginal title. So, what he says is not only *obiter dicta*, but perhaps may be regarded also as having been said *per incuriam*."

149 Above note 7.

150 This conclusion was reached by Vickers J. in *Tsilhqot'in Nation*, above note 25: see above note 105.

151 See cases and articles cited in notes 41–43, above in this chapter. In *Tsilhqot'in Nation*, however, Vickers J. held that provincial laws infringing Aboriginal title are not referentially incorporated by s. 88 because that section only makes provincial laws apply to "Indians," not to "Lands reserved for Indians": see above note 25.

152 Possible examples are the family, community, and economic interests identified by Dale Gibson in Chapter 8.

153 See text accompanying notes 37–38, above in this chapter.

decision.[154] This could mean that the Aboriginal rights of status Indians alone are exposed to justifiable infringement by provincial laws, through the operation of section 88.[155] If so, one has to wonder how the honour of the Crown in right of Canada is served by a statutory provision that singles out status Indians and subjects their Aboriginal rights to unequal treatment by exposing these rights to provincial infringement.[156]

---

154 While treaty rights and Métis Aboriginal rights would have the same interjurisdictional immunity protection, treaty rights enjoy the additional protection of s. 88 and federal paramountcy. However, this may not make any difference, as the interjurisdictional immunity and s. 88 protections may be equivalent: see text accompanying notes 121–22, above in this chapter.

155 See cases cited in notes 41–43 and 151, above in this chapter.

156 This unequal treatment could be avoided by judicial reconsideration of whether, after the enactment of s. 35 of the *Constitution Act, 1982*, provincial laws that infringe Aboriginal rights can be referentially incorporated by s. 88: see the articles cited in note 43, above in this chapter. Recent decisions invoking the honour of the Crown could be relied upon: see *Haida Nation v. British Columbia (Minister of Forests)*, [2004] 3 S.C.R. 511; *Taku River Tlingit First Nation v. British Columbia (Project Assessment Director)*, [2004] 3 S.C.R. 550; *Mikisew Cree First Nation v. Canada (Minister of Canadian Heritage)*, [2005] 3 S.C.R. 388; and discussion in Brian Slattery, "Aboriginal Rights and the Honour of the Crown" (2005) 29 Sup. Ct. L. Rev. (2d) 433.

‹ 12 ›

The Métis Nation's Self-Government Agenda: Issues and Options for the Future[1]

JASON MADDEN

A. INTRODUCTION

Major changes are afoot with respect to the Métis[2] reality in Canada as evidenced by a number of positive political and legal developments, including, the 2003 Supreme Court of Canada decision recognizing and affirming the constitutional rights of the Métis.[3] Over the next decade, courts will continue to elaborate on the relationship between the Métis people and the Crown, as well as the nature and scope of Métis rights. Governments and the Métis will be required to work together in order to move forward on reconciliation, as mandated by section 35 of the *Constitution Act, 1982*, and the honour of the Crown.

---

1 This paper is based on a presentation given by Jason Madden at a national symposium on Crown–Métis Relations co-hosted by the Law Commission of Canada and the Métis National Council. It is largely based on an earlier paper co-authored by Jason Madden, John Graham, & Jake Wilson, "Exploring Options for Métis Governance in the 21st Century," available on the Institute on Governance's (IOG) website, online: www.iog.ca/view_publication.asp?publicationItemID=223. The paper has been updated and modified to better suit the publication resulting from the National Symposium.

2 This paper focuses on non-land-based governance structures of the Métis Nation as represented by the Métis National Council and its provincial Métis organizations from Ontario westward; it does not deal with the realities of Métis living north of 60, Métis living on the Alberta Métis Settlements, or other groups that claim to represent "Métis."

3 *R. v. Powley*, [2003] 2 S.C.R. 207 (S.C.C.) [*Powley*].

It is a certainty that the coming years will herald major advancements with respect to the Métis agenda. What is unclear, however, is what form these advancements will take. How will the process of registration of the Métis citizens and rights-holders evolve? How will Métis choose to implement their rights? How will the Métis people relate to the Canadian state? How will the Métis people govern themselves? How will Métis jurisdiction be addressed? Métis people, the public, and governments, at all levels, have great interest in how these important questions will be addressed.

Despite the urgency of these questions, and in contrast to the governance issues relating to First Nations, relatively little has been written or researched on Métis self-government or contemporary Métis governance structures in Canada. This paper attempts to identify some of the issues the Métis people and their elected leadership should consider in order to be prepared for and take advantage of emerging opportunities for the Métis self-government agenda. The paper does not focus on extensively setting out or arguing the legal basis for Métis self-government in Canada. Instead, it focuses on Métis governance issues, internal and external, that should be addressed in order to move the broader Métis self-government agenda forward. While addressing these issues may not be as "exciting" or "sexy" as lofty discussions on Métis self-government, the author believes they are essential for laying the foundation for implementing Métis self-government in Canada. Simply put, strong governance structures and institutions are needed into order to create the environment and conditions for effectively implementing Métis self-government.

This paper begins by briefly exploring the concepts of governance. It goes on to provide a brief historical overview of the Métis Nation, describe current Métis governance systems, outline a series of governance challenges, and then present some best practices. From there, it provides an overview of some of the rationales for Métis self-government, which is central to driving governance development. Next, fundamental governance issues that Métis will need to address as they move their self-government agenda forward are explored. Within each of these governance issues, the paper attempts to identify the issues at play and presents options or, in some instances, specific proposals for further consideration and reflection.

Finally, it is important to note that while the paper does make suggestions and proposals, it will ultimately be up to the Métis people, through their respective democratic governance structures and institutions, who will decide how the Métis self-government agenda moves forward. The paper is meant to act as a helpful catalyst for initiating and focusing those discussions with a view to advancing the Métis self-government agenda.

B. UNDERSTANDING GOVERNANCE

Understanding exactly what is meant by the term *governance* is an important starting point for this paper. Two sets of governance issues will be addressed. On the one hand, governance in *organizational* space refers to the relationships between elements of an organization — for example, between a board, an executive director, and staff in a not-for-profit organization, or in the case of the Métis self-government, between the executive, legislative, and judiciary branches of an emerging set of governments. On the other hand, Métis governance must be seen in the *societal* space it occupies. In this context, governance needs to be seen as something broader than government. Rather, it is best understood as a process whereby societies make their important decisions, and determine whom they involve in the process and how they are accountable. In this dynamic process are a number of players in the overlapping and interconnected spheres of government, civil society, private sector, and media. These varying players make one another accountable for their decisions, allow opportunities for citizens to participate in governance in varying ways, identify and create potential leaders, and find the most effective and efficient means to achieve goals. Effective governance systems require the full development of *all* governance spheres — not just government — and the achievement of balance between them.

Governance processes consist of several formal elements — agreements, procedures, conventions, policies, institutional arrangements — which are most easily observed and analyzed. But there are also a number of less tangible factors, such as history, culture, technology, and traditions — factors that also influence how decisions are made. For governance systems to meet societies' needs, the formal elements need to reflect these less tangible, but important historical, cultural, and traditional factors. For this reason many Western governance institutions imposed on colonized societies have proven deeply problematic. It is important to note, however, as David Newhouse of Trent University points out, that "tradition is a guide not a jailor." As they emerge, governance systems — like democracy itself — should also be dynamic, adapt to modern circumstances, and take advantage of new technological possibilities.

1) Governance in an Aboriginal Context[4]

In the Royal Commission on Aboriginal Peoples (RCAP) final report, nine key aspects of Aboriginal traditions of governance were identified: the centrality of the land, individual autonomy and responsibility, the rule of law, the role of women, the role of elders, the role of the family and the clan, leadership and accountability, and consensus in decision-making.[5] In a similar vein, Haudenosaunee (Mohawk) political theorist Taiaiake Alfred, from Kahnawake, has outlined eight characteristics of strong Indigenous communities: wholeness with diversity, shared culture, communication, respect and trust, group maintenance, participatory and consensus-based government, youth empowerment, and strong links to the outside world.[6]

These Aboriginal ideas of governance emphasize particular qualities that distinguish them from non-Aboriginal conceptions of governance. Traditional Aboriginal governance systems have valued consensus rather than simple majority rule; a unique view of and respect for the roles of elders, women, and youth in society; a vision of the *rule of law* rooted in spiritual learnings and oral traditions rather than written legislation; leadership derived from adherence to common culture, community identity, and the promotion of collective well-being; a holistic view of people's place in nature and a deep respect for the land and all its creatures; and governance institutions rooted in families, kinship, and

4 The IOG, in its considerable work on the topic of governance, has produced five principles of good governance. This information is available online: www.iog.ca/publications/policybrief15.pdf. These five principles share some important parallels with aspects of Aboriginal governance set out in the RCAP final report.

5 Royal Commission on Aboriginal Peoples, *Report of the Royal Commission on Aboriginal Peoples: Restructuring the Relationship*, vol. 2 (Ottawa: Supply and Services Canada, 1996) Part 1 at 116 [RCAP, *Restructuring the Relationship*].

6 Gerald R. Alfred, *Peace Power, Righteousness: An Indigenous Manifesto* (Don Mills, ON: Oxford University Press, 1999) at 82.

community structures which may not resemble the formal institutions of European cultures. Within these concepts, this paper will examine Métis governance.

C. UNDERSTANDING MÉTIS GOVERNANCE

Understanding the governance structures of any society must include a grasp of the history and evolution of the collectivity in question. This is particularly important in the Aboriginal context. Often, events (internal and external) dramatically shape and change the identity and cohesion of Aboriginal peoples. Governance structures and institutions react and adapt to these realities. The Métis are not an exception to this proposition; therefore, a brief historical overview of the Métis Nation's development is essential to understanding their current governance structures.

1) The Métis Nation[7]

The Métis Nation, as an Aboriginal people, evolved out of the initial relations of European men and Indian women who were brought together as a result of the early fur trade. While the initial offspring of these relations were individuals who simply possessed mixed European and Indian ancestry, continued relations between these cultures made way for a new and distinct people—the Métis. Beginning as early as the 1700s, distinct Métis settlements arose along the freighting waterways and Great Lakes of Ontario, throughout the historic Northwest, and as far north as the McKenzie river.[8] Métis settlements were generally organized around a mixed economy—economic trading combined with a subsistence-based lifestyle—with the use of resources being largely dependent on their geo-

7 Parts of this section are from other papers and documents written by Jason Madden for various sources.

8 For a more detailed review of the history and evolution of the Métis Nation and its communities, see Royal Commission on Aboriginal Peoples, *Report of the Royal Commission on Aboriginal Peoples: Perspectives and Realities*, vol. 4 (Ottawa: Supply and Services Canada 1996) Part 5 at 5 [RCAP, *Métis Perspectives*]. For a helpful collection of academic writings on Métis emergence in North America, see Jennifer S. H. Brown & Jacqueline Peterson, eds., *The New Peoples: Being and Becoming Métis in North America* (Winnipeg: University of Manitoba Press, 1985).

graphic location (e.g., parklands, grasslands, or woodlands).[9] As a result, Métis have historically been recognized for their ability to rapidly adapt to their environs in order to sustain themselves, their families, and their communities. An interesting first-hand assessment of this characteristic can be found in the writings of Alexander Ross who was a visitor to the Red River in the early 1800s. Ross observed, "[t]hey [Métis] are not, properly speaking, farmers, hunters, or fisherman; but rather confound the three occupations together, and follow them in turn, as whim or circumstances may dictate. They farm today, hunt tomorrow, and fish the next, without anything like a system; always at nonplus, but never disconcerted."[10]

While specific Métis settlements were established at fixed locations, which were often strategic subsistence, trading, and freighting points, a broader Métis identity evolved as a part of the extensive fur-trade travel network, ongoing seasonal rounds, and growing kinship connections between the fixed settlements.[11] This group identity evolved from more than just a mixing or adaptation of two divergent cultures. Through a process known

---

9 For writings describing Métis "mixed economies" depending on territory and resources available, see Arthur J. Ray, *Final Historical Report on Métis Economy in Sault Ste. Marie for* R. v. Powley (unpublished); Frank Tough, *The Importance of Freshwater Fisheries to the Métis of Western Canada: A Report for* R. v. Laviolette [unpublished], and Nicole St. Onge, *Saint-Laurent, Manitoba: Evolving Métis Identities* (Regina: Canadian Plains Research Centre, 2004).

10 Alexander Ross, *The Red River Settlement: Its Rise, Progress and Present State* (1856; repr., Winnipeg: Helen Doherty, 1984) at 193. The authors credit finding of this quote to Tough, above note 9. It is also interesting to note that in *Powley*, the Métis use of resources around Sault Ste. Marie was described by experts and accepted by the trial judge as "opportunistic." It depended on such factors as season, availability, location, and needs.

11 In his testimony at trial in *Powley*, Dr. Arthur Ray provided a helpful description to understand this concept:

> . . . these [Métis] communities get moved around with changing political boundaries and so on, but, so that there are nucleated settlements beginning to emerge, but there's also this larger Métis community that may or may not be present in any one of those communities at any point in time . . . . [T]here is a movement back and forth in the area [Sault Ste. Marie], people coming and going. There are ties to the Red River in the West, but it isn't all one way, it's backward movement as well.

See *R. v. Powley*, [1999] 1 C.N.L.R. 153 (Ont. Ct. Prov. Div.) (Evidence, Testimony of Dr. Ray, Excerpts from Trial, Vol. II at 234 and 306). *Powley* trial transcripts are available online: www.metisnation.org/harvesting/Powley_Case/court.html.

as "ethnogenesis," a distinct Métis culture, language (Michif), dress, music, and way of life emerged. Dr. Arthur Ray, one of the experts in *Powley*, emphasized the need to appreciate this point in his testimony at trial:

> The problem with the term Half-breed or mixed-blood is . . . [i]t implies that just half of this and half of that is what a Métis is. It overlooks the fact that the Métis culture was a creative result of a mixing of those two in language, art and song and a way of life, so it wasn't just half this and half that and I think that would be the major point that I would make.[12]

Another important element of this emerging identity was that the Métis no longer saw themselves as extensions of Indians or European communities, but as a distinct Aboriginal group who operated and asserted themselves as such. In the early 1800s, one of the first examples of this Métis collective consciousness occurred. The Métis of the Red River, led by Cuthbert Grant, protested the arrival of the Selkirk settlers whose agriculture focus threatened their traditional lifestyle. An initial 1815 treaty[13] between the Hudson's Bay Company (HBC) and the Métis lessened tensions for a period; however, in 1816, upon the arrival of a new HBC governor and more settlers, the Battle of Seven Oaks ensued. Grant and the Métis killed the HBC governor and a number of settlers. As a result, the settler colony left. In victory, the Métis Nation flag was raised in an act of nationalism as a "new nation" sentiment grew among Métis.

Throughout the 1800s, the Métis settlement at Red River continued to evolve as a highly visible, cohesive, and populated centre for Métis culture and nationalism. However, the mobility of the Métis people through well-established Métis settlements throughout the Northwest and the ongoing development of Métis institutions, such as brigade routes and buffalo hunts, also contributed to the ever-increasing nationalism of the Métis. These realities led to the Riel-led Red River resistance of 1869 and the negotiations between the Métis and Canada, resulting in the *Manitoba Act, 1870*.[14] Further, Métis living at other fixed settlements launched collective actions to assert their identity and rights. From the Mica Bay uprising near Sault Ste. Marie (1850) to the Rainy Lake Half-Breed Adden-

12 Testimony of Dr. Ray, *ibid.* at 286.

13 A copy of the treaty is reprinted in D. Bruce Sealey & Antoine Lussier, *The Métis: Canada's Forgotten People* (Winnipeg: Pemmican, 1975) at 39–40.

14 (U.K.), 33 Victoria, c. 3.

dum to Treaty 3 (1875) and numerous rights and land petitions throughout the Northwest — Fort Qu'Appelle, Cypress Hills, St. Laurent, and Green Lake — the Métis, as a distinct collective, were consistently a presence in Canada's nation-building exercise. In 1885, another one of these assertions led to the well-known Battle of Batoche. Although ultimately unsuccessful at Batoche, this assertion, in response to Canada's ongoing expansion westward, led to the establishment of Métis scrip commissions throughout the Northwest in an attempt to deal with Métis claims.

It is equally important to note that Canada's response (or in some cases a lack thereof) to Métis collective actions underlie many of the current challenges that exist between the Métis Nation and Canadian governments. For example, while Canada proceeded to deal with Indians as collectives through negotiating treaties and setting aside land bases — that is, reserves — for them, its policy towards Métis was substantively different.[15] By and large, the Métis were dealt with as individuals rather than as an Aboriginal people with collective rights and interests. Canada's administration of the Métis land provisions of the *Manitoba Act, 1870*, and the Métis land and money scrip system implemented through the *Dominion Lands Act 1879*[16] and various Orders-in-Council provide evidence of this. These individual-based systems were fraught with maladministration, sharp dealings, and outright fraud. They resulted in Métis becoming a landless Aboriginal people by the end of the 1800s.[17]

15 Commenting on the moral, legal, or constitutional soundness of Canada's policy approaches to the Métis is beyond the scope of this paper.

16 S.C. 1879, c. 31.

17 Currently, Métis are challenging the constitutionality and legality of these systems in the courts. See *Manitoba Metis Federation v. Canada (Attorney General)*, 2007 MBQB 293. In this civil action, the Manitoba Metis Federation and several Métis defendants asked the Manitoba Court of Queen's Bench to make a series of declarations based on the historic record leading to and following the events at Red River in 1869–70. These included declarations that (1) Canada and Manitoba failed to fulfill their obligations to the Métis that are set out in the *Manitoba Act*, (2) Manitoba's taxation of Métis lands granted pursuant to s. 31 of the *Manitoba Act* was unconstitutional, and (3) in 1870 Canada and the Métis reached a treaty. In 2007, Justice MacInnes, of the Manitoba Court of Queen's Bench, denied the Manitoba Metis Federation's claim in its entirety. The case has been appealed to the Manitoba Court of Appeal and will likely end up before the Supreme Court of Canada in the next few years. Another case, *Morin et al. v. Canada et al.*, Saskatoon, File No. 619/1994 (Sask. Q.B.), which is a land claim filed on behalf of the Métis of Northwest Saskatchewan, is still in the discovery stage with no date set for trial.

Moreover, the political events of 1885 dramatically reduced Métis assertions against the Canadian state. The very public prosecution, imprisonment, and hanging of Louis Riel as a traitor dampened the public presence of the Métis. RCAP made the following observation about the Métis during the post-1885 period:

> Some Canadians think that the Métis Nation's history ended on the Batoche battlefield or the Regina gallows. The bitterness of those experiences did cause the Métis to avoid the spotlight for many years, but they continued to practise and preserve their culture and to do everything that was possible to pass it on to future generations.[18]

Even in the face of this adversity, some Métis continued to gather and organize politically. The Union Nationale Métisse de Saint-Joseph was created on 17 July 1887 at St. Vital, Manitoba, to write the Métis record on the events that took place in 1870 and 1885.[19] From the late 1800s to the early 1900s, Métis living throughout the Northwest repeatedly petitioned the government to recognize their rights and lands.

2) Contemporary Manifestations of Métis Self-Government

Beginning in the 1920s, increasingly visible Métis political movements began to emerge once again to assert the rights and existence of the Métis. In 1928, a small group of Métis in the Cold Lake area began to meet. This group, led by Charles Delorme, created L'Association des Métis Alberta et Les Territoires du Nord-Ouest, which evolved into the Métis Association of Alberta (now the Métis Nation of Alberta).[20] Similarly, the Saskatchewan Métis Society (now the Métis Nation — Saskatchewan) was formed in 1938. The Manitoba Metis Federation was created as a federation made up in part by local Union Nationale councils as well as Métis throughout all of Manitoba. These political movements, along with others from Ontario and British Columbia, led to a revitalization of

18 RCAP, *Métis Perspectives*, above note 8 at 227.

19 For more information on the formation of Union Nationale Métisse de Saint-Joseph, see A.-H. de Trémaudan, *Hold High Your Heads (History of the Métis Nation in Western Canada)*, trans. by Elizabeth Maguet (Winnipeg: Pemmican, 1982).

20 For more information on the political history of Alberta Métis, see Joe Sawchuk, Patricia Sawchuk, & Theresa Ferguson, *Métis Land Rights in Alberta: A Political History* (Edmonton: Métis Association of Alberta, 1981).

Métis Nation self-government aspirations. Many of these political movements and their initial structural manifestations form the underlying frameworks for contemporary Métis governance structures.

Beginning in the 1950s in Canada, a new Aboriginal political awareness began to emerge. The deplorable socio-economic conditions facing Aboriginal peoples caught the attention of politicians as well as the public at large. Aboriginal peoples, as well, began to use the courts to seek redress.

The Métis Nation was a key player in this new momentum. The Métis joined with non-status Indians and other Aboriginal peoples in forming regional political organizations to draw attention to Aboriginal issues. These organizations were brought together under a national organization — the Native Council of Canada (NCC). However, even within these pan-Aboriginal organizations the Métis Nation maintained a distinct agenda.

In 1982, all Aboriginal peoples were successful in securing the recognition and protection of Aboriginal and treaty rights in the Canadian Constitution. In particular, this event was a triumph for the Métis Nation, with the explicit recognition of the Métis as one of Canada's three Aboriginal peoples within section 35(2) of the *Constitution Act, 1982*.[21] Following the 1982 amendment, four First Ministers Meetings (FMMs) were to be held to elaborate on and agree to additional changes needed to address and implement the new Aboriginal provisions of the Constitution.

Before these meetings, Métis leadership from the Prairies led a drive to separate from the NCC in order to form a Métis-specific national representative body. In March 1983, the Métis National Council (MNC) was formed. After negotiating an out-of-court settlement with Canada (flowing from an injunction application to stop the prime minister from holding the FMM), the MNC assumed a full seat at the FMM table to represent the Métis Nation.

Aligned with this national direction, the NCC's organizations from Ontario westward began to reorganize in order to form Métis-specific organizations. Today, these organizations include the Métis Nation of Ontario (MNO), Manitoba Metis Federation (MMF), Métis Nation — Saskatchewan (MNS), Métis Nation of Alberta (MNA), and Métis Nation British Columbia (MNBC), which make up the Métis National Council.

21 Being Schedule B to the *Canada Act 1982* (U.K.), 1982, c. 11.

3) An Overview of Contemporary Métis Governance Systems

The section above provides a brief historical overview of the Métis Nation. Several important factors within this history have shaped and continue to shape present-day Métis governance. Some of these factors are as follows:

- The result of historic Crown (federal and provincial) policy vis-à-vis Métis lands have left Métis, by and large, a landless people;[22] therefore, a majority of Métis governance structures have evolved off a land base.
- Until recently, both the federal and provincial governments denied the existence of Métis rights. As a result, federal and provincial governments have limited the scope of Métis self-government discussions to cultural preservation, program and service delivery, and limited institutional capacity development. Moreover, these governments continue to recognize Métis governance structures only as "organizations" rather than as "Aboriginal governments" with jurisdiction. While government policies slowly catch up to the emerging law, these current policy realities affect Métis governance developments.
- Métis have historically and continue to have consequential populations in urban areas. As a result, Métis have significant capacity, institutions, and a presence in urban centres (e.g., Sault Ste. Marie, Winnipeg, Edmonton, Saskatoon, and Vancouver) in relation to other Aboriginal peoples.
- Neither the federal nor provincial governments have maintained or supported Métis identification systems or registries; therefore, the exact population of Métis in Canada is unknown and existing Métis membership systems vary in scope and credibility from province to province.
- Métis governance structures have largely evolved on a province-wide basis based on mandates received through ballot box elections and assemblies. As a result, significant institutional capacity is at the provincial level while the capacities of local communities vary.

22 Notable exceptions are the Métis Settlements in Alberta, which are beyond the scope of this paper. For more information on the Alberta Métis Settlements, see Chapter 15 for the paper by Catherine Bell and Harold Robinson.

- Jurisdictional positioning between the federal government and provinces on what level of government has jurisdiction for Métis has limited Métis moving forward on self-government and socio-economic initiatives.

Based on these and other factors, Métis governance structures have evolved with the following layers:

a) Local — Locals and Community Councils

Locals and Community Councils are the foundation of Métis governance structures. They are created to represent Métis people at the local level. Local governance structures provide a mandate and feed into the larger regional and provincial based structures, as well as the national one.

b) Provincial — Provincial Organizations

By and large, the role of provincial Métis organizations is twofold: (1) to politically represent the Métis people within their respective province by advocating for and negotiating on their behalf and (2) to undertake cultural and socio-economic programming and services for Métis people living within their respective province. Even though there are differences between each provincial organization's structure, there are some consistent elements, as well:

- Each provincial Métis organization maintains a membership list, or, in some cases, a registry of Métis citizens within its respective provincial boundary.
- Each provincial Métis organization has a governance structure that allows for various types of interests to be effectively represented and balanced within the Métis Nation: these include local interests (through locals and community councils); specific groups, such as women, youth, and elders; provincial; and national.
- Each provincial Métis organization's leadership is democratically selected through province-wide ballot box elections, held at regular intervals.
- Between elections, the provincial Métis organization's accountability to members is maintained by holding annual assemblies at which the leadership reports back to constituents.

- These governance structures incorporate women, youth, and elders into decision-making processes.
- An elected provincial president acts as the chief spokesperson for the Métis people within their respective province.
- Annual assemblies give members an opportunity to be updated on activities as well as provide input and direction to the elected board of directors in between general elections.
- Program and service delivery infrastructures (affiliate corporations and internal administration among them) provide cultural and socio-economic initiatives to all Métis people within the province.

The following provides a visual overview of how provincial Métis organizations are structured:

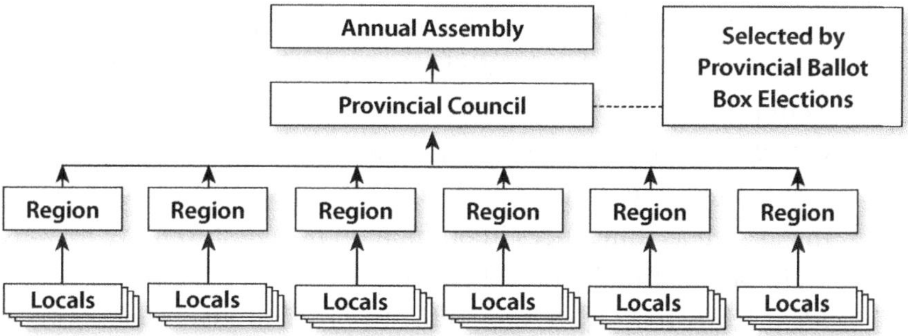

c) National — Métis National Council (MNC)

The MNC is formed by the provincial Métis organizations coming together to mandate a national governance structure. It is often described as "the sum of its parts" with the president of each provincial Métis organization sitting as a member of the Board of Governors, along with a national president, who is elected by the MNC's General Assembly every two to three years.

The MNC has established two secretariats — Métis National Youth Advisory Council and Women of the Métis Nation — which participate in the affairs of the MNC on behalf of women and youth. As well, the MNC has a Métis Nation Cabinet. The MNC president appoints ministers who are accountable for specific ministries, and these ministers play a supportive and collaborative role with the president and the Board of Governors in order to pursue various sectoral initiatives on behalf of the Métis Nation.

4) Current Métis Governance Challenges

The following is a list of some of the key governance challenges the Métis Nation faces. As such, they provide an underpinning for the remainder of the paper which provides options and suggestions for addressing some of these challenges.

- *Communicating the argument for Métis self-government to the public at large:* Notwithstanding key victories, such as the Supreme Court of Canada's decision in *Powley*, the Métis Nation still faces challenges in gaining public familiarity and acceptance, and making its agenda clear.
- *Addressing misconceptions on the Métis agenda held by other governments*: There is a need to overcome some of the misconceptions, often held by the federal and provincial governments, that Métis seek identical rights and benefits to that of First Nations, for example, that they seek Indian "status."
- *Clearly articulating a vision of implementing Métis self-government*: Throughout the Métis Nation, there is a lack of understanding as well as differences in opinion on how best to move forward on implementing Métis self-government.
- *Identifying and registering Métis*: In order to give Métis governments maximum legitimacy, a nationally consistent set of registration criteria and acceptance processes, along with credible objectively verifiable identification systems will be indispensable — a major challenge, given the varying stages each provincial Métis organization is at in implementing a credible system and the high degree of regional autonomy.
- *Clarifying local, regional, provincial, and national roles*: As Métis make advances on their self-government agenda, there will be an increased need on delineating who is responsible for what among local, regional, provincial, and national bodies. Development of constitutions that are regionally and nationally in sync will be extremely helpful for moving forward on Métis Nation self-government. As well, the question of what is a "Métis community" as set out by the Supreme Court of Canada in the *Powley* case may influence what level of Métis governance structures other governments deal with on various issues, consultations and negotiations among them.

- *Building a Métis public service*: Recruiting, training, and retaining a strong Métis public service is a challenge faced by Métis organizations. Common problems include the inability to compete with salaries offered in private and public sectors, a lack of clear protocols between politicians and officials, a lack of internal communications and human resources policies, job security issues with changes in leadership, the ability to offer competitive compensation packages, and training on how the Métis self-government agenda relates to program delivery.
- *Resolving the question of legislative jurisdiction*: The Métis have long sought acknowledgment by Canada that they are "Indians" for constitutional purposes in section 91(24) of the *Constitution Act, 1867*,[23] and thus a federal responsibility. What would this mean and equate to? Are there other strategies to better address the jurisdictional limbo Métis currently face?
- *Establishing new fiscal arrangements*: Unlike First Nations living on-reserve, Métis pay income tax, although only a fraction of the services they consume are delivered by Métis governments. As Métis governments assume a greater range of functions from Canada and the provinces, new fiscal relationships will be required to support these roles.
- *Determining a land base for Métis*: While a form of Métis self-government is possible off a land base, many Métis believe acquiring a greater land base is essential. How would this look and operate? Would lands be set aside for cultural and ceremonial purposes? Could compensation address land issues in urban centres? Where would a land base in fee simple be practical?
- *Building checks and balances among Métis governments*: Power in the Métis Nation currently rests inordinately at the provincial level, and the national organization has little authority to coordinate initiatives nation wide or to consider appeals of province-level decisions.
- *Building governance capacity at all levels*: Unlike the experiences of other Aboriginal peoples, most Métis communities have not been provided adequate resources to operate local governance struc-

23 *Constitution Act, 1867* (U.K.), 30 & 31 Vict., c. 3, reprinted in R.S.C. 1985, App. No. 5.

tures. For the most part, the concentration of capacity and power has been at the provincial level, while the national, regional, and local levels have varying levels of capacity to undertake governance functions.

- *Considering greater cooperation with other parties*: There have been historical differences between the Métis Nation and other Aboriginal political and service delivery organizations claiming to represent Métis or urban Aboriginal peoples. While there have been important reasons for the divergent views, could any future governance approaches accommodate the possibility of closer cooperation between these groups on common goals?
- *Better integrating the growing range of Métis program delivery vehicles*: Similar to how other governments are able to focus efforts to target the needs of their populations, Métis governance structures must be able to improve coordination and integration between their delivery structures. Moreover, in recent years, in some provinces, a decentralized model of governance (that is, affiliates with separate board of directors and no accountability to the larger body politic) has proven problematic. Efforts should be made to horizontally manage limited resources and possibly establish single-window delivery of Métis services, such as labour market training, business development and financing supports, and child and family services, under one roof for cost efficiency and convenience.

5) Some Best Practices in Métis Governance

While significant governance challenges face the Métis Nation, there are also successes that merit consideration as future initiatives are contemplated and developed. Some of these are as follows:

a) Devolution of Child and Family Services to Métis in Manitoba

In 1988, the Manitoba established the Aboriginal Justice Inquiry (AJI) to examine the relationship between the Aboriginal peoples of Manitoba and the justice system. The AJI also looked at the historic treatment of Aboriginal peoples by the Manitoba child and family services system. In its final report, issued in 1991, the AJI concluded that the mainstream child and family services system did not serve Aboriginal peoples well and recommended changes. One of these recommendations was to establish a mandated province-wide Métis agency to deal with Métis child and family services, along with separate agencies to address the needs of First Nations.

In 1999, the Manitoba government announced its commitment to address the AJI's recommendations and established the Aboriginal Justice Implementation Commission (AJIC) to review the report and identify priority areas for action. In its first report, the AJIC recommended that Manitoba enter into agreements with the Assembly of Manitoba Chiefs and the MMF to "develop a plan that will result in First Nations and Métis communities developing and delivering child and family services." By August 2000, Manitoba and the MMF signed an agreement establishing a joint initiative to "recognize a province-wide Métis right and authority" for child and family services.

Through a three-year joint implementation process, known as the Aboriginal Justice Inquiry—Child Welfare Initiative (AJI-CWI), a collaborative and incremental approach was taken between the MMF and Manitoba in order to establish a Métis Child and Family Services Authority (which has province-wide responsibility for Métis child and family services), Métis Child, Family and Community Services (the agency which is responsible for service delivery based on the direction of the Métis authority), as well as a Métis Family and Community Institute, which undertakes policy development and research for the Métis community on child and family issues. At the same time, similar approaches were undertaken with First Nations jurisdictions.

On 13 September 2003, the Métis Child and Family Services Authority received its formal mandate from the Manitoba government to oversee Métis child and family services province wide. As well, the Manitoba *Child and Family Services Authority Act*,[24] which is the legislative basis for the new Métis and First Nation authorities, was proclaimed on 24 November 2003. In 2005, Métis Child, Family and Community Services began to take on its first cases and now delivers community-based family services to Métis throughout the province to prevent circumstances that are likely to place children and families at risk, to assist families in

24 Manitoba *Child and Family Services Authority Act*, C.C.S.M. c. C90.

resolving issues that place children at risk, and to ensure that children in agency care are able to maintain appropriate and safe family relationships.

This initiative is the first of its kind for Métis anywhere in Canada. It establishes a new standard with the legislative recognition of Métis responsibility over child and family services. Further, it demonstrates that jurisdictional issues can be easily overcome through political will and by Métis and provincial governments working together.[25]

b) Implementing a Centralized Registry System for Alberta Métis

In 1991, the MNA made the decision to centralize its membership system in its head office in Edmonton. Although Métis could still obtain applications for membership at the local level, it became standard practice that all completed applications were then forwarded to the MNA's head office for review, final approval, and the issuance of a MNA membership cards. This centralized system allowed the MNA to ensure that the criteria for membership, such as completed and signed application form and genealogy documentation, were met in a uniform manner.[26]

Today, within this centralized system, the MNA has more than 45 000 members. Beginning in 2004, with federal resources dedicated for implementation of the *Powley* decision, the MNA began a process of re-registration of all members in order to issue citizenship cards based on the new national definition of Métis, adopted by the Métis National Council. All MNA members are now required to reapply for citizenship. Once an applicant's file is complete in terms of genealogy, statutory declaration of Métis self-identification, and so on, a new bar-coded, security-featured, photo identification card is issued by the MNA.

In 2007, the MNA had re-registered approximately 8400 of its members who met the new citizenship requirements set by the MNC. It is expected that the re-registration process will be complete in the next few years. As a result of this process, Métis and governments will have certainty and confidence that all new MNA card holders have objectively verifiable proof of their self-identification and Métis ancestry.

---

25 This initiative is discussed at length by Harvey Bostrom, Alison Rogan, and Richard Asselin in Chapter 14.

26 More information on the MNA's Registry is available online: www.albertametis.com/MNAHome/mna-membership.aspx.

In addition, the MNA continues to strengthen its registration process. It has streamlined the application process with regional intake clerks and the creation of standardized family trees for registration review. Appeals on citizenship issues are heard by an independent Métis Judicial Council. Further, the MNA has a working relationship with Indian and Northern Affairs Canada to verify that Métis citizens are not registered as Indians under the *Indian Act*. As a result of this work, the MNA has the most comprehensive and verified Métis citizenship registries in Canada.

At the time that the MNA moved towards a central registry, this system was a significant departure from other provincial Métis organizations, which continued to allow locals to issue membership cards on behalf of the provincial organization. The remaining Prairie Métis organizations are at various stages of moving towards more centralized systems. The MNO has implemented a centralized registry since its creation in 1995, and the MNBC instituted a centralized registry in 2005.

c) Establishing a Métis Post-Secondary Education Institute in Saskatchewan

In 1980, the Gabriel Dumont Institute (GDI) was established as the educational arm of the Métis Nation — Saskatchewan (MNS). Since its inception, GDI has focused on "education through cultural research as a means to renew and strengthen the heritage and achievement of Saskatchewan's Métis."[27] It is the only wholly Métis-controlled, accredited post-secondary institution of its kind in Canada and is overseen by a board of directors that includes the MNS's minister of Education, along with Métis representatives from throughout the province. A majority of GDI resources come from the Saskatchewan government.

Currently, GDI develops and publishes Métis-specific curriculum and historical education materials; trains Aboriginal teachers through the Saskatchewan Urban Native Teachers Education Program (SUNTEP); maintains libraries and information services for students; administers a scholarship program; and delivers programming contracted from the province's universities, colleges, and technical institutes. It has offices and offers services in Regina, Saskatoon, and Prince Albert and employs more

---

27 Gabriel Dumont Institute, *2002/03 Annual Report* (Saskatoon: Gabriel Dumont Institute, 2003) at 5.

than 100 staff and faculty (part and full time). GDI serves about 700 adult students each year. In the 1990s, GDI also established Dumont Technical Institute (DTI), which deals with adult upgrading and training as well as Gabriel Dumont College (GDC), which delivers the first two years of an arts and science program to students anywhere in Saskatchewan.[28]

Today, more than 650 teachers (First Nations and Métis) have graduated from GDI with bachelor of education degrees. In 2001, a comprehensive evaluation further confirmed GDI's success. As of the spring of 2001, GDI had graduated 544 teachers. Of these teachers, 79 percent were female (428) and 21 percent were male (116). Overall, GDI has a 90 percent placement rate for all of its graduates. In 2001, 71 percent of graduates were still employed in the K–12 system.[29]

GDI is an example of a win-win-win partnership between Saskatchewan and the Métis: the Métis community is able to build its own educational institution to enhance its cultural identity, individual Métis are able to access post-secondary education in a culturally appropriate way and secure gainful employment, and the province benefits from Métis teachers who are able to contribute to the educational and labour-market needs of Saskatchewan.

d) Federal Devolution of Labour Market Programming to Métis

In the early 1990s, when the government of Canada was divesting its role in labour-market programming to provincial jurisdictions, a decision was made to devolve an Aboriginal allocation of labour-market programming to First Nations, Métis, and Inuit jurisdictions.

In 1996, National Framework Agreements were signed with the national organizations representing the three constitutionally recognized Aboriginal peoples; namely, the Assembly of First Nations (First Nations), the Métis National Council (Métis), and the Inuit Tapirisat of Canada (Inuit). These Agreements were enabling documents for Human Resources and Skills Development Canada[30] (HRSDC) to begin the process of administrative devolution of Aboriginal labour market programming to

28 Additional information on GDI is available online: www.gdins.org.

29 Gabriel Dumont Institute, above note 27 at 17.

30 This federal department was then known as Human Resources Development Canada (HRDC).

the identified regional affiliates[31] of these national organizations. These regional affiliates entered into subsequent Regional Bilateral Agreements with HRSDC for responsibility to deliver labour market programming to their respective constituencies.

In 1999, this process was renewed through the five-year Aboriginal Human Resource Development Strategy. This time, the MNC signed a Métis Accord on Human Resources Development and subsequent Métis Human Resource Development Agreements (MHRDAs) were signed with each identified Métis provincial organization. MHRDAs serve province-wide constituencies, and they have all accordingly been required to establish a delivery structure that reaches Métis throughout the province concerned.

Collectively, since 1996, these Métis delivery structures have successfully administered well over $300 million in labour-market support services by making strategic investments to meet the training and employment needs of Métis people (approximately $43 million annually from Ontario west). MHRDAs support more than eighty-five points of entry from Ontario west for Métis to access labour-market programming in urban, rural, and remote communities. The provincial organizations are responsible for the overall management of their respective MHRDA, while programming and funding decision-making is based at the community level. This type of developmental platform has enabled strong governance and sound financial management infrastructures to be developed, implemented, and sustained. As well, these infrastructures lower overall administration costs further by the sharing of office space and administration with other federal and provincial programs delivered by Métis.

Within the Métis Nation, this devolution model is considered an overwhelming success. For example, for the period 1999–2003, more than 25 000 Métis were served through MHRDAs; and close to 10 000 of those clients found employment as a result of these interventions.[32] Further, these MHRDAs have established effective partnerships with

---

31 For the MNC, these affiliates included the MNO, MMF, MNS, MNA, and MNBC. A special provision was also included for the Métis Settlements in Alberta.

32 Métis National Council, *Moving Forward: Results of Métis Constituency Consultations on the Renewal of the Aboriginal Human Resources Development Strategy* (Ottawa: Métis National Council, March 2003) at 26–27.

private sector employers, universities, and training institutions to improve Métis positioning in the labour market: for example, the MNO established a $4.2 million bursary trust at thirty-two colleges and universities in Ontario, the MMF established a recruitment initiative with such employers as Maple Leaf Foods, Manitoba Hydro, and others; and the MNA partnered with First Nations in urban centres for cost-shared delivery. MHRDAs have also successfully incorporated youth initiatives from both Aboriginal Human Resource Development Strategy (AHRDS) funding and resources provided by the Department of Canadian Heritage through the Urban Multi-Purpose Aboriginal Youth Centres program into their infrastructures.

e) Ensuring Good Governance through a Community Charter System in Ontario

One ongoing challenge faced by Métis has been the lack of formal recognition, by all levels of government, of Métis self-government structures and institutions. Unlike First Nations bands, which are recognized as legal entities under the *Indian Act*,[33] Métis do not yet have such recognition. The result has been Métis governance structures and institutions having to incorporate under federal or provincial not-for-profit or societies legislation in order for governments to deal with them or to channel monies.

Often, these corporate constraints frustrate Métis self-government aspirations. For example, Métis governance structures now have numerous incorporations at the provincial, regional, and local levels. However, based on corporate law, these incorporations are "their own masters." This makes it difficult to have direction or decisions in one corporation uniformly implemented in all associated corporations. For example, although locals may be affiliated with a provincial body, each local has the authority under its own bylaws to issue membership cards. Further, provincial bodies do not have the authority to step in if a board of directors misappropriates Métis community assets or local elections are not held.

In 1994, when the MNO was formed, it adopted an approach to remedy some of the incorporation issues it had witnessed in Ontario and other

33 *Indian Act*, R.S.C. 1985, c. I-5.

provinces. The MNO developed a Community Charter Agreement,[34] which it enters into with each MNO community council. Through the Agreement, the local community does not have to incorporate separately and could use the MNO's incorporation number in exchange for ensuring it fulfilled the terms of the Charter Agreement. These include:

- community councils using the MNO's central membership list for identifying Métis members;
- community councils holding regular local elections for leadership;
- community councils ensuring that regular public meetings are held;
- community councils maintaining financial statements, with assets remaining in the name of the community council.

The Charter Agreements also provide for a dispute resolution mechanism between the MNO and a community council if issues arise. The MNO's Charter Agreements have proven themselves invaluable in ensuring that the provincial body can intervene when problems, such as contested elections, financial irregularities, and a lack of public meetings, arise within the community.

Initially, other levels of governments did not recognize the MNO's Charter Agreements. In 1996, the government of Ontario agreed to formally recognize the MNO Charter Agreements for administrative and funding purposes. The federal government soon followed suit. Today, provincial and federal government funding flows directly to the community councils while the MNO ensures that Charter Agreement terms are fulfilled.

f) Partnerships with First Nations and Aboriginal Service Delivery Organizations in Ontario and Manitoba

A lack of recognition and respect for Métis jurisdiction is often a legitimate make-or-break issue for Métis when working with other groups and stakeholders. This issue can often frustrate making progress on potential initiatives as well as cause extensive divisiveness within the Aboriginal community.

34 A sample of the MNO's Charter Agreement is available online: www.metisnation.org/gov_bodies/Councils/home.html.

Some provincial Métis organizations have moved forward on delineating their jurisdiction with other bodies in order to build a cooperative and collaborative atmosphere in the province and urban centres.

- In 2002, the MMF signed a Protocol agreement with the Manitoba Association of Friendship Centres (MAC). It commits to regular meetings between the respective groups at a provincial and local level. In the Protocol, MAC recognizes that the MMF is the legitimate political representative of the Métis people in Manitoba and has the sole responsibility to move forward on the Métis self-government agenda. In turn, the MMF recognizes that the MAC is a service delivery organization providing services to Métis people in Manitoba and supports MAC's continued efforts. Moreover, the Protocol commits the parties to coordinating service delivery efforts for Métis people where possible.
- In 2004, the MNO signed a Political Protocol with the Chiefs of Ontario (COO).[35] The Protocol recognizes the MNO as the representative body of the Métis Nation in Ontario and COO as the representative body of First Nations at a provincial level in Ontario. It commits to a government-to-government relationship and sets out a schedule for regular MNO–COO meetings at a leadership and officials level. The Protocol also states that where appropriate the parties will work collaboratively on issues.

g) Building Métis Self-Sufficiency through Economic Opportunities for Alberta Métis

The Métis Nation of Alberta (MNA) has focused significant efforts on engaging in economic opportunities with a view to moving towards Métis economic self-sufficiency in the province. Some of its strategies include these:

- Since 1988, the MNA's capital corporation (Apeetogosan [Métis] Development Inc.) has lent out more than $32 million to Métis entrepreneurs starting and expanding their businesses in the province. In total, more than 800 businesses have been created through Apeetogosan's support. These businesses have created jobs and op-

35 A copy of the MNO–COO Protocol is available online: www.metisnation.org.

portunities for Métis individuals, communities, and the Alberta economy.[36]

- In June 2002, the MNA acquired a double telescopic drilling rig through a partnership with EnCana Corp. and Lakota Drilling Inc. After the repayment of loans and Métis people receiving training on the operation of the rig over a five-year period, the MNA expects Métis in Alberta to play an expanded role in the oil and gas sector. Further, the profits from the rig can support the self-government aspirations of Alberta Métis.
- The MNA is in the process of establishing Métis Crossing at Victoria Landing (a national historic site) as a Métis cultural heritage centre. The centre's plans call for an interactive adventure and learning experience on Métis culture and history; a training and conference facility; a "live" education site; a theatre for drama and musical productions; and a traditional farming experience. Organizers expect that the project will be fully completed by 2008 and will become a self-sustaining enterprise for Alberta's Métis from tourist dollars, campground fees, meetings, and conferences.

h) Implementing Métis Self-Government in Saskatchewan

In 1993, as a part of moving forward on Métis self-government, Saskatchewan Métis adopted a political constitution. This constitution, the first of its kind in the Métis Nation, established the Métis Nation—Saskatchewan (MNS) as a self-governing entity outside of the Saskatchewan *Non-Profit Corporations Act*.[37] Further, the Constitution established a Legislative Assembly, which includes representation from all Saskatchewan Métis locals as the supreme authority within the MNS with the mandate to enact legislation and regulations; a Senate to oversee citizenship and elections; and the Provincial Métis Council as the cabinet responsible for all MNS affiliates, departments, programs, and ministries. The MNS also maintained a corporate secretariat for the sole purpose of carrying out the council's administrative duties.[38]

---

36 More information on this protocol and other negotiations by the MNO to establish nation-to-nation relationships is available online: www.metisnation.org/nations/home.html.

37 Saskatchewan *Non-Profit Corporations Act*, S.S. 1995, c. N-4.2.

38 Copies of these documents are available from the Métis Nation — Saskatchewan.

Building upon the MNS's self-government agenda, in 2002, the government of Saskatchewan proclaimed *The Métis Act*.[39] The Act had three principal purposes: (1) to recognize the distinct culture and heritage of the Métis people and their contribution to Saskatchewan; (2) to establish a bilateral process for negotiations between Saskatchewan and the MNS; and (3) to legally recognize the MNS's corporate secretariat outside of the Saskatchewan *Non-Profit Corporations Act*. *The Métis Act* is the only one of its kind in Canada.

D. THE RATIONALES FOR MÉTIS SELF-GOVERNMENT

While this paper is not meant to extensively review the legal arguments for Métis self-government, it is important to recognize that the arguments, or rationale, for Métis self-government are key drivers in the evolution of Métis governance structures and institutions in Canada. There are numerous legal, policy, and moral rationales for implementing Métis self-government in Canada. Over the past few decades, the case for Métis self-government has grown stronger. Recent court victories in favour of the Métis, a resurgence of Métis pride and culture, evolving Métis governance structures with increased capacities and stability, a clearer vision and articulation of Métis self-government aspirations, and increased political attention to Aboriginal issues have all been positive developments for the Métis.

Of all these rationales, the ever-increasing recognition that Aboriginal peoples possess the inherent right of self-government has served as an important driver for change. International law has already recognized that this right exists.[40] While the Supreme Court of Canada has not yet recognized an all inclusive Aboriginal right of self-government,[41] there is strong support for the proposition that Aboriginal peoples in Canada

---

39 *An Act to recognize contributions of the Métis and to deal with certain Métis Institutions*, S.S. 2001, c. M-14.01.

40 *International Covenant on Civil and Political Rights*, GA Res. 2200A (XXI) at 52, UN Doc. A/6316 (1966); *International Covenant on Economic, Social and Cultural Rights*, GA Res. 2200A (XXI), 21 UN GAOR, Supp. No. 16 at 49, art. 1; *Declaration on the Granting of Independence to Colonial Countries and People*, UN GA Res.1514 (XV), 15 UN GAOR, Supp. No. 16 at 66 (1960).

41 *R. v. Pamejewon*, [1996] 2 S.C.R. 821.

possess self-government rights. RCAP, academics, and, to date, one lower court[42] have all recognized that Aboriginal self-government is a necessary protected right in order to achieve section 35's promise to Aboriginal peoples. Further, since 1985, federal policy[43] has recognized that the inherent right of Aboriginal self-government is an existing right protected by section 35 of the *Constitution Act, 1982*.[44] Provincial and territorial governments have adopted varying policies on how they approach Aboriginal self-government and relations in their respective jurisdictions.[45]

Similar to other Aboriginal peoples, the Métis Nation has long asserted it is a rights-bearing Aboriginal people possessing the inherent right of self-government. In its final report, RCAP supported this assertion.[46] More recently, in support of this position, the Supreme Court of Canada affirmed in *Powley* that Métis have existing Aboriginal rights protected by section 35 of the *Constitution Act, 1982*. The Supreme Court held that section 35 is based on a "commitment to recognizing the Métis and enhancing their survival as distinctive communities"[47] and that the Métis are a full-fledged rights-bearing people. Based on *Powley*, lower courts have increasingly been recognizing the harvesting rights of Métis from Ontario west.[48] Since Métis rights, like all Aboriginal rights, are

42 See RCAP, *Restructuring the Relationship*, above note 5 at 202–13; Brian Slattery, "Aboriginal Sovereignty and Imperial Claims" (1991) 29 Osgoode Hall L.J. 681; John Borrows, "Constitutional Law from a First Nations Perspective" (1994) 28 U.B.C. L. Rev. 1; Patrick Macklem, *Indigenous Difference and the Constitution of Canada* (Toronto: University of Toronto Press, 2001); and *Campbell v. British Columbia (Attorney General)*, [2000] B.C.J. No. 1524 (S.C.), where the British Columbia Supreme Court upheld the self-government provisions of the Nisga'a Treaty, partly based on the Nisga'a people's inherent right of self-government.

43 Minister of Indian Affairs and Northern Development, *The Government of Canada's Approach to the Implementation of the Inherent Right and the Negotiation of Aboriginal Self-Government* (Ottawa: Indian and Northern Affairs Canada, 1995).

44 *Constitution Act, 1982*, being Schedule B to the *Canada Act 1982* (U.K.), 1982, c. 11.

45 For example, see the government of Alberta's *Aboriginal Policy Framework*, online: www.international.gov.ab.ca/documents/final_strengthrelations.pdf; or the government of Ontario's *New Approach to Aboriginal Affairs*, online: www.nativeaffairs.jus.gov.on.ca/english/news/brochure.html.

46 RCAP, *Métis Perspectives*, above note 8 at 232.

47 *Powley*, above note 3 at para 13.

48 *R. v. Laviolette*, 2005 SKPC 70; *R. v. Belhumeur*, 2007 SKPC 114. See also *R. v. Morin*, [1996] 3 C.N.L.R. 157 (Sask. Prov. Ct.), aff'd [1998] 1 C.N.L.R. 85 (Sask. Q.B.).

collective rights, it is necessary for the rights-bearing group to assume a role in the management and regulation of the right (that is, a function of self-government). Prior to and following *Powley*, all of the provincial Métis organizations have taken on this self-government function in some way, as it relates to harvesting rights.[49] In some jurisdictions, these Métis systems have been recognized by provincial governments.[50]

Without a doubt, over the next decade, ongoing litigation will further delineate the nature and scope of Métis rights. Current federal and provincial policies of ignoring or denying Métis rights and only recognizing Métis governance structures as organizations, rather than as Aboriginal governments will have to be revisited in order to keep up with legal and political developments. Key to this evolution must be a willingness, first, on the part of other governments to work and share with Métis in order for them to implement their unique self-government aspirations, and second, on the part of the Métis people to grapple with and address important self-government issues they face.

There is also increasing support for the rationale that, from a policy perspective, Aboriginal self-government makes sense. After fifteen years of research, the Harvard Study on American Indian Economic Development has concluded that First Nations economic self-sufficiency is closely linked to practical sovereignty, capable governing institutions, and culturally matching government institutions to Indigenous concepts on how authority should be organized and exercised.[51] Central to this study is the finding that when First Nations have a sense of ownership and control over their own destinies, improvements in quality of life indicators result. While this type of specific research in relation to Métis has not yet

49 In 1994, the MNS passed its *Métis Wildlife and Conservation Act*. Since 1995, the MNO has issued Métis Harvesters cards based on its MNO Harvesters Policy. In 2005, the MMF adopted *Interim Métis Laws of the Hunt* and began issuing MMF Harvesters cards. In 2007, the MNA adopted a province-wide MNA Harvesting Policy; it will be issuing harvester identification stickers in future years.

50 In July 2004, the MNO and Ontario government entered into a Métis harvesting accommodation agreement which relies on the MNO's Harvesters card system. For history and details of this agreement, see *R. v. Laurin*, [2007] O.J. No. 2344 (Ct. Just.).

51 For more information on and publications from Harvard Project on American Indian Economic Development, see online: www.ksg.harvard.edu/hpaied.

been undertaken, the conclusions reached can be easily applied to the realities faced by many Métis communities.

Moreover, Métis governance structures and institutions already have a long history of effectively delivering to their own people as well as other urban Aboriginal peoples. Currently, provincial Métis organizations administer well over $125 million annually in combined federal and provincial programs and services.[52] Best practices and outcomes can be cited in all areas where federal or provincial investments have been made;[53] however, there are significant gaps in some areas — for example, health, justice, and education — and varying investments from province to province. These gaps result in a patchwork of programming and an inability of Métis governance structures and institutions to address the holistic needs of Métis citizens. Often, Métis face "silo" programming in urban, rural, and remote communities and are shuffled between uncoordinated delivery agencies. From a policy perspective, the failings of the current programmatic approach are readily apparent. As a result, a strong case can be made that Métis would benefit from a more coordinated, self-government framework.

Finally, another rationale for implementing Métis self-government is that it reflects Canadian values and traditions. In the *Quebec Secession Reference*, the Supreme Court described Canada as an experiment in "reconcil[ing] diversity with unity."[54] Throughout its history, Canada has recognized the value of a multiculturalism policy which allows distinct identities and cultures to survive and flourish. For example, one of the oldest ethnic communities in Canada, the Montreal Jewish community, has a history of institution building stretching back over 200 years. Current programs span family and children services to education and culture to services for seniors with annual budgets in the tens of millions of dollars. Equally impressive, as a second example, is the rich array of institutions developed by the Franco-Manitoban communities with some thirty to forty active community organizations that host cultural

52 See Métis National Council, *Snapshot of the Nation: An Overview of the Métis Nation's Governance Structures and Institutions* (Ottawa: Métis National Council, 2001). Note that this figure does not include programs and services delivered by regional or local Métis organizations (such as community councils and locals).

53 See Section C(5), above in this chapter, for some notable examples.

54 *Reference re Secession of Quebec*, [1998] 2 S.C.R. 217 at 244.

events, promote economic development, and provide services in a wide range of areas.[55] In a similar vein, Métis communities seek to deliver services to their people in a culturally appropriate manner and to promote their culture, language, and traditions through their own institutions. Canada's diversity has always been one of its strengths. A strong argument can be made that supporting Métis self-government contributes to Métis self-sufficiency and to the Canadian federation overall.

E. EXPLORING OPTIONS FOR MÉTIS GOVERNANCE

With an understanding of good governance, the history of the Métis Nation, contemporary Métis governance structures, and the rationales for Métis self-government as important backdrops, the author believes there are five key governance areas the Métis Nation will have to grapple with and develop strategies on in order to make real progress on its self-government agenda over the next decade.[56]

1) Identifying Métis Nation Citizens and Métis Rights-Holders

If the Métis Nation is going to advance its self-government agenda in the next decade, the MNC and its provincial Métis organizations must have well-defined and verifiable constituencies. Undoubtedly, two of the first questions to be raised in any future Crown–Métis self-government negotiations will be these: Who are you negotiating for? How will any arrangement be ratified? Vague or unverified representation claims will be non-starters. Moreover, addressing issues of who can access Métis-specific services and who can participate within Métis governance structures (for example, by voting in elections or holding office) are all central to ensuring fairness, accountability, legitimacy, and voice in Métis governance structures. In recognition of these realities, the MNC and its provincial Métis organizations have undertaken much work in this area.

---

55 For more information on these two communities and others, see Institute on Governance, "Ethnic Minorities in Canada: A Governance Perspective," March 2000, online: www.iog.ca/publications/ethnic.pdf.

56 It should be noted that these identified areas are not exhaustive, but have been identified based on interviews conducted as a part of the paper co-authored with J. Graham and J. Wilson for the IOG, as well as the author's work with Métis organizations at the national and regional levels.

As a starting point, it is important to set out the distinctions between the terms *membership*, *citizenship*, and *rights-holders* as used in this paper. Membership requirements are set out by legally incorporated bodies or associations. For example, membership in a political party can be obtained based on the meeting of certain requirements, such as being over age sixteen, filling out a form, and paying a fee. Further, each legal part of the political party — riding associations, provincial wings of party, national party — can set its own requirements for membership. In this way, membership is very different than citizenship in an Aboriginal people or nation. Simply filling out a form and paying a fee does not equate to citizenship. Citizenship requires proof of shared identity, culture, and acceptance by the larger collective based on criteria set by the collective itself. Individuals or smaller parts of the collective do not set the terms for citizenship. This right inheres in the larger collective. Finally, the term *rights-holder* relates to citizens that may have specific rights, as a part of the larger collective. Not all citizens may have the same rights. For example, all citizens may have the right to vote or hold office in an Aboriginal nation, but one particular settlement in the larger nation may have a constitutionally protected commercial fishing right based on historic practices, customs, and traditions on a specific lake. The citizens living at that settlement may have a commercial fishing right, but that does not mean that all members of the larger collective have a right to commercial fishing everywhere in the nation. As a result, rights-holders may be a subset of all citizens, as it relates to specific rights.

With that said, in the Métis context, two major developments have affected how Métis citizenship issues are being addressed. The first is the Métis Nation's adoption of a "National Definition of Métis for Citizenship within the Métis Nation." The second is the Supreme Court of Canada's decision in *Powley*. In order to better understand the implications of these developments the sections below provide background information on each.

a) National Definition of Métis for Citizenship in the Métis Nation

In the past, a major stumbling block for Métis identification was the reality that there was not one uniform definition of Métis across the Métis Nation. With each provincial Métis organization having jurisdiction for its respective membership, there were variations in definitions as well as application requirements (a centralized registry versus local communities issuing memberships, documents required). While there was some consistency in the key elements of these definitions — self-identification, ancestral connection, and community acceptance — varying practices often frustrated Métis individuals moving from province to province. Contrary to a citizenship-based model, where criteria and procedures are set by a larger collective, each provincial Métis organization pursued a membership-based approach.

Further, the political realities of these Métis governance structures have evolved over the years: after breaking away from the NCC in the 1980s, there were still many non-status Indians who were members of provincial Métis organizations. Naturally, membership requirements within these organizations have not been static so as criteria evolved over the 1980s to 1990s, some individuals who used to be members are no longer being eligible. Finally, the lack of provincial or federal resources to support sustained work on these membership lists has resulted in varying levels of integrity and capacity within the systems.

In September 2002, in a move to address these issues outlined above and to move towards a self-government model based on citizenship rather than membership, the MNC, at a General Assembly, adopted a "National Definition of Métis for Citizenship within the Métis Nation."[57] Following this ratification by the larger collective, each of the MNC's affiliated provincial Métis organizations undertook a process to incorporate the national definition into their respective bylaws or constitution. As of September 2003, a uniform definition for citizenship within the Métis Nation has been put into place from Ontario westward.

The National Definition's companion acceptance process was adopted, in principle, by the MNC General Assembly; however, it has been agreed that additional consultations on the document were to be undertaken and brought back to a future Assembly. Many of the contentious issues (outlined below in the paper) still need to be addressed in order to move forward on ratifying a final acceptance process.

57 "Métis" means a person who self-identifies as Métis, is distinct from other Aboriginal peoples, is of Historic Métis Nation ancestry, and is accepted by the Métis Nation. For full definition, including defined terms, see MNC's website, online: www.metisnation.ca/who/definition.html.

b) The Supreme Court of Canada's Decision in the *Powley* Case

While the Métis Nation, like other Aboriginal peoples, maintains that only it has the right to define its citizenship, it is undeniable that the Supreme Court of Canada's decision in *Powley* has had some effect on Métis identification issues. The Court did not set out a comprehensive definition of who is Métis,[58] but set out a "test" to identify a rights-bearing Métis community and who is eligible to exercise such a rights-bearing Métis community's constitutionally protected rights. Specifically, the Supreme Court set out three criteria to determine who is an eligible Métis rights-holder: self-identification, ancestral connection, and community acceptance.

The Supreme Court made several additional points of importance to Métis identification issues:

- *Métis Are Not Just Mixed-Blooded Individuals:* The Court held, "[t]he term "Métis" in s. 35 of the *Constitution Act, 1982* does not encompass all individuals with mixed Indian and European heritage; rather, it refers to distinctive peoples who, in addition to their mixed ancestry, developed their own customs, and recognizable group identity separate from their Indian or Inuit and European forebears."[59] This point dispels the often-held notion that Métis are any mixed-blooded individuals or group in Canada. More simply put, non-status Indians are not Métis and losing Indian status does not make you Métis by default.
- *The Geographic Scope of a Métis Community:* The Court defined "Métis community" in a broad sense by holding that a "Métis community can be defined as a group of Métis with a distinctive collective identity living together in the same geographic area and sharing a common way of life".[60]
- *Urgency in Identifying Métis Rights-Holders:* The Court gave strong direction to all levels of government to get on with the task of supporting Métis identification systems. Specifically, the Court held, "[t]he development of a more systematic method of identifying Métis rights-holders for the purposes on enforcing hunting regulation

58 *Powley*, above note 3 at para 12.

59 *Ibid.* at para. 10.

60 *Ibid.* at para. 12.

is an urgent priority. That said, the difficulty of identifying members of the Métis community must not be exaggerated as a basis for defeating their claims under the Constitution of Canada."[61]

- *An Objectively Verifiable Process:* The Court said that there must be an "objectively verifiable process" to identify Métis rights-holders. Directions were given to Métis groups for their membership requirements to become more standardized; however, governments were also directed to support this work. "Objectively verifiable" does not mean the government arbitrarily assesses who is Métis. Nor does it mean that Métis registration systems cannot be subject to review or assessment. As such, "objectively verifiable" Métis identification systems will be key to the legitimacy and credibility of systems.[62]

c) Outstanding Issues and Challenges Relating to Métis Identification

In assessing the state of current Métis identification processes and systems, several layers of issues and challenges must be addressed by the Métis Nation. Specifically, identifying the geographic scope of the Métis Nation's Homeland and which settlements are a part of this distinct Aboriginal nation remains an issue. While, to date, the Métis Nation has defined the general parameters of its Homeland,[63] it has not specified just how far its territory spans and which areas and settlements are a part of the larger nation. Moreover, the MNC's National Definition is somewhat cyclical in how it identifies the Historic Métis Nation and the Historic Métis Nation Homeland.[64]

---

61 *Ibid.* at para. 49.

62 *Ibid.* at para. 29.

63 MNC literature generally describes the Homeland as including the three prairie provinces and extending into Ontario, British Columbia, the Northwest Territories, and parts of the northern United States.

64 In the National Definition, the "Historic Métis Nation" is defined as being comprised of Métis or Half-breeds who resided in the "Historic Métis Nation Homeland." The "Historic Métis Nation Homeland" is then defined as "the area of land in west central North America" used and occupied by Métis or Half-breeds. The definition provides no further precision on "Métis Nation" or "Métis Nation Homeland."

In the future, it may become challenging to claim that the Métis Nation is a distinct Aboriginal people based on a common history, identity, culture, and language, while the nation itself has not delineated its settlements and territory. Moreover, on a practical level, it will also be increasingly difficult for registrars within provincial Métis organizations to answer whether someone is of Historic Métis Nation ancestry when the geographic boundaries of the nation are undefined. As a result, deciding whether an applicant from one settlement outside the Métis Nation's Prairie core is in or out becomes a somewhat arbitrary decision, rather than something based on the Métis Nation's inherent right to define its citizenship. Clearly, work on indicators for recognizing settlements as a part of the Métis Nation, research on settlements, and mapping of the Métis Nation Homeland are needed.

Further, the need to identify and recognize rights-bearing Métis communities and their traditional territories will also be part of addressing this preliminary challenge. To date, most governments have relied heavily on the Supreme Court's statement in *Powley* that Métis rights are "site-specific"[65] to narrow the scope of Métis claims. For example, in some jurisdictions, a "Métis community" and "site-specific" have been interpreted to mean a discrete physical settlement or a town. Conversely, Métis assert that an expansive definition of community must be used. Many Métis leaders consider the nation, in its entirety, as a rights-bearing community. To date, in lower court decisions applying the *Powley* decision, judges have been adopting a regional approach to the identification of a Métis community.[66] Regardless of the differing positions, it is clear that more research and traditional land-use studies need to be undertaken in order to develop a principled and factual basis for identifying rights-bearing Métis communities. Flowing from this work, complex issues relating to mobility and community acceptance will also have to be addressed.

---

65 *Powley*, above note 3 at para. 12.

66 For judicial findings on contemporary rights-bearing regional Métis communities, see *Laviolette*, above note 48 (community includes northwest Saskatchewan and covers approximately 40 000 square kilometres) and *Belhumeur*, above note 48 (Métis community includes the Qu'Appelle Valley and environs and covers approximately 30 000 square kilometres).

Finally, public education and awareness on the Métis Nation being a distinct and culturally coherent Aboriginal people is needed. Part of this task is ensuring that Métis are not equated with the population of mixed-race, non-status Indians or others. Misconceptions in the general public over Métis identity and why Métis have rights have been a major obstacle to political progress on the Métis agenda. Part of this may be due to the fact that Canada's political system tends to centralize power in the populous centre of the country, where the Métis are less prevalent. Other factors may include a lack of diligence on the part of the media to get the facts, apathy from the public at large with respect to Canadian and Aboriginal history, the lack of a clear, public-oriented message from Métis, and the diffusion of the Métis population within the Canadian electoral system.

The second group of Métis identification challenges relate to the more technical, but equally important task of registering citizens. In the wake of the *Powley* decision, for the first time ever, the federal government has made dedicated registry funding available to the MNC and provincial Métis organizations to identify rights-bearing Métis.[67] As a result, significant effort has been dedicated to establishing or enhancing provincial Métis identification systems.

As provincial Métis organizations continue their work on establishing these systems, outstanding national issues need to be addressed; if addressed in each province instead, different systems that are not ultimately consistent or even compatible could be created. For example, as these provincially based systems continue to develop their "own way of doing things" to address unresolved issues, it will become increasingly difficult to change their business practices or policies. The following are some of the Métis identification issues that remain unresolved:

- *Ratifying an Acceptance Process for Métis Registration:* As discussed above, although the MNC General Assembly has adopted an in-

67 Within the 2004 federal budget, $20.5 million was committed for *Powley*-related work. The 2005 federal budget committed to another $30 million over two years (2005–2007) for ongoing *Powley*-related work. In 2007, the funding was extended for one year. This *Powley* funding is set to be evaluated and reviewed by the federal government in the winter 2007/2008 in order to determine whether future funding will be provided.

principle acceptance process, it has not been formally ratified. There continues to be a need to move forward on adopting an acceptance process since each region is now addressing issues that are within the process on their own: document requirements, adoption, and being on another Aboriginal registry among them.

- *"Grandfathering" of Existing Members:* The issue of whether existing Métis membership card-holders who do not meet the new Métis citizenship requirements should be grandfathered into the new membership list is an issue. For example, some founding members of these provincial Métis organizations have always culturally identified as Métis; however, they do not have Métis Nation ancestry or took Bill C-31. The current definition of Métis and the proposed acceptance process do not provide a means to accept these individuals.
- *Control over Applications and Cards:* In some provinces, the issue of who has control over citizenship and registration has not been resolved. For example, some locals want to maintain complete control over citizenship applications and issuance of cards, rather than moving to a centralized provincial registry.
- *Adoption:* The issue of adoption remains contentious. Currently, the national definition of Métis does not provide for adoptees being accepted as Métis. However, within the in-principle acceptance process, children adopted at birth can become citizens of the Métis Nation. This issue cuts to the heart of whether being Métis is a racial or cultural concept. If the latter, adoptees and their children should not be distinguished from "birth" Métis in terms of their voting rights, rights to run for office, right to harvest, or the status of their own children. Further, in *Powley*, the Supreme Court accepts that adoptees can be rights-bearing Métis through the ancestrally connected branch of its test.[68] On the other side of the argument, individuals express concerns about adoptees automatically becoming Métis citizens even though they have no Métis ancestry or connection to the Métis Nation.
- *Community Acceptance:* The role of local, regional, and provincial bodies in accepting Métis citizens needs to be uniformly addressed.

---

68 *Powley*, above note 3 at para 32.

Some jurisdictions undertake community acceptance on a provincial basis — that is, if you meet the requirements for registration, you are deemed to be accepted by the registrar — while others still require locals to accept new citizens through meetings at the community level. Ensuring consistency and meeting the community acceptance requirement set out in *Powley* is important.

- *Bill C-31:* There are individuals who culturally identify as Métis, but who registered as status Indians under the *Indian Act* in the advent of Bill C-31. Currently, these individuals have no legal means to be removed from the *Indian Act* registry. Based on current policies that are being implemented, namely, that Métis citizens cannot be registered on another Aboriginal registry, provincial Métis organizations will not register these individuals and are removing registered Indians from newly created citizenship lists. There are strong arguments on either side of this issue. Registered Indians who culturally identify as Métis argue that if Métis identity is based on a common culture, why should a racist and external piece of legislation such as the *Indian Act* define Métis citizenship? These individuals also point to their inability to remove themselves from the *Indian Act* as a factor that should be considered. On the other side of the argument, Métis who have never tried to get Indian status take the position that these individuals made a choice and are now a part of the Indian community. Many lifelong Métis become upset by these individuals having the ability to "double dip" or come back to the Métis community because it appears that Métis are making gains. It should be noted that the MNC's in-principle acceptance process addresses these issues directly by refusing registration to anyone who is already on another Aboriginal registry.
- *Compatibility:* As each provincial Métis organization moves forward on implementing identification systems, there is concern that, if a national registry is ever established, the database systems being established will not be compatible. This issue is also of concern to Métis who move between provinces and will either be able to seamlessly transfer their citizenship or have to reapply in each province.
- *Separate Cards for Citizenship and Harvesting:* Whether there should be separate cards for citizenship and harvesting is an issue

that is being dealt with differently between provincial Métis organizations.

- *Security of Métis Cards:* Ensuring that highly secure, fraud-proof cards are produced will be essential to the integrity of the systems. Currently, a majority of these cards are far from secure.

Addressing these issues in a timely manner will be critical to the Métis Nation. Without a doubt, provincial Métis organizations need to ensure that these registration processes are of the highest integrity because dependable Métis citizenship cards and registries have many crucial uses — not least of which include exercising Métis rights, voting in Métis elections, participating in Métis political processes, and accessing Métis programs and services.

Moreover, because so much of the future legitimacy of these provincial Métis organizations and the assertion and exercise of Métis rights will rest on the integrity of these registries, there is a strong argument for nationally consistent and stringent approaches to registration. Without this, a non-Aboriginal person might be able to use a false or wrongly issued Métis citizenship card to harvest or access Métis-specific programs, or a particular Métis local or region could register large numbers of non-Aboriginal people for electoral or funding purposes. Such situations could create conflict or attract negative media coverage, adversely affecting the reputation of the *entire* Métis Nation and the credibility of *all* Métis identification systems. The media will not likely distinguish between the quality of each provincial Métis organization's card system — the black eye will likely be on all Métis cards. Thus, there are serious needs, both internal to the Métis Nation and external, to ensure a level of credibility in all identification systems.

Given the sensitivity of decisions around delineating the Métis Nation Homeland, identifying rights-bearing communities, and the registration of Métis individuals, it will be essential to establish clear processes that are insulated from political considerations, that include adequate checks and balances, and that allow for appeals. Such processes are critical to the fairness principle of good governance. The elements listed below are some of the governance initiatives the Métis Nation may want to consider to achieve this good governance goal.

2) National Métis Citizenship and Elections Commission

One approach with respect to Métis identification might be to institute a nationally consistent system administered by a national Métis citizenship and elections commission, which would be made up of a national commissioner (who would act as chair of the commission), along with provincial registrars. This commission would be tasked with ongoing reviews of the registry systems and electoral processes as well as making recommendations to Métis leadership and assemblies for improvements to the systems. All members of the commission would be non-political, arms-length officers of their respective Métis organizations. As well, an independent, arms-length Métis Nation auditor-general would be responsible for regularly auditing the provincial systems and electoral processes in order to ensure confidence in the systems. Details of such an approach could include the following:

- *Establishment of a national Métis citizenship and elections commission and Métis Nation auditor-general*: A commission and auditor-general, as outlined above, would be established through legislation passed by the MNC General Assembly and subsequently ratified by all provincial Métis organizations. The legislation would outline roles and responsibilities, mandates, appointment and removal procedures, and reporting requirements.
- *A consistent national system with regular independent audits*: The provincial registrars, with guidance of the national commissioner, would agree on a nationally consistent approach to registration of members, to include the types of documents required, roles and responsibilities of the various officials involved, and the nature of identification cards and registry systems. The independent auditor-general would then conduct audits of provincial registries and applications processes based on agreed-to checklists of needed documents and policies to ensure that the system agreed upon is indeed enforced.
- *National Métis identification card with regional affiliation*: Each region's card would be highly secure, standard nation wide, and indicate the individual's affiliation with a particular provincial Métis organization as well as with the Métis Nation as a whole (MNC).

- *Centralized provincial registries*: All files as well as electronic information in a database would be securely housed within a provincial registry. Efforts would be made to ensure all information was in digital format rather than cumbersome paper files. Locals and community councils can assist with application intake and may also have a role within accepting local members; however, a centralized registry will be established and maintained. Along with proof of residency in the jurisdiction concerned, the citizenship rolls would provide the basis for voting rights at all levels. Citizenship lists would also serve as electoral lists with chief electoral officers and provincial registrars working closely together during provincial elections.
- *Virtual national registry*: Because Métis registered in one province could become resident in another province and wish to retain political voice as well as access to programs and services, a national registry of Métis citizens is required (in order to prevent "shopping around," people denied Métis citizenship would also be listed). Only the provincial Métis organizations would have the authority to add or remove affiliated members, although the national commissioner would provide administrative support for the database (including, by monitoring INAC's Indian and Inuit registries, recommendations to the provincial organizations that they remove Métis who gain such status). It would thus function like a chest with five keys.
- *Selection of provincial registrars, chief electoral officer, national commissioner, and auditor-general*: To ensure their political independence and integrity, the registrars, commissioner, chief electoral officers, and auditor-general should be politically independent and appointed by a resolution of their respective Métis assemblies and the MNC General Assembly, and would serve lengthy terms (perhaps five to ten years). They would be removable only for cause, by the provincial or national president, after a majority vote by the particular assembly.[69]
- *A one-time reapplication*: In order to make stronger and more credible identification systems, there would be a one-time reapplication

69 This selection process is akin to that for Canada's chief electoral officer.

for all members across the Métis Nation based on the new national definition and agreed-to registration procedures.[70] This nation-wide process may alleviate some of the political fallout for leaders in specific regions asking their members to reapply. A national as well as regional communication strategy would be undertaken to explain to members the need to reapply and what is required. In addition to public announcements, all members of existing lists would be contacted regarding the new registration requirements.

- *Acceptance process*: In order to make the proposed one-time re-application process effective, an acceptance process (which addresses the outstanding issues canvassed above) must be ratified through political processes. This acceptance process would then guide the work of the national citizenship and elections commissioner and provincial registrars.
- *Appeals process*: Appeals of provincial decisions on citizenship or elections could be made to the national Métis citizenship and elections commission, which would establish procedures and mechanisms to hear appeals consistent with fairness and transparency. Any constituted appeal panel would not include the provincial registrar from the province whose decision is being appealing. A similar principle would be applied to appeals from provincial elections.
- *Reporting*: Members of the national citizenship and elections commission would be required to report regularly to the MNC Board of Governors, provincial boards, and assemblies on its activities. A national annual report along with provincial reports on activities would be a requirement. As well, the commission would make recommendations for changes to existing citizenship and elections policies as well as its enabling legislation through ongoing internal and external reviews.

a) National Panel on Identifying the Métis Nation Homeland

In order to assist the Métis Nation in delineating the geographic scope of its traditional territory, there is a need to establish a fair, principled, and

70 Some provincial Métis organizations with well-established centralized registries may not require the reapplication of all members; just those who do not have enough documentation on file to meet the Métis Nation's national definition and acceptance process requirements.

fact-driven process. While the decision of identifying which communities are a part of the Métis Nation ultimately rests with the Métis people, a transparent process will assist the political bodies in getting to a point where they can make these difficult and contentious decisions.

- *Agreeing to criteria for identifying a "people"*: Although there is no universally accepted definition of a *people*, domestic and international jurisprudence has generally taken a very broad view of the term. Without being exhaustive or essential, objective elements include common language, history, culture, kinship, race or ethnicity, way of life, and territory. In addition, a subjective element, whereby a people identifies itself, is necessary.[71] Since the Métis Nation largely bases its self-government and rights claims on being a distinct Aboriginal people, it would seem logical to use these well-recognized indicators to assess which communities are a part of the Métis Nation. Through a consultation process, key indicators could be agreed to which would then assist the assessment process.
- *Establishing a Métis Nation Homeland review panel*: In order to undertake the assessment of communities based on the indicators agreed to by the political bodies, a blue-ribbon Métis Nation Homeland review panel would be assembled. This panel would consist mainly of independent experts in the field, such as academics and professors. The panel could also include elders to assist or guide the experts in their work. The task of the panel would be to assess communities (historically and in contemporary times) based on the agreed to indicators and make recommendations based on fact-based research and visits to the communities. The panel would then table a final report with the Métis Nation for consideration.
- *Doing a political review of the panel's report*: The final step in the process would be for the Métis Nation's political bodies to review and decide whether to accept all, some, or parts of the panel's re-

---

71 *Reference re Secession of Quebec*, above note 54 at 278 and 281–82; Ronald Lambert, "Does a Canadian People Exist," S.C.C. File No. 25506 (3 March 1998) (QL db CSRQ, d=49); and RCAP, *Restructuring the Relationship*, above note 5 at 169–78 and 184.

port. As stated above, decisions in relation to nationhood ultimately lie with the people themselves; therefore, members would have the opportunity to provide comments on the panel's final report and whether to accept its recommendations.

F. CONSTITUTIONAL DEVELOPMENT AND DELINEATING THE ROLES AND RESPONSIBILITIES OF MÉTIS GOVERNMENTS

Another unresolved self-government issue within the Métis Nation is the development of a Métis Nation Constitution. Central to any constitutional reform is the need to delineate what the chief functions of Métis government might be and which of the four levels of Métis government might handle them — national, provincial, regional, and local.

Currently, most Métis governance functions are carried out at the provincial level: provincial Métis organizations handle the bulk of Métis program funds; manage most cultural, historical, linguistic, and educational facilities; coordinate the exercise of harvesting rights; conduct registration; appoint members to the MNC's General Assembly; and are the focus of the most high-profile elections. It seems likely that most of these responsibilities would stay as they are. That said, there are a few areas — particularly citizenship and elections — in which improved national coordination and the possibility of appeals to the national level would benefit the nation as a whole; there are also a few areas in which capacity building at the regional and local levels could improve service delivery and ensure that Métis are engaged and consulted in relation to their rights and interests vis-à-vis natural resources and economic development within or around their communities.

The need to delineate the roles and responsibilities between Métis governments is an important exercise that must be undertaken in order to move forward on constitutional development. To date, the MNC's development of a Métis Nation Constitution has been stalled. Factors such as unanswered questions on the boundaries of the Métis Nation Homeland, the lack of a reliable enumeration of Métis in order to make determinations based on representation by population, limited resources to undertake constitutional work, and concerns from Métis leadership that power may be substantially redistributed between the national and provincial bodies are all challenges. Further, some provincial Métis organizations are in the process of undertaking their own governance reform or constitutional development; therefore, the development of a national constitution is seen as a daunting and unwieldy task. Irrespective of these challenges, achieving some form of agreement on the division of powers between the Métis Nation's governance structures and institutions will be critical in figuring out how Métis self-government negotiations will move forward.

The following outline proposes a set of roles and responsibilities for the four levels of Métis government, along with explanations that could assist discussions vis-à-vis constitutional development.

1) Roles and Responsibilities Shared by All Four Levels

- *Promotion of Métis Nation identity and culture*: All four levels of government should be involved in defending and promoting Métis culture, including language, history, traditions, arts, values, heritage, traditional knowledge, spirituality, and way of life. Efforts to maintain interest, understanding, and involvement within the nation — particularly among youth — as well as in the general Canadian population are equally important. In considering the current activities of the various organizations, it appears that there could be a greater national role in this regard, one that could be achieved through national historical, educational, linguistic, or artistic organizations, or through higher profile national gatherings. Important institutions, such as the Gabriel Dumont Institute, have been established at the provincial level, but there is little reason the national organization could not connect to these and build on them in order to better reach out to all Métis Nation citizens and increase the national profile of the Métis Nation.
- *Negotiations on Métis rights and self-government*: Dependent on the nature and scope of negotiations, specific or multiple levels of Métis governments may be engaged, for example:
    - » lead-up negotiations to a First Ministers Meeting, which would be undertaken by the MNC based on the direction of provincial Métis organizations;
    - » negotiations involving specific land or resource development, which would need to involve affected local Métis communities with

possible support from regional and provincial Métis governments that possess increased capacity and expertise in these areas.

2) National Roles and Responsibilities

- *Advocacy and legal coordination around rights*: Because of the high cost of legal processes and the need for coordination, because Métis rights nationwide are in many ways affected by court rulings on the subject, and because of the need for expertise in the area, the MNC should continue to play a lead role in advocacy, and in supporting and coordinating legal pursuits related to Métis rights.
- *Intergovernmental and international forums*: The MNC should represent the Métis at forums such as First Ministers Meetings and other important federal–provincial meetings, as well as at international meetings of Indigenous peoples or other international forums relating to rights and other issues.
- *Liaison with the federal government*: The MNC would continue to play a major role in (a) coordinating national negotiations and agreements around federal initiatives relating to the Métis or to Métis-specific policy and (b) maintaining ongoing relations vis-à-vis existing federal programs, in particular, around federal programs managed by Métis organizations, such as the Aboriginal Human Resource Development Strategy (ARHDS) and Aboriginal Language Initiative (ALI).
- *Communications to members on issues of national concern*: The MNC and the national president should be seen and regarded as the national voice of the Métis Nation in order to avoid confusion and mixed messages among Métis leadership on issues of national concern.
- *Auditing provincial registries and electoral processes, ensuring accountability, and resolving intergovernmental disputes*: A Métis Nation auditor-general could play a valuable role in holding the MNC, as well as provincial Métis organizations, to account for the stewardship of the money of the Métis people, including through value-for-money audits of financial statements and special examinations of particular programs. As well, this type of arms-length and well-respected Métis institution could be called upon by other governments when administrative issues arise. Instead of a third

party, who is often unfamiliar with the issues, conducting a review, an independent auditor-general could investigate and make findings and recommendations. Proactive measures such as this could also help to avoid strained or severed relations between Métis organizations and governments when issues arise. Moreover, the auditor-general could make findings with respect to governments not fulfilling their obligations to provincial Métis organizations: these might pertain to late payments to Métis organizations and disputes on funding guidelines. Finally, as discussed previously, the auditor-general would audit provincial registries and electoral systems.

- *Coordination of research activities*: The MNC could be tasked with coordinating and becoming a clearinghouse of research and academic study on the Métis Nation and Métis communities; part of this role would be to ensure that information is accessible to the Métis community at large.
- *Equalization of revenues among provincial Métis organizations*: Depending on the form of the fiscal agreements forged between the federal and provincial governments and their Métis counterparts, there could be a role for the MNC to manage the sharing of revenues between have and have-not provincial Métis organizations. The Métis organizations that provide and those that receive revenues under this system may well be different from the have and have-not provinces of the Canadian federation; their status may also change over time. While controversial for some, equalization is a common feature of most federal systems worldwide and is generally seen as essential to maintaining the unity of the nation over the long term. It can also help residents of resource-dependent regions — which include many Métis people — weather periodic economic downturns.

3) Shared National and Provincial Roles and Responsibilities

- *National commission on Métis citizenship and elections*: As outlined in the section above, the Métis Nation could establish an arms-length national commission consisting of a national commissioner and provincial registrars who would work together to ensure integrity and consistency within the Métis Nation's registries and electoral processes.

- *Coordinating relations with other Aboriginal peoples*: In part because of its Ottawa location, the MNC can play a lead role in coordinating advocacy efforts and other issues with the leadership of the other national Aboriginal organizations representing First Nations and Inuit. Provincial Métis organizations would take a lead on establishing relationships and possibly coordinating efforts at a regional level with tribal councils or First Nations provincial bodies.
- *Fiscal agreements with provincial and federal governments*: The provinces will be more inclined to engage the Métis Nation in a serious manner if they see their neighbours taking similar initiatives. Consequently, the MNC can play a useful role in supporting and coordinating the activities of the provincial Métis organizations as major agreements — particularly on fiscal relations — are concluded with the federal and provincial governments.

4) Shared Local, Regional, and Provincial Roles and Responsibilities

- *Receipt of citizenship applications*: As discussed above, it is important to allow Métis members different channels to submit applications for citizenship. In some cases, gaining the signature of the local and/or regional president could be a useful way to demonstrate "community acceptance" before the application is passed on to the provincial registrar for final approval. As well, local bodies could assist applicants in completing their membership applications. On the other hand, families who have moved to another region and lost personal ties to their ancestral community, but can still demonstrate through other means that they have retained their culture should be able to apply for citizenship directly to the provincial registrar, with the necessary genealogical and other evidence.
- *Communicating to members*: All three levels of Métis government would have the responsibility to ensure that members are informed of activities and initiatives that affect them. Specific communications tools for each level of Métis government could be agreed to. For example, provincial bodies could publish quarterly magazines or papers and maintain a website for members, regional bodies could publish regional newsletters, and locals and councils could hold regular information meetings.

5) Provincial Roles and Responsibilities

- *Liaison with provincial governments*: Just as the MNC would take the lead on federal initiatives, the provincial organizations would have the chief role in negotiating agreements with provinces in such areas as education, youth, and child and family services.
- *Maintaining a provincial registry*: As described above, arms-length provincial registrars should be appointed to approve individual applications for Métis status and to handle appeals of local or region-level decisions.
- *Communications on issues of regional concern*: In order to avoid confusion and mixed messages among Métis leadership on issues of regional concern, the provincial Métis organization and provincial president should be seen and regarded as the provincial voice of the Métis Nation.
- *Advocacy pertaining to natural resources*: Because natural resources are provincial jurisdiction and the provinces differ widely in their willingness to engage Aboriginal communities in consultation on forestry, mining, oil and gas, and other natural resources, advocacy efforts pertaining to revenue sharing or other opportunities around natural resources development are best left to the provincial Métis organizations.
- *Program and service regulation, oversight, funding coordination, and some delivery*: Provincial Métis governments are already involved in coordinating funding, regulating, and overseeing the delivery by regional or local Métis governments of programs and services. In some cases, the programs and services are delivered directly by the provincial organization. The principal programs and services that the provincial organizations govern or might seek to govern, are as follows:
    - » child and family services;
    - » some aspects of justice and corrections programming (particularly around young offenders, probation, and community reconciliation);
    - » youth programs (such as youth councils and summer camps);
    - » some aspects of education programming (especially culturally appropriate special education, curriculum development, stay-in-school programs, mentorship programs, adult education and employment training, and scholarship funds);

 - » labour market programs (such as counselling, skills upgrading, and access to apprenticeship opportunities);
 - » health (such as long-term and personal care workers, prevention programs, education and awareness on diabetes, prenatal nutrition, infant health, responsible gambling, addictions, and residential schools survivors);
 - » economic development (such as Métis-controlled business ventures, resource sharing agreements, impacts and benefits agreements);
 - » financial services (such as a credit union or other lending institutions); and
 - » housing programs (such as building and maintaining social housing, and repair programs).
- *Coordination and oversight of harvesting activities*: Provincial Métis organizations should play a lead role in coordinating and overseeing harvesting activities. For example, as is currently the case in Ontario, this would involve appointing local coordinators of harvesting activities (in the MNO's case, captains of the hunt) to implement the provincial Métis government's harvesting policy and any agreement with provincial departments. This coordinating role should remain at the provincial level because the nature of Métis harvesting practices varies from province to province, and because the most important linkages are with provincial rather than federal ministries. The only national role in this regard should be that of the commissioner, who could oversee the integrity of the provincial harvesters' registries (but not make decisions on individual cases) as well as liaise with the federal government on its limited role in the area of harvesting.
- *Appeals from program-related disputes*: Many government programs have appeal mechanisms so that citizens denied program benefits have a means of airing their grievances. The provincial Métis organizations could assume that role, perhaps by establishing an ombudsman-like function or some other dispute resolution mechanism.

6) Regional Roles and Responsibilities

- *Delivery of programs and services*: Depending on the level of capacity present in the regional organization, provincial Métis organizations could delegate many of the tasks of delivering programs and services, such as those listed above, to regional organizations. These regional organizations should remain creatures of the provincial organization, constituted by it and financially accountable to it, though with their own democratically elected leadership. Indeed, efforts should be made to enhance the delivery capacity of these regional organizations as well as their accountability to the Métis communities through Charter Agreements, similar to MNO and MNBC.

- *Coordination of resource-related opportunities*: If Métis communities succeed in gaining a greater stake in natural resources development, there may be a role for regional organizations in distributing royalties or managing opportunities around jobs, contracting, training, or business ventures, particularly where the project affects multiple communities.
- *Aggregated governance functions for groups of communities on a land base*: The Metis Settlements General Council and the Metis Settlements Appeal Tribunal handle a range of regulatory appeals, and oversight functions, and deliver a number of programs and services to the eight disparate Settlements, which each have their own local governments delivering municipal-like services. If other Métis communities on a discrete land base are established elsewhere, or if the existing Settlements choose to integrate with the other Métis Nation governance structures, it may be necessary to establish clear jurisdictions for aggregated regional Métis governments to serve such communities.

7) Local Roles and Responsibilities

- *Delivery of programs and services*: As with the regional bodies, where capacity exists, the provincial organizations may engage local organizations in the delivery of certain programs and services, such as those on the list above.
- *Local governance of geographically specific communal rights*: Local authorities appointed by the provincial organization should coordinate the exercise of harvesting rights at the local level, and in accordance with provincial Métis harvesting policies and relevant agreements with government departments.

- *Provision of local government functions on a land base*: As in the case of the Métis Settlements, if any land-base communities are newly established or absorbed into the Métis Nation governance system, clear jurisdiction for municipal-like government functions for these local authorities should be established.

8) Independent Métis Judicial or Dispute Resolution Institutions

- *Dispute resolution between various levels of Métis government*: There may be a need to establish an independent body, such as a senate, to resolve any disputes between the MNC and provincial Métis organizations, rather than resorting to courts based on the interpretation of corporate bylaws. As well, this body could be responsible for interpreting legislation or any eventual Métis Nation constitution.
- *Final level of appeal for identified citizenship or election disputes*: This non-political independent institution could also act as a final level of appeal in citizenship and election disputes, which would be first heard by a national Métis citizenship and elections commission.

In order for constitutional development to move forward, members need to come to some agreement about who does what. Once there is general agreement in this area, constitutional development will become an easier exercise: all bodies will have a clear sense of what they do and how they interrelate with other levels of Métis government. Until there is a level of comfort between the parties in this area, constitutional development exercises will continue to be stalled. Similarly, until the unresolved identification issues that were outlined above are addressed, national constitution development will remain a difficult and challenging task. There also needs to be a clear understanding of who the constitution includes.

G. STRENGTHENING GOVERNANCE AND ADMINISTRATION

As the national and provincial Métis organizations continue to grow, the need to strengthen governance and administration becomes more and more pressing. Governance deals with the roles and responsibilities of elected leaders and how they interact with the Métis civil service, or bureaucracy. Administration deals with more internal matters, namely, day-to-day program delivery, accounting for results, recruitment, retention, training, and financial checks and balances.

Clearly, stable, long-term funding for Métis groups is a solution to many of the problems in the areas of governance and administration. That said, funding will not be the panacea for all of these issues. For one thing, there is a widespread need for improved understandings of the roles that political leaders and board members can play and how these relate to those of staff.

One initiative that could be implemented is ensuring all newly elected or re-elected Métis leaders go to a leadership training "boot camp." Similar to what newly appointed federal ministers go to, this type of session could provide Métis leaders with information on what their political roles and responsibilities are versus administrative issues, how to interact with staff, dispute resolution techniques, how not to expose the organization to legal liability (e.g., labour law issues, harassment) as well as team building with other elected colleagues.

An equally important challenge facing the Métis Nation is building a strong and productive civil service. Numerous challenges vis-à-vis recruitment and retention of competent staff persist in Métis organizations:

- an inability to offer competitive compensation packages to qualified candidates (significantly lower salaries than federal or provincial governments, a lack of pension plans, a lack of defined grids for salary reviews, and so on);
- an inability to offer long-term employment contracts to qualified candidates due to the project-based nature of funding received from other governments;
- a lack of effective and ongoing training for staff in order to upgrade skills throughout their careers;
- a lack of job security due to the political nature of these organizations where there may be elections every three or four years and political factions on provincial boards; and
- a lack of clearly defined organizational structures, job descriptions, expectations, and career planning within the organizations.

These issues contribute to some qualified individuals not seeing a career with the Métis Nation as a long-term option. With this comes high "churn" within the organizations, often leading to a lack of stable corporate knowledge as well as sustainable strategy development and implementation.

One suggested initiative is having one of the Métis Nation's educational institutions assume the role of developing training modules to address a variety of these governance and administration areas — there could be a Métis Nation Centre of Excellence in Governance and Administration. An advisory board, with representation from each provincial Métis organization, would provide direction to the centre. Courses in finance, governance, reporting, skills upgrading, dispute resolution, and so on would be developed and incorporate a Métis-specific perspective. Further, a Métis Nation 101 course would be helpful for new employees and leaders to better understand the Métis Nation's history, overall organizational structure, and political agenda. Ideally, this centre would become a forum where best practices in governance and administration are shared rather than each provincial Métis organization having to invest the time and resources to develop its own approach to these issues.[72]

One final comment on the timing and nature of the Métis Nation's self-government agenda is in order.

To date, First Nations and governments have pursued self-government in what some have called a "big bang" approach — that is, negotiate a full range of jurisdictions and then implement. Such an approach entails lengthy negotiations.[73] In addition, and perhaps more seriously, many First Nations have assumed jurisdiction in areas where they had little or no capacity or governance experience. The suite of regulatory functions relating to safe water comes to mind.

The Métis Nation may wish to learn from this experience. Taking a more evolutionary approach to self-government would ensure that governance and administration capacity and experience are in place prior to

72 For example, finance staff from Ontario west could compare the pros and cons of existing financial practices and software to develop a system that fits the needs of the Métis Nation.

73 For example, the United Anishnaabeg Councils began their self-government negotiations in the late 1980s and reached a final agreement not long ago; the agreement was subsequently rejected by two of the four communities.

assuming formal, jurisdictional responsibilities; the Métis Nation could take on jurisdiction a sector at a time. A notable example of this is the best practice of devolution of child and family services to the MMF. The MMF had to marshal much of its resources and attention to this sector in order for the negotiations and transfer to be successful. It is questionable whether the transfer would have succeeded had the MMF attempted to build institutional capacity and human resources on a multitude of fronts at the same time. This type of methodical and measured assumption of jurisdiction may be a more effective means for the Métis Nation to achieve success.

H. THE PLACE OF THE MÉTIS IN THE CANADIAN FEDERATION

The long-standing position of the Métis Nation has been that section 91(24) of the *Constitution Act, 1867*,[74] includes Métis in assigning legislative jurisdiction to the federal government for "Indians and Lands reserved for Indians." The federal government maintains the position that Métis are not included in section 91(24) and that provinces have primary responsibility for Métis. Provincial governments take an opposing view and assert the federal government has responsibility for all off-reserve Aboriginal peoples. Many well-regarded academics and legal commentators agree with the Métis Nation's position.[75]

Unfortunately, litigation of this issue has proven to be costly, time consuming, and open to delays and stall tactics by both levels of government.[76] Contrary to bold political statements of wanting to tackle

---

74 Above note 23.

75 Peter Hogg, *Constitutional Law of Canada*, 4th ed. (Toronto: Carswell, 1997) at 540; Clem Chartier, "'Indian': An Analysis of the Term They Used in s. 91(24) of the *British North America Act, 1867*" (1978–1979) 43 Sask. L. Rev. 37; Catherine Bell, "Who Are the Métis People in Section 35(2)?" (1991) 29 Alta. L. Rev. 351; Bradford W. Morse & John Giokas, "Do Métis Fall within Section 91(24) of the *Constitution Act, 1867*?" in Royal Commission on Aboriginal Peoples, *Aboriginal Self-Government: Legal and Constitutional Issues* by Patrick Macklem (Ottawa: Royal Commission on Aboriginal Peoples, 1995); Don McMahon & Fred Martin, "The Métis and 91(24): Is Inclusion the Issue?" in *Aboriginal Self-Government: Legal and Constitutional Issues, ibid.*

76 For example, in Métis rights litigation in Saskatchewan, at trial, the Saskatchewan Crown admits that Métis are "Indians" for the purposes of s. 91(24) and then

jurisdictional issues head on, both levels of government often resort to a wait-and-see approach on this important issue.[77] As a result, Métis find themselves being volleyed back and forth between levels of government. They see federal acknowledgment of jurisdiction as key to moving forward on their agenda for the following reasons:

- Only the federal government has the jurisdictional competency to enter into treaties with peoples and this is what the Métis Nation seeks to negotiate with Canada.
- Section 91(24) recognition would break the current log jam in that neither the federal nor provincial governments are willing to negotiate seriously with the Métis on issues relating to land and self-government for fear of compromising their constitutional positioning.
- The federal government would have clear authority for legislation vis-à-vis Métis and could no longer use the jurisdiction uncertainty as an excuse for inaction.
- It would make it more difficult for federal government departments to deny Métis access to much needed programs and services that are provided to other Aboriginal peoples on a policy basis.
- Such recognition would serve as a unifying factor among the five provincial Métis organizations that make up the Métis Nation and focus relationship efforts federally.
- Métis would have a door to knock on within the Canadian federation to have their issues addressed without hearing the excuse of the federal government having "no mandate" to negotiate with them.
- One level of government must have jurisdiction to deal with the Métis, and it is logical that all three constitutionally recognized Aboriginal peoples are within federal jurisdiction.

---

argues that Métis claimants cannot introduce evidence on s. 91(24) in order to obtain a decision on the issue because the question is moot and uncontroversial between the parties. This tactic seems to contradict Saskatchewan's political assertions on s. 91(24) because it forestalls obtaining certainty on Canada's jurisdiction vis-à-vis Métis. See *R. v. Laviolette*, [1996] S.J. No. 378 (Q.B.).

77 For example, the MNC has consistently requested, to no avail, that Canada refer this issue to the Supreme Court of Canada as a reference question. Similarly, provinces from Ontario west have refused to refer the question to their respective courts of appeal.

- Inclusion would place the Métis on the same footing with Canada's other Aboriginal peoples and create equity in relations between the Métis and the Canadian federation.
- In recent times, the federal government has been in a financial surplus position and more able to make financial investments in its areas of jurisdiction in comparison to most provincial governments.
- Recognition would have important symbolic value to the Métis, who are often referred to as Canada's "forgotten people."

Very likely, the Métis will ultimately be legally successful on the section 91(24) issue; however, there are some on-the-ground realities and four specific factors that make a review of the current positioning, on the part of all parties, a recommended course of action.

- Governments remain reluctant to engage too much or make Métis-specific investments for fear of compromising their positions; nonetheless, the socio-economic needs of Métis individuals and communities are pressing.
- Métis leadership is reluctant to be seen as too willing to focus on practical arrangements which puts jurisdiction aside. Programming arrangements, however, can address the pressing socio-economic needs of Métis individual and communities.
- Obtaining a Supreme Court of Canada decision on the section 91(24) issue is at least a decade away; however, being legally vindicated that far in the future will not address immediate needs.
- Having the "stars align" politically in order for the federal government to acknowledge jurisdiction for Métis does not seem likely any time soon.

In light of these factors, a case can be made for a different political approach over the next decade while the litigation proceeds. This approach would eschew recognition of Métis people under either section 91(24) or section 92 (the heading on powers for provinces), but rather call for new constitutional space to be created for the Métis Nation based on its own inherent jurisdiction.

What are the arguments for such a new approach? There are several, some principled and some pragmatic. On the principled side, the Métis Nation's argument for occupying its own unique constitutional space rests squarely within section 35 of the *Constitution Act, 1982*. If section 35 recognizes the inherent right to self-government for Métis and other Aboriginal peoples, what is the logic in seeking either section 91(24) or section 92 recognition? The inherent right suggests that eventually the Métis people and their governments should have their own jurisdictions recognized (as a third order of government) with intergovernmental relationships and arrangements with both the federal and provincial governments to solidify this. Although ideally the Métis Nation would like one level of government to take the lead on this, is it not a possibility that through bilateral, trilateral, and multilateral processes, Métis jurisdiction could be carved out?

Similarly, it is becoming increasingly evident that, in this complicated world where "everything is related to everything else," the notion of water-tight, jurisdictional compartments in a federal state makes less and less sense. It is difficult to imagine a major policy undertaking by either level of government that doesn't require considerable intergovernmental cooperation. And for this reason, ongoing federal–provincial committees of ministers with corresponding shadow committees of officials abound in just about every major policy domain. The same challenge of intergovernmental coordination would face any self-government arrangements negotiated with the Métis. Thus, this argument suggests Métis recognition under both sections 91(24) and 92, or alternatively under its own heading.

On the practical side, time is of the essence to address many of the socio-economic challenges facing the Métis, such as a burgeoning youth population and a health crisis in Métis communities. Irrespective of how section 91(24) is finally decided, Métis desire and need intergovernmental relationships with both levels of governments. Starting to build those relationships now, based on the Métis Nation's jurisdiction to do so, makes sense, and such relationships will most likely not be prejudiced by any future decision on section 91(24). For example, it is unlikely that the federal government will attempt to set aside an existing Métis–provincial self-government arrangement because it is found to have jurisdiction for Métis. A future finding of federal jurisdiction could serve to enhance existing Métis–provincial partnerships by adding federal contributions.

Eventual section 91(24) recognition may also provide an excuse for provincial governments to reduce, if not minimize their involvement with the Métis. This result would be unfortunate, especially in light of current statistics. For example, in 2003/04, provincial investments to the Métis Nation accounted for close to 40 percent of total funding received by provincial Métis organizations.[78] The current ambiguity allows for both federal and provincial governments to work with the Métis for socio-economic policy reasons. So, far from breaking the current log jam, section 91(24) recognition might serve only to rearrange the logs.

Yet another practical argument would question whether it is in the best interests of the Métis to emulate the section 91(24) status of Indians and Inuit. For First Nations communities, a strong argument can be mounted that section 91(24) status is a major impediment to realizing effective, self-governing entities. Why is this so? The answer is that the federal government does not have in place the governance infrastructure for many of the key jurisdictions that First Nations want to assume. Take, for example, something as basic as drinking water. There is no federal "Safe Drinking Water Act" or any of the regulatory machinery to ensure that First Nations have drinking water regimes comparable to those that exist in the provinces. For a group of First Nations, let alone single entities, building this capacity is an enormous undertaking.[79] And safe water is only one of a dozen jurisdictions ranging from waste management to environmental protection to health and education systems in which the federal government has only limited capacity or involvement. The First Nations experience is clear: effective self-government regimes can be built only with the active involvement of both the federal and provincial governments and the lack of comparable provincial regimes on Indian reserves represents a significant capacity-building challenge.

---

78 *Snapshot of the Nation*, above note 52.

79 An example of the effort involved to create such a regime can be found with the Navajo, a tribe of over 120 000 occupying a reserve the size of West Virginia. The U.S. Environmental Protection Agency (EPA) worked with the Navajo over a seven-year period to develop their own EPA so as to have the capacity to administer the U.S. safe water acts.

I. CRAFTING A SOUND GOVERNMENT-TO-GOVERNMENT RELATIONSHIP

Whatever the outcome of the jurisdictional status of the Métis, it is evident that the MNC and provincial Métis organizations will need to work cooperatively and effectively with both federal and provincial governments. So, this leads to the next important set of issues: what constitutes sound intergovernmental relationships in a federal state like Canada?

A possible answer to this question might be found by looking to the principal elements encompassed in the Social Union Framework Agreement (SUFA),[80] which was signed in 1999 by Canada's federal, provincial, and territorial governments (with the exception of Quebec) after two years of negotiations. Some elements worthy of emulation might be the following:

- *Developing a common vision to which governments are committed*: In the opening paragraphs of the Agreement, the SUFA signatories provide a compelling vision of what they intend the partnership to achieve:
  - » to treat all citizens equally;
  - » to meet citizens' needs equally and effectively with social programs and services of reasonably comparable quality anywhere in the country;
  - » to promote the full and active participation of all in the country's social and economic life;
  - » to work in partnership with stakeholders and to ensure opportunities for citizen input;
  - » to ensure adequate, affordable, stable, and sustainable funding for social programs; and
  - » to respect Aboriginal, treaty, and self-government rights.
- *Establishing principles on how the relationship is to be conducted*: The SUFA, for example, commits the partners to joint planning and the sharing of information; respecting each others' constitutional jurisdictions; collaborating on the implementation of joint initiatives; treating all of the partners in an equitable fashion; and providing advance notice of new initiatives.

80 A copy is available online: www.socialunion.gc.ca/news/020499_e.html.

- *Reviewing the relationship after a set time*: On this point the SUFA provides for leaders to participate in a full review of the Agreement after three years and to ensure input and feedback from citizens and stakeholders.
- *Establishing ongoing machinery to manage the relationship*: The SUFA provides for a ministerial council mandated to "support sector Ministers by collecting information on effective ways of implementing the agreement and avoiding disputes and receiving reports from jurisdictions on progress on commitments."
- *Ensuring transparency in the relationship*: In the Agreement, governments agree to (i) "Publicly recognize and explain the respective roles and contributions of governments"; (ii) "Make eligibility criteria and service commitments for social programs publicly available"; (iii) "Report publicly on citizens' appeals and complaints, ensuring that confidentiality requirements are met"; (iv) "Monitor and measure outcomes of . . . social programs and report regularly to . . . constituents on the performance of these programs"; and (v) "Share information and best practices to support the development of outcome measures, and work with other governments to develop, over time, comparable indicators to measure progress on agreed objectives."
- *Developing an approach for dealing with disputes*: Throughout the SUFA, there are commitments that should reduce the likelihood of disputes, including agreements to provide for "information sharing, joint planning, collaboration, advance notice and early consultation, and flexibility in implementation." In the event of a dispute, the Agreement states that the parties will utilize "joint fact-finding" as a dispute resolution device; that a written fact-finding report will be submitted to the governments involved; and that governments may seek the assistance of third parties ". . . for fact-finding, advice or mediation."
- *Ensuring high-quality collaboration among the partners*: The SUFA enshrines a number of important practices, including these:
  - » to undertake joint planning;
  - » to collaborate on implementing joint priorities through developing joint objectives and principles, clarifying roles and responsibilities, and being flexible;

- to give one another advance notice prior to implementation of a major change in a social policy;
- to offer to consult before implementing new social programs and programs that are likely to affect the other parties; and
- to ensure some degree of funding predictability by having the federal government consult with the other parties at least one year prior to renewal or significant funding changes.

In a Métis Nation context, these elements of the SUFA would need to be modified to take into consideration the special constitutional status it enjoys within the Canadian federation. For example, any government-to-government relationship would need to recognize Aboriginal and treaty rights protected by section 35 of the *Constitution Act, 1982*, and the fiduciary relationship that exists between the Crown and Aboriginal peoples.

One type of forum to initiate such discussions could be a Métis Nation multilateral process, in which the MNC, all five provincial Métis organizations, the federal government, and the provinces from Ontario west would participate.[81] This type of Métis Nation multilateral process already exists to some extent, but it is focused on harvesting and has been fledgling. A re-mandated multilateral process with clear mandates from all parties could provide an effective means to address government-to-government relationship issues in a Métis context. The Métis Nation multilateral process could also be expanded to include other agreed-upon subjects for negotiations — for example, health and justice. Further, these sector-specific discussions could link into federal–provincial processes to ensure that Métis perspectives are heard at existing federal–provincial tables.

1) Métis Government Revenues

Effective governments require revenue sources that match their responsibilities, and Métis governments would be no exceptions. So what might these sources be?

81 This Métis Nation multilateral process is proposed in the signed Canada–Métis Nation Framework Agreement. A copy is available online: www.metisnation.ca/press/framework_agreement.pdf or www.ainc-inac.gc.ca/nr/prs/m-a2005/02665mnc_e.html.

The starting point is international experience that strongly suggests the importance of governments taxing their own citizens in order to achieve high levels of accountability and performance. This relates to the fact that citizens' sense of "ownership" of their government is built on paying part of their incomes to it and developing expectations of what to get in return. Indeed, one expert in public finance, Professor Emeritus Robert Bish of the University of Victoria and the former co-director of its Local Government Institute, is emphatic on this point. He identifies Norway as the only country he knows that receives a large share of its revenue from a source other than taxes (in this case, oil revenues) and whose government services have not deteriorated.[82]

Métis people, of course, already pay considerable taxes to their local, provincial, and federal governments. One estimate, based on 2001 census figures, is that Métis Nation citizens paid $550 million in federal tax in 2001.[83] This number does not include provincial taxes, GST, or corporate and business taxes from Métis-controlled companies. Following negotiations with federal and provincial governments, likely in the context of a self-government agreement, it is conceivable that a portion of the federal and provincial income taxes of Métis people collected by the federal government through the personal income tax system could be paid to Métis governments.[84] This would follow the federal government's current practice of collecting provincial taxes and handing these to the provinces and would be based on Métis citizenship — hence, yet another reason for having in place a Métis registry system of unquestioned integrity.

It is important to be clear that this portion of income tax paid by Métis citizens would not be a grant for which Métis governments would be accountable to the federal government. Rather, the accountability relationship would be from the Métis governments directly to their own tax-paying citizens. Again, the parallel here is with the provinces and

---

82 Robert Bish, as quoted in the report of the Institute on Governance, "Workshop on Tribal Councils, Scale and Aggregation, Summary Report" (Ottawa: Institute on Governance, 2003).

83 Métis National Council, *Canada-Aboriginal Peoples Roundtable: Accountability Policy Paper* (Ottawa: Métis National Council, 2005), online: www.metisnation.ca/pres_pubs/MNC_Roundtable_Compilation.pdf.

84 Should the Métis Nation achieve a land base, collecting property tax would be another possible source of revenue.

their direct accountability to their citizens for how they spend revenues from their tax points.

There are also other potential means for Métis governments to collect their own source revenues. For example, should Métis governments acquire land as part of a claims settlement, then rents from natural resources use or extraction could be an important revenue source. User fees might be another possibility, especially under the following circumstances:

- Services have characteristics of a private good, that is, bought and sold in the marketplace (examples include drinking water, public transit, and use of national parks).
- Individual beneficiaries are easy to identify.
- There are no significant effects (spillovers) on other citizens who do not receive this service.
- Operating and capital costs can be measured.
- The user fee is easy to administer.

Another own source revenue might be dividends paid by a Métis-owned commercial business. Several such businesses already exist — for example, an oil drilling business in Alberta referred to in the best practices subsection of this paper. In addition, Métis governments could be recipients of a portion of provincial revenue from gaming operations such as now occurs in Saskatchewan or alternatively, be issued gaming licences.

Finally, as in the case with provincial and local governments, Métis governments would need to rely on transfers from other governments. Métis organizations are already significant recipients of federal and provincial program funding. With few exceptions, however, these funds are directed to specific delivery organizations incorporated under provincial, not-for-profit legislation with their own boards of directors. Furthermore, the funding is accompanied by strict conditions.

The long-term direction of these transfers should move from one of a government department transferring funds to a specific program delivery organization to that of a government transferring funds to another government, much like federal–provincial transfers. The box below indicates the nature of the evolutionary change.

Current	Future
Multiple departments transfer funds to program delivery organizations, each governed separately	Single government-to-government transfer
No opportunity to set own priorities or move funds between programs	Métis governments to determine funding levels among programs subject to some constraints
Funding highly conditional	Métis governments to meet certain broad standards
Significant reporting burden with many reports	Single annual report
Single-year time horizon	Multi-year time horizon

Some First Nations, especially those that have entered into self-government arrangements, have funding relationships with the federal government with characteristics similar to those in the second column; Métis governments, at some future point, should enjoy similar relationships with both federal and provincial governments. That said, the importance of the Métis developing sound governance practices and having their own accountability mechanisms, such as an auditor-general and other checks and balances, cannot be understated.

One option Métis people might wish to consider is establishing their own certification system for sound governance and management of all Métis entities. Developed in partnership with federal and provincial governments, the certification system might result in a variety of benefits for those organizations obtaining certification, such as a reduction in the reporting burden or eligibility for longer term agreements. Further, certification would boost the confidence of the private sector and government agencies in working with Métis entities and pinpoint weaknesses that required attention.[85] Finally, by focusing on the positive (an ever increasing percentage of Métis entities meeting the certification standards)

85 For more details on how such a certification system might work in an Aboriginal context, see John Graham, "Policy Brief #8: Getting the Incentives Right: Improving Financial Management of Canada's First Nations" (May 2000), online: www.iog.ca/publications/policybrief8.pdf. It is noteworthy that the *First Nations Fiscal and Statistical Management Act*, S.C. 2005, c. 9, recently adopted by the federal Parliament, authorizes the newly created First Nation Financial Management Board to develop a voluntary certification system for the financial management of First Nations.

rather than the negative findings of audits, such a system would help boost public confidence.

J. CONCLUSION

These are propitious times for the Métis Nation. For a variety of reasons, there are now and will continue to be significant opportunities to make progress on the Métis self-government agenda and on improving the well-being of the Métis people. Nonetheless, to make the most of these opportunities, the Métis people will need to grapple with some critical governance issues.

The purpose of this paper has been to identify and analyze some of the most important of these governance concerns. The paper is not intended to be prescriptive. Its objective is to provoke discussion and debate both by the Métis and within various governments as a way of making progress on the Métis agenda.

A number of priority areas emerge when looking at the current state of Métis governance. First among these is the need to make progress on Métis identification and registration. This task includes identifying the scope of the Métis Nation and its rights-bearing communities as well as the registration of Métis individuals. This area will be key to realizing Métis self-government in a real way because so much will depend on having credible registries in place. The registries are the bases of knowing who the Métis Nation represents and negotiates on behalf of, ensuring credible elections results, and being able to identify Métis socio-economic needs based on data. With this in mind, several initiatives may warrant further discussion with the Métis Nation:

- the establishment of a national panel on identifying the extent of the Métis Nation Homeland to make recommendations to the Métis Nation's political bodies;
- the establishment of a national Métis citizenship and elections commission, headed by a national commissioner; and
- regular audits on the system for registering members of the Métis Nation by an independent Métis Nation auditor-general.

A second set of priorities revolve around constitutional development. Such initiatives would need to address the following issues, among others:

- roles and responsibilities of the various levels of Métis government — national, provincial, regional, and local;
- the Métis Nation's vision for its place within the Canadian federation; and
- generation of revenues for Métis governments.

To make progress on some of these constitutional issues, the Métis Nation requires a consultation process to engage all levels of the nation, including individuals, local communities, and provincial leaders. These consultations must be transparent, broadly based, and driven by a political willingness to listen to take into account the results, even if they reflect a redistribution of power and authority.

A third priority area is to continue the development of the Métis Nation's governance and administrative capacity. Much has been accomplished over the past decade and Métis organizations can point to many exemplary practices. Nonetheless, much remains to be done and further work on developing a longer term capacity-building strategy or Métis-specific training approaches would produce important dividends for the future.

Finally, continuing to develop effective intergovernmental relationships with the federal and provincial governments remains a priority. A new approach to dealing with intergovernmental relations may be warranted. Maintaining a strategy similar to that employed in the pre-*Powley* era or not adjusting an approach to meet the priorities of a new government may not be extremely effective in moving the Métis agenda forward. As a part of reviewing the Métis approach to intergovernmental relations, the Métis Nation's desired place within the Canadian federation should be debated and a strategy, which includes addressing issues such as jurisdiction, determined.

The above priority areas represent an ambitious agenda, one that will require considerable political will and energy to launch. However, in order to make substantive progress on the Métis Nation's self-government agenda for the 21st century, focused and sustained effort in these governance areas will be required.

‹ 13 ›

Métis Self-Government: Reflections on the Way Forward

FRED CARON

A. INTRODUCTION

In this paper I approach the question of Métis self-government from three vantage points: that of the recent past, the present, and the future. I will seek to situate Métis self-government within the constitutional history of the past two decades, suggest how I believe the *Powley*[1] decision and other developments have changed the legal landscape in respect of Métis self-government, and offer some thoughts on where Métis self-government might move in the years ahead. It is not my intention to be prescriptive, but rather, to stimulate further thinking on the part of Métis representatives, provincial and federal government officials, advocates, and others. For this reason, the paper poses some key questions that I believe will need to be addressed primarily, but not exclusively, by the Métis parties to this discussion, in order to move forward toward a meaningful exercise of self-government for the Métis people.

B. FROM CHARLOTTETOWN TO *POWLEY*: A COMPRESSED HISTORY

I turn first to consider where we have come from on the Métis self-government front. The Aboriginal self-government debate writ large has

1 *R. v. Powley*, [2003] 2 S.C.R. 207 [*Powley*].

mainly been a debate about rights: whether Aboriginal peoples have a right of self-government within the meaning of section 35(1) of the *Constitution Act, 1982*,[2] what the scope of that right might be, and who the holders of the right would likely be. Given that so many advances for Aboriginal peoples over the past three plus decades have resulted from movement on the legal front, either through constitutional amendment or court decision, it is hardly surprising that the discourse has been framed in terms of legal rights. Nevertheless, it can be helpful to set aside the rights discourse, if only briefly, to consider what lies at the core of the self-government project.

1) The Charlottetown Accord

In my view, the movement to recognize, articulate, and implement Aboriginal self-government is about achieving a realignment of power sharing and decision making within the federation among federal, provincial, and Aboriginal governments and institutions, as well as a realignment of the lines of accountability between these political entities and their constituents. Implicit in this realignment is the need to re-establish Crown–Aboriginal relationships on a more respectful and collaborative footing. When viewed from this perspective, it may be easier to understand the central struggle that lay at the heart of the various attempts, in the 1980s and early 1990s, to amend the constitutional text to provide explicitly for an inherent right of self-government, as exemplified by the Charlottetown Accord.[3] I am referring, here, to the debate over whether a right of self-government depended for its exercise, or even its existence, on the content of negotiated agreements (the *contingent right* approach), or whether the right was fully enforceable independent of government agreement (the *inherent* approach).

For their part, federal and provincial governments believed that such a significant realignment of power sharing should be negotiated among

2 (U.K.), 1982, c. 11.

3 The accord was signed 28 August 1992 in Charlottetown, Prince Edward Island, after intensive negotiations involving the federal, provincial, and territorial governments, and representatives from the Assembly of First Nations, the Native Council of Canada, the Inuit Tapirisat of Canada, and the Métis National Council. It was defeated on 26 October 1992 in referenda held nationally and in Quebec.

the very parties (or their representatives) that would ultimately have to exercise those powers, and not proclaimed by the judiciary through a series of legal judgments. Underlying this position was a real concern about what self-government would mean in practice. To be sure, there was also a desire on the part of federal and provincial governments to have some control over the outcomes of self-government deliberations, rather than having such outcomes imposed upon them, and by extension, upon Canadian society as a whole.

By contrast, Aboriginal representatives to the Charlottetown process were unanimous in their view that constitutional amendment was not about the creation of new rights, but rather the recognition of existing rights: as an existing right, the inherent right of self-government could not be dependent for its exercise on the agreement of other governments, but must be fully enforceable by Aboriginal peoples upon amendment of the constitutional text. Quite apart from the legal merits of this view, Aboriginal representatives must surely have been concerned — as a mirror image to the concerns of federal and provincial governments — about leaving control over the very exercise of self-government to parties that could frustrate Aboriginal aspirations by under-funding negotiations, by impeding the success of negotiations, or simply by refusing to negotiate at all.

The way around this impasse between federal and provincial governments, on the one hand, and Aboriginal representatives, on the other, was ultimately found in the proposed *delay on justiciability*, designed to ensure that the parties would have a five-year period in which to reach some negotiated understandings about Aboriginal self-government before the courts could begin adjudicating on the scope and content of an inherent right of self-government. The Charlottetown Accord included two other related features, namely, an ongoing commitment to negotiate on the part of all parties, and a context clause describing the purpose and contours of Aboriginal self-government, both of which would have to be taken into account by the courts before making any final rulings on the scope and content of an inherent right.

What was so significant about these aspects of the Charlottetown Accord was that they reflected the parties' recognition of the need for reaching common understandings about what self-government would mean in practice before setting it in motion. (Nonetheless, it was naive to think that five years would suffice to establish meaningful precedents on Aboriginal self-government.) While a discourse of rights has proven to be essential in achieving Aboriginal aspirations, if Aboriginal self-government is to be lived, not merely written or argued about, it requires the parties to ask and answer difficult and sometimes inconvenient questions along the way.

To summarize, then, the Charlottetown Accord represented a marriage of sorts between *rights recognition* and what I would call *self-government actualization*, or making self-government real on the ground. The deal would have offered foundational and invaluable legal recognition of the existence of an inherent right of self-government within the Canadian constitutional regime. At the same time, however, that legal recognition was inextricably linked to the need for parties to reach negotiated understandings about self-government in practice.

As an aside, it is interesting to note that the *contingent right* logjam that had plagued constitutional discussions for over a decade was, in the end, broken by the proposals of a representative of the Métis National Council. I mention this fact not gratuitously, but because I believe it illustrates that Métis representatives have historically exhibited a unique combination of creativity and pragmatism, and because these characteristics will be critical as we move forward on the road towards Métis self-government.

Had the Charlottetown Accord become law, it would have established that the Métis belonged to the Aboriginal peoples of Canada and thereby had the inherent right of self-government. It is at least arguable that recognition of a Métis right of self-government would have eased the way towards recognition that the Métis also had other Aboriginal rights under section 35(1), perhaps obviating the need for the *Powley* litigation. The Charlottetown Accord would also have resolved the jurisdictional disputes between the federal and provincial governments by clarifying that the Métis are included within Parliament's jurisdiction under section 91(24).[4] That said, it bears emphasizing that the Charlottetown Accord would not have answered the myriad of legal and practical questions that existed then and that still exist today about how Métis self-government can work in practice given the realities of Métis life in Canada. The Char-

---

4 The Charlottetown Accord would have added a provision to the Constitution to clarify that s. 91(24) of the *Constitution Act, 1867* (U.K.), 30 & 31 Vict., c. 3, reprinted in R.S.C. 1985, App. II, No. 5, applies to "Aboriginal" peoples, which includes the Métis.

lottetown Accord would not have eliminated the need to reach negotiated understandings about the scope and content of a Métis right of self-government (what powers and responsibilities are included), its attribution (what entities hold the right), and its exercise (how and over whom Métis polities would exercise their governance powers in practice).[5] In essence, these are the same types of issues facing all Aboriginal peoples and groups who assert rights of self-government, though admittedly, the specifics are in some instances more challenging for Métis people.

2) The Inherent Right Policy

In the wake of the failed Charlottetown Accord, the federal government took a new policy approach to Aboriginal self-government. Adopted in 1995, the *Government of Canada's Approach to Implementation of the Inherent Right and the Negotiation of Aboriginal Self-Government* (the "Policy")[6] represents another, albeit more modest, marriage of rights recognition and self-government actualization. The Policy recognizes the existence of an inherent Aboriginal right of self-government within the meaning of section 35, allowing the parties to act "as if" the constitutional text had been modified to include an inherent right (the *rights recognition*), while eschewing a rights definition approach in favour of reaching negotiated understandings of how self-government will work in practice (the *self-government actualization*). The goal of the Policy is thus not to

5 It is worth noting that, despite the proposed amendment to s. 91(24), the effect of the Charlottetown Accord, when read together with the Métis Nation Accord, would not have been to remove provincial governments from the equation. On the contrary, the Métis Nation Accord recognized that provinces were essential partners in the *actualization* of Métis self-government. The Métis Nation Accord was negotiated during the deliberation of the Charlottetown Accord. For more details, see Chapter 4, volume 5 of the *Report of the Royal Commission on Aboriginal Peoples* (Ottawa: Minister of Supply & Services, 1996). The need for significant provincial involvement in this regard flows not merely from federal and provincial jurisdictional positioning, but from the reality that most Métis people in Canada reside in urban settings, on provincial lands, a fact that would not change merely by clarifying that the Métis come within federal jurisdiction under s. 91(24). The importance of provincial participation is discussed further, below.

6 The Government of Canada's Approach to Implementation of the Inherent Right and the Negotiation of Aboriginal Self-Government, online: www.ainc-inac.gc.ca/pr/pub/sg/plcy_e.html (accessed 17 March 2008).

avoid the rights angle entirely, but to sidestep the likely intractable legal debates on scope and content of an inherent right, preferring to focus energy and resources on negotiated agreements that would stipulate how self-government would operate.

To take an obvious example of how the Policy strives to avoid a legal morass, consider that, while in its earliest pages the federal government recognizes "the inherent right of self-government as an existing Aboriginal right under section 35 of the *Constitution Act, 1982*," the Policy is noticeably silent as to who might hold such a right. The Policy does not distinguish among Indian, Inuit, or Métis peoples; it also does not recognize which collectivities among these peoples might hold the right now acknowledged in section 35. Needless to say, this silence has become an enormous sticking point in self-government negotiations across the country. How can governments negotiate the scope and content of an inherent right with Aboriginal groups if they are not even prepared to acknowledge that the Aboriginal groups with which they are negotiating have such a right?

The silence of the Policy in respect of rights attribution was no accident. Policy drafters knew well that the exercise of attributing the inherent right (as any other Aboriginal right) to individual Aboriginal collectivities would raise many questions, would require considerable research, and in the end, would pose legal risks should the parties "get it wrong." In this sense, the attribution issue is representative of the risks of a rights definition approach. This approach requires the expenditure of valuable time and resources in pursuit of agreements that define the existence, attribution, scope, and content of Aboriginal rights that will likely prove elusive. Aboriginal peoples may, quite legitimately, resist any agreement that seeks to limit their rights when Crown recognition of such rights is still relatively recent and when the jurisprudence, which has been largely responsible for articulating and protecting Aboriginal rights, is still so young and full of promise. In the result, much time is taken away from considering the practical realities of Aboriginal self-government, the nuts and bolts of good governance, and the roles and responsibilities of the negotiating parties to ensure that the self-government project ultimately serves to improve the quality of life for Aboriginal people.

If the issue of rights attribution to specific collectivities has not proven to be an obstacle in Métis self-government negotiations, it is only because the Métis had, until *Powley*, faced the even bigger hurdle of governments' resistance to recognize that they have any existing Aboriginal rights within the meaning of section 35. Now that the *Powley* decision has upheld the existence of Métis Aboriginal rights, discussions about attribution of an inherent right of self-government to Métis collectivities may be more likely to occur. I will consider the impact of *Powley* on Métis self-government below. My point here is to underscore the challenges posed by adopting a rights recognition and definition approach to the negotiation of self-government arrangements. Where the parties are able to set aside their respective legal views on the existence, scope, and content of the inherent right, focusing their energies on what the exercise of self-government will mean in practice, they are more likely to achieve workable arrangements in a timely fashion.

Where did the Métis fit within the Policy? The Policy falls far short of the legal promise of the Charlottetown Accord by not resolving the section 91(24) debate and not stipulating clearly that the Métis have an inherent right of self-government; however, in my view, it leaves the Métis people in much the same position as the Charlottetown Accord would have left them in respect of the *actualization* of Métis self-government. In other words, the realization of Métis self-government under the Policy will depend on the answers to key questions on where Métis communities can be identified and how they are constituted; how self-government can take shape in an increasingly complex urban context; and how to ensure good governance for the Métis in light of the stage of development of Métis governing bodies and institutions. Even under the Charlottetown Accord package of amendments, though, these questions would have needed addressing.

C. ADDING *POWLEY* TO THE SELF-GOVERNMENT MIX

This brings us to the central question of how the seminal *Powley* decision changes the state of play in respect of Métis self-government. *Powley* has undoubtedly altered the legal landscape for Métis people in important ways, some of which remain to be clarified in the coming years; however, there can no longer be any doubt about the existence of Métis Aboriginal rights within the meaning of section 35. I would argue that, as a result of *Powley*, the Métis may have Aboriginal rights of self-government on the same or similar legal bases as First Nations or Inuit peoples. Of course, the courts have not yet ruled definitively on the existence of an inherent right of self-government as an Aboriginal right recognized and affirmed by section 35(1), and many legal questions remain as to the shape and meaning of such a right. That said, the case law indicates that the Métis could establish an inherent right of self-government — assuming it is available as a section 35 right and that they can meet the relevant legal tests.

If the Métis are on the same legal footing as First Nations and the Inuit in respect of the existence of an inherent right of self-government, how would this change the application of the Policy to Métis self-government? Perhaps the most obvious change is that the Métis could now argue for upfront recognition of an inherent right of self-government as a precondition to self-government negotiations. They could argue, as do many First Nations, that they do not come to the table empty-handed, but with an existing, inherent right of self-government protected by section 35. The Métis could insist that governments recognize this right in an open-ended way in negotiated agreements.[7] Again, however, the attribution of an inherent right to specific Aboriginal collectivities (individual groups within Indian, Inuit, or Métis) poses significant challenges to the parties. These challenges would be even greater in respect of Métis attribution, as we are not as advanced in knowing who, among the Métis people, might be the holders of an inherent right — patterns of social and cultural organization are different among the Métis. For example, would the inherent right be held by a Métis community, on its own, or as part of the Métis Nation? If the right is held by the Métis Nation, what does this mean for the practical exercise of the right by smaller groupings that comprise the Nation? If, on the other hand, the inherent right is properly held at the community level, what constitutes a Métis community, where do such communities exist in Canada, and what is the makeup of their citizenship? While *Powley* provides some direction as to the nature of Métis communities, more work must be done in this regard before we

7 A Métis collectivity could also make a unilateral assertion of its inherent right of self-government. Like First Nations and Inuit groups, Métis groups could simply exercise what they believe to be their right and defend any challenges to that exercise through the courts. I do not deal with a possible unilateral assertion in this paper because I have chosen to focus on the development of self-government arrangements through negotiations, which I believe to be a more constructive and collaborative approach to realizing self-government.

would be able to identify the Métis communities that might hold an inherent right of self-government.

These and other questions are already under consideration in respect of the attribution of other Métis Aboriginal rights. Arguably, though, the issues are even more pressing when the Aboriginal right in question is that of self-government. Unlike Aboriginal hunting and fishing rights, which pertain to activities that may be undertaken individually or with others, a right of self-government involves the collective exercise of significant power over the lives of individual citizens. It is all the more important, then, to be sure of where that power vests before attributing an inherent right to a specific polity.

In my view, it is premature to consider attribution of an inherent right of self-government to specific Métis political entities. Moreover, Métis self-government aspirations will not be advanced by taking a legalistic approach to negotiations. Experience demonstrates the difficulty of reaching agreement on legal definitions of Aboriginal rights. Achieving legal definitions of a Métis inherent right would likely be all the more challenging given the absence, in most cases, of a defined land base, the range of views of provincial governments — still necessary parties to self-government negotiations — and the complexity of defining self-government in an urban context.

This is not to suggest that, within the process of negotiating self-government, there is no room for recognition of any specific rights. The courts have told us that the Métis have Aboriginal rights, just as they have told us that the fundamental purpose of section 35 is to reconcile those rights with Crown sovereignty. If reconciliation is to mean anything in respect of Métis self-government, it must mean that governments have to find respectful and creative ways to recognize Métis rights, while advancing understandings of how Métis self-government can work. Rights recognition, however, need not take the form of unqualified statements about the existence and attribution of rights. The mere fact of negotiating self-government in good faith might reflect government recognition of rights. Similarly, providing assistance to Métis organizations and representatives to undertake needed research and developmental work that will advance understandings about Métis self-government might constitute recognition of Métis rights. Where formal statements about rights recognition are perceived as essential to negotiations, consideration could be given to according general recognition to a Métis right of self-government within the meaning of section 35 without attributing that right to any specific Métis polity. Such statements could, in turn, be tied to the negotiation of a self-government agreement outlining particular self-government arrangements. By this I mean to suggest that formal rights recognition should follow, rather than precede, the achievement of negotiated understandings of what Métis self-government means in a given context and how it will work in practice.

Another significant change that results from *Powley* is that, with some caveats, it may now be possible to negotiate jurisdiction for the Métis. The Policy distinguishes between jurisdiction, defined as "law-making authority," and authority, defined as something less than law-making authority and usually denoting the design and delivery of programs and services. It also distinguishes between Aboriginal governments, defined as the governing bodies of land-based Aboriginal groups, and Aboriginal institutions, defined as bodies that serve Aboriginal people. Under the Policy, the exercise of jurisdiction is effectively restricted to governments, while Aboriginal institutions are limited to the exercise of authority. The Policy does not directly exclude the possibility of Métis exercising jurisdiction; by tying the concept of jurisdiction to governments of land-based Aboriginal groups, however, the Policy effectively excludes most Métis, who are not land based, from exercising jurisdiction. This leads to the conclusion that the Métis can only have institutions and through those institutions, can only exercise authority, not jurisdiction. The Policy was intentionally crafted in this way because of the prevailing views of governments at the time: (1) the Métis did not have Aboriginal rights within section 35 and thus could not have an inherent right of self-government, and (2) a fuller form of self-government could really only be practised by Aboriginal peoples on defined land bases. This reality did not then, and still does not, pertain to most Métis people.

It seems to be a generally accepted principle that an inherent right of self-government includes jurisdiction, that is, the power to govern through the making and enforcement of laws. In the wake of *Powley*, and for the reasons suggested above, I believe a strong case could be made for the negotiation of jurisdiction as well as authority in respect of Métis self-government. While this view would seem to contradict the definitions of the Policy which limit jurisdiction to land-based governments, the precise terms of the Policy would likely have to give way to developments in the jurisprudence and resulting changes in our legal thinking. That said, many important questions — both legal and practical — would remain to be addressed about the scope, content, and exercise of jurisdiction by Métis people under the Policy or under any other policy. Some of these questions relate to the exercise of jurisdiction by any Aboriginal peoples, be they Indian, Inuit, and Métis, while others pertain largely to the Métis.

The first question that will arise relates to the entity that exercises jurisdiction. At present, the Policy contemplates the exercise of jurisdiction only by land-based *governments*. While it may be possible to deviate from the requirement of a land base, it is more difficult to contemplate the exercise of jurisdiction — law making and law enforcement authority — by something less than a government. What political entities within the Métis Nation would constitute governments both capable and empowered to exercise jurisdiction over their citizens? The fact that federal and provincial governments have, to date, been prepared to recognize only Métis institutions, not Métis governments, is noted in a thoughtful paper by Jason Madden, John Graham, and Jake Wilson (the "IOG paper").[8] While the authors cite some of the difficulties that have been occasioned by governments' unwillingness to recognize Métis governments, they do not appear to disagree with the basic idea that something more than an institution or organization is required for the exercise of jurisdiction.

Assuming that we could determine the existence of Métis governments, we would then need to determine over whom jurisdiction would be exercised. There are essentially two types of jurisdiction: territorial and personal. Territorial jurisdiction applies in respect of a known territory or land base, embracing all individuals located in that territory; personal jurisdiction applies to individuals independently of their location. If we assume for the purposes of this discussion that, for the foreseeable future, Métis self-government in most cases will not be exercised over a land base that equates to an Indian reserve, then Métis jurisdiction would be personal, not territorial. In the result, the exercise of Métis

8 Institute on Governance, *Exploring Options for Métis Governance in the 21st Century* by Jason Madden, John Graham, & Jake Wilson, September 2005, online: www.iog.ca/publications/2005_metis_gov.pdf [IOG paper].

jurisdiction would require a clear determination of Métis citizenship in order that the application of Métis laws could be easily known. We know, however, that significant work remains to be done to answer all of the various questions in the Métis citizenship debate.[9]

While most Métis do not reside on reserve-like land bases, there are northern communities in which the Métis comprise a majority of the residents. Here, it may be feasible to contemplate public government arrangements, similar to those that work for the Inuit. To the extent that we can negotiate public government, it may be possible to conceive of Métis jurisdiction as a combination of both territorial and personal jurisdiction. One can imagine a Métis majority public government in which jurisdiction over education is exercised over the entire territory covered by the government, with some education laws or particular programs that apply solely to Métis individuals residing within that territory.[10]

Within the discussion of Aboriginal self-government, jurisdiction is crucial. The concept is associated with notions of inherency—the idea that the power emanates from the Aboriginal group rather than as something transferred or given to it. It is therefore seen as a measure of *real* self-government. By contrast, authority is seen as a delegated power, reflecting a lesser form of self-government. Nothing, however, dictates that jurisdiction cannot be delegated or that authority cannot be inherent. Similarly, it does not follow that in any particular case, the scope and content of jurisdiction will exceed the scope and content of authority, or that powers will be more meaningful if characterized as the former rather than the latter, or that decisions made pursuant to jurisdiction will be

9 The IOG paper, *ibid.*, identifies some contentious issues remaining to be resolved. These include ratifying an acceptance process, grandfathering existing members, control over applications and cards, adoption, community acceptance, Bill C-31, compatibility of database systems if a national system is ever established, adoption of separate cards for membership and harvesting, and card security. In the words of the authors, "... because so much of the future legitimacy of these provincial Métis organizations and the exercise of Métis rights nationwide will rest on the integrity of these registries, there is a strong argument for nationally consistent and stringent approaches to registration." See IOG paper, *ibid.* at 36.

10 It should be noted that the Inherent Right Policy has, from its inception, seen the possibility of Métis self-government exercised through forms of public government. Perhaps, in the wake of the *Powley* judgment, the parties may be more inclined to explore this type of self-government seriously.

more likely to provide good governance than those made pursuant to an exercise of authority. In my view, whether Aboriginal governance in any given case is effective in advancing community goals and well-being, and whether it is ultimately meaningful in the lives of those governed will not be determined by semantic characterizations of the Aboriginal powers or views about their source.

I believe that *Powley* and other legal and political developments compel us to be more open to the possibility of recognizing or otherwise providing for Métis jurisdiction. At the same time, it will be essential in each case to consider whether jurisdiction will result in more effective and responsive Métis governance or whether other forms of authority may be more realistic and appropriate. In other words, it would be a mistake to pursue jurisdiction in order to imbue Métis self-government with more importance or credence in the eyes of federal and provincial governments and other Aboriginal peoples.

That the initiatives taken in Métis communities matter more than determining whether they are based on jurisdiction or authority is exemplified by the Manitoba Métis. Indeed, the IOG paper resounds with references to the art of the possible and the practical. As an example, the paper references the success of the Manitoba Métis Child and Family Authority, which operates pursuant to the *Manitoba Child and Family Services Authority Act*:

> Through a three-year joint implementation process, known as the Aboriginal Justice Inquiry—Child Welfare Initiative (AJI-CWI), a collaborative and incremental approach was taken between the MMF and Manitoba in order to establish a Métis Child and Family Authority, which has province-wide responsibility for Métis child and family services, a Métis Child and Family Agency, which is responsible for service delivery (*e.g.*, counselling, case management, etc.) based on the direction of the Métis authority, as well as a Métis Family and Community Institute, which undertakes policy development and research for the Métis community. At the same time, similar approaches were undertaken with First Nation jurisdictions.
>
> On September 13, 2003, the Métis Child and Family Authority received its formal mandate from the Government of Manitoba to oversee Métis child and family services province-wide. As well, the Manitoba

> *Child and Family Services Authority Act*, which is the legislative basis for the new Métis and First Nation authorities, was proclaimed on November 24, 2003. Since this time, the Métis Child and Family Agency has begun to take over service delivery and cases as offices and staff capacity come on line. It is expected that the Métis authority and agency will fully assume all responsibilities and cases by the end of 2005.
>
> This initiative is the first of its kind for Métis anywhere in Canada. It establishes a new standard with the legislative recognition of Métis responsibility over child and family services. Further, it demonstrates the jurisdictional issues can be easily overcome through political will and by Métis and provincial governments working together.[11]

This arrangement for child and family services seems to defy easy categorization as consisting of either *jurisdiction* or *authority*, inherent or delegated powers. And yet, it appears to hold much promise in respect of its governance possibilities.

In this discussion about rights, jurisdiction, and authority, it is important to underscore that moving along the road to self-government will require the active participation of provincial governments. Beyond the reality that the provinces control most of the lands on which Métis reside is the inescapable fact that many areas that would fall to self-government touch upon or intersect with areas of provincial jurisdiction. Putting aside the jurisdictional disputes over section 91(24) for the moment, I would observe that self-government for all Aboriginal peoples cannot operate in a vacuum; individuals do not live in silos, and the Aboriginal governments and institutions that govern and serve them cannot govern and serve them well if the business of self-government is not harmonized with surrounding environments. Indeed, this point was addressed eloquently in the IOG paper:

> . . . it is becoming increasingly evident that, in this complicated world where "everything is related to everything else", the notion of water tight, jurisdictional compartments in a federal state makes less and less sense. Indeed, it is difficult to imagine a major policy undertaking by either level of government that doesn't require considerable intergovernmental cooperation. And for this reason, ongoing federal prov-

11 Above note 8 at 20–21.

> incial committees of Ministers with corresponding shadow committees of officials abound in just about every major policy domain. The same intergovernmental co-ordination challenge would face any self-government arrangements negotiated with the Métis.[12]

I would go even further and suggest that the need for intergovernmental coordination does not apply solely in respect of Métis self-government, but is a requirement of most self-government arrangements negotiated with First Nations, as well. The federal government insists on provincial participation in any self-government negotiations under the Inherent Right Policy that may touch upon provincial interests or jurisdictions. A review of the range of potential subject areas that may be negotiated under the Policy reveals that few matters can be discussed without engaging the provinces.

D. WHERE DO WE GO FROM HERE?

In the preceding pages I have offered my perspective on the recent past as well as the present as it relates to Métis self-government. Of course, I do not have a crystal ball and am no better placed than many others to predict the future course of self-government for Métis peoples or for any other Aboriginal peoples. That said, I continue to believe that the future of Métis self-government remains promising: it is an inevitable part of our evolution as a federation and it will be pursued by Métis leaders with wisdom and creativity. In this concluding part of the paper, I offer some thoughts on the key issues that will have to be addressed as part of this exercise. In doing so, I refer to many points about Métis governance issues raised by Madden, Graham, and Wilson in the IOG paper.[13]

1) Membership and Elections

Establishing clear rules to determine eligibility for Métis membership,[14] processes to adjudicate disputes over membership, and systems for recording the state of that membership are clear priorities for the Métis.

12 *Ibid.* at 54.

13 *Ibid.*

14 Use of the term *membership* in this paper is intended to include notions of both membership and citizenship.

The need for such systems can hardly be doubted: if governance jurisdiction and authority are to be exercised in respect of individuals, it must be clear who and where they are. This information is necessary for a variety of purposes, most notably to determine the scope of governance authority, to ensure accountability in respect of that governance, for policy, program, and service design and delivery, and to establish workable funding arrangements to support that governance. In recent years the Métis National Council and its provincial affiliates have made real strides in developing registration systems that are principled, credible, and reliable — in the current vocabulary, systems that are *objectively verifiable*. But significant work remains to be done, and the federal government is prepared to assist.

A companion piece to membership is that of leadership selection or elections. How various Métis representative bodies choose their leadership will have an impact on their legitimacy within the broader Métis community, as well as their ability to speak for their constituents in the challenging negotiations that lie ahead. In this regard, the IOG paper contains an interesting suggestion about the establishment of a national Métis citizenship and elections commission, one that we may wish to explore further in the months ahead.[15]

2) Governance Structures

Defining and establishing the range of bodies and structures that will exercise governance, be they governments, organizations, institutions, or authorities, will also require further work. Ensuring a good fit between governing entity and governance functions is essential to the self-government enterprise. The IOG paper notes that there is significant institutional capacity at the provincial, rather than the community level, but states that communities are the foundation of Métis governance structures. How this reality can be made to realign with the governance needs of distinct areas of self-government, such as education, is part of the exercise of matching governing body to governing function.

---

15 We may also wish to explore the possible creation of a national panel on identifying the Métis Nation Homeland as a vehicle for clarifying the scope of Métis Aboriginal rights.

While there may be a desire to move beyond the recognition of Métis organizations to recognition of Métis governments, the fundamental task in each case should be identifying the appropriate body to exercise the intended governance functions. Whatever changes may have been wrought by *Powley*, they do not include the unquestioned assumption that Métis political organizations should now be recognized and treated as governments; it must be determined that those organizations are needed and intended to function as governments. Once decisions are made as to the type of body appropriate to fulfill particular governance functions, there will have to be processes of institution building to establish those bodies on a sound footing.

3) Roles and Responsibilities

A discussion of the roles and responsibilities between various levels of Métis governing bodies[16] should also include consideration of whether, and if so, how Métis programs and services can be delivered more effectively through aggregations within or across provinces. I see this as important developmental work and part of the overarching governance structure piece referenced above. The exercise of delineating roles and responsibilities will be critical to furthering Métis self-government aspirations, both in terms of reaching consensus among Métis polities on the way forward and for better informing other governments and public sector actors about how Métis representative bodies are constituted and how they operate.

4) Capacity Building

Canada is committed to assisting the Métis with a range of capacity-building initiatives. In this regard I have noted that the IOG paper identifies the need to develop more expertise at the civil service level. Here, again, I think it is important to target capacity-building energies to developing bureaucracies that fit the governance needs of the sector in question.

The issue of capacity building relates directly to the negotiations approach adopted. The Métis may wish to use the *Powley* judgment as a

16 See IOG paper, above note 8.

springboard for obtaining the broadest possible array of powers or they may prefer to fashion their brand of self-government more incrementally, to build their self-government institutions and programs from the ground up. The approach taken will determine the capacity building that is necessary and most valuable. In this regard, I was encouraged by some of the thoughts expressed in the IOG paper on the value of *incrementalism*:

> To date, First Nations and federal and provincial governments have pursued self-government in what some have called a "big bang" approach — that is, negotiate a full range of jurisdictions and then implement. Such an approach entails lengthy negotiations. In addition, and perhaps more seriously, many First Nations have assumed jurisdiction in areas where they had little or no capacity or governance experience. The suite of regulatory functions relating to safe water comes to mind. The Métis Nation may wish to learn from this experience by taking a more evolutionary approach to self-government by ensuring that governance and administration capacity and experience are in place prior to assuming formal, jurisdictional responsibilities or by taking on jurisdiction a sector at a time. A notable example of this is the best practice of devolution of child and family services to the MMF. The MMF had to marshal much of its resources and attention to this sector in order for the negotiations and transfer to be successful. It is questionable whether the transfer would have succeeded had the MMF attempted to build institutional capacity and human resources on a multitude of fronts at the same time. We suggest that this type of methodical and measured assumption of jurisdiction may be a more effective means for the Métis Nation to achieve success.[17]

5) Harmonization and Urban Realities

I have spoken about the need for harmonization with surrounding jurisdictions, most notably the provinces. Another aspect of harmonization is the complexity of creating workable self-government arrangements that respond to the diverse needs and realities of urban Aboriginal people. It is no secret that a majority of Métis people today reside in urban centres, large and small, interspersed with other Aboriginal people and with non-

17 *Ibid*. at 51.

Aboriginal people. In addition, demographic studies confirm increasing levels of mobility into, within, and out of urban centres. This reality makes the design and implementation of meaningful self-government arrangements more challenging than it would be in the case of more homogeneous groups with a defined land base. And it makes the need for harmonization with a range of entities, from provincial and municipal governments, to Aboriginal program and service delivery organizations, to non-Aboriginal community service vehicles, all the more urgent.

To quote a paper on urban Aboriginal geographic trends, "[t]he size, characteristics and distribution of Aboriginal people shape dimensions of self-government — that is, they create some opportunities and impose some limits."[18] In other words, while the *Powley* decision and other developments have energized the movement towards Métis self-government, given current realities and demographic trends, Métis aspirations must be tempered and guided by a sense of what is possible in an urban environment.

These observations are not intended as a recipe for inaction. On the contrary, they represent a call for real creativity to respond to the complexity of the urban environment. As an example, given the difficulty of carving out Métis jurisdiction within a mixed Aboriginal population, consideration could be given to developing models of jurisdiction or authority sharing among a range of Aboriginal groups within the same urban setting. One can imagine a province-wide education authority for urban Aboriginal people that contained within it Métis-specific programming, or an Aboriginal social services delivery mechanism that targeted Métis-specific needs alongside off-reserve First Nation needs. Cooperative jurisdictional arrangements may hold the key to developing more efficient and effective self-government programming in an urban context because they would reflect and serve economies of scale.

I offer a final observation on urban realities in the context of Métis self-governance. There appears to be a perception in some quarters that monies available for any initiative — education and culture, housing, social services, human resource development — should simply be divided among First Nations, Inuit, and Métis bodies. Doing this may not always

18 Evelyn Peters, "Geographies of Urban Aboriginal People in Canada: Implications for Urban Self-Government" in M. Murphy, ed., *Reconfiguring Aboriginal-State Relations* (Kingston, ON: Institute of Intergovernmental Relations, Queen's University, 2005) 39–76.

make sense in an urban context, where, for example, Inuit, Métis, and First Nations children need protection, or Métis, Inuit, and First Nations individuals struggling with substance abuse may be virtually indistinguishable from one another in terms of the help they require.

E. CONCLUSION

The *Powley* decision opens up some new possibilities to establish a stronger legal basis for Métis self-government. At the same time, meaningful self-government opportunities are unlikely to be found through intractable legal debates about rights and more likely to be created by furthering our understandings of how Métis self-government can be achieved on the ground. The road to accomplishing this will require an investment of time, energy, and resources on the part of the federal government, provincial governments, Métis organizations, scholars, and self-government workers in the field. In this regard, the federal government has been very committed to assisting the Métis to do the research, developmental work, and capacity building that will lay solid foundations for Métis self-government.

For all of its uniqueness, the journey towards Métis self-government shares much with the journey towards all other forms of Aboriginal self-government, and indeed, with the path towards better and more responsive governance for all peoples. In this it requires the courage to ask difficult questions and to be clear in our deliberations and negotiations about what we need and can reasonably accomplish. It is possible to be so artful in the language of negotiated agreements that the results do not ultimately reflect the negotiators' intent. For example, our discourse is peppered with references to "government-to-government" relationships, yet most of us would be hard-pressed to explain precisely what we mean by that phrase or how its use can be expected to change realities on the ground. It is my hope that negotiations towards Métis self-government in all its forms will be characterized by both imagination and realism, and will remain focused on the objective of making Métis self-government work for Métis people. Only then can self-government truly improve the lives of the Métis in measurable ways, enhancing their membership in their communities and their participation in the broader Canadian society.

< 14 >

The Aboriginal Justice Inquiry–Child Welfare Initiative: Creating the Métis Child and Family Services Authority

HARVEY BOSTROM, ALISON ROGAN, AND RICHARD ASSELIN

A. INTRODUCTION

There is no common understanding among Métis, federal, and provincial governments on what Métis self-government means. The lack of clarity as to which government has jurisdiction and responsibility for Métis people and uncertainty about the nature of Métis Aboriginal rights fuel this disagreement. One thing is certain; the uncertainty will prevail for the foreseeable future.

Instead of focusing on a definition of what Métis self-government is, what powers and responsibilities are included in it, and what entities hold the right of self-government, the provincial government has focused its energy on improving the well-being of Manitoba's Métis through an evolving process of new relationships, relationships that are often expressed as Métis institutions. Since the 1980s, the Manitoba government has supported the development of several key Métis institutions and devolved or delegated the delivery of provincial programs and services; it continues to build partnerships with the Manitoba Metis Federation (MMF) that allow it to support the improved social and economic well-being of Métis in a culturally appropriate manner. The province has supported the development of Métis institutions in cultural development, housing, education, economic development, and most recently, in child and family matters. Consistently, three conditions have emerged as necessary for successful institution building: political will, strong relationships, and organizational capacity.

This paper focuses on the processes that the government of Manitoba used to build political will and relationships with the MMF and the role that organizational capacity within the MMF played to support Métis institution building. The processes leading up to and including the creation of the Metis Child and Family Services Authority and agency will be used to demonstrate the importance of these three factors.

1) Change Drivers

A driver of change is a factor that has the potential to bring about systemic reform. Change drivers are not simply individual champions of reform, but rather the interaction between structural features, agents, and institutions. Structural features include natural and human resources, economic and social structures. Agents are individuals and organizations pursuing particular interests. Institutions, which can be both formal and informal, include the rules structuring the behaviour of agents. Links run in both directions between structural features and institutions, as well as between institutions and agents.[1]

Legislation, policies, and the ways that relationships exist between organizations (and the individuals representing them) and the public they serve make up the "institutional framework." Actions by individuals and organizations (agents) can affect the institutional framework, which, in turn, affects human and natural resources, and economic and social structures (structural features). In the same way, structural features have an impact on agents in a way that is mediated through institutions. The effectiveness of both the formal rules — legislation, policies, regulations, and so on — and informal relationships, as in levels of trust between parties and reciprocity, is therefore central to understanding the change processes and the impacts they will have.

A focus on change directs attention to the underlying and longer term factors that affect political will, relationships, and organizational capacity for reform, as well as factors that affect the incentives and capacity for changes that would be likely to benefit Métis children and families. It requires that a realistic investigation of circumstances grounded in experience, rather than in preconceived solutions, be the point of departure. It also re-

1 Oxford Policy Management, *Drivers of Change: Reflections on Experience to Date* (Oxford: Oxford Policy Management, 2003).

quires adopting a longer term perspective, while at the same time, looking for short- and medium-term opportunities to support strategic change.

a) Building Métis Institutions

The government of Manitoba has backed Métis aspirations of self-government by supporting the development of Métis institutions. Métis institutions referred to in this paper are the organizations that hold authorities delegated by the province[2] to deliver programs and services in specific sectors for the benefit of Métis.[3] Protocols may exist for these institutions to influence provincial policy, as well as regulatory and legislative changes. Over the past twenty years, the MMF has built institutions in key social and economic sectors for its constituents and done so on an evolutionary basis.

b) Role of Political Will in Building Métis Institutions

As discussed in this paper, political will is the sustained commitment of politicians and administrators to invest the necessary resources to create Métis institutions. It is the willingness of these individuals to undertake systemic reform and implement legislative and policy changes despite opposition. Commitment, leadership, and responsiveness to the needs and aspirations of Métis are key components of political will.

A sustained and evident commitment by politicians and administrators is a necessary ingredient if changes that affect the development of Métis institutions are to take place in any meaningful and ongoing fashion. When this commitment comes from political mechanisms,[4] it is often based on evidence of systemic benefits from proposed changes; however, evidence is not always sufficient. Commitment also depends on a sustained belief of leaders in their ability to muster adequate support to overcome resistance from stakeholders who oppose change.

A major shift in the way programs are developed and delivered for Métis requires decision makers to respond to the needs and ambitions of

---

2 Canada has delegated considerable authority to the MMF as well. This discussion, however, deals only with Manitoba's approach.

3 Other Manitobans may also receive services through Métis organizations delivering provincial programming.

4 Commitment to change may also come from legal mechanisms, but that is not discussed in this paper.

individuals, to their organizations, and to the evidence that creating Métis institutions will benefit Métis citizens. Ultimately, political responsiveness requires a relationship of accountability between Métis citizens, their representatives, and the organizations that create policy and regulations, and provide services. It is crucial that advocates of Métis institution-building have a way to influence and call to account politicians and other leaders, administrators, and front-line workers.

In a more general sense, leadership includes the intelligence and vision of individuals, their organizational skills, innovativeness, and a willingness to take risks, make hard choices, and set priorities.[5] Leadership is needed at all levels and regions if change is to be achieved. Political and senior administrators must exercise their leadership to establish and maintain Métis institutions as a priority, to ensure that commitments to change are followed through, and to counter both opposition and inertia. These are the individuals with the authority and resources to develop the organizational structures necessary to create institutions. Equally important to the process is ensuring that program managers and specialists are also driving the process forward and not stopping it in its tracks.

c) Role of Relationships in Building Métis Institutions

Strong relationships built on trust, empathy, and respect form the foundation upon which all other work can occur. Relationships are the formal and informal connections that pull the many parts of a complex activity together under one banner. At the same time, good relationships help overcome conflict, an inevitable product of change. Building relationships usually involves time on the ground with community members and a lot of listening. Some people are suited to achieving effective outcomes and some are not.

The relationships underpinning the Aboriginal Justice Inquiry–Child Welfare Initiative (AJI-CWI) were built through tripartite self-government negotiations, bilateral working relationships to foster the delegation or devolution of programs and services, and the creation of provincial legislation that clarified the relationship between government and Métis

5 Oxfam Great Britain, *Making It Happen: Political Will for Gender Equality in Education*, Education and Gender Equality Series, Programme Insights (December 2005) at 2, online: www.oxfam.org.uk/what_we_do/issues/education/downloads/edPaper5.pdf.

institutions. Manitoba focused on relationships that were, and continue to be, evolutionary in nature, that is, relations that build upon historical successes and rely on the knowledge gleaned from lessons of the past.

d) Role of Organizational Capacity in Building Métis Institutions

Mature organizations are characterized by their stability, their ability to evolve and adapt to change, and governance structures that separate transactions with the public from political functions. The MMF needed to demonstrate this organizational maturity before the province could consider devolving the delivery of child welfare functions.

The MMF has adopted organizational models that keep program delivery at arm's length from the political leadership, ensuring the continuity of programs through successive presidents. It has been able to test various models of Métis governance, while adapting traditional philosophies and approaches with contemporary circumstances and needs as it builds Métis institutions. This approach has allowed the federation to build up its organizational capacities to deal with an increasing scope of complex issues that prevail in the Métis community. It has provided leaders with an opportunity to gain the confidence and support of their people by working together to design Métis governance structures that meet members' day-to-day concerns. It also provides the MMF with the opportunity to define working relationships with Métis locals, other Métis affiliates, and the Métis National Council, as well as municipal governments, the province, and Canada. Finally, its institutions separate political and administrative functions through the creation of corporations and authorities.

B. EVENTS LEADING UP TO THE ABORIGINAL JUSTICE INQUIRY–CHILD WELFARE INITIATIVE

> "Europeans assumed the superiority of their culture over that of any Aboriginal peoples. Out of that misconception grew the European conviction that in order for the Indians to survive, they would have to be assimilated into the European social order."[6]

---

6 Jean Barman, Yvonne Hebert, & Don McCaskill, eds., *Indian Education in Canada: The Legacy*, vol. 1 (Vancouver: University of British Columbia Press, 1986)

> "There was no publicity for years and years about the brutalization of our families and children by the larger Canadian society. Kidnapping was called placement in foster homes. Exporting Aboriginal children to the U.S. was called preparing Indian children for the future. Parents who were heartbroken by the destruction of their families were written off as incompetent people."[7]
>
> —*Anthony Wood, Gods River, Manitoba, 1989*

During the 1960s, 1970s, and 1980s, provincial and federal child welfare agencies removed a substantial number of Aboriginal children from their families and placed them in primarily non-Aboriginal homes, often outside of their home communities and sometimes out of the country. As the *Report of the Aboriginal Justice Inquiry of Manitoba* pointed out, more than 3400 Aboriginal children were shipped to adoptive parents between 1971 and 1981. In 1983, the Canadian Council on Social Development found that Aboriginal children were highly overrepresented in the child welfare system and in Manitoba, making up 50 to 60 percent of children in care.[8] Responding to what they viewed as cultural genocide, Aboriginal leaders and citizens put intense pressure on government to change the system. More than two decades of work that would culminate in the creation of the Métis Child and Family Services Authority and agency began.

In the early days, the governments of Manitoba and Canada focused on First Nations child welfare. Over time, Métis issues were identified and addressed. However, not until the Aboriginal Justice Inquiry (AJI) was struck in 1988 to investigate the relationship between the justice system and Aboriginal peoples in Manitoba were issues and solutions for Métis child welfare explored in the context of developing a Métis child welfare authority.

The creation of the Métis Child and Family Services Authority and agency was the product of a significant history of commissions and tripartite agreements that built the political will and relationships necessary

---

at 2, quoted in Manitoba, Public Inquiry into the Administration of Justice and Aboriginal People, *Report of the Aboriginal Justice Inquiry of Manitoba: The Justice System and Aboriginal People*, vol. 1 (Winnipeg: Public Inquiry into the Administration of Justice and Aboriginal People, 1991) at 512 [*Report of the Aboriginal Justice Inquiry of Manitoba*].

7 *Report of the Aboriginal Justice Inquiry of Manitoba*, *ibid.* at 519.

8 *Ibid.* at 520.

to support such a radical change in Manitoba's approach to Aboriginal child welfare. It was predicated on the past success of the MMF to build institutions that were stable and had effective governance structures in place. Finally, it was influenced by socio-economic circumstances that demanded a dramatic shift in the way services were provided.

1) Building Political Will

a) Indian Child Welfare Sub-Committee and Early Tripartite Agreements

In 1977, the governments of Canada and Manitoba established a tripartite[9] working committee on Aboriginal child welfare to address the serious problems that existed between Aboriginal peoples and the child welfare system. The Indian Child Welfare Sub-Committee learned from Aboriginal communities that it had to deal with the unique legal, political, and social circumstances of First Nations citizens and communities. Foremost among the issues identified was the need to preserve Indian identity in terms of language and culture within the framework of tribes, bands, communities, extended families, and individuals.[10] Although the working group dealt with First Nations, its final report determined that Aboriginal child welfare needs were a matter of urgent priority and all initiatives to address these priorities had to involve, "Indian people . . . at all levels and in all aspects of child welfare services."[11] First Nations' response to existing child welfare systems became change drivers for the restructuring of the system.

The Sub-Committee determined that a common legal base throughout Manitoba was needed to integrate the statutory provisions for all family-related services to registered Indians. It recommended that regional child welfare agencies be set up for Indian reserves, controlled by band chiefs and councils. It also recognized that implementation of the plan needed to be flexible and priority given to developing facilities that were close to home.

---

9 *Tripartite* refers to three-way relationships, usually between the two levels of government (federal and provincial) and a third party. In this instance, the third party was the Manitoba Indian Brotherhood.

10 *Report of the Aboriginal Justice Inquiry of Manitoba*, above note 6 at 521.

11 *Ibid.*

These findings became the foundation for a series of tripartite agreements that established Aboriginal child welfare agencies. Signatories to agreements were Manitoba, with constitutional responsibility to provide child welfare services; Canada, with fiduciary responsibilities for First Nations; and First Nations themselves. Agencies were limited to exercising their authority on reserve. From the early 1980s to 2001, twelve fully mandated[12] First Nations Child and Family Services agencies were established in Manitoba, and all sixty-three First Nations in Manitoba[13] now receive services from their own First Nations Child and Family Services agencies. The Indian Child Welfare Sub-Committee also contributed to an Aboriginal leadership organized around the issue of child welfare.

b) The Kimelman Report: No Quiet Place

In 1980, First Nations and Métis leaders mounted a robust campaign against the practice of adopting Aboriginal children out to families not living in the local community and often not even living in the province and country.

The government of Manitoba responded first by prohibiting all out-of-province adoptions and then appointed Kimelman C.J. to conduct an inquiry into the Aboriginal child welfare system and how it affected Aboriginal people. The Chief Judge recommended changes to Manitoba's child welfare legislation to ensure that a "child's best interests" would include a consideration of cultural and linguistic heritage. He further recommended increased involvement of parents in programming and increased emphasis on preventive measures.[14]

The "Kimelman Report" was the first investigative report to raise issues about the impacts of the child welfare system on the Métis. It contributed to the development of collaborative relationships between community and regional child welfare offices and MMF locals in areas such as foster care, whereby Métis foster families were recruited to care for Métis children.

---

12 *Mandated* means the delegated authority to apprehend children under the *Child Welfare Act*.

13 The sixty-three First Nations agencies referred to are all "on-reserve." "Off-reserve" child welfare agencies serving Aboriginal children and families did not exist at this time.

14 *Report of the Aboriginal Justice Inquiry of Manitoba*, above note 6 at 523–26.

The report demonstrated and furthered political will. It also established relationships between the government of Manitoba and the MMF on child welfare issues.

c) The Aboriginal Justice Inquiry

In 1988, the Aboriginal Justice Inquiry (AJI) was commissioned to examine the relationship between the Aboriginal peoples of Manitoba and the justice system. The report, submitted in 1991, included an analysis and observations regarding the historical treatment of Aboriginal peoples by the social service system and, in particular, the child welfare system of the province. Commissioners found that Aboriginal peoples living off-reserve were not well served by the existing child welfare system; at the same time, it found that tremendous advances were being made by First Nations providing services on-reserve. The AJI recommended the following changes to the child welfare system:

- Establish the office of Child Protector, as recommended by Kimelman C.J., to protect the interests of children, to investigate any complaint into the practices of any child welfare agency, and to be responsible to the legislature.
- Provide Aboriginal and non-Aboriginal child and family services agencies with enough resources to enable them to provide the full range of direct and preventive services mandated by the *Child and Family Services Act*.
- Legislate rights to culturally appropriate services.
- Establish a mandated Métis child and family services agency serving Métis and non-status children across Manitoba.
- Expand the authority of existing First Nations agencies to provide services to members living off-reserve.
- Establish an Aboriginal child and family services agency in the city of Winnipeg to handle all Aboriginal cases.

The AJI examined a very complex issue and provided recommendations on how government could address them. However, shortly after the AJI was created, the government changed.[15] Several of the AJI recom-

15 The Progressive Conservative (PC) Party, led by Gary Filmon, defeated the Howard Pawley New Democratic Party (NDP) government in 1988. The PC government remained in power until 1999, when the NDP, led by Gary Doer, was voted into office.

mendations were acted upon in a manner consistent with the government priorities of the time. However, the recommendations to expand First Nation authority to off reserve and to establish a Méts CFS were not implemented.

d) Aboriginal Justice Implementation Commission

In 1999, a renewed commitment to address the AJI's recommendations surfaced. Political will was strong. The government established the Aboriginal Justice Implementation Commission (AJIC) to advise it on methods of implementing the AJI recommendations. Specifically,

> The AJIC was mandated to address only those AJI recommendations that touch upon areas for which the Manitoba government is responsible and accountable. The AJIC was also instructed to have regard . . . to the reports of the Royal Commission on Aboriginal Peoples (RCAP) . . . .[16]

The Commission made family and child welfare a priority and recommended that "the Government of Manitoba seek to enter into agreement with the Assembly of Manitoba Chiefs and the Manitoba Metis Federation to develop a plan that would result in First Nations and Métis communities developing and delivering Aboriginal child welfare services."[17] It was on the basis of this recommendation and the considerable commitment and efforts of the Métis, First Nations, and provincial leadership that the AJI-CWI was born.

2) Building Relationships

At around the same time that the First Nations child welfare system was being reformed through tripartite agreements, the MMF entered into tripartite self-government negotiations (TSN) with the governments of Canada and Manitoba (1987). This forum fostered enduring bilateral arrangements between the MMF and Manitoba in various social and economic sectors. Both processes supported the development of institutions, including the Metis Child and Family Services Authority.

---

16 Aboriginal Justice Implementation Commission, *Final Report and Recommendations* (Winnipeg: Aboriginal Justice Implementation Commission, 2001) at 1.

17 *Ibid.*, Appendix I, Recommendation 10.1.

Tripartite self-government negotiations are covered by formal Memoranda of Understanding (MOU). Although the precise wording of the agreements has changed, the general objectives have remained the same:

1) Reach agreements on establishing institutions of self-government for Métis people in Manitoba;
2) Improve Métis individual, family and community self-reliance; and,
3) Develop and coordinate policies and mechanisms that enhance devolution of programs and services.[18]

What makes the TSN process successful is the communication and advocacy it fosters. The structures, processes, consultations, and financing arrangements that have been agreed to by the parties make this possible.

The TSN process is managed by a Joint Management Committee (JMC), made up of representatives from the MMF, Canada, and Manitoba. Specific projects are the result of multi-year work plans reflecting the priorities of the Métis people of Manitoba. After consultations with the relevant departments and agencies by government representatives, primary relationships between line departments and the MMF are created to get the projects running.

Regular quarterly meetings of the JMC ensure that any difficulties the MMF is experiencing with projects and more specifically, partnerships with line departments are addressed. Overall, the TSN process has successfully provided a vehicle within which Métis priorities can be communicated to governments, forging partnerships between the governments of Canada and Manitoba, and in devolving programs and services.

Early on in the TSN process, Métis child welfare issues were tabled as priorities. The MMF wanted to expand their Family Support Program, an advocacy support program established as a product of Chief Judge Kimelman's Report, to a fully mandated child and family services program. These issues were later communicated to the Aboriginal Justice Inquiry and again to the AJIC.

18 2001 Memorandum of Understanding between the Government of Canada, Government of Manitoba, and Manitoba Metis Federation on Tripartite Self-government Negotiations.

3) Building Organizational Capacity

The MMF had consistently created and managed large organizations and institutions prior to the devolution of authority for child welfare.

Between 1989 and 2001, the MMF created

- the Community Housing Managers of Manitoba as an institution addressing housing,
- the Louis Riel Institute as an institution addressing education,
- the Metis Human Resources Development Agreement as an instrument addressing training and labour-market development,
- the Louis Riel Capital Corporation and Manitoba Metis Community Investments Inc. as institutions addressing economic development, and
- the Metis Family and Community Institute as an institution addressing child, family, and community development.

Different mechanisms were used to create these institutions, including provincial legislation, devolution of programming, and ongoing funding agreements between Manitoba and the MMF, and Canada and the MMF.

4) Impact of Environmental Factors

In 2001, the government of Manitoba, faced with escalating costs for child welfare services and a dissatisfaction with the care provided among Aboriginal peoples off-reserve, found that

- a disproportionate number of Aboriginal children were in care,
- Aboriginal children were more likely to come into care and less likely to be returned to their families than non-Aboriginal children,
- many Aboriginal children were placed in non-Aboriginal homes, often away from their community, and subsequently lost connections to their families, communities, and identities, and
- high rates of Aboriginal children in care ended up in the correctional system.

The social and economic costs and outcomes of the existing child welfare system provided further impetus to the government of Manitoba to make significant changes to the system, including a change in the way authorities and resources were allocated.

C. THE ABORIGINAL JUSTICE INQUIRY–CHILD WELFARE INITIATIVE

In early 2000, the government of Manitoba received direction from Cabinet to proceed with the AJI-CWI. The vision for the new and very different child welfare system would be developed through the cooperation of all parties to the initiative.

Through negotiations with First Nations and Métis representatives, the Province of Manitoba signed three separate three-year Memoranda of Understanding with the MMF, the Assembly of Manitoba Chiefs (AMC), and Manitoba Keewatinowi Okimakanak (MKO) between February and July 2000. All four parties subsequently signed the Child and Family Services Protocol. The Protocol agreement established the partnership as the four parties agreed to a joint process, using a consensus model of decision making. These agreements established the AJI-CWI.

The primary goal of the AJI-CWI was to recognize and acknowledge a province-wide Métis and First Nations right and authority to control the delivery of child and family services for their people, wherever they resided in the province. The partners envisioned a system that ensured that First Nations and Métis child and family services respected their values, beliefs, customs, and traditions. The new system would also provide the basis for reducing the number of Aboriginal children in care.

Broad and systemic changes to the child welfare system, the people working in and affected by the system, and the rules that directed its activities were needed. Further, the people working on the AJI-CWI quickly realized that these changes would have an effect on one another. The process was highly dynamic.

The partnership faced a series of challenges that had to be overcome and accommodated on an ongoing basis. First among these were the cultural and political differences among the parties which had the potential to create misunderstandings before participants had an opportunity to establish credibility with one another. Participants recognized the need for an interest-based and collective approach at all stages of the initiative to overcome potential polarizations among the parties. Manitoba insisted upon one joint process among First Nations, Métis, and government. Having this ensured the development of compatible systems within the new child welfare systems, while also ensuring that all parties were treated equitably, without side deals made with any individual party.

Adding further complexity was the broad range of stakeholder groups with interests in relation to the system which had to be dealt with effectively. One major stakeholder group was the Manitoba Government and General Employees Union (MGEU) representing the interests of public employees working in child welfare agencies. Its concerns were addressed through a labour adjustment strategy prepared by the government of Manitoba and the MGEU: the strategy honoured existing obligations to the public employees, while insisting that the process take into account a fair and effective transfer of human resources that would allow each authority and agency to provide quality and culturally appropriate services.

The government lacked the resources to commit significant new funds to ongoing operations of new child welfare institutions, and except for transitional costs, required that the new institutions function within existing budget. However, existing budgets could be reallocated in a way that achieved equitable funding and parity of service throughout the province. This measure also served to address some of the disparity of resources for First Nations and Métis.

1) Change Process: Milestones

In the Protocol Agreement that established the original partnership, committees and groups were set up to guide the restructuring processes. These agents of change developed the processes that would create the Métis and First Nations Child and Family Services authorities and agencies. Consensus among all parties — the MMF, AMC, MKO, and the Manitoba government — was a guiding principle for the change agents or organizations.

a) Organizational Structure

The Protocol Agreement established an Executive Committee, a Joint Management Committee (JMC), and an Implementation Committee, each with balanced representation from all of the parties, and in the case of the JMC, Métis women and Winnipeg Child and Family Services. The Executive Committee, comprised of the political leadership from signatories to the Protocol agreement and respective MOUs, was responsible for overseeing and directing the initiative as a whole.

The four parties assigned senior officials to the JMC to produce and oversee the implementation of a detailed plan to restructure Manitoba's child and family services system based on the recommendations of the AJI report. To do this, the JMC created and directed an implementation sub-committee and working groups; set terms of reference, timelines, and monitoring processes; and ensured that key stakeholders were consulted during the development of the implementation plan. The JMC was responsible for implementing the plan based on the direction provided by the Executive Committee.

Reflecting the same balanced representation as the JMC, the Implementation Committee, composed of the representatives of the four parties, was established to create, coordinate, and manage working groups. Using a consensus model for all decisions, the Implementation Committee developed specific policy and process proposals with respect to every aspect of the new legislative structures and processes. This culminated in a single work plan submitted to the JMC and Executive Committee.

The working groups maintained both a keen task orientation and aggressive timelines. In the fall of 2000, 200 people came together for a massive orientation and received a mandate to conduct the research and planning necessary to create new child welfare institutions. The working groups, which were given ninety days to meet their objectives, met, on average, two or three times a week. The core membership of the working groups was composed of the same balanced representation as the JMC and the Implementation Committee. However, these groups were also tasked to consult with the various external/internal stakeholder groups who would or could be affected by the restructuring of the child and family services system.

Seven working groups[19] were created to research and analyze the features of the child and family services system that would be affected by the restructuring, prepare options, and make recommendations on all

19 These were the Research, Interjurisdictional/Intersectoral Issues, Financial, Human Resources, Service Delivery, Legislation, and Technology working groups.

aspects of the devolution process. Working groups had to consider broad operational changes. While the new child welfare service-providers needed individual governance processes that considered and reflected the specific nature of the communities where they would be applied, they also needed to be integrated. Innovative prevention and early intervention programs that emphasized a holistic approach, as well as protocols and service agreements that could be used with collateral care providers, were prepared.

Managing human resources through the transition was a key success factor. Issues included education and training needs of staff for the new Métis (and First Nations) authority and agency and a workforce adjustment strategy for existing employees.

New funding models and visions that promoted the development and restoration of families and the devolution of funding decision making were prepared with a view to identifying appropriate and adequate funding options. However, except for transitional expenditures, the new institutions had to function within existing budgets. Combined with the reality that the child welfare practices of the day supported maintenance rather than prevention functions, these were challenging tasks. Working groups focused on reallocating budgets to achieve equitable funding and parity of service throughout the province.

All of these changes required integrated database systems that would link all online registries, provide human resources, and serve financial, infrastructure, and case management functions.

Finally, groups addressed the changes that would be needed in *The Child and Family Services Act* and *The Adoptions Act* to enable the creation of new mandates. Changes to Foster Care Regulations and Residential Care Licensing Regulations were defined and amendments were recommended.

b) Conceptual Plan

The efforts of the working groups resulted in 350 recommendations which were submitted to the Implementation Committee in December 2000. The committee consolidated the recommendations under eight essential themes as well as the systematic development of consensus proposals related to all of the themes between January and June 2001. The Conceptual Plan, completed in July 2001, outlined the strategic design principles and concepts that would structure the AJI-CWI. It focused on the governance model for the new system and referenced service delivery systems.

The Conceptual Plan phased in the creation of the new child and family services institutions:

Phase 1: Working groups (completed December 2000)
Phase 2: Development/Approval of Conceptual Plan (July 2001)
Phase 3: Public feedback process, design teams, and detailed implementation plan completed (November 2002)
Phase 4: Implementation (June 2005)
Phase 5: Stabilization (December 2006)

c) Public Consultation

"Promise of Hope: Commitment to Change," a vision document based on the Conceptual Plan, described the main features of the proposed system. It also provided information on the public feedback process that took place in August and September 2001.

A press conference in August 2001 signalled the beginning of public consultations with the release of the vision document and public feedback activities.[20] In addition to the public feedback process, Phase 3 included the development of a detailed implementation plan based on the Conceptual Plan and public feedback. As part of the public feedback process, twelve town hall meetings and focus groups took place on reserves and in communities across Manitoba.[21] Interested groups and individuals were encouraged to submit written feedback. Focus groups were held to secure feedback from stakeholders in the system, including youth in care, adults who had been in care, birth family members of children in care, foster parents, and women's organizations. The results of the public consultation were used to inform the implementation plan.

20 AJI-CWI, Press Release, "Restructuring of Child and Family Services System Reaches Next Step: Vision Document Released to Generate Public Feedback" (9 August 2001), online: www.aji-cwi.mb.ca/eng/news_release_vis.html.

21 Communities and reserves included Brandon, Churchill, Cross Lake First Nation, Cross Lake, Garden Hill First Nation, Garden Hill, Opaskwayak Cree Nation, The Pas, Pinaymootang First Nation, Fairford, Portage la Prairie, Sagkeeng First Nation, Pine Falls, St. Boniface, Swan River, Thompson, and Winnipeg.

d) Detailed Implementation Plan

Prepared by the Implementation Committee, this plan was the work plan for implementing the new Aboriginal child welfare system. Putting together the plan involved a variety of teams, committees, and individuals from the MMF, First Nations, child and family services agencies, and other organizations. Each party established a steering group. These committees met monthly or as needed to have input on the issues being discussed. A highly technical document, the plan was well over 200 pages, with hundreds of task items; it was essentially designed as a project management tool.

2) Key Governance Transformations

Four essential components of governance needed to be changed in order to restructure the child welfare system: powers and duties needed to be reallocated, resources needed to be reallocated, the workforce needed to be transformed, and the service system itself needed to be transformed.

a) Reallocation of Powers and Duties

The primary mechanism used by the government of Manitoba to reallocate powers and duties was legislation. Provincial legislation was proclaimed in November 2003 to support the devolution of responsibilities from the province (Child and Family Services Support Branch) to the Métis, First Nations, and general authorities. It called for a child welfare system built on the principle of culturally appropriate services for Métis children and families. The Act, which falls under provincial jurisdiction, has resulted in Métis having expanded and increased authority over what happens to their children and families anywhere in the province. Because Métis were significantly involved and instrumental in its preparation, Métis interests and values are explicitly recognized. The government and partners have also agreed to cooperate in a broader review of all child welfare legislation in Manitoba once the restructuring is stabilized.

The "Authority" is the organization that took over many of the provincial functions of the Child and Family Services Support Branch. Of the four new authorities created by the AJI-CWI, one was Métis. While the MMF appoints the board of directors for the Métis Authority, the

Authority operates at arms-length from the political organization. Core funding for all authorities was first received in late summer 2002.

The Child Protection Branch acts as the arm of the provincial minister in oversight, monitoring, and compliance functions. The province sets laws, foundational policies, and standards, and provides funding to authorities. Authorities design, manage, and oversee their service delivery systems, set culturally appropriate standards, mandate and fund agencies. Agencies develop, deliver, and manage programs and services.

b) Reallocation of Resources

"Budgets follow the work" was the primary principle that guided the reallocation of resources among the new authorities. Regional Transfer Tables were created and included each of the four authorities, the province, the sending agency, and the receiving agency/agencies. Transfer tables had two components: a Case Transfer Table to design the case transfer process and a Resource Transfer Table to determine how and what human resources, budgets, and physical assets would be transferred.

Resources were reallocated based on the results of the transfer plan and on what currently existed there. For example, in one region, 36 percent of the families requested that responsibility for services be transferred to a First Nations Authority. Thirty-six percent of existing non-Aboriginal staffing and funding resources were transferred to the First Nations Authority. Actual transfer occurred when the work physically moved. Authorities determined the levels of funding that would be made available to their service-providing agencies.

Work has now begun to find a new model for the province to fund the authorities. The objective is to provide funding that encourages prevention, rather than child-in-care maintenance.

c) Workforce Adjustment

Two workforce issues needed to be addressed by the Resource Transfer Tables: training Métis and First Nations people for the approximately 400 new jobs in the child welfare authorities and agencies, and ensuring that a plan was in place to accommodate existing child welfare workers in the new system. A Master Human Resource Agreement, which took about two years to negotiate, was signed by the authorities and agencies to guide the workforce adjustment strategy.

Early on in the process, the government of Manitoba negotiated a Workforce Adjustment Agreement with the unions. A secondment strategy was a key element ensuring that the Métis and First Nations agencies had qualified staff available while training was under way. It also ensured a labour force adjustment that reduced the number of redundant workers and, where a collective agreement existed, involved the union in the process.

d) Service System Transformation

Transforming the child welfare system required that every child and family case, every foster home placement, and every resource and asset was counted and transferred smoothly from non-Aboriginal to Métis and First Nations agencies. The undertaking was huge. The on- and off-reserve service system that was transformed included about 6000 children in care, 8500 active family files, and 4000 foster families.

All components of the service system needed to be included in the transfer: intake, authority determination protocol, abuse services, children in care, foster care, family support services, and management information systems.

The authority determination process that was developed created a process for intake workers to determine where a family would go for service. Generally, a family receives service from an agency of the culturally appropriate authority. However, families could choose which authority would provide oversight to the services they received. The process, applied to all existing cases, is now part of the regular intake process and is a regulation under the legislation.

The transfer changed the criterion of who provided a family with service from where they live to who they are. Table 14.1 shows that at the end of the process, 82 percent of Aboriginal families using child welfare services were transferred to Aboriginal authorities.

Table 14.1: Service System Transformation: Cases by Authority

Ethnicity of Family Members	Total Cases	Aboriginal Authority		Non-Aboriginal Authority	
		Number	Percent	Number	Percent
Aboriginal Only	4019	3296	82%	723	18%
Aboriginal and Non-Aboriginal	949	399	42%	550	58%
Non-Aboriginal	2195	33	1.5%	2163	98.5%

In a system of concurrent jurisdiction, coordination is important. In October 2006, a separate agency to do joint intakes, the "Joint Intake and Response Unit" (JIRU), was put in place in Winnipeg to handle all intakes on behalf of all Authorities and their agencies, with abuse services provided by a jointly managed unit attached to the JIRU. Outside of Winnipeg, abuse services are being coordinated amont the various agencies. On a reserve, these services are provided by the First Nation agency.

Each authority sets standards, is responsible for designing a foster care system, and hears appeals. Since agencies continue to license foster homes, control of planning for Métis children is put back with Métis families and communities.

e) The Future

With the transfers complete, the move is now on to transform the child welfare system. This process will include developing funding models that support implementing new approaches to child protection, incorporating Métis and First Nations helping or support methods, emphasizing early intervention and prevention as front-end services, and supporting the use of "least intrusive" measures.

Discussions about restructuring the residential care system encompass privately operated group homes and treatment centres. These discussions began in 2006.

The AJI-CWI created a legislated relationship that ensures an appropriate demarcation of the parties' responsibilities and fosters effective cooperation between the province, Métis Authority and agency, the MMF, and Métis people. The statute has provided a means for Métis people to access culturally appropriate services for Métis children and families. It has also given Métis the statutory right to take part in the development of changes to child welfare policies, regulations, and standards — a larger Métis workforce will result from the AJI-CWI. It has provided an opportunity to get increased provincial and federal resources. As well as contributing to improved Métis well-being, all of these are important elements that could contribute to Métis organizational capacities.

D. LESSONS LEARNED FROM THE AJI-CWI

Change that empowers is usually driven by a myriad of factors. These factors are not simply individual champions of reform, but the interaction that takes place between organizations, people working in these organizations as well as people who influence them, people who are served by the organizations, socio-economic circumstances, and the rules that guide the interactions among all of these. The AJI-CWI provides a clear example of how these drivers of change together overcame jurisdictional uncertainty, acknowledged the Métis authority for child and family well-being, and devolved authority as far as it could be devolved under our existing constitutional framework. This section provides a brief overview of the factors that supported change.

1) Success Factors for Organizational Changes

The AJI-CWI was all about partnerships between the provincial government, Métis, and First Nations, with elders, with communities, with agencies, with foster families, with parents, and with youth. The partnerships were about making decisions, specifically, who was making decisions.

There were several principles that the government of Manitoba had to put in place to ensure the success of the AJI-CWI. First, it had to uphold the equality of all partners at the table even though all of the power and the resources rested with the province. Without the government constantly redressing power differentials and ensuring an equal voice, the focus may well have slipped from child welfare into a conflict over power. Further, partnership was predicated on consensus as the model of decision making. This meant that government partners would not invoke solutions to an issue; instead, there would be enough discussion to allow for consensus. When it came to doing things differently, the government could neither hide behind policy and bureaucracy nor make side deals with any partner. Transparency was a key element of success.

Among Métis and First Nations, there were also several factors that contributed to the success of the AJI-CWI. The Aboriginal partners had to be willing to "push the limits" and take risks; they also had to have a focus on the future. While all parties acknowledged the wrongs of the past, effort was to focus on making changes for the future. Issues of the past had to be accepted or put aside in order to move forward with the AJI-CWI. Success often relied on viewing the initiative as a long-term process, with success measured incrementally — all-or-nothing approaches would not have worked. Finally, Métis and First Nations partners, at all levels, had to have confidence in their legitimate role and ability to participate fully without allowing themselves to feel intimidated by government officials and organizations that, along with holding most of the power, had most of the resources in the areas of child welfare, organizational and change management.

Foremost among success factors for all partners was their commitment to working in good faith, in a manner that was respectful of one another and the relationships with others. Complementing this was the recognition that different and unconventional views were equally valid to those held in the status-quo. It was important for all to realize that professionals were not the only expert resources in the child welfare field.

Approaching the transformation of the child welfare system as an interest-based process, not as a positional process was significant.[22] Similarly, partners needed to view changes as win-win solutions, not as "gains" to be won at the expense of another party. Recognizing that some of the work would be completely new, that mistakes would be made, and that all of the process would not be perfect was critical. An innovative attitude that enabled participants to learn from mistakes, while recognizing that the systems would never be "perfect," was crucial. Innovation is typically based on creative responses to challenges or needs and often matches best strengths against best opportunities to produce breakthrough solutions that will improve quality of life. The AJI-CWI required a new approach to governance and institutions, one that had never been put in place anywhere in Canada.

Finally, all partners needed to accept the existence of barriers — monetary barriers, attitudinal barriers, time constraints, human resources

22 In interest-based negotiations, parties avoid taking "positions" because arguing over positions may lead to entrenchment and rigidity. Instead, decisions are made jointly on what issues need to be addressed. The interests of each party are discussed on each issue. The parties jointly develop options to satisfy interests. Participants must be willing to discuss a variety of options on the understanding that they are not making commitments, but discussing hypothetical possibilities. Parties then evaluate various courses of action on the issue. They compare each option against agreed-upon standards, postponing final commitment on each issue until the end of the process.

issues, and so on — and that these needed to be treated as obstacles to get around, not as blockages precluding work.

2) Success Factors for Formal and Informal Relationships

Two fundamental processes shaped both the formal and informal relationships between the partners in the AJI-CWI.

The first was the task-oriented, program management approach taken to the initiative at its outset. Specific responsibilities and tasks with aggressive completion dates were developed and documented jointly among all parties. Commitments to these plans at the highest political and organizational levels were also critical to ensuring that the inevitable conflicts of partnerships could be resolved and the forward momentum of change could continue.

Accountability, both to the leadership and the public, was built into the system as an important factor galvanizing ongoing support for the initiative. Accountability was shown through the completion of projects and phases.

The second process that reshaped the "rules" of child welfare was the creation of the *Child and Family Services Authority Act*. The new legislation realigned powers, duties, and responsibilities as close to the Métis as was and is legally possible. The Act has resulted in Métis having expanded and increased authority over what happens to their children and families anywhere in the province. Métis interests, culture, and values are recognized in the legislation.

Finally, all partners recognized that the AJI-CWI is an iterative and evolving process. New legislation defining child welfare in Manitoba remains as a future project.

3) Success Factors for People, Culture, Social and Economic Environment

Early on in the process, the government of Manitoba negotiated a Workforce Adjustment Agreement with the unions. Adoption of a secondment strategy ensured that the Métis and First Nations agencies had qualified staff available, while training was under way. The agreement also ensured a labour force adjustment that reduced the number of redundant workers, and where a collective agreement existed, involved the union in the process. Without these assurances, a successful transition would not likely have occurred and services for children and families in need would likely have been inadequate. Either condition would have jeopardized the implementation of the initiative.

Except for process and transitional costs, the government of Manitoba was constrained in its ability to increase the budgets allocated to child and family services. The transition to the four authorities model, therefore, had to be done within existing funds without incurring many incremental costs. Clearly communicating this constraint to all partners and including it in all planning and implementation processes was vital to the success of the AJI-CWI.

E. CONCLUSIONS

The AJI-CWI was founded upon and relied on political will dating back to the 1970s, the relationships built between the province and the MMF, and the organizational capacity of the MMF. It depended on Métis and First Nations leaders effectively communicating their outrage at existing child welfare practices to the provincial (and federal) political leadership who then created commissions of inquiry on the Aboriginal child welfare system. Each of these commissions carefully explored issues of Aboriginal child welfare and provided sophisticated direction to the government of Manitoba on how it could address them. The impartial and independent commissions also prepared the public to accept the new structure by raising the profile of the issues involved. These recommendations provided a foundation upon which the AJI-CWI and the Métis Authority and agency rest.

The relationship between the government of Manitoba and the MMF was strengthened by the TSN process, which also fostered the development of institutions in housing, education, and economic development, as well as family and community services. The MMF developed the organizational capacities necessary to take on the responsibility for delivering child welfare services, while forging relationships with the government of Manitoba that would facilitate the AJI-CWI processes.

At the point where political will, strong relationships, and sufficient organizational capacities converged, the AJI-CWI became possible, and the processes employed to implement the dream became a reality.

Although Manitoba recognizes that resolving jurisdictional uncertainty and the nature of Métis Aboriginal and treaty rights are important, it has also focused its efforts on building Métis institutions that will provide concrete support to improve the quality of life for Métis Manitobans. The creation of the Métis Child and Family Services Authority and agency is one example of this.

‹ 15 ›

Government on the Métis Settlements: Foundations and Future Directions

CATHERINE BELL AND HAROLD ROBINSON

A. INTRODUCTION

The Métis Settlements of Alberta are Canada's only legislated, land-based Métis government. About 7000 Métis live on eight Métis settlements in central and northern Alberta. Together, settlement lands total approximately 1.25 million acres (or 505 102 ha). Understanding the unique landholding and governance structure on the settlements requires consideration of the historical, legal, and political contexts for negotiation; settlement government and justice objectives; and the ultimate goal of creating a practical, flexible, and functional regime in which governmental institutions respond to the experiences and needs of the people. Similarly, the strengths and weaknesses of this system of government are best measured by the extent to which institutions and policies of Métis settlement government promote the well-being of the settlements affected.[1] However, the Métis settlement scheme and history of its develop-

1 The approach advocated is similar to the "well-being" approach applied to an early analysis of settlement legislation by Tom Pocklington. In that analysis, he also discusses the impact of the model on other citizens of the province. He considers not only issues of political autonomy, but also specific areas of well-being, such as political health, administrative skills, and self esteem. See, for example, Tom C. Pocklington, *The Government and Politics of the Alberta Métis Settlements* (Regina: Canadian Plains Research Centre, 1991). See also Catherine E. Bell, "Métis Self-Government: The Alberta Settlement Model," in John. H. Hylton, ed., *Aboriginal Self-Government in Canada*, 2d ed. (Saskatoon: Purich, 1999) at 330. For a more

ment also offer interesting lessons for others engaged in self-government negotiation and implementation.

The foundational principles and framework for transfer and allocation of Métis settlement lands and resources, protection of settlement lands, and executive, legislative, and judicial branches of government are found in the 1989 Alberta–Métis Settlements Accord (the Accord) — a bilateral agreement between the government of Alberta and the then Federation of Métis Settlements. Legislation was enacted in 1990 to implement negotiated agreements in these areas and, as acknowledged in amendments to the original legislation, "for the purpose of enabling the Métis to attain self-governance under the laws of Alberta."[2] Although settlement leaders advocated recognition of Métis Aboriginal rights to land and government at constitutional conferences and dealings with the province, this rights-based strategy was eventually set aside: they wanted to avoid provincial negotiations being mired in the complex legal issues that resulted in the failure to reach a national agreement on the existence and scope of Métis constitutional rights. Negotiating a unique, results-oriented, made-in-Alberta approach to self-government was seen as the most practical means to achieve concrete results for settlement members.

At the core of the settlement model is an understanding that what is important is not that "ideal institutions are created" but that the Métis Settlements and Alberta government are committed "to the ideal of continued co-operation in adapting institutions to meet new challenges."[3] Unlike rights-based agreements, certainty and extinguishment of Ab-

---

detailed discussion of matters raised in this chapter, including Métis Settlement government, land rights and administration, historical and political context, self-government justice objectives, and the Metis Settlements Appeal Tribunal and decisions, see Catherine E. Bell, *Alberta's Métis Settlement Legislation: An Overview of Ownership and Management of Settlement Lands* (Regina: Canadian Plains Research Centre, 1994); and Catherine E. Bell & the Metis Settlements Appeal Tribunal, *Contemporary Métis Justice: The Settlement Way* (Saskatoon: Native Law Centre, 1999).

2 *Métis Settlements Amendment Act*, S.A. 2004, c. 25, s. 41 (Assented to 11 May 2004, with sections applying to the Appeal Tribunal awaiting proclamation. These are ss. 3(b), 3(d), 10–18, 24–27, and 43.) [MSAA].

3 Alberta, Task Force to Review the Mandate of the Metis Settlements Appeal Tribunal, *Metis Settlements Appeal Tribunal Mandate Review Task Force Report* by Co-chairs Denis Ducharme and Fred V. Martin (Alberta: Intergovernmental and Aboriginal Affairs and Metis Settlements General Council, 1999) at 1.

original constitutional rights is not central to the agreement reached. Indeed, only with the 2004 amendments was the goal of self-governance clearly articulated. Due to concern about issues of jurisdiction and potential impact on Aboriginal rights, a paragraph was included in the *Constitution of Alberta Amendment Act, 1990*, to clarify that the Métis Settlements legislation is not to be construed so as to abrogate or derogate from Aboriginal rights.[4] Despite this intent, the legislation raises complicated constitutional questions. Further, although certain provincial mechanisms are adopted to protect the settlement land base and ensure the continued existence and makeup of the Metis Settlements General Council (MSGC or General Council), the binding effect of these mechanisms on future governments is debatable. Thus, the success of this system is largely dependent on its flexibility and the cooperation and goodwill between the parties affected.

Paradoxically, one of the key ingredients for the success of this model — its ability to adapt to experience, change, and the needs of the settlements — is also a fundamental weakness. As provincial statutory entities with delegated authorities, the institutions of Métis government are vulnerable to unilateral change. However, settlement members have adopted a pragmatic response to this by achieving what is possible within a delegated framework and looking to new opportunities for increased protection and control. As with any relationship, the partnership between MSGC and Alberta has had its ups and downs, but generally, intergovernmental relations have been positive and respectful of Métis political autonomy in negotiated fields of jurisdiction.

Over the past fifteen years, government institutions for regional and local Métis settlements have assumed jurisdiction in a wide range of areas. Significant progress has been made on the ground in the areas of community, and social and economic development. Jurisdictions of the MSGC have been expanded and the office of the Métis Settlements Ombudsman (MSO) has been established. Some proposals to expand Metis Settlements Appeal Tribunal (MSAT) jurisdiction and the creation of the MSO resulted from a joint initiative to review MSAT's mandate (MSAT Task Force). Other changes are in response to the continuing demand for good government by settlement members and the natural

---

4 R.S.A. 2000, c. 24.

evolution of new structures and approaches that will improve local and central governance and thereby enhance local autonomy; however, some changes are under negotiation. Other changes, such as the unilateral increase in regulatory powers of the minister, requirements for General Council policies on such matters as its personnel manual and rules for meeting (Robert's Rules), creation of an executive committee for MSAT, and changes to the role of the MSAT chair, seem inconsistent with the trend to greater autonomy set out in the Accord.

Essential to the functioning of any government is adequate financing and strong economic development. Métis settlement government is currently financed in ways including a financial commitment of $310 million allocated over seventeen years commencing 1 July 1990; revenues from surface and sub-surface development of settlement land; the ability to charge fees, dues, and levies on settlement and non-settlement members for services provided, permits, licences, and other authorizations; and the ability to access federal and provincial grants available to other Aboriginal and municipal governments. Taxation powers over interests in settlement lands also exist.

As of 2007, the unconditional funding provided as part of the original Accord package is no longer available. To prepare for this, the MSGC and Alberta initiated the Transition Assessment and Planning (TAP) Project in 2004. Together, the partners have taken stock of the progress made over the first fifteen years of the Accord. In the planning and development phase, work has had the focus of identifying new approaches to promote continued progress towards the Accord goals of improved land security, self-governance, and economic self-sufficiency.

Today, Métis constitutional rights are being addressed in legal and political forums and federal jurisdiction over Métis is again receiving serious consideration. The *Powley* decision recognizing the existence of Métis Aboriginal rights and the creation of the office of the Federal Interlocutor for Métis and Non-Status Indians have opened avenues of negotiation that were not available when the original Accord was negotiated in the late 1980s.[5] In response, the MSGC has negotiated a new provincial harvesting agreement for hunting, trapping, and fishing outside of settlement lands (similar to an agreement negotiated by the Métis Na-

---

5 *R. v. Powley*, [2003] 2 S.C.R. 207 [*Powley*].

tion of Alberta Association). The MSGC is also creating a database of traditional land-use activities and ancestral connections to historical Métis communities through a grant provided by the Federal Interlocutor's Office. In order to improve the federal government's awareness of the settlements, the MSGC opened up an outreach office in Ottawa in 2005.

The purpose of this chapter is to outline the basic structure and operations of Métis Settlement government and changes that have occurred, or are proposed, to the initial settlement scheme, financing, and operations of government over the last fifteen years. We conclude with reflections on practical issues in the exercise of government functions and complicated questions that arise as we enter a new era of Métis Aboriginal rights. What we present is not the end of a history of negotiations, but part of an ongoing journey towards new partnerships between the Métis Settlements, and federal and provincial governments.

B. HISTORICAL AND POLITICAL CONTEXT

Pursuant to federal policy, in the late 1800s Métis people in Manitoba, and later Saskatchewan and Alberta, were offered treaty if they lived among and were accepted by First Nations or scrip (a certificate redeemable by individual Métis for land or money).[6] Métis who were not eligible for treaty were offered scrip only. These processes failed to protect the collective existence of Métis in communities and to provide them with enough lands and resources to sustain themselves. As a result, some Métis in

6 The issue of entitlement to land as a result of problems arising in the scrip distribution system is the subject of ongoing litigation in Alberta, Saskatchewan, and Manitoba. There are many academic commentaries on the scrip distribution system. See, for example, Paul Chartrand, *Manitoba's Métis Settlement Scheme of 1870* (Saskatoon: Native Law Centre, 1991); Thomas Flanagan, *Métis Lands in Manitoba* (Calgary: University of Calgary Press, 1991) at 35–55; Joe Sawchuk, Patricia Sawchuk, & Theresa Ferguson, *Métis Land Rights in Alberta: A Political History* (Edmonton: Métis Association of Alberta, 1982); Douglas Sanders, "Métis Rights in the Prairie Provinces and the Northwest Territories: A Legal Interpretation" in Harry Daniels, ed., *The Forgotten People: Métis and Non-Status Indian Land Claims* (Ottawa: Native Council of Canada, 1979) at 5; Douglas Sprague, "Government Lawlessness in the Administration of Manitoba Land Claims, 1870–1887" (1980) 10 Man. L.J. 415; and Douglas Sprague, *Canada and the Métis, 1869–1885* (Waterloo: Wilfrid Laurier Press, 1988).

Manitoba migrated west to join other Métis communities in central and northern Saskatchewan and Alberta. In northern Alberta, Métis communities of Ojibwa, Cree, and Chipweyan descent also emerged near, or within the present geographical boundaries of, some contemporary Métis settlement communities. Concerned about some of the more destitute Métis populations in Alberta and after the Northwest Métis resistance of 1885, Father Albert Lacombe approached the federal government to set up a farming colony in northern Alberta for the benefit of the Métis. St. Paul des Métis was established in 1895, but ten years later declared a failure and opened up for settlement. Only a small number of Métis claims in the area were recognized.[7]

Métis from the colony joined others throughout the province struggling to survive.[8] Although some succeeded in establishing farms in southern Alberta, those who remained in central Alberta lived in tents along road allowances and tried to make their livings as farm hands. In addition to suffering from poverty, many Métis lacked schooling, housing, medical services, and social relief. As wildlife resources were depleted or disrupted by settlement, malnutrition became an issue for those in the north. Non-status Indians of mixed blood whose fate was similar were, for the purposes of federal and provincial policy, referred to as "Half-breeds." At the time, this term was used interchangeably with "Métis."

This was the situation during the negotiations over the *Natural Resources Transfer Agreements* (NRTAs). Although these agreements in-

---

7 For more extensive discussion of the circumstances leading to the creation of St. Paul des Métis, see Joe Sawchuk *et al.*, *ibid.* at 172–78; and George F. Stanley, "Alberta's Half-Breed Reserve St. Paul de Métis 1896–1909" in A. S. Lussier & D. B. Sealey, eds., *The Other Natives: The Métis*, vol. 2 (Winnipeg: Métis Federation Press and Editions Bois-Brûlés, 1978) 105–7; Bell, *Contemporary Métis Justice*, above note 1 at 1–14.

8 The following discussion of the history leading to the Ewing Commission and its hearings and outcomes draws on these sources: Commission, A. Gaz. 1934. 941 in Native Affairs Secretariat, *Alberta's Métis Settlements: A Compendium of Background Documents* (Edmonton: Alberta Native Affairs, 1984) [*Ewing Commission*]; Murray Dobin, *The One-and-a-Half Men: The Story of Jim Brady and Malcolm Norris* (Vancouver: New Star Books, 1981; Regina: Gabriel Dumont Institute, 1987) at 88–106; and Joe Sawchuk, *The Dynamics of Native Politics: The Alberta Experience* (Saskatoon: Purich, 1998) at 53–55; and including testimonials from settlement members see Bell, *Contemporary Métis Justice*, above note 1 at 7–14; and Pocklington, above note 1 at 12–21.

cluded a provision to protect the "Indian" lifestyle of hunting, fishing, and trapping, its application to any or all Métis has been a matter of political debate, with Métis people arguing for inclusion. Settlement Métis also take the position that the Crown's duty to address scrip claims was a trust encumbering federal lands and that Alberta acquired land under the NRTA subject to this trust. Although still a contentious issue, the relevant provision in the Manitoba NRTA, identical to Alberta's NRTA, has been interpreted by the Supreme Court of Canada to exclude the Métis.[9]

During this time many Métis moved to the Fishing Lake area to join families who had settled on forest reserve land.[10] Perceived threats to the continued existence of this settlement arising from the NRTA resulted in the creation of the first Métis regional political organization in Alberta (later to become known as the Métis Association of Alberta, or MAA). After a 1931 meeting of 200 Métis representing six communities, Jim Brady, Malcolm Norris, and Joseph Dion (an enfranchised Indian) submitted a petition with more than 500 names to the Alberta government on behalf of the Métis: the Métis sought help in obtaining land, education, medical care, and free hunting and fishing permits. The government responded with a questionnaire, completed by more than 1000 Métis and non-status "Half-breeds," addressing issues such as failure to receive scrip and homestead lands, ownership of livestock, and attitudes towards farming. Shortly thereafter the MAA was formed. The primary goals of the organization, approved by thirty-two councillors representing as many communities, were to see that adequate provision was made for "homeless and destitute families," including education and medical services.[11] These

---

9 *R. v. Blais*, [2003] 2 S.C.R. 207 [*Blais*]. Before this decision, case law in Alberta supported the inclusion of some Métis who "live an Indian way of life" (sustenance hunting, fishing, gathering). See *R. v. Ferguson*, [1993] 2 C.N.L.R. 148 at para. 19 (Alta. Prov. Ct.). For a more in-depth treatment of this issue and arguments against *Blais*, see Frank Tough, "The Forgotten Constitution: The *Natural Resources Transfer Agreements* and Indian Livelihood Rights, ca. 1925–1933" (2004) 41 Alta. L. Rev. 999 at 1000–1; Frank Tough, "Introduction to Documents: Indian Hunting Rights, *Natural Resources Transfer Agreements* and Legal Opinions from the Department of Justice" (1995) 10 Native St. Rev. 121; and Catherine Bell & Clayton Leonard, "A New Era in Métis Constitutional Rights: The Importance of *Powley* and *Blais*" (2004) 41 Alta. L. Rev. 1049 at 1063–67.

10 Dobin, above note 8 at 56.

11 *Ibid.* at 63.

issues "were contained, depended upon, and were expressed in one clear and unmistakable demand: the demand for land."[12]

As the federal government asserted "Half-breeds" were a provincial responsibility, Métis leadership focused on pressing the provincial government into action.[13] The province appointed the Ewing Commission to look into the "problems of health, education, and general welfare of the Half-breed population of the province."[14] Although all Métis executive members emphasized social welfare needs in their submissions, Brady and Norris also argued that Métis had rights to land arising from the failure of the scrip system and an independent economic base for Métis self-determination. The Commission viewed the latter position as a leftist radical opinion and the chair refused to hear rights-based arguments.

The Commission operated on the assumption that if Métis had rights to land by virtue of Aboriginal ancestry, such rights were extinguished by the scrip system. It recommended allotment of Crown land for the creation of farm colonies to be free from intrusion by white settlers, a paternalistic system of local governance consisting of elected advisory boards and provincially appointed settlement supervisors; and preferential rights to the Métis in harvesting fish, game, and furs. The Commission also recommended that girls be educated in homemaking skills, boys in agriculture, and both in writing and arithmetic.

Following these recommendations, the province enacted the *Métis Population Betterment Act*, later known as the *Métis Betterment Act*. Although similar to federal Indian legislation in many respects, it differed in others. The preamble to the *Métis Betterment Act* recognized that it was in the public interest that the ways and means of giving effect to the Ewing Commission recommendations should be arrived at by "means of conferences and negotiations." Somewhat disillusioned by the Commission recommendations, Brady pulled back from political life, which resulted in Norris also not negotiating. Tomkins and Dion worked with the

12 *Ibid.*

13 Pocklington, above note 1 at 11–12; Sawchuk *et al.*, *Métis Land Rights in Alberta*, above note 6 at 188–90; and Fred Martin, "Federal and Provincial Responsibility in the Métis Settlements of Alberta" in David Hawkes, ed., *Aboriginal Peoples and Government Responsibility: Exploring Federal and Provincial Roles* (Ottawa: Carleton University Press, 1989) 255.

14 *Ewing Commission*, above note 8, Tab 2.

province and, despite the emphasis on agriculture, selected lands for the colonies (later known as the settlements) in areas where Métis had traditionally sustained themselves. Their belief in the goodwill of the government, a leadership vacuum in the MAA, challenges to the creation of the colonies in favour of individual titles, and the priority of securing a land base were likely reasons they placed less emphasis on administration and governance of the colonies than Brady and Norris.[15]

In the administration of the legislation, the occurrence of several events resulted in a call for new arrangements. The original vision was for cooperative settlement management, but by the 1950s the system had become very top-down with supervisors appointed without consultation and accountable only to the minister of Welfare. By the 1960s, more administrative power was delegated to the settlements and unworkable sections of the *Métis Betterment Act* were ignored. However, increased administrative power also resulted in uncertainty about the extent of settlement powers, their status to enter into binding legal relationships, and the continual need to involve the Métis Development Branch in contractual and other arrangements. Of particular significance was the disestablishment of four colonies without consultation or consent (Touchwood, Marlboro, Cold Lake, and Wolf Lake). At the time only one was occupied by Métis, but the province's unilateral action generated concerns about security of the Métis land base. Further, Métis believed the province was more concerned with developing oil and gas under settlement lands than acting for the "betterment" of the Métis.

In 1972, a task force was established in response to these concerns. It recommended that the settlements move towards a form of local self-government and that land be set aside perpetually for their benefit. In 1975, the Alberta Federation of Métis Settlements, a representative body of the remaining eight settlements, formed. The Federation began litigation on behalf of settlement members, accusing the province of misappropriating resource revenues that, pursuant to Orders-in-Council under the *Métis Betterment Act*, were to be placed in trust for the benefit of the Métis.[16] Following the task force report, the Métis Development Branch

15 *Ibid.* at 104–9; Bell, *Contemporary Métis Justice*, above note 1 at 14.

16 The *Métis Settlements Population Betterment Act* is cited as *The Métis Population Betterment Act*, S.A. 1938, c. 6. As amended by S.A. 1940, c. 6, in s. 8(j), it provided that the minister could make regulations whose purpose is "the advancement

adopted a policy to devolve more responsibility to settlements, which, by then, had assumed administrative powers for delivery of local housing, education, and economic and cultural programs. Two years later an investigation into seizure of settlement files during natural resource litigation led the provincial ombudsman to recommend that a new joint Métis–provincial commission be formed to review the administration of the *Métis Betterment Act*.

After consultations with settlement members, the MacEwan Committee made many recommendations designed to enhance Métis control, protect Métis culture, and provide adequate financial resources to build viable communities. Unanimous recommendations included securing a permanent land base, increasing local government over settlement lands, clarifying legal status, and allowing greater control by settlement members over social and economic development. The Federation included Aboriginal rights to land and government in their submissions and subsequent negotiations with the province.[17] The Committee proposed that new legislation recognize Métis Aboriginal ancestry and their distinct role in the history and culture of Alberta, but matters of Aboriginal rights were viewed as outside the Committee's provincial mandate.[18]

At this time, the Federation was also involved in national conferences held to clarify Aboriginal rights recognized and affirmed in section 35

---

and betterment of any Settlement Association, or any members thereof, or the administration of the affairs of any Settlement Association." Pursuant to this section, Order-in-Council 1785/43 was promulgated providing for the creation of a Métis Population Betterment Trust Account funded by natural resource revenues accrued from settlement lands. Litigation over whether the wording of the relevant section, and subsequent related regulations, included sub-surface resources, provided significant impetus for negotiation on the part of Alberta during a time when other provinces denied jurisdiction and refused to negotiate with the Métis. See Bell, *Alberta's Métis Settlement Legislation*, above note 1 at 9–10.

17 See, for example, Alberta Federation of Métis Settlements, *Métisism: A Canadian Identity* (Edmonton: Alberta Federation of Métis Settlements, 1982).

18 Alberta, Joint Metis–Government Committee to Review the Metis Betterment Act and Regulations, *Foundations for the Future of Alberta's Métis Settlements: Report of the MacEwan Joint Committee on the Métis Betterment Act and Regulations* by Dr. G. MacEwan, Chair (Edmonton: Alberta Municipal Affairs, 1984) at 11 and 59. For a general discussion, see Pocklington, above note 1 at 141; and Bell, *Alberta's Métis Settlement Legislation*, above note 1 at 11–14.

of the *Constitution Act, 1982*.[19] During these conferences, identification and membership became contentious issues that were never resolved and both federal and provincial governments denied jurisdiction over the Métis. At the root of provincial concerns was the potential impact of Métis claims on provincial lands, revenues, and resources. Further, to the extent that Métis Aboriginal rights were acknowledged, governments asserted they had been extinguished through scrip distribution. Although Federation representatives appreciated that other Métis people had little success in negotiating with provincial governments, the Federation was in a unique position to develop a relationship with the government of Alberta. Alberta had responded positively to the MacEwan Committee recommendations and was prepared to negotiate pursuant to its jurisdiction over property, municipal governance, and civil rights.[20] Also, even if the federal government had jurisdiction, there was no guarantee it would be exercised. Concerns about federal reluctance to exercise jurisdiction proved true in subsequent negotiations. A similar position for recognition of joint jurisdiction was maintained by settlement leaders and the government of Alberta during negotiations of the failed Charlottetown Accord.[21]

The MacEwan Report, released in 1984, gave rise to a fresh set of negotiations and eventually a resolution by the Lougheed government to protect settlement land through an amendment to the *Alberta Act*.[22] However, this critical resolution was conditional upon settlements developing fair and democratic procedures for membership and land allocation.[23] Resolution 18 also called for transfer of fee simple title to Métis government, delegated self-government jurisdictions exercised by institutions proposed by the Métis, and introduction of new legislation to replace the old regime. Ensuing negotiations, conducted without

---

19 *Constitution Act, 1982*, being Schedule B to the *Canada Act 1982* (U.K.), 1982, c. ll.

20 *Constitution Act, 1867* (U.K.), 30 & 31 Vict., c. 3, ss. 92(13) and (18), reprinted in R.S.C. 1985, App. II, No. 5.

21 For more detailed discussion of these issues, see Bell, "Métis Self-Government," above note 1 at 331–33.

22 Originally the *Alberta Act*, 1905, 4-5 Edw. VII, c. 3 (Can.), now identified as part of the Constitution of Canada by s. 52(2)(b) of the *Constitution Act, 1982*, being Schedule B to the *Canada Act 1982* (U.K.), 1982, c. 11.

23 Alberta Legislative Assembly, *A Resolution Concerning an Amendment to the Alberta Act*, No. 18 (3 June 1985).

prejudice to Aboriginal and treaty rights, resulted in the signing of the Alberta–Métis Settlements Accord. Hundreds of community and Métis government meetings were held throughout the Accord process. In the end, 77 percent of those who voted supported the Accord. The greatest opposition came from members of Paddle Prairie who were concerned about implications of the Accord on their Aboriginal rights; they felt that all title and jurisdiction to enact laws affecting settlements should rest at the settlement level.[24]

Contemporary governance goals flowing from this history are land security, local autonomy, and self-sufficiency. The Accord was implemented in 1990 with the enactment of four pieces of legislation: The *Metis Settlements Act* (MSA), *Constitution of Alberta Amendment Act* (CAA), *Métis Settlements Land Protection Act* (MSLPA), *and Métis Settlements Accord Implementation Act* (MSAIA).[25] Eight settlement councils and one central authority, the MSGC, have the powers of a natural person in law and enjoy delegated authority to pass policies and bylaws in relation to land, membership, governance, and matters related thereto. Another key feature was the creation of the Metis Settlements Appeal Tribunal (MSAT).

The leadership agenda in the early 1930s, through to the Alberta–Métis Settlements Accord, and today continues to focus on results without prejudicing potential legal rights. What follows is a discussion of some of the main features of the original land and governance system followed by changes brought about through, and proposed by, the 2004 *Métis Settlements Amendment Act.*

C. GOVERNMENT AND MEMBERSHIP

There are four key features of settlement government: settlement councils, the MSGC, the minister responsible for administering the Act, and MSAT. Settlement councils are comprised of five elected members from

---

24 Pocklington, above note 1 at 151–52.

25 *Metis Settlements Act*, R.S.A. 2000, c. M-14, as am. S.A. 1998, c. M-14.3 and by the *Métis Settlements Amendment Act*, S.A. 2004, c. 25 [MSA]; *Constitution of Alberta Amendment Act, 1990*, R.S.A. 2000, c. C-24 [CAA]; *Métis Settlements Land Protection Act*, R.S.A. 2000, c. M-16 [MSLPA]; and the *Métis Settlements Accord Implementation Act*, R.S.A. 2000, c. M-15 [MSAIA].

the settlement and exercise bylaw powers similar to a municipality.[26] Settlement councils can also enact bylaws relating to membership and land allocation, as well as other jurisdictions given to them under MSGC policies (e.g., surface access, allocation of settlement share of sub-surface royalties). Bylaws must comply with MSGC policy and be given three separate readings by a settlement council, presented at a public meeting, and approved by the majority of settlement members in attendance. These governments also run local programs and services, such as water systems, garbage pick-up, housing, and economic development. Matters such as election procedures, resignations, disqualifications, delegation of authority, and conflicts of interest are modelled on provincial municipal law.[27]

The MSGC is the central government composed of members from each settlement council and a four-person executive elected by the forty settlement councillors for a total of forty-four members.[28] It has delegated jurisdiction to enact policies binding on settlement councils in specified areas of collective interest formerly within the jurisdiction of the province, manage collective settlement funds, and hold fee simple title to the settlement land base under letters patent.

Within General Council are also several committees to carry out the responsibilities of the MSGC. The Strategic Training Initiative (STI) is primarily concerned with delivering training programs to settlement residents under the federal Aboriginal Human Resources Development Agreement. The tripartite unit was established to negotiate agreements with Canada and Alberta. Various standing advisory committees, including Land and Resources, Finance, and Governance, and the MSGC Board, enable the MSGC to attend to its executive functions as holder of letters patent, partner in co-management processes, and manager of the Future Fund, $100 million at time of writing.

26 Bylaw powers cover a range of areas, including matters of internal management, health, safety, welfare, public order, fire protection, nuisance, pests, animals, airports, advertising, refuse disposal, parks, recreation, control of businesses, water, sewage, development levies, and land use planning. See Sch. 1 to MSA, *ibid.*

27 Structure, function, and jurisdiction of settlement councils are elaborated in MSA, *ibid.* ss. 8–71, and bylaw powers are elaborated in Sch. 1.

28 Structure, function, and jurisdiction of the MSGC (Metis Settlements General Council) are elaborated in MSA, *ibid.*, ss. 214–32.

The *Metis Settlements Act* (MSA) only provides a framework for settlement government and jurisdiction. Many of the settlement laws are found in MSGC policies, ministerial regulations, settlement bylaws, and decisions of MSAT. General Council has jurisdiction to enact, amend, or repeal policies and model bylaws after consultation with the minister in a range of areas: these include membership and residency; finance; land and resource development and allocation; creation, transfer, and devolution of interests in settlement lands; administration of estates; and taxation, levies, and fines.[29] Policies inconsistent with provincial laws, subject to a few exceptions noted in the MSA, are of no effect to the extent of being inconsistent with provincial law. This has resulted in numerous consequential amendments to legislation to enable its application to the interests created under the MSA, such as dower and family relief legislation. Policies, published in the *Alberta Gazette*, have the force of law within the settlements after ninety days from the date of submission to the minister, provided that the minister does not veto the policy, or a portion of it. Although unpopular with settlement government, the veto power has yet to be exercised. Particularly important in negotiations was preservation of traditional lifestyles and the ability to enact policies relating to hunting, fishing, trapping, and gathering in the settlement area. As these are given priority over other provincial law, they are developed with the minister and approved by the Lieutenant Governor in Council.[30]

29 Several policies have been enacted by the MSGC concerning business activities, assessments and levies, financial allocation, public utilities, and business property contributions. Important ones relating to lands and resources include the Non-Renewable Surface Resources Policy (G.C.P. 9807), A. Gaz. 1999.I.266; Timber Policy and Model Timber By-Law (No. 9806), A. Gaz. 1999.I.243; Mineral Projects Policy and Model By-Law (No. 9603), A. Gaz. 1992.I.919; Land Policy (No. 90003), A. Gaz. 1992.I.2592; and Hunting, Fishing, Trapping and Gathering By-Law (No. 90001) O.C. 642/90, A. Gaz. 1991.I.1719 [HFTG]. The mineral projects policy is being revised and new hunting agreements are being negotiated in light of *Powley*.

30 Under the HFTG bylaw, hunting and fishing for food during any season, and trapping, are limited to licensed settlement members. Pursuant to settlement bylaws, special permits can also be issued to families of members and non-members. Members can also gather wild plants within the settlement area during any season. Licences and permits are issued by settlement councils. Alberta policy for Métis harvesting off settlement lands has been in flux since the *Powley* decision, above note 5. Currently, a settlement member can also hunt for sustenance within 160 km of the settlement if he or she is a resident of Alberta and meets the criteria

The desire to protect Métis values also resulted in the incorporation of community consultation and consensus requirements into bylaw-making powers of settlement councils, the composition of the MSGC as an "all council," and the original process for enacting General Council policies.[31] The practice of MSGC is to develop policies through its committees and institutions and to circulate them to affected third parties and settlements after first reading. Policies are posted in settlement council offices after the second reading.[32] The MSA also requires that most policies have unanimous support by MSGC members before being adopted and implemented. At the time, this provision was central to the decision of the Paddle Prairie Métis Settlement to support the Accord.

General Council also works together with several central governance institutions and corporations. These include the Settlement Investment Corporation (SIC), Settlement Sooniyaw Corporation (SSC), Land and Membership Registry, and Region 10 Child and Family Services Authority (CFSA). The SIC is a $4-million company that provides settlement members with small business loans. The SSC was established to promote economic development through business incubation and promotion of joint ventures and new partnerships, but was largely silent during the first fifteen years of the Accord. This will change as the settlements are now poised to move from investing in critical infrastructure and housing to investing in people and business. The Métis Settlements Ombudsman (MSO) and new authorities anticipated in the TAP proposals are discussed later in this paper.

Before leaving structures of government, mention should be made of the Transition Authority (comprised of the minister of Intergovernmental Affairs and the president of the MSGC) and Transition Commis-

---

set out in *Powley*: self-identification as Métis, ancestral connection to a historic Métis community in Alberta, and acceptance by a contemporary Métis community in the province.

31 For a discussion of traditional and contemporary community values and the challenge of incorporating traditional values into the settlement scheme, see Bell, *Contemporary Métis Justice*, above note 1 at 43–52.

32 Ken Noskey, president, MSGC, presentation to the Royal Commission on Aboriginal Peoples at Elizabeth Métis Settlement (16 June 1993) at 68, available on CD-ROM: Royal Commission on Aboriginal Peoples, *For Seven Generations: An Information Legacy of the Royal Commission on Aboriginal Peoples* (Ottawa: Libraxus, 1997).

sion created to assist in the transition from government administration through the Métis Settlements Branch to self-government. The Transition Commission was also responsible for certain aspects of training, financial management, and maintaining the Métis Settlements Land and Membership Registry. Intended to expire after seven years, it was extended for four years by agreement of the MSGC and the minister. With the exception of the Land Registry, currently administered by the province, MSGC has assumed many of the former powers of the Transition Commission. Under the TAP Project, however, the relationship of the MSGC and of Alberta to all Métis institutions is being reviewed; some may be brought under the General Council umbrella, while others will remain at arm's length.

Four significant changes to this system have been brought about by the 2004 amendments:

Under the original system, settlement councillors were elected annually for staggered terms of three years with at least one new councillor appointed each year. The original rationale for this system was to ease the settlements into the role of government and to ensure consistency of experienced and new councillors. However, the system proved unworkable in the operations of government because local decision makers were always in election mode. Consequently, as of October 2004, elections were changed to every three years, and all councillors have a term of three years. Terms of office that expired before this date were extended and those that expired after were deemed to end with the election.[33] New election provisions were to be reviewed jointly or independently no later than 31 December 2005. At the time of writing, the review was under way.

A second change is the mechanism by which the MSGC enacts policy. The requirement of unanimity proved problematic in practice because it gave every settlement a de facto veto over critical policy development, without providing an effective dispute-resolution mechanism to deal with the inevitable disagreements. The MSA was amended by Alberta so that all policies and amendments could be passed by special resolution (six of eight settlements). A further amendment enabled the MSGC to develop a new review policy that enables settlement councils that oppose

33 MSAA, above note 2, ss. 3–14 and 42.

a policy to apply to the MSAT on the grounds that a newly passed policy unfairly discriminates against their members.[34]

Further, under the original MSA, the minister exercised regulatory power to clarify application of the Act,[35] but only at the request of General Council. The minister may now make regulations of his/her own motion in areas of MSGC policy jurisdiction. However, such regulations expire on the earliest of the coming into force of MSGC policy, two years, or the day on which they are repealed.[36] Although well intentioned, this power has the potential to significantly undermine the autonomy of the General Council by having the minister set priorities for policy development. It is hoped that this provision, too, will operate only as a safety net, and like the minister's veto power, not be exercised. In keeping with the spirit of flexibility and commitment to cooperation, this change and others in the Act are subject to review, both through the TAP Project and through the Act itself. The MSGC may make proposals to change the Act or regulations that are "directed to the creation of a more effective and culturally appropriate structure for self-governance" and set out "workable alternatives" to existing structures and institutions.[37]

Finally, under the MSA, a Métis person is defined as "a person of aboriginal ancestry who identifies with Métis history and culture."[38] Applications to settlement council must be accompanied by proof of Métis identity, which could include affidavits of two Métis recognized as elders. Applications could not be approved if an applicant was a registered Indian or Inuk unless he or she was removed from the registry or was registered under the age of eighteen, lived on the settlements, had one or both parents as members of the settlement, and a bylaw was passed approving membership. With the 1985 amendments to the *Indian Act* (Bill C-31), some settlement and non-settlement Métis regained Indian status sometimes without knowing how this could affect their existing

34 Metis Settlements General Council Review Policy (G.C.P. 0408), A. Gaz. 2005.I.316.

35 Examples include the *Land Interests Conversion Regulation*, Alta. Reg. 362/91; *Métis Settlements Land Registry Regulation*, Alta. Reg. 361/91; and *Transitional Membership Regulation*, Alta. Reg. 337/90.

36 MSAA, above note 2, s. 40.

37 *Ibid.*, s. 41.

38 MSA, above note 25, s. 1(j); and regarding applications, proof of membership, and registered Indians and Inuit, ss. 74–84.

and potential membership in the settlements or their inability to remove themselves from the Indian register once status was granted.[39] This issue was dealt with, in part, by a Transitional Membership Regulation requiring each settlement council and the minister to provide the Transition Commissioner with a list of existing members as of November 1990. Members on both lists were affirmed as members; those deemed of uncertain status could apply to the Appeal Tribunal to confirm or deny membership based on whether they were treated as members under previous legislation — fairness dictated that membership be maintained.[40] MSAT can also hear appeals from membership denials, several of which have involved consideration of Bill C-31 status. On some settlements, this issue has also been litigated and continues to result in the denial of membership, residence, and other services.

In addition to the above processes, the MSGC can now enact its own policies and criteria to determine whether an Indian or Inuk can become a settlement member. General Council did not seek this jurisdiction, has not enacted a policy on this issue, and is reluctant to do so because of the divided and strongly held opinions of different settlement councils. However, through workshops and its traditional-use studies, the MSGC is examining the underlying principle of what it means to be a member of the Métis Settlements. Rather than focusing on the legalistic definitions contained in federal statutes, which inevitably create division, the MSGC is focusing on the elements that unite community members, such as common cultural practices, language, and the settlements' own unique history and development.

D. LAND RIGHTS AND THE LAND REGISTRY

Fundamental components of the Accord are greater control over settlement lands and the creation of a secure land base for the Métis. These goals can be accomplished through transfer of title, two protective legislative enactments, jurisdictions delegated to MSAT and MSGC, and the

39 *An Act to Amend the Indian Act*, S.C. 1985, c. 27, and see Bell, *Contemporary Métis Justice*, above note 1 at 21–22 and 67–71.

40 For elaboration, see Bell, *Alberta's Métis Settlement Legislation*, above note 1, and Bell, *Contemporary Métis Justice*, *ibid.* at 25 and 66–71, respectively, citing sample MSAT decisions.

co-management agreement for mineral rights appended to the MSA. Fee simple title is held by the MSGC by way of letters patent (including beds and shores, road allowances, and highways, but excluding water, mines, and minerals). *The Métis Settlements Land Protection Act* (MSLPA) confirms the terms of the letters patent, restricts rights of expropriation to interests less than fee simple and includes mechanisms to resolve disputes, prevents the giving of fee simple as security for a debt (other interests are addressed in the Land Policy), and requires consent of both the affected settlement and MSGC for entry to settlement land to exercise sub-surface rights. It also prohibits alienation of a fee simple interest without the consent of the Crown, MSGC, and the majority of members of the affected settlement, and a majority of all settlement members is necessary before any of this land can be sold to non-settlement members.

The *Constitution of Alberta Amendment Act* (CAA) also provides some security by preventing changes in the MSLPA, alteration or revocation of MSGC ownership under the letters patent, and dissolution or changes to the composition of the MSGC without the MSGC's agreement. However, the ability of one provincial government to bind another on matters relating to enactment, repeal, and amendment is a matter of debate. Although contemporary academic opinion suggests a distinction must be drawn between binding the substance of, and procedures for, enacting legislation and that the latter is acceptable, this is not clear in law.[41] Because federal involvement would make it more difficult for the province to amend or repeal its constitution, and provincial constitutions are instruments that form part of the Canadian Constitution, the MSGC and Alberta sought greater protection through federal involvement in the amending process. To date, the federal government has denied this request on the opinion that it is a wholly provincial matter covered by section 45 of the *Constitution Act, 1982*,[42] which allows provinces to enact laws to change provincial constitutions.

MSGC policy provides for a unique system of landholding on the settlements and acquisition of leasehold and lesser interests by non-set-

---

41 For elaboration, see Bell, *Alberta's Métis Settlement Legislation*, *ibid.* at 81–82. See also R. Elliott, "Rethinking Manner and Form: From Parliamentary Sovereignty to Constitutional Values" (1991) 29 Osgoode Hall L.J. 215.

42 Above note 19.

tlement residents.[43] Métis title to settlement land is held by settlement councils unless Métis title to a specific parcel is registered in the name of a settlement member in the Métis Land Registry. Métis title gives the holder exclusive rights to use, occupy, improve, and grant lesser interests to settlement and non-settlement members in accordance with MSGC policy and settlement bylaws, and transfer *inter vivos* or on death to other members of the settlement. Title is acquired through conversion under the *Land Interest Conversion Regulation*, inheritance, or application to the settlement council. Provisional Métis title provides exclusive use and occupation for five years with the ability to renew for another five. The Land Policy anticipates members with converted equivalent interests or subsequently acquired provisional Métis title will make improvements the settlement council deems necessary to acquire Métis title. Métis title is limited to 175 acres (about 71 ha); however, settlement council can grant allotments of up to 167 additional acres necessary for farming, ranching, or business purposes. The nature of an allotment is similar to leasehold under common law.

Métis settlement lands do not form part of the provincial land titles system, but are administered through a unique registry created to enable registration of collective and individual interests, lesser interests of non-settlement members, and estate instructions. Like other registry systems, it is intended to provide proof of entitlement and public notice of interests in settlement land, facilitate efficient disposition, indicate priorities of interest holders, and provide compensation for loss arising through errors or unauthorized registrations. Unlike the federal Indian registry system, the Métis land registry system closely resembles provincial land titles systems and has generally not hindered commercial development through lack of clarity or priority of interests. As a joint initiative of the General Council and the province, it was intended to promote Métis control through the appointment of a registrar and local staff to monitor and record the transfer of interests. As discussed earlier, at the time of writing, the function of the registrar had been temporarily assumed by the Department of Aboriginal and Northern Affairs (Alberta). However,

43 The source for this discussion is the Metis Settlements General Council Land Policy (G.C.P. 90003), A. Gaz. 1992.I.2625, reproduced in Bell, *Alberta's Métis Settlement Legislation*, above note 1.

settlement members still have an active role monitoring the creation of new interests and preparing documents for registration.

A fundamental component of the landholding system is control by Métis government over renewable surface-resource development and increased participation by the Métis settlements over sub-surface development. Significant oil and gas deposits and surface resources (including timber, peat, gravel, and marl) are found under and on settlement lands. Settlement council has the sole authority and responsibility for managing the non-renewable surface resources of the settlement area.[44] However, the management of these resources must benefit the community and minimize damage to wildlife resources and the environment. Should a dispute arise as to whether the surface resources are being properly managed, an adversely affected party (including the MSGC) can ask MSAT to review a settlement council's decision.

Schedule 3 to the *Metis Settlements Act* provides for the co-management of sub-surface resources under settlement land. The Co-management Agreement enables the MSGC to propose terms and conditions on public offerings of resources under settlement lands. These terms and conditions have now become standard, and among other terms on such matters as environmental protection, cultural impact, and employment, require successful bidders to offer participation rights of up to 25 percent to General Council and the affected settlement, and to commit to negotiating overriding royalties (which range from 3 to 10 percent). While the participation rights and overriding royalties were managed for a time by an oil and gas company incorporated by the MSGC, RESCO, these rights are now directly managed by the General Council in concert with affected settlement councils. As set out in the MSGC Oil and Gas Resource Sharing Policy,[45] the MSGC and affected settlement split the overriding royalty down the middle (12.5/12.5 percent) and the MSGC receives the first 3 percent of any negotiated overriding royalty.

---

44 Métis Settlements Non-Renewable Surface Resource Policy, above note 29, s. 2.2.

45 Metis Settlements General Council Oil and Gas Sharing Policy (G.C.P. 0502), A. Gaz. 2005.I.2180.

E. DISPUTE RESOLUTION

One way to improve justice for Aboriginal peoples is to minimize incompatibilities by making the system more sensitive to particular cultural traditions, laws, and justice objectives. Doing this means increasing Aboriginal input, representation, laws, traditions, and values in dispute resolution while correspondingly reducing complexity, formality, and rigidity of process. Tribunals can lend themselves to these objectives because they are created to adjudicate issues requiring expert knowledge and to implement policy goals. The expertise of the Metis Settlements Appeal Tribunal (MSAT) includes knowledge in Accord negotiations and intent of the legislation, the landholding and registry system, membership matters, community practice and custom, and land and resource development. Tribunals can also be given broad discretion and remedial powers to help implement the self-government and justice goals of the legislation that creates them. For example, MSAT can provide for any means of alternative dispute resolution it considers appropriate and has a wide range of remedial power including "any remedy, that in all circumstances, fairness requires."[46] With greater emphasis now placed on alternative processes, approximately two-thirds of appeals brought before the Appeal Tribunal since 2005 have been resolved in this manner without a hearing and imposition of an MSAT order.

Specific justice goals of settlement members arising from the administration of former Métis legislation are inextricably linked to self-government goals. These include "providing an internal check on the exercise of government power; resolving disputes that arise in the interpretation of Métis legislation and settlement laws; and providing fair, impartial, and accessible justice to settlement members."[47] If necessary, by leave of the Court of Queen's Bench, its decisions may be enforced as a judgment of that court. A tribunal can also take on extra-judicial functions that assist in the resolution of disputes, such as investigation, research, and educational functions. This capability may make it more desirable than a court. All of these functions are performed by MSAT and its staff, an important consideration given the differing levels of resources, education,

---

46 MSA, above note 25, s. 190(1)(o). The structure, jurisdiction, and operations of MSAT are elaborated in MSA, ss. 180–232.

47 Bell, *Contemporary Métis Justice*, above note 1 at 7.

comfort, and familiarity of legal process by disputants. Finally, tribunals also have procedural flexibility that enables them to create procedures more grounded in and responsive to the culture of a specific community and to utilize alternative processes that share common ideologies with Indigenous systems.

MSAT has extensive jurisdiction over settlement land, membership, and surface rights (formerly exercised by the Alberta Surface Rights Board). Unlike other tribunals, it also has jurisdiction arising from written consent of parties to a dispute and its jurisdiction is dynamic, increasing through delegations under new policies and bylaws. Through its surface access jurisdiction, MSGC policy, bylaws, and the co-management and other mineral agreements, MSAT jurisdiction extends to non-settlement members, mainly but not exclusively oil and gas companies. Like a court, MSAT has the ability to interpret and enforce legislation.[48] It has also contributed to the development of a unique contemporary Métis common law. Although not bound by previous decisions, the decisions, where possible, fuse together legislation, common law, custom, and community practice and offer some predictability for resolution of disputes. MSAT also has unique features not commonly shared with other tribunals: these include jurisdiction over alternative dispute resolution; the ability to hold hearings on settlement lands; joint review processes and accountability to two governments; and input of affected constituencies into its design and operation.

Creating a tribunal was viewed as a practical response to self-government aspirations as it was not possible to engage the federal government in the creation of a settlement court or to achieve agreement on inherent jurisdiction. Because the federal government was not prepared to negotiate and under section 96 of the *Constitution Act, 1867*,[49] they have jurisdiction to appoint judges to superior courts, the only option available was creation of a quasi-judicial tribunal with delegated jurisdictions in areas of provincial responsibility. The challenge was to invest MSAT with sufficient powers so it could act like a Métis court while at

---

48 Some of this analysis draws on arguments that MSAT is more analogous to a Métis court. These were developed by Fred Martin, lead negotiator for the Federation, "Self-Government and the Métis Settlements" (paper presented at the Faculty of Law, 20/20 Celebration, 18 September 1992) at 8 [unpublished].

49 Above note 20.

the same time include enough safeguards so that it could survive a section 96 challenge. Safeguards include minimizing, but retaining supervisory powers of the superior court, inclusion of extra-judicial functions, such as research and investigation, and inclusion of judicial functions and remedial powers which can be defended as necessarily incidental to a novel social policy goal.[50]

Like lower courts, the decisions of MSAT are subject to appeal on questions of jurisdiction and law to the Alberta Court of Appeal, and challenges can be made to its jurisdiction before or during a hearing. As of December 2005, 167 orders had been issued, only eight had been appealed (one withdrawn), and only one has been challenged on jurisdiction. Subject to one exception, the experience of MSAT has been judicial deference to its decisions and understanding of the broader political purpose it serves. For example, in the *Paddle Prairie Métis Settlement* case, Picard J. upheld a verbal agreement for transfer of an interest in settlement land and acknowledged that "the policy and intent of the legislation is to put power in the hands of Métis people to deal with lands disputes within the framework of the Act."[51] Similarly, in *Paramount*, a case concerning a challenge by an oil and gas company to Métis jurisdiction, Wilkins J. noted that the province developed a "unique legislative regime which is intended to assist the Métis people in achieving self-sufficiency and local autonomy" and later in the decision "to enable the Métis people to govern their own relationships in matters concerning their lands."[52]

---

50 This and other criteria set out in *Reference re Amendments to the Residential Tenancies Act (N.S.)*, [1996] 1 S.C.R. 186 at para. 74 and *Reference re Residential Tenancies Act 1979 (Ontario)*, [1981] 1 S.C.R. 714 at paras. 41–44; and elaborated in Bell, *Contemporary Métis Justice*, above note 1 at 52–53.

51 *Paddle Prairie Métis Settlement v. Metis Settlements Appeal Tribunal*, [1998] A.J. No. 863 at para. 7 (C.A.). The exception is a decision of Trussler J. concerning the status of the settlement member to challenge a subdivision appeal, in which MSAT held that because settlements are held for the benefit of all settlement members and all settlement members are directly affected by subdivision applications, they should have status to challenge them. Justice Trussler held that this was too wide a definition of "directly affected" and that MSAT must look at each case to determine if an individual is directly affected. See *Anderson v. Metis Settlements Appeal Tribunal*, [1994] 2 C.N.L.R. 15 (Alta. C.A.).

52 *Paramount Resources Ltd. v. Metis Settlements Appeal Tribunal*, [1999] 3 C.N.L.R. 199 at para. 47 (Alta. Q.B.).

The current structure of the Appeal Tribunal consists of a chairman appointed by the minister from a list provided by MSGC, three members appointed by MSGC, and three appointed by the minister. Important for support of oil and gas companies was the creation of the Existing Leases Land Access Panel (ELLAP) consisting of a chair appointed by agreement of MSGC and the minister, two members appointed by MSGC (usually two of the three already appointed), one by the Ministry of Energy, and one by industry associations. This panel deals with access matters arising under leases in existence before 1 November 1991 and has authority to issue right of entry orders and compensation orders. The Land Access Panel (LAP), consisting of at least three members appointed by the chair with agreement of MSGC and the minister, exercises jurisdiction formerly exercised by the surface rights board in relation to all other surface and sub-surface development. Other panels of MSAT include the Land panel, the majority of whom must be tribunal members appointed by MSGC, with jurisdiction to hear all other matters relating to settlement land; and the Membership panel, the majority of whom must be MSAT members appointed by the minister.

It is beyond the scope of this paper to review all of the changes that have occurred in the evolution of this system; however, two important events are worthy of note: (1) the MSAT Task Force (equal representation from the settlements and government) and (2) amendments proposed in 2004. The Task Force held public meetings on each settlement and heard representations from experts who had worked on projects involving MSAT and representatives of the oil and gas industry. Concerns raised included difficulties caused by unanimity provisions of the MSA; limited jurisdiction over civil matters; MSAT jurisdiction over settlement council decisions and MSGC policy; lack of jurisdiction over election issues and removal of councillors from office; MSAT's inability to provide support in criminal cases (for example, justice committees); politicization of the appointment process and the need for more settlement representation; the need for settlement council approval before members can agree to MSAT jurisdiction; misconduct by elected councillors; timeliness of MSAT's decisions and its consequential ability to deal with expanded jurisdiction; and use of legal counsel. The oil and gas industry supported MSAT's role, but called for "a clearer statement of the purpose of MSAT," consolidation of LAP and ELLAP, more detail in Appeal Tribunal decisions, and the right to appeal compensation awards, public availability of MSAT decisions, and "fair and impartial membership."[53]

The Task Force made several important recommendations relating to MSAT, adopted in amending legislation yet to be proclaimed. A new section 187.1 proposed that MSAT exercise its powers "with a view to preserving and enhancing Métis culture and identity and furthering the attainment of self-governance by Métis settlements under the laws of Alberta." MSAT jurisdiction would be extended to include validity of elections and the right to hold office (formerly exercised by the Court of Queen's Bench) and to review MSGC policy regarding assessment and taxation of interests in settlement land on request. Acting on a report from the ombudsman or minister and after a hearing, MSAT would also have jurisdiction to dismiss a settlement council, councillors, employees, and officials, or direct specific actions to be taken. LAP and ELLAP have not been consolidated, likely in the interest of maintaining a majority of settlement members, but their jurisdiction to terminate right of entry orders has been clarified. MSAT can also bring its own application to the Court of Queen's Bench for an opinion on a question of law or jurisdiction, and can act jointly with another board, commission, or other body if considered expedient or in the public interest. The Task Force did not recommend extending jurisdiction in other areas, but called for these matters to be considered in implementing recommendations from the provincial justice summit and subsequent reviews of MSAT. Recommendations that MSAT determine if settlement council approval is necessary for exercising consensual jurisdiction over members and that MSAT be designated a friend of the court to assist in issues relating to the settlements were not adopted.

The 2004 amendments also propose changes to the composition of MSAT and the process for appointing chairs, vice-chairs, and members.[54] Membership includes three full-time members and eight part-time members from each settlement, persons appointed by the minister, and a newly created Selection and Review Committee composed of the chair and vice-chairs. Of the three full-time members, one is appointed

53 *Task Force Report*, above note 3 at 4.

54 MSAA, above note 2, s. 23, regarding the ombudsman, and with respect to MSAT, ss. 7, 16–19, 22, 24–35, and 43–46.

as MSAT's chair by the minister on recommendation of the Selection and Review Committee and the other two, appointed by MSGC and the minister, are vice-chairs. Appointments would be made in accordance with criteria, if any, established by MSGC policy. The chair and vice-chairs also form an Executive Committee, which may make rules on procedure for conducting MSAT business and administrative matters relating to its quasi-judicial functions, processes for hearings and appeals, and ethical conduct. Many of these functions, although not specified in the MSA, were formerly exercised by the chair. Amendments would also clarify that alternative dispute resolution processes apply to jurisdictions acquired under policies and bylaws and can be made mandatory by the Executive Committee.

The Task Force also called for an independent conduct advisor office to address complaints against settlement councillors, as this was not considered compatible with MSAT's primarily judicial role. In response to this recommendation, the minister was given regulatory power to establish the office of the Métis Settlements Ombudsman (MSO). Pursuant to this power, an ombudsman office was created and is accountable to the minister of Aboriginal and Northern Affairs (Alberta). The 2005/2006 Annual Report indicates that, from the creation of the MSO in September 2003, 1033 complaints and requests for information were received. Of the 354 complaints received in 2005/2006, the largest number related to housing, employment, professional conduct, and nepotism. Of the 293 complaints relating to administrative fairness and conflict of interest, 197 were not in the form of formal complaints or supported with enough evidence to investigate, 18 were withdrawn, 64 were resolved informally, 11 resulted in referrals or facilitated resolution, and only 2 went to mediation or arbitration. Not all complaints were legitimate while others revealed a range of concerns, including mismanagement of funds, administrative unfairness in provision of services, unfair hiring practices, and the need for forensic audits on some settlements.[55] The existence of these types of problems is common to all governments and even more understandable in this context given the size of the settlement popula-

55 Métis Settlements Ombudsman, *Annual Report* (1 April 2005–31 March 2006) at 13 and 16, online: www.metisombudsman.ab.ca/PDF/2005%20Annual%20Report.pdf.

tions; constant turnover in settlement government; education levels in regard to governance rules, operation, administration, and other matters; and the need for capacity-building resources. Over time and with the new changes to election procedures, it is hoped that the number of complaints will decrease.

F. FINANCING MÉTIS GOVERNMENT

The preamble of the Alberta–Métis Settlements Accord aims for the settlements "to achieve . . . economic self sufficiency." How to do that is a key question being explored in the TAP Project. Below in Table 15.1 are the key findings from the Stage 1 TAP Report concerning the settlements' socio-economic situation.

Table 15.1: Findings — Stage 1 TAP Report (11 May 2005)

• Settlement Councils provide many more services than a regular municipal government, including membership, land allocations, housing, education, oil and gas operations, investment decisions, business development and management, and participation in General Council meetings. • Over the first 15 years of the Accord, the emphasis has been on infrastructure and housing, not economic development per se. • Settlement members now have a higher level of education and employment than they did before the Accord. However, members still trail Albertans in terms of education, engagement in the workforce, and individual and household income.	• It is difficult to get a conventional loan to start a business on the settlements. It is also difficult to find qualified people to manage and work in a settlement business. Lack of marketing and coordination services also hampers business development on the settlements. • With some work, institutions such as the Settlement Sooniyaw Corporation (SSC) and Settlement Investment Corporation (SIC) could provide the expertise and (non-political) framework needed for an economic diversification effort. • Working with regional partners will help the economic growth efforts by tapping into existing pools of expertise, business networks, capital, and increasing marketing power.

The settlements and their members face a number of challenges, including workplace discrimination, politics mixed with commercial transactions, land that cannot be used as collateral, services and infrastructure that are expensive to set up and maintain, and limited linkages to today's technology. With limited economic activity on the settlements, most members work off-settlement. The resulting Labour Outflow Model may work for individuals, but communities suffer because members and revenues are absent. Some people are making more money, but that doesn't translate into the local council having money unless they introduce ways to translate individual income to local government revenue.

As identified through the TAP Project, a possible starting point for appropriate development is the Community Development Model. This model invites community members to explore the traditions and practices that positively set settlement communities apart from surrounding municipalities. It draws attention to communal resources, such as ecological attractions, recreation facilities, and cultural events. The Community Development Model builds on western and traditional capacities that are essential to building successful Métis communities. These range from improved education and business supports to reclaimed language and cultural practices.

With these cultural benchmarks in place, the foundation is set for the next stage of community development. The Corporate Development Model sees community members translating the mix of western and traditional capacities into new business partnerships and new companies. The development envisioned by this model anticipates support through business incubation, training in entrepreneurship, loan guarantees, and direct financial, logistical, and marketing assistance for new or growing businesses. The goal is to graduate successful, financially sound firms that can compete in the regional economy. While successful application of the Corporate Development Model would represent a significant step forward, it is not the final step. Ultimately, the goal is to facilitate participation in the global economy.

The TAP findings and the models for economic development provide three lessons: (1) economic development takes time and you have to ensure that what you do in the short term works towards a longer term vision; (2) economic development takes place in an increasingly global environment and will require that businesses are run like businesses, not as by-products of local government; and (3) economic development is not the same as building fiscal capacity to run local government because much economic development is done by private individuals and companies.

As evidenced by the Stage 1 TAP findings, in which settlement councils are all things to all people, the proposed models for community and economic development present a serious challenge to the settlements' legislated governance structure. In particular, they call for a shift in the pervasive culture of reliance through which members have come to depend on a small group of individuals to deliver not only core services, such as water and road services, but to also deliver training grants, jobs, and social housing allocations.

G. NEW DIRECTIONS

Looking forward necessitates first looking back at the 1989 Alberta–Métis Settlements Accord. This critical document committed Alberta and the MSGC to the shared goals of settling the oil and gas lawsuit, securing settlement lands, establishing self-governance, and achieving economic self-reliance. In the MSGC's opinion, the last three goals of land security, increased autonomy, and economic sustainability are not end points, but starting points in a continuing partnership. In 2004, the TAP was established by the MSGC and Alberta government to determine how far the settlements have advanced towards the Accord goals and to jointly develop new action plans and agreements wherever the goals remained unmet.

The Stage 1 TAP Report, released May 2005, found that tremendous progress (especially with respect to new housing, roads, gas and water services) was made over the past fifteen years, but more needs to be done to achieve Accord goals. Of particular importance is the finding that continued progress will be impossible unless there are changes that enable increases in local employment, revenues, and business and cultural opportunities. Stage 2 of the TAP Project is intended to identify the changes and new partnerships needed to make sure the settlements continue to move forward.

The chairs from each settlement were invited to work on the Stage 2 planning process and to form a new group, called the Accord Review and Renewal Council (ARRC). Together, settlement leaders are working hard to develop new and improved ways for the settlements and Alberta to meet the Accord goals of security, autonomy, and prosperity. However, rather than taking a top-down approach, ARRC is committed to talking with settlement members about the developmental models under consideration: community meetings were under way at the time of writing to get member feedback on new models for housing, economic development, governance, and the delivery and payment systems for core services.

From the community meetings held so far, many members are concerned that the final payment under the Accord will spell the end of the settlements. While it is true that the last payment under the *Accord Implementation Act*[56] was scheduled for 1 April 2006 (which covered the 2006/07 fiscal year), this did not spell the end of the settlements. Further, the land protection framework and governance powers, including the MSGC's statutory authority to make budgets, pass laws, and negotiate participation interests in oil and gas activities, stayed in place. However, like municipal governments and districts, securing ongoing funding through provincial municipal grant and other provincial and federal support in designated program areas remains crucial to self-governance and the economic viability of the settlements.

The MSGC is trying to avoid a rights-based approach to this issue and is working with the Alberta government to develop appropriate plans for community viability and prosperity. To this end, the General Council signed a Goals and Guidelines Agreement with then-minister Pearl Calahasen to work together on future planning. To further solidify the Alberta government's commitment to the planning process, the MSGC also secured the premier's commitment through an Affirmation Agreement on 1 November 2005. [57]

Although the settlements' main partnership rests with the government of Alberta, the General Council has also made concerted efforts to enhance and expand its relationship with the federal government. With its tripartite office entering the tenth year of operations, the MSGC has accessed over $5 million in federal grants and more than $2 million in new grant money in one year alone. The MSGC's new satellite office in Ottawa is intended to increase awareness of the settlements among federal politicians and officials and to monitor key activities and trends within the federal government.

---

56 MSAIA, above note 25.

57 Both documents can be found on the MSGC's website, online: www.msgc.ca/media/agreement_0805130015.pdf and www.msgc.ca/media/affirmation_agreement.pdf, respectively.

H. CRITICAL REFLECTIONS, EMERGING ISSUES, AND CONCLUSIONS

The structure and operation of Métis settlement government has generated many challenges and raised broader legal questions in need of further exploration. Practical problems include issues of generating prosperity when the usual prerequisites to growth, such as education, business acumen, and access to capital, are in short supply and the ever-present challenge of ensuring effective and accountable government in small remote communities that are often dominated by extended families. Another practical challenge is finding the appropriate method and forum to ensure maximum community participation in decision making. Although printed information is circulated to members, MSAT has visited communities to educate them about its functions; hearings are public and held in communities; and law-making processes include community participation. Ironically, some communities are meeting less frequently than in the past. Although committed to traditional values of community participation and consensus, the development and ensuring enactment of MSGC policies has been slow, difficult, and labour intensive, sometimes bringing progress to a standstill. As Ken Noskey, former president of the MSGC, acknowledged, "there are circumstances in which consensus need not mean unanimity" and where there is division of opinion, "all communities, no matter how highly they value consensus, require some mechanism whereby division of opinion will not make decision-making come to a halt."[58]

Other cultural institutions, such as reliance on elder opinion, have also been affected. For example, the original vision for dispute resolution was for each settlement to have an elder advisory and appeal committee. However, it soon became apparent this was unworkable given the extension of MSAT jurisdiction beyond local matters, the need for specialized knowledge in addition to the cultural expertise of elders, and the fact some members had lost touch with the role of elders in dispute resolution. In the end, elder expertise was incorporated into membership provisions of the MSA and potential participation in dispute resolution processes through appointments to MSAT by the General Council. Despite the potential avenues for participation, the failure to include

58 Noskey, above note 32 at 72–73.

specific institutions of Métis eldership in the legislation may have indirectly contributed to decline of their traditional dispute-resolution roles. In recognition of this, MSGC has hosted a series of Elders conferences, some settlements have created advisory committees, and MSAT has developed a mediation model which incorporates participation by elders if desired by settlement members.

There are, of course, many objections that can be raised against relying on tribunals as a means to achieve Aboriginal justice objectives. Tribunal decisions are subject to review by non-Indigenous courts, governed in the main by non-Indigenous laws, and only give effect to Indigenous laws when non-Indigenous governments determine such laws should be considered. The hierarchy of decision making, dominant role of non-Indigenous law and normative values, and ability of non-Indigenous governments to alter jurisdiction and processes runs contrary to goals of those who seek a separate justice system and their own system of checks and balances to constrain potential bias and abuse of authority. The reality of the federal and political environment in which the settlements operate, however, does not support separate justice, nor was this considered in Accord negotiations as necessary to make justice more accountable to settlement members.[59]

Recognition of Métis Aboriginal rights to hunt and the broader implications of *Powley* raise issues about the eligibility of settlement members to exercise Aboriginal constitutional rights, rights to commercial hunting and sustenance hunting outside of settlement lands, reconciliation of mutual interests and legal rights, and legal characterization of the Accord, to name a few. In *Powley*, the Supreme Court of Canada recognized a Métis Aboriginal right to hunt for food and articulated a process for proving Métis Aboriginal rights to hunt, fish, and trap for sustenance in a specified geographical area.[60] The decision also stands for the broader proposition that Métis rights (asserted independent of claims to title) are

59 For further discussion, see Catherine Bell & David Kahane, eds., *Intercultural Dispute Resolution in Aboriginal Contexts* (Vancouver: UBC Press, 2004).

60 For elaboration of these arguments, see Catherine Bell, "Towards an Understanding of Métis Aboriginal Rights: Reflections on the Reasoning in *R. v. Powley*" in Joseph Magnet, Dwight Dorey, & Russel Barsh, eds., *Aboriginal Rights Litigation* (Markham, ON: LexisNexis Butterworths, 2003) 387; and Bell & Leonard, "A New Era," above note 9.

sourced in particular practices, customs, and traditions integral to a distinctive Métis community and its relationship to the land at the date of effective European control over a particular Métis community and area. Therefore, *Powley* also provides a general framework to prove rights, other than title, claimed in a specified geographical area inhabited by a contemporary community asserting a historical, practice-based right. As Arthur Pape, co-counsel for the Powleys, stated after the victory: "The court has now made it possible for . . . interests in land, in resources, in self-governance to in fact be enjoyed and operate for the benefit of the Métis people, as the Constitution has extended similar kinds of protections to First Nations and Inuit."[61]

A challenge in identifying the historical foundation of Métis rights, and contemporary communities entitled to exercise those rights, is the impact of social, political, and economic forces on the formation and sustainability of Métis identity and communities. The Court acknowledges this in the flexibility it applies to community identification and issues of continuity.[62] However, it also sets out certain criteria for Métis identity for the purpose of exercising section 35 harvesting rights and calls for membership requirements in contemporary Métis political organizations to "become more standardized so that legitimate rights-holders can be identified."[63] In practical terms, this may mean identifying those members who meet the judicial definition of a Métis person given in *Powley*; conducting land use and other studies to establish reasonable continuity of activities and connection of existing members to a historic Métis community in a given geographical area at the date of effective European control; doing historical research on periods that may qualify as the date of effective European control; and considering whether members who cannot trace ancestry to a particular historic Métis community have sufficient ancestral connection by "birth, adoption, or other means."[64]

61 Quoted in Cristin Schmitz, "Historic SCC Ruling Affirms Aboriginal Rights of Métis" *The Lawyers Weekly* (3 October 2003) 1 at 24.

62 Individuals must self-identify as Métis and have an ancestral connection to a historic Métis community by "birth, adoption or other means." *Powley*, above note 5 at para. 32. However, in assessing the historical foundations of a right, focus should be on continuity of the practice grounding the right, not continuity of community.

63 *Powley*, *ibid.* at para. 29.

64 See above note 62.

The criteria given in *Powley* raise some interesting, but not insurmountable, challenges for the Métis settlements. For example, the definition of a Métis under the *Metis Settlements Act* is "a person of aboriginal ancestry who identifies with Métis history and culture" and membership criteria are broad enough to include some who are of Aboriginal ancestry, but are not necessarily descendants of a distinctive historic Métis community.[65] Secondary literature on the settlements and research conducted pre-*Powley* in the settlements suggests that many members are descendants of distinctive Métis communities and of Métis for whom the scrip distribution system failed. Those who are not, identify as Métis and at some point acquired status, becoming accepted as part of the Métis settlement community through application of legislation or a history of family connections dating to the original purpose and creation of the first colonies. Pragmatic, personal, and economic consequences arise in attempting to distinguish among members for existing governmental relations, consultation mechanisms, reconciliation of statutory and constitutional rights, and life within the settlement communities. It is difficult to conceive of disentitling settlement members from exercising rights enjoyed by other settlement members when they identified as Métis prior to Métis rights recognition in the Constitution, are legally recognized as such by statute, and are accepted by a contemporary Métis community with a clearly defined territory and identifiable representative government. It may well be that this type of situation is what the Supreme Court had in mind when it suggests that "an individual's self-identification need not be static or monolithic" as long as it is not "recent in order to benefit from s. 35" and ancestral connection can be proved by "other means." Indeed, equitable and legal arguments can be developed to support this conclusion.[66]

Another complication may arise in identifying the relevant geographic land base. Some settlement lands set aside in 1938 (after the date a court would likely consider to be the assertion of effective control) were selected on the basis that Métis communities were established in those areas; however, other factors came into play. These include availability of fish and suitability of land for agricultural purposes. Thus,

65 MSA, above note 25, s. 1(j); and see also ss. 74 & 75.

66 *Powley*, above note 5 at paras. 31 & 32.

traditional territories over which hunting, fishing, trapping, and other practices were exercised may not always coincide with, and may extend beyond, settlement areas. Given the migratory nature of the Métis, these areas may overlap with other contemporary Métis or other Aboriginal communities that trace land use and ancestry to the geographic area in question. Failure to establish exclusivity does not vitiate a First Nation or Inuit claim to harvesting rights in a given area and should not for the Métis. This challenge requires more consideration of references in *Powley* to rights being located in a community's traditional hunting grounds. As Jean Teillet explains, "In *Powley*, it was not necessary for the court to determine whether the Métis community at Sault Ste Marie formed part of a larger Métis people that extended over a wider area such as the Great Lakes because the Powley/LaSage family had always lived in the environs of Sault Ste Marie and because Steve Powley shot his moose within minutes of Sault Ste Marie."[67] Also of interest is *Laviolette*, in which the Provincial Court of Saskatchewan identified the relevant geographic area as all of northwest Saskatchewan, rather than just fixed settlements with significant Métis populations, based largely in part on Dr. Frank Tough's evidence that Métis in the area had a regional consciousness based on trade and family connections and were highly mobile.[68]

Although Alberta entered into an Interim Métis Harvesting Agreement (IMHA) with the MSGC for members to hunt, fish, and trap for sustenance on unoccupied Crown lands in Alberta, this and the IMHA entered into with the Métis Nation of Alberta (MNA) were not renewed in light of significant opposition by non-Métis interest groups. Given the membership criteria and history of these Métis organizations, as a practical matter, these agreements assumed that the vast majority of members in these organizations met the *Powley* criteria for Métis identity; they did not require that each Métis person who is a member of the MNA or a Métis Settlement prove identification for the purpose of exercising rights under the agreement. Like the lower courts in *Powley* (upheld by the Supreme Court) and *Laviolette*, the interim agreements took into account the historical migratory lifestyle and regional consciousness of the

67 Jean Teillet, *Métis Law Summary 2007* at 11, on the Pape Salter Teillet website, online: www.pstlaw.ca/resources/MLS-2007-FINAL.pdf.

68 *R. v. Laviolette*, 2005 SKPC 70.

Métis in defining areas where harvesting rights could be exercised. However, despite these influences, the IMHAs acknowledged in their preamble that there is "uncertainty in the law relating to Métis Harvesting in Alberta" and provided in paragraph 4 that they do not "affect, abrogate, or derogate from, or recognize or affirm any constitutional or Aboriginal rights of the Métis Settlement General Council or its members." The IMHAs were chanllenged in *R. v. Kelley*,[69] on the basis that they granted more rights than recognized under section 35(1) of the *Constitution Act, 1982*,[70] and therefore are contrary to equality provisions found both in section 15 of the *Charter* and the *Alberta Bill of Rights*.[71] However, on appeal, the Alberta Court of Queen's Bench held that the IMHAs were accommodation agreements flowing from section 35 and therefore legally enforceable.[72] These challenges to the IMHAs underscore numerous issues that need to be explored in their application to the settlements, including the importance of clarifying the concept of community and territory applicable to the exercise of Métis rights in Alberta. Given the diversity of case law on this issue, this may not be resolved until these issues are again before the Supreme Court.

Another issue that arises from *Kelley* is the ability of a province to enter into agreements or terminate or limit the exercise of Métis Aboriginal rights by other means. The IMHAs specifically indicate they are not concerned with this, but could they be if the parties wished it? The question is complicated because it is not clear who has jurisdiction over Métis Aboriginal rights and indeed, the decision of the Supreme Court in *Blais* may have significant ramifications for the ability of a province to terminate Aboriginal harvesting rights through regulation.[73] The complications of jurisdiction are discussed in detail elsewhere by the author and in this volume. They are raised here simply to demonstrate another area the settlements must explore in developing new paths for negotiation. Further, a finding that Métis are solely within federal jurisdiction has ramifications for assessing the constitutional validity of provincial legislation that singles out Métis.

69 *R. v. Kelley*, [2006] 3 C.N.L.R. 324 (Prov. Ct.).

70 Above note 19.

71 R.S.A. 2000, c. A-14.

72 *R. v. Kelley*, [2007] 2 C.N.L.R. 332 (Alta. Q.B.).

73 *Blais*, above note 9. See also Bell, "A New Era," above note 9.

Experiences responding to the 2004 amendments and some provisions in those amendments, although well meaning and perhaps necessary, raise issues of meaningful participation and negotiation; they could also have significant implications for Métis autonomy. Even if settlement autonomy remains intact, concern about long-term sustainability of the settlements has arisen — there are questions about the enforceability of government obligations under the Alberta–Métis Settlements Accord in the post-2007 era. Add to this the outstanding need for constitutional amendment to permanently protect the Métis land base, and one begins to understand the mounting pressures on the MSGC.

However, to understand the MSGC, one must also consider that whatever the legal or political milieu, the great constant of settlement leadership and settlement members has been their unwavering practicality and pragmatism. While this does not exclude pursuing a rights-based agenda (sometimes the most practical approach to addressing critical issues), it does mean that the settlements will look first to conferences and negotiations to develop lasting solutions to the challenges of the day.

Author Biographies

Richard Asselin has worked in various roles in the human services sector in Manitoba for more than twenty-five years. These roles include program evaluation, early childhood programming, disability inclusion, and service integration/case management. Since 2000, Asselin has served as a leader within the policy and implementation team that restructured and devolved child welfare services to First Nations and Métis control.

Catherine Bell, B.A., LL.B., LL.M. Catherine Bell is a professor of Law at the University of Alberta, teaching in the areas of property law, Aboriginal legal issues, and alternative dispute resolution. She is the author of numerous articles and book chapters principally focused on Métis and First Nations constitutional rights.

Charlotte A. Bell, B.A., LL.B., Q.C. Charlotte Bell is general counsel in the Aboriginal Affairs Portfolio of the federal Department of Justice. She has served as lead counsel to the Nisga'a Treaty Litigation team and on other complex cases involving Aboriginal rights and fiduciary responsibilities.

The Honourable Harvey Bostrum, B.A. (Hons.). Harvey Bostrum has served as the deputy minister of Aboriginal and Northern Affairs in Manitoba since 2001. Before that appointment, he was executive director of the Aboriginal Affairs Secretariat in the Department of Aboriginal and Northern Affairs in that province.

Alfred (Fred) E.N. Caron, B.A., LL.B., Q.C. Fred Caron is assistant deputy minister, Office of the Federal Interlocutor for Métis and Non-Status Indians. He began his career with the federal government in 1975 as a policy analyst at Indian and Northern Affairs Canada. He subsequently joined the federal Department of Justice, where he held various senior positions, including senior general counsel, Native Law Section.

Paul L.A.H. Chartrand, B.A., LL.B. (Hons.), LL.M., I.P.C. Paul Chartrand, Indigenous peoples' counsel, of the Indigenous Bar Association, is a professor of law at the University of Saskatchewan and adjunct professor at the University of Victoria. He is one of twelve children of J. Aime Chartrand — a Métis trapper, fisher, and carpenter, from the Métis community of Saint-Laurent, Manitoba — and his wife, Antoinette. His teaching areas and publications are in law and policy pertaining to Aboriginal peoples.

Dale Gibson, B.A., LL.B., LL.M. F.R.S.C. Dale Gibson, retired professor of law (University of Manitoba and University of Alberta), writes and practises as a consulting barrister in the area of public law. He is the author of several books and many articles chiefly about constitutional law and legal history. He served as constitutional adviser to several governments, as well as to the Royal Commission on Aboriginal Peoples.

Jason Madden, B.A., LL.B. Jason Madden is a Métis born and raised in northwestern Ontario. His family resides in the historic Treaty 3 Halfbreed adhesion area near Rainy Lake. Former general counsel to the Métis National Council in Ottawa, he returned to private practice in 2006 and is now based in Toronto. His practice focuses largely on Métis legal and governance issues.

P. Mitch McAdam, LL.B. P. Mitch McAdam is the director, Aboriginal Law, in the Constitutional Law Branch of Saskatchewan Justice. He has been involved in several prosecutions related to Métis hunting and fishing rights. He has also represented Saskatchewan in the Supreme Court of Canada in such cases as *Powley*, *Blais*, and *Morris*.

Kent McNeil is a distinguished research professor at Osgoode Hall Law School in Toronto, where he has taught since 1987. He is the author of numerous works on the rights of Indigenous peoples, including two books: *Common Law Aboriginal Title* (1989) and *Emerging Justice? Essays on Indigenous Rights in Canada and Australia* (2001).

Bradford (Brad) Morse, B.A., LL.B., LL.M. Brad Morse is a professor at the University of Ottawa, Faculty of Common Law, where his teaching subjects include Aboriginal Law, Property Law, and Trusts. Morse formerly served as executive director of the Native Legal Task Force of British Columbia and as research director, Aboriginal Justice Inquiry of Manitoba. He is former chief of staff to the Honourable Ronald A. Irwin, minister of Indian Affairs and Northern Development.

Albert C. Peeling is a lawyer practising in the area of Aboriginal rights in Victoria, British Columbia. He has participated in some of the leading cases in Aboriginal rights, including *Delgamuukw v. B.C.*, and has been involved in negotiations on behalf of Aboriginal peoples with both government and industry. Peeling taught Aboriginal law at the University of Victoria, and has written on Aboriginal rights and title, governance, and constitutional law.

Arthur J. Ray, Ph.D., F.R.S.C. Arthur Ray is L.G. Pathy Visiting Professor of History and the Program in Canadian Studies at Princeton University and a former Woodrow Wilson Center fellow. He has also taught history at the University of British Columbia. Ray is the author of several books, articles, and chapters on Aboriginal history and is often engaged as a consultant in Aboriginal and treaty rights matters. He has appeared as an expert witness in numerous Aboriginal law cases.

Harold Robinson, LL.B. Harold Robinson is a Métis lawyer who specializes in Aboriginal law and policy. His experience includes coordinating hearings and writing decisions for the Metis Settlements Appeal Tribunal. Robinson has also directed federal–provincial relations for the Métis Settlements of Alberta and Alberta Aboriginal Affairs and Northern Development. He has devoted his energies to advancing the interests of the Métis Settlements of Alberta. His full-time job, other than being a husband and father of two boys, is executive director of the Metis Settlements General Council.

Alison Rogan served the public for sixteen years in Nunavut and the Northwest Territories before joining the government of Manitoba in 2005. Shaping and implementing appropriate governance processes, improving Métis relations, and promoting community development have been central to her career. Rogan works on Métis policy and strategic initiatives for the government of Manitoba.

Mark L'Hirondelle Stevenson, M.A., LL.B. Mark Stevenson is a Cree-Métis lawyer working for First Nations clients on treaty negotiations, specific claims, corporate law, and forestry-related issues. Stevenson worked with the Privy Council in Ottawa and was deeply involved in the Aboriginal constitutional process from 1983 until 1987. He then worked as legal counsel for the Ontario Native Affairs Secretariat. Stevenson has also worked with the British Columbia Ministry of Aboriginal Affairs. He is a former commissioner of the Law Commission of Canada and a past president of the Indigenous Bar Association.

Jean Teillet, B.F.A., LL.B. A partner in the law firm of Pape Salter Teillet, Jean Teillet is a great niece of Louis Riel. A member of the bars of Ontario, Manitoba and Northwest Territories, and British Columbia, she practises Aboriginal rights law with a particular emphasis on Métis rights law. She has acted as counsel for Aboriginal groups in several Supreme Court of Canada cases, including *Taku River Tlingit First Nations v. B.C.* She was counsel for the Powleys at all levels of court in the landmark Métis harvesting rights case *R. v. Powley*. She is also involved in negotiations of land claims agreements for First Nations and in negotiations on Métis harvesting rights.

Frank Tough, Ph.D. Frank Tough is a professor of Native Studies, former director of the School of Native Studies at the University of Alberta, and former head of the Native Studies Department at the University of Saskatchewan. He has published articles and chapters on such subjects as Aboriginal rights and the transfer of Rupert's Land, the economic policies at Indian Affairs after 1870, Indian economic behaviour and the use of fish by the Métis, and the *Natural Resources Transfer Agreements*. Tough has also engaged in archival research for the Royal Commission on Aboriginal Peoples and served as the principal investigator of the Métis claim to lands and resources in northwestern Saskatchewan. He has appeared as an expert witness in several court cases concerning treaty and Métis Aboriginal rights.

Table of Cases

Index

Printed and bound by CPI Group (UK) Ltd, Croydon, CR0 4YY

15/09/2026

14962403-0002